W9-ABY-167

TOMORROW IS ANOTHER DAY

Winner of the
Jules F. Landry Award
for 1980

Tomorrow Is Another Day

The Woman Writer in the South, 1859 – 1936

ANNE GOODWYN JONES

LOUISIANA STATE UNIVERSITY PRESS
Baton Rouge and London

DESIGNER: Joanna Hill
TYPEFACE: Primer
TYPESETTER: G & S Typesetters, Inc.
PRINTER: Thomson-Shore
BINDER: John H. Dekker and Sons

LIBRARY OF CONGRESS CATALOGING IN
PUBLICATION DATA

Jones, Anne Goodwyn.
     Tomorrow is another day.

     Bibliography: p.
     Includes index.
        1. American fiction—Women authors—History and
criticism.   2. American fiction—Southern States—
History and criticism.   3. Women in Literature.
4. Southern States in literature.   5. Women authors,
American—Southern States.   I. Title.
PS374.W6J6   813'.4'099287   80-29123
ISBN 0-8071-0776-X
ISBN 0-8071-0866-9 (pbk.)

To my mother and father

Contents

Illustrations

Preface

This book is about seven white southern women who, before the Southern Literary Renaissance, tried to come to terms with their experience by writing fiction and succeeded—at least in the practical sense of surviving to another day as professional writers. They are: Augusta Evans, Grace King, Kate Chopin, Mary Johnston, Ellen Glasgow, Frances Newman, and Margaret Mitchell. All seven were raised to be southern ladies, physically pure, fragile, and beautiful, socially dignified, cultured, and gracious, within the family sacrificial and submissive, yet, if the occasion required, intelligent and brave. The tension between the demands of this cultural image and their own human needs lay close to the source of their creativity; that tension is expressed thematically in their fiction, often as the conflict between a public self and a private one or in the imagery of veils and masks.

In fact, the very act of writing itself evoked within these women a sense of self-contradiction, for southern ladies were expected to defer to men's opinions, yet writing required an independent mind. The wide variance in the quality of their fiction and in the depth of the understanding and control they gained in their lives attests in part to that self-division. Because I am interested in the relationship between their experience and their creativity, I have chosen to discuss in this book those of their works that most directly address the question of southern womanhood. The works are: Evans' *Beulah* (1859); King's *Monsieur Motte* (1886, 1888), "Bonne Maman" (1886), and "The Little Convent Girl" (1893); Chopin's *The Awakening* (1899) and several stories; Johnston's *Hagar* (1913); Glasgow's *Virginia* (1913) and *Life and Gabriella* (1916); Newman's *The Hard-Boiled Virgin* (1926) and *Dead Lovers Are Faithful Lovers* (1928); and Margaret Mitchell's *Gone With the Wind* (1936). These fictions differ dramatically in popularity as well as quality. Evans' and Mitchell's novels were best sellers; Newman's were barely known. I have been less interested in these differences, however, than in the common terms in which these various writers articulated their experiences and envisioned their ideals. Popular or obscure, artisan or artist, they confronted fundamentally similar experiences in strikingly similar ways, despite their historical and geographical differences. In their fiction, all criticize the ideal of southern womanhood point by point in similar ways, and by means of similar imagery, plotting, characterization, and narrative point of view. Some ultimately retreat from the critique, some envision alternative ways to define men and women and to organize community, and some find their material to be the stuff of tragedy.

The ideal of southern womanhood that informed these women's lives and fictions not only often conflicted with their actual human needs but also contained its own internal ambiguities and contradictions. When the image exhorts both intelligence and submission, both bravery and fragility, conflict seems inevitable. Such ambiguities are, of course, at the very heart of the literary imagination: one thinks of Edna Pontellier swimming to her death to be free, or of Quentin Compson saying, "I dont hate [the South]. . . . *I dont! I dont hate it! I dont hate it!*" Literature therefore seems a particularly appropriate place to look for reflections upon southern womanhood.

But that ideal did not serve only as a norm for individual behavior; it became also a central symbol in the South's idea of itself. With all her paradoxes, the southern lady has represented the best of the South. Southern women thus confront a particularly tenacious image of true womanhood. Chapter One begins with an investigation of the sources, ideological use, and persistence over time of the image of the southern lady in the mind of the South. It then offers some historical and some speculative material concerning the conditions in which the southern woman who wrote found herself, and introduces in more detail the seven writers to be discussed. Each subsequent chapter is devoted to the experience of a single writer and the close analysis of one or more of her works. Finally, the conclusion gathers together some of the threads that have appeared in the fabric of the individual works.

Every book is shaped by its writer's experience and predilections; this one is no exception. I grew up in the South, and thus I have known firsthand both the appeal and the threat of becoming a southern lady. Like many southern white women of my generation, I felt the fissures of southern life as personal rifts, ultimately requiring personal choices. The image of the lady awed and angered me; I went to the cotillions and to the civil rights marches, enjoying the privileges of southern white womanhood while pursuing the contradictory dream of freedom and equality. When I chose to go to graduate school, the now flourishing study of women's history and literature had just blossomed. This book owes its very existence to the excitement and the work of the many people who have contributed to that endeavor. Inspired by their example, by coursework in southern literature, and by W. J. Cash's *The Mind of the South*, I decided to seek out the mind of the southern woman as she told her own story in fiction. My own immersion in the culture about which I have written brings with it the special awareness as well as the special ignorances associated with such a stance toward a subject for intellectual inquiry.

Both my historical research and my experience of living outside the South lead me to issue a caveat at the outset: southerners and northerners seem to have—often unbeknownst to them—differing images of the southern woman. A. D. Mayo, a northerner, spent some time in the South and wrote after the Civil War about the "grotesque misapprehension of Southern womanhood" in the Northeast:

> The Southern woman was pictured there as an object lesson of feminine self-indulgence and laziness—a sort of barbaric queen, surrounded by her dusky satellites, who anticipated her every whim. Her pet activities were furious secession politics, ultra fashionable excesses, with an occasional cyclone of jealousy or passionate rage over one of the inevitable outbreaks that, like tropical earthquakes, relieved the stagnation of her monotonous home life. . . . Ignorant of letters, art, and music, with no capacity for literary production or interest in the great movements for the elevation of humanity that so profoundly excited the serious society of other States and nations, she was pictured rather as the heroine of the sensational novel.

An entirely unscientific sampling of opinion here in Meadville, Pennsylvania, in 1980, produced contemporary versions of the southern woman that show interesting parallels to Mayo's. She is supposedly either hedonistic, sensuous, fertile, warm, mysterious, lusty—in a word a voluptuary apparently making up with her body for what she lacks of Puritan backbone—or alternatively, she is impulsive yet repressed, a mindless tease who wants men but not sex. As southern readers will immediately note, the South had—and has—a different idea. That idea, as articulated by southern men and (often differently) by southern women, is the subject of this book.

I hope this book will serve not to close but to open questions about the study of southern women and southern literature. In what context can southern white women best be seen—regional, racial, or sexual? Is their history most characteristically southern, white, or female? Less easily answered, I expect, is what role these writers played in southern literary traditions. As foremothers, how did their work affect that of Eudora Welty? Flannery O'Connor? Carson McCullers? Or did it at all? In what relation does this heritage of literature by southern white women stand to that of their brothers and fathers and sons? Of the black women and men about whom they wrote? And finally, how have these women begun to disentangle the knot of race, class, and sex whose complex relationships in the South created an ideal so profoundly significant to their own experience? To what extent do their efforts and their insight inform us about patterns and themes in American literature more generally and in the literature of women around the world?

Acknowledgments

I am indebted so deeply to the many people who have helped in the creation of this book that to speak of a single author seems illusory.

For the example of their passionate commitment, I would like first to thank two former teachers, Julia Randall Sawyer and C. Hugh Holman. In their differing ways and places, they taught me the complex pleasures of literature. With my own students I continue to enjoy those pleasures: to them, too, thanks.

Research took me to the libraries of the University of North Carolina, the University of Georgia, and the University of Virginia; in each place I found people who were invariably knowledgeable, friendly, and eager to help. I am especially grateful to those in the Southern Historical Collection in Chapel Hill, the Rare Books and Georgiana collections in Athens, and the Alderman Library in Charlottesville. Stephens Mitchell, Margaret's brother, very kindly allowed me to interview him in Atlanta during the summer of 1976, and the Faculty Development Committee at Allegheny College generously provided a travel grant in the summer of 1978 that allowed further research. Allegheny College has two remarkable reference librarians, Dorothy Smith and Don Vrabel; their generosity and acuteness saved me much time.

I had wonderful luck in finding people to undertake the large and at times labyrinthine task of typing this manuscript. At different stages, Jan Cutshall at Allegheny College, Fred and Martha Gilbert in Meadville, and Muriel Dyer in Chapel Hill demonstrated remarkable capacities for patience, flexibility, endurance, and occasional mindreading, in addition to their uncommon typing skills. My thanks to them, and to Lawrence Pelletier and David Baily Harned for making funds available to cover some of the costs of typing and indexing.

My luck extended as well to the people I encountered at Louisiana State University Press. Margaret Fisher Dalrymple's painstaking and supportive copyediting has kept me on my toes, and Beverly Jarrett's enthusiasm for this project has kept me going. Thanks to them, to Joanna Hill, Production Manager, to Eleanor Ransburg for her help with further typing, and to Cindy Crawford, Marilynn Poe, and Kim Rye for their help in proofreading.

Many other people also agreeably read and commented on sections of this manuscript at various stages of its growth. Here I would like particularly to thank Barbara Adams, Jim Bulman, Bruce Clayton, Alice Gertzog, Aurelia Hogan, Mary Kelley, Lloyd Michaels, Darden Pyron, Jeff Steinbrink, and Kate Wayland-Smith for their careful, perceptive, and invariably helpful readings. I am especially grateful to Lewis Leary, Maggie O'Connor, and Lee Smith Seay, who read the work in its entirety more than once.

The dedication of this book suggests my debt to my mother and father. Here I thank them for their numerous acts of practical assistance, for their willingness to entertain a manuscript during my visits home as an extra (and demanding) guest, and for the gift of their love of language. To my sisters Polly and Claiborne, and to my friends scattered everywhere, thank you for aid, comfort, loyalty, and distraction.

Louis D. Rubin, Jr., teacher, adviser, scholar, and friend, has given more than any other single person to the making of this book. For seventeen years, first at Hollins College and then in Chapel Hill, his persistent faith in me, his perfect honesty, and his love of living and working have shaped my own life and work. In particular, he has patiently read through all the transformations of this book with, in addition to everything else, an almost infallible ear for the garbled metaphor. Thanks once more to him and to Eva Rubin, for their generosity and their humor.

The errors that remain after all this help are my own.

I wish to acknowledge the following for their kind permission to quote extensively from published works:

University of Chicago Press for Anne Firor Scott, *The Southern Lady: From Pedestal to Politics, 1830–1930*, copyright © 1970 by University of Chicago Press.

From *Virginia* by Ellen Glasgow, copyright 1913, by Doubleday, Page, and Company; renewed 1941 by Ellen Glasgow. Reprinted by permission of Harcourt Brace Jovanovich, Inc.

From *Life and Gabriella: The Story of a Woman's Courage* by Ellen Glasgow, copyright 1918, 1946, by Ellen Glasgow. Reprinted by permission of Harcourt Brace Jovanovich, Inc.

Houghton Mifflin, Inc., for Mary Johnston, *Hagar*, copyright 1913 by Houghton Mifflin.

Alfred A. Knopf, Inc., for Walker Percy, *The Moviegoer*, copyright © 1961 by Noonday Press.

Louisiana State University Press for Grace King, *Grace King of New Orleans: A Selection of Her Writings*, edited by Robert Bush, copyright © 1973 by Louisiana State University Press, and for Kate Chopin, *The Complete Works of Kate Chopin*, edited by Per Seyersted, copyright © 1969 by Louisiana State University Press.

Stevens Mitchell Literary Rights for Margaret Mitchell, *Gone With the Wind*, copyright 1936 by Macmillan Company.

John C. Ruoff for "Southern Womanhood, 1865–1920: An Intellectual and Cultural Study," Ph.D. dissertation, University of Illinois, 1976.

From "The Women" from *The Blue Estuaries* by Louise Bogan. Copyright © 1968 by Louise Bogan. Reprinted by permission of Farar Straus and Giroux, Inc.

Selections from *The Hard-Boiled Virgin* by Frances Newman reprinted by permission of Liveright Publishing Corporation, copyright 1926 by Boni & Liveright, Inc.,; copyright © renewed 1954 by Louis Rucker.

Selections from *Dead Lovers Are Faithful Lovers* by Frances Newman reprinted by permission of Liveright Publishing Corporation, copyright 1928 by Boni & Liveright, Inc.; copyright © renewed 1955 by Louis Rucker.

TOMORROW IS ANOTHER DAY

Gary Kissick

CHAPTER I   **Dixie's Diadem**

Southern men have toasted and celebrated southern womanhood since the South began to think of itself as a region, probably before the American Revolution. The lady, with her grace and hospitality, seemed the flower of a uniquely southern civilization, the embodiment of all it prized most deeply—a generosity of spirit, a love for beauty. Lucian Lamar Knight looked with nostalgia in 1920 at the ideal southern woman:

> The Confederate woman. Imagination cannot dwell too tenderly upon a theme so inspiring. Reverence cannot linger

too fondly at so pure an altar. The historian's pen . . . has not portrayed her superior, if, indeed, her equal; nor may we expect to find it in all the hidden future. It took the civilization of an Old South to produce her—a civilization whose exquisite but fallen fabric now belongs to the Dust of dreams. But we have not lost the blood royal of the ancient line; and in the veins of an infant Southland still ripples the heroic strain. The Confederate woman, in her silent influence, in her eternal vigil, still abides. Her gentle spirit is the priceless heritage of her daughters. The old queen passes, but the young queen lives; and radiant, like the morning, on her brow, is Dixie's diadem.[1]

But real southern girls who aspired to become ladies found behind the rhetoric a complex and sometimes contradictory set of values. For the image wearing Dixie's Diadem is not a human being; it is a marble statue, beautiful and silent, eternally inspiring and eternally still. Rather than a person, the Confederate woman is a personification, effective only as she works in others' imaginations. Efforts to join person and personification, to make self into symbol, must fail because the idea of southern womanhood specifically denies the self.

In that, southern womanhood is not alone. It has much in common with the ideas of the British Victorian lady and of American true womanhood. All deny to women authentic selfhood; all enjoin that women suffer and be still; all show women sexually pure, pious, deferent to external authority, and content with their place in the home. Yet southern womanhood differs in several ways from other nineteenth-century images of womanhood. Unlike them, the southern lady is at the core of a region's self-definition; the identity of the South is contingent in part upon the persistence of its tradition of the lady. Secondly, and perhaps for that reason, the ideal of southern womanhood seems to have lasted longer than the other ideas. On a recent trip to the South, a journalist asked about "women's liberation" at a small party in what he called a typical medium-sized southern city. "The three women replied cautiously," he wrote. "One said she didn't like it 'if we're talking about the thing that calls itself women's lib now.' Another said she felt that *in some cases* women doing the same work as men should get the same pay. Two of the men came on as classical chauvinist pigs and the other kept quiet." The journalist discovered later that one woman was a supervisor in a business, another worked in a federal agency, and the last was a systems analyst and computer programmer.[2] Not only has it lasted to the present, but in a third divergence from other womanly ideals, southern womanhood has from the beginning been inextricably linked to racial attitudes. Its very genesis, some say, lay in the minds of guilty slaveholders who sought an image they could revere without sacrificing the gains of racial slavery. And finally, the image itself seems, if not radically different from, at least an extreme version of the nineteenth-century lady. For instance, it emphasizes fragility and helplessness to the point that protecting the southern lady seems to the southern gentlemen both essential and appealing. And the class—aristocratic—that the image of the lady represents receives a stronger emphasis in the South than elsewhere.[3]

Investigating southern womanhood, then, might take us in some respects into the heart of American, even Western, experience. For the image meshes profoundly held assumptions about sex with strongly felt class aspirations, beliefs about race, and patriotism for one's homeland. If, to put it another way, woman everywhere has been "made to represent all of man's ambivalent feelings about his own inability to control his own physical existence,"[4] in the American South woman represented as well his ambivalent feelings about social class, race, and national identity. Very little work has been done on this subject, either in the more traditional histories of the South or in the newer histories of women; southern women and southern womanhood are not yet part of mainstream history.[5]

My own purpose in this work, however, is not so much to investigate the concept of southern womanhood as such, as it is to examine certain of its literary manifestations. Since literature for many years constituted almost the only profession that a southern lady of good family not driven by dire economic necessity might pursue without being thought by her society to have in effect "desexed" herself, works written by southern women might offer an especially insightful way of looking at the matter. How did the southern author who was female portray members of her own sex? How did she view their engagement with the needs for intellectual and emotional fulfillment within the context of a society that decreed a particular role for them, a role that in important ways might clash with the very impulses that prompted the southern woman writer to *be* a writer?

In this chapter I have gathered what seem to me the most intriguing historical insights available concerning the origins of the concept of southern womanhood, its place in the "mind of the South" (that is, in southern identity), and its effects on roles for men and for women. Finally, I will consider some questions that connect language, literature, and southern women; and I will introduce the seven writers whose works and lives this book primarily concerns.

At the end of Walker Percy's first novel, *The Moviegoer*, Binx and Kate have married. If it were a traditional comedic resolution, the harmony between man and woman should symbolize a larger harmony within their society and even within the universe. And, indeed, their affection gives the reader hope. But in Percy's novel, tradition takes a disturbing and peculiarly southern turn. Binx has had at best a tenuous hold on his identity, and Kate has been near psychic collapse. Binx's latest identity is that of the traditional southern gentleman. He has asked Kate to run an errand for him, and she responds with the helplessness of the traditional southern lady:

> "I wouldn't know what to ask for!"
>
> "You don't have to. I'll call Mr Klostermann and he'll hand you an envelope. Here's what you do: take the streetcar, get off at Common, walk right into the office. Mr Klostermann will give you an envelope—you won't have to say a word— then catch the streetcar at the same place. It will go on down to Canal and come back up St Charles."
>
> "I don't have any money."
>
> "Here."
>
> She considers the quarter in her palm. "Here's the only thing. It's not that I'm afraid." She looks at a cape jasmine sticking through an iron fence. I pick it and give it to her.
>
> "You're sweet," says Kate uneasily. "Now tell me . . ."
>
> "What?"
>
> "While I am on the streetcar—you are going to be thinking about me?"
>
> "Yes."
>
> "What if I don't make it?"
>
> "Get off and walk home."
>
> "I've got to be sure about one thing."
>
> "What?"
>
> "I'm going to sit next to the window on the Lake side and put the cape jasmine in my lap?"
>
> "That's right."
>
> "And you'll be thinking of me just that way?"
>
> "That's right."
>
> "Good by."
>
> "Good by."
>
> Twenty feet away she turns around.
>
> "Mr Klostermann?"
>
> "Mr Klostermann."

> I watch her walk toward St Charles, cape jasmine held against her cheek, until my brothers and sisters call out behind me.

And so the novel ends. Kate depends on Binx not just for guidance and money; her very existence itself is a function of his imagination, of his thinking of her "just that way." Wary of self-expression, invented and sustained by Binx, she acts for him as well. Like the cape jasmine she holds, Kate is lovely and fragile, the flower of the South. Moreover, her traditional role permits his. For as a southern gentleman, Binx may now make decisions, take responsibility, be gentle but authoritative. At the end of the novel, then, both are climbing into the shell of southern tradition in the hope of surviving the middle of the twentieth century.

Southern traditions—for the white and wellborn, the lady and gentleman—by no means constitute the center of Percy's interest in *The Moviegoer*. Yet as part of their contemporary searches, both Binx and Kate have to decide what to do with the weight of the southern past. Binx's characterization at the end of the novel implies that he has accepted the particular burden of the southern gentleman, a burden that his Aunt Emily earlier in the novel hoped he would accept: "More than anything I wanted to pass on to you the one heritage of the men of our family, a certain quality of spirit, a gaiety, a sense of duty, a nobility worn lightly, a sweetness, a gentleness with women—the only good things the South ever had and the only things that really matter in this life." Binx prefers such an identity to joining the "very century of merde . . . where needs are satisfied, [and] everyone becomes an anyone."

Kate, on the other hand, asserted her own identity earlier in the novel precisely when and because she aimed for the anonymity of Chicago or Modesto or Fresno, away from the place of her past. Binx explained it then: "When it comes to a trip, to the plain business of going, just stepping up into the Pullman and gliding out of town of an evening, she is as swift and remorseless as Della Street." "I'll tell you what," she had said to Binx, sounding "very happy." "You go lie down and I'll take care of it . . . I'll fix everything." Under way, though, she found that "what I want is to believe in someone completely and then do what he wants me to do." She agreed to marry Binx on the condition that "we are together a great deal and you tell me the simplest things . . . like: Kate, it is all right for you to go down to the drug-store." So, at the end, the plain business of going to Mr. Klostermann on the streetcar requires the careful support of her husband. And though she does it "uneasily," Kate has become not just "anyone" but a southern lady, an identity she has tried to escape.

It is sad and ironic that the very traditions whose uncomfortable acceptance permits Binx and Kate to escape the anonymity of what Binx calls "scientific humanism" should deprive Kate of the chance to seek identity and autonomy while offering Binx that very opportunity. For the tradition of the southern lady, though not of the southern gentleman, is a tradition that specifically denies the self. Though she lacks the regal demeanor of the Confederate woman, Kate has won Dixie's Diadem: effacing herself, she becomes Binx's creation.[6]

As an image, southern womanhood has been the crown of Dixie at least since the early nineteenth century; it originated earlier, with the development of a planter class in the South in the seventeenth century.[7] Roughly interchangeable with the image of the southern lady or (for the young unmarried) that of the southern belle, southern womanhood was born in the imaginations of white slaveholding men. Thus southern womanhood was linked directly to fundamental southern questions of race, class, and sex, and, as Sara Evans has said, "revealed more about the needs of white planters than about the actual lives of women, white or black."[8] For example, George Fitzhugh clarified the ideal in 1854 by using the language of the master-slave relationship: "Let [woman] exhibit strength and hardihood, and man, her master, will make her a beast of burden. So long as she is nervous, fickle, capricious, delicate, diffident and dependent, man will worship and adore her. Her weakness is her strength, and her true art is to cultivate and improve that weakness. . . . In truth, woman, like children, has but one right, and that is the right to protection. The right to protection involves the obligation to obey." Clearly such a woman—like the slaves to whom Fitzhugh consistently compares her—is designed to serve the needs of her secular "lord and master."[9]

The persistence of southern womanhood through the vicissitudes of southern history is only now being investigated, but the ideal has clearly played at least two historical roles. First, it has been at the heart of the ideology of the South, embodying the values by which southerners have defined the region's character through Civil War and Reconstruction, New South and modernism. Wilbur Cash and, more recently, John C. Ruoff have argued that southern womanhood eventually became "identifi[ed] with the very notion of the South itself."[10] Thus a "violation of Southern Womanhood was also, *ipso facto*, a violation of the South. Conversely, an attack upon southern civilization and culture was an attack upon Southern Womanhood."[11] But the terms must be understood with caution. The ideology of the South, like Wilbur Cash's "mind of the South," means primarily the ideology of the South's white men of means. The only group with the education and social sanction for undertaking such self-analysis, white men of the upper classes shaped community vision as well as public policy. Women thus did not participate significantly in making the ideology of the South in which their own idealization played so persistent a part.

But the image of the southern lady, though it might have meant the same thing to white southern husband and wife insofar as they saw themselves as southerners, meant radically different things in their daily experiences. In a second historical role, the idea of southern womanhood has exerted through time tremendous power to define actual roles for southern (perhaps all American)[12] women of the white middle and upper classes. The relationship between image and reality became the central fact in many southern women's lives; indeed, their very identity depended on it. More than just a fragile flower, the image of the southern lady represents her culture's idea of religious, moral, sexual, racial, and social perfection. Pious—whether aristocratic Episcopalian or middle-class Methodist—the ideal southern lady also acts as a moral exemplar. She embodies virtue, but her goodness depends directly on innocence—in fact, on ignorance of evil. She is chaste because she has never been tempted; in some renditions she lacks sexual interest altogether. Because it is unthinkable for her to desire sex, much less sex with a black man, and because the white man protects her from the black man's presumably uncontrollable sexual desire, her genes are pure white. Thus, Jacquelyn Hall says, "as absolutely inaccessible sexual property, white women became the most potent symbol of white male supremacy."[13] Finally, she serves others—God, husband, family, society—showing in her submissiveness the perfection of pure sacrifice. Ironically, this model of perfection cannot stand alone; she needs Christ for salvation and, on earth, the pedestal of male economic support and the protection of the walls of a southern gentleman's home. "The weakness and dependence of woman was thrown into bold relief by [the gentleman's] virility and mastery of his environment," said Anne Firor Scott. "Husbands were frequently referred to in the words used for God: Lord and Master."[14]

Historians speculate variously about the origins and function of the concept of southern womanhood in southern ideology. In the knot of race, sex, and class, some find one thread clearer than others. Thus some scholars point to the white man's feelings about slavery, some specifically to miscegenation, some to anxieties about societal order, and some to Western patriarchy as the source of southern womanhood. But, in general, historians agree that the function of southern womanhood has been to justify the perpetuation of the hegemony of the male sex, the upper and middle classes, and the white race.

Anne Scott sees the base of the pedestal in racial slavery: "Because they owned slaves and thus maintained a traditional landowning aristocracy, southerners tenaciously held on to the patriarchal family structure. . . . Any tendency on the part of any of the members of the system to assert themselves against the master threatened the whole, and therefore slavery itself." Thus, Scott continues, it was "no accident that the most articulate spokesmen for slavery were also eloquent exponents of the subordinate role of women."[15] Similarly, Cash finds racial supremacy at the origin of the image: "This Southern woman's place in the Southern mind," he says, "proceeded primarily from the natural tendency of the great basic pattern of pride in superiority of race to center upon her as the perpetuator of that superiority in legitimate line."

But the white woman could perpetuate white superiority only because of what Cash calls her "remoteness from the males of the inferior group," a remoteness not paralleled in the relationships between white men and black women. Proud of his presumed racial superiority, the white man—according to this theory—felt guilt and fear about his sexual use of black women: guilt vis-à-vis the white woman, that is, and fear for his own self-image. "The [white] woman must be compensated, the revolting suspicion in the male that he might be slipping into bestiality got rid of, by glorifying her," argues Cash.[16] Lillian Smith, too, sees the origin of southern womanhood in this "race-sex-sin spiral": "The more trails the white man made to back-yard cabins, the higher he raised his white wife on her pedestal, when he returned to the big house. The higher the pedestal, the less he enjoyed her whom he put there, for statues after all are only nice things to look at. More and more numerous became the little trails of escape from the statuary and more and more intricately they began to weave in and out of southern life."[17]

Insecurities of a less sexual sort led southerners to create the pre–Civil War plantation novel and to place the lady at its gracious center, according to William R. Taylor. And, to judge by their popularity, such novels struck a responsive chord. Despairing at southern social and economic decline (a decline apparent particularly in the Tidewater and in contrast to the greatness of the Revolutionary past) and fearing "social dissolution" (particularly in the forms of an open society and a dismembered family), southerners "grasped for symbols of stability and order to stem their feelings of drift and uncertainty and to quiet their uneasiness about the inequities within Southern society." But southern men, Taylor argues, could not associate feeling, introspection, or moral awareness with masculinity. The popular plantation novels solved this problem "without robbing the Southern gentleman of his manhood. The Southern answer to this question lay in the cult of chivalry—in having the Cavalier kneel down before the altar of femininity and familial benevolence."[18]

Yet giving moral authority to the woman was, as Sara Evans points out, the "weak link in the image of the Victorian southern lady. Ultimately it made no sense to place women in charge of piety and morality and then deny them access to the public sphere where immorality held sway."[19] Certain pre–Civil War southern men, Taylor says, "began regretting the moral autonomy which they had assigned to women" and returned, like George Fitzhugh, to insist upon a rigid hierarchy that made woman, slave, and yeoman subject to the Cavalier.[20] Southern womanhood was only one part, then, of an inflexible abstraction into which these men hoped to fit an alarmingly organic society. Scott, too, points to fear of social instability as a reason for the persistence of "the complementary images of the soft, submissive, perfect woman and of the strong, commanding, intelligent, and dominant man in the face of an exigent reality that often called for quite different qualities." Facing growing threats from outside before the Civil War, the South had to quash any internal changes as threats to stability, she points out, including, of course, changes in the definitions of lady and gentleman.[21]

More positively, Eugene Genovese implies that the role and image of woman developed as the South invented its own view of the ordered society, a view that not only justified slavery but offered alternatives to significant moral limitations implicit in bourgeois society. Fitzhugh, in this sympathetic interpretation, believed that slavery served the interests of the black slave (and the white woman in her slave relation to man) better than could the isolation and vulnerability of bourgeois society, in which slave and woman become mere property, cut off from a loving and dutiful master. Thus "slavery, marriage, religion, are the pillars of the social fabric."[22]

Yet another argument finds the origin of southern womanhood in the Western patriarchal tradition, antedating and then reinforcing racial slavery. Southern settlers brought with them from England a belief in patriarchal values, says John Ruoff. These values made the man the source of family authority, the family the source of societal order and stability, and the planter class the source of authority within society. Then, as early as the seventeenth century, a native southern aristocracy developed an "ethos of leisure and consumption" that "stipulated that women should perform an essentially ornamental function in society." The development of the master-slave relationship thus reinforced and was reinforced by the prior notion that the husband held absolute authority in the home. And slavery required that the wife continue to be a passive, obedient, and beautiful symbol of her husband's wealth and power. Thus the idea of southern womanhood, according to Ruoff, "supported the patriarchal defense [of slavery], but did not originate in it."[23]

Sara Evans points to Europe for the myths about women that southern colonists brought along with their patriarchal social and familial assumptions. Those basic Western myths polarized women into the "virgin, pure and untouchable, and the prostitute, dangerously sexual." The clustering of images—goodness and light with virginity, evil and darkness with sexuality—seemed to be reified and therefore confirmed when white planters owned black slave women. Race and sex thus fused to create in the "white lady" the southern version of the nineteenth century's cult of true womanhood. And the dynamic of white patriarchy produced the images of black womanhood as well, argues Evans: "Responsibility for the rape of black women was laid at the feet of the victim, who, it was said, was naturally promiscuous. Finally, the black mammy became the nurturant, all-giving mother figure, beloved because she threatened the hierarchy of neither race nor sex."[24]

Despite these historians' hypotheses, definitive interpretations of the pre–Civil War sources and continuing function of southern womanhood will have to wait until more research has been done. Already, however, the miscegenation argument has lost cogency, for it seems clear now that miscegenation took place largely in towns—yet the men who propounded the myth of southern womanhood came not from towns but from the rural planter class. My own guess would support Evans and Ruoff; patriarchal values not only antedate but seem to have persisted beyond slavery, guilt over miscegenation, and regional social decline. Nevertheless, it is the peculiar relation of patriarchal attitudes toward women with the development of a slave society that produced, in the early nineteenth century, both the South's most intense period of self-definition and the refinement of the image of the lady as the slaveholder's ideal: his daughter, his mother, his wife. Traveling through the South, Carl Carmer watched southern college men carry out one of the rituals of university dances, called the "Key-Ice." As he describes it, the lights go out, fraternity members "march in carrying flaming brands," and finally "four acolytes attend a long cake of ice. Wheeled in on a cart, it glimmers in the torches' flare. Then the leader . . . lifts a glass cup of water and begins a toast that runs: 'To Woman, lovely woman of the Southland, as pure and chaste as this sparkling water, as cold as this gleaming ice, we lift this cup, and we pledge our hearts and our lives to the protection of her virtue and chastity.'"[25] The year was 1934. From marble statue to block of ice: shaped by that tradition, southern women found southern womanhood a procrustean bed.

"Someday someone is going to be bold enough to write fully and completely about the Southern white women through slavery up to the present," wrote Jessie Daniel Ames in 1931, "but that day is far off."[26] And so it is, even now. Nevertheless, it is possible to take a brief look at the persistent appearance of the image of the white lady as a central element in the history of the dominant South's idea of itself. From before the Civil War, when—as we saw—it originated as part of the South's self-definition, through Reconstruction, and into the developing New South, southern womanhood has appeared as an element in the ideology of every period in southern history.

An early challenge to the image as it had developed during the antebellum period came during the Civil War, when southern women played an active role, "carrying on as if they had always been planters, business managers, overseers of slaves, and decision makers."[27] Many worked in hospitals; some even disguised themselves as men and went into military camps. Already the image had included the "weak link" of moral autonomy. This newly revealed experiential strength brought fear into the hearts of men who worried about the "Amazon" and the "strong-minded female." But the concept of southern womanhood simply incorporated the new strength to create the oxymoronic ideal of the woman made of steel yet masked in fragility, like Melanie Wilkes. Thus the threat was apparently removed and the concept of southern womanhood retained its patriarchal character, for such strength was to be exerted only within the home and only to serve the husband, the family, and the South.

How did this incorporation take place? In an 1891 *Century* article called "Southern Womanhood as Affected by the War," Wilbur Fisk Tillett grapples with the problem. He begins with the antebellum image: "In native womanly modesty, in neatness, grace, and beauty of person, in ease and freedom without boldness of manner, in refined and cultivated minds, in gifts and qualities that shone brilliantly in the social circle, in spotless purity of thought and character, in laudable pride of family and devotion to home, kindred, and loved ones—these were the qualities for which Southern women were noted and in which they excelled." He then carefully adds the wartime virtues: "That the Southern woman of ante-bellum times lacked those stronger qualities of character and mind that are born only of trials and hardships and poverty and adversity may be granted." By implication, of course, those "stronger qualities" have only improved southern womanhood. And indeed Tillett sees women's wartime strength entirely as it affected men: the wife "inspired the despairing husband," the sister "inspired her soldier brother," and the maiden "inspired her disheartened lover." Thus his position on the women's movement is predictable: "So far as this movement may have any tendency to take woman out of her true place in the home, to give her man's work to do and to develop masculine qualities in her, it finds no sympathy in the South." One of the southern women whom Tillett quotes in his article reveals, probably unconsciously, the degree to which such incorporation of new strength into the old ideal served the needs of the defeated and despairing southern men after the war. Whereas, before the war, for the white woman to work meant, she said, "injuring or entirely forfeiting [her] social standing," now such a woman would lose respect if she refused to work and "settled herself as a burden on a brother, or even on a father." [28]

At its worst, this paradoxical image supported the notion of woman as a spoiled child, tyrannical in the home and helpless outside, or as a hypocritical deceiver, sweet as sugar on the surface and scheming within. At its best, it added to the prewar role of woman as moral authority the experience of autonomy, preparing a tradition into which a woman like Jessie Daniel Ames could later step, from which she could push the circumference of woman's sphere beyond the walls of the home, and because of which she could begin to unravel the South's tangled knot of race, sex, and class. From the Civil War until the present, many southern women would, instead of rebelling, strategically exploit this divided image so that they could think of themselves and be thought of as ladies while undertaking even the most radical critique of their society and actions to change it. Others, however, found the oxymoron self-divisive and stressful.

But to return to the South's ideological use of the southern lady: after the Civil War, two variants of the Lost Cause [29] used an identical idea of southern womanhood for conflicting ends. Those who advocated a return to the patriarchy of the Old South expressed their irreconcilability with the North by pointing to the "uncompromising stance of southern women toward the Yankees"; in literature, the southern woman's refusal to marry a Yankee symbolized the "last stand of the South against the North." But those who advocated reconciliation with the North, proponents of the New South, also used the image of the southern lady to advance their case. In that literature, the southern lady marries the northern charmer, then persuades him to agree with her political ideas. In both cases the woman plays the same role: she preserves the culture of the South, thus in effect she is the soul of the South. [30]

Through the late nineteenth and early twentieth century, the idea of southern womanhood continued to play a central part in southern thinking. Trying to bring back the prewar social order, southerners instituted legal racial segregation and voting restrictions for blacks and poor whites, because these two groups threatened traditional political and social authority. When political equality was effectively blocked, attention moved to social order. Since southern white womanhood symbolized the "purity and sanctity of the family," and since the family provided one's class, status, and honor, as well as a "model for the operation of southern society," the potential debasement of the family through sexual or marital connections between southern upper-class white women and blacks or lower-class whites threatened the elite dominance of society. Moreover, for a black man to rape a white woman was seen as a symbolic attack on the social and political authority that suppressed him. In addition, the black man's presumed incapacity to control his passions demonstrated to white men the evil effects of his (also presumed) lack of a pure home life: the black man's failure to respect his own wife and mother, white men felt, was the cause for disorder, crime, and social chaos.[31] Thus in southern womanhood, here extended to black women, were lodged all the forces of civilization. And in this way, despite the low incidence of actual rape or even of accusations of rape,[32] the defense of southern womanhood became a rallying cry for lynch mobs across the region.

The almost uniform refusal of the former Confederate states to ratify the Nineteenth Amendment attests further to the persistence of the image of the lady in southern ideology throughout the period. Southern men predictably "equated ballots for females with a terrifying threat to society."[33] Now southern womanhood was invoked not only against New South industrialization or against black men but against the women themselves. Although racist arguments opposing the vote were probably voiced more often, the inconsistency of the image of women voting with the image of the lady garnered its share of the verbiage. Writing in 1899, Laura S. McAdoo traces the continuing effects of chivalry on the women of her region. Chivalry blights woman's education, she says, since men fear "strong-mindedness"—"You are to propagate no individual ideas. You are simply to follow what is laid down," she reports one young woman teacher being told by her superintendent. Chivalry further demoralizes the working woman through pitying her for being too unattractive to be rescued from such a fate. And it distorts southern mothers, continues McAdoo, who "are prone to live entirely in the lives of their children, giving themselves over to the domestic life, and glorifying in their subordination of self."[34] Even the Populist movement failed to crack the perfect mould. The Farmers' Alliance, for instance, which dedicated itself to equality and offered women within its structure a pragmatic and equal working relationship with men, had blossomed, flowered, and virtually died by 1900. Moreover, as Julie Jeffrey interprets the North Carolina branch, the alliance ultimately sought to keep women within a prescribed role on the farm, doing hard work for low or no wages.[35] In short, the "new woman" of the period never became the ideal of southern womanhood: instead, the lady lived on.

Nor was the new woman of the twenties to modify seriously the image of the lady. Although some of the most famous flappers came from the South—Zelda Sayre Fitzgerald grew up in Montgomery, Alabama—their sexual emancipation stopped short of challenging the patriarchal image of the lady, as William Chafe has pointed out.[36] W. J. Cash thinks that "in the bottom of the minds of even the most flauntingly 'emancipated' of these youths, the old sentimentality and Puritanism bred in their bones from birth still lurked, and often started up to torture the young woman with longing for the old role of vestal virgin, the young man with longing for the old gesturing worship of a more than mortal creature—to make them continually restless with the subconscious will to escape into being more nearly whole again."[37] Whether he is right or not about the depth of sexual emancipation, Cash reveals his own assumed equation of southern lady and southern integrity.

In this period of general political conservatism, southerners invoked the ideal of southern womanhood to oppose the theory of evolution, arguing that teaching it was just as certain to break down southern morals—"destroying the ideal of Southern Womanhood"—as it was to breed Communism.[38] Southerners also invoked the image against child labor regulations and other woman-supported reforms; the Louisville *Herald* ironically warned women away from such political action by appealing to their ladylike sensitivity and good manners: "The woman voter is making herself felt in ways not chartered for her. . . . there are times when one may gauge the need for one's activity and curiosity by the ungracious manner of one's reception."[39]

And in 1930, twelve southerners published *I'll Take My Stand*, a celebration of agrarianism against industrialism and—in certain essays—of a traditional southern aristocratic ideology. In John Donald Wade's portrait of the representative agrarian, Cousin Lucius, women play a familiar role. Beloved and strong, Lucius' mother carries culture and the arts through poverty and defeat. In college, Lucius joins a fraternity "dedicated to God and ladies." After years of marriage, he thinks that his wife, "who was at best but a frail creature, was the strongest hope he knew for the perpetuation of that bright tradition"; hence her character demands "a sort of worship." And Caroline indeed has the good sense to defend her tippling husband at their fiftieth wedding anniversary party against the ladies who "were not shadowed—nor glorified—by a sense of tragic vision, and [who] were not capable—not indeed aware—of philosophic honesty, but [who] were good and angry with Cousin Lucius and [who] went to Cousin Caroline and told her that she should curb him." Caroline sweetly diverts their energy. Yet despite all this womanly perfection, Cousin Lucius can't see his way clear to supporting woman's suffrage, for, "despite his fervor for justice, he was sure that the practice of a perfectly sound 'right' often involves the practicer, and with him others, in woes incomparably more galling than the renunciation of that right."[40] Perfect woman is too morally weak to vote.

Nor did southern habits vanish after World War II. In the discussion preceding the Civil Rights Act of 1964, southern men once again used the image of southern womanhood to argue against reform, this time against the end of segregation. Eliza Heard wrote an appeal to southern women in 1962 to "rise up all over the South . . . and proclaim to these white men that we will no longer stand for them to take our name in vain to keep segregation." Yet, as she continues her argument, it, too, has a familiar ring. Women are chaste, pure, and virtuous enough, she says, to keep the race pure *without* segregation, so to argue against segregation for its risk to southern womanhood is, perforce, to insult and exploit pure, white, southern womanhood. "None [of the southern women] I know has ever entertained the slightest idea of taking either a Negro husband or a Negro lover. I never knew personally a southern white woman who was raped," she says. If she did not do so herself, Heard must have thought that her audience shared the old ideal of the lady.[41]

Even today, the South is nearly solid once again in its refusal to ratify an amendment that challenges its traditional notions of sex roles. Former Senator Sam Ervin of North Carolina appealed to the tradition of the southern lady and gentleman when he wrote in 1978, opposing the extension of the ratification deadline for the Equal Rights Amendment, that "a ratified ERA would invalidate laws imposing upon husbands the primary duty of supporting their wives, laws imposing upon fathers the primary duty of providing food for their helpless and hungry children."[42]

Thus the idea of southern womanhood, which Anne Scott maintains "stretched across the whole South,"[43] also stretches across time in the southern mind with fewer variations than one might expect. For what John Ruoff notes about the period from 1865 to 1920 is true beyond that time: when significant changes in both role and status took place for

American women generally, the "dominant themes are stability and order rather than change for southern [white] women of the upper and middle classes."[44] Thus "Southern women of the 1880s and the 1920s shared behavior patterns whether they lived in Memphis or Mobile, in Richmond or Atlanta, or in smaller towns scattered across the South.[45]

The idea of southern womanhood can be found in the middle not only of the "mind" of the South but also in the psyches of particular southern men. Has the image of the lady in fact enhanced their roles, as seemed the case with Binx Bolling? Or do their identities suffer, too?

The position of the southern white man has never been an easy or a simple one. Even before the Civil War, he had become, as William R. Taylor has shown, a national stereotype: the "gay, pleasure-loving and generous-hearted Southerner won admiration for his indifference to pecuniary drives and his reputedly greater familiarity with polite culture and genteel ways; yet he, too, early became a cautionary figure in tales which revealed him as weak, vacillating and self-indulgent, or wild, vindictive and self-destructive," a Southern Hamlet or Hotspur. Emerson's version of the stereotype demonstrated the distance of the southern man from the northern intellectual community: an "accomplished Southerner," to Emerson, was "as ignorant as a bear, as irascible and nettled as any porcupine, as polite as a troubadour, and a very John Randolph in character and address."[46]

In addition to becoming an object for northern admiration or disgust, the white southern man had been—whether consciously or not—inwardly damaged or divided by the moral contradiction between his Jeffersonian faith and his practice of slavery. Louis Rubin has suggested, using the example of the planter-sportsman William Elliott, that antebellum southern literature "remained an affair of surfaces" precisely because men like Elliott could not write honestly of what they knew and simultaneously continue living as they did.[47] Taylor found a "condition of paralysis brought on by conflicting loyalties—they finally could not believe in either their own regional ideals or those of the country as a whole . . . the result was confusion, indecision and a kind of gnawing dispiritedness."[48]

The prewar decline in the power and influence of the South added to this sense of moral unease to leave men feeling cut off and ineffective. Southern women had meanwhile gained—at least in popular novels— not only moral autonomy but final authority on the matriarchal plantation. In fact, women were beginning to "speak out in their own names," challenging the "patriarchal role which the planter had assumed for himself and many of the values which he thought of himself as embodying."[49] And finally, unlike his Yankee brother, the southern man, who took such pride in his knightly bravery and physical prowess, suffered military defeat.

Feeling these pressures, many men—like George Fitzhugh—resorted to the assertion of patriarchal dominance and authority, subordinating, in the pattern of southern chivalry, women, children, blacks, and nonslaveholding whites to their own control. Thus, as his traditional sources of masculine identity eroded, the southern gentlemen seemed to turn more and more often to the domestic patriarchy to find himself, fastening even more firmly to the dual image of woman as the lodestar of perfect southern virtue that Cousin Lucius worshipped and as the fragile and submissive lady who needed his help and his strength, and could not withstand the polls.

Individual men responded to the image as did individual women, personally and idiosyncratically. Yet whatever the idiosyncratic response, most men throughout these periods assumed completely that the cult of southern womanhood was self-evidently true. So profound was this assumption, Bruce Clayton points out, that during the period 1880–1920, a period when white male intellectuals in southern universities challenged the southern "savage ideal" of unquestioning conformity and when women got the vote, practically no evidence can be found of these liberal men's concern for women's suffrage or for the larger issue of women's rights.[50]

Self-interest helped to keep at bay any doubts about the assumption that the southern lady was real. For if the image of the southern lady cost anyone, it was not, at least on the surface, the husband. On the contrary, southern womanhood served to permit an apparently flattering and expansive role and self-image for the white southern man. John William DeForest, sent from Connecticut to South Carolina during Reconstruction, linked chivalry with masculinity when he said that "the central trait of the 'chivalrous Southron' is an intense respect for virility." Virility, in turn, meant physical strength, courage, and competence, coupled with a firm sense of one's authority. "If you will fight, if you are strong and skillful enough to kill your antagonist, if you can govern or influence the common herd, if you can ride a dangerous horse over a rough country, if you are a good shot or an expert swordsman, if you stand by your own opinions unflinchingly, if you do your level best on whiskey, if you are a devil of a fellow with women . . . [the southern man] will grant you his respect."[51] No southern lady could be imagined doing any of these things; the polar opposition of her qualities to his thus confirmed his virility. But if she did show, for example, self-reliance, his identity came into question. Belle Kearney's father was, she reported, a fine example of the old-fashioned southern gentleman. After the Civil War, when Belle told him she intended to teach school in order to support herself, her father exclaimed, "making a desperate effort to control the quaver in his voice and to hide the tremor of his eyelids that revealed the storm in his heart, 'you *forget* that I am able to give you a support. You forget that you are my only daughter. Do you mean to tell me that you are going to teaching? I will *never* consent to it.'" (Her mother, she adds, "believed in me utterly. She was my devoted, changeless, unquestioning ally.")[52] And, arguing against women's suffrage in 1913, Conway Whittle Sams said, "Authority has declined far enough in this country. . . . About all that is left is domestic authority."[53] No wonder, as Scott suggests, "man's image of woman changed more slowly than women's view of themselves."[54]

Yet along with the tenacity with which southern men held to the notion of southern womanhood appears a persistent sense of fear, even suspicion, that the notion will not work, that behind the marble mask lies a monster. Scott finds such fear in the great amount of "time and energy [that southern men spent] stating their position."[55] "Stripped to its barest essentials," William Taylor said, "the deference shown to [southern women before the Civil War] in the form of Southern chivalry was the deference ordinarily shown to an honored but distrusted servant."[56] When that servant becomes her own boss, as Kearney's father's reaction indicates, the effect on her men could be devastating. As late as 1928, according to Ernest R. Groves, even the "new" man "who glories in his wife's outside success is aware of the belittling remarks made about him and the common suspicion that he does not amount to much."[57]

An extreme but revealing expression of that fear came from an Episcopalian clergyman at the University of the South. Robert Afton Holland argued that, historically, the "safeguards of the hearth broken away from, [woman] has recognized no barriers beyond, and has led men to lengths of iniquity," for "the woman who does not rightly obey her husband, will not obey the god who enjoins her submission." Once out of the home, woman becomes a horrific animal, acquiring "bigger hands, bigger feet, higher cheek bones, lanker limbs, flatter chests, hook noses, lips thin and tight"—rather like the caged parrot to which Holland compares woman. Freed, as in the Paris Terror, women are rapacious: "the reddest tongue that hung from [the Commune's] many red-frothed mouths was the tongue of woman athirst for the lives of women." For woman "knows no half-measures," her "one earnest gait is a gallop," and if she "undertook legislative reform, it would be . . . by tantrums, frenzies, explosions. . . . The ballot once in [women's] hands, they would be less content and more rapacious than ever." The dangers of women ruling are best seen in Elizabeth I, says Holland. When she grew old, her "great counsellors . . . had done what they could to cage the leopard in her character, and had kept it behind the bars which it bent with many a mad leap; but now the bars were broken." So the nation "prayed for her death . . . as every other nation has done and will do for the woman who tries to rule it." Holland makes the reason perfectly clear: a home is a "province within the State, a minor realm with authority to be recognized as authority, and with laws to be obeyed as laws." Thus the "suffragette" attacks the very core of societal order, for she "hates household authority and law, and would put argument in their place except when she loses her temper and has a fit of personal despotism." Holland's vision of disorder extends to economic devastation: "she would insist on her rights first in the household . . . anti-husband newspapers, companies, caucases [sic], and at his expense."[58] Holland's imagery and his threats are reminiscent of the ways in which, before the Civil War, white southern men envisioned the world if blacks were freed: dangerous, disorderly, and terrifying. Insofar as his anxiety may stem from a recognition of the energy, anger, and aggression threatening to crack from within the marble mask of southern womanhood, Holland's vision is acute. Yet insofar as his anxiety shapes itself into monstrous images, Holland only adds to the long Western tradition of imagining woman as angel or monster, virgin or whore, a tradition whose acceptance by southern women puts still more stress beneath the marble surface. Nor does the image do much for Holland's own apparent rationality and emotional maturity. In such a case, the destructive effects of the image of the lady appear to take their toll on men.

There were healthier exceptions, but they were exceptions. The Farmers' Alliance, as shown, voiced a commitment to equality; one alliance publication said the group had "come to redeem woman from her enslaved condition, and place her in her proper sphere. She is admitted into the organization as the equal of her brother . . . the prejudice against woman's progress is being removed."[59] Anne Scott finds that activist women in the twenties found "in almost every instance groups of men were working to the same ends, and frequently there was co-operation."[60] Earlier, men like Desha Breckenridge in Kentucky, Luke Lea in Tennessee, and Walter Clark and Josephus Daniels in North Carolina had supported women's suffrage.[61] Walter Hines Page made the connection between chivalry and lynching in his 1893 article, "The Last Hold of the Southern Bully."[62] Edwin Mims devoted a sympathetic and informative chapter to "The Revolt Against Chivalry" in *The Advancing South* (1926). And Belle Kearney's father—who had been so shaken by her wish to be her own support—showed remarkable flexibility once he accepted that "*his* daughter might desire to enter the field of active modern workers." Eventually, in fact, he presided over an Equal Rights Club and, according to his daughter, consulted her opinion on "important affairs" and "did all in his power to further my projects."[63]

Yet the southern man of Holland's class had, as his own profession indicates, several fields for his actions. Even though the number of fields might shrink, identity did not hang solely on being either a "devil of a fellow" or, as for Binx Bolling in *The Moviegoer*, "gentle" with women. For most southern women of the same class, the situation differed. Whereas southern manhood could be demonstrated by obtaining an ideal southern woman, southern womanhood had to be shown by becoming one. The difference in psychic cost is clear. "When the belle, abdicating her throne of social dominion, yielded herself to the program of the plantation lord, [she] found that matrimony locked the door and threw away the key, locked a door so thick that not even the cry of pain could ever penetrate to the outer world," suggested Francis Gaines in 1925. Constantly chaperoned, economically dependent, denied development, the actual lives of women became part of the "vast unsaid" left out of the plantation literature that Gaines discusses, a literature that extolled southern womanhood in its defense of the southern way of life.[64]

Confronted with an image of themselves that was at odds with their experience, southern women have responded in several characteristic ways throughout southern history. The rare ones have rejected the necessity even to pretend to conform, have radically criticized their society, and have often left the South, in body if not in mind. The Charleston Grimké sisters moved North—Sarah in 1821 and Angelina in 1829—and, from that "refuge," at times addressing the southern white women at home, directly attacked the "assumptions upon which southern society based its image of women," including, of course, slavery. In fact, Sarah's *Letters on the Equality of the Sexes* were, according to Anne Scott, the "earliest systematic expression in America of the whole set of ideas constituting the ideology of 'woman's rights.'"[65] Sara Evans has shown that the 1960s feminist revival found its roots, too, in the South. Once again southern white women—this time in the civil rights movement—saw the connection between racial and sexual oppression, thus providing the initial impulse toward contemporary feminism.[66]

At the opposite extreme from outright rebellion, some women have determined to shape themselves entirely into the ideal. "We owe it to our husbands, children, and friends," wrote Caroline Merrick to a friend in 1859, "to represent as nearly as possible the ideal which they hold so dear."[67] At the extreme, such women blanked out their perceptions and repressed their feelings until they lost, almost entirely, a sense of self. A diarist describes her state of mind: "My way of late has been hedged up and my mind has seemed sunken with a state of apathy from which I can with difficulty arouse myself." Though she blames her malaise on her "own neglect of duty and fearful transgression of God's Holy law,"[68] she may be suffering from the lack of self-respect that Sarah Grimké saw to be a result of "being educated from earliest childhood, to regard [herself] as [an] inferior creature."[69] Educated, on the other hand, into the belief that they were simultaneously perfection itself, some real southern women found it hard to admit and harder to rectify such "besetting sins [as] a roving mind and an impetuous spirit."[70] "To repress a harsh answer, to confess a fault, and to stop (right or wrong) in the midst of self-defence, in gentle submission, sometimes requires a struggle like life and death; but these *three* efforts are the golden threads with which domestic happiness is woven," taught Caroline Gilman.[71] And religion simply drove the point home still more firmly: woman was inferior to man; she could find salvation only by attaining the virtues of self-abnegation and humility, by, in a word, accepting her inferiority and abdicating her self.

It is no wonder that one diarist confessed, "Lord I feel that my heart is a cage of unclean beasts";[72] that is just the perception that Robert Holland had of woman. A "good" woman tried to destroy the beast. After a year of marriage to Binx, Kate Bolling is "sleek as a leopard" but continues to pluck self-destructively at the thumb she has shredded into "spikes of feathered flesh."[73] On the other hand, a few women, as the Grimkés had done in fact, rebelled in imagination against the restrictive bonds of slavery and womanhood. Kate Chopin's earliest sketch tells the story of an "animal born in a cage," well fed, well rested, and narcissistically self-centered. One day the cage door accidentally opens. The animal crouches in a corner, "dreading the unaccustomed." The "spell of the Unknown" finally prevails: "a bracing of strong limbs, and with a bound he was gone." Outside, the animal risks being hurt—he tears and wounds his skin, almost tastes the "noxious pool," fights for his food—but he never returns to his cage. Instead, he joins the real world, "seeking, finding, joying, and suffering."[74] The young Chopin called her sketch, surely intending the parallel to slavery, "Emancipation."

More typically, though, southern women neither freed the beast nor killed it in its cage. Instead, they made for it a sort of sheep's clothing, a public persona, a mask of sorts that coexisted with but did not always correspond to the woman's inner self. Such self-division produced guilt both about what they felt was the wolf within and about the inevitable hypocrisy involved in concealing it. In her wide reading of southern women's diaries, Anne Scott found that "the biblical verse most frequently quoted [therein] was from *Jeremiah*: 'The heart is deceitful above all things and desperately wicked: who can know it?'"[75] Nevertheless, Caroline Gilman enjoins upon her reader, "[A woman's] first study must be self-control, almost to hypocrisy. A good wife must smile amid a thousand perplexities, and clear her voice to tones of cheerfulness when her frame is drooping with disease."[76] The narrator of Chopin's novel *The Awakening* finds something more heartening than wickedness, perplexity, or disease beneath the mask, yet she still recognizes "the dual life—that outward existence which conforms, the inward life which questions."[77] But of course questioning—that "roving mind"— also had to be kept within the cage, not only because it threatened the very structure of southern society, but because intelligence itself, in woman, "distressed more than it pleased. When [men] did not openly condemn, they treated it with insulting condescension."[78]

Southern women trusted that inner self only to diaries, to letters and conversations with close (usually women) friends, and—casting its voice through yet another mask—to fiction. Writing and speaking the truth of feeling and experience in these relatively safe modes allowed women to avoid either the literal alienation of physical departure or the psychological alienation of selflessness or madness. Transforming their self-division into language kept them from isolation and radical repression; transforming language into fiction let them imagine alternatives as well.

But the southern woman faced more than conflict between image and reality. She found herself at the center of the paradoxes that informed her own southern culture, yet she had experience and a point of view that diverged in some ways sharply from those of her southern white father, husband, brother, and son. Caught between white supremacy and female inferiority, her loyalties to her race might well conflict with her loyalties to her sex. She was torn, too, between her love for the men and boys central in her life, her pride at what she symbolized for them, and her perhaps buried anger at the repressiveness implicit in their reverence and the fear implicit in their habit of commanding her. Most likely identifying herself strongly as a southerner, her sympathies would be entirely on the side of the Confederacy or the Lost Cause, yet she would become, as "Confederate woman," a symbol in place of a self.

Her experience and point of view set her off, too, from her Yankee sisters. Where the northern woman could oppose slavery with relative ease, the southern woman felt an identification with the slaves and yet knew she was at the same time their oppressor. Where the northern woman could (in Gerda Lerner's variation on Simone de Beauvoir) "see man as 'the other,' "[79] the identification of the southern woman with the southern white man in mutual grief over the destruction and loss of the war and in mutual fears during Reconstruction might well retard that perception. The Yankees often became her "other." Unlike her northern counterpart, battling materialism, acquisitiveness, and the social horrors of industrialization, the southern woman fought agrarian and urban poverty after the war. Unlike her Puritan sister, she grew up in the Church of England. Where the northern woman stayed consigned to the increasingly work-free home, the southern woman gained the self-reliance and sense of competence that comes from useful work during and after the Civil War.

Where the "American" woman, then, faced no radical shift in role but rather a gradual regression into powerlessness, the southern woman after the war had to shift roles entirely in the face of the returning man's desire to re-create a stable society. If his vision urged him to hold on to the Lost Cause, she had to relinquish her actual role and retreat into the passivity that the cause called for. If, on the other hand, his method of finding a stable society meant endorsing the New South, going whole hog for the "progress" characterizing the rest of the country, she had to relinquish her actual role and become, like her northern counterpart, the hostage to an earlier code of values. And the virtual absence of significant immigration into the South, along with an inherited ideology of caste and belief in aristocratic values, made the society in which she participated very different from that of her middle-class northern sister.

Although one could speculate further, it seems reasonable that the conflict for the southern woman between her identity as southerner and her identity as female was likely to produce an intensification and an important variation of the conflicts felt by women across the country. But though her style might look different from her Yankee sister's, both were dancing to someone else's music. Both confronted a cultural image of themselves that served someone else's needs. And if a particularly southern theme is community—the development and perpetuation of a group of people who share fundamental assumptions and values, likes and dislikes—then the southern woman might find, in this respect, a community of mind with other American women that spoke at times more directly to her own experience and aspirations than the southern community for which she was the focal center and crown.

But for now, let us focus on image and reality, southern womanhood and southern women. In the South, the conflict between image and reality took its purest form in the years before the Civil War. During that period, the southern lady became a walking oxymoron, gentle steel, living marble. Although the ideology depicted them as passive, submissive, and dependent symbols of leisure, these women found that actual experience involved long days of hard active work making administrative decisions that determined how the household ran. "The popular delusion is that the ante-bellum Southern woman, like Christ's lilies, 'toiled not,'" remembered Belle Kearney. "Though surrounded by the conditions for idleness she was not indolent after she became the head of her own household. Every woman sewed, often making her own dresses; the clothing of all the slaves on a plantation was cut and made by negro seamstresses under her direct supervision, even the heavy coats of the men; she ministered personally to them in cases of sickness, frequently maintaining a well managed hospital under her sole care. She was a most skillful housekeeper, though she did none of the work with her own hands, and her children grew up around her knees; however, the black 'mammy' relieved her of the actual drudgery of child-worry."[80]

Where the image had her needing the economic protection of her husband, reality found her chafing, as did Mary Boykin Chesnut, at her economic dependence. "Why feel like a beggar, utterly humiliated and degraded, when I am forced to say I need money? I cannot tell, but I do and the worst of it is, this thing grows worse as one grows older. Money ought not to be asked for, or given to a man's wife as a gift. Something must be due her, and that she should have, and with no growling as to the need of economy, nor amazement that the last supply has given out already."[81]

Where the ideal southern woman was chaste as that cake of ice, many women felt a natural physical attraction to their husbands and even possessed a "humor so earthy as to contradict the romantic tradition of universal refinement among Southern ladies," says Bell Wiley.[82] When such feelings were suppressed, it may often have been because southern women knew the consequences of sexual passion: almost yearly pregnancies for them and, for some, their husbands' philandering with black women. The fertility rate of southern women consistently exceeded that of women in New England and the Middle Atlantic states. Childbirth and diseases of reproductive organs accounted for 10 percent of the southern female deaths in the 1860 census.[83] An affectionate husband, General William Dorsey Pender, wrote to his pregnant wife in 1863 that he "did sincerely hope that you had escaped this time, but darling it must be the positive and direct will of God that it should be so." He nevertheless enclosed pills that were purported to cause abortion.[84] Yet, Scott points out, "in the face of the idealization of the family and the aura of sanctity surrounding the word 'mother,' only in private could women give voice to the misery of endless pregnancies, with attendant illness, and the dreadful fear of childbirth, a fear based on fact."[85]

Where the ideal woman lived in presumed ignorance of it, miscegenation aroused this commentary from Mary Chesnut:

> I wonder if it be a sin to think slavery a curse to any land. Men and women are punished when their masters and mistresses are brutes, not when they do wrong. Under slavery, we live surrounded by prostitutes, yet an abandoned woman is sent out of any decent house. Who thinks any worse of a Negro or mulatto woman for being a thing we can't name? God forgive us, but ours is a monstrous system, a wrong and an iniquity! Like the patriarchs of old, our men live all in one house with their wives and their concubines; and the mulattoes one sees in every family partly resemble the white children. Any lady is ready to tell you who is the father of all the mulatto children in everybody's household but her own. Those, she seems to think, drop from the clouds. My disgust sometimes is boiling over. Thank God for my country women, but alas for the men! They are probably no worse than men everywhere, but the lower their mistresses, the more degraded they must be.[86]

Where the ideal woman was a repository of culture and the arts, her actual ignorance of worldly reality (which the image called innocence) was maintained by the low quality of education available for women in the South. Though he wrote after the Civil War, A. D. Mayo here describes the prewar "miseducation" of southern girls: "Trifled with at school, [she] goes out into a hotbed of perilous flattery. From the hour when she receives her lying diploma, in a cloud of 'illusion,' . . . lifted on the tide of inflated masculine rhetoric, . . . her life wavers in a mirage of self-delusion. Out of that realm of falsehood she emerges, often too late, at thirty, with broken health, bowed under the cares of a family she is incompetent to rear . . . and the most melancholy feature of the case is that the girl is not to blame for all this, but is the victim of a system of miseducation."[87] Sarah Grimké wrote in 1852 that "the powers of my mind have never been allowed expansion; in childhood they were repressed by the false idea that a girl need not have the education I coveted."[88] Indeed she *could* not have it: even after a few female institutions tried to shape their offerings to match the men's colleges, "the greater number of southern educational institutions for women were directed at making young girls into ladies."[89] Men and women consistently supported men's institutions at the cost of women's; although the first women's colleges in the nation were founded in the South, endowments were low, and women faculty there worked longer hours for less pay and at lower rank than their male colleagues.[90]

Nevertheless, women did read—in private and at home. They read Darwin, Emerson, Margaret Fuller, Madame de Staël; they even passed copies of *Uncle Tom's Cabin* from woman to woman. Caroline Merrick, born in 1825, called Margaret Fuller D'Ossoli a "large-souled woman."[91] And they read the novels that southern women wrote: one Georgian "announced her resolution to resume the study of Latin under the inspiration of Augusta Evans' *St. Elmo*."[92] Moreover, running their households required women (like the fictional Ellen O'Hara in *Gone With the Wind*) to learn bookkeeping, healing, biology, and numerous other semiacademic skills.

The ideal woman remained a pious Protestant. And in fact evidence of any widespread (if private) religious skepticism is rare. Bell Wiley notes that, after an early resurgence of interest in the church, "during the last two years of the war ministers often complained about shrinking congregations and the waning of interest in spiritual activities." Wiley attributes this decline in women's zeal to lack of clothing, transportation, and hope for military victory.[93] Though it seems that analysis of the culture would have revealed the connection between patriarchal society and patriarchal religions (black literature consistently shows this perception) and though women clearly disliked Pauline theology, few women went so far as to leave the church. Perhaps, as Scott suggests, they needed the consolation of religion more than they wanted to see what it did to them; perhaps the perfect mesh between what God and man said about woman made religious questions taboo; perhaps the lack of education prevented the development of the habit of intellectual analysis; perhaps they believed in spite of their awareness. In any case, Scott found that "Elizabeth Avery Meriwether stood practically alone among the diary-keepers and memoirists when she asserted . . . that at an early age she had rejected immortality on her own initiative."[94]

Thus each element of the image—leisure, passivity, dependence, sexual purity, submission, ignorance (with the possible exception of piety)—failed to correspond to the reality of women's lives, and for women to undertake to match the ideal must have required creativity and persistence.

In their relations to the peculiar institution of the South, however, women were less eager to conform to the official ideology. The relations between white women and slaves were significantly different from other white-black relationships. White women took on a nurturing role, clothing and nursing the slaves as well as supervising their work. They in turn had been raised by slave women who served as mother surrogates and role-models. Irving H. Bartlett and C. Glenn Cambor have argued that the two-mother system may have perpetuated idealized southern womanhood by producing white women who are "dependent on and locked into perpetuating an authoritarian system" and hence are willing to accept the paradoxical combination of overvaluation and devaluation that characterizes the treatment of southern women. Such a system reveres the white mother yet deprives her of her sexual and maternal identity, leaving her a child-wife, and forces the black woman into a paradoxical position, strong and dependent, responsible and subservient. "Each image was paradoxical and something far less than that of a mature, autonomous, and well integrated woman," they argue; this "perpetuated the underdeveloped personality structure which we associate with the stereotyped feminine ideal," and which, in turn, responds well to external authority. It is an ideal, they note, "significantly different from the national [feminine] norm."[95]

In any case, between white woman and black there was a good deal of love and not a little hostility. The white woman's love was in part for those with whose lives she was intimately and daily connected; the hostility was in part for the fearful responsibility entailed on her by the slave relation and its attendant anxieties. Ultimately this led many southern white women privately to oppose slavery itself, a conviction far more widely spread in diaries and letters than one might expect. And, further, many white women began—also privately—to make connections between the condition of slavery and the requirements of southern womanhood.

Particularly close relationships developed between white and black women. Sarah Grimké, as usual, took her actions further than the norm: as a girl, she taught her "little waiting-maid" to write. "The light was put out, the keyhole screened, and flat on our stomachs before the fire, with the spelling-book before our eyes, we defied the laws of South Carolina." They were caught.[96] More typically, a Virginia white woman tried to free her slave woman friend Amanda and "keep her in the state, contrary to the law," because of her strong feelings for the black woman. Another went into mourning when her slave Rose died.[97]

But southern women, sensing the paradox, also hated the bondage of slaveowning. "Slaves are a continual source of trouble. . . . They are a source of more trouble to housewives than all other things, vexing them and causing much sin," said one lady to her diary. Another asked, "Will the time *ever* come for us to be free of them?" Yet another, after the war, said, "I was glad and thankful—on my own account when slavery ended, and I ceased to belong body and soul to my negroes." Both affection and distaste thus led to opposition to slavery. One woman saw that "in some mysterious way I had drunk in with my mother's milk . . . a detestation of the curse of slavery laid upon our beautiful southernland."[98] Another identifies with the male slave in her imagination: "Think what it is to be a Slave!!! To be treated not as a man but as a personal chattel . . . compelled to know that the purity of your wife and daughters is exposed without protection of law to the assault of a brutal white man!! Think of this, and all the nameless horrors that are concentrated in that one word *Slavery*."[99] Abolitionist Sarah Grimké's imagination re-creates the "women . . . bought and sold in our slave markets to gratify the brutal lust of those who bear the name of Christians. . . . if . . . a woman desires to preserve her virtue unsullied, she is either bribed or whipped into compliance, or if she dares resist her seducer, her life . . . has actually been sacrificed to the fury of disappointed passion."[100] Another confessed to her diary in 1859 that "Southern women are all, I believe, abolitionists."[101]

As southern white women began to make the connections, the vocabulary of slavery crept into their own self-description. "What a slave a holiday makes of a mistress! Indeed, she is always a slave, but doubly and trebly so at such times." "They say the Senator [Sumner] avoids matrimony. 'Slavery is the sum of all evil,' he says, so he will not reduce a woman to slavery," recounted Mary Chesnut. She added, "There is no slave, after all, like a wife." Later, she found it necessary to distinguish African slavery from other forms, since "all married women, all children and girls who live on in their fathers' houses are slaves!"[102]

Miscegenation too bound white women to black women in opposition to the bonds of slavery. "I saw slavery in its bearing on my sex," wrote Elizabeth Lyle Saxon. "I saw that it teemed with injustice and shame to all womankind and I hated it."[103] Scott elsewhere finds it significant that white women put the blame for miscegenation, not on black women, but on white men.

The effect on individual marriages of all this conflict between women and their society's central tenets must have been complicated. Hostility certainly appeared: "What a drag it is sometimes on a woman," said one usually happily married woman, "to 'lug about' the ladder upon which man plants his foot and ascends to the intellectual haven of peace in ignorance of the machinery which feeds his daily life."[104] No doubt those who saw the connection between masculine identity and the ideal of southern womanhood felt torn still more deeply when tempted to jump from the pedestal, for to do so would surely evoke a husband's anger or—for some a worse result—make him feel hurt and diminished. Actually, what is remarkable about this complex network of feeling and idea, of region, race, and sex, is that women still loved their men and men their women with this kind of love: "I would give anything to be near you or with you," wrote one woman. Her husband replied, "If it were possible I would go in quest of you." [105]

Born in 1826 near Natchez, Mississippi, Varina Howell Davis, whose husband Jefferson presided over the Confederacy, comes close to embodying the paradoxes of the image of the southern lady before and during the war. In an 1849 letter to her husband of four years, she asks him to take care of himself "for your Winnie, your thoughtless, dependent wife. . . . Winnie is Husband's baby and baby is your devoted wife, Winnie Davis." Speaking five years later of her youngest child, she sees no contradiction between being a baby and being a lady: the baby is "so soft, so good, and so very lady-like," she says. Davis opposed women's suffrage, and all her life declared she believed in the mental superiority of men.

Yet this is the same woman who, in a letter to General John S. Preston, called herself a "revolutionary," hoping he would excuse the "expression of a habitude of free thought to me so dear and intimate." She goes on to argue for a loose construction of the Confederate Constitution. Varina Davis advised her husband on military and political matters, and, according to Bell Wiley, "probably influenced him far more than he realized." Near the end of the war she realistically faced the inevitable—as apparently he could not—by selling family clothing, china, and silver, and arranging to exchange the Confederate dollars she received for gold. And while her husband was in prison after the war, she traveled to Washington to see President Johnson on his behalf. Though she "grew stronger with the passing of years," as Wiley suggests, she never rejected, challenged, or tried to reshape the image of the southern lady. [106]

Changes that occurred during and after the Civil War were largely modifications of these prewar patterns, not radical redefinitions of roles. During the Civil War, women worked in ordnance plants, textile mills, garment factories, and government offices. Aristocrat Mary Darby recalled "when pay-day came, the first time I had ever worked for wages, how mean I felt when I went up and signed for my pay. Rose Wilkinson . . . next to me . . . laughingly said, 'Never mind Mary, I too felt that way at first but you will get beautifully over the feeling and find yourself going up demanding it as your right.'" The pay, nevertheless, was lower than men's for equal work.[107] One man remembers that such women found the "habit of command" to their liking: they could not forget "how pleasant life had been when all the men were gone."[108] Many of the men who came home after the war were despondent and broken, and the women drew on their own strength to help heal their men and restore the order of society. Caroline Merrick remembered, "The women in every community seemed to far outnumber the men; and the empty sleeve and the crutch made men who had unflinchingly faced death in battle impotent to face their future."[109]

Yet these changes in the realities of southern life were merely incorporated, as we have seen, into the image of southern womanhood. The gentle lady's newly exposed steel did not automatically allow her access to education, to the professions, or to equality under the law. Yet, when they could, women maintained the independence afforded by the war. After her family's fortune had improved, one daughter was ordered home from teaching school. She "announced firmly that independence was to be preferred to a dependent respectability."[110] And another daughter, Belle Kearney, began her own school at home, as we saw.

Nevertheless, as the vitality of the Lost Cause ideologies demonstrated, the tradition of the lady was far from dead. The idea of her purity still remained crystallized in ice in 1910, when a southern white man observed that the southern white man sought sex with black women "to ease . . . in some measure the frustration that came to him through the code of conduct he himself had imposed upon his own womankind."[111] Even in 1937, John Dollard saw that the ideology had made southern white women "untouchable" and that "sexual behavior toward [them]" had to occur "against a personal sense of guilt."[112]

Domesticity, too, held its own in the postwar ideology. Although some southern women, like their northern counterparts, began in the last quarter of the century to move out of the home by means of women's organizations, nevertheless, by comparison with the North, "New Womanhood never attained a large following in the South."[113] The United Daughters of the Confederacy and other Civil War memorial organizations offered the first opportunity to organize and to locate activity outside the home with, paradoxically, the stated purpose of preserving traditions. Church auxiliaries and mission groups worked in a similar way and grew at an astounding rate: during the 1880s, membership in the Southern Methodist Woman's Board of Foreign Missions increased tenfold, from 5,890 in 1878 to 56,783 in 1888. These churchly societies began to seek reforms in the very areas one might have predicted from the prewar experience of southern women: education, labor, race. A synthetic example came in 1901 when the Methodist Woman's Board sought to add, to a black college's curriculum, a girls' industrial training program and, to its faculty, women professors. The persistence of the ideal of southern womanhood, however, was apparent in the arguments against creating the office of deaconess and, still more, when the Methodist General Conference, "without consulting the women who had built [the] organizations," in 1906 simply put the women's church societies under the control of a "male-dominated Board of Missions."[114] Such experiences led one woman to write, in 1910, that "we are in a helpless minority in a body where the membership is largely made up of men opposed to independence of thought in women."[115]

John C. Ruoff sees these postwar white southern women's organizations in concentric circles, with the least number of women involved in the central circle. The largest circle includes the church societies; next come women's clubs; third, reform organizations like the WCTU; and finally, the suffrage movement. The women's clubs that survived in a "region noted for hostility towards women's clubs,"[116]—Mrs. J. C. Croly notes that *club* was still a frightening word in 1884 in New Orleans— educated members both directly, in their literary programs, and indirectly, since they gave women a location and a communal identity separate from both house and church, the two foci of the southern patriarchy. And indeed such women's clubs were seen by southern men as a serious threat to the home, as their national historian, Mrs. Croly, implicitly notes: "Southern women are especially home-keepers. It was a tradition that they be guarded and kept from contact with the outside world. A 'club' was a plunge which carried with it only the idea of something dreadful to their minds, and particularly to the minds of the men of their families."[117]

If literary clubs seemed threatening, reform organizations were even more so. As Scott has demonstrated, the reform interests of southern women in the Women's Christian Temperance Union widened from alcohol abuse to venereal disease, infant mortality, labor conditions, prison conditions, and, ultimately, suffrage. Yet clearly the prescription remained, and with it the life behind a mask: the WCTU "provided a respectable framework in which southern women could pursue their own development and social reform without drastically offending the prevailing views of the community about ladylike behavior."[118]

Similarly, arguments against suffrage—like Holland's—"drew heavily on the old image of southern woman in danger of becoming unfeminine if she dared to step out of her natural sphere."[119] Ruoff contends that the women in his most radical circle went beyond the pale for southern ladies, violating the "basic canons of Southern Womanhood by leaving the home and addressing crowds. Such activities tended to undermine the basis of authority and stability in society."[120] Certainly suffrage was unsuccessful in the South, and the ERA has to date fared no better. In a predictable paradox, it was a southern woman who engineered the Republican party's 1980 platform decision to drop support for the ERA. Nevertheless, many southern women tried various tactics, including the appeal to racism, to win support for the vote. Again the paradox appears: southern women argued that the radical step of women voting needed to be taken to maintain the status quo ante bellum in the South. And whether from a belief in that southern ideology or from a sense of the strategic, some women turned publicly against blacks as a race, despite a history of more complex relationships. Certainly the necessity for suffragists to appear at all times like ladies was seen directly, clearly, and repeatedly as the sine qua non of the southern strategy.

Though these organizations permitted some steps outside the home, they were small and tentative ones, taken with decorum. The virtue of dependence, like domesticity irrelevant during the war, reasserted itself after the war as an ideal. Although many women did go to work to earn money because of postwar poverty and because so many southern men had died or been disabled during the war, their choice of work was severely restricted. The respectable professions for women—teaching, sewing, and writing—all "took on some of the respectability of the home, and far from challenging traditional role models tended to support them." Moreover, teachers and authors were told or encouraged to follow formulae—rote teaching, sentimental plotting—that effectively quashed the potential to provoke thought, putting these women instead into the service of tradition. Even during the period 1870–1900, in the "kinds of jobs liable to be held by white women of the middle and upper classes, the South continued to lag well behind the North in the number and proportion of women engaged."[121] In 1910, 7.4 percent of the working women in the South were in white-collar occupations, compared to 16.4 percent nationally. By 1940, those percentages had moved to 30.5 percent and 41.5 percent, respectively. And the birthrate in both rural and urban South was the highest in the nation in 1910.[122] As long as the sole justification for women working was necessity, and as long as southern men found their pride in supporting their women, little change could be expected.

Despite the perpetuation in force of the old ideology of southern womanhood, education for women did show some growth in two direc-

tions. Normal schools developed to prepare women for the vocation
of teaching, and a few liberal arts colleges for women began to set
down roots. Such education—rote though it often was—did establish a
groundwork for women to work for money in the professions. But by
1910, only 1 out of 28 women college students in the nation was a
southerner; by 1942 the ratio was 1 in 8.[123] One southern woman who
did receive a man's education at the University of North Carolina at
Chapel Hill spent the rest of her life, according to her daughter, "forever
discontented with the ordinary round of women's activity." "Too much
mental activity in a woman is still considered a nuisance," wrote Hope
Summerell Chamberlain in 1938. In her mother's day, "it was a monstrous excrecence [sic] upon a womanly personality. Accordingly, neither then nor later did Mother talk much of her mental excursions."[124]

Change was slow. Many women continued to identify with the image; one argued against suffrage because, she said, women in Louisiana did not need the ballot to "protect any of our just rights and privileges. . . . Every Southern woman has a protection and champion in
every Southern man."[125] Only in 1979 did Louisiana rewrite the classi-
fication of husband as "head and master" of the household. And when
women did get the vote, many of the women leaders in the South discovered themselves shut out of power, while lawmakers instead "reared
up" artificial rubberstamp women as leaders, "not to lead women but to
fool them."[126] Between the extremes of collaboration and open rebellion,
many women still chose a middle ground behind the mask: "In public,
women continued to defer to men [in the Progressive movement], but
in their private correspondence they described their own efforts as
more practical than those of men."[127]

Time after time, both optimistically and pessimistically, individuals
have argued that the southern lady tradition is dead. Nell Battle Lewis,
an outspoken North Carolina feminist and journalist, believed it was
over in 1925: "The idol, thank God, is broken beyond repair. For, graceful though it may have been, romantic though it certainly was, it was
only an image after all. And whatever its artificial beauty, it lacked the
beauty of life. In its place is a woman of flesh and blood, not a queen nor
a saint nor a symbol, but a human being with human faults and human
virtues, a woman still only slowly rising to full stature, but with the sun
of freedom on her face."[128] Lewis' vision was optimistic. As Scott says,
and as contemporary experience shows, the image "live[s] on," at the
least as a style to "ward off criticism of unladylike independence or to
please men."[129] Ruoff's emphasis is the correct one: "stability," he contends, "was the dominant theme [in the years he covers, between the
Civil War and World War I]. Those changes which did occur were

largely within the context of Southern Womanhood rather than in opposition to it." [130]

The life of Jessie Daniel Ames, as told by her biographer, Jacquelyn
Hall, shows both the possibilities and the limits of southern womanhood during the early twentieth century. Ames consciously used—and
modified—the image of the southern lady for political and for personal
purposes, to fight racism and to forge her own identity. She always
thought of herself as a lady and used ladylike tactics. Yet she is remembered now because she organized, administered, and shaped an organization that spoke for four million southern white women who opposed
lynching. In the twenties, these women "articulated an ideal of interracial female solidarity grounded in shared maternal values. In the 1930s,
they based a dramatic disavowal of the 'false chivalry' of lynching on
the use and modification of the symbolism of the southern lady."

Born in East Texas in 1883, Ames married at twenty and by thirty-
one was a widow with three children. She returned to her hometown,
helped her mother in business there, and plunged into suffrage work.
By 1919 she had become the first president of Texas' League of Women
Voters. While working for reform legislation, her concern for the condition of black people grew, and by 1929 she was director of woman's
work for the South-wide Commission on Interracial Cooperation. And
in 1930, seeing in lynching "cultural assumptions as degrading to
white women as they were oppressive to blacks," [131] she founded the Association of Southern Women for the Prevention of Lynching, a "sub-
versive affair," Lillian Smith called it, as "decorously conducted as an
afternoon walk taken by the students of a Female Institute." [132]

Unlike the Confederate woman Varina Davis, Ames increasingly saw
and consciously sought to revise the limits of southern womanhood,
particularly in its connotations of fragility, helplessness, and dependence. Ames and her women reforged some of the bonds of southern
womanhood that had brought black slave and white mistress together
before the Civil War.

Having gained control of the image, Ames fought efforts of men in
the antilynching campaign to use the image in other and sometimes
insulting ways, yet she did not directly challenge the image itself. Lillian Smith notes that ASWPL ladies were "conventional, highly 'moral'
women, who would not have dreamed of breaking the letter of their
marriage vows or, when not married, their technical chastity." And
along with the prewar closeness of black and white women, the ambiguities of those relationships also reemerged in this movement; white
women tended to mix "maternalistic," sometimes noblesse oblige, attitudes with a "hint of identification." Finally characteristic of women of

this period, Hall says, they were "prepared by habit and experience to act out their discontents and moral impulses not through solitary intellectual effort, career ambitions, explicitly feminist protest, or private rebelliousness, but through church-based female institutions." Ames died in 1972, "virtually unnoticed," yet having seen another group of southern white women unite in opposition to racial (and eventually sexual) discrimination, inspired by liberal theology in the churches, in the civil rights movement in the South.[133]

To have a voice is to have some control over one's environment. To have the vote, for example, is to have a voice in and therefore some power over the political world. But in another sense—a sense familiar to writers—to have a voice is to have a self. Learning to express the self in language is intimately related to learning to be. Thus voicelessness may imply selflessness both in the familiar and in the more sinister meaning. For southern women, particularly, the quality of voice reveals the condition of selfhood. With the exception of outspoken women like the Grimkés and psychological mutes like the little convent girl in Grace King's story of that name, southern women speak through the mask. As an element in the ideal, talking became a social skill, not a means of self-expression. The relationship between Kate Chopin's "inward life which questions" and the "outward existence which conforms"[134]—a relationship whose companionability can be eased by language—is therefore complicated for these women by their felt need to sustain the divided self. To be "fearlessly direct"—as Gabriella soon learns in Ellen Glasgow's novel—is to be impossibly vulnerable. Thus much that went on behind the mask remained unuttered—unuttered, that is, in the larger world. Ernest Groves suggested in 1928 that "the rapidity with which women have aged in the past, their invalidism, mental breakdown and early death have been in part because of the strain of concealing irritation that was not permitted self-expression."[135] Even if written in diaries or letters, as long as those feelings and perceptions remained limited to the woman's private world, they could have little significant effect on the man's public world.

If, then, "open complaint about their lot was not the custom among southern ladies,"[136] it was in part because those ladies well recognized the penalty for serious public speaking. To speak out against speechlessness was literally as well as logically impossible, even for those who, like Delia W. Jones, gathered together the courage to try. Arguing that "in addition to [women's] known and confessed ability to *talk*, we would also like to *think*, and be taught how to direct thought so as to *talk* more wisely," she prepared a speech favoring education for women for the

North Carolina Education Association in 1859. But since she was a
woman she was not allowed to deliver her paper herself: a man spoke
for her.[137]

Southern white men recognized the power of language, as the laws
against slaves learning to read and write demonstrate. Scott tells the
story of the antebellum minister "who had refused permission for a
woman's prayer meeting on the ground that if the women were alone,
'who knows what they would pray for?'"[138] More common than his
blunt honesty was reference to biblical precedents. In 1888 a Virginia
gentleman argued against allowing Baptist women to form a group: "An
independent organization of women naturally tends toward a violation
of divine interdict against woman's becoming a public religious teacher
and leader—a speaker before mixed assemblies, a platform declaimer, a
pulpit proclaimer, street preacher, lyceum lecturer, stump orator, *et id
omne genus.*"[139] The reference, time and again, is to Paul.

Predictably, women found it terrifying at first to speak out. That antebellum minister mentioned above had no cause to fear a South Carolina
Presbyterian group when they prayed together, because the women at
first were "so shy that they could only recite the Lord's Prayer in unison.
[But] they soon grew bolder. They progressed to sentence prayers, delivered seriatim, until finally more than half of them were willing to lead
the prayer."[140] Later, the WCTU gave women the chance to go much further: to give public speeches. In one state, the WCTU was thought to
have "brought hundreds of Georgians to recognize the fact that woman
could speak in public and not only retain her womanly dignity and gra-
ciousness but become in the hands of God a mighty agency for good."[141]
Women's clubs, too, permitted speech: Mrs. J. C. Croly remembers
"that clubless past of our grandmothers. Have you ever considered their
voiceless condition, and been thankful in your day and generation?"[142]

This early optimism that speaking in public with seriousness could
remain consistent with southern womanhood was not borne out entirely by experience, as the "real" suffrage leaders, cited earlier, learned.
The inconsistency is implied in Belle Kearney's description of northerner Julia Ward Howe, speaking on "Woman's Work" in New Orleans.
Kearney was interested in the subject of Howe's talk: "Since beginning
to teach, every question that relates to the attainments and possibilities
of women was of intense interest to me." But Howe was also the first
woman Kearney had heard speak before the public, so she listened and
watched with special concentration. "For many years an earnest desire
had possessed me to behold a genuinely strong-minded woman,—one
of the truly advanced type. Beautiful to realise she stood before me! and
in a position the very acme of independence—upon a platform deliver-

ing a speech!"[143] But as long as the tradition of southern womanhood required dependence, submission, and deference, southern women would find it hard to retain the image yet speak the truth out loud. When Caroline Merrick delivered a speech supporting women's suffrage before the Louisiana Constitutional Convention in 1897 at the age of seventy-two, she was "scared almost to death!" She proposed that her son-in-law read the speech for her. But when a friend pointed out that "you do not wish a man to represent you at the polls; represent yourself now, if you only stand up and move your lips." She replied, "I will. You are right."[144]

In the light of the tradition of women's silence, then, Binx Bolling's assuring Kate that she "won't have to say a word" may have less than therapeutic effect. Certainly many southern women, though they have a reputation for gracious social employment of language, have remained in some sense like Kate, speechless by choice. One way to circumvent the barrier between private thought and public utterance, between diary and platform, is fiction. Fiction seems to offer its own excuses; after all, it's only a story. Seen in this light, fiction can become a strategy for speaking truths publicly—but only for those who choose to hear and believe that stories can be true.

Southern women exploited the possibilities of fiction as a mask just as they did, in life, the mask of southern womanhood. In the plots, a heroine's rebellious urge toward autonomy could be punished at the end or placed behind the veil of an acceptable formula. Many novels and stories contain a split between two sets of values, corresponding to the private and public selves of their southern women authors. And many heroines who were authors, "like the authors themselves, retreated behind pseudonyms, into asylums, or within cities when they took up the pen." Or an author could disguise her economic independence and intellectual assertiveness by working at home, refusing public attention, and thus maintaining a "womanly" life style. Though with time authors become more self-conscious as artists and their works show fewer splits, still the "independent, self-declarative life of the writer"[145] places the woman who writes into a special class that is in certain respects outside the norms of southern society, even southern literary society. Disproportionately few marry; still fewer have children—and such expectations form the very marrow of the tradition of the southern lady. Yet the South has always welcomed and praised its women writers—Grace King, who never married, nevertheless became the center of New Orleans' cultural community.

The woman writer in the South, then, participates in a tradition that defines her ideal self in ways that must inevitably conflict with her very integrity as an artist: voicelessness, passivity, ignorance. Some writers, like the Grimkés, simply defy the definition. Some, like Augusta Evans, shape the truth of their stories into an artifice of convention. Some, like Kate Chopin, find in the conflict the material for a masterpiece. And, like all writers everywhere, each seeks to find and articulate her individual voice in the face of the terrible pressure toward uniformity, by seeking and speaking with the authority of her experience.

Sandra Gilbert and Susan Gubar, in their important book *The Madwoman in the Attic*, argue persuasively that all women writers experience a radical "anxiety of authorship," anxiety focused not, like that of men who write, on conflict with a literary father, but on the act of writing itself. Gilbert and Gubar show first that the Western tradition has defined the writer on the basis of sex, as a paternal ruler of the fictive world he makes and therefore owns: the author is, in short, a patriarch, the pen a penis. Her very body, then, suggests to the woman that she cannot "author." Moreover, the male writer creates plots that reflect male experience and images of woman that reflect male hopes and fears. When the female would-be writer reads those texts, she sees herself as either an angel, frozen into the selfless attitude of an objet d'art and forever worshipped, or extruded into an ugly and filthy monster, forever hated and feared. The woman who writes must therefore find her own plot, her own images, and her own voice. And that plot is the *quest* for her plot, her story, her self. Yet because they must survive within a patriarchal society, women writers may "attempt to transcend their anxiety of authorship by *revising* male genres, using them to record their own dreams and their own stories *in disguise*," producing literary works that are palimpsestic as a "necessary evasion." [146]

Gilbert and Gubar built upon the earlier work of several other feminist literary scholars, among them Elaine Showalter. In *A Literature of Their Own*, Showalter articulates her understanding of women's writings as the productions of a female literary subculture. As has happened in other subcultures, such as black America, she argues, women's writings have undergone three stages (at least in nineteenth- and early twentieth-century England): "First, there is a prolonged phase of *imitation* of the prevailing modes of the dominant tradition, and *internalization* of its standards of art and its views on social roles. Second, there is a phase of *protest* against these standards and values and *advocacy* of minority rights and values, including a demand for autonomy. Finally, there is a phase of *self-discovery*, a turning inward freed from some of the dependence of opposition, a search for identity." Showalter calls these stages "feminine," "feminist," and "female." [147] Gilbert and

Gubar concern themselves in their volume with writers of the "feminine" stage who have imperfectly internalized the dominant values and hence protest, but do it covertly.

Having baldly summarized these complex and important ideas, let us now look briefly at the history of southern women writers. Do the concepts of "anxiety of authorship" and palimpsestic art, of subcultural persistence and the stages of evolution help to clarify the life behind the southern woman's mask? Asked another way, are southern women writers part of the female subculture's mainstream? What follows is speculative and suggestive.

There is reason to answer *no.* As writers, southern white women have had an active and highly visible history since colonial times. In numbers alone they outdistanced men before the Civil War. They held their own literary revival of sorts after the war, contributed significantly to the local color movement, and shared fully and richly in a long Southern Renaissance that, some say, is still with us. Moreover, as we saw, the community in the South has historically accepted and praised its women writers. Yet enthusiasm for their high percentage of southern literary efforts must be dampened by a recognition of southern literary expectations.

The relationship between literature and sexuality took a different shape in the South from that in New England, a shape that reflects a differing image of the man. Already we have seen the southern gentleman defined as gentle and genteel, leisurely and cultivated, a lover of beauty, goodness, and grace. In those respects, he resembles more nearly the southern—indeed the Western—notion of womanhood than he does the patriarch. Moreover, pushed out of the main currents of American history, defeated in battle, the southern gentlemen shared a powerlessness with northern clergy that, as Ann Douglas showed in *The Feminization of American Culture,* linked the clergy in an alliance with women.[148] Although one response of the southern elite might have been a strong assertion of literary authority, in fact the reverse took place, for reasons that will become clearer shortly. Instead, women became not only the perfect embodiments of beauty—Jay Hubbell lists numerous southern male writers, including Edgar Allan Poe and Mark Twain, who exhibit something "akin to the Renaissance literary worship of woman as embodying the spirit of beauty and goodness"[149]—but also the appropriate vehicles for the expression of beauty in language. Gentlemen learned to appreciate a beautiful poem by a beautiful woman.

The difficulty, as one might guess, lay in the definition of beauty implicit in the dominant southern culture. Like the lovely creature who best represented and naturally created it, beauty was fragile and ethe-

real, or sensuous and pleasurable, but it was finally irrelevant to the serious business of life. In 1850, Henry Timrod complained that in the
South "literature is still regarded as an epicurean amusement; not as a
study, at least equal in importance, and certainly not inferior in difficulty, to law and medicine." [150] Poe shows in "Israfel" his despair at the
failure of beauty to enter the world of human experience; he further
connects beauty with women in contradistinction to life in his theory
that the highest beauty is the death of a beautiful woman. And Ellen
Glasgow later called the southern attitude, as C. Hugh Holman says, a
"'confederacy of hedonism,' a kind of refusal to use literature seriously,
or to view it as a serious vocation. Literature was almost an avocation to
the [male] Southern writer before the Civil War, something that he did
for ladies' books." [151] It is plausible that a man's taking literature seriously would threaten still more profoundly his already ambiguous
sense of sexual identity, an ambiguity whose anxiety he staved off
by worshipping woman and deferring to her mysterious beauty and
goodness.

Whatever the relationship between literature and sexuality, that between literature and southern slaveholding society left little likelihood
that southern men, patriarchs on the plantation, would undertake the
rule of the republic of letters. The early South's lack of literature has
been attributed to the South's lack of interest in the movement to forge
a national literature; the South's failure to develop its own publishing
firms and successful magazines; and the southern man's life, busy with
plantation and politics, spending his linguistic time on eloquence, not
writing. On a more profound level, as Louis Rubin has suggested, the
avoidance of creating serious literature paralleled an avoidance of the
moral ambiguities of the slaveholder's experience. Serious contemporary literature forces the writer to face his or her experience; southern
white men turned to the tested classics, to paeans to the South, and to
what they saw as the beautifully safe and patriotic productions of the
ladies, in these ways tacitly refusing to explore their own lives.

Lewis Simpson has appropriated Eugene Genovese's interpretation
of the world the slaveholders made in order to understand the literary
Sahara that was the South. Genovese's belief, as we saw, is that the
southern patriarchal and paternalistic ethos developed not from the European inheritance but from "the plantation regime itself. The confrontation of master and slave, white and black, on a plantation presided over by a resident planter for whom the plantation was a home
and the entire population part of his extended family generated that
ethos." Moreover, Genovese insists, the absence of the cash nexus from
human relationships—"to have a world without marketplace values,

you must have a world without a marketplace at its center"—and the substitution of organic, personal, human relationships offers a critique of bourgeois society that "still [has] something to offer" us. (Interestingly, Genovese's chart contrasting bourgeois marketplace society assumptions with those of the slave society could almost be labeled—at least for New England—the contrast between male values and those assigned to the female, with "male" substituting for "bourgeois." For instance, bourgeois "possessive individualism" upholds freedom from dependence, a "masculine" value, whereas the slave society, as Genovese sees it, endorses dependence—clearly a "feminine" value. The bourgeois can alienate his capacity to labor, as a man can work, but in the slave society [says Genovese] one can alienate all of himself—as can a woman in marriage. Although the parallels are here simplified and approximate, they are suggestive enough once again to connect the southern male slaveholder with the imagery of American womanhood.) [152]

Simpson picks up Genovese's threads to note that "the pursuit of the 'Confederate Dream' meant a drastic repudiation of the artistic and literary tradition of Western literature." In his "quest for an independent intellect" grounded in his "unique historical community," the southern man of letters cut himself off from his "proper home in the Republic of Letters" and withdrew from "the homeland of the western literary mind . . . the source of literary authority and fraternity." Despite the consequent loss of the dialectic between European tradition and American modernity, Simpson concludes, the southern writer discovered in the plantation ethos the central theme of that dialectic: the "nature of man in relation to community . . . in the recognition that the intricate bonds of community may be as much of hate as of love." [153] Simpson's theory helps to explain the lack of a need in the South for a national literature as well as the lack of parallelism in the development of southern and "American" literature. Yet it is apparent that Simpson speaks exclusively of the male writer in the South: the very language, "authority" and "fraternity," demonstrates this. Nevertheless, the argument once again locates in the history of southern literary men an experience analogous in certain respects to that of Western literary women: cut off from the Western tradition, seeking to develop their own subcultural ethos, they produced—partly as a result of these pressures—what is almost universally called flawed literature.

Finally, though, the similarities between southern men and Western women fade in the light of the difference made by a rigid southern patriarchy that subjected women, blacks, children, and nonslaveholding white men to the control and authority of the slaveholding man. If only in his subculture, he ruled patriarchally. And if that authority was not exerted in writing literature, it appears in the equation of woman, beauty, literature, and irrelevance. Handing women literary control meant little loss of power if such authority could not extend to addressing significant realities of experience, and if instead it had to be spent in defending the South or indulging in feeble and decorative romanticism of the kind that led Paul Hamilton Hayne to attack "subliterary novels of Southern women" as "The Fungous School."[154]

Thus southern white men, struggling, for the most part probably unconsciously, with their own conflicts, never defined themselves as literary authorities in the manner of a Milton or even an Emerson. Nevertheless, because they retained cultural dominance, they could call the very making of contemporary literature trivial—or worship it, and then go on their way, Lillian Smith might add, to the trails behind the big house. Ellen Glasgow was to call this habit "evasive idealism" and spend a lifetime exposing it.

For these reasons, then, southern women have avoided in certain respects the "anxiety of authorship" and instead felt the ambivalence of being central to a fundamentally nonserious literary tradition. Despite the ambivalence, the rewards for women writers were several. Women could and did in fact write for money, in great numbers, and for this activity receive the acclaim of their communities, male and female. In this way a tradition of female authorship developed, complete with supportive ties among women writers across time and space. Jay Hubbell, historian of southern literature and always a sympathetic reporter of the role of literary women, pointed out in 1954 that "the numerous Southern women writers who emerged in the [eighteen] forties and fifties continued to write after the war, and their influence is seen in the work of the women writers who followed them."[155] One indication of the continuity of that tradition appears in the numerous anthologies of southern women writers edited by southern women—to name only two, Mrs. Julia D. Freeman published in 1860 (as "Mary Forrest") *Women of the South Distinguished in Literature*; and Mrs. Mary T. Tardy, as "Ida Raymond," produced *Southland Writers* in 1870, reprinted in 1872 as *Living Female Writers of the South*. Southern women made a practice of editing their foremothers' diaries and journals. And they have been central to southern literary groups. Frances Newman and Emily Clark, with other women and men, formed a group around *The Reviewer* in Richmond in the 1920s; Josephine Pinckney and Beatrice Ravenel were active in the 1920s South Carolina Poetry Society. And, interestingly, one particular figure—the image of the strong, imaginative, and experienced woman as teacher—can be found in the literature of southern women from the diary of Mary Chesnut to the fiction of Eudora Welty.

These southern women writers, however, did not limit their literary self-definition to the South. They turned to England for models; they chose Elizabeth Barrett Browning's *Aurora Leigh* and Charlotte Brontë's *Jane Eyre*, Fanny Burney and Maria Edgeworth. More remarkably, many southern women looked North to read *Uncle Tom's Cabin* and Emerson, by no means always unsympathetically. Which brings the argument full circle: for southern women found an identity, not just with women outside the South, but with the very books their brothers hated. Here may be located another thread in the curious paradox of southern women, conservative as an ideal and often radical in feeling, soft and gentle in manner with a vein of iron within. Figures are impossible here, of course, but one can suggest the outlines of a tradition of liberalism—often veiled rather than direct—in southern women's writings. It is a tradition that grew in the soil of the South's historical endorsement of southern women as writers and of the southern woman's own rejection of the tradition of patriarchy. Its hallmarks include the critique, implicit or direct, of racial and sexual oppression, of the hierarchical caste and class structures that pervade cultural institutions, and of the evasive idealism that pushes reality aside. And it parallels the tradition of southern women in radical social action that Jacquelyn Hall and Sara Evans discuss.

One early piece of evidence of this tradition might be Angelina Weld's "Appeal to the Christian Women of the Southern States." In it, Weld develops an argument based on strong women models, on female courage and truth-telling, on a rational reading of the Bible. And—despite her geographical distance—she addresses a community whose bonds as women she still shares, unlike the connection she has severed with the slaveholding South.[156] That tradition would be carried on by Kate Chopin, in her treatment of women's sexuality and freedom, and by Ellen Glasgow, who, "for want of other explanation, sometimes thought she was born a rebel."[157]

Yet this more liberal tradition is only part of the female mind of the South. More often, anything that felt radical was suppressed, masked, or transformed into the familiar paradox of the strong southern woman arguing for her own fragility. The purpose of this book is to begin drafting a map of that mind, searching in the fiction for patterns of imagery, characterization, plotting, narrative stance, and theme that seem to persist over time and over various regions of the South.

Many of the works discussed here have never been examined with much care or with an eye to the probable effects of sexual and regional identity. I have therefore looked at short stories and novels written by these seven women with the tools both of close analysis and of feminist criticism. It might be argued that the very fact that the seven women studied here wrote fiction at all separates them from the majority for whom they presumably speak and binds them together as artists in ways more significant than even sex or race or region. This is in fact unlikely, given their professional attitudes toward writing and their personal roles as southern women writers, both of which tended to blur the distinctions between life and art. Thus an interpretive historical and biographical study of each writer accompanies the critical analysis. The relationships among various writers' themes that emerge in the art thus are placed into a context that should show how close to their experience as southern women these writers found the sources of their fiction.

I have chosen writers who span the South spatially and temporally, yet who focus in the works here discussed on the nature of southern womanhood. And I stopped before I came to probably the finest of all, the writers of the Southern Renaissance and beyond, such as Eudora Welty, Flannery O'Connor, Katherine Anne Porter, and Lillian Hellman. For I wanted, in this book, to search out their roots.

The writers and their works are, in chronological order, Augusta Jane Evans' *Beulah* (1859); Grace King's *Monsieur Motte*, "Bonne Maman," and "The Little Convent Girl" (1886 and 1888; 1886; 1893); Kate Chopin's *The Awakening* (1899); Mary Johnston's *Hagar* (1913); Ellen Glasgow's *Virginia* (1913) and *Life and Gabriella* (1916); Frances Newman's *The Hard-Boiled Virgin* (1926) and *Dead Lovers Are Faithful Lovers* (1928); and Margaret Mitchell's *Gone With the Wind* (1936). Other novelists during the period and other works by most of these writers could and should be studied. Some introductory words about the lives of these writers, then, should help to explain why these women were chosen.

All of the writers in this study were white, and all southern, both by birth and by continued residence. All came from upper-middle-class families, as indicated by their fathers' professions: four were lawyers, three businessmen. They represent (with the caveat that Louisiana is, in some ways, like no other southern state) what Hugh Holman calls the "three Souths"—the Tidewater, the Piedmont, and the Deep South.[158] Glasgow and Johnston were Virginians; Newman, Mitchell, and Evans Georgians; King was a lifelong Louisianian, and Chopin spent her married life (and set most of her fiction) there. Three were born before the Civil War, four after; Margaret Mitchell, the last, was born as the century turned. Almost to a woman, their childhoods were in significant ways unsettled: the father died, the family lost its money, or the mother died. Most were Protestants. Chopin, however, was raised a Catholic, Glasgow and Mitchell turned away from religion, and Johnston moved into mysticism. Their educations varied from Catholic to public schools; three were educated at home, and more helped themselves to their fathers' libraries to educate themselves. Four never married; Mitchell married twice and had no children; Chopin's husband died after twelve years of marriage and six children; and Evans married late (aged thirty-three) to a man twenty-seven years older than herself. Almost to a woman, they traveled—to New York and to Europe, for the most part. Yet all of them stayed, sometimes reluctantly, citizens of the South. These writers provide, then, a composite for the typical experience of the southern white woman of some means.

Three subjects, however, need to be explored more deeply: their identification with the South, their views on being artists, and their attitudes towards domesticity and womanhood. Almost every writer felt a strong regional identification, sometimes with the specific section of the South that was hers, but always with the idea of the South, the South as a region of mind. Augusta Evans wrote the fervidly pro-Confederate *Macaria* (1863) and indicated in letters her pro-South loyalty. Despite the fact that her fiction lent itself to characterization as "local" (New Orleans) color, Grace King repeatedly expressed her identification with the cause of the South in her autobiography, *Memories of a Southern Woman of Letters* (1932). Perhaps because she spent much of her life in St. Louis, Kate Chopin never showed a deep loyalty to the South—as some indication, she never worked seriously with historical fiction—yet the importance of the region is clear in more subtle ways in her fiction. Ellen Glasgow set out to write a "social history" of Virginia, revealing there and in her prefaces to the Old Dominion edition of her novels (1929) that she considered herself to be as clearly southern as she was female. Mary Johnston, too, showed by writing fiction about the Civil War how her regional identity counted. Frances Newman's novels repeatedly use the term *southern lady* and pit southern ladies against those of other regions. And Margaret Mitchell, of course, found her subject in her region; her letters and interviews, too, reveal an absorbing concern with being a southerner. However they manifested them, all of these women found their identities strongly shaped by their region; however angry or despairing about its limitations, they never entirely lost their loyalty to the South.

In the light of the ambiguous position of the southern woman writer, it is interesting to speculate as to why these women wrote. Almost all gave publicly stated reasons for beginning to write that had nothing to do with their own desires, talents, or powers. And when it came to getting a book published, or dealing with copyright difficulties, or working out contracts, or collecting royalties, from Evans to Mitchell they often relied on men as "fronts." Evans' first book was written as a gift for her father; she later persisted in claiming a moral purpose as primary for her work. King said that she wrote her first story (when she was thirty-two) because Richard Watson Gilder, editor of *Century* magazine and publisher of much of George W. Cable's work, challenged her to do what she claimed George Washington Cable did not: portray the South accurately. Chopin began to write when she was thirty-seven, only after her husband had died; she virtually stopped following the public rejection of *The Awakening*, only ten years later. Glasgow, unusual in this sense, said in her memoirs that she had wanted to write as early as the age of seven. Johnston began writing because her family needed money, as Evans' family had earlier. Newman began writing as young as age ten; she later confessed that she cultivated her intelligence because she thought she was physically unattractive. Mitchell provides most clearly the paradox for the southern woman writer: although she wrote naturally from the time she could write at all, continuing to produce plays, stories, novelettes, and novels through much of her life, she said that she never made any effort to publish. Moreover, when she married John Marsh, she quit her job as a journalist. She began *Gone With the Wind* only, she claimed, because she had an ankle injury; her husband complained that she had read all the books in the library and would have to write one if she wanted to continue to read during her convalescence. And *Gone With the Wind* was published only after it was almost wrested from her hands.

Nearly every writer, then, gave a public reason for writing that had little to do with conscious decision; this may indicate their perception of the ignominy attached to the serious woman writer. Yet almost every writer in this group (Newman is the exception) wrote very popular books; Mitchell's is still close to the all-time bestseller. The fact that they received wide readership indicates that the writers in some ways expressed and reinforced the popular sentiments of their times. With some novels, at least, they touched a pulse that beat in the body social; like most popular novelists, they may have soothed instead of measuring it. Certainly they were, with the exception of one or two writers and one or two novels, part and parcel of the culture they described. They did not deviate enough—despite stepping outside the role in order to publish—either to receive the anathema of the community or, quite possibly, to write excellent fiction. Yet precisely because, unlike Sarah Grimké, they kept their roots in the South, these writers better represent the mind of the southern woman.

Domesticity was the cornerstone of all the other "virtues" of southern womanhood, not only because leaving the home might present experiences that would crumble the rest of the image, but also because of the southern emphasis on family and kinship for identity. Thus it is important to see how these writers handled, in their lives, the ideas of family and home. Although none of them fully participated in the female norm of marriage and motherhood, most found the extended family essential to their own psychic happiness. And most set up homes in which relatives, real or surrogate, lived.

Evans always lived with members of her family, first her own parents, then her husband and stepdaughter, and, after her husband's death, with her brother. When King traveled, it was invariably with a sister or to stay with a family—the Warners, the Clemenses. And when she was in New Orleans, she stayed in the family home with her parents and, after their deaths, with her sisters. Chopin married at nineteen and produced, unlike the others, her own "home." Yet even while Oscar Chopin lived, she refused to play the role of housewife, taking "long, solitary jaunts," smoking cigarettes, dressing unconventionally, rejecting the literal typical home in a different manner. With the exception of five years in New York, Glasgow lived in her family home in Richmond and relied for years on her sister Cary for emotional support. Johnston lived with her family after her mother died when she was nineteen; she took over the household and traveled extensively with her father until his death. Then she and two sisters built a home in Warm Springs, Virginia, where she lived until her death. Newman lived most of her life in Atlanta, setting up house with her black "mammy" and her nephew, for whom she was a guardian. Mitchell withdrew from Smith College when her mother died; she came home to run the household for her father and brother and stayed there even after she married Berrien K. Upshaw. Later she left the family home to live in a series of apartments with her second husband, but she never left Atlanta, where her father continued to make demands on her time and attention until his death.

Thus, although these women varied from the norm either by not marrying, by not having children, or by modifying the typical family and home, they all participated in the southern valuation of both by creating some form of family arrangement, often with their "kinfolks."

Women writers typically vary from the norm that a woman marry and have children. In *Silences*, Tillie Olsen cites woman writer after writer who, in the last century and until very recently in this, never married or, if married, was childless. Those who married either did so late or had servants. Olsen ascribes this correlation not to the "moldy" theory that babies are woman's true art (hence writing a substitution for the childless), but to the training of all Western women to "place others' needs first, to feel these needs as their own," and to the special circumstance of mothering, which is being "instantly interruptible, responsive, responsible." [159] These seven southern women writers, with the help of southern traditions of family networks, managed to live out a form of domesticity that gave them freedom to write yet kept them with their kin.

All of these women wrestled in the fiction to be examined here with their own condition and character as southern women, with the expectations implicit in the ideal of the southern lady, and with what was for them the acutely paradoxical nature of writing itself. For most of them, Dixie's Diadem felt more like a burden than a charm. As Jessie Daniel Ames put it, somewhat melodramatically, "the crown of chivalry . . . has been pressed like a crown of thorns on our heads." [160]

CHAPTER II   # Augusta Jane Evans
Paradise Regained

During the period 1820–1870 and beyond, "woman's fiction," or "sentimental," or "domestic" fiction, was written by a dozen or so American
women—one of them Augusta Jane Evans—for an eager audience of
other American women. The novels were overwhelmingly popular, and
through this movement, "authorship in America was established as a
woman's profession, and reading as a woman's avocation."[1]

These novels and novelists were the target of attacks both from serious writers, like Nathaniel Hawthorne, and from genteel moralists.

Constance Fenimore Woolson, writing to Paul Hamilton Hayne concerning a novel (*Infelice*) by Augusta Jane Evans, asked, "What in the world *can* any cultivated reader see in that mass of words, words, words?"[2] Explaining to his publisher why he wanted to stay abroad, Hawthorne wrote as one reason to William Ticknor that "America is now wholly given over to a d—d mob of scribbling women, and I should have no chance of success while the public taste is occupied with their trash—and should be ashamed of myself if I did succeed. What is the mystery of these innumerable editions of the 'Lamplighter,' and other books neither better nor worse?—worse they could not be, and better they need not be, when they sell by the 100,000." But it was not just the marketplace that troubled Hawthorne. He objected, too, because "generally women write like emasculated men, and are only to be distinguished from male authors by greater feebleness and folly."[3] If Hawthorne did not know the "mystery" of these novels' success, the American Library Association thought it did, and found the writing anything but feeble. In an 1881 national survey of authors who were "sometimes excluded from public libraries for reason of sensational or immoral qualities," ten of the nineteen on the list who wrote for adults were domestic novelists. Among them was Augusta Jane Evans, now Wilson.[4]

This apparently paradoxical contemporary response—the attack from the right *and* the left, as it were—has been paralleled by what Mary Kelley called "strikingly dissimilar, even contradictory" responses from literary and social historians over the past forty years.[5] Almost all agree that the nature of womanhood takes the thematic center of these books. But they disagree on whether the conventionality of the novels is a mask hiding a rebel within or simply the expression of the novelist's convictions. They also disagree as to the import or the message of the novels: some see them confirming established values, some criticizing society, and some carrying a more personal vision.

Did the domestic novelists adopt a literary mask of conventionality, both in the novels and in their lives? Ann Douglas Wood has argued that they did, in an effort to circumvent the "conventional set of preconceptions as to why women should write and what kind of literature they could write." Those expectations of the literary woman enjoined the timidity and dependence that characterized, of course, the ideal woman generally. Yet since writing is an act of psychological and economic assertion, these women had to mask and hallow their work, argues Wood, for example by claiming to be agents of some more powerful force, such as God. Such disclaimers created the paradoxical notion that "they were somehow hardly writing at all."[6] Similarly, say critics of this persuasion, the novels themselves wore masks of femininity, officially endorsing, perhaps in plot or narrative intrusions, the values their authors were expected to embody. But behind the mask, image patterns, for example, might suggest radical divergence from ideal womanhood. Thus a marriage might serve as both a conventional ending and a mask for female victory over the male.

On the other hand, Nina Baym contends that the mask *is* reality, that there is no contradiction between the writers' private lives and beliefs and those of their public personae and their audience. She sees a "moderate, or limited, or pragmatic feminism, which is not in the least covert but quite obvious . . . [but] constrained by certain other types of [Victorian] beliefs that are less operative today." Those beliefs, she says, led these writing women to interpret experience not in class or caste terms but as personal relationships; to deny the body spiritual possibilities and hence try to transcend sexuality; and to have a "nonandrogynous certainty that men and women were essentially different." Profoundly Victorian, according to Baym, they believed that duty, discipline, self-control, and sacrifice were "not only moral but actually useful strategies for getting through a hard world." Given these beliefs, Baym finds no discrepancy between these novels' mask and reality. In fact, "the happy marriages with which most . . . of this fiction concludes are symbols of . . . resolutions of the basic problems raised in the story."[7]

One's position on the internal consistency of these novels, on the role of the mask, is bound up with one's understanding of the relationship between the novelists and their culture. The earliest critics, like Herbert Ross Brown and Fred Lewis Pattee, found the novelists consciously purveying society's conservative view of woman as happily and properly domestic, the dutiful appendage to man, and at the same time, allowing their readers a moment of romantic escapism.[8] This view is perfectly consistent with the view that these writers were essentially not serious artists, but skilled professionals eager to make money by telling the public what it wanted to hear. Nina Baym, with her belief that the novels constitute overt but unspectacular feminism, treats the novels more sympathetically than earlier critics but essentially shares their stance. Though no buried Jane Austens are here, she says, she finds a seriousness of moral concern and energy and a subtlety of development that Brown and others missed. Nevertheless, she finds no contradiction between medium and message: the pleasures of the plot, as the heroine triumphs over adversity, are the point.[9]

Other recent critics—and one earlier critic, Helen Waite Papashvily, who published *All the Happy Endings* in 1956[10]—find social criticism often veiled, but occasionally barefaced, in the novels. Papashvily saw the women writers using their novels to express an otherwise dangerous hostility to men, hostility based on the experience of oppression. Thus, says Papashvily, they tend to wound, emasculate, or otherwise damage their male characters, transforming the traditional view of the happy marriage into a victory for the female. Dee Garrison found the novels opposing an authoritarian society by creating a "new heroine— sensual, active, defiant," by allowing major characters to criticize parental and clerical authority, and by finding the "social structure" itself responsible for the ills they decry.[11]

Mary Kelley, objecting that the writers were "not antagonistic to males per se, but to the individualistic and materialistic values of their time which men were thought to embody more than women," contends that the novelists began by seeking to add strength to the domestic ideal through showing the power for good that could be wielded from the hearthstone. Their prescription for women, however, could not be filled; "the defects of man and the burdens of domesticity made it difficult if not impossible to create the idealized home and family." So, for Kelley, the novels end in protest; for "instead of reformer, woman ends up the victim."[12]

Despite the development of this body of writing about woman's fiction of the nineteenth century, it is still hard to find close literary analyses of the works, and practically impossible to locate any speculation about differences between northern and southern writers. Yet a closer look at the novels might in itself begin to reveal the individual, regional, and other differences that tend to be glossed over in the interest of generalization. And on the second point even this brief survey should suggest that certain hypotheses are more likely to speak to southern experience than others. For example, the notion that these novelists sought to invent a womanhood powerful enough to battle materialism and individualism would seem less likely for southern than for northern writers, simply on the basis of economic differences. If one accepts Genovese's theory, the southern ideology had far more to do with the slave relations than it did with northern bourgeois values; in fact, it countered those values, though it was not designed to do so. Leaving Genovese aside, the fact that agrarians launched their attack on materialism and acquisitiveness in *I'll Take My Stand* as late as 1930 gives some slight indication of how much later the problems attendant upon industrialization came South.

Nor, for example, in the light of the history of division and masking that typifies southern womanhood, would we expect a straightforward, middle-class assertion of the female will. And those nineteenth-century beliefs that Nina Baym cites are not entirely applicable to southern women. As part of their culture, they in fact did see in terms of class and caste. Well aware of the feminized image of the southern gentleman, they thought, if not androgynously, in a manner that parceled out male and female characteristics differently from the North. And their already entirely transcendent sexual image might conceivably have led them to want to descend a bit from the pedestal of purity on which southern men had placed them.

Nathaniel Hawthorne did find one of those d—d scribbling women whose work he respected. To describe *Ruth Hall*, by "Fanny Fern" (Sara Parton Willis), Hawthorne used some very interesting metaphors: "I must say I enjoyed it a good deal. The woman writes as if the Devil was in her; and that is the only condition under which a woman ever writes anything worth reading . . . when they throw off the restraints of decency, and come before the public stark naked, as it were,—then their books are sure to possess character and value."[13] Hawthorne's metaphors go to the heart of American womanhood—piety and purity—to emphasize, perhaps unintentionally, the difficulty of being a serious woman writer. For a man to write like the Devil or go metaphorically stark naked was hardly the norm, as the career of Herman Melville certainly demonstrates. Yet how much more difficult to do either when the very role one is given—as woman, as writer—is to save men and women from the devil and to deck out the world with beautiful fiction.

Only a close look at the numbers of novels written by southern women in this period—nearly half the writers were southern by birth or adult residence—can answer these questions. But a close analysis of one novel, *Beulah*, can both suggest directions and demonstrate the value of applying careful literary analysis to popular fiction.

> "Beulah Benton, do you belong to the tyrant Ambition, or do you belong to that tyrant Guy Hartwell? Quick, child; decide!"
>
> "I have decided," said she. Her cheeks burned; her lashes drooped.
>
> "Well?"
>
> "Well, if I am to have a tyrant, I believe I prefer belonging to you? [*sic*]"
>
> He frowned. She smiled and looked up to him. . . .
>
> "Have you learned that fame is an icy shadow? that gratified ambition cannot make you happy? Do you love me?"
>
> "Yes."

"Better than teaching school and writing learned
articles?"
"Rather better, I believe, sir." [14]

Written, like other domestic novels, for a predominantly female readership, *Beulah* ends in a triumphant dramatic statement of the southern women's creed. Beulah submits to her husband-to-be, calling him
"sir" like a child, and gives up the world to take her place in his home.
But she still has one job left to do: she must convert Guy to Christ.

Augusta Evans draws it all together in the final scene. Dr. Guy Hartwell, his own heart now healed by the power of Beulah's love, sits
quietly. His hand lies gently on her hair; she sits in an attitude of deference below him, her Bible on his knee, her hand on her Bible, and her
eyes looking "reverently" into her husband's "noble face" (440). She is
trying, quietly but strongly, to talk him out of his pantheism: "Sir, can
you understand how matter creates mind?" she asks (440). While Hartwell ponders, the narrator—clearly the author—ties off her emblematic
scene with a final sentence that is an invocation: "May God aid the wife
in her holy work of love" (510). No longer will Beulah teach or write;
instead she will do "holy" work, fulfilling a responsibility to others that
came with submission, the submission to Christ. Finally, no longer is
her work of the intellect. It is a work of love, of the heart—of, in fact, the
"woman's heart" (117).

It all seems so clear, and so predictable for "woman's fiction." Yet despite Evans' efforts to prepare us for it, such a conclusion comes as a
shock. For Beulah's growth has been away from submission—personal,
intellectual, or religious. True, Beulah has gone to extremes: she has
stubbornly refused to accept help—much less orders—from men; has
hoped to win the world's glory through her writing; has called herself a
"woman" rather than a lady; has come to the very edge of atheism. She
has invited rebuke, too, with words like these, to a woman friend:

> "Don't talk to me about woman's clinging, dependent na-
> ture. You are opening your lips to repeat that senseless simile
> of oaks and vines; I don't want to hear it; there are no creep-
> ing tendencies about me. You can wind, and lean, and hang
> on somebody else if you like; but I feel more like one of those
> old pine trees yonder. I can stand up. Very slim, if you will,
> but straight and high. Stand by myself; battle with wind and
> rain and tempest roar; be swayed and bent, perhaps, in the
> storm, but stand unaided, nevertheless." (117)

So one could see Evans in the conclusion simply turning the tables, an
entirely predictable literary convention, and allowing Beulah to find her

true happiness in a situation that was the exact opposite of the one she had so ardently—and wrongly—sought.

But in fact the novel has, until its end, moved toward a more complex, less harmonious, and finally less didactic vision of character than the conclusion suggests. The end does not just turn the tables; it turns back the forward motion of the novel, denying the implications of the previous 430 pages rather than fulfilling them. For in *Beulah*, Evans had articulated an early version of the southern woman's vision of the self and the world. The force of the narrative is centrifugal. It presents polar opposites, then draws in, centers, unifies. For instance, Beulah has tried out her mind and tried out her heart; she has relied on herself and relied on others; she has seen nature stormy and seen nature calm. Thus, at the end of the novel, one looks for synthesis, a via media. And so does the narrator: midway, for instance, she asks for "an ardent love of nature as far removed from gross materialism or subtle pantheism on the one hand as from stupid inappreciation on the other." Yet she doubts the possibility: "Oh! why has humanity so fierce a hatred of medium paths?" (235).

However, the conclusion of *Beulah* chooses not the middle path but the road most taken. The conclusion is not a resolution but a forced stop; the novelist stuffs her implications into the conventional formula for the domestic novel, just as Beulah ultimately submits to the formula for the "true woman." But this novel founders as vision and as art for another reason as well: it runs up against profound and perhaps unanalyzed assumptions that characterize southern society. Although the southern lady protagonist questions the accuracy of Genesis and doubts the objective existence of God, she—and her creator—question only rarely and tentatively certain notions current in their society about the natures and proper relationship of men and women.

Although little in the novel directly reveals its southern roots—there is no plantation, there are no slaves—Augusta Jane Evans lived in a culture that, by the time of her birth in 1835, had already begun to diverge from the American norm. In the 1830s and 1840s, southerners "beg[a]n to think of themselves as a separate people with their own culture and way of life," [15] and Evans, apparently unequivocally, shared in this identification of herself as a southerner.

Evans was born the first child to a family whose heritage and experience in some ways reflected larger historical movements. Though her parents came from South Carolina planter aristocracy, Evans' father ran a general store in the frontier town of Columbus, Georgia, where she was born. By 1836, Matt Evans had built a southern mansion, Sherwood Hall; in the 1840s, "floods, Indian depredations, and the commer-

cial panic brought him to bankruptcy."[16] Like many others, the family
headed west by covered wagon to Texas. But security was not to be
found there. After having moved at least three times within the state,
the Evanses returned to Mobile, Alabama, when Augusta was fourteen.
There, poverty never left them—until she began to publish her novels.

Evans was always to see herself as her father's protector. She wrote
that, with the success of *St. Elmo* in 1866, she had "accomplished the
darling desire of her heart: to free her father from the burdens of care
and financial embarrassment."[17] Yet this was the same father who, as
Helen Papashvily understands it, had "lost his capital, his wife's wedding portion and their home" before Augusta could make her rightful
debut into the "best society in the South" for which she had the "en-
tré."[18] Add to this the predominant notion, seen in Belle Kearney's story,
that the man was expected to be the protector, not the protected, and
we have grounds to speculate that Evans felt a certain ambivalence
about her father.

Harper published *Inez* in 1855, when its author was twenty. Never
the huge success of her later works, *Inez* still had fourteen printings by
1912, by eight different publishers. *Inez* attacked Catholicism through
lengthy intellectual arguments, many of which turn on the notion that
it is foolish to follow authority blindly.

After this attack on Catholicism, Evans began the questioning of her
own Methodist fundamentalism that took novelistic shape in *Beulah*.
She had always been a voracious reader; though she had practically no
formal education, her mother taught her at home, and Evans apparently felt a much stronger influence from her than from her father. According to Hubbell, Evans in turn "took immense satisfaction in the letters she received from reclaimed infidels and from culture-hungry
young people who asked her what books they ought to read."[19]

Beulah was turned down at first by the publisher D. Appleton. Not to
be daunted, Evans rustled up a "necessary male escort" in the form of a
cousin and headed for New York.[20] The people at D. Appleton claimed
the manuscript had been mislaid; it was shortly found, and the two
southerners left to see J. C. Derby of Derby and Jackson. Derby refused
to pass judgment on the novel by himself; he took it home to his family,
who read and loved it. As a result, *Beulah* was published in 1859 and
became an immediate success.

Sometime during this period Evans met and became engaged to a
"pious young journalist" named James Reed Spaulding.[21] Within a year,
however, she broke off their engagement; he was a northerner, and her
political differences with him, she felt, would make marriage impossible. Those political differences emerged quite clearly back home during

the Civil War and in her next novel. Evans nursed wounded soldiers at Camp Beulah (named after her novel, as was a home guard contingent); while she sat at the bedsides of the soldiers, she wrote *Macaria*. This novel, she wrote to General Beauregard on March 17, 1863, was "dedicated to the *Army of the Confederacy*."[22] Despite its attacks on the Yankee character, the novel—published in Richmond on brown wrapping paper because of the paucity of supplies—sold so well in the North that Federal officials felt it had to be burned. A copy had been sent to Derby by blockade runner; after the war, again in New York to speak to Derby, Evans received a considerable sum of Yankee money for her Confederate novel.

Evans' identification with the Confederate cause seems to have been profound. She gave up a marriage to it. Her letters further attest to her faith: in 1861, she wrote to L. Virginia French that "I am an earnest and uncompromising Secessionist. . . . For fifteen years, we of the South have endured insult and aggression; have ironed down our just indignation and suffered numberless encroachments, because of our devotion to the 'union': because we shuddered and shrank from laying hands on the magnificent Temple which our forefathers reared in proud triumph."[23] After the war, she wrote to J. L. M. Curry that "I believe I loved our cause *as a Jesuit his order*; and its utter ruin has saddened and crushed me, as no other event of my life had power to do."[24] As late as 1867, she refused to meet a Federal officer carrying a letter of introduction from a friend because of her "determination to hold no social intercourse with persons who drew their sword against *a cause*—for which, I would gladly have sacrificed my life."[25] Temple, Jesuit, sacrifice—Evans uses the language of faith to express her political passion.

Neither religious nor regional faith, however, found expression in her most famous and most popular novel, *St. Elmo*. Although she had thought of writing a history of the Confederacy, Evans decided to write this novel instead, a novel so popular that a special edition was "limited to 100,000 copies."[26] *St. Elmo*—a later version of *Beulah*—takes its clearly autobiographical heroine Edna Earl through the trials of work and love. Like Beulah, after gaining national success as a "moral" writer, Edna finally gives up her career to marry. Her man, dark, experienced, Byronic St. Elmo, has reformed and become a minister. Like *Beulah*, *St. Elmo* traces the development of the heroine through thought to religion, reinforcing once again the suspicion that Evans herself enjoyed a freedom of thought that she publicly condemned in her novels.

St. Elmo, however, adds a new theme to the old one of reason versus faith. That theme is antifeminism. Edna delivers this passionate political oration:

America has no Bentham, Bailey, Hare or Mill, to lend countenance or strength to the ridiculous clamor raised by a few
unamiable and wretched wives, and as many embittered,
disappointed old maids of New England. . . . I think, sir, that
the noble and true women of this continent earnestly believe
that the day which invests them with the elective franchise
would be the blackest in the annals of humanity, would ring
the death-knell of modern civilization, of national prosperity,
social morality, and domestic happiness! and would consign
the race to a night of degradation and horror infinitely more
appalling than a return to primeval barbarism.[27]

Consciously, then, Evans seems to have accepted the prescription of
her region for her sex; her faith in the South, specifically, sets her
against Yankee feminism. Yet she seems unaware of the irony that
Edna's rather pretentious language reveals unladylike erudition, political passion, and oratorical instincts.

Two years later, Evans married Colonel Lorenzo Madison Wilson, a
rich neighbor who was older than her own father. During her marriage,
she published only two novels, *Vashti* (1869) and *Infelice* (1875). After
Colonel Wilson died, she wrote *At the Mercy of Tiberius* (1887), *A
Speckled Bird* (1902), and finally *Devota* (1907). According to Fidler,
she "believed that any woman should put her domestic duties first"
after marriage, so she "assumed management of Ashland, her husband's estate, with its servants, gardens, and five greenhouses, and
cared for an adolescent stepdaughter."[28] Hubbell astutely notes another
likely explanation for the reduction in both quality and quantity of her
work after marriage and before her husband's death: Colonel Wilson
"tried to prevent her from working too hard at her writing. Until after
his death in 1879, she published comparatively little. Perhaps, impressed though he was by the success of her novels, Mr. Wilson did not
quite approve of his wife's writing novels."[29] Papashvily, quoting from a
"contemporary biographer," has a different version of Wilson's motives:
"Because of her delicate health Mr. Wilson objected to her writing . . .
and she discontinued it and devoted herself to the decoration of her
homes and grounds." But then a $25,000 check came as an advance
against any novel she might send her publisher, and "Mr. Wilson was so
pleased he displayed the check all over Mobile and his wife put on 'the
fetters of literary bondage' once again."[30]

A definitive biography of Evans has yet to be written; when it is, it
should treat the conflicts Evans must have felt about marrying at thirty-
three, and after national success at writing, a man twenty-seven years

older than herself and paternalistic in the old style. Recent research into nineteenth-century women's ailments, too, should help us understand Evans' recurrent allergies and insomnia. It is quite possible that these illnesses were another ploy, for, in search of relief, Wilson took her traveling. Under the umbrella of protection, Evans continued to journey. In any case, Evans lived with her brother Howard for her last fifteen years; she died, not of hay fever or her heroine's "brain fever," but of a heart attack, the day after her seventy-fourth birthday in the eighth year of the new century.

When *Beulah* appeared in 1859, Evans was compared favorably with George Eliot and the novel considered "one of the best American novels." [31] Marion Harland, another popular novelist of the period who was also writing "woman's fiction," pronounced it "the best work of fiction ever published by a Southern writer" and added, still more generously, "no American authoress has ever published a greater book." [32] Nearly a best-seller, in its first nine months 22,000 copies were printed.

Yet apparently Evans had not been writing to a mass audience. Rather, she spoke to intellectuals (like herself) faced with contemporary skepticism, reading Carlyle and Feuerbach. She intended the novel as a "fictional confession" of her own "ordeal of skepticism," resolving to "combat skepticism to the day of my death, and if possible, to help others to avoid the thorny path I have trod ere I was convinced of the fallibility of human Reason." [33]

Nevertheless, Evans' novel sold to the many readers of women's fiction. According to her biographer, "she professed to be pleased that her audience was composed of unsophisticated commoners who follow the dictates of their heart and conscience, even in matters of art." [34] Why would such folk pay money for a novel about the life of the mind? Baym suggests that "even though the religious question is important, it is clearly subordinated to the larger pattern of conventional women's fiction." [35] Yet, despite the generally poor quality of education available to women in the South at this time, many middle- and upper-class women were managing to gain some exposure to the important intellectual questions of their day, perhaps through reading in their fathers' libraries. Perhaps, then, the intellectual content of Beulah's journey found interested women readers; perhaps the audience was not so unsophisticated as Evans believed.

Certainly readers looking only for what Baym sees as the conventional fictional pattern—the deprived heroine who makes it on her own [36]—would have to skip long passages in this novel. Conversation after conversation concerns ideas, and characters feel ideas with passion. A typical passage, though brief, shows that intensity: "'Yet you accept Emerson's "compensation." Are you prepared to receive his deistic system?' Cornelia leaned forward and spoke eagerly" (237).

The novel tells the story of Beulah's growth to adulthood—it covers ages thirteen to twenty-four—and the principal ordeal, the journey she takes, is a journey into the mind. Evans sets up Beulah in the beginning as what seems to be the ideal little woman of domestic fiction. A sober asylum orphan, she loves and prays to God; she mothers her blond little sister Lilly and her dark friend Claudia; she is repressed, repressing, and very orderly; and, though the world calls her ugly, she stoically turns to study in hopes of becoming a teacher.

Because they are beautiful, Lilly and Claudia are adopted by the fashionable Graysons, thereby splitting Beulah's family; because she is ugly, Beulah has to take a job as nurse for the wealthy Martin family. Mrs. Grayson won't even let Beulah visit her sister, whereupon Beulah hurls a coin at their door and curses her: "May God answer their prayers as she [Mrs. Grayson] has answered mine!" (30). Lilly soon dies, and the attending doctor, Guy Hartwell, rescues Beulah from the faint she falls into as she looks at the body. He has seen her before, at the Martins' house; this time, he asks her to "be my child; my daughter" (43). Although she refuses, he prevails, takes her home, bathes her feet, and doctors her through brain fever. His envious sister May Chilton (whose daughter Pauline is Beulah's age and Guy's putative heiress) tries to kill her, but Beulah survives both the disease and the murder attempt and turns fourteen. Guy then argues: "Now Beulah, I have saved you, and you belong to me" (54). Although she rejects this transaction—she hates dependence—Beulah agrees to stay with him long enough to get an education and enters Madame St. Cymon's private school with her energetic new friend Pauline Chilton. She meets another friend at school, "sweet and angelic" Clara Sanders. But after Mrs. Chilton tells her friends that Beulah is a "beggarly orphan," a "wretched object of charity" (87), Beulah runs back to the asylum, infuriated at the implication that she cannot take care of herself. The "ebon" servant Harriet (whose efforts to serve her Beulah has resisted) tells Guy the truth; he sends May and Pauline to New York and, threatening to cut them off entirely unless she returns, persuades Beulah to come back and keep him from being "lonely." Meanwhile, Beulah has missed this man: "if she had dared to yield to the impulse that prompted, she would have sprung to meet him and caught his hand to her lips" (105). But she does not yield and agrees to return to him on the condition that she now attend public school (it is cheaper). Once again she refuses adoption, arguing that she is self-sufficient.

With these stipulations, she settles into the life at the doctor's rather lavish estate. Drawn to his library, despite his warnings, she continues reading and enters the "vast Pantheon of Speculation" (123) through the stories of Poe, then De Quincey. At a concert with her guardian, which she has entered clinging to him "with a feeling of dependence utterly new to her" (136), she overhears a conversation about her: the people say that she is ugly and that Hartwell will probably marry her. Again inflamed, she vows to herself: "Support myself I will, if it costs me my life" (141). Thus when Guy again tells her she can repay her debt to him, not by the money earned from teaching, but by becoming his adopted child, it is no surprise that Beulah says, "I will not" (148). Cold and bitter, Guy leaves for New York; Beulah is too "proud" to leave him a note or to ask for a friendly goodbye and moves out immediately into a boardinghouse.

As her school's valedictorian, Beulah delivers a talk called "Female Heroism," which argues simultaneously and with no apparent sense of contradiction that "the female intellect was capable of the most exalted attainments . . . of cop[ing] successfully with difficulties of every class" and that woman has a "peculiar sphere, her true position [as] . . . ornaments of the social circle, angel guardians of the sacred hearthstone, ministering spirits where suffering and want demanded succor; . . . qualified to assist in a council of statesmen, [but only] if dire necessity ever required it" (144). She immediately gets the chance to prove her own heroism when yellow fever hits the town and, helping old Dr. Asbury, she nurses the sick. Guy returns in time to help, too; Beulah feels a new capacity to share the "dread weight of responsibility" (174), but he is cold. Beulah interprets Guy's "freezing manner": "He wants to rule me with a rod of iron, because I am indebted to him for an education and support. . . . I will repay him every cent he has expended for music, drawing, and clothing!" (180).

At the orphanage, Beulah's good friend and soul mate Eugene had read "Excelsior" with her and dreamed of a future as a lawyer. Adopted by the wealthy Graham family and sent to Europe, where he has disappointingly studied the mercantile profession at his adoptive father's behest, he now returns showing signs of "dissipation"—drinking. His adopted sister Cornelia, who is dying of heart disease, gives up her arrogant ways and tries to befriend Beulah; she too is a seeker and hopes Beulah can help her through her intellectual quest. After spending Christmas with Cornelia, Beulah's "pity" for her turns from contempt (that Cornelia is weak and needs Beulah's strength) to compassion. Not so for Guy: when he once again asks her to come back, Beulah replies "Never, sir!" and he speaks like God to a proud angel: "Fierce, proud spirit! Ah! It will take long years of trial and suffering to tame you. Go, Beulah! You have cast yourself off. It was no wish, no work of mine" (212).

Beulah is not too proud, though, to ask for intellectual help. But Dr. Asbury can give her none, because he is "too unsettled" to "direct others" (254); and Dr. Hartwell offers her an either/or choice: "pantheism or utter skepticism—there is no retreat" (275). When she rejects that choice, arguing that "there is truth for the earnest seeker somewhere" (275), he tells her, "Child, you are wasting your energies." She retorts, "Sir, I am no longer a child! I am a woman, and—" "Yes, my little Beulah," he replies, "and your woman's heart will not be satisfied long with these dim abstractions" (276).

Undaunted, Beulah continues to teach, think, write, and publish: she walks downtown, heavily veiled, and persuades a publisher to accept and even to pay for her work. In one article, she argues that "the love of beauty and intellectual culture" can satisfy the soul (296). Guy again urges her to quit, saying she is miserable and lonely. Beulah, however, moves on. She reads theology and philosophy and finally engages in a "desperate struggle," when, "alone and unaided," she "wrestle[s] with some of the grimmest doubts that can assail a human soul." The struggle within her soul takes her to the very "verge of chaos" (301). There she cries "Oh! how is each so solitary in this wide grave of the All? I am alone with myself. Oh Father! oh Father, where is thy infinite bosom, that I might rest on it?" (301). She does not find it.

Beulah's alienation deepens when her childhood friend Clara, who had shared the boardinghouse life, decides to leave. "My isolation will be complete," says Beulah (302). Shortly afterward, she sets up housekeeping with old Mrs. Williams, the matron at the asylum, in a small cottage no bigger than a "pigeon-box" (312). It seems her hopes are fulfilled: "For years she has been a wanderer, with no hearthstone, and now, for the first time since her father's death, she was at home. Not the home of adoption; nor the cheerless room of a boarding house, but the humble home which labor and rigid economy had earned for her" (315). There, she follows a simple plan: she teaches, takes walks, writes, and works in her garden. She is content.

But others around her are not. Pauline Chilton, who has married a minister, has marital problems. As she writes to Beulah, "He is tyrannical; and because I do not humor all his whims, and have some will of my own, he treats me with insulting indifference" (316). And Cornelia Graham dies, going into the dark unredeemed and alone. Beulah asks what good all that speculation did for Cornelia and begins to doubt that her own intellect is so "vastly superior to those who for thousands of years" had asked the same questions (326). Yet when kindly Mrs. Asbury offers her help, Beulah refuses, "No, no. No one can help me; I must help myself" (337). Her writing having gained renown, she no longer publishes incognito.

One more time Guy comes to see Beulah. Confessing that he is no longer merely a "friend," "pleading tenderness" in his "dark, fascinating eyes" (341), he proposes marriage. "Now I ask you to be my wife, to give yourself to me." Beulah says it is impossible: he is lonely, she believes, but does not really love her; moreover, she loves him only as a friend and protector. Guy immediately assumes it is ambition that prevents her from accepting him and predicts "you will drain the very dregs rather than forsake your tempting fiend, for such is ambition to the female heart. . . . Remember when your health is broken and all your hopes withered, remember I warned you and would have saved you, and you would not" (343). Having given her another either/or choice—marriage or estrangement—Guy leaves, saying, "Oceans will soon roll between us" (344). Beulah goes back to her desk to finish an article proving that "woman's happiness was not necessarily solely dependent on marriage. That a single life might be more useful, more tranquil, more unselfish . . . to female influence she awarded a sphere (exclusive of rostrums and all political arenas) wide as the universe and high as heaven" (345). Now, though, it seems "weary work"; after she finishes it, she weeps.

During the next week Beulah meets someone who seems to be the perfect man for her: Reginald Lindsay has a fine intellect, is a converted Christian, and is not egotistical. They enjoy talking, and the "expression of resolute endurance" leaves Beulah's face (345). Guy departs for the Orient and sends his dog Charon to Beulah; Dr. Asbury (who has said, "Child, keep Guy at home!" [352]) sends Guy's portrait for her to keep. She hangs it above her desk. As she looks at it, she analyzes why she turned him down: she "loved him as a child adores its father; but how could she, who had so reverenced him, consent to become his wife? Besides, she could not believe he loved her . . . she could not realize that he, who so worshiped beauty, could possibly love her" (355).

Eugene Graham, meanwhile, has married the belle of the town, duplicitous Antoinette Dupres. His dissipation grows as Antoinette's mask drops to reveal a woman with no truth in her. One night, driving drunk, he loses control of his horse and falls out of the carriage, injured. As it happens, Beulah's cottage is nearby; he is taken there, where she nurses him back to health of body and of spirit. He decides to go back to his original dream to pursue the law and lavishes all his attention on his little daughter, while Antoinette pursues her unfaithful life.

Lindsay continues to visit Beulah, arguing in conversations that to know God one must be God, which is impossible. Beulah, for her part, has "lost faith in ratiocination" but not in reason: "reason is divine" for "by spontaneous apperception" it "grasps truth" (376). Lindsay persists: if so, why are there so many individual faiths? Beulah develops a dislike for his imperturbability and his constant attention; Charon confirms this instinct by growling at him. Lindsay argues against Beulah in print, her first critique; she assures him that criticism will not hurt true friendship. Finally, he proposes; she turns him down but feels "unworthy" and "undeserving" (348). Immediately thereafter, she rehearses (once more) the stages of her intellectual journey and asks, "Was her life to be thus passed in feverish toil and ended as by a leap out into a black, shoreless abyss? Like a spent child she threw her arms on the mantelpiece and wept uncontrollably" (386). Finally, she begs "My God, save me! Give me light! Of myself I can know nothing!" (387). The stars—God's light—look in.

Four years later, Beulah still lives in her little pigeon-box, still teaches (she has been promoted to principal), and still gardens. Her writing now, though, is not for fame, as it was, but to show others the way out of speculation. When someone asks why she does not love Guy, she replies only that her heart is not the tool of her will; yet now she remembers, says the narrator, only his kindness and none of his bitterness. She is, in short, "very lonely, but not unhappy" (395), with a face that Christianity has made "quiet" and "serene," but not "sparkling" (396).

Eugene, meanwhile, has pursued the same ambition that Beulah has turned into Christian service. He has political hopes and oratorical skills and divides his time between his child Cornelia and his work.

The Asburys have kept Guy's possessions locked for five years in a third-floor room of their house. Among them are the melodeon that Beulah used to play and a portrait of his stunningly beautiful first wife. One day Mrs. Asbury tells the story: Creola Labord had been only a bit more than a child, daughter of a poor family in New Orleans, when Guy had seen her and fallen in love. She married him because her family needed money, but she stayed in love with her first fiancé. When Guy found out, his rage turned Creola insane; months later, she died, and Guy had not trusted a woman since. Yet Guy's "heart must have an idol" (402). So—says Mrs. Asbury—he took Beulah home. Beulah asks for the key to this locked upstairs room.

Mrs. Williams dies, leaving Beulah alone in their little house. Both Dr. Asbury and Reginald Lindsay say it will not do for Beulah to stay there alone; she does not question this and moves in with the Asburys, insisting upon paying a boarder's fee. Lindsay offers his hand again; to prove that his love is genuine, when she turns him down, he offers to track down Guy for her, since that is (he thinks) what she wants. She denies it. Pauline writes to explain how she solved her marital difficulties: she simply puts on the role of the demure matron in public and romps and plays at home, at least when her husband permits. Beulah, too, must put on a new face with the move (which she regrets) to the Asburys; she learns to be more sociable and yet still yearns for her solitude. She disciplines herself so that she has time to fit in her new "family"; she walks to the graveyard and remembers Cornelia, Lilly, and Mrs. Williams, and to Guy's former home to see the chaos that uncontrolled nature has made of his house and gardens.

Another suitor pursues her, this time a real "catch," in "society's" eyes. Beulah refuses to see him. Her former orphanage friend Claudia is the social belle of the season and has become so arrogant and tyrannical due to the indulgence of the Graysons that she spurns Beulah on the streets. But then Mr. Grayson, in a financial hole, shoots himself, and all Claudia's fashionable friends desert her and her mother. Only Beulah and Mrs. Asbury help. Beulah, in fact, gives them the $5000 Cornelia had left her and sets up Claudia in a job teaching art. The "world" now eulogizes Beulah for her writing; even her looks have improved, so that she is "noble" if not "handsome" (427). Yet she grows daily more joyless.

One rainy day, Beulah climbs up to the third-story room to play Guy's melodeon. While she is worrying about him, Charon jumps up and whines with pleasure. She turns around and finds Guy leaning against the door, arms folded. She reaches out for him; he does not move, she hesitates, then she embraces him anyway. She says she has prayed for his return. Finally, he returns her embrace, and asks her—as we have seen—which tyrant she wants.

After she chooses him, Guy asks,

> "Beulah, do you cling to me because you love me? or because you pity me? or because you are grateful to me for past love and kindness? Answer me, Beulah."
> "Because you are my all."
> "How long have I been your all?"
> "Oh, longer than I knew myself" was the evasive reply.
> (432)

Guy then tells her to give him her hand; she does so, and he "claims" it: "Is it mine?" (433). She says yes, and Guy *becomes* light: "his face kindled, as if in a broad flash of light; the eyes dazzled her, and she turned her face away" (434).

On the day of their wedding, though, Beulah begins to feel apprehensive. She knows his "passionate exacting" nature and, remembering Creola, tells him that she is afraid. When he asks why, she merely looks at his face: "She saw the expression of sorrow that clouded his face; saw his white brow wrinkle; and as her eyes fell on the silver threads scattered through his brown hair, there came an instant revolution of feeling. Fear vanished; love reigned supreme" (437).

"Reader, marriage is not the end of life," says the narrator at this point. But it is just about the end of the novel. In a brief summary of the months after their wedding, we see Dr. Hartwell open up, relax, learn to laugh; and we see Beulah, "conscious of the power she wielded" (438) over his psyche, trembling "lest she failed to employ it properly" and thinking she had been far too proud of her intellect: "I . . . put so much faith in my own powers; it was no wonder I was so benighted" (438). Now, her faith in reasoning to the world behind the veil of God having left her, she puts her faith in reasoning about the physical world: science, as material progress, will not only give "all that a merely sensual nature could desire" (438), but will also "link hands" with religion. Finally, she pities the souls who leave the ark of God to embark on the "toys of man's invention," for they, by "deliberate[ly] rejecting the given light," have only "bitter darkness" (439). Since Beulah herself has seen the light and climbed back into the ark, with her mate and in her place, she can now help keep the boat afloat and on its course to eternal shores.

So why are we not happier with Evans' story? When it was first published, Henry Timrod wrote to Rachel Lyons that he was "disappointed in the treatment of the bold speculations in *Beulah* . . . and expected a more artistic construction of the philosophical debate. Beulah's transition from scepticism to Faith is left almost unaccounted for. How much I should like to have my own doubts settled in the same satisfactory, yet most inexplicable manner!"[37]

Evans answered Timrod indirectly when she wrote to Rachel Lyons. Yet in that letter she simply restates the intellectual conclusion, still not explaining the "transition":

> The preponderance of the Rationalistic element in Beulah's organization necessitated her speculative career. . . .
> Beulah constituted her Reason the sole criterion of truth, but found on all sides insolvable mysteries—found that unaided by Revelation which her reason had ignored that [sic] she

was utterly incapable of ever arriving at any belief. . . . discarding the belief that Reason alone could discover the truth, she rested her spent soul in the Ark of Faith! whereby she was enabled to receive the sublime teachings of *Inspiration*.[38]

Yet that "transition"—as opposed to its result, or its intellectual content—is precisely what puzzles the narrator within the novel, as well as Henry Timrod. Observing Clara Sanders' mysteriously emergent strength (she has realistically relinquished her infatuation with Guy and taken control of her life), the narrator muses on the sources of strength. Granting that the ultimate source is God, yet, she wonders, "who shall unfold the process? . . . how, and by whom, is the key applied?" (213).

Evans' narrator suggests it may be our "loved dead," acting as angels, or perhaps a "sudden tightening of those invisible cords which bind the All-Father to the spirits he has created" (213). The cords that bind Beulah to the "All-Father" in her conversion are reminiscent of the "bonds of womanhood" that, in Nancy Cott's phrase, "bound women together even as [they] bound them down."[39] For the fact is, though the motives for Beulah's conversion may be unclear to the reader, and though they may have been unclear even to the conscious Evans, they are right there in the text and will take us to the heart of the novel.

Beulah submits to God only hours after she has turned down Reginald Lindsay's proposal of marriage. Lindsay has been described, as we have seen, as the perfect man. He is intelligent, educated, thoughtful, one of few whom Beulah can call "companion." Moreover, he is—unlike Guy—neither egotistical nor philosophically skeptical: he is an educated Christian. And he loves her; in fact, he proposes again after four years of patient waiting.

But Beulah rejects this paragon. Immediately after he leaves, she castigates herself: "A burning flush suffused her face as she exclaimed: 'Oh, how unworthy I am of such love as his! how utterly undeserving!'" (384). Her guilt, here expressed as self-deprecation, is profound. In rejecting the perfect man, she has symbolically expressed her continuing rejection of the All-Father, whose human expression in Christ was male and whose nearest approximation in Beulah's world is this man. She punishes herself, falls on her knees, and weeps uncontrollably, repeating twice that she is a mystery to herself and begging God to save her and give her light. Thus "her proud intellect was humbled" (387). Like Noah's dove, she says, she "cannot explore and fully understand [the ark's] secret chambers" but, also like that "exhausted bird," she seeks "safety in the incomprehensible" (386). Thus her search ends, the chambers of the self remain locked, and she gives her key—her questioning mind—to God.

But one suspects that Lindsay is turned down for personal as well as artistic reasons. The contrast between the relationship of equality possible with a man who takes her protagonist's work seriously and that of patriarchy actually achieved at the end of the novel indicates a direction from which Evans must shy away.

There is no doubt that Evans consciously believed that Beulah made the right choice; Beulah's language recapitulates almost word for word that in Evans' letters to a young minister who helped her through her own crisis of faith.[40] Yet Evans' imagination drew, in the novel, a sketch that, when the layers of southern expectations are scraped off, describes a process of growth to identity and a set of social values well worth the work of uncovering.

Evans' mask, as writer, is the mask of duty to others; behind that mask lies the life of the mind. In a letter to her friend Janie Tyler, Evans expresses her commitment, as author, to the self-abnegating purpose of helping others. She denies any personal interest and invokes, interestingly, a now-familiar theory of art that emphasizes the split between autobiography and art:

> I could smile at your estimate of me [that metaphysics must be the novelist's passion], if I were not aware that you predicated it from a by-no-means uncommon error that an author's mental or moral idiosyncrasies are clearly indexed in his or her books. Pardon me if I insist that this is an unsafe criterion. . . . If I have given much time and attention to the abstruse speculation of metaphysicians, it was because I feared their ethical creed was insidious and deleterious to earnest, unsettled young thinkers, and I strove to combat their arguments for love of my countrymen and women, rather than through fondness for their vexed and tortuous paths.[41]

This is, of course, the same mask Beulah wears as a Christian author.

Evans' authorial cover as didactic storyteller parallels and perhaps reflects her lifelong habit of explaining her controversial acts as really sacrificial. As an adult, she loved to tell how, at age three, she had stolen a pair of red shoes. But, she claimed, it wasn't really stealing; the red shoes were for her baby brother.[42] That pattern became conscious strategy when at nineteen she wrote her first novel, *Inez*. Aware that her parents might object to her "accepting money for writing," she plotted with an old slave named Minervy to provide oil to write by at night, to "destroy evidence of her night's labors," and to hide the manuscript during the day. But Evans' mother suspected something and, "during an interview with Augusta, accompanied with much squirming and many endeavors to avoid confession," learned about the book.[43] The plot thickened; conspiring now with her mother, Augusta Evans did not tell her father about her book until—in an ingenious deployment of the sacrificial mode—she gave him the completed manuscript as a Christmas gift. Like the red shoes story, this was one the adult Evans loved to tell. And Evans' attitude toward the public at the outset of her career was consistent with that toward her father: aware of the moral stigma then attached to novels, she "planned to give her own compositions such religious fervor that any opposition to the form would quickly disappear among her readers."[44] We have seen already, in her reply to Timrod's criticism, that Evans maintained the red shoes stance with *Beulah*: I am only writing it, she said, to help my readers.

However, masks can distort one's own vision as well as hide one's identity: "A man only sees that which he brings with him the power of seeing," thinks Beulah during a conversation with Cornelia. Augusta Evans must have squinted mightily to see *Beulah* fitting the straight-laced pattern of the domestic hope. Within the novel, the kind of doubleness she experienced in her personal life takes shape in two images, mask and veil. And the novel speaks more truly than its author could.

The word *mask* appears most frequently to describe the worst female character, Antoinette, and in this simplest sense is a symbol of duplicity. Covered by her mask of beauty, Antoinette tricks Eugene into marrying her: "Her pretty face veils her miserable, contemptible defects of character" (232), says Beulah. Cornelia says she has "probed [Antoinette's] mask of dissimulation" (332). But Eugene learns the truth quickly: "I did not expect it so soon," says Cornelia. "I fancied Antoinette had more policy. She has dropped the mask. He sees himself wedded to a woman completely devoid of truth" (320). Beauty and policy combine to create an effective but unethical mask. In this context, then, the mask is employed as a weapon.

However, it is not just truthless characters who wear masks. Beulah herself is "closely veiled" when she "set[s] off for the business part of the city" carrying "under her shawl a thick roll of neatly written paper" (249). After she lifts her veil, she debates with the publisher, very assertively arguing for southern literature and pay for her articles; then Beulah "lower[s] her veil, and most politely he bow[s] her out" (251). Hawthorne's praise of the nakedness of good female prose comes to mind. Here again, the veil hides, but in this scene it conceals a woman writing in an honest search for truth, as Hawthorne saw Sara Parton

Willis'. Evans leaves it to her readers to understand why Beulah must be veiled; they—if not Hawthorne—surely knew how risky it was for a woman to write. And, of course, Beulah puts on yet another mask—the pseudonym of "Delta"—when she begins to publish. Only after the world approves of her work does she publish under her real name, the face and the mask becoming one. So a veil or a mask can be a shield as well as a weapon, protecting one's feelings from exposure.

Masks can also protect others from one's own unpleasant or inappropriate feelings. Here, for instance, the narrator points out that "though well-nigh exhausted . . . Beulah never complained of weariness, and always forced a smile of welcome to her lips when the invalid [Eugene] had his chair wheeled to her side" (367). When Beulah first meets Pauline after her return, she "found it rather difficult to withdraw her fascinated eyes from Pauline's lovely face. She knew what was expected of her, however" (210), so she compliments Pauline's fiancé.

Whether masking is praised as kindness to others and protection for self or blamed as duplicitous, the novel moves, not toward unmasking, but toward, first, self-awareness and, second, ethical "policy"—that is, the conscious and responsible choice of masks. The two are linked. Eugene, for instance, wears an ethical mask when he lies to Cornelia, giving her the impression that he prefers Beulah to Antoinette. Yet because he is fooling himself, this mask also blinds Eugene to the truth. Someday, Beulah says to him, Antoinette will "tear the veil from your eyes" (285). Early in the novel, Evans milks the metaphor for pathos: "it was touching to note the efforts [Beulah] made to appear hopeful; the sob swallowed, lest it should displease him; the trembling lips forced into a smile, and the heavy eyelids lifted bravely to meet his [Eugene's] glance" (40). Because Beulah begins to emerge from the condition of victim—coming out from behind the veil to show and know the truth—and because she learns to manipulate her masks, the extreme self-pity indulged in this passage disappears from the novel. A good mask, finally, reveals truth but leaves the face behind the mask aware and in control. Thus onlookers can trust that, though the truth be partly concealed, it is not malevolent.

But not just people in this novel are veiled or masked. So is the truth, and so is God. Reginald warns Beulah against trying to "lift the veil of Isis" (349), and, in her final statement, Beulah herself says about philosophy that "the torch of science will never pierce and illumine the recesses over which Almighty God has hung his veil" (439). No longer will she try to find the truth behind the mask; she will, instead, act in the faith that the truth is beneficent, that God is not like Antoinette.

Early in the novel, two stanzas from Longfellow's "Psalm of Life" attract Beulah. One ends, "And things are not what they seem"; so the mask and veil imagery just discussed shows. The other stanza ends with the imperative, "Be not like dumb, driven cattle, / Be a hero in the strife" (12). Most of the novel deals directly and indirectly with the question of human identity, cowed or heroic. Beulah notes late in the novel that "from childhood this question of 'personal identity' has puzzled me." When orphanage and adoption are seen as metaphors, they indicate a similar interest on Evans' part. If one is orphaned, then forces in the environment seem to Evans to be separated from those of heredity, so that identity becomes wholly contingent upon experience. Since an orphan also lacks family experience, she or he may be more capable of envisioning alternatives to that structure—or more vulnerable to its appeal. Separated from the conventional sources of identity, then, the orphan becomes a kind of litmus test for the rest of society. When adopted, Eugene loses his high standards and Claudia her high spirits and loyalty; they both fall victims to the materialistic values of their new families, hence their identities change. In resisting adoption, and in insisting on repaying every cent Dr. Hartwell spends on her, Beulah resists the conventional definition of the self as a "dumb, driven" member of a wealthy family and strikes out on a different path, to be a hero in the strife.

Although Evans wrote about a woman and for women, her *Bildungsroman* contains evidence that she saw it as showing the path for both men and women, that she saw her vision as universal or, as Beulah says, "absolute." Hints can be found in the plot: women and men undergo similar trials, intellectual and emotional. Guy must learn to trust a woman as Beulah must learn to trust a man. Male doctors serve others in the home, as do women. Female teachers and writers leave the home, as do men.

Characterization of men and women, too, emphasizes similarities. Although Guy sees a difference between men and women—"Man may content himself with the applause of the world and the homage paid to his intellect; but woman's heart has holier idols" (343)—he himself is not content with applause and homage. In fact, Mrs. Asbury points out that he took Beulah in because "the heart must have an idol" (402)—for the man, the lady on the pedestal. Both men and women, in her view, need human as well as Godly "idols."[45] Guy and Beulah are more alike than different in another way; according to Dr. Asbury, they are both "as proud as Lucifer and as savage as heathens" (254). "Congenial natures" (290), to Beulah—and Evans—make the best marriages, and congeniality really means similarity. Similar people even look alike, though they may be of different sexes: in Pauline and Guy the "dazzling transparency of the complexion was the same, the silky nut-brown hair the same, and the classical chiseling of mouth and nose identical" (268). And little Cornelia looks like her father, "having the same classical contour and large, soft, dark eyes" (390). The best individuals combine male and female characteristics; one notes the "feminine delicacy of [Guy's] hands" (47). And thus in action, characterization, and physical description, Evans tries to make her story everyone's story.

It doesn't work, though. For one thing, most men are not doctors and most women are not writers; on the contrary, the men in Evans' novel more often write erudite sermons and serve their own "ambition," and the women write personal letters about marriage and serve men. Thus the possibility for men to learn to give and for women to learn to assert themselves—metaphorically, for men to learn to enter the home and for women to leave it—is a remote one. Evans' instinct that this is so appears in her refusal to allow Beulah to marry Lindsay, whose similarity is not of pride but of mind, and in the imbalance of her last scene, with Beulah below and Guy above. It appears also in her choice of point of view, almost exclusively female, though not entirely restricted to Beulah; only two or three times in 440 pages does a sentence tell the reader what Eugene or Guy actually felt and thought. Almost always the reader is told only what they *seem* to feel—that is, one is shown only the mask.

With that caveat, then, let us look at Evans' version of the *Bildungsroman*. Beulah states a principal theme in a passionate speech: life is not "merely to eat and drink, to sleep and be clothed . . . a constant effort to keep soul and body together." Rather "there is truth for the earnest seeker somewhere—somewhere!" (275). Life is a quest for something more than survival. Several metaphors broaden Beulah's statement: the "hunt" (238) for a creed, the "ordeal" (257) of the hero, the "maze" (167) of the intellect, the "labyrinth" of the mind. Overwhelming the other journey metaphors is that of the journey across the sea; the poem most often quoted is Coleridge's "The Ancient Mariner." The sea can be calm or high with waves; it can be sunny or tempest-tossed. But more important than its condition is the mode of travel upon it: in Noah's ark—the Christian tradition; in the "gilded toys of man's invention" (387)—speculative philosophy; or in one's own body, as a swimmer, relying on oneself.

In the center of the novel, Beulah undergoes for the first time the kind of experience that will later send her to her knees begging for and ultimately finding God's light. She asks herself, in the dead of night, alone with her books,

> "What am I. . . . Am I my own mistress, or am I but a tool in the hands of my Maker?" . . . In the solitude of her own soul she struggled bravely and earnestly to answer those "dread questions". . . . The clouds grew denser and darker, and, like the "cry of strong swimmers in their agony," her prayers had gone up to the Throne of Grace. Sometimes she was tempted to go to the minister of the church. . . . But the pompous austerity of his manners repelled her . . . and gradually she saw that she must work out her own problems. . . . In her reckless eagerness, she plunged into the gulf of German speculation. (217–18)

This is the only passage in the novel where swimming appears as a metaphor; more clearly than elsewhere, Beulah here articulates her conflict as one between autonomy and passivity, and she rejects as fallible even God's emissary the minister. Later, of course, she finds Lindsay a nearly perfect companion in her quest, but at this early stage she chooses to trust herself over other fallible guides, even after praying to God, and takes the plunge into the gulf hoping to swim alone. "Temptation" here is not to bite the apple of knowledge, but to give it up.

Evans could not sustain such a metaphor. Inevitably, Beulah's gulf turns into "a howling chaos . . . about to ingulf her." Finally unable to pray, "blindfolded" by *Sartor Resartus*, she "threw herself down to sleep with a shivering dread, as of a young child separated from its mother and wailing in some starless desert" (219). Alone and lost in the dark: that image, for Evans, is finally too terrifying to confront. The risk of loss of identity is expressed in the single word *ingulfed*. Several times Beulah again feels lost, storm-tossed, or on the edge of an abyss; that abyss or dark gulf becomes in the novel metaphorically linked with death, and each time Beulah faces it she turns back, seeking either the "gilded toy" of someone else's ideology or the "ark" of a community of believers. It is noteworthy, then, that this early passage ends with the metaphor of a child separated from its mother. Only once in the novel does Beulah call herself "woman," and that is when she is still, in her "reckless eagerness," swimming in the gulf of speculation. As we have seen, the condition for her ultimate salvation is to become as a little child, and indeed, at the moment she finally accepts Guy Hartwell, he addresses her as "child." The ark of faith admits its passengers only in pairs; the convention of marriage thus parallels the convention of faith, and the pairs are unequally matched.

The sea, then, is the metaphoric medium of the quest; the vehicle, faith; and faith in one's body is shown to be clearly inferior to faith in an ark, given the travel conditions. One of those conditions is darkness. When Beulah searches, the darkness is unrelieved; what seem to be stars go out "when the telescope of her infallible reason [is] brought to bear upon the coldly glittering points" (285). Yet when she chooses the ark, those stars shine in on her. The stars are God's light; that they pierce the darkness like holes in cloth links this metaphor to that of masks. If she trusts that the stars are perforations in God's mask, and if she believes that light is ultimately good, then she can believe in a benevolent God.

But here we can trace a complication that keeps Evans from creating a universal *Bildungsroman* describing a path suitable for both men and women. For Evans the southerner merged patriarchal religion with patriarchal society. This can be seen in the extension of these metaphors to the depiction of Guy Hartwell, Beulah's final "tyrant." Early in the novel, Harriet, Guy's slave, compares his will to the sea: "Haven't you been here long enough?" she asks Beulah, "to find out that you might as well fight the waves of the sea as my master's will?" (64). One could argue that in choosing the ark of faith, Beulah chooses the one way she can survive in Guy's sea. But why swim in it at all? The answer is clear in the description of Guy's response when Beulah gives herself to him: "his face kindled, as if in a broad flash of light; the eyes dazzled her, and she turned her face away" (433). There can be no question about it. This is God's light, and Beulah will, in Miltonic style, love the God in Guy. And well she might: "a man without religion is to be pitied; but, oh! a Godless woman is a horror above all things" (328).

Like the Ancient Mariner, alone on a wide, wide, sea, Beulah has blessed the water snakes and they have turned lovely in her eyes. Clearly, though, such a pattern for a *Bildungsroman* depends on profound divisions between the sexes. If, behind his Byronic mask, Guy is like God, then why does he need to journey at all? And if men more generally are God's representatives on earth, then women are wrongheaded to swim into the gulf alone; instead, they should seek their proper mate. Yet a closer look at the pattern of the quest and the map of the psyche that are implicit in the novel's structure and metaphors will show further that Evans was herself split on the issue.

There are roughly four stages to Evans' fictional quest: passivity, rebellion, autonomy, and friendship. Passive persons rely on outside authority; the world of fashion, bought into with a man's money, provides the outside authority for several passive characters "who are in the habit of determining the gentility of different persons by what they have, not what they are" (283). Antoinette's is "such a beauty as one sees in wax dolls—blank, soulless, expressionless" (209), because she relies on outside norms, like clothing, for her identity. When she first meets Beulah, she "scan[s] Beulah's countenance and dress with . . . cool impertinence" (209), and by the end of the novel she is "dressed superbly . . . as extravagantly as she chose" (389). Passivity has its drawbacks; Antoinette "almost feared" Eugene—another outside authority—"shrank from his presence and generally contrived to fill the house with company when she was, for short intervals, at home" (389). The narrator asks "woman" directly, "When will you sever the fetters which fashion, wealth, and worldliness have bound about you?" (389), using an image of bondage consistent with Evans' depiction of fashion as destructive because its authority is external to the self.

More powerful than the dictates of fashion is an authoritarian individual. When Eugene passively accedes to his adoptive father's choice of a mercantile career, Beulah contends that "his adoption was his ruin. Had he remained dependent on his individual exertions he would have grown up an honor to himself and his friends" (309). In the process of defining herself, Beulah spends most of the novel fighting to keep out of the hands and home of that "tyrant" Guy Hartwell; Guy meanwhile persistently phrases his offers of help in language that makes it clear that his help implies possession of her. Pauline, already a self-defined individual, finds that her marriage to an authoritarian minister, the "master of her destiny" (289), is miserable. Her eventual "solution" schizophrenically yokes together Pauline's real self with the self required by Ernest, the outside authority:

> I began in sober earnest to be all my husband wished me . . . in short became quite a demure pastor's wife. Occasionally my old fondness for fun would break out . . . but Ernest was very good, and bore patiently with me, and now I am as prim and precise as any old maid of sixty. At home I do as I like; that is, when Ernest likes it too. I sing, and play, and romp with the dogs and kittens; but the moment the door bell rings, lo! a demure matron receives her guests. . . . My husband loves me better than everything else beside, and what more could I desire? (408)

In Pauline, a child coexists with an "old maid"; there is no adult here. Although Evans apparently intends Pauline as proof (for Beulah) that compromise can make a happy marriage, she succeeds instead in proving the destructiveness of authoritarian relationships.

Authoritarian individuals in the novel themselves use outside authorities, like religion. Whips, wielded by Antoinette and Guy, symbolize those characters' reliance on force. Yet such individuals, Evans implies, are weak at the center. When Eugene is in this phase, Beulah knows that "weakness . . . prompted much of his arrogance and egotism" (119). And Guy's weakness is his dependence on unequivocal love from a woman. Thus victims are shown as exerting power over their masters through service. The most prevalent form of service is nursing, for the most common expression of weakness is illness. Eugene falls ill, needs Beulah to nurse him, and as a result drops his arrogant ways, returning to his ideals. Ernest Mortimor's change of heart toward Pauline comes when he is "suddenly taken very ill. . . . his illness was 'the blessing in disguise'; he forgot all our disgraceful bickerings, and was never satisfied unless I was with him" (407). Beulah's recognition of her "power" over Guy after their marriage is a recognition of the power of service; having received her love, he is now vulnerable to her. On the other hand, just as Beulah rejects direct authority, she also rejects this more subtle exertion of power over her. She will not let Guy rescue her—for then, as she knows, he would possess her, just as she finally, nervously, possesses him.

Whether victim or master, then, stage one of the quest places the individual self ultimately in the hands of another. Evans' ambivalence about this stage—which is, of course, the stage in which the novel ends—comes from, on the one hand, her instinct that this is the earliest stage of the quest and, on the other, her acceptance of yet a third outside authority: God. Like fashion, and like the authoritarian individual, God is outside the self, masked behind the night, not immanent in nature or (especially) in people, though His light may shine through them. Master of every destiny, He too rescues sick souls. Yet unlike these other forms of power, God's does not cover weakness; He is invulnerable.

Most important for our purposes, God is the All-Father to His children: "Blessed be the holy tones," says the narrator, "which at least once a week call every erring child back to its Infinite Father!" (263). God is male and parental; His word defines reality. Most of the men in the novel are also parental, and their words, like God's, define reality. The men define themselves as realists—Eugene tells Beulah, "I grapple with realities now . . . and you refuse to see things in their actual existence" (193), and Guy calls Beulah the "last embodiment of effete [by which he means idealistic] theories" (127). The men also take it upon themselves to define women. Dr. Asbury thinks nature "intended" women to be "thorough housewifes," not "too fashionable" to look after their men, or so extremely charitable that they forget that true charity "begins at home" (252). When Beulah lives happily with Mrs. Williams in their cottage, Dr. Asbury sees her "bury[ing] herself out there with an infirm old woman for a companion" (313); he makes it clear, after Mrs. Williams' death, that "It will not do, child, for you to live there by yourself" (402). For his part, Guy identifies women with children and dogs. He compliments Beulah by saying she has "more intellect than all the other women and children in the town!" (266). And his heart is touched when he sees Beulah and Charon lying on the rug asleep together (124). Of course, it is Guy who argues that a woman's heart needs holier idols than ambition (343) and that ambition is far more debilitating to women than it is to men.

As we saw in her final scenes, Evans consciously agrees with her male characters; the red shoes are for her brother. Yet within the novel, she repeatedly undercuts their authoritarian words and acts, reserving only God as the authoritative father figure. Thus Beulah's cry—"am I but a tool in the hands of my Maker?"—gets to the heart of Evans' own doubts about men as the makers, the authors, of women.

Evans doesn't simply undercut outside authority, though. She envisions alternatives to following that authority. Stage two of the quest is to rebel. Beulah defies almost every voice in the community by not returning to Guy. She rebels against the power of service, too. To the slave Harriet, she says, "I have not been accustomed to have someone always waiting on me, and in future I shall not want you" (64). Perfectly symbolizing her rejection of the authority of fashion, Cornelia sends her new clothes downstairs so that her visitors can see them: "Don't leave a rag of my French finery behind . . . and tell Miss Julia she will please excuse me" (297). As victims of fashion cannot, Cornelia separates her self from her clothes.

Yet rejecting outside authority does not alone invent a self. In stage three, one makes autonomous choices. Beulah's decision to rent the pigeon-box cottage falls into this category; so does her writing and her publishing. As she pursues both choices, her identity unfolds and her happiness grows. Eugene's decision to pursue a law career is autonomous, once Beulah's nursing helps free him from the fetters of fashion; he eventually grows into a political power. Similarly, Clara's decision to leave town, based on a recognition that Guy will never love her, is autonomous. The narrator recognizes that such decisions are rare and noteworthy; it is Clara's independent decision that prompts the narrator to ask what the "process" of acquiring such strength could be.

But autonomy, for Evans, almost by definition can lead to isolation. How can an independent, self-sufficient person join the human community? Evans envisions a fourth stage, which she calls friendship, and which puts the autonomous individual into a sympathetic, nonexploitative, and honest relationship with others that leads to mutual growth. When Beulah first talks with Cornelia, she is coldly intellectual, lecturing rather than discussing ideas. Through their talks, though, Beulah learns from Cornelia; she sees, for instance, that Cornelia has for Eugene a "degree of intense love such as Beulah had supposed her incapable of feeling" (242). As a result, what had been contemptuous pity for a weak person grows into genuine compassion for a respected friend, and what had been isolated study becomes a dialogue. Similarly, because Reginald Lindsay cares about ideas, Beulah can relax with him: discussing "some of the leading literary questions of the day . . . her mouth lost its expression of resolute endurance" (347). As Evans sees it, friendship does not conflict with, but rather depends upon, the autonomy of individuals. When Cornelia asks Beulah to give her some of Beulah's "calm contentment, some of [her] strength," Beulah replies, "I am your friend, Cornelia; I will always be such; but every soul must be sufficient for itself. Do not look to me; lean upon your own nature; it will suffice for all its needs" (233). Because autonomy is predicated, service to a friend is no longer a strategy for power; Beulah takes no advantage of nursing Eugene. Finally, honesty is essential to Evans' version of friendship. Beulah is blunt with Cornelia, telling her she is "weak," and blunt with Eugene, telling him he is "rushing down to an awful gulf" of alcohol. "I have risked your displeasure—I have proved my friendship!" she concludes (293). Because he is truly a friend, Reginald can criticize Beulah's writing; she knows he will be calm, dispassionate, and fair. Honesty, mutual support, autonomy: as Beulah says, "the claims of true friendship are imperative" (377).

Yet—as the ending indicates—there is a fifth, and final, stage. For Evans must have her characters join not just the human community in general but the southern community in particular. To do that, illusions of parity must be dropped.

For women characters, various bird images express some of these stages of growth. Clara defends her lack of intellectual curiosity by saying that "an unfledged birdling cannot mount to the dizzy eyries of the eagle," whereupon Beulah urges her to "come out of your warm nest of inertia! strengthen your wings by battling with storm and wind!" (215).

But the autonomous eagle is isolated : urging Beulah to rest, Guy says that he "might as well try to win an eagle from its lonely rocky home" (341). And when she rejoins the community of faith, Beulah sees herself as "like Noah's dove," back from a lonely journey into the unknown.

Given these images of female growth, one is not surprised when Evans shows Guy as—of all people—St. Francis, feeding the birds:

> He was bare-headed and the sunshine fell like a halo upon his brown, clustering hair, threading it with gold. He held, in one hand, a small basket of grain, from which he fed a flock of hungry pigeons. On every side they gathered about him— blue and white, brown and mottled—some fluttering down from the roof of the house; two or three, quite tame, perched on his arm, eating from the basket; and one, of uncommon beauty, sat on his shoulder, cooing softly. (266)

This "singularly quiet, peaceful scene . . . indelibly daguerreotype[s] itself" on Beulah's mind. No wonder: the scene combines the image of man as God with the image of woman as bird, putting them into the relationship that Evans' culture endorsed and Evans' protagonist resisted for most of the novel—a relationship of dependence. Guy has, one remembers, said to Beulah, "it will take long years of trial and suffering to *tame* you" (my italics).

Even more appropriate—given stage five—is this biographical footnote. After Evans had reaffirmed her own faith, following her personal period of skepticism, she wrote a letter expressing her feelings to the clergyman who had helped her see the light:

> I give it over and admit that I do not and cannot know anything, save as God wills I should. Like a caged bird, I have quit fluttering madly against the bars, and am waiting for the appointed hours, when food is to be given my soul. Where is the sense of beating yourself to death, unavailingly. My proud nature you know . . . and imagine what a fierce, bitter conflict it cost me ere I could bring my spirit to rest on the Ararat of dependence of a "blind faith." . . . Like a sick child after a violent spasm, I am willing to be quiet, almost anywhere.[46]

A sick child, a caged bird—these are powerful images, but they are obviously not images of triumph, not even of healthy compromise. They are images of defeat. Personally sickened by her capitulation to "blind faith," Evans could find here no hopeful image. In her novel, she offers more: there are no cages, and there is a choice of flight images—moth, eagle, Guy's pigeon, Noah's dove. Yet in the surface plot, the mask, the choice lies only between the domesticated pigeon and the returning dove. Thus the bird imagery expresses Evans' double vision that could see strength in flight but settled personally for what she felt to be a religious cage, a vision that in her novel offers more images for flying in the texture of the novel than are permitted into the plot.

Evans sets up a number of antitheses in her novel: pride and humility, isolation and sympathy, intellect and heart, independence and dependence. From the surface plot, the reader can catch the author's intended resolutions, meant for an audience of pre–Civil War southerners: women should humble themselves so that their hearts can feel sympathy and their wills can permit dependence on husband and God. Yet submerged in the metaphoric structure, as her imagery shows, lies another, quite different, message. There, Evans' imagination works against a simple antithetical vision. After all, one remembers, it is Guy who thinks in polar opposites in the novel, showing its methodological flaw.

But Evans doesn't adumbrate just stages of social growth on that submerged level. She also presents a model of psychic growth—feelings, intellect, body—mostly through her depiction of Beulah's growth. Beulah learns to be aware of, to express, and to control her feelings; she learns to question, reason, analyze, observe; and she learns to accept her body and to use it as a medium for self-expression. These rather surprisingly modern "lessons," however, are undercut by Evans' conclusion. At the end, Beulah represses threatening feelings, relinquishes her independent mind, and uses her body only as a concealing mask for her real self.

At the outset of the novel, Beulah barely knows what her feelings are. Repressed and self-destructive, she does not shed a tear when Lilly is taken away, and she exerts power only through martyred service to the Martins. Soon, though, she becomes directly aware of her feelings; consumed with anger, she rages at the Graysons and argues with May Chilton. Her love for Guy is not as easy for her to see as was her anger; of all her feelings, this is most hidden from her own awareness. When Clara mopes after Guy, infatuated, Beulah consciously feels only pity for her. She tries to keep Guy from knowing how Clara feels, explaining to herself that she is protecting Clara, but actually protecting her own unadmitted interest in Guy. Beulah rejects with disproportionate energy the suggestion that Guy loves her: "'It is utterly false from beginning to end! He never had such a thought! never! never!' cried Beulah, striking her clenched hand heavily on the table" (198). Later, after Guy has proposed marriage, she comes a bit closer to understanding her own feelings; she knows now that "she could not believe he loved her . . . could not realize that he, who so worshipped beauty, could possibly love her" (355). Only when Guy is gone for four years does she become aware that she cares for him. And when he does finally return to ask, "Do you love me," she replies, simply, "yes." After the wedding, though, Beulah feels again the fear that kept her from recognizing her love for Guy. But instead of confronting her ambivalence—a task harder than confronting her love—Beulah merely represses her fear.

In the course of the novel, Beulah not only learns to understand but also to express her feelings. On one occasion, while she is still living with Guy Hartwell as his ward, she welcomes him home eagerly, forgetting "her wounded pride . . . only remember[ing] that he was sitting there in the study. . . . She felt as if she would like very much to smooth off the curling hair that lay thick and damp on his white, gleaming brow, but dared not." She does, however, offer him tea; when he refuses, she "bit her lip with proud vexation, and, taking her geometry, left him" (125). Several times similar scenes appear; only at the end of the novel does Beulah take the risk of fully expressing her feelings of warmth. When Beulah first sees Guy, she

> sprang into the doorway, holding out her arms, with a wild, joyful cry. "Come at last! Oh, thank God! Come at last!" Her face was radiant, her eyes burned, her glowing lips parted.
>
> Leaning against the door, with his arms crossed over his broad chest, Dr. Hartwell stood, silently regarding her. She came close to him, and her extended arms trembled; still he did not move, did not speak. . . . She looked up at him so eagerly; but he said nothing. She stood an instant irresolute, then threw her arms around his neck and laid her head on his bosom, clinging closely to him. He did not return the embrace. (430)

She must, implies Evans, let her love out, despite his coldness. And she is rewarded: finally, he "put his hand softly on her head, and smoothed the rippling hair" (431).

Throughout the novel, animals and children are given this capacity to express their feelings. Not only does Charon supply the role of emotional barometer, barking at the people whom Guy and Beulah dislike and jumping up on those they like, but the diction of little children like Claudia and Pauline is alive and imaginative in ways that other language in the novel is not. Since women are compared to animals and children, explicitly by Guy and implicitly in the action, Evans implies that emotional expressiveness is a characteristic of the true woman.

Surely that is the author's point in this final scene, when Beulah has finally let her warm heart rule her icy reason. Yet when Guy and other men extend to women other characteristics of animals and children, particularly their lack of intellect, their submissiveness to authority, and their lack of self-control, women are as a class devalued. Only the virtual absence of blacks from the novel, one suspects, prevents the completion of the southern equation.

But Evans does not make that extension. Rather, she covertly shows how women can control their feelings. One function of the mask was to control one's feelings by disguising them. Horses best symbolize the energy and power of emotion in the novel. Eugene, drunk, loses control of his horse entirely and gets hurt. Antoinette whips hers into submission, riding them daily until the spunk is gone from them. Behind her mask is a blank. But Beulah—in a scene at the very center of the novel—controls some runaway horses by anticipating their movements and using the reins. "Curb the rushing horses she did not hope to do; but, by cautious energy, succeed in turning them sufficiently aside to avoid . . . collision. . . . She stood up in front, reins in hand, trying to guide the maddened horses. Her bonnet fell off; the motion loosened her comb, and down came her long, heavy hair in black, blinding folds." She says to some men on the street who try to grab the bits, "'Stand back—all of you! You might as well catch at the winds!' . . . and with one last effort, she threw her whole weight on the reins and turned the horses into a cross street" (223). This image, of great force reined in by courage, intelligence, energy, and assertion, is that of a hero; "There are no more like her," says Cornelia. It is also the image of emotion brought under proper control, neither repressed like Antoinette's horses nor wild like Eugene's, but finally placed in creative tension between expression and control. No wonder, for Beulah, "duty is a vast volcanic agency" (117).

By the end, Beulah's creative tension turns into repression, as we have seen; she marries the Guy with the whip. Similarly, her intellectual growth lands her not behind the reins but rather in the "All-Father's bosom." Books symbolize mental development. Thus both the experience of reading books and the content of those books play significant roles in Evans' *Bildungsroman*. At the end, of course, Beulah turns to one book, the Bible, as she turns to one man and one God, rejecting all others.

The library, as the source of books and therefore of knowledge, takes on mythic proportions. It is forbidden, like the apple in Eden: Guy-as-God warns Beulah-Eve, suggestively, "Don't read my books promiscuously. There are many on those shelves yonder which I would advise you never to open. Be warned in time, my child" (131). Yet Guy-as-Adam has already fallen himself: "Do you want to be just what I am? Without belief in any creed! hopeless of eternity as of life! . . . If not, keep your hands off my books!" (132). And Guy-as-Satan encourages her, giving her free access to the library and telling her to "come to [him] for explanation" (122). The vaguely sexual implications of the language are borne out by the immature Asbury girls' fear of their father's library. And the religious metaphor is cemented by Mortimor's sermon warning that "much study is a weariness of the flesh," and that "only from the pages of Holy Writ could genuine wisdom be acquired" (264–65).

Beulah falls, of course, first for Poe's "recondite psychological truths . . . eluding analysis" and then for Emerson, Carlyle, Goethe, and dozens more. She reads through the nights, gaining in critical capacities as she goes. The issues raised in these books bear directly on her quest for identity. "How was her identity to be maintained . . . could there be consciousness without bones and muscles?" she asks early in the novel (135). As Beulah moves into the "troubled sea" of philosophy, approaching the "deepest blackest gulf" of atheism (274), pantheism suggests that she is identical to God; geology and ethnology suggest that identity is contingent not upon God as revealed in Genesis but upon natural law, as revealed in science. Yet ultimately she gives up the intellectual quest because of "the old trouble": "How far was 'individualism' allowable and safe?" (383). The choice of adjectives is significant. For when Beulah's thinking takes her into paths that might permit her confidence as an independent thinker, she rejects her thoughts; when pantheism suggests that she is part God, she rejects it. Evans does not give a convincing philosophical argument—even through Lindsay—against Beulah's ideas, as Timrod pointed out. Instead, apparently plagued by the same questions, Evans reverts after her character's conversion to the same old arguments within Beulah's mind, despite narrative statements that Beulah has changed. One senses that Evans' objections to Beulah's free thinking have more to do with how "allowable and safe" it is to pursue an independent intellectual life than they do with rational arguments. And the imagery we have already seen—the fear of being alone in a stormy night sea, the yearning of the child for the bosom of the All-Father—contribute to that sense.

But this conflict was inevitable; many nineteenth-century readers "felt that a Southern lady should refrain from discussing the subject"[47] at all, much less coming down on the side of the individual. And Emerson, one remembers, was regarded with a baleful eye by many southern men.[48] What is remarkable is not that Evans finally capitulated; rather,

it is the seriousness with which she—and Beulah—pursue the intellectual issues presented in the novel. As Nina Baym has said, Evans could
feel as passionate with her mind as she could with her heart.[49]

Beulah's passion for ideas leads her to the edge of an abyss she will
not leap into, just as she has achieved and then sacrificed a degree of
complexity and independence in her emotional growth. A similar pattern can be seen in the development of her attitude to her physical body.
Evans sets up the body as an explicit thematic concern by making
Beulah ugly—at least, ugly to herself. Beulah has "a pair of large gray
eyes set beneath an overhanging forehead, a boldly projecting forehead, broad and smooth; a rather large but finely cut mouth, an irre-
proachable nose . . . and heavy black eyebrows which, instead of arch-
ing, stretched straight across and nearly met" (2). Beulah hides her
face repeatedly because it is, she thinks, so ugly; even as late as Guy's
proposal, her reason for thinking he cannot love her is that he loves
beauty—as southern men do—so much. Yet by the time Guy returns,
"time had changed her singularly." She "was now a finely formed, remarkably graceful woman, with a complexion of dazzling transparency
. . . the dark gray eyes, with their long, jetty, curling lashes, possessed
an indescribable charm, even for strangers. She had been an ugly child,
but certainly she was a noble-looking, if not handsome, woman" (427).
Her carriage and her confidence are new, and they affect her appearance. She cares more about her grooming, putting flowers in her
hair or in her dress; and she has stopped castigating herself about her
looks. Perhaps Beulah no longer accepts her culture's definition of the
beautiful woman as her own norm. In any case, thanks to her emotional
and intellectual growth, Beulah now sees herself as subject, not object.
Hence she stops her self-deprecation for being ugly in the world's eye.
Yet the narrator seems determined also to find qualities in Beulah's actual body that she had not noticed before; certainly those lashes are not
new. Inner growth, apparently, is not enough to suit the world's definition of beauty. Probably more important, Beulah must achieve beauty in
whatever manner before her body can be fit into the values of the community as her mind and heart have already been shaped.

Beulah learns not only to accept her body but also to use it as a medium for expressing her inner self. One element of that self is her sexuality. Many critics, reasonably, think sexuality is absent from novels of
this sort; Nina Baym argues that nineteenth-century women wanted to
transcend, not express, their sexuality.[50] Yet the scene of Guy's return—
he posed like an early Bogart, she trembling, lips parted—seems erotic
enough. Tellingly, though, that description of female sexual passion is

followed by this one of the male variety: "She felt his strong frame quiver; he folded his arms about her, clasped her to his heart with a force that almost suffocated her, and bending his head, kissed her passionately" (431). Rather than being erotic, this passage emphasizes the superior physical force—and the consequent threat—of the man. And it is immediately after this nearly suffocating embrace, one notes, that Guy gives her the choice between those two "tyrants," ambition and himself. So heterosexual passion is complicated, too—by now, predictably—by Evans' sense of fundamental sexual differences.

In fact, sexuality—rather loosely defined—actually appears all the way through the novel, quite overtly, and in the most unlikely places. The same language that describes heterosexual passion also appears in love scenes between father and daughter, between sisters, between female friends, and between male friends:

[Cornelia] sprang into [Eugene's] lap, and threw her little, snowy arms about his neck, kissing him rapturously, and passing her fragile fingers through his hair. . . . He returned her caresses with an expression of almost adoring fondness, stroking her curls with a light, gentle touch. The evening was warm, and large drops stood on his forehead. She noticed it, and standing on his knees, took the corner of her tiny, embroidered apron, and wiped away the moisture, kissing the forehead as she did so. (390)

Beulah sat down on the edge of the blue-curtained bed, and drew her idol [Lilly] close to her heart. She kissed the beautiful face, and smoothed the golden curls she had so long, and so lovingly, arranged, and as the child returned her kisses, she felt as if rude hands were tearing her heart-strings loose. (15–16)

The touch of [Clara's] fingers sent a thrill through Beulah's frame, and she looked at her very earnestly.

Clara Sanders was not a beauty in the ordinary acceptation of the term, but there was an expression of angelic sweetness and purity in her countenance which fascinated the orphan. (72)

[Dr. Asbury] sprang up, nearly knocking his wife down, and looked around the room. Dr. Hartwell emerged . . . Dr. As-

bury bounded over a chair and locked his arms around the
tall form, while his gray head dropped on his friend's shoulder. (435)

This diffused sexuality may be an unconscious rebellion against the
conscious prescription for the woman of dependence on the husband.
As has been shown, the ideal woman must give up reason for faith in
God the "All-Father," give up her will to obey her husband's, shape her
disciplined heart and her body to conform to the image of a child and of
ideal beauty, relinquish her personal ambition in order to help her man;
since she has had to give up so much to the male, it is understandable
that she might fear, resent, or reject his superior physical power. Thus
she might diffuse her own sexuality into relationships that threaten less
centrally her sense of her own identity. In the scenes that seem nearly
erotic to the twentieth-century reader, the two participants are emotionally "safe"; the father unambivalently loves his child, the young girl
her sister, and the friend her/his friend. Notably, the only scene of equal
heterosexual passion occurs between Eugene and Antoinette at a
dance. And Beulah is appalled: "He held his lovely partner close to his
heart, and her head dropped very contentedly on his shoulder. He was
talking to her as they danced, and his lips nearly touched her glowing
cheek. On they came . . . Beulah looked on with a sensation of disgust,
verily she blushed for her degraded sex" (281).
    In that light, Beulah's "species of fear, of dread" (436) that pervades
her wedding ceremony is further explicable. When, immediately after
she looks at Guy's silver-threaded hair and sorrowing face and suddenly,
miraculously, her fear transposes into love, it may be because he is no
longer a stereotypical sexually adult male, but a fatherly androgyne.
    Every example has shown characters using their bodies to express
their feelings. And, predictably, this capacity is learned, not given, particularly in situations where there is conflict and emotional risk. That is
the case, of course, with Beulah and Guy; her emotional confidence is
expressed invariably by her capacity to touch Guy when she feels affection for him. Again, though, the end of the novel negates whatever
growth has taken place. For in her final subservient position, at Guy's
feet, Beulah denies rather than expresses her actual sense of both emotional and religious power over Guy; she masks her truth by falsifying
the language of her body.
    Evans seems herself unaware of the strongly physical reason she has
given Reginald Lindsay for falling in love with Beulah. When he first
meets her, she has been picking ripe berries; her cousin Georgia fas-
tens purple blossoms in Beulah's hair; and they sit down to stem the

berries. "Soon their fingers were stained with the rosy juice of the fragrant fruit. All restraint vanished" (347). It is no wonder that when Reginald proposes to her he says, "Since the evening I first saw you with your basket of strawberries, I have cherished the hope that I might one day be more than a friend" (383–84).

Evans' imagination here again seems truer than her didactic commitment, for to this very rare sensuous detail she instinctively connects emotional freedom—"all restraint vanished"—linking the two types of expressiveness. For ultimately, at the end of the internal journey, mind, heart, and body are all in connection. In Evans' narrator's terms, "heart" and "will" must work in concert, neither dominating the other, and both expressing themselves through the body.

One overriding metaphor expresses both the quest for integration of mind, heart, and body, and the quest for a right relation to authority. Evans' notion of internal order, in which all elements of the self are integrated, permitting the growth of an authoritative self, expresses itself in the image of the home. That metaphor cannot be identified with the family, for the asylum and the pigeon-box are two of the happiest homes in the novel. Rather, as a limited, controlled space, the home becomes a symbol of an individual's internal harmony or disintegration and of a community's authoritarian or democratic values.

When Pauline as a child fantasizes that in her house "I mean to paste in great letters over the doors and windows, 'Laughing and talking freely allowed!'" (71), she expresses a value essential to her own open self. When she is an adult, she is caged by her rigid husband and—appropriately—becomes a prim matron at the door of her house while she stays laughing within. Like Antoinette's face with its misleading mask, Pauline's household is headed for crisis because it is inconsistent with itself. In Mrs. Martin's house, where Beulah works as a nurse, the chaos and disorganization result in danger to the inhabitants; the baby is picking up loose pins and needles. No adult is at home; metaphorically, there is no authority in Mrs. Martin's psyche. Similarly, Dr. Hartwell's house goes to pieces while he is gone; animals graze in the gardens and all his favorite shrubs are uprooted, for he has deserted his space.

Other badly organized homes reflect distorted values. Cornelia is shut off upstairs into her sick room while fashionable society comes and goes below; cause and effect are obscure. Similarly, Guy's melodeon, his picture of Creola, and (in the reconciliation scene) Beulah herself are locked into a third-floor room at the Asburys' house while intellectual society carries on below. Cornelia is an intellectual radical, the melodeon symbolizes art, and Creola went mad; none of these, one infers, can be admitted into polite or even intellectual society. It is no surprise that the attic would then be the place where (in the reconciliation scene) Beulah first expresses her sexuality to Guy. Later, downstairs, she is far more prim.

Two ideal homes present themselves: Beulah's "pigeon-box" and the asylum. Beulah's dream, achieved with her cottage, which she shares with Mrs. Williams, was "laboring, conquering, and earning homes for ourselves"; the journey of the hero becomes a metaphorical search for a home. The cottage is just the right size for Beulah, provides just the distance and privacy she needs, and is what she calls her only real home in the novel. There is one exception: the asylum, where Mrs. Williams was, be it noted, the matron. Offering a communal and interdependent life where everyone both works and plays, where Eugene and Beulah could be friends as equals and dreamers, the asylum remains throughout the novel a symbol of the ideal home. But it—like the pigeon-box—is vulnerable to forces beyond its control; just as her society's mores for women prevent Beulah from staying in her little house after Mrs. Williams' death, so the tyrannical board can have its way with any individual orphan's destiny. The only home with a future, in *Beulah*, is Noah's ark.

Beulah searches for Beulah land, for Jerusalem, for her home, throughout the novel. *Beulah land* is a traditional term, too, for the South. Like Bunyan's pilgrim, she finds a land of peace and rest at the last—or so Evans wants us to believe. In a rare moment of self-revelation, Guy tells Beulah early in the novel that geographical journeying gets him nowhere: "I pack my trunk, embark, and finally wake up in Naples, and there beside me is the stern fact, the sad self, unrelenting, identical, that I fled from. . . . My giant goes with me wherever I go" (108). Beulah's psychic journey into her own sad self takes her back, full circle, to her beginnings, to her name; *Beulah* means, in Hebrew, "married woman." Just so: Evans rests her point.

And if there were any doubts left in her readers' minds about the proper relationship of wife to husband, Evans was to answer it in the following poem, with which, seven years after *Beulah*, she concluded *St. Elmo*. St. Elmo addresses Edna Earl:

> My wife, my life. Oh! We will walk this world,
> Yoked in all exercise of noble end,
> And so through those dark gates across the wild
> That no man knows. My hopes and thine are one;
> Accomplish thou my manhood, and thyself
> Lay thy sweet hands in mine and trust to me.[51]

By trusting her husband to navigate the "wild," Edna will survive; by "accomplish[ing his] manhood," she will give him an identity.

I disagree, then—at least for this novel—with Mary Kelley's argument that the enemy is materialism and individualism; I agree with Nina Baym that the real story is a female *Bildungsroman* rather than social criticism. Yet more fundamentally, Kelley is right: in this novel, the prescription (for individual female growth) does turn to protest and finally, depressingly, to capitulation. And I do not share Baym's optimism that "Hartwell's return finds each of them finally ready for the other. For both of them marriage will be a compromise, as it must be; but Hartwell is prepared to compromise at last, and Beulah no longer equates compromise with defeat."[52] It is difficult to see mutual compromise dramatized in the final scenes of *Beulah*.

Augusta Jane Evans found herself split between an inner vision and a desire to conform. That inner vision develops a female *Bildungsroman*, promising psychic integration and an interdependent relationship with one's community. But Evans' mask was that of the southern woman writer; the actual community for which and within which she wrote held strongly patriarchal values concerning religion, women, and the structure of society itself. Thus when Evans forces her *Bildungsroman* to fit the social expectations that it must, she has to convert her speculative protagonist to an All-Father God and shape her character into that of the child-wife who can serve as idol for a southern gentleman. Marriage, as it is depicted in this novel, then, does solve one of the problems raised by the novel: how can a woman best survive in the southern community? Yet instead of solving, it simply exacerbates the other central theme of the narrative: how can a southern woman grow? And at the end, instead of healthy compromise, Beulah finds herself divided again, concealing her adult self behind the mask of a child. Converted from the devil, clothed with propriety, she has become the very type of the woman writer Hawthorne so despised.

CHAPTER III   # Grace King
That Great Mother
Stream Underneath

Grace King was born in 1851, 1852, or 1853: the sources vary.[1] In any case, she was old enough to experience and remember vividly the period of Civil War and Reconstruction; much of her work is set in New Orleans during the latter period. "It had been her grand theme," says Robert Bush, ". . . defending the character of New Orleans and upholding the quality of its traditions."[2]

By 1853, both its economic and its social history had made New Orleans a city more European than most American cities, more sophisticated than most southern cities. Since the colonial period, its port had served to export goods from that vast section of the continent with access to the Mississippi; by 1835, New Orleans' exports exceeded those of New York, and by 1840 the city's population was exceeded only by those of New York, Baltimore, and Philadelphia. Although its economic and demographic position deteriorated during the immediate prewar period, New Orleanians seemed "complacent . . . tranquil and undisturbed."[3]

Moreover, the city mixed and separated racial and national groups to form a kaleidoscope unique in the nation. Originally settled by the French and Spanish, New Orleans produced the Creoles, highest in the city's social scale, self-segregated from the rest of the town, and often French-speaking. White Americans coming from South and North increasingly dominated the economic and political life of the city after 1803. Blacks in the city presented as wide a variety of cultures as did the whites, from the West Indians' indigenous life-style, to the mulattoes, some of whom were free (though without all the perquisites of full citizenship), to the quadroons and octoroons (the name indicating the number of black ancestors), who formed a caste of their own.[4] Needless to say, the relationships among these groups provided a complexity of conflicts and resolutions that made New Orleans almost a perfect city for a writer.

Grace King's principal subject matter was found in the society of the Creoles—the descendants of European aristocrats, the "best men under Bienville"—and their successors.[5] George W. Cable, another New Orleans writer, described the Creole character as it appeared just before the French ceded Louisiana to the Americans:

> [The women] were much superior to the men in quickness of wit, and excelled them in amiability and in many other good qualities. . . . [The men] are said to have been coarse, boastful, vain; and they were, also, deficient in energy and application, without well-directed ambition, unskilful in handicraft—doubtless through negligence only—and totally wanting in that community feeling which begets the study of reciprocal rights and obligations, and reveals the individual's advantage in the promotion of the common interest. Hence, the Creoles were fonder of pleasant fictions regarding the salubrity, beauty, good order, and advantages of their town, than of measures to justify their assumptions.[6]

Cable exhibits his own bias here, but certainly one of those "pleasant fictions"—and one of the city's traditions—was the definition of the sexes. "If it were not for the South," wrote Grace King, "the terms gentleman and lady would fall out of our vocabulary, which would contain only man and woman."[7] The Creole definition apparently differed only slightly from the South's, probably in being more obviously European. In discussing the Creole man during the Civil War, Cable at any rate saw him as "little different from the Southerner at large, . . . gallant, brave, enduring, faithful."[8]

Grace King was not herself a born-to-the-blood Creole. Her father came to the city in the 1830s. A lawyer, William King was a southerner, born in Georgia, raised in Alabama, and educated at the University of Virginia; he demonstrated his loyalty to his region during the Civil War by refusing to take the oath of allegiance to the Union after New Orleans fell to Federal troops in 1862. Grace's mother, King's second wife, Sarah Ann Miller, also came from Georgian stock and retained her Protestant heritage. But she was born, like her daughter, in New Orleans and grew up in the middle of its French-speaking, Catholic, Creole society.[9]

New Orleans was one of the first southern cities to fall to Federal troops during the Civil War. For the rest of her life, Grace King remembered vividly the hardships of the war and the occupation of the city by Federal troops. As a loyal Confederate, William King was forced to flee the city to escape imprisonment, leaving behind his wife and children. Mrs. King "saw her opportunity to open a boarding-house for Federal officers."[10] Later she finagled a passport into the Confederacy through one of these officers, and the family escaped to their plantation, L'Embarras, near New Iberia, where they survived minimally until the end of the war. Then they returned to the city, "completely dispossessed of their city property and obliged to live in crowded quarters among working-class people opposite Jackson Barracks."[11]

Grace King, though raised a Presbyterian, was educated, like her mother, mostly in Catholic Creole schools; after the war, she won a prize in French, competing with her native-speaking classmates. When she finished the Institut St. Louis, Heloise Cenas taught her "Carlyle, Ruskin, a serious study of English . . . Keats . . . Wordsworth. . . . This was beyond the curriculum of a girls' school at that time in New Orleans," remembered King in 1932. She was never to give up the "intellectual life" (*MSWL*, 89–90). And in the life of the Creoles, where she found "more individuality and certainly more sensuous appeal,"[12] she set her fiction.

King never married. After finishing school, she assumed her share of responsibility in the management of the Kings' large and sociable household and spent the rest of her life living and traveling with members of her immediate family.[13] Her father died in 1881; she continued to live with the "charming raconteuse," her mother, whose death in

1903 deeply affected her daughter, and with two unmarried sisters, who enabled Grace to write by taking over many household tasks and offering secretarial help.

After the war, Grace King's family lived at "various temporary addresses" until 1904, when the children bought a house on Coliseum Place in which one brother and three sisters lived for the rest of their lives. To King, buying this house was

> of solemn significance—the great landmark of our lives—
> the attainment of what our Father worked so nobly for—the
> hope and prayer of Mimi [her mother]—a permanent home
> for the family. What a track of life behind us; since the day
> that the family quitted their home under the compulsion
> of Butler's orders, leaving their furniture—pictures . . .
> souvenirs—behind them . . . . How we have struggled and
> worked—fallen down, gotten up again—to toil on . . . striv-
> ing with others—striving with the villainous temper of one
> another . . . suffering what anguish of mind & heart—in the
> midnight hours of wakefulness—in consequence thereof—
> the home . . . we are where we were forty years ago! at the
> point from which the war drove us back.[14]

The house represented the end of a long search for the place she had started from: the past, the traditions, and the life lost with the war. No wonder she was, as Edmund Wilson wrote Robert Bush, "offended" by Joseph Hergesheimer when he asked her, "Where did you pick up all these beautiful things?"[15] One earned one's past.

One also earned one's way in the world. When her father died, King felt obliged to seek a career, hoping for financial independence. The first step she took toward a career of letters came during the winter of 1885. Julia Ward Howe, who was then visiting New Orleans, led a literary discussion group called the Pan-Gnostic League; that winter, Grace King read a paper for it titled "The Heroines of Novels." During the same year, she met *Century* magazine editor Richard Watson Gilder at a party. To him, she claimed (as many New Orleanians thought) that George W. Cable had "stabbed the city in the back, we felt, in a dastardly way to please the Northern press." Gilder challenged the Creoles to do better. She "later asked herself, 'Why, why, do we not write our side?'" climbed the stairs to her bedroom, and wrote "Monsieur Motte." Thus, says Bush, "outrage . . . first drove her to her pen." To defend "our side," she portrayed sympathetic black-white relationships, especially between women, that she hoped put the lie to Cable's more pessimistic treatment in *The Grandissimes* (1880). King's defense of the established point of view characterized her career to its end, when she had become a "literary heroine of the state" and her home a social center in New Orleans. Cable, on the other hand, was barely forgiven by the city.[16]

Grace King sent "Monsieur Motte" anonymously to Gilder; it was rejected. But, again at a party, she made another fortuitous connection: Charles Dudley Warner. "I had dragged through a long evening talking 'scraps,'" she later wrote. "But I watched my opportunity & scratched it when it came."[17] Soon she and Warner were close friends; encouraged, she mailed the story to him, and he submitted it to *New Princeton Review*, where it appeared in January, 1886. In 1888, with three more sections, it appeared as a novel. Ironically, one positive review in a New York newspaper attributed the anonymously published story to George W. Cable.[18]

In 1906, writing to Warrington Dawson, Grace King remembered *Monsieur Motte*: "A first novel, you know, is a first revelation of one's self. As you once wrote me, it writes itself. Criticism is useless upon it because one can write a first novel only once. Never again will you be so much possessed by your characters. Hereafter you must be content with possessing them—but you will be freer to do as you please."[19]

It is "near mid-day in June," in New Orleans, at a girls' school for boarders and day students called the Institut St. Denis. The graduating seniors (class of 1874) are nervous, about to take their final exam in French history. A black woman tries to get into the gated schoolyard; she is carrying the toilette for "Mamzelle Marie," but the white woman inside, maintaining a "quarrel involving complex questions of the privileges of order and the distinctions of race,"[20] is making entry difficult.

Thus opens the short story "Monsieur Motte," published in 1886 as Grace King's first fiction. The story's plot hinges on the irony that there is no Monsieur Motte. Marcélite, the quadroon bringing Marie Modeste Motte's toilette, has saved enough money from her earnings as a hairdresser to the Creole elite to board and educate Marie in the Institut, hoping that Marie won't remember her earliest years. As a baby, Marie escaped in Marcélite's arms from the family plantation after the deaths of both her parents during the Civil War. Marcélite (later called the "magician") has invented a mysterious "uncle" who has "supported" Marie. But now, at Marie's impending graduation, Marcélite is faced with the logical conclusion to her long fiction: Marie wants to go home to her uncle.

Having managed to enter the school, Marcélite prepares her "*bébé*" for the festivities with even more than her accustomed solicitude;

Marie, however, cries when her questions about "Uncle" are evaded. Meanwhile, the school's principal, the widowed Madame Eugénie Lareveillère, worries about the awarding of prizes, the graying of her hair, the graduation fête, and her relationship to the amiable notary, Monsieur Armand Goupilleau. Marie, she decides, has won the prize in French history after the "trying" Monsieur Mignot's test. Marcélite approaches Madame Lareveillère, almost ready to confess her invention, but her effort is thwarted, in part by circumstance. She goes back outside the gate, leans against the forbidding wall of the school, throws her apron over her head, and spends all evening against the wall.

The girls, excited about their futures as belles, look forward to the appearance of Marcélite, who is to prepare their coiffures. But the next day Marcélite does not come: the boarders and the teachers must appear at the event *sans coiffure*. Marie suffers more than the others; not only does she confront the emotions she has suppressed concerning her own orphanhood, but she feels the absence of Marcélite, the one person of all who should help her through the ritual of moving from adolescence to womanhood.

The great evening comes. Talent and beauty find their rewards; and each girl leaves with her family from the room and the school—except Marie, who scans each parting man for her "uncle." The last man to leave simply picks up a fan left behind by one of the girls and walks out. This night, alone in the large dormitory room, Marie faces more clearly still the implications of her aloneness; in anger she strips off all her clothes (forgetting the history prize crown) and finally sleeps.

The next morning, Madame asks for Marcélite. There has been no word from her. To Madame's surprise, Marie is still at the school. Together, they search out the school's records for Monsieur Motte: there is no address. Madame, in desperation, sends for her friend Monsieur Goupilleau (whom she publicly claims to look upon as a "father"). Goupilleau, who is secretly in love with Eugénie, sends for the city directory. Still no Monsieur Motte.

Suddenly, a noise—apparently a struggle—is heard outside Madame's room. It is Marcélite, now a "panting, tottering, bedraggled wretch" (91); she begs help from Goupilleau and finally tells the truth, thinking Marie can't hear: "It was me—me a nigger, that sent her to school and paid for her—" (92). Marie overhears; she nearly collapses, and Marcélite interprets this to be her shock that she has been supported by a "nigger." Marcélite herself has spent the night under a bed in the dormitory, hearing Marie's cries for her and afraid to go to her. Marie now stands up to say that she wants to go home with Marcélite. "A white young lady like you go live with a nigger like me!" responds

Marcélite in horror (94). Marie claims she is "not too good" for that; Marcélite interprets this to mean that Marie believes she is Marcélite's biological daughter.

In a one-page resolution to the plot, Goupilleau intervenes. He says he will be a father to Marie; Madame Lareveillère adds that she will be her mother. Marcélite then pulls out the prayer book she has carried inside her clothing for seventeen years, the proof that Marie is indeed a pure white Motte. The papers are, says the narrator, "unanswerable champions for the honor of dead men and the purity of dead women" (95). All the white people agree that it is *"par la grâce de Dieu"* that the papers survive; Goupilleau takes Madame's hand and ends the tale by affirming the old values: "They say, Eugénie, that the days of heroism are past, and they laugh at our romance." We are not told what will happen to Marcélite.

This was King's original conception, designed to respond to Gilder's challenge that some New Orleanian tell the truth about the Creoles if they objected to Cable's version. In letters, Grace King explicitly stated that her aim in "Monsieur Motte" had to do with the female gender, black and white. "It seems to me," she wrote to Charles Dudley Warner, "white as well as black women have a sad showing in what people call romance."[21] Later, she wrote to Warner that she "love[d] to dwell on this . . . holy passion of the Negro women, for it serves to cancel those other grosser ones, with which they are really victimized by their blood. And besides I think it highly honorable to the Southern women that they could be so served and loved by slaves."[22]

"Monsieur Motte" gives us an authorial voice surer of itself as a writer, more detached and more careful in its imaginative ordering of experience than Evans'. The title itself demonstrates authorial irony and introduces the major theme of a reality (or its absence) that hides beneath the apparent, a theme that is supported carefully and subtly by other elements in the fiction. The romance of Madame Lareveillère and Monsieur Goupilleau, for instance, is a "subterranean passage for friendship." Like the truth about Monsieur Motte and Marcélite, this buried truth is unearthed at the conclusion of the tale. And with symbolic appropriateness, something close to nakedness parallels the disclosure of the real, in Marie's deserted anguish (84) and Marcélite's final revelation (91). In keeping with the theme that the truth conflicts with what appears is the careful narrative control over what the reader and what the characters know. The narrator keeps the final revelation from both reader and characters until the scene of Marcélite's disheveled return, when all learn, simultaneously, what is true.

King develops a corollary theme—journey from one realm of understanding to another, deeper one—through symbols. Primary, of course, are the wall and door of the school, out of which most of the girls pass at graduation, through which Marcélite must be allowed to bring Marie's toilette, and on which Marcélite falls in a heap in her despair over how to handle the fact of Monsieur Motte's nonentity. The boarders and the day students—*internes* and *externes*—reinforce the notion that there are two worlds, radically different in kind. The *externes*, each from an individual home, come, to a girl, well coiffed to the fête; the *internes*, all in one communal family, must make do without the help of Marcélite, and they show it. ("What is the matter with your hair?" ask the *externes* [83]). Marie is separated even from that group. When, left alone after the fête, she sees a man come in and thinks he must be her uncle, the fan he retrieves (instead of her) underlines Marie's separation from both the frivolity ("when they opened their . . . fans . . . it was like a cloud of butterflies hovering and coquetting about their own lips") and the internal unity of the group of girls who "always do the same thing at the same time" (82–83). King neatly weaves her themes—the two worlds, the conflict of reality and appearance—by the simple choice of one profession. She could have given Marcélite a type of work irrelevant to the meaning of the story—washerwoman, nurse, housekeeper. But Marcélite is a hairdresser: she is essential to the school's students and faculty, showing where the real values of the school lie—in appearance.

Yet with all this care and artistry, one still senses difficulties, a sense of false resolution or irresolution, by the time the story ends. That ending is almost as crammed as is the end of *Beulah* with lucky revelations. And some problems are not resolved at all. What is the meaning, for example, of Marie's comment that "I am not too good" to live with Marcélite? Is this a sign of maturity on Marie's part—does she use the word "good" ironically, showing her consciousness of the false divisions of race? Or is it self-deprecation? Does it come (as Marcélite thinks) from Marie's belief that she is in fact Marcélite's daughter and that, since she is therefore also black, she is "not too good"? King never clears this up. More important, the future for Marcélite is equally unclear. She is in many ways the central character in the story, but she is left out of the triangle of familial resolution. One doesn't even know why she looks as roughed-up as she does. Has she been drunk? Beaten up? Gone on a self-destructive rampage? Why, in fact, has she not anticipated the problem with Monsieur Motte before now? And, since she had the packet of papers all along, why did she feel there was a problem at all? One might guess these problems were symptomatic of Marcélite's anguished torment about giving up her "*bébé*," perhaps of her refusal to admit the necessity to herself. But at the forefront of the concluding paragraphs, instead of Marcélite's agonized mind, we see the happy end for the white folks.

Part of the difficulty here can be answered by speculating that King, like Evans, has stepped into waters from which she must retreat. Although the author's stated intent is to "bring us all nearer together blacks and whites,"[23] the degree of that proximity becomes fuzzy. By creating the nasty white lower-class Jeanne as a foil for Marcélite, King demonstrates that it is not class but race that keeps Marcélite an outsider: she must stop the imaginative exploration of black-white relations at a point short of equality. Marie cannot be allowed to live with her real, if not biological, mother. A closer look at King's depiction of women, men, and society should shed light on this racial issue.

King posits her major female characters in the story against not the ideal but the typical. And the typical white southern female is exactly what the Institut St. Denis is designed to produce. Like Evans' fashionable lady, the students care about beauty above all ("A woman's first duty is to be beautiful," says our ironic narrator [76]). Hence trips to the shops are the girls' only forays into the outside world, the most beautiful girls are placed center front on the graduation platform, and the future holds "a debut in society, a box at the opera, beautiful toilettes, balls, dancing, music" (75).

But beauty requires dependence, not only on money but also on the people who make one beautiful. The typical girl, then, is pampered and dependent. She is protected, even ignorant: the gates are built of "the heavy cypress timber and iron fastenings, prescribed by the worldly, or heavenly, experience of St. Denis as the proper protection of a young ladies' boarding school" (57). The sex, thus protected, is still further shielded and isolated from reality, since womanhood "usually warrants justice in leaving one eye at least unbound" (55).

The ultimate goal of these soon-to-be belles is, of course, marriage and motherhood. After the "romances and poetry," the "nascent passion," the "vague apprehensions," comes the "great unknown but instinctive prophecy" (62) that we have seen implied on the previous page: school academic prizes had to be earned only because "*noblesse oblige*, that the glory of maternal achievements be not dimmed in these very walls where their mothers . . . strove for laurel crowns" (61). The cycle must continue, and that "nascent passion" must be saved for the one man who deserves it, to maintain the "purity" (95) that is also essential.

For these young women, education is not substance but surface. "Personally they could not imagine any state or condition in life when knowledge of French history would be a comfort or cosmography an assistance; but prizes were so many concrete virtues which lasted fresh into grandmotherhood" (61). The "very idea" of "no more study, routine, examinations" intoxicates the girls; they "efface with cheerful industry every trace of their passage through the desert of education" (80).

Such women, too, must of necessity remain in important ways child-like. When Marie, who says easily that her life "depends" on her uncle and who weeps over the loss of her supposed protector, looks at her trunk, the narrator (now in Marie's mind) says "What more credible witness than a coffin or a trunk?" (81). Passage, journey, movement, and hence growth—all are linked to death.

This is no place for hard women. The girls are tender towards one another, supportive and sensitive; they have learned already how to help one another by what is essentially fabrication. All know the convention of the "migraine" for the reality of personal difficulty. Fondness and affection, the network of "best friends," tie the girls together as individuals and as a group. Religion, too, is presupposed and never denied. But these graceful, tender girls are also overt racists. "The more I brush," says one, "the more like a *nègre* I look" (81). The convent girls, King seems to say, are prepared in the best way to fit as good Creoles into their class, their race, and their gender: they will be belles, then wives, and then mothers, all the while remaining essentially children themselves, thanks to the protection that permits ignorance. In short, "they had a grace of ease, the gift of generations; a self-composure and polish, dating from the cradle. Of course they did not romp, but promenaded arm in arm, measuring their steps with dainty particularity; moving the whole body with rhythmic regularity, displaying and acquiring at the same time a sinuosity of motion" (60).

Posited against this "typical" white woman, albeit possessing some of her qualities, are Madame Lareveillère, Marie Modeste Motte, and the narrator herself. Madame Lareveillère is alone and widowed, running a school with apparent success. We see her making decisions (about prizes) in the full awareness of the relationship of money to merit: "No one but a schoolmistress," says the narrator, "knows the mental effort requisite for the working out of an equation which sets good and bad scholars against good and bad pay. Why could not the rich girls study more, or the poor less?" (69). An independent and educated woman, she nevertheless has an intimate relationship with a man—and a man who is not, unequivocally, her protector.

Marie, too, differs from the typical. She is forced by the circumstance of Marcélite's apparent desertion to confront herself, to go on that journey that looked so much like death itself. We are prepared for this difference by her description as a "proud, reserved, eager, passionate spirit" under the chrysalis of the apparent languor, apathy, and lassitude that are fashionable (62). It is no surprise, then, that when she recognizes her own solitude in the "shelter" of the night, she feels a "woman's indignation and pity over it. The maternal instinct in her bosom was roused by the contemplation of her own infancy. . . . and she wept, not for herself, but for all women and all orphans" (84). King wants us to notice the choice of "woman," not girl, and she follows this scene of Marie's partial insight with another. Marie "bounded up, and with eager, trembling fingers tearing open the fastenings, she threw the grotesque masquerade, boots and all, far from her on the floor" (84). There is hope for her, one is led to think; loss has produced insight, and self-pity given over to anger, causing her to reject the role as represented by her clothing. Moreover, Marie goes to bed with her gilt-paper crown still on, the only clothing left—and her prize for winning the French history contest.

Finally, the narrator herself demonstrates qualities not found in the "typical" woman. She has a good dose of irony, as we have seen. And her knowledge of an "outside" (largely economic) world lends further credence to this narrator's experience and education: describing a little girl's leaping for a bell-pull, for instance, she says "the operation involved a terrible disproportion between labor invested and net profit" (59).

But independence, growth, insight, and strength are mitigated in all three. Madame Lareveillère, for instance, must be told what a city directory is: she is that isolated, that ignorant of the larger world. Also, she falls easily into racism when Marcélite fails to appear. She calls her a "great, big, fat, lazy good-for-nothing quadroon" (85). And she perceives Marcélite's "desertion" of her customers as approaching "tragic seriousness": "The being deserted in a critical moment by a trusted servitor, dropped without warning by a confidante, left with an indifference, which amounted to heartlessness . . .—this, and not the mere trivial combing, was what isolated and distinguished Madame Lareveillére in her affliction" (82). Her overreaction shows that even Madame's independence is shaky at best.

Marie, it seems, has really journeyed, really become an adult human, for near the end of the story "her eyes [are] too old for her face" (93). When Marcélite returns, Marie hears (through a symbolically consistent half-open door) the truth about "Monsieur Motte" and, when she asks to go home with Marcélite, acts with quiet assertion and decisiveness in the face of knowledge. Were she in fact to do so, we might have a heroine who has grown to freedom from even the societal dictate of racism.

But the third significant woman, the narrator, snatches her created Marie from the outside world, as it is most extremely embodied in the

home of a black woman, and puts her into the arms of Madame Lareveillère and under the "protection" of Monsieur Goupilleau. Moreover,
the narrator brings religion back on the scene: it is a prayer book that
confirms for all the "honor of dead men and the purity of dead women,"
i.e., Marie's legitimate birth to white people. To cap it off, of course, the
narrator makes a pseudofamily of the white folks and ends her story
with Monsieur Goupilleau's pungent remark: "They say, Eugénie, that
the days of heroism are past, and they laugh at our romance!" (95).

Clearly the heroism is ascribed to all, including Marcélite: that is one
way King challenges Cable. And it is Marcélite who, more than any
other woman in the story, embodies the ideal that King adumbrated in
her depiction of Marie and Madame and embodies herself as narrator.
Marcélite is strong, intelligent, independent, and self-supporting, fully
capable of love (particularly maternal love), yet able to show her anger
in astonishingly assertive ways. But Marcélite is black. How can a white
southern woman put her authorial voice into a black woman?

Once considered, King's choice seems perfectly appropriate. Marcélite is a woman who, possessing all the qualities and more that are
valued elsewhere in the story, whether by implication or assertion,
is also irretrievably oppressed. Here is Marcélite, the strong woman,
speaking to the notary: "'Master! Oh master! Help me!' All the suffering and pathos of a woman's heart were in the tones, all the weakness,
dependence, and abandonment in the words" (92). The narrator has
chosen to describe this plea, not as that of a slave, or even of a black, but
of a woman. The association between blacks and all females is clear. A
strong woman in a situation of insoluble oppression may turn her anger
to herself. Marie, for instance, does this when she says, at the height of
her resilience from the blow of desertion, "If she [Marie] could die then
and there! that would hurt her uncle who cared so little for her, Marcélite who had deserted her!" (84). It is just what Marcélite, too, has
apparently done in her night-long vigil by the wall and in her chaotic
and distraught appearance in the last scene. Marcélite's self-abuse has
been seen earlier: she calls herself "'nigger, nigger, nigger' (trying to
humiliate and insult herself)," explains the narrator (68).

Not only does the narrator associate Marcélite's behavior with that of
all women, but she also articulates what she thinks is Marcélite's point
of view:

> Her untamed African blood was in rebellion against the re-
> ligion and civilization whose symbols were all about her in
> [Madame's] dim and stately chamber,—a civilization which
> had tampered with her brain, had enervated her will, and
> had duped her with false assurances of her own capability.

> She felt a crushing desire to tear down, split, destroy, to surround herself with ruins, to annihilate the miserable little weak devices of intelligence, and reassert the proud supremacy of brute force. She longed to humiliate that meek Virgin Mother; and if the form on the crucifix had been alive she would have gloated over his blood and agony. She thirsted to get her thin, tapered, steel-like fingers but once more on that pretty, shapely, glossy head. (73)

The narrator carefully condemns such feelings as "untamed" and alien. Nevertheless, that same "religion and civilization" have had similar effects on Madame and Marie, making Madame to a degree isolated and dependent on Monsieur Goupilleau and rousing Marie to anger, ripping their symbols off her body. And like the white women, Marcélite has participated in its devices, deceiving her beloved *bébé*. Thus it is likely that King's emotional identification went strongly into the creation of Marcélite, for she represents in the extreme the condition of the white southern woman. But King founders in her conclusion precisely because she cannot carry out this imaginative leap to its conclusion. She must see the alien civilization as black, not male.

And those comments are direct. Madame Lareveillère calls men "egoists" who help women only when they want to, and she doubts whether Marie will receive Monsieur Motte's inheritance because "one is never sure about men" (74); she gives Marie a woman-to-woman talk: "You see, *ma fille*, this is a lesson. You must not expect too much of the men: they are not like us. Oh, I know them well. They are all *égoïstes*. They take a great deal of trouble for you when you do not want it, if it suits them; and then they refuse to raise their little finger for you, though you get down on your knees to them" (87). Her bitterness is clear, and the narrator supports it by making the one male teacher we see, Monsieur Mignot, a man of "diabolical temper" (56).

Hostility toward men is mitigated, though, not only by the introduction of the perfectly "feminized man" Helen Papashvily mentions, but by his treatment as something more than a maimed creature for woman to dominate.[24] The only man with a significant role in the story, Monsieur Goupilleau has the "eyes of a poet and the smile of a woman" (89); he is far shorter than Marcélite; his hands are "kind, tender, and little"; his eyes "glistened with tears" at Marcélite's story. Madame Lareveillère has been careful to describe him to Marie as "a father, and he treats me just as if I were his daughter. I go to him as to a confessor. . . . He is just like a father, I assure you, and very, very old" (88). But the reader knows that she is portraying him thus in order to cover up the "romance," to make it appear "innocent." Yet what is their real relationship? They are friends. He provides the "subterranean passage for friendship" that "all unmarried women, widows or maids" have and that "sometimes offers a retreat into matrimony" (88). And the reader is told, in the rest of this passage, that Madame's real feelings for the man are far more adult than those of a daughter. So Monsieur Goupilleau is a genuine friend, who might flavor the friendship with romance.

But King introduces into the last scene, once again, elements of the "typical" man that confuse the issue. He is the one who must send for the directory—he knows the "real" world outside. He must rescue the ladies from the unknown "assault" when Marcélite arrives: "But danger called him outside," says the narrator; "he unloosed the hands [Madame's] and opened the door" (90). It is he, not she, who opens a door, a symbol that has increasingly been used to separate truth from appearance, the "outside" from the protected "inside." And, finally, when the dénouement occurs, he assumes the traditional paternal role to his "daughter," Marie: "I shall protect her; I shall be a father to her—" (94).

In almost the last line of the story, we feel we are back at the end of *Beulah*. Monsieur Goupilleau "hazarded the bold step of taking both her [Madame's] hands in his," the symbol for the protection a husband will afford a wife when he takes her metaphorical hand and she, his name.

As was the case in *Beulah*, the community, as symbolized by the home, takes strange forms in "Monsieur Motte." The ideal seems at first to be the nuclear family. Little attention is paid to larger communities, and Marie expresses throughout the need for a mother and a father. On page 63, the narrator says "the young woman was motherless [despite Marcélite]. She had an uncle, however, who might become a father." Again, Marie says "I want to go home so much, and to see him [uncle]!" (67). She has never seen the man or the place, yet she calls it "home." Later, "if she were as old as that trunk, she would have known a father, a mother, and a home!" (81). After graduation, she still wears a "light shawl she had thoughtfully provided to wear home. Home!" (84). Yet all these quotations come *before* her "journey" into what the narrator calls "womanly" insight and behavior; one may guess, then, that the "family" as a model for adult community is to be dismissed.

The need for a community is met, however, in other ways in the story. The community of the school itself, like Beulah's asylum, seems to provide for the family needs of the girls: "Relieved from the more-or-less restraining presence of the day scholars, the boarders promenaded in the cordial intimacy of *home* life" (75, my emphasis). And the thrust of the story indicates that "home" is defined by the emotional ties a person has; this is why Marie wants to go "home" with Marcélite. Home is not defined even by class or race, but as a community of feeling.

As in *Beulah*, emotional ties are expressed physically. But, again, this leads to a rechanneling of sexuality. The most obvious and most powerful feeling is maternal love, a love that benefits the "mother" as much as the "child." Marcélite's love for Marie is so important to the black woman that she sees its end as her own death (69). And Madame's maternal feelings for Marie give Madame herself a new sense of existence. The mother-daughter bond is as crucial a form of relationship as exists in the story, and that bond is in no way dependent on biological motherhood, as is clear from the two mother figures in the story.

Yet Marcélite's love for Marie is rendered not just physically but sexually:

> She [Marie] felt the hands patting her back and the lips pressed against her hair; but she could not see the desperate, passionate, caressing eyes, "savoring" her like the lips of an eager dog.
>
> "Let us try them on," said Marcélite.
>
> She knelt on the floor and stripped off one shoe and stocking. When the white foot on its fragile ankle lay in her dark palm, her passion broke out afresh. She kissed it over and over again; she nestled it in her bosom; she talked baby-talk to it in creole; she pulled on the fine stocking as if every wrinkle were an offence, and slackness an unpardonable crime. How they both labored over the boot,—straining, pulling, smoothing the satin, coaxing, urging, drawing the foot! What patience on both sides! What precaution that the glossy white should meet with no defilement! (64)

Although King's point is to show the reader the depth of Marcélite's "holy passion," a love that Marie only guesses at, and although her readers certainly found nothing odd—as *Beulah*'s did not—in the passage, it is important to notice that the language used could well be found today in a romantic novel of sexual passion. Further, the comparison of Marcélite to a dog implies that blacks could be passionate, could wish for the unattainable; but that they would always be thwarted—like dogs who can never reach their masters' "level." Insofar as the black woman is the white woman's "double," then, the scene warns women of both races that to allow even a desire for their male "masters" to penetrate the defense of repression would only increase vulnerability; one becomes a helpless puppy.

Predictably, then, sexual passion between a woman and a man is infused, as in *Beulah*, with a sense of inequality. The "first thrill" of Monsieur Goupilleau's "first passion" is felt when Madame "held him fast

with her two little white hands on his arm. '*Mon ami*, I implore you!'"
(90). She doesn't want him to risk rushing to the door to see what the
ruckus is. Of course, his thrill comes in part from her touch and in part
from her caring about his safety. But the "implore" is oddly similar to
Marcélite's "Master! Help me!"—an appeal to someone who has the
power to reject the plea. Perhaps, then, he is also "thrilled" by her vulnerability. But more important, this is not a very erotic passage by comparison with those describing Marcélite. Nor is the final scene when he
"hazards the bold step of taking both her hands in his . . . recollecting
the tender pressure on his arm" (95). Those hands are practically in kid
gloves, as are the author's; adult male-female passion is described in
language that to a modern reader, ironically, better befits the touch of a
parent. The reversal seems complete.

Although there are differences, Evans' and King's imaginations thus
far seem to focus on certain themes that are central to these southern
women writers. Imperfectly orchestrated, perhaps, in both instances,
the writers imagine a woman who is strong, independent, expressive,
honest, intelligent, the mistress of her fate—and pose her against foils
who are puppets to fashion, to conventions, to men, even to religion.
Marcélite is a "threatening idol" (72) to Christians. But both writers
want their protagonists to have a relationship or relationships with men
that are both conventionally and emotionally satisfying. Evans gives
Beulah the intelligence of her husband, as well as his artistic apprecia-
tion; King gives Madame Lareveillère a man who, in some ways, is like
Madame herself. The key seems to be not identity (though close to it)
but enough shared characteristics for the man and woman to be friends.
For both, though, that friendship is damaged by its elements of sexual
inequality. And, finally, both writers seem to find some kind of solitary
journey essential for a woman's development. But both reject ultimate
isolation from any "community" (however defined) as a means of self-
definition or happiness.

Neither writer has been able to offer this vision without qualification
or confusion, and both seem largely unaware of the submerged implications. But this failure is, if unhappy, understandable: that vision rejects
the dominant social pressures of the nineteenth century that defined
woman, man, and the community in ways that would prevent each author's ideal from becoming actual—and perhaps her book from being
published.

After "Monsieur Motte" appeared in Sloane's *New Princeton Review* it
was, according to its author, "well received. It pleased the public, the
quiet, unsensational public of the eighties" (*MSWL*, 65). Sloane wrote
asking that she "relate what happened afterwards to the heroine, Marie

Modeste" and, said King, "I immediately agreed. It gave me no trouble, although it was a new episode to me. I wrote three additional chapters, which brought Marie Modeste through a love story to a happy marriage in the most conventional manner" (*MSWL*, 66). Once again, King's memoir says far less than does her imaginative work (though we may suspect some irony in her emphasis on the "conventionality" of the work). I have suggested that the real heroine of the story "Monsieur Motte" is not Marie but Marcélite. And although both Sloane and King emphasize the development of Marie, the following three sections find her once again dramatically in the background. Her mind, her actions, and her dialogue are rarely shown us, and their formulaic elements make her the least interesting of the characters.

Grace King came up with an eight-page transition from "Monsieur Motte" to Part II of *Monsieur Motte*. The implied comic resolution at the end of the story has not, in fact, occurred; Madame Lareveillère, Marie Modeste, and Marcélite are alone in the empty school through the summer. Marie Modeste sees her future as "only a blank space, or a world thick with strangers, aliens."[25] The disappearance of Monsieur Motte has not only deprived her of her motivation for work—"all her efforts had been made to please him some day"—but has taken away "her world, her house, her family, her nurse, her friend, her almost mother, with him" (105). Marie is still on her long and dark passage between childhood and womanhood; she is mourning the loss of the one and deprived of conventional images for the other.

Marcélite has utterly changed. "Unmasked, stripped of disguise, [she] ha[s] indeed lost her nerve and audacity" and only plays the "part of a faithful servant." To Marie, this means more alienation, since she does not recognize "this wretched substitute crouching, cringing, trembling before her, unnaturally." For Marcélite, the loss of her mask means the loss of her own power ("As Monsieur Motte what could she not do?") and the loss of Marie's confidence and trust. She can no longer hold up her head before the white servant Jeanne, who barred her from the school at the beginning of the story; she loses her "old volubility"; and she becomes fiercely inarticulate in her grief, "like some wild animal that cannot tell its pain." Split between her inner sense of identity ("Oh my *bébé*!" she thinks, "it's your nurse!") and her changed public image and status, she begins to "reproach God, and vaguely to rebel against the shadow on her skin as casting the shadow on her life" (105–107). The animal imagery, the inarticulateness, the split between inner and outer selves—all suggest that, connecting race with sex, King continued to cast her own voice through Marcélite.

As for Madame Lareveillère, she ponders Marie's experience, interpreting it as the common condition of women. Women are "fine vases" that disappointments crack; "We ought all to be sold as bargains—damaged goods. I am sure we are all cracked somewhere; the fracture may be hidden, but never mind, it is there, and every woman knows just where it is, and feels it too" (108). All three women in this community, then, are on their private, separate journeys. As individuals, they all deviate from their culture's norm of southern womanhood, but, King suggests, together they participate in the archetypal experience of their sex.

Monsieur Goupilleau—who continues to drop in for daily visits—argues against Madame's notions about women. He does not deny the reality of disappointment, as he might, but rather attempts to redeem it. Goupilleau considers that when God wants to "put the finishing, the perfecting touch to a woman, he simply sends her in youth some misfortune." Silently, he looks at Madame Lareveillère, proof of his thesis; to her, he claims that a perfect "fine vase" would be an entirely "unbearable creature" (109). Thus that element of woman's suffering that derives specifically from the conflict between the image of southern womanhood and the reality of experience (a conflict that Grace King sees as between typical and atypical southern girls) need not, Goupilleau implies, persist. For he argues—radically—against the perfect mold itself, the fine vase, the marble lady. King here verbalizes her own rebellion against the shadow on her life by disguising herself as a white man, and, like Marcélite with Monsieur Motte, she gains power and "audacity" with that mask. So the conflicts specific to Marie Modeste, the young white girl who must grow to adulthood in the South, are in this transition passage felt inarticulately by a black woman and then articulated by a white man.

Each chapter that follows centers upon a single major event, but the bulk of the writing is often only tenuously related to the central plot. Part II, "On the Plantation," takes Marie with Madame Lareveillère and Marcélite to the plantation of Madame's once close schoolgirl friend, Mademoiselle Aurore. Aurore, as devout a Catholic as she is a spinster, runs Bel Angely with her brother Félix. The action of the story moves towards Eugénie's decision to marry Monsieur Goupilleau, but most of the pages take us into the minds of four women: Aurore, Marcélite, Eugénie, and Marie. Aurore, distressed by her brother's attack of sciatica at sugarmaking time and by her young Indian-black "favorite," Gabi, who has let a pig tear up the daily mail (in which sat a letter from Monsieur Goupilleau professing his love for Madame Lareveillère), spends most of her time worrying. Marcélite, caught between the blacks on the plantation (with whom she does not identify) and her "child" Marie, agonizes over Marie's "apathetic *white* silence. Oh for one moment of equality and confidence!" (150). Eugénie is torn between her experienced recognition of woman's lot and her romantic love for Monsieur Goupilleau. Marie drifts through the story, gazing at moonlight and reconciling herself to the loss of her fantasy of Monsieur Motte.

For most of the story, the women talk to one another, perform various activities on the plantation, and talk, through interior monologues, to the reader. Then Monsieur Goupilleau appears—thinking, of course, that his letter has arrived. After the misunderstanding is cleared up, with much embarrassment to this man who can write about love but not talk about it, he proposes. Eugénie Lareveillère accepts, he leaves, and the section ends with an open reconciliation between the two older white women, whose emotional and experiential divergence from one another has been the subject of many of their private thoughts.

Thus the definition of womanhood comes from the author's pitting these four against one another, by age, race, and experience. Eugénie says, "Our lives are surprise-boxes to us women; we never know what is going to come out of them: our own plans, our own ideas count for nothing" (158). Aurore replies: "Ah yes, men are more fortunate. . . . There is something sure, something stable in a man's life. Look at Féfé [her brother Félix]. I do not say he has not had griefs, disappointments, misfortunes even, in his life, but they did not change it, only interrupted it a minute; with me, those things take away my life itself" (159). Each woman has used a method to circumvent this fate. Aurore's is not just religion; it is more specifically the replacement of the "visions of youth," of the "gratification of desire," by "a crucifix and Golgotha" (127). Madame has moved from an early, very traditional marriage and a sense that marriage is "duty," through a period of self-sufficiency heading the school, to the present, when she sees love and duty in conflict and finally decides to let her love for Goupilleau win. Marcélite opposes religion, funneling her energies into a maternal love for Marie. And Marie, the innocent among the four, deals with her first confrontation with actuality by much private thought and by dreams of a future that for the other three is already past.

How does the author, then, envision woman? By using these multiple points of view and by providing a partial reconciliation among them in her plotting, King seems to endorse certain values. Nurturance (except for Marie) is expressed by all of them—in fact, it causes, says Aurore, woman's life to be different from man's. Despite their differences, too, all of these women are compassionate; all think through their lives and in their thinking are, for a time, alone. All are honest in the expression of feeling and thought: this honesty permits the conclusion. All endure, stoically or half-humorously, their lots.

The men show a familiar pattern. Félix, the businessman, is the least sympathetically treated character. He is not only an unadulterated materialist, but he is compulsive about his work and most unpleasantly dominates all who come within his purview. On the other hand, Armand Goupilleau retains the androgynous characteristics we saw in "Monsieur Motte." He has "those wonderful, eloquent eyes of a recluse poet," even though he is a notary; his words are "timid, hesitating" (169). He, too, shares with Eugénie the belief that love, not duty (in this case, to parent Marie) should form the basis of a relationship: "He had offered the love of his lifetime, he had asked for love. Was she to give him duty, self-sacrifice?" (170).

The community envisioned by "On the Plantation" again transcends expectable lines of class, age, race, and sex. Although there is a fairly clear emphasis on a female community, united by bonds of differently experienced but mutual oppression, the larger community—the community of good folk—consists of characters who share the values of honesty, love for persons rather than objects, experience from which one has learned, nurturance, compassion, strength of character. The description of the black women on the plantation shows the transracial nature of this "community": they "defy concealment," show "savage grace."

Part III, "The Drama of an Evening," sets up two parallel dramas, and once again that of Marie Modeste takes the background. It is "carnival" time in New Orleans, and most of the action takes place at a soirée where a Madame Fleurissant's daughter is to make her debut "into the great world out of the little world of school" (182). After introducing us to the flutter of the girls—a theme that is touched upon periodically and not without irony—the narrator brings to the front of the stage two new characters, the Parisian Madame Montyon and her Creole stepson Charles. Most of this section shows Madame Montyon in her rude, callous—in King's view—and "masculine" efforts to extract the money owed her by various of the genteel poor Creoles, who pay to give their daughters debuts but do not pay the rent. The subsidiary plot shows Charles rejecting his stepmother and falling in love with Marie Modeste, who falls for him at the same time. During the evening, he meets his old nurse, the quadroon Nourrice—now a poor, ugly, desperate, half-crazy old woman. Reconciling his memories of her soft protection and care with her present terrifying wildness, Charles gives her money and a home, rejecting simultaneously his stepmother's maternal role towards him and her un-Creole materialism.

Meanwhile, Morris Frank—not Creole and not gracious—bumbles into the ball, eager to meet a wife for his prospering plantation. (In the next section one learns that he is the son of the overseer at the old Motte plantation and that, now living in the Motte home, he has been aspiring to join Creole culture while he stares at the portraits of the lovely Creole Motte women.) Madame Montyon's comments on the Creoles' debts so insult one young man at the ball that he demands a duel with her son. Marcélite and Monsieur Goupilleau appear in minor roles—Marcélite as hairdresser to the debutantes and "mother" to Marie, and Goupilleau as the notary through whom Madame Montyon must funnel her avarice. The section ends when Madame Montyon discovers the scheduled duel and writes an apology to prevent it. In the apology she accepts what have been seen as the Creole values, reversing her earlier stand to say that moneyed debts are *not* debts of honor. The narrator gives the last line to Monsieur Goupilleau: "Ah, gratez la femme, et vous trouverez la mère!" Roughly translated, it means "Scratch a woman, and you will find a mother" (260).

The definition of womanhood and the theme of the collection have been complicated by the introduction of what appears to be a female Félix. Although Madame Montyon is almost consistently treated as a villain, unlike Félix she has one redemptive quality: maternal love. It is, of course, her maternal love that saves her stepson from the duel, the Creoles from financial disaster, and herself from total opprobrium. But there are buried elements that make the reader guess the author felt at least ambivalent about this businesswoman. Apparently Madame Montyon has suffered some mysterious but great "amount of shame" from Arvil, the man whose inheritance she is now trying to collect. Moreover, the narrator tells us that it was only her money that bought her, late in life, a husband and a son, Charles. She loves that son, too, although he unpleasantly reminds her more than once that she is not his "real" mother. Apparently King's ability to create a fairly complex woman (compared to the far more simply awful Félix) conflicted with the didacticism she wanted to express about business values.

Although the debutantes are treated with some light irony, and although the narrator makes it clear that the girls are terribly innocent, lack confidence, and live in the ignorance produced by youth and present bliss, they are generally treated sympathetically: "They have not changed in the least,—only the fashion of their dresses" says one grandfather (209). It is partly because they unconsciously carry the past into the present, and more because their ritual is central to the Creoles' concept of love, that the girls (particularly, of course, Marie, who has now undertaken the typical southern feminine experience) are treated with sympathy. Other characters, however, tend to undercut the optimism of this vision: Odile, for example, is a young married woman who now feels only *ennui*, who barely sees her husband at the ball, and about whom the gossipy Tante Pauline says, "Poor Odile! but she would marry him; she was warned enough! I heard she threatened to kill herself or go in a convent. The threats of a girl of seventeen—bah! And that is what is called having a husband!" (204). Too, the debutantes dance "round and round in the circle bounded by the rows of darkly-clad chaperons, as if they did not see them, their anxious, calculating faces, their sombre-hued bodies, or their sombre-hued lives" (204–205). The narrator seems torn between the beauty of the girls' hopes and innocence on the one hand and the knowledge of experience on the other. She intrudes into the story: "Her [any debutante's] first illusion goes when the young girl finds her own Eden neither the brightest nor the best, nor an individual creation; the last goes when she finds that she is not the only woman in it, but that Eves are under every tree" (229). Yet the Creole value of love, not flirtation, is upheld. Marie's evening is described as a psychic journey from the typical "American" method of flirtation, where one pretends to love in order to get the man to fall genuinely in love, to the Creole "method": the risk of actually loving a man.

Black women come to the ball, too. But they must be neither seen nor heard; they sit, separated, and observe. Probably because of this, they know more than anyone else at the party; they possess not mere information, but insight about the characters themselves. Of course, they are powerless to use this knowledge in any way but in forming the characters of their protégées, their girls. There the black women contribute importantly; it is to them that the girls turn for approbation and support. Nourrice, of course, has felt the same concern for Charles, and King demonstrates her valuation of Nourrice's nurturance not just in the name but in her plotting, when she has Charles choose Nourrice as his more genuine mother. Consciously, King probably applauded the degree to which her black women have internalized the definition of them provided by whites; she shows that internalization by having the black women attack Madame Montyon for selling Nourrice on the grounds that Madame Montyon thought she was "too good to own slaves"—an attitude the black women themselves consider false and insultingly patronizing.

Once again, the men who appear seem to share in the values of the "good" women. Charles is sensitive, charitable, supportive, stoic (he leaves to help Nourrice just when his romance with Marie is blooming, risking its loss at that vulnerable moment). Monsieur Goupilleau once again shows that he values love over money, acts "stoically" (246), and refuses to let his small stature define or limit his character, for he will try to recoup the Motte plantation.

Morris Frank would seem the likely setup for a villain: son of an overseer, outsider to the Creole culture, upwardly mobile, pragmatic, and business-directed. Yet as becomes clear in the next section, King refuses to follow the stereotype, again placing humane values above divisions of society.

This third section is called "The Drama of an Evening" and is set in an antebellum ballroom. Ironically, it is here that King comes closer to dealing with the problems that faced the postwar society about which she writes. Although imperfectly resolved, the conflict between the need for money and the need for the "old" values of honor, love, and black-white community is clearly expressed. Signs of King's times include the comment that Monsieur Goupilleau, in marrying Eugénie, has married "up"; the somewhat complex development of Madame Montyon's "business" values; Goupilleau's efforts to provide Marie with a dowry—her plantation; and the gently ironic treatment of the genteel poor as having "the attitude that expresses an effort to keep on a level with elevated principles, the attitude generally of the poor in pocket" (240). In short, King seems to envision a community that, although it recognizes the pragmatic necessity of material well-being, places other values above it, values that transcend race, class, and sex. She might have written a better story had she refused the temptation to resolve this conflict, as she does in the last section, by an authorial fiat that seems less realistic than wished-for.

Part IV fulfills what King had called the "most conventional" plotting by giving us the "Marriage of Marie Modeste." Once again, however, the plotting shows the strength of King's commitment to realism—until its conclusion.

Eugénie, now Madame Goupilleau, surprises Marie and Charles (to her chagrin) while they are, apparently, embracing. The conflict between fantasy and real, between old and new southern codes, is felt within her mind at that point:

> She had planned it otherwise, and far better,—this scene,— with a minute particularity for detail which only an outsider and a schemer in futurity can command. The young man would come to her first, of course, with his avowal, as etiquette prescribes. She would go to Marie herself, and delicately, as only a woman can, she would draw aside the veil from the unconscious heart and show the young girl the dormant figure of her love there,—love whose existence she did not dream of. . . .
> But the event always fools the prepared. (265)

Eugénie's fantasy is that of the sentimentalist; it is extremely interesting that King would see it as the dream of an "outsider" and a "schemer in futurity," a businesswoman. For this puts the sentimental old style into the hands, not of the old aristocrat, but of the capitalist in Madame's nature, the side of herself that has rejected this very dream of romance for herself. Both—the last line above implies—are unrealistic fictions. In any case, Marie, still held by the dream of first love, tells Madame that they plan to marry. King makes no effort at all to conceal the sensuality that is part of their love: "Behind [Madame], discretion was again violated and outraged. The hands of Marie and Charles met of themselves, first accidentally and then purposely, and would not part. . . . [Marie's] lips parted as if again in the tremor of caress" (267–68).

Madame Montyon, as one might expect, objects to a "dowerless bride" and urges her stepson to rethink his decision. King enters rather fully into Charles' mind in a long passage in which Charles tries to comprehend his cynical stepmother, manages to empathize with her point of view, and finally gains the authority to speak in "intonations unknown before to him" (276), to state unequivocally his intention to marry Marie. Madame Montyon retaliates by working out an elaborate marriage contract that, like most, goes "against the women, the poor women! That is the way with Eugénie there. Old Lareveillère made a marriage contract against her; she had nothing of her own, and all her life there he has held her" (312).

Meanwhile, Marie's bridesmaids form a female chorus to accompany what all perceive as the major rite of initiation for the girl-woman. Marie herself ponders the event through several pages, ending in an expression of gratitude to God. In this way, says the narrator, she is unlike the typical girl, who, her life plotted out for her from birth, thinks only of "the costly presents, the beautiful dress, the new-fashioned wreath . . . what they will do after marriage, sending their thoughts along blushing paths" (290).

Marcélite brings Marie a wedding present, the many gold dollars she has saved since Marie moved in with the Goupilleaus. This is the only way she thinks she can express her love. Marie is faced with a decision. Should she take the money from a Negro, breaking with racist tradition and reinforcing Marcélite's identification of honor with money? Or should she refuse it, abiding by tradition, and showing that love alone is enough? Here King finds the potential for real dramatic conflict. Marcélite sees Marie's vacillating expression and reacts with violence, accusing her of not accepting the money because Marcélite is black. "Even God will not help a negro!" she says (299). It is "the first confession of the galling drop in her heart. Gay, *insouciante*, impudent, she had worn her color like a travesty. Who would have suspected her?" (299). Marie accepts and wants to show the gift to Eugénie. But Marcélite, "effacing majestically all trace of emotion," immediately reaffirms the white prescription by refusing to let Marie show her that "you take money from me!" (300).

Armand Goupilleau has discovered that Morris Frank's father, the overseer, had taken the plantation by some chicanery, apparently pretending there were no more Mottes, although he knew Marie might still live. The innocent, trusting Morris, overwhelmed at the discovery of his father's dishonor, is reassured by Goupilleau's insistence that bad blood does not get passed along. Now, though, he feels he must give up the place he wants so strongly as his home—for he must make "restitution."

Marie Modeste, to everyone's surprise, refuses to sign the contract, to take Madame Montyon's money. She "gives" and "wants" "nothing but love" (318). Into the scene comes Morris Frank, who walks over to Marie and tells her the plantation is hers. Marcélite saves Frank's face by (apparently) lying: she claims neither he nor his father knew that the Motte baby was alive. Finally, at the wedding, Marcélite, not Eugénie, walks behind Marie, "gives her away," and performs all the functions of a mother and a father, finally accepted as the parent she always was.

The last two paragraphs, tacked on by the narrator's intrusion— "Time still carries on the story, life still furnishes the incidents; there is no last chapter to the record" (327)—provide the happy resolution that has in some ways been prepared for and in other ways conflicts with the preceding narrative. Morris Frank, Charles Montyon, Marie Modeste Motte, their children, and Marcélite all "live well, happily, prosperously together" at the Motte plantation, "for in giving hearts, God assigned destinies" (327).

Contrived though this resolution is, it does accurately fulfill the sentiments shadowed forth in the four sections of *Monsieur Motte*. It gathers together—without regard to race, class, and sex—the people who embody most fully and clearly the good "heart"—the androgynous values that King would like so much to see prevail. Had she pursued the implications of the racial, sexual, social, and economic conflicts touched upon in the work, King might well have written a first-rate novel. As it stands, though, *Monsieur Motte* shows us what a more realistic writer than Evans, but one no less southern and female, envisioned as her ideal. Countering the pleasant fictions of her world with the actual experience of individuals, particularly women, King demonstrates through Marcélite's story that "with the truth [comes] the substance of what fiction had supposed" (277).

In 1886, less than a year after writing "Monsieur Motte," Grace King wrote "Bonne Maman," or "Grandmother." It is a story peopled solely by black and white women, reversing and transforming their roles. The white patrician grandmother, "at bay, every nerve tingling with haughty defiance at the taunts and jeers of despising conquerors"[26] and determined to support herself ("as the men had fought, let the women suffer against overpowering odds" [87]), refuses to go to France after the fall of the Confederacy and settles in a former slave's cabin in the center of the quadroon section of town. There, in virtual isolation—she has renounced all friends and relatives "bravely to assume the penalty she had dared" (86)—she raises her grandchild Claire Blanche and tries to support the household by taking in sewing. Claire has been to a convent school where she refused to accept the pious definition of reality, listening instead to "'ces diables de l'enfer' out there shooting their cannons" (70); now, though, they have lived together for three years with a black woman, Betsy. Betsy gets her food from the gutters at twilight—"for [her] the darkness has no terrors, the loneliness no trepidations" (95)— and stays because the two white women depend on her as a link to the outside world. Claire and Betsy conspire to serve "by fair means or foul, the proud old lady glorying in her lofty ideas of self-support" (97).

When the story opens, Claire is surreptitiously sewing a gaudy dress for a black woman, who comes in to demand that the girl finish it in time for a "moonlight picnic" that night. She criticizes Claire imperiously: "Lord knows there's white people enough to do sewing, and glad to get it" (79). Meanwhile, Bonne Maman discovers that Claire is finishing her embroidery and that she is therefore no longer really supporting herself. Recognizing that she will soon die, the old lady confronts for the first time the realistic consequences of her "heroic" gesture: she will leave Claire alone with no friends and no family, "cut off . . . even from certification of her own identity" (98). Bonne Maman thinks: "This, then, was to be the end of a life conducted on principles drawn from heroic inspirations of other times. The principles were the same, but human nature had changed since women's hearts were strong enough not to break over bullet wounds, sabre cuts, and horse-hoof mutilations, when women's hands were large enough to grasp and hold the man-abandoned tiller of the household. It has all gone wrong" (85). Her intended martyrdom, her "retaliation against fate," will not "solace [Claire] in those conditions for which ancestral glories, refinements, and luxuries had but poorly equipped her" (88).

As a child on the plantation, Bonne Maman had been given a black baby to raise as her "doll," her child, and her slave. She freed Aza before the war but now remembers the little slave's fidelity. Aza was a "devil," "impertinent, pushing, and perfectly fearless," but she "followed [her mistress] around like a little dog" (73).

Later that night, Claire, blooming into adolescence, comes in from a rare trip out of the yard. She is exhilarated by going out, by the sunset, and by the smells. Her exhilaration is sensuous: "'I wish I could walk up there in all that pink and blue and gold; walk deeper and deeper in it, until it comes up all around and over me!' She drew a long, quivering breath. . . . 'The night jasmine . . . makes me feel faint with its sweetness . . . it is so good to go out on the street, bonne maman. It makes one feel so gay, so fresh, so strong'" (90). Finally, she is exhilarated by the black music she hears. "She . . . danced round and round, as if caught in its melodious wheels, until it left her panting and glowing. 'When I hear music like that, bonne maman, it is as if my blood would come out of my veins and dance right there before me. . . . I want so much to get up and follow it, out, out, wherever it is, until I come to the place where it begins fresh and sweet and clear'" (91).

But Betsy warns Claire that this music is not for white women: "Them niggers over there don't play no music excepting for devils to dance by, and that piano don't talk nothing fittin' a young white lady to listen to" (92). Claire replies that she had only said she wanted to dance, not that she would. The reader remembers her rebellious attitude at the convent school, where they always "scold[ed] you because you were not some one else, always punish[ed] you because you were what you were" (70), and where the good girls literally died. Claire's Huckleberrian moral is: "Goodness doesn't stand a convent and war as well as badness" (72).

Bonne Maman dies before she can summon the family; Claire is inconsolable. Black crepe hangs outside, symbolizing that the house is open to any who want to mourn. Among the visitors is a fierce, sensual, confident black woman—the woman who, as madam, runs the brothel where the music comes from. It is Aza. She is heartbroken at the sight of her "Nénaine" dead; but Betsy rebukes her, as a prostitute, and sends her away. Then Aza seeks out "like a fiery cross" (113) all "Nénaine's" friends and kin who have, all these years, thought the two white women were in France. The story ends as a traditional funeral procession—including former slaves like Aza—takes Bonne Maman to her grave; Claire goes off in the arms of her new-found relatives, and, in the final paragraph, Aza goes back to the quadroon neighborhood: the dance music is just beginning.

The implications of this story are confusing. Certain elements seem predictably, sentimentally southern: the loyal slave, the reconciliation with lost family, the defiantly prewar funeral procession. From this point of view, the black woman for whom Claire sews is to be blamed; we are meant to sense the injustice of an aristocratic white lady working for "uppity" blacks. And from this point of view, Claire's sensuous response to the music and Aza's confident sensuality indicate only the danger and immorality of blackness.

But other elements in the story defy these conventional southern morals. Bonne Maman, for instance, finds that the slave's cabin where she has lived to perpetrate "the deepest insult she could inflict upon the world" (89) looks "kindly, protectingly, at her," and she sees it "for the first time as . . . a home" (89). Secondly, when Bonne Maman despises Betsy's forwardness with Claire, our sympathies are with the black woman; for the grandmother has been exposed as acting out of false heroics, whereas Betsy has been shown sympathetically as a loyal, courageous, and realistic woman. Such a depiction flatly contradicts what Grace King wrote in a letter praising her region: "The South stands out for the heroic against the successful."[27]

More prominently, if King had intended the links between Claire's coming of age, her going "outside," the black music, and Aza's house to serve as a warning, elsewhere she implicitly celebrates those links. She does so in the tone of a speech like this of Claire's: "'It doesn't cost anything,' she interrupted furiously—'it doesn't cost anything to listen to music, to know people. I don't have to work for it, like bread and meat; and, grand Dieu, how much better it is!' Two tears rolled from her hot eyes" (93). King celebrates the links between black and white culture further by connecting Claire's rebellious realism to survival and the "good" convent girls' piety to death. In showing Aza's capacity to be both madam and savior, to dance and to pray, King implies a less than unambiguous condemnation of prostitution. Finally, had King clearly intended these connections as a warning of the dangers to white women of proximity to black culture—in a story whose "morals" are everywhere explicit—she most likely would have made her point crystal clear. Instead, the story ends with Aza's point of view, in a description of her "in her slavish dress, worn for the last time. The piano had already commenced its dances" (99). The implication is that, homage having been paid to the old ways, Aza will continue in the new. And if Claire is to continue her journey to adulthood, the metaphor implies, she will have to keep listening to the music.

Surely, though, Grace King would never have accepted such an interpretation. For, just as Evans wore the authorial mask of Christian persuasion, Grace King wore the mask of a righteous defender of southern traditions, including the tradition that white and black cultures do not meet on the street, dancing. Since King was so fully a part of the established New Orleans white social and literary world, it is even less plausible to think that she was aware of the submerged shadowy "other" side of her story than it is to assume that Evans might have been. And apparently her audience missed it entirely.

For modern readers, though, it is difficult to miss or to misunderstand the implications of another story, "The Little Convent Girl," which King wrote in 1893, eight years after "Bonne Maman" and nearly at the end of her prolific fiction-writing period. During the years between, she had not only published widely,[28] but she had also traveled and made friends with literati elsewhere in the United States and in France. In 1887, she paid her first visit to the homes of Charles Dudley Warner and Samuel Clemens in Hartford, Connecticut. There she was fascinated with Harriet Beecher Stowe, "in spite of her hideous, black, dragon-like book that hovered on the horizon of every Southern child."[29] And she made a friend of Livy Clemens, Mark Twain's wife. In 1891–92, King spent her first long period in Europe, mostly in Paris, which she called a "delightful place to work."[30] She joined the salon at the home of and became a close friend of Madame Marie Thérèse Blanc ("Th. Bentzon"), a protégée of George Sand and critic for the *Revue des Deux Mondes*. She joined the congregation of Pastor Charles Wagner, an Alsatian Protestant who preached a Thoreauvian life of simplicity and love of nature. And she lobbied for her fellow southern writers, Lafcadio Hearn and Sidney Lanier, who were virtually unknown in Europe.[31]

At the end of this lengthy European stay, Grace King spent a month with the Clemenses in Florence; when she returned to the United States, her *Balcony Stories* were being prepared for publication. Among those stories is "The Little Convent Girl," another story of black and white women, but this time—unlike King's earlier prolix style—startlingly clear, simple, and taut, a nearly perfect tale. And it seems now to be a nearly perfect allegory of the life behind the southern lady's authorial mask.

The little convent girl has so little self that the reader never knows her name or hears her speak. After years in a Cincinnati convent, she "never raise[s] her eyes except when spoken to . . . walk[s] with such soft, easy, carefully calculated steps that one naturally [feels] the penalties that must have secured them." Even the curl has been "taken out of [her hair] as austerely as the noise out of her footfalls."[32] Further repressing any self-expression, she "keep[s] her lips well shut, the effort giving them a pathetic little forced expression" (151). And a thick black veil prevents both revelation from within and the entrance of anything from outside.

Separated from her mother almost since birth, she has vacationed only with her father, who forbade any communication between the two women "on account of some disagreement between the parents." But now he is dead, and she is eighteen. It is time to leave the convent, and "the first thing that the girl herself wanted to do was to go to her mother" (151). The little convent girl has been placed on a Mississippi steamboat to journey downriver from Cincinnati to New Orleans to live with her mother. On the boat, her self-denying habits are matched by her passivity. She stays all day in her cabin, crocheting lace, unless someone comes to "fetch her out in front." "She could not do anything of herself; she had to be initiated into everything by someone else." She eats only convent food, despite the "field for display the boat's table at mealtimes affords" (150–51).

But "it is a long voyage from Cincinnati to New Orleans" (151). At first, when shut up in her cabin, she thinks the noise of landing is shipwreck, death, and judgment; she prays for "her sins! her sins!" (152). Then the captain brings her "out in front" to see the boat make a landing, and the little convent girl begins to respond to her initiation to the world. "Then she got to liking it so much that she would stay all day just where the captain put her, going inside only for her meals. She forgot herself at times so much that she would draw her chair a little closer to the railing, and put up her veil, actually, to see better" (152). To describe the risky landings that the girl sees, the narrator uses language of noise, color, movement: "dangling roustabouts hanging like drops of water from [the gangplank]—dropping sometimes twenty feet to the land, and not infrequently into the river itself . . . the black skins glistening through torn shirts, and white teeth gleaming through red lips, and laughing, and talking" (152). "Surely," the narrator concludes, "the little convent girl in her convent walls never dreamed of so much unpunished noise and movement in the world!" (152).

At nights the little convent girl is taken to the upper deck, to which she must climb "steep stairs." The effort to "keep the black skirts well over the stiff white petticoats," to prevent a "rim of white stocking" from being seen, obsesses her; coming down, she "cling[s] to each successive step as if [she] could never, never, make another venture . . . the one boot would . . . hesitate out, and feel and feel around, and have such a pause of helpless agony as if indeed the next step must have been wilfully removed" (153).

Eventually, choosing the pleasures of this new hint of life over the risk of exposure and even death, she lets the pilot "get her up into the pilot house" where he "would talk of the river to her" (153). It is there that she "forgot herself for the first time in her life, and stayed up until after

nine o'clock. Although she appeared almost intoxicated at the wild pleasure, she was immediately overwhelmed at the wickedness of it, and observed much more rigidity of conduct thereafter" (154).

But there must be an end to this journey. The little convent girl prepares herself as rigorously for the landing—whisking her dress "as if for
microscopic inspection," scrubbing her fingernails until they are sore,
and smoothing her hair until the "very last glimmer of a curl disap-
peared"—as "some good people" are prepared, says the narrator, for
death (154). And in fact, of course, she is killing her incipient self with
goodness.

The little convent girl's mother comes to meet her; the captain looks
at her again and again, takes her to her daughter, and can think of saying to the girl only "Be a good little girl" (155). They leave, "hands
tightly clasped" (155), and the girl does not look right, left, or even once
("what all passengers do") back at the boat. As mother and daughter
leave, all the crew look at the mother and exclaim, "Colored!"

A month later, the boat is back at New Orleans. Early in the morning,
embarrassed but "bold and assured enough," the mother brings her
daughter by the hand to see the captain: "She is so quiet, so still, all the
time, I thought it would do her a pleasure." But the captain fails to see
or hear the submerged meaning. The girl has let go her mother's hand
to shake the captain's. After the visit, she follows her mother down the
gangway. Halfway down, she jumps or falls ("no one was looking") and
drowns, pulled down by her stiff white petticoats.

Although the story's surface plot has to do with "a girl's first knowledge that her mother is black,"[33] its thematic center has to do with that
girl's aborted journey to her self. The little convent girl's black mother
represents her hidden self, a double that she represses in herself by
straightening her curls. Bold and confident where her daughter is terrified, speaking where her daughter is silent, the black woman shows
what the girl could have become. "Forgetting" her fictitious convent
"self," as she does at least twice on the boat, the girl might have had
more "pleasure," made noise, moved, worn colors, like her mother.

Doubling fascinates King in this story. Of the tales the pilot tells the
little convent girl, we hear only this one:

> It was his opinion that there was as great a river as the Mis-
> sissippi flowing directly under it—an underself of a river, as
> much a counterpart of the other as the second story of a
> house is of the first; in fact, he said they were navigating
> through the upper story. Whirlpools were holes in the floor of
> the upper river, so to speak; eddies were rifts and cracks. And

> deep under the earth, hurrying toward the subterranean
> stream, were other streams, small and great, but all deep,
> hurrying to and from that great mother-stream underneath,
> just as the small and great overground streams hurry to and
> from their mother Mississippi. (154)

The girl is fascinated, and no wonder. Her own "underself" lies beneath
her starched clothes, her heavy veil, and her straightened hair. The
story is "almost more than [she] could take in" (154). But when she
dies, she goes down into a whirlpool. "Perhaps," says the narrator, "it . . .
may have carried her through to the underground river, to that vast,
hidden, dark Mississippi that flows beneath the one we see; for her body
was never found" (156). This implies that in drowning herself the girl
may have saved herself. And in going under, she does expose—for the
first time—a "flutter of white petticoats, a show of white stockings"
(156), revealing what she had so tried to conceal, dragged down by
death to the "vast, dark" deeper river of self. Unable to accept consciously the fact that her mother—hence her self—is black, she affirms
that awareness by the manner of her dying.

Just as the river has its underself and the girl her unknown dark
mother, so do sights and sounds—so central to the girl's awakening—
have doubles, hidden and, by implication, deeper. On the boat, noises
are loud and sights are colorful; the men shout at one another to be
heard and to exert power. Because he is accustomed to this loudness
and color, the captain cannot hear the mother or see the daughter when
they come to visit: "There was, perhaps, some inflection in the woman's
voice that might have made known, or at least awakened, the suspicion
of some latent hope or intention, had the captain's ear been fine enough
to detect it. There might have been something in the little convent girl's
face, had his eye been more sensitive—a trifle paler, maybe, the lips a
little tighter drawn, the blue ribbon a shade faded. He may have noticed
that, but—And the visit of 'How d' ye do' came to an end" (156). The
narrator's own caution in the passage ("perhaps," "might have been")
reveals itself as irony in the light of the metaphoric doubling elsewhere
in the story. Of course, says the narrator's "underself," there was another
reality to be seen and heard, but only by those who are "fine" and "sensitive," not limited by the perceptual expectations of the male world, that
colors be bright, and sounds loud.

Confirming one's sense that King has created an allegory not just of
the southern woman but of the southern woman writer in a man's
world, language itself takes a thematic role in this story. The tone of the
men's language is fortissimo, its diction curses and swearing, reflecting
the male world: forceful, direct, and defiantly antireligious. But the very

presence of the little convent girl transforms that language. When she first hears the cursing, she turns pale and retreats from the deck, refusing to come out until the captain "guarantees his reassurance" (152). Thereafter, the mate "change[s] his invective to sarcasm" (153). Even the captain "forgets himself" one day when the boat runs aground, but when he sees the "little black figure," his voice sticks "as fast aground in midstream as the boat had done" (153).

The girl, then, has power over male language, but it is only destructive power. When the captain adopts her apparent values, he too forms a second self, not under but over his real self. Like the girl, he forgets that repressive self when confronted by the energy of actuality. And when he remembers that self, the narrator compares his sudden stop to the ship's accident, suggesting its destructiveness. The mate, more subtly, responds to the girl's repressive power by directing his true speech into another channel. But "at night," says the narrator, "or when the little convent girl was not there, language flowed in its natural curve, [the male] swearing like a pagan" (153).

What, then, is the "natural curve" of women's language? We never hear the voice of the girl directly; her lips stay "well shut." When she does "relax the constraint over her lips," we are told, out comes a prayer (152). If "pagan" is natural, this is unnatural. Yet there is hope; when she does speak to others (only when spoken to), it is in the "wee, shy, furtive voice one might imagine a just-budding violet to have" (150). Could that flower survive, we might hear a woman's voice. But shut up (in both senses) in her cabin, she creates only lace, innocuous and merely decorative, and she radically misinterprets the sounds from the world outside.

Nevertheless, the woman's voice can be heard in the story. The girl's mother "spoke with an accent, and with embarrassment" (156); she speaks in the dialect of her black subculture: "She don't go nowhere, she don't do nothing" (156). And there is, we saw, "perhaps some inflection" in her voice that hints of a deeper level of meaning. By implication, in a world noisy with men's language, even the "bold and assured" voice of the adult woman is different, the language not only of an outsider but of an inferior. When Grace King finished her first story, she wrote to Warner, "I am afraid of my English."[34] And a letter from Sherwood Anderson to King confirms that an idea of separate male and female literary worlds existed in King's circle: "We . . . have been such truculent fellows. There has been so much of meeting flair with flair. Always however I have known and loved a gentler tribe of the ink party here—of which you, in my mind, have always been one—and have hoped some day to merit what would make me acceptable to gentler people too."[35] Anderson sounds much like the boat's mate.

Unable or unwilling to speak her mother's tongue, the little convent girl dies speechless. Black mother, white daughter: here King allowed her imagination the freedom to make Marcélite into Marie's actual mother, to pursue the sound of Aza's music. But she could not carry out the implications of both earlier stories to let her white girl survive in the black community. Insofar as the little convent girl accepts the orthodox white view, to have a black mother and therefore to be a black girl confirms and deepens her sense of deserved inferiority, her conviction that she has sinned. That conviction sends her off the gangplank to her death. Yet insofar as the girl accepts the hidden values of that deeper Mississippi, of the self that began to come out on the boat, to have a black mother is to reconcile herself with the alienated part of herself— hair, speech, motion, even, of course, "color." And that more profound intuition sends her off the gangplank into the whirlpool of a deeper life.

Impossible though it was for Grace King—so thoroughly was she a part of the traditional white South—to let that "violet" grow in a home with her literally and psychologically real mother, she also found it impossible unequivocally to let her grow pale and wither away. So King sent her little convent girl, not to Heaven, but beneath the bottom of the river, to that other "great mother stream" below.

Monsieur Motte and "Bonne Maman" came at the beginning of King's most productive decade; "The Little Convent Girl" came at its end. After *Balcony Stories*, she published no fiction, with the exception of a trickling of uncollected stories, for twenty-three years. Committed to her intention to tell the story of her South, she turned from the metaphoric imagination to write the history and biography of the region and its famous men. She wrote the biography of Jean Baptiste le Moyne, founder of New Orleans (1892); a textbook history of Louisiana (1894); *New Orleans, the Place and the People* (1895); *De Soto and His Men in the Land of Florida* (1898); and *Stories from Louisiana History* (1905). Then Macmillan editor George P. Brett asked her to write a "romance of the Reconstruction period," like Thomas Nelson Page's work. But, says Bush, "to her the Reconstruction period was one of cruel memories of economic struggle and humiliation rather than love stories between northerners and southerners or repressive measures of one race against another."[36] So she began an unromantic novel about families during Reconstruction that she eventually rewrote five times for Brett, who nevertheless rejected it. She said it "consumed years of my life & bled me of spirit & energy."[37] In 1913, literary critic Edward Garnett read the manuscript in London; only in 1916 did he write about it, assuming in an *Atlantic Monthly* article that the novel had already appeared in print.

The novel, *The Pleasant Ways of St. Médard*, was finally published by Henry Holt in 1916. Though it sold poorly, the reviews were good; Robert Bush says it "may be her masterpiece."[38]

King returned to history with *Creole Families of New Orleans* (1921). Her final novel, *La Dame de Sainte Hermine* (1924), received no public attention. King's last work was her autobiography, posthumously published as *Memories of a Southern Woman of Letters* (1932). That work, points out her biographer, "brought out the polite side of Grace King the lady rather than the perceptive and critical writer at her best."[39] In her last words, then, King spoke from behind the mask that she had begun to remove in at least the three stories discussed in this chapter. Marie, Claire, the little convent girl: all are about the same age, all begin a journey to womanhood, and all stop short.

As is the case with all the writers considered in this study, one may at best show the parallels between art and life and then guess at the degree of contingency of artistic expression upon the artist's experience. Though it would be clearly reductionistic to see the rather sad conclusion to Grace King's early ambitions as the result of her difficulties in being both a southern lady and an artist, it is equally clear that those difficulties played a large part in it. In 1906, she was still struggling, certainly, with the relationship between life and art, a relationship she saw as paralleling that between reality and the ideal, thus that between southern women and southern womanhood. To Warrington Dawson she wrote, "Shall I or my experience be master in my stories? My 'ideal' or my knowledge—my instinct for art—or my duty toward the real."[40]

Until the publication in 1973 of Robert Bush's *Grace King: A Selection of Her Writings*, very little critical attention had been paid to her work—unless it was to include her with Kate Chopin and Cable in a group of "local colorists." Jay B. Hubbell, for instance, does not discuss her work at all in *The South in American Literature*. The *Literary History of the United States* spends one paragraph on her, calls "Monsieur Motte" a "girlish, theatrical piece," and sums up her career by saying that "Miss King carefully avoided controversial matters, stepped softly, and sought everywhere to tone down the more garish, but always more interesting, portraits which Cable had drawn." And Ann Douglas Wood has agreed that, along with other women Local Colorists, she rejected sentimentalism but "had nothing to put in its place but its negation."[41] In fact, Grace King's place in literary history seems to have been irrevocably etched by her statement that Cable libeled her people. Yet King's fiction, as I have suggested, consistently treats the lives of women, white and black; this, not the defense of the Creoles, seems to have been her real subject. In the title of her autobiography, *Memories of a Southern Woman of Letters*, King generically defines herself as a southerner, a woman, and an artist. That might, in fact, be the order in which she herself ranked her identity. Certainly southern came first. In any case, the three facets of her being deserve separate treatment.

Yet it is hard to treat the three separately, for Grace King's artistic life was strongly social: never a writer who took to her desk in solitude, King the southerner valued the conversation and the community of artists and other intellectuals as much as and at times even more than their written words. Moreover, in New Orleans, Hartford, and Europe, her self-perception as a female interfered with but sometimes aided her career as an artist. Furthermore, her artistic motivation was strongly informed by her southernness; in a 1905 letter to Warrington Dawson, for example, she urged that "the South must *write* itself to the front of the nation—its old place." [42]

However, we must try to separate these aspects of King's personality, for in that analysis we will find some of the conflicts central to her fiction. It is clear that King identified herself as a Creole within New Orleans—that is, as an aristocrat—despite her American heritage. Miss Katherine Pope described her: "She speaks French like the French, has from girlhood been closely connected with the Creole element of New Orleans society, knows intimately the descendants of the Spanish and French who for generations held high place in the councils and social life in Louisiana." [43] And her decision to write the biography of the Sieur de Bienville and the histories of Creole families further substantiates the claim that King felt herself intimate with the Creoles. But King identified herself far more frequently, and far more strenuously, as simply southern. As Bush says, "She held loyalty to the tribe as a primary moral rule." Her "usual conclusion," he adds, "was that the South was . . . richer than the North in spiritual values." [44] Writing to Livy Clemens about the Warners, she said: "Ah my dear! they show me the want—the actual want—of a grief—in a loss in their lives. They have grown old in increasing prosperity—they have *succeeded*—and they are typically American in their enjoyment of it." [45] When in France, she went to visit an artists' colony, whose members she describes as "all Southern in sympathy" (*MSWL*, 149). Among the last scenes in her *Memories*, and the last in her life, is a nostalgic trip through Virginia, from Lee's Lexington to Richmond to Williamsburg.

Two areas in which her self-identification as southern must have had important consequences are race and sex. Bush sees King's attitude toward blacks as highly conventional: "both kindly and paternalistic, patronizing and apprehensive." [46] Although King consciously and, if put to the test, politically held to this racist southern heritage, its rebellious opposite was apparent especially in her fiction. Imaginative identification with blacks may have produced conflicts with her conscious beliefs. Speaking of King's failure to retract in her *Memories* her youthful attack on Cable, Edmund Wilson has said: "There was evidently in this stubbornness of the Southerner in sticking to an official position even when it must lead to conscious falsity an element of the strategy for which George Orwell . . . has coined the word 'doublethink.' The point of view of Grace King who read [French religious scholar Ernest] Renan (and who liked to be thought to look like him) existed in a different compartment from that of the loyal upholder of the orthodox Confederate creed, and they moved side by side, simultaneously, along two parallel tracks."[47] It is this cognitive dissonance, perhaps, that finds its relief in King's fictional treatment of blacks—particularly, in the three stories already discussed, of black women.

Bush notes that though "she loved the South, [she] had strong misgivings about the thoughtlessness of southern men to women."[48] Yet consistent with her conscious endorsement of New Orleans traditions, Grace King played the role of the southern lady and did so with no apparent reservations: in her letter responding to William Sloane's acceptance of "Monsieur Motte," King said (perhaps less than ingenuously), "I am too much of a woman not to dwell more on the sentiment that you cared enough for me to take so much trouble—than on the immense practical advantage your intermediation has been to me."[49] Her "feminine" need for support seems clear, too, in her memoirs: men "take charge" of her trip abroad (*MSWL*, 103); she is "hurt" when Parisian men do not "interfere" for her in a subway incident (*MSWL*, 139); her heart is "won" by a man who, in discussing Cyrano, lays his hand on her arm and says, "*Mais, ma chère enfant*" ("But, my dear child," *MSWL*, 147); she remembers "for thirty years" a "young and handsome gentleman" who helps her with a broken bag of grapes (*MSWL*, 169). More deeply, when Branch, her brother and financial supporter, died, she was left distraught: "What were we to do without him! What could we do! He was the head of the family. . . . Everything was dark and confused before us. We became not only frightened but demoralized" (*MSWL*, 237). At the time, Grace herself was (probably) fifty-four.

This expressed dependence on men—more precisely, on chivalric men—was enhanced by King's deferential demeanor toward men. Describing to her nephew the day she received the doctor of letters degree from Tulane, King said, "If I had been younger & foolish, my head would have been turned. But I managed to keep it in the proper position on my shoulders—& answered compliments with compliments, & very deftly turned the tables on the complimenters."[50] In her *Memories*, she recalls

her first meeting with William Sloane—"The creator of my new life"—
as being a bit frightening: "I was thrown by him into a state of helpless
timidity, so impressive I found him. Tall, handsome, serious, and formal,
he made me feel honored by his consideration and courtesy" (*MSWL*,
81). She was usually quiet in the presence of those she almost worshiped: with the Clemenses, "I, as usual, sat by silent, in a shy dream"
(*MSWL*, 85). Perhaps because she so thoroughly internalized the definition of the modest, self-effacing southern lady, there threads through her
autobiography a consistent self-deprecation. She refers to her own life
and those of her sisters as "*little* lives" (*MSWL*, 339, my emphasis).
After the publication of her *Bienville*, Charles Gayarré's comment
("What could anyone of today write about Bienville?") immediately
makes her feel "very small and insignificant with my little store of gathered items" (*MSWL*, 181). At every public appearance, from her first at
the Pan-Gnostic League to the last at the Louisiana Historical Society's
honorary program, King reports suffering fear, embarrassment, and a
temptation to reject celebrity: "I gossiped along in a leisurely way, forgetting, as ladies will, in their talk, the passing minutes; nevertheless
the story [her speech at the society's tribute to her] came to an end with
much kind applause, and the event of the evening, which I had been
unconsciously delaying, took place, the presentation of a loving cup"
(*MSWL*, 297). The very last line of her memoirs attests to her rather
overdone self-deprecation: "Truly the reward was out of proportion to
merit, the crown too large for the wearer's head!"

Grace King embodied not only the dependence, the deference, and
the self-deprecation of the southern lady; she also shared her stoicism.
She refused once to disrupt a dinner simply because she had received a
telegram announcing her uncle's death. And at least at several points
she placed her loyalty to her family above that to literature: "What, after
all, was literary success in comparison with good family ties?" (*MSWL*,
97).

Yet we find elements first of confusion and then of rebellion against
her feminine role, conflicting as it must have with her needs as an artist. Madame Blanc, whom she describes as one of her closest friends
and with whom she spent much time, King sees as "masculine" in appearance; she "talked with the aplomb of a man" (*MSWL*, 122). Describing Ernest Fenollosa's wife—he was a prominent Orientalist—she
notes proudly that this Mobile, Alabama, lady "showed herself his
match, not helpmate, in mind" (*MSWL*, 210). Before sailing from Europe, she watches the "sturdy women stevedores walk up and down the
gangway with heavy loads on their backs . . . it was most interesting"
(*MSWL*, 323). And the man she seems, in *Memories*, to have admired
most—Charles Wagner, the Parisian minister—she admires precisely

for his "feminine" qualities: nurturance, humility, concern for others' welfare, self-sacrifice.

One way of resolving any confusion about being a southern lady is to revert to a staunch defense of the image. Here she compares Jane Carlyle to women of the South: "we thought if Mrs. Carlyle had lived in the South after the Confederate War, she would have known what real hard times and poverty were. We compared her life with the heroic patience and endurance of our mother and of Mrs. Gayarré, who wrote no journals and kept no records of their feelings, and who would as soon have thought of accusing God as their husband of ill treatment, though God knows they had known to the full the bitterness of disappointment and despondency" (*MSWL*, 160). Another alternative would be to turn to feminism. King never did, but she inserted this curious note in her autobiography: "Isabella Hooker lived not far away [from the Warners]; a tall, handsome woman, who talked to me about 'Woman's Rights' and converted me to her point of view" (*MSWL*, 77). Much later, in England, a suffragist rally rates only a mention that King's wraps and umbrella were taken away.

Yet the portrait of Grace King's mother—the one who would never accuse her husband—in the first, probably best, chapter of *Memories* is that of a woman who is commanding, ingenious, courageous, intelligent, capable of anger. Probably it is important that her husband was not there when Mrs. King appeared this way to her daughter. Moreover, she was only carrying out his orders: she "must get to the plantation and deliver her charge to her husband, who had laid his commands upon her when he left the city" (*MSWL*, 15). Later, King says that "in truth, she always echoed his opinions and seemed to have a horror of forming her own" (*MSWL*, 30). Her father, says King, adhered to a "standard of cold, stern repression of feeling as a measure of good breeding" (*MSWL*, 31). It is speculation, surely, but it is quite possible that Mrs. King's skills and fame as a storyteller came in part because a southern lady was forbidden to state more directly either feelings or opinions. The perfectly repressed, perfectly well-bred little convent girl does not even tell stories.

Surely King's unusual education had much to do with her later commitment to the life of the mind, yet her description of the typical education (which she underwent before going to Madame Cenas) shows no sign of regret at the clear gender distinctions:

> Impoverished ladies throughout the city, dressed in mourning, most of them were making their bread and meat by teaching. They opened schools and gave gratuitously, if need be, to the measure of what they had learned in the days

of plenty. French, English, music, and drawing were furnished with their accompaniments of refinement and good
manners. . . .

And there was the Jesuit College for the boys who needed
classical studies. (*MSWL*, 24)

King was later to satirize just such "female education" in her portrait of
the young San Antonio ladies' schooling in *The Pleasant Ways of St.
Médard*. Later, King comments—again without expressing much feeling—that "the boys of our quartette—we older children—entered
training for business careers, the two girls for young ladyhood and society" (*MSWL*, 46).

Literary gender distinctions, of course, pervaded the culture. King
makes such distinctions herself: "She [Julie K. Wetheril] was well
known for her verses, exquisite and dainty and evanescent, quite in
contrast to her literary articles, which were 'masculine,' as we used to
call them, in their clear and strong decision" (*MSWL*, 57). The assumption that supposedly sex-linked character traits could also be seen in
writing produced conflicts for Grace King as a woman artist choosing to
live the life of a professional writer. As early as the age of ten, she says,
she resolved to become a writer; yet her ambivalence in presenting her
first written piece, "The Heroines of Fiction," is clear:

When my name was announced in due course of routine for
a paper, I shrank back in consternation from the ordeal and
had to be coaxed and persuaded by my friends to stand in the
group of the previous brave volunteers. When I saw there
was no escape from it, I went home miserable, but at the
same time determined to stand the test for which, in truth, I
had been waiting secretly. . . . A rather caustic review it
must have been, and an arrogant one. I read it at the club
meeting in a trembling voice and could hardly believe my
ears when I heard expressions of compliment. (*MSWL*, 58)

When "Monsieur Motte" came out, King was careful to preserve her anonymity for at least a year, like so many of her female literary predecessors. Yet at the same time that she denigrated her work as "arrogant"
and hid behind the shield of anonymity, she was developing a sense of
vocation and commitment. "By this time I felt that I had thoroughly established myself as a story writer and began to detach myself from all
other duties," said King. This was after only one published volume. Yet
on the same page of her memoirs, she describes her other, unpublished
work as "lowly aspirations" and herself as "plodd[ing] sturdily on" with
her "little stor[ies]" (*MSWL*, 67). This ambivalence ran through her lit-

erary life. After translating some letters of George Sand, she immediately accepted Warner's "severe scolding for translating them . . . he
was ashamed that I should even think of submitting them to an editor. I
meekly put them away and said no more about them, although in comparison with what magazines publish at the present time [1932] they
are mere icicles" (*MSWL*, 153–54). Yet, in an earlier letter to her sister,
King mocked the Tulane University president's attitude toward women
writing in the "ludicrous effort on his part to come down to the occasion. He tried to be very grateful for the volumes of *women's* books,—
complimented books & women's work in general, vague, terms—&
then by a happy thought finished up by an eulogium of Mrs Howe & her
accomplished daughter . . . then gave us a peep at Boston & the position the women occupied there."[51] Although at one point she describes
herself as a vessel for her art (it "took possession of me . . . it carried me
along" [*MSWL*, 187]), at another she gives the credit to her own heart—
but at the cost of her brain: "My heart took charge of my pen and succeeded as the heart always does in writing when untrammeled by the
brain" (*MSWL*, 379). At still another point, she finds herself in clear
and decisive control: "Upon one thing I was determined, to avoid moral
and pedagogic comment" (*MSWL*, 204).

When King learned that a Tulane University professor was writing a
school history at the same time she was, she "dared the risk of rejection, but would not withdraw" (*MSWL*, 218). Yet later, she submitted to
a wholly unjust rejection of that very history and, moreover, considered
her history a "humiliation" (*MSWL*, 332), taking the blame for what
was actually a school superintendent's dishonesty. And the self-de-
meaning words continue through her story of her literary life; she describes a fairly late period in her career as "the end of my little quiver"
and turns to the "goodness that lies at the heart of the publishing auto-
crat" to encourage her to go on (*MSWL*, 234). One remembers, again,
that the little convent girl was entirely dependent on the men in the
boat to initiate and to protect her.

Writing once to Fred Pattee, King emphasized that "Harris & Page of
course wrote from a different standpoint;—that of the white *gentleman*
as I write from the standpoint of a white lady."[52] That her standpoint
produced conflicts is clear. And it may have informed the last several
years of her life, years when her art seemed to die within her. King
wrote a sad note about the death of George C. Préot in 1901, sad more
for what it tells of her own state of mind than for its grief over his death.
She has seen him earlier in the summer and remembers:

> He told me that I had grown so much pleasanter—more
> agreeable—that I used to be so nervous—striving—never

seemed at peace—unhappy. I told him, that I was happier, since I had got rid of all my hopes—and had my future behind me—that I strive no more—for there was nothing new that could give me the pleasure. I sought this—and he became rather sad too. He said my last story was too sad—he asked me why I did not write gayer stories—more cheerful. I told him I could only write of life as I knew it—but that I thought that story extremely amusing ("Making Progress"). He thought it was the best one that I had written.

He was the only one who ever helped me in my writing. He was the first one who thought I could write. I remember how much pleased he was with my "Heroines of Fiction" that I read at the Pangnostics—and how he came around to persuade me to publish it—and to go regularly into writing.[53]

That tone of failure, of giving up in order to be pleasant, informs both King's comments about and the content of her last work. She describes the *Memories* as "interminable"; she will finish them "this winter" (1930) "unless they finish me first" (*MSWL*, 404). Indeed the *Memories*, as writing, are flawed. Her narrative identity is more contingent than ever; this is evident in the apparently uncontrolled shifts of person, from first to third to first again. Increasingly there appears a preoccupation with anonymity after death. Dream, memory, and mystical experience become confused. And we read the story of a writer, insomniac too often, repeatedly turning to nature for solace, and looking, in scene after scene, throughout her memoir, down upon or out a window on life.

CHAPTER IV

Kate Chopin
The Life Behind the Mask

Of the writers discussed in this study, with the exception of Ellen Glasgow, Kate Chopin is the only one whose life and work are today the subjects of widespread serious critical work. Although she is also the only writer not born in the South (Kate Chopin was born in St. Louis, Missouri), no quick conclusions can be drawn. For St. Louis was a town that, as Per Seyersted describes it, "had a definitely Southern and Gallic atmosphere" when an American "influx," and later Irishmen and Germans, made the city into a frontier town.[1] Kate O'Flaherty's father Thomas, an Irish immigrant from County Galway, was killed in 1855 when she was four. Her mother came from a French Creole heritage, and much of Kate's rearing took place in the hands of her great-grand-mother, Victoria Verdon Charleville, who was born in St. Louis in 1780. Although Madame Charleville instilled in her charge some of the values of the traditional southern lady, she also taught her to face life without self-consciousness or embarrassment and with courage and decisiveness, lessons that were deepened at the Catholic academy Kate attended later. There, in addition to the typical concentration on religion, domestic skills, and deportment, she learned intellectual discipline and vigor. When the Civil War began, Kate was ten; although St. Louis was under firm Union control, the entire Chopin family took the side of the Confederacy, and little Kate "tore down the union flag from the front porch when the Yanks tied it up there" and was apparently almost arrested.[2]

After the war, Kate Chopin played the role of the belle with apparent success but without wholehearted enthusiasm. A division between her inner and her outer selves that persisted through her life can be seen in an early diary entry, which discusses the "art of making oneself agreeable in conversation" by saying absolutely nothing and simply responding appropriately to the subjects suggested by "your antagonist."[3] Of course, this is part of the self-effacement included in the southern lady prescription; that the young Chopin herself pondered over other elements in that prescription is clear in another diary entry, a passage copied from the novel *The Woman's Kingdom* that urges women to take the power and the responsibility for making the "internal comfort" of a family. Until they do this—and Kate underlined these words—"it is idle for them to chatter about their rights."[4] Her persistent concern with the inner condition of woman and its potential for conflict with the prescription for ladylike behavior appears fully expressed in her 1899 novel *The Awakening*, the subject of which one reviewer called "the life behind the mask."[5]

At nineteen, Kate O'Flaherty married twenty-five-year-old Oscar Chopin, whom she had met when he came from New Orleans to investigate business practices in St. Louis. From all accounts (including her own poetry), the marriage was a happy one. The Chopins lived in New Orleans, his home, until business losses forced them to move to Cloutierville in Natchitoches Parish. In 1883, less than three years after opening his general store there, Oscar Chopin died, leaving Kate with six children. She was then thirty-one. During their marriage, Kate had acted out a growing independence of spirit. Even on their honeymoon, for instance, she had strolled about alone in Germany and drunk a glass of beer in a beer garden; back in New Orleans, she had continued her walking, exploring the city's riches. Simultaneously, she acted out the role of society woman and busy mother—a role that required a weekly reception day, like Edna's in *The Awakening*. Meanwhile, Oscar fulfilled the expectations of his race and class by joining the White League, formed to resist Radical Reconstruction, and by taking part in the Battle of Liberty Place (1874), a riot that cost forty lives.[6] Later, in Cloutierville, Kate Chopin seems to have been universally social and popular, her house a community focal point. When Oscar died, she took over the management of his work and the plantation. Like Thérèse Lafirme in *At Fault*, apparently she learned much, working through her grief and building her confidence.

Despite Chopin's success as a widow and mother in Louisiana, her own mother's urgings that she bring the children home to St. Louis were heeded; the family moved there permanently a little over a year after Oscar's death. Mrs. O'Flaherty herself died in 1885, leaving her daughter overcome with grief. Chopin's doctor Frederick Kolbenheyer (who might have been a model for Dr. Mandelet in *The Awakening*) helped her by visiting, talking, and suggesting that she write. At thirty-seven she wrote her first published piece, "Wiser Than a God," the story of Paula von Stoltz, a pianist who gives up a "good" marriage possibility for a successful career as an artist. Chopin continued writing and publishing short stories, and by 1890 she had completed her first novel, *At Fault*.[7]

The central story in *At Fault* concerns Thérèse Lafirme, left at thirty by the death of her husband with the responsibility for a four-thousand-acre plantation. "She felt at once the weight and sacredness of a trust, whose acceptance brought consolation and awakened unsuspected powers of doing."[8] When David Hosmer appears to offer money in exchange for cutting timber from her land, Thérèse at first rejects the invasion of her privacy and then, for business reasons, agrees. The relationship between the healthy, beautiful, and sensible widow and the quiet, grayed, and overly serious man develops through friendship to love. But David's sister Melicent, visiting for the summer, lets slip that her brother has been divorced. Confronted by Thérèse, Hosmer agrees that it was "the act of a coward" (*CW*, II, 769) to leave his alcoholic wife with only the money to support her habit. He goes back to St. Louis, remarries Fanny Larimore, and takes her away from her seedy hedonistic life to the plantation in Louisiana. There, Fanny faces difficulties. Though she responds to the balmy environment, and though she justly complains about David's dislike for her and his love for Thérèse (both of which he nobly tries to conceal), she lacks "any determined effort of the will" and "any resolve to make the best of things" (*CW*, II, 801). She turns again to alcohol; on a trek to get more, she is washed down the river in a storm and drowns. David leaves, and Thérèse continues to run her plantation, taking several months off for trips to Paris and to New Orleans. On a train, the two meet again; both are still in love, and they return to the plantation to marry. Thérèse says, "a little hopelessly," "I have seen myself at fault in following what seemed the only right. I feel as if there were no way to turn for the truth. Old supports appear to be giving way beneath me. They were so secure before . . . do you think, David, that it's right we should find our happiness out of that past of pain and sin and trouble?" (*CW*, II, 872). David Hosmer replies that "the truth in its entirety isn't given to man to know . . . but we make a step towards it, when . . . we learn to know the living spirit from the dead letter" (*CW*, II, 872). The implication is that Thérèse erred by invoking a legalistic set of values in her assessment of David's divorce; elsewhere, it is implied (though not so strongly) that David erred in following blindly the dictates of his beloved Thérèse.

A subplot shows a parallel love affair between the St. Louis girl, Melicent, and a Creole, Thérèse's nephew Grégoire. Grégoire adores Melicent in the old romantic way, and Melicent begins to respond to his advances. But Grégoire murders a man who sets fire to David's sawmill, and Melicent never forgives him. Both leave the plantation; Grégoire is killed far away in a brawl, and Melicent eventually finds herself as an intellectual of sorts.

Chopin's apparent intention in both plots was to demonstrate the pernicious effects of unforgiving and legalistic morality; such righteousness may be more at fault than the sins—whether desertion or murder—it decries. Yet Chopin's novel does not make the point simply or easily. Fanny is carefully developed as the passive product of a pernicious environment, suggesting that Thérèse could be right and that a change of place could help. Thérèse's injunction to David comes as much from apparent sympathy for Fanny's married situation as it does from legalism: "You married a woman of weak character. You furnished her with every means to increase that weakness, and shut her out absolutely from your life and yourself from hers. You left her then as practically without moral support as you have certainly done now, in deserting her. . . . A man owes to his manhood, to face the consequences of his own actions" (*CW*, II, 768–69). Chopin seems to imply that the wisdom and tolerance gained from an understanding of life's realities—and not just its moral codes—lead ultimately to true fulfillment and communication. As the story develops this point, it moves each of the four major characters, Thérèse and David, Melicent and Grégoire, from a form of innocence to experience, though only the older couple learns from that experience. Their learning brings happiness as well as wisdom; the resolution to their story shows Thérèse and David joyful and playful, sensual and loving. Here is David trying to persuade Thérèse from going to supper:

> "Then let me tell you something," and he drew her head down and whispered something in her pink ear that he just brushed with his lips. It made Thérèse laugh and turn very rosy in the moonlight.
>
> Can that be Hosmer? Is this Thérèse? Fie, fie, It is time we were leaving them. (*CW*, II, 877)

Lewis Leary summed up the achievement of *At Fault* accurately. "Mrs. Chopin," he wrote, "evidently had something which she wanted to say about self-fulfillment, its possibilities and its cost, which she would say better . . . in *The Awakening*."[9]

Chopin returned to the short story after *At Fault*, polishing her subject and her technique and publishing over a hundred stories in both adult and children's publications like *Atlantic Monthly* and *Youth's Companion*. She wrote quickly, once her idea had formed, in a room swarming with children, their friends, and their activities. Then, in 1899, she finished *The Awakening*.

The novel caused quite a furor, and even in her private self, Kate Chopin seems to have been completely unprepared for the reaction. Reviews called it immoral, erstwhile friends deserted her, she was turned away from the St. Louis Fine Arts Club, and the novel was banned from local libraries. Though—probably inspired by her work on the novel—she had written a fine and even more shocking story ("The Storm") before the novel was actually published, probably the only good piece she wrote after *The Awakening* debacle is "Charlie." She never talked to her close friends about the issue; she simply wrote less fiction, and wrote less surely. In 1904 she died at fifty-two of a brain hemorrhage.

It is Chopin's remarkable perception of woman—Seyersted calls it an "existential" vision—that, with her artistry, has brought her works under serious contemporary scrutiny. And it is clear that, both in her life and in her work, Chopin's perception of what it meant to be a woman was informed in part by traditionally southern prescriptions and experience. In one of her columns written apparently at the request of the *Criterion*, for example, Chopin lightly and ironically discusses the vogue for women to write their memoirs; the occasion was the publication of another southern woman's memoirs, and Chopin's purpose is to praise fiction over autobiography. Although Chopin begins with a straight face ("I find it quite natural that a woman should want to write her memoirs, and enjoy doing so" [CW, II, 715]), she soon introduces a tone that delicately mocks such efforts. Her own memory, she says ironically, "retains only the most useless rubbish, while all recollections of those charming episodes—those delightful experiences which I, no doubt, shared in common with others of my age and condition—had completely deserted me" (CW, II, 716). Her "condition" was, in part, southern; a woman raised with that region's expectations might well ask "whether I received much attention, and whether I was a great belle or not; that sort of thing. Do you remember if I ever met any people of distinction?" (CW, II, 716–17). Although it is clear that the lack of concern Chopin's persona shows here by her "failure of memory" is, *ipso facto*, a rejection of the role of belle, it is equally clear that it is a southern definition of womanhood being rejected. An interesting note follows, given *Beulah*'s use of horses. The writer asks her male friend, whose memory has "unerring precision and cock-sureness" (CW, II, 716), if he remembers the time the horses ran away with her and threw her down an embankment. He reminds her that this happened to her cousin, not her. Since the point of the essay is to suggest (albeit through humorous self-effacement) the superiority of fiction to fact, it is doubly interesting that Chopin would choose to cast herself as the lead in this "fiction" about female powerlessness. Chopin goes on to reject the "*pleasant little* past events . . . [that] give sparkle" (CW, II, 716) in order to stick to "inventions," presumably like this one. And she does so by constructing an intentionally ironic tale. By the end of her conversation with her gentleman friend, she "submissively" accedes to *his* suggestion that she stay with fiction, having manipulated him, from behind her mask, to tell her to do the very thing she wants to do.

That Chopin persisted in leading an extremely active social life in St. Louis—"her home was . . . always full, particularly on Thursday, which was her 'day'"—suggests that she perpetuated her role as southern lady in life as well; in fact, Seyersted states quite clearly that "she had been reared with the Creole notion that publicity was a bad thing, particularly for a lady, and the general idea that a woman could be satisfied with her home." He adds that she "inherited" "aristocratic manners and . . . perfect etiquette." [10]

Thus it seems evident that Chopin grew up in and accepted certain elements of the South's definition of the lady. "According to all accounts, she was a perfect wife and mother," says Seyersted. Yet "under the surface, however,—and even unknown to herself . . . she identified deeply with Edna Pontellier" (CW, I, 29). The divided self that must have resulted has been interpreted, in the case of Edna Pontellier, as schizoid.[11] In the case of Kate Chopin herself, Seyersted sees that divided self as necessitating a compromise: "Kate Chopin did everything she could to further her local and national success, while retaining her womanly modesty and hiding her secret aspirations from everyone—except Kolbenheyer."[12] But that compromise came at a cost. For example, though she gave readings to "society" people, she confided to her diary at one point, "Aren't there enough ladies & gentlemen sapping the vitality from our every day existence! are we going to have them casting their blight upon art." "Things which bore me and which I formerly made an effort to endure are unsupportable to me," Chopin wrote, adding that she found her consolation in nature. Apparently some of those boring things were social requirements: "I am losing my interest in human beings; in the significance of their lives and actions. . . . I want neither books nor men. They make me suffer. Is there one of them can talk to me like the night—the summer night?"[13] Behind the mask, alienated though she felt, her concern with womanhood led her to see deeper into the role of woman, says Seyersted: she saw "the idea of male supremacy and female submission as so ingrained that women may never achieve emancipation in the very deepest sense. Furthermore, she also looked beyond this emancipation, and there she saw the horror of an unsupported freedom. This, and her awareness of how woman in particular is a toy in the hands of nature's procreational imperative, lend a note of despair to such works as *The Awakening*" (CW, I, 32).

Two late stories demonstrate Chopin's hopeful vision of woman in ideal relation to man and to society and her rather gloomy feelings about the possible realization of that vision. "The Storm" presents the vision. Written after *The Awakening* but before its publication, it continues the story of Alcée Laballière and Calixta, first seen in "At the 'Cadian Ball." By now each has married into his class; Alcée's Creole wife Clarisse has gone to Biloxi with their babies for a vacation, and Calixta's Cajun husband Bobinôt has gone to the store with their son. A storm comes up just as Alcée passes Calixta's house. He goes in out of the rain, and the two finally make love. Chopin's description of the scene is explicit and natural, showing both people sexually assertive and both laughing and happy:

> They did not heed the crashing torrents, and the roar of the elements made her laugh as she lay in his arms. . . . The generous abundance of her passion, without guile or trick-

ery, was like a white flame which penetrated and found response in depths of his own sensuous nature that had never
yet been reached.

When he touched her breasts they gave themselves up in
quivering ecstasy, inviting his lips. Her mouth was a fountain of delight. And when he possessed her, they seemed to
swoon together at the very borderland of life's mystery.

He stayed cushioned upon her, breathless, dazed, ener-
vated, with his heart beating like a hammer upon her. With
one hand she clasped his head, her lips lightly touching his
forehead. The other hand stroked with a soothing rhythm his
muscular shoulders. . . .

The rain was over. . . . He turned and smiled at her with a
beaming face; and she lifted her pretty chin in the air and
laughed aloud. (*CW*, II, 595)

After Alcée leaves, Calixta is pleased to see her son and husband; in fact
she is more relaxed with them than they expected of the normally
"over-scrupulous housewife" (*CW*, II, 596). Alcée writes to Clarisse
that he is willing for her to stay longer at Biloxi; she in turn is happy to
stay where she is, for she is now feeling again "the pleasant liberty of
her maiden days." And so "the storm passed and everyone was happy"
(*CW*, II, 596).

Through her entry into the various points of view of those concerned
with this act of adultery, Chopin asserts the possibility that *The Awakening* denied: sex, even outside marriage, can be enjoyed without personal guilt and without at least immediate harm to the others to whom
one is emotionally and legally bound. In fact, Chopin implies, freeing
sexual passion from conventional restraints puts it into its natural place
and therefore frees and enriches the lives of every person in the "community" of the story.

By sharp contrast, "Charlie," written after the psychic devastation of
the furor following the publication of *The Awakening*, diffuses sexuality
into relationships that preclude its performance and moves instead to
an examination of socially determined gender roles. "Charlie," the tomboy of widower Laborde's seven daughters, gallops on the levee on a big
black horse, cuts her hair short, wears "trouserlets," fishes, shoots,
writes poems, invents Tom Sawyer-like fantasies, and idolizes her father. As for him, "in many ways she filled the place of that ideal son he
had always hoped for" (*CW*, II, 644). Mr. Laborde is astonishingly
youthful in appearance, with deep blue eyes, a clean-shaven face, and a
quiet and tolerant disposition. One day, Charlie, practicing her shooting

and, as usual, missing her schooling, accidentally hits Firman Walton in the arm as he emerges from the woods. Walton, who has come to Les Palmiers on business with her father, is charmed by the oldest girl Julia, who is beautiful, dainty, an "angel," and who sits in her dead mother's place at the table. But it is Charlie, not Julia, who falls in love with him.

Though the shooting incident finally convinces her father that Charlie must wear dresses and even be sent away to school to become a lady, he finds it "dismal" to see her in "unfamiliar garb." When she is in New Orleans at school and has determined to become superwomanly, he comes to see her, "hungry for her" (*CW*, II, 661). They spend a secret day together, buying things, wandering around, and sitting near the lake "feeling like a couple of bees in clover" (*CW*, II, 662). The narrator says about the father and daughter that "such exceedingly young persons could not be expected to restrict themselves to the conventional order" (*CW*, II, 661).

Although Charlie fails at dance, music, and painting—the proper "clothing" for a young lady—she succeeds as a poet, winning the school poetry prize. When her father is seriously and permanently injured in an accident at home, Charlie is filled with grief and despair that "she would perhaps never see him again as he had been that day at the lake, robust and beautiful, clasping her with loving arms when he said good-bye in the soft twilight" (*CW*, II, 663), and she comes home to help care for him and the plantation. Then Julia announces her engagement to Firman Walton; Charlie feels Julia is a hypocrite, hates her, and calls her "no sister of mine" (*CW*, II, 667), clearly expressing her own infatuation with Walton. But her "girlish infatuation which had blinded her was swept away in the torrents of a deeper emotion, and left her a woman" (*CW*, II, 667). She burns her poems, takes off her mother's engagement ring and gives it to Julia, then tells her father that she has been "climbing a high mountain" and has "seen the new moon" (*CW*, II, 667). Volunteering to be his (now literally missing) "right hand," she seems likely to marry a local boy, Gus Bradley, whose shyness and plodding unimaginativeness have prevented him from telling her of his long-standing love. Despite his drawbacks, Gus is a responsible, decent man; Charlie throws away her "creams" and dresses, puts on her old riding habit and tomboy manners, and tells him she has always "liked" him and is liking him more and more. She will be free to run the plantation as she chooses. The last line is her father's: "I only wanted to know if you were there" (*CW*, II, 669–70).

This story, following as it does both *The Awakening* and "The Storm," shows a troubled imagination. Chopin deprives her heroine of both objects of her sexual love. Her father's blood is obviously too close, and

Walton chooses the perfect southern lady instead of the unconventional but clearly more intelligent and interesting Charlie. (There is no hint whether Chopin's description of the father-daughter relationship is conscious. There are, however, hints of a rather androgynous love; Charlie is a masculinized girl, and Chopin describes the two using the image of two bees in clover, whereas the conclusion to *The Awakening* joins the "male" bees with the "female" pinks.) Though Chopin gives Charlie independence, power, and control, she does so by making her over into a "man"—by giving her not just the internal attributes but the behavior and dress that society deemed masculine, even to guns and spurs. The implications seem to be that sex, love, and independence are mutually exclusive for a woman. She must either become "masculine" and lose her sensual life, or become "feminine" and lose her independence; in fact, to have independence a woman *must* become "male." Given Chopin's work before April, 1900, when she wrote "Charlie," it is a saddening conclusion.

As an artist, rather than as a southern lady, Chopin seems to have been most strongly affected by her culture's definition of woman in the way she created her public, nonfictional persona. Though one finds occasional protest against the treatment of women artists, her public tone is most often self-deprecation; if there is irony, it is subtle and not sharp. A rather overt expression of discontent came in an article Chopin wrote for the St. Louis *Post-Dispatch*:

> Many readers would be surprised, perhaps shocked, at the questions which some newspaper editors will put to a defenseless woman [writer] under the guise of flattery.
>
> For instance: "how many children have you?" This form is subtle and greatly to be commended in dealing with women of shy and retiring propensities. A woman's reluctance to speak of her children has not yet been chronicled. I have a good many, but they'd be simply wild if I dragged them into this. I might say something of those who are at a safe distance—the idol of my soul in Kentucky, the light of my eye off in Colorado, the treasure of his mother's heart in Louisiana—but I mistrust the form of their displeasure, with poisoned candy going through the mails.
>
> "Do you smoke cigarettes?" is a question which I consider impertinent, and I think most women will agree with me. Suppose I do smoke cigarettes? Am I going to tell it out in a meeting? Suppose I don't smoke cigarettes. Am I going

to admit such a reflection upon my artistic integrity, and thereby bring upon myself the contempt of the guild?

In answering questions in which an editor believes his readers to be interested, the victim cannot take herself too seriously. (*CW*, II, 723)

Although her last sentence seems rather serious in tone, and although Chopin has rather neatly captured the bind of the woman artist in her discussion of cigarette-smoking, even in this mild protest she creates a persona who accepts women's prescribed attitudes towards children, uses conventional clichés to describe her feelings about her children, and hints at a self-deprecation that is clearer in other articles. We have seen self-deprecation already in her essay on writing one's memoirs. In another essay, entitled "On Certain, Brisk, Bright Days," Chopin denies that she has the habit of writing and takes far less than seriously the imagined questions about where, when, what, and why she writes: "I write in the morning, when not too strongly drawn to struggle with the intricacies of a pattern, and in the afternoon, if the temptation to try a new furniture polish on an old table leg is not too powerful to be denied. . . . I write because of [a spontaneous expression of impressions gathered goodness knows where] and to seek the impulse for writing is like tearing a flower to pieces for wantonness. . . . I am completely at the mercy of unconscious selection" (*CW*, II, 721–22). But Chopin's self-deprecation, her insistence that writing means the same thing as sewing or polishing furniture to her, her demonstration that she is like any other normal woman—domestic, impulsive, irrational—may be her form of self-defense. Chopin well knew that her public would expect this sort of language from a woman writer. On the other hand, it is in fact true that she wrote at odd times and maintained a household that was both filled with activity and socially "accepted." Thus it is possible that Chopin here argues implicitly for the validity of a nonmasculine method of and attitude toward writing.

There are hints elsewhere of Chopin's rejection of what she saw as a "masculine" dedication to efficiency and to an externally imposed order. In order to write, she says, she had to break such rules as those for apportioning one's day, "shattering the 'household duties' into fragments of every conceivable fraction of time, with which [she] besprinkled the entire day as from a pepper-box"—this added to the "harmonious discord" and "confusion" which had "reigned my days before I listened to the Voice" and "which seems necessary to my physical and mental well-being" (*CW*, II, 702–704). The "Voice" is that of the "preacher" who teaches rules that make her "stagnant and miserable." Hence Chopin

seems to follow an interesting path that leads from her public acceptance of the definition of woman (as self-effacing, flighty, etc.), to her
use of this role as an ironic persona (as in the essay on writing one's
memoirs), to her affirmation of certain of those womanly characteristics
as essential to her art.

But it is difficult to sort out the irony from the serious, the negative
definition of "feminine" from the positive one of "womanly." In discussing the work of Ruth McEnery Stuart, for instance, Chopin's stance for
her column was that Stuart herself was so charming, so honest, so humorous, so free of anger—so womanly a woman—that Chopin could
not "take her seriously"; they spent the entire interview simply enjoying one another (CW, II, 712). By *seriously* Chopin means self-impor-
tantly: "I had met a few celebrities, and they had never failed to depress
me," but she says she might have known that "a woman possessing so
great an abundance of the saving grace—which is humor—was not
going to take herself seriously, or to imagine for a moment that I intended to take her seriously" (CW, II, 712). Although Chopin praises
Stuart for the womanliness of her work, she says that it has a "whole-
some, *human* note" with "nothing finical or *feminine* about it," and
adds that few of "our women writers have equalled her in this respect"
(CW, II, 711, my emphases). Apparently *feminine* and *womanly* are,
for Chopin, very different and even antithetical terms. When it came to
the point, however, that Chopin felt she had to publish a retraction for
The Awakening, she resorted once again to the ironical use of the feminine persona: "Having a group of people at my disposal, I thought it
might be entertaining (to myself) to throw them together and see what
would happen. I never dreamed of Mrs. Pontellier making such a mess
of things and working out her own damnation as she did. If I had had
the slightest intimation of such a thing I would have excluded her from
the company. But when I found out what she was up to, the play was
half over and it was then too late." [14] Here the irony is available only to
those who give Chopin enough credit to be able to see it; others might
well swallow the bait offered by this exceedingly "feminine" and passive
description of the ways of a female artist and by its subtle appeal to the
mores that prescribed for women self-deprecation and a concern for polite society.

Publicly, then, Chopin was fully conscious of the implicit contradictions between lady and artist and made the best of them, largely
through irony. More privately, her views on art were, in fact, quite serious. She took as models Walt Whitman, Guy de Maupassant, Sarah
Orne Jewett, and Mary Wilkins Freeman, for very specific reasons. All

wrote of "life, not fiction" as she said of Maupassant; all saw the shape and form of writing as essential to meaning. Further, Maupassant "had escaped from tradition and authority . . . had entered into himself and looked out upon life through his own being . . . and told us what he saw. . . . He did not say, as another might have done, 'do you see these are charming stories of mine . . . study them closely . . . observe the method, the manner of their putting together—and if you are moved to write stories you can do no better than to imitate.'" [15] Not only had he himself escaped from tradition, then, but he refused to let himself become one—except to urge, like Whitman, that each writer see life through his or her own eyes. It is no surprise that a woman who found herself in a web of strong traditions would hear the voice of such a writer when she looked to her own art and her own most private self.

So strong was Chopin's need and desire to affirm the individual vision that she rejected not just society but social movements, including those whose goals might most nearly resemble her own. *At Fault* exposes the reformer's impulse when Thérèse insists that David take back his alcoholic wife. Reform—particularly temperance work—was a realm dominated during the nineteenth century by women. It provided, as we saw, one of the few public arenas in which they could work. Chopin, however, apparently found the independence that such work afforded women not appealing enough to counter her repugnance for its content. In "Miss McEnders," Chopin again details her objections to the "feminine" reforming instinct. Georgie McEnders, a busy reformer who is engaged to be married, discovers that her dressmaker Mademoiselle Salambre has an illegitimate child. To teach the seamstress a moral lesson, Georgie cancels her order—despite the fact that she has just read a paper to the Woman's Reform Club called the "Dignity of Labor for Women." "Almost too white-souled for a creature of flesh and blood" (*CW*, I, 205), Miss McEnders "draw[s] an invisible mantle of chastity closely about her" (*CW*, I, 206) and believes in "discipline," hating "unrighteousness." But Mademoiselle Salambre is not to be so easily stopped. She knows the intimate life of almost everyone in town. So she comes to Miss McEnders' house to tell her that she wouldn't touch her work, because, whereas there is "not a mouthful of bread that she had not earned" for herself, both Georgie's father and her fiancé are less than honest themselves (*CW*, I, 209). The dressmaker tells Georgie to "meddle no farther with morals until her own were adjusted" (*CW*, I, 210). Georgie goes out on the street to ask passersby who lives in her house; everyone tells her it is Horace McEnders, who made his money in the Whiskey Ring—or might even have stolen it. Apparently her fi-

ancé's morals are equally tainted. Georgie throws the "spotless" bou-
quet of white spring blossoms he has given her into the "wide, sooty,
fire-place" (*CW*, I, 211) and weeps bitterly.

Despite the story's obvious attack on reformers and self-righteous-
ness, the story does have an ethic of its own. Georgie's morals are un-
tested, virginal; Mademoiselle Salambre, on the other hand, has vast
experience but still maintains an ethic, not of sexual morality, but of
personal integrity. She is the character who in fact embodies the dignity
of labor for women—and for men; implicit in the story is the belief that
working for oneself rather than living as a parasite upon others (as do
the two men, and Georgie herself) is a mark of dignity. Thus Chopin
here invokes a code of her own—by implication, a code that includes
honesty, self-sufficiency, and experience. There is no hint, however,
that Chopin ever thought such values could be gained through social
movements.

Nor could they be gained through directly didactic literature. As an
artist, Chopin rejected Emile Zola for his "mass of prosaic data, offensive and nauseous description and rampant sentimentality" and for "the
disagreeable fact that his design is to instruct us." She argued that it
was "unpardonable" for an author to speak through his main character
(*CW*, II, 698). Chopin disliked Thomas Hardy for the same reason: his
characters were, she said, "so plainly constructed with the intention of
illustrating the purposes of the author, that they do not for a moment
convey an impression of reality" (*CW*, I, 24). About *Jude the Obscure*,
she said "the book is detestably bad; it is unpardonably dull; and immoral, chiefly because it is not true" (*CW*, II, 714). As was the case in so
many areas of Chopin's life, she faced an apparent paradox: to argue
against moralizing is to presume an ethic of one's own. It is doubtful
that she ever resolved this artistic conflict; yet she seems to have held
consistently to the belief that the personal vision, whatever it may be,
comes first and that "there is far too much gratuitous advice bandied
about, regardless of personal aptitude and wholly confusing to the individual point of view" (*CW*, II, 704). Hence, she said, "I am more than
ever convinced that a writer should be content to use his own faculty,
whether it be a faculty for taking pains or a faculty for reaching his
effects by the most careless methods . . . and if he is content to reach
his own group of readers who understand and are in sympathy, without
ambition to be heard beyond it, [he will] attain, in my opinion, somewhat to the dignity of a philosopher" (*CW*, II, 704–705). Thus Chopin
as an artist circumvented as best she could the restrictions placed both
by the definition of ladyhood and by the popularity, particularly in the
woman writer's tradition, of didacticism.

Chopin's southernness, unlike that of many other writers, took no prominent place in her imagination or her life; at least she did not define herself, as Grace King did, by her region. After her fervent pro-Confederate actions when she was a child during the Civil War, Chopin hid "whatever views she held on Southern problems . . . behind a serene objectivity," says Seyersted. Yet once again we see a woman writer from the South finding in the black people of the South a sympathetic subject. As Seyersted says:

> Kate Chopin undoubtedly had her own set of standards, and they were rather at variance with those of the Gilded Age. One reason she loved children and her Natchitoches people was their directness and lack of sophistication and their unconcern with status and wealth. The Creoles and the Cajuns, and even more the Negroes and the vagabonds, were unambitious and unsmitten by Yankee speed and financial and social push, and they could therefore be more genuine and spontaneous, more natural and wholesome, and live for a hedonistic enjoyment of the present, all of which were true values of Mrs. Chopin.[16]

Elsewhere, he maintains that the "fact that she gave only a few early stories to certain Southern issues which necessarily affected her suggests that she wanted to free her mind of them and move on to more timeless or immutable matters" (*CW*, I, 26). Nevertheless, granted that Chopin's concerns more centrally had to do with what she saw as the almost immutable and far from regionally limited relationship between woman and man, the symbols she chose to invest her subject with imaginative power come from her southern experience. Hence it is not surprising to find, in "Athénaïse," the clear parallel between the experience of a white woman and that of slaves. Cazeau, Athénaïse's husband, is stern; he is seen with jangling spurs and snarling dogs like a stereotyped slaveholder. Cazeau himself makes the unconscious connection when he remembers, just as he passes an oak tree with his wife (whom he has retrieved from an escape to her parents), that this was the very spot where his father had let a recaptured runaway slave rest for a minute. Athénaïse herself, "not one to accept the inevitable with patient resignation," continues to rebel against "distasteful conditions" (*CW*, I, 433). One of those is masculinity: "I can't stan' to live with a man; to have him always there; his coats an' pantaloons hanging in my room; his ugly bare feet—washing them in my tub, befo' my very eyes, ugh!" (*CW*, I, 431). So her brother Montéclin (just as patriarchal as Cazeau has been) spirits her off, this time to New Orleans, where she

lives in a boardinghouse, plans to look for work, and meets the journalist Gouvernail.

Gouvernail predictably falls in love with Athénaïse, but she sees
him only as a friend. Yet even Gouvernail, the most sensitive and (to
Athénaïse) feminized of men (his hands seem to her "remarkably white
and soft for a man's" [CW, I, 444]), acts possessive with Athénaïse (CW,
I, 447). So again she uses her brother as a protection against the development of a possibly sexual relationship. Like Cazeau after his insight
at the oak tree, Gouvernail takes a liberated view: "So long as she did
not want him, he had no right to her" (CW, I, 450). But all is to no avail,
for Athénaïse discovers she is pregnant. Not only is she filled with ecstasy, but "the first purely sensuous tremor of her life swept over her" at
the news and the thought of Cazeau (CW, I, 451). She goes home, now
"know[ing] her own mind," to her husband.

But the anticipated baby is a deus ex machina. And for a story whose
apparent purpose is to show the stages of a woman's sexual awakening,
from repulsion to brotherly asexuality to sensuality, in "Athénaïse" Chopin weaves into her fabric the themes of mastery and possession far less
explicably than she does in The Awakening. Though Cazeau has rejected his identification with slavemasters, and though Athénaïse has
awakened to her attraction for Cazeau, the final note is a somber, possibly ironic evocation of the parallel to slavery. "A little negro baby was
crying somewhere. As Athénaïse withdrew from her husband's embrace, the sound arrested her. 'Listen, Cazeau! How Juliette's baby is
crying! Pauvre ti chou, I wonder w'at is the matter with it?'" (CW, I,
454). In "The Storm," Chopin uses the language of possession to describe the act of sex: "he possessed her" (CW, II, 595). And in The
Awakening, the core of the tragedy has to do with the links between possession and sexuality. The cry of that baby will chain Athénaïse, Chopin
suggests here, as Cazeau alone could never do.

If, as Nancy Cott claimed, Sarah Grimké's choice of "bonds" revealed
her southern heritage, certainly Chopin's choice of "Emancipation" for
the title of the early work written before her marriage and discussed in
Chapter One reveals the same roots. The freedom gained by the animal
in the sketch is the freedom of the slave or the woman.[17]

Other sketches and stories deal more directly with blacks and slavery.
"A Little Free-Mulatto" tells of the difficulties experienced by a girl
whose mixed race permits her no world, no friends—until her family
moves to "L'Isle des Mulâtres" where everyone is "just like herself"
(CW, I, 202). The problem raised by the sketch, of course, is that happiness for such an alienated person can be found only on an island. "The
Bênitous' Slave" tells the story of old Uncle Oswald, who searches for

and finally finds "his" family, the white people who had owned him before emancipation and with whom he finds happiness by repeating his old role. Hence it can easily be seen as a very conventional apology for slavery. Yet in another sense, the story is about Oswald's persistence in getting what he wants, and about identity, for he feels his very name includes the name of the owner.

An odd sketch, "A December Day in Dixie," tells of the reactions of a man who is on a train going South toward home when a brief snowstorm covers the land. A first-person narrative, the sketch shows not just the narrator but the entire community expressing various kinds of imagination and even insanity because of the snow; the businesslike voice of the traveler's seat mate provides the counterpoint. By the end of the sketch, the snow is melting, and the man goes home to his "dear wife" and to a "southern day." The implication seems to be that the intrusion of an alien, specifically a northern, element into southern life temporarily frees that life; its departure shows the conventions still intact.

"Nég Créol" seems, like "The Bênitous' Slave," to endorse the traditional southern view of slavery, for old Chicot continues to serve the impoverished remnant of his old "family," Mamzelle Aglaé, and when she dies he cries "like a dog in pain" and puts a "little black paw" on her stiff body. Chopin, however, complicates this stereotyping. She tells the story from his point of view, noting that for most people his departure is like the "disappearance from the stage of some petty actor whom the audience does not follow in imagination beyond the wings." Of course, Chopin does precisely what she says most audiences do not—the last line shows him center stage. Moreover, her portrayal of the last Boisduré, Aglaé, is far from attractive; she whines and complains constantly to Chicot, using him both psychologically and economically. It is Chicot who has the intelligence and the loyalty that create character.

Once again, Chopin's use of black people in "A Dresden Lady in Dixie" can be seen as stereotyped. In order to cover for the little Cajun girl Agapie, Pa-Jeff, who is black, claims he stole the plantation mistress' Dresden figurine. He does it because, despite Agapie's one act of theft, she has spent days caring for him in his old age. Loyalty and kindness, then, along with the ability to act altruistically without any public reward, are attributed to blacks, providing a clear contrast to Miss McEnders' self-serving righteousness.

"La Belle Zoraïde," a story within a frame, still further complicates the issue of race and shows even more clearly that Chopin is using blacks as an objective correlative for her feelings about oppression. In the frame story, Loulou, the black nurse to Madame Delisle, bathes her mistress and tells her a bedtime story: Zoraïde, a *café-au-lait* slave, falls in love with the handsome pure black Mézor. Their respective owners do not permit their marriage; in fact, Mézor's owner sells him away. But Zoraïde has his child, a healthy girl who, Zoraïde's owner tells her, dies at birth. Eventually Zoraïde goes crazy, forming a "baby" out of some old rags. When her mistress brings back her real child, Zoraïde rejects her, clinging to her rag doll in now-unalterable suspicion and insanity. Clearly the author's sympathies are with Zoraïde, both for her sensual love for Mézor and for her maternal love for Mézor's child. Equally clearly, Chopin spares no sympathy for the white people in the framed story; it is their prejudice about degrees of color and their insensitivity in selling Mézor that change Zoraïde the beautiful to Zoraïde "la folle." In the frame story, the white mistress, clearly affected by the story, makes the comment that it would have been better had the child died, apparently missing the point by concentrating not on Zoraïde's but on the child's fate. Hence the apparent implications of the frame's plot—a black woman happily serving a passive white mistress—are undercut not just by the internal story, but by the thoughts of that white mistress, and the line between oppressor and oppressed is clear in both tales.

In a somewhat confusing story, "In and Out of Old Natchitoches," Chopin follows the fate of a white schoolteacher who refuses to allow a mulatto child into her schoolroom. Chopin dispenses with the mulatto family by sending them to the "Isle des Mulâtres." But the schoolteacher, Mademoiselle Suzanne St. Denys Godolph, is apparently punished for her actions. After she spends some time in New Orleans and develops a relationship with a man named Hector, the very man who had sent the little mulatto to her school comes to claim her for his wife. (He is a "modern" cotton planter, apparently a Creole on the way back up the ladder). One could see this story as Suzanne's punishment for acting like a slaveowner by being herself put into a form of slavery. In any case, again Chopin's sympathies lie, not with the prejudiced whites, but with the freer whites and the mulattoes.

One of the most famous of Chopin's stories, "Désirée's Baby," again uses received notions about blacks. Désirée, believing that she has black blood, as does her child, walks off into the woods, never to be seen again. Yet the death comes at least as much from her recognition that her husband will never love her again as it does from racism. And the ironic twist at the end of the story—it is her husband who had slaves as ancestors—seems designed more to punish the despotic Armand than to endorse the valuation of blacks as inferior.

Finally, "Ma'ame Pélagie" focuses on a different southern experience.

Pélagie lives with her considerably younger sister Pauline in a tiny cabin near the ruin of the family's antebellum mansion. She is saving every penny to rebuild the house; it is clear that she plans to rebuild not just the house but the dream that the house represents to her, the dream of the elegance, the luxury, the ease, and the romance of the Old South. Her plans are changed, however, by the summer visit of their niece La Petite, who like her aunt Pauline, grows pale and deathlike in the atmosphere of Pélagie's dream world. Pélagie, recognizing that La Petite will soon leave them and that her sister Pauline will die if she does, spends an agonized night in the ruins of the old house and comes back having decided to spend her money to build a new house, neither a mansion nor a cabin, but a sensible home. She does; in the new house, Pauline drops years from her face and La Petite moves in to live permanently. But Ma'ame Pélagie, unlike the younger women, cannot adjust to the change; instead she stands "alone" and "erect," growing far older than her years because her soul "stayed in the shadow of ruin," but retaining the dignity of her sacrificial choice. The story is Chopin's only direct statement about the Old South and the New; clearly allegorical in nature, it gives sympathy to those who live in the dream of the past, but makes it clear that life is in the present and in a new, less romantic set of values.

Chopin, then, did concern herself with the South, though she did not identify herself with it. Like other southern women writers, she made connections between blacks and women; like others, she found the Old South an impossible and, in certain senses, an undesirable dream. Most of her work, however, is not regional in concern. As she said about the Western Association of Writers, "there is a very, very big world lying not wholly in northern Indiana" (CW, II, 691–92). These writers, she said, in clinging to the past and to convention, fail to see that larger world, which is "human existence in its subtle, complex, true meaning, stripped of the veil with which ethical and conventional standards have draped it" (CW, II, 692). Moreover, she saw not just southern, but American experience generally as repressive of great art: American writers might equal the French, she said, "were it not that the limitations imposed upon their art by their environment hamper a full and spontaneous expression" (CW, I, 24). Seyersted notes that one of Kate Chopin's friends "observed that she might have developed earlier as a writer, had her environment been different" (CW, I, 29). And that environment, as we have seen, was that of the particular southern version of the American experience. For Chopin, then, though the South provided some of her important metaphors, community at its deepest level must have become that community of readers who understood and were in sympathy, of artists in her chosen tradition, and of the few persons who were able to see beyond the mask of her divided self.

That divided self was perhaps best expressed in the conflicts experienced by Edna Pontellier in *The Awakening*, and in the psychic fissures expressed by Kate Chopin in her creation of three women who might have been one—Edna, Adèle Ratignolle, and Mademoiselle Reisz. For in her 1899 novel, Chopin drew most clearly the portrait of women, and particularly artists who were women, in the South.

The story needs little recapitulation; by now it is familiar. Edna Pontellier, on a summer visit to Grand Isle with her commuter husband and two little boys, responds to the lush setting, the Creole style, and the attentions of Robert Lebrun by a gradual awakening of her senses, her sexuality, her emotions, and her selfhood. Robert, aware that this "American" girl-woman is taking him seriously and that he is responding on a level deeper than that of his normal flirtations, leaves for Mexico. Back in New Orleans, Edna begins to act on her growing feelings of emancipation. When her children and husband leave for a period of time, she rents a little "pigeon-house" nearby, throws a huge, lavish dinner at the family house, and moves. Meanwhile, she has kept up with two radically different women friends, Mademoiselle Reisz, an artist-pianist who lives alone and acerbically, and Madame Ratignolle, a completely charming and almost completely self-effacing "mother-woman." Although Edna longs for Robert, more immediate attention is received from Alcée Arobin, a roué-about-town with whom she first expresses her awakened sensuality. Edna tries to develop her talents as a painter, but she never commits herself to it; her real commitment is to self-discovery. When she learns that Robert has returned, the self-discovery seems complete, but after an eventual temporary reunion, she leaves to sit through Madame Ratignolle's latest childbirth only to return to her pigeon-house and find a note from Robert saying "Good-bye—because I love you." She thinks through the night, decides that if she did not want Robert she would simply want some other man and that she must "think of [her] children," then goes back to Grand Isle. There she walks into the sea, the seductive sea where she had learned to swim the summer before, and drowns herself.

The Awakening has evoked widely diverging views both of Edna Pontellier as protagonist and of Kate Chopin's stance as author. Emily Toth sees the book as "embodied feminist criticism": "In its picture of the particular limitations placed upon women, the novel belongs to the tradition of feminist criticism a century ago,"[18] in particular John Stuart

and Harriet Taylor Mill's analysis of the condition of women. Otis
Wheeler found the novel a "tough-minded critique of the Victorian
myths of love" and further a "rejection of the pervasive nineteenth-century faith in the individual."[19] And in his fine critical biography, Per
Seyersted finds Chopin focusing on the "truly fundamental problem of
what it means to be a woman, particularly in a patriarchy."[20] Those who
fall more or less into this camp then laud Edna's life as in some sense
heroic and see Chopin as taking a position that is sympathetic to Edna's
experience. Whether one emphasizes Edna's suicide as a tragic failure
to break the bonds of the past in order to live with her freedom, or as an
expression of power and a triumphant union with the sensuous sea, a
birth, Edna's experience can be cherished as striking into new territory
and leaving some markers.

On the other hand, a number of critics have found that Edna's
changes are not heroic but neurotic: self-indulgent, childish, finally re-
gressive. She shows us, they say, not the route out of the past but the
map of a disintegrating mind. "The awakening of Edna Pontellier is in
actuality a reawakening," says James Justus; "it is not an advance toward a new definition of self but a return to the protective, self-evident
identity of childhood."[21] Cynthia Griffin Wolff argues that, with her suicide, "Edna completes the regression, back beyond childhood, back into
time eternal."[22] When the book appeared in 1899, Willa Cather found
Chopin's theme "trite" and "sordid" and Edna the victim of "the over-
idealization of love," "expecting an individual and self-limited passion to
yield infinite variety, pleasure, and distraction."[23]

Indeed, the debate began with first publication of the novel; critics of
that time, however innocent of psychoanalytic theory they may have
been, saw Edna as either a woman who, awakened to passion, "could
not forget her womanhood and, to save the remnants of it . . . swam out
into the sunkissed gulf, and did not come back,"[24] or as "one individual
out of that large section of femininity which may be classified as 'fool
women,' . . . the woman who learns nothing by experience and has not
a large enough circle of vision to see beyond her own immediate desires."[25] The New Orleans *Times-Democrat* took a moral view and
damned Edna both for "failing to perceive that the relation of a mother
to her children is far more important than the gratification of a passion
which experience has taught her is . . . evanescent" and for ignoring
the "moral obligation which peremptorily forbids her from wantonly
severing her relations with [Léonce], and entering openly upon the independent existence of an unmarried woman." Yet the reviewer notes
that "it is not altogether clear that this is the doctrine Mrs. Chopin intends to teach, but neither is it clear that it is not." He finds an "under-

current of sympathy" for Edna and "nowhere a single note of censure of her totally unjustifiable conduct."[26]

A third set of modern critics have followed the avenue suggested by this *Times-Democrat* reviewer, focusing on narrative technique in order to separate Chopin's view of the action from Edna's. Ruth Sullivan and Stewart Smith argue that Chopin "chose to use a complex narrative stance in which Edna is presented alternately as an unusual woman with significant problems admirably dealt with and as a narcissistic, thoughtless woman, almost wantonly self-destructive." Finding Chopin partial to the "romantic vision of life's possibilities" represented by the first stance, rather than to the "alternate stance for a realistic understanding and acceptance of human limits," Sullivan and Smith argue that the author never makes up her mind, portraying both "the feminist's heroine" and "an impulsive somewhat shallow self-deceiver" in "unresolved tension." These authors, however, themselves take a stand that is essentially with what they call the "realists": "Edna never really becomes a free woman because she confuses impulsive action with liberation and because she never understands herself or her own wishes and goals." Her failure they attribute largely to the absence of a mother.[27] Jane Tompkins, noticing as well that the "novel is built on a bipolar axis, the extremities of which might be labeled . . . 'realism' and 'romanticism'" finds that the narrator's tone can distinguish her two voices, so that "we become accustomed to their alternation." Tompkins agrees that Chopin offers no "clue to where she stands" or to what she makes of the impossibility of choosing between "chasing after spirits of the Gulf and redecorating the house on Esplanade Street." Yet she hypothesizes that Chopin withheld her hand because "direct self-revelation was foreign to her fictional mode, and far too risky," and because her theme was in fact "revolutionary in a socio-political sense." "Edna's dramatic death by drowning mitigates the force of social criticism accumulated in the novel by implying that the heroine's rejection of life was solely romantic, directed against mortality itself, rather than against specific social institutions."[28] Thus Tompkins, I think, finally favors the first group of critics, who see Edna as a hero.

Sullivan and Smith conclude that the "complex narrative technique encourages its readers to project their own fantasies into the novel and to see Edna as they wish to see her."[29] But there is, of course, more than just an inkblot on the pages of Chopin's novel: its complicated linguistic structure imposes obvious limits on the reader's projective freedom and offers correctives to inaccurate reading.

Yet each reader does choose which words and patterns to emphasize. Another productive line of inquiry has emphasized the specifically female elements in Chopin's imaginative creation. Per Seyersted pointed out that the novel "covers two gestations and births . . . a finely wrought system of tensions and interrelations set up between Edna's slow birth as a sexual and authentic being, and the counterpointed pregnancy and confinement of Adèle."[30] Peggy Skaggs adds that these themes relate the very "structure of the novel" to the "basic, natural rhythm of the human gestation cycle."[31] By comparing the treatment of time here with that in *Sister Carrie*, Emily Toth finds that "the rhythm of *Sister Carrie* is purposeful, causal, and linear [whereas] . . . *The Awakening* is lyrical, epiphanic, concerned with moments of consciousness rather than with upward striving." Where Dreiser's novel "follows a masculine model of incremental public success," Chopin's "is more concerned with the private or feminine sphere, with the growth of awareness in its central female character who in effect gives birth to herself." Unlike the male—and capitalist—view that "time is money," female time is biological with Madame Ratignolle and social in Edna's "languorous days at the seashore and impulsive wanderings in New Orleans." For, unlike Léonce, Edna, "like other female heroes, is supposed to find her identity through relationship with significant others" rather than through significant work.[32]

I would like to pursue this last line of inquiry further. Chopin's novel, seen as a female *Bildungsroman*, shows some striking similarities to *Beulah* in imagery, in areas and patterns of growth, and in the reasons for its lack of resolution and failure to complete itself. Beulah finally could not sustain her rebellion against the symbol of ultimate patriarchal power and authority who was God, and with whom she identified Guy. The risks of utter alienation and isolation—and the implied threat of physical harm—were too great. Symbolically expressed, she chose not to swim in the sea alone in the dark. Yet of course this is precisely Chopin's symbol for Edna's growing sense of power and self-control, both in her first frightening but exhilarating night swim and in her (daylight) suicide swim. But swimming as control or power fails in *The Awakening* as well, as Edna knows it must; nature (Adèle has just proved it) always "wins" in the long run. However, Edna does not see the experience as a contest between self and nature, as the masculine world in the novel envisions power and control. Instead, she grows powerful at the same time as, and because, she becomes one with the sea, responding to its caresses. The self affirms and expresses itself in the act of merging with the other; the sea and Edna are, in this sense, like two lovers. Beulah surrenders to Guy's sensual pull; Edna responds to the touch of the sea. The appeal of this Whitmanesque[33] alternative to the prevailing values of conflict and competition is mitigated by Edna's death and by the suspicion that less romantic and less final resolutions were available to her. Why couldn't she have gone, like Huck Finn, into the *territory* ahead of the rest? I think it is because Edna has been unable to find, on the land, any image of freedom that is not derived from an essentially masculine and capitalistic value system and thus can serve as a satisfactory model for her growth into womanhood. So, as she grows more independent, she sees herself as more masculine; yet as she awakens to her sexuality, she sees herself as more womanly. As a result, she experiences what seems unresolvable conflict between womanhood and freedom.

Compounding these difficulties are her background and training as a woman. Charlotte Perkins Gilman wrote in *Women and Economics* (1899) that the "inevitable result of the sexuo-economic relation" was to produce "such psychic qualities born in us [women] all," as "an intense self-consciousness, born of the ceaseless contact of close personal relation; an inordinate self-interest, bred by the constant personal attention and service of this relation" and a "childish, wavering, short-range judgment, handicapped by emotion."[34] Although Edna does not express all the qualities that Gilman names in the full passage (Gilman includes maternal passion and moral sensitiveness), as a southern (Kentucky) woman she has been trained into precisely the qualities that will impede her growth and deprived of certain skills that would permit it.

If this is so, it is ironic that critics should damn Edna Pontellier and sometimes Kate Chopin by using the very values that Edna sought to escape from or transcend. "Needless to say," says James Justus, "an aimless and unguided drift is not the state appropriate for the willed forging of a new identity."[35] Justus' assumption not only ignores the difference Toth pointed out between masculine and feminine growth and hence time models; it actively invokes the masculine model to denigrate the female one. Justus' anxiety about Edna's aloneness (he sees it as a form of solipsism) is stated more mildly by John R. May, who sees "a withdrawal into solitude that poses as a quest for freedom."[36] Yet, for a woman defined solely by social relations, Edna's quest for freedom is rather well undertaken in her quest for solitude; as Margaret Culley argues, "because of her sex, Edna Pontellier experiences not only dread in the face of solitude, but also delight."[37] Without assuming that anatomy—or geography—is destiny, then, one can find elements of male and female experience in the South to be both what enables and what thwarts Edna's growth toward maturity.

Like Beulah's, Edna's growth moves from passive acceptance of outside authority to rebellion against it, then toward autonomy and friendship, neither of which is fully achieved. Like *Beulah*, *The Awakening* expresses the idea of growth through the metaphor of a solitary sea journey. Edna swims into the literal gulf, whereas Beulah swam into the gulf of speculation. As Beulah finally climbed into the ark of faith, so Edna, in the story she relates to Dr. Mandelet, envisions "a woman who paddled away with her lover one night in a pirogue" (*CW*, II, 953). Appropriately, Edna's hope for salvation is romance, as Beulah's was faith. Unlike Beulah, Edna learns that her belief in romantic love is an illusion; she thus carries on her journey alone and with no boat. Edna even looks remarkably like Beulah; she is "handsome rather than beautiful," with "eyebrows a shade darker than her hair . . . thick and almost horizontal, emphasizing the depth of her eyes" (*CW*, II, 883). Her body, less feminine than Adèle's, is "long, clean and symmetrical . . . there was no suggestion of the trim, stereotyped fashion-plate about it." She has, too, a certain "noble beauty . . . which made [her] different from the crowd" (*CW*, II, 894).

At the beginning of the novel, Edna has led an essentially passive life; when, in chapter 11, she stubbornly stays outside despite Léonce's orders, she "wondered if her husband had ever spoken to her like that before, and if she had submitted to his command. Of course she had; she remembered that she had" (*CW*, II, 912). The clanging spurs of the cavalry officer in her younger romantic fantasy symbolize male authority (as they do in "Athénaïse"), particularly the southern man's physical dominance over animals (horses) and slaves (in "Athénaïse"). Edna's father, a former colonel in the Confederate army who believes that "authority, coercion, are what is needed. . . . to manage a wife," had "coerced his own wife into her grave" (*CW*, II, 954). As a child in his family, Edna had moved deeper into the South, from Kentucky to Mississippi. Only one memory surfaces of early rebellion to these authorities: she remembers running across a green meadow away from her father's Presbyterian church. Submission to the authority of both man and church shapes the lives of "mother-women" like Adèle Ratignolle; the home is a "temple" (*CW*, II, 968) in which those "ministering angels" "flutter about with extended, protecting wings," serving, "idolizing" their children, and "worshipping" their husbands. Again, as in *Beulah*, religious, domestic, and patriarchal authority are identified. Though woman is the angel in the house, man is its Creator: Léonce Pontellier buys objects to place in his home as his "household gods" (*CW*, II, 931).

When Edna rebels, then, it is to defy those authorities that she has earlier passively followed. She refuses to obey Léonce's orders to go inside, refuses to obey her father's order that she go to her sister's wedding, runs away from the Catholic church at Chênière Caminada as she had run away from the Presbyterian church when a child. Moreover, she rebels against the symbols of that constellation of masculine, materialistic, and religious values: she stomps on her gold wedding ring, she leaves the societal "procession" by deserting her Tuesday afternoon receiving hour, she objects to Léonce's buying more things for the house, and she chooses to move into a simple small home, the pigeon-house, which is no temple at all. Her final dinner at the big house symbolically embodies her rebellion. To pay for it she uses Léonce's money; during the evening a "heathen" [38] ritual takes place crowning Victor Lebrun as an Oriental god of sensuality, a "graven image of [female] Desire" (CW, II, 973). And through it all, Edna sits at the head of the table, "the regal woman, the one who rules, who looks on, who stands alone" (CW, II, 972). Having invented this countersymbol for the home as God's temple, Edna leaves; she calls herself, quizzically, a "devilishly wicked" woman (CW, II, 966). But by the end of the novel, Edna rebels against not just individuals and institutions, but against the structure of nature itself. "With a flaming, outspoken revolt against the ways of Nature, she witnessed the scene of torture" as Adèle gives birth (CW, II, 995).

As with *Beulah*, though, rebellion is insufficient for autonomy; it forces Edna to define herself as exactly opposite to that against which she rebels (thus if not an angel her only choice is to be "devilish"). Edna must invent a self-defined existence. She tries to do this with her painting, which, says her teacher, "grows in force and individuality." Painting also earns her the money to live in the pigeon-house where she can experience "freedom and independence" (CW, II, 963). Finally, Edna's autonomy is expressed in her ability to swim, another experience that gives her a sense of power and self-control (CW, II, 908).

Yet her efforts at autonomy fail. It is no accident that, just after her first exultant swim alone, Edna feels for Robert the "first-felt throbbings of desire" (CW, II, 911); similarly, her departure for the pigeon-house is "hastened" (CW, II, 967) immediately after Arobin gives her the "first kiss of her life to which her nature had really responded" (CW, II, 967). Autonomy and sexuality thus are linked. But her sexuality drives her back into bondage—to men, as possessors (Robert) and masters (Alcée), and ultimately, through childbirth, into bondage to nature itself. (Interestingly, it is precisely because Edna lacks the novel's "masculine" values that her efforts toward autonomy through painting fail; unlike Beulah, "devoid of ambition and striving not toward accomplishment," she "draws satisfaction from the work itself" when she paints. She is also, apparently as a result, vulnerable to nature: "When the weather was dark and cloudy Edna could not work" [CW, II, 866].) Edna seems, then, to face a choice between autonomy and sexuality.

Moreover, her inability to find autonomy through work is traceable to her rejection of the values of acquisition and public success. The alternative that Edna imagines—satisfaction from the work itself—is too unrealistic to be effective.

Friendship, the image of ideal community found in *Beulah*, also appears in *The Awakening*. The Creole community, in fact, encourages openness; responding to the "candor of [Adèle's] whole existence, which everyone might read" (*CW*, II, 894), Edna verbalizes her own inner self and feels "intoxicated" with the "unaccustomed taste of candor. It muddled her like wine, or like a first breath of freedom" (*CW*, II, 899). Freedom through community: precisely *Beulah*'s image of friendship. How important it is, then, that Edna and Robert talk about themselves to each other, "each . . . interested in what the other said" (*CW*, II, 884). For here lies Chopin's opportunity to resolve the conflict between autonomy and sexuality; she can have her two characters articulate conflicting values through speaking candidly, as friends. In fact, that is what happens both when Robert decides to leave (*CW*, II, 909) and when he returns. Edna at least has learned her lesson well; she speaks to him with perfect honesty from her "inner life which questions" (*CW*, II, 893). How fully Chopin envisioned this possibility for resolution and why it fails will be treated later.

Other people also seem to offer Edna the honesty, support, and freedom of friendship. Adèle, of course, speaks with candor; it is she, in fact, who first "awakens" Edna's sense of her body:

> Madame Ratignolle laid her hand over that of Mrs. Pontellier, which was near her. Seeing that the hand was not withdrawn, she clasped it firmly and warmly. She even stroked it a little, fondly, with the other hand, murmuring in an undertone, "*Pauvre chérie.*"
>
> The action was at first a little confusing to Edna, but she soon lent herself readily to the Creole's gentle caress. She was not accustomed to an outward and spoken expression of affection. (*CW*, II, 897)

Mademoiselle Reisz is equally open with her home, her feelings, and her ideas. Yet because both women's support of Edna entails their hopes that she will change in specific and radical ways, Edna's ultimate freedom—her autonomy—is restricted. As an indication that Edna sees Mademoiselle Reisz more as an authority than as a friend, her last thoughts of Mademoiselle Reisz envision the pianist laughing, even "sneer[ing]" at Edna's suicidal swim.

Again as in *Beulah*, birds provide imagery that seems to parallel these stages of growth. In their cages, the mockingbird passively imitates what he hears, and the parrot defiantly screeches "*allez-vous en! Sapristi!*"—words that are equally imitative, though defiant. Otis Wheeler notes that when "mòther-women" are described as angels who extend their wings over "their precious brood," the "confusion of angel and chicken imagery is not insignificant."[39] Exactly like Beulah, Edna moves into what looks like a "pigeon house"; she will be domesticated but, unlike the chicken, able to fly. (Seyersted interprets the image to imply a "place of cooing love.")[40] But birds in flight (like Beulah's eagle) must, according to Mademoiselle Reisz, "have strong wings" in order to "soar above the level plain of tradition and prejudice" (*CW*, II, 966).

Listening to a "short, plaintive, minor strain" played on the piano by Madame Ratignolle, Edna imagines a "figure of a man standing beside a desolate rock on the seashore. He was naked. His attitude was one of hopeless resignation as he looked toward a distant bird winging its flight away from him" (*CW*, II, 906). Edna called this image "Solitude"; the bird is certainly an image of freedom as well. And when she herself walks down to the beach for her final swim, a "bird with a broken wing was beating the air above, reeling, fluttering, circling disabled down, down to the water" (*CW*, II, 999). Like the bird's, Edna's wings are broken; Mademoiselle Reisz had felt her shoulder blades when she told her about the artist bird, to see if her wings were strong.

Also like *Beulah*, *The Awakening* envisions growth as movement from within to without, from ignorance to awareness to expression of feelings, thoughts, and body. Yet Beulah is a professional intellectual and teacher; Edna is a painter. Appropriately then, Edna's intellectual growth is more accurately the growth of her pictorial imagination. Where Beulah uses analytical intelligence to question reality, Edna uses her imagination to paint pictures of reality and then tests her fantasies on experience.

Edna begins to "recognize her relations as an individual to the world *within* and *about* her" (*CW*, II, 893, my emphasis). But at the outset she sees those worlds as very different: the "outward existence . . . conforms" and the "inward life . . . questions" (*CW*, II, 893). So in order to "cast aside that fictitious self which we assume like a garment with which to appear before the world" (*CW*, II, 939), she must first "loosen a little the mantle of reserve that had always enveloped her" (*CW*, II, 893). Adèle in fact sews just such envelopes for her own children's clothing; the pattern is "fashioned to enclose a baby's body so effectually that only two small eyes might look out from the garment" (*CW*, II, 888). Appropriately, when Edna goes to visit, Adèle is folding the laundry.

KATE CHOPIN 163

The clothing imagery, then, undercuts the notion that Creole society is utterly candid. Although Edna learns, especially from Adèle and Robert, how to express her feelings, she fails to see or, finally, to accept the limits that Creole society sets on expression. Robert knows, and leaves Grand Isle; Adèle knows, warns Robert to leave Edna alone, and cautions Edna to "think" before expressing herself.

Edna first learns that she is entering a "new and unfamiliar part of her consciousness" when Léonce comes home late at Grand Isle, wakes her up, and insists that she must attend to what he says is Raoul's high fever. Thoroughly awake, she goes outside and begins to cry—but does not know why. Some days later, when he orders her to "come in the house instantly," her "will . . . blazes up, stubborn and resistant" (*CW*, II, 912). The mist clears off from the shapes of her unfamiliar feelings; crying reveals itself as anger. As more and more impulses come into her consciousness, she relinquishes her earlier efforts to repress them: in church, when a "feeling of oppression and drowsiness" comes over her, her "one thought is to quit the stifling atmosphere of the church and reach the open air." She gets up and leaves—although "another time she might have made an effort to regain her composure" (*CW*, II, 916). As seen earlier, Edna learns to voice her feelings at the same time she is learning that she has the feelings in the first place. Thus she speaks of Robert when he leaves, even though "she had all her life long been accustomed to harbor thoughts and emotions which never voiced themselves" (*CW*, II, 929). Thus, too, it is a step forward when she admits to Mademoiselle Reisz that she loves him: she can feel and speak what had been unspeakable. The degree of her evolution is measured by her change when she sees Robert in Catiche's garden. Intending to be "indifferent and reserved" when she meets him, she instead tells him just what she feels: she is angry at his neglect. She says, "I suppose this is what you would call unwomanly; but I have got into a habit of expressing myself" (*CW*, II, 990). But Edna's candor is not Creole candor; Robert, thinking ahead, believes she is "forcing [him] into disclosures which can result in nothing, as if you would have me bare a wound for the pleasure of looking at it, without the intention or power of healing it" (*CW*, II, 990). For the Creole, expression of feelings is not in itself a good (as Edna sees her painting to be); instead, one must calculate risks, anticipate consequences. Edna herself may be thinking this way when she does not accept the chance to say what she feels to Dr. Mandelet, for, rather than offering a possible resolution for the conflicts in the novel, Dr. Mandelet is part and parcel of the values Edna rejects. In the very conversation in which he offers his help, he addresses her as "my dear child" and seems to feel that she should have been protected from seeing Adèle's suffering. Thus, perhaps, Edna senses that the consequence of speaking her feelings will be assimilation, and so she turns down the chance.

On the whole, though, Edna learns only how to know and say what she feels; she does not learn the freedom of the discipline of self-control. Similarly, her awareness of her body moves from apparent ignorance of it to the capacity to express her self through her body, yet stops short of a sense of the power of self-control. As we saw, Madame Ratignolle opens Edna to her sense of her body; on the *chênière* after leaving church with Robert, Edna explores it as though it were a new-found land:

> Edna, left alone in the little side room, loosened her clothes, removing the greater part of them. She bathed her face, her neck and arms in the basin that stood between the windows. She took off her shoes and stockings and stretched herself in the very center of the high, white bed. How luxurious it felt to rest thus in a strange, quaint bed, with its sweet country odor of laurel lingering about the sheets and mattresses! She stretched her strong limbs that ached a little. She ran her fingers through her loosened hair for a while. She looked at her round arms as she held them straight up and rubbed them one after the other, observing closely, as if it were something she saw for the first time, the fine, firm quality and texture of her flesh. She clasped her hands easily above her head, and it was thus she fell asleep. (*CW*, II, 917–18)

When she awakens, Edna looks at herself "closely in the little distorted mirror. . . . Her eyes were bright and wide awake and her face glowed" (*CW*, II, 918). Presumably a healthy awareness of her body contributes to that glow.

Of course, Edna's awakening to her own sexuality provides a major theme in the novel. Despite marriage and children, Edna has apparently never felt anything more sexual than the fantasy thrills of kissing the photograph of a tragedian. Gradually she feels "throbs" of desire for Robert and is fully awakened by Alcée's kiss. Although Edna regrets that "it was not the kiss of love which had inflamed her" (*CW*, II, 967), she continued to unfold, always in response to the men's initiation. She feels attracted to Victor, for instance, when he looks at her "with caressing eyes. The touch of his lips was like a pleasing sting to her hand" (*CW*, II, 974). She enters into a full-blown affair with Alcée and finally recognizes that sexual attraction is as changeable as circumstance: "Today it is Arobin; tomorrow it will be some one else" (*CW*, II, 999). Yet she has demonstrated the capacity to control her sexual choice at least once, for, when Robert came to the pigeon-house, it was she who "leaned and kissed him—a soft, cool, delicate kiss, whose voluptuous sting penetrated his whole being—. Then she moved away from him. He followed, and took her in his arms, just holding her close to him. She put her hand up to his face and pressed his cheek against her own. The action was full of love and tenderness" (*CW*, II, 991). Even though she can initiate this lovingly sensual scene, she cannot force him to stay; and, of course, he does not.

Just as Edna cannot finally control her sexuality, she cannot—finally—control her thoughts. Many critics have noticed that the narrator of *The Awakening* distances herself from Edna by telling us what Edna does not know.[41] A favorite device imagines her thoughts as "somewhere in advance of her body, and she . . . striving to overtake them" (*CW*, II, 910; see also p. 995). It is no surprise when Robert tells her "he had often noticed that she lacked forethought" (*CW*, II, 914); when she moves to the pigeon-house without a "moment of deliberation, no interval of repose between the thought and its fulfillment" (*CW*, II, 967); and when Adèle tells her that she acts "without a certain amount of reflection" (*CW*, II, 979). Yet Edna does begin to catch up with her thoughts. Sitting with Adèle on the beach early in the novel, she tries to "retrace her thoughts" and, as a result—though Madame Ratignolle claims it is "really too hot to think, especially to think about thinking"—discovers the connection between that little girl walking through a Kentucky summer meadow "as if swimming" and Edna now. "Oh, I see the connection now!" Edna exclaims (*CW*, II, 896). The effort to "think" leads to the recognition and confession that this summer, like that one, Edna feels idle, aimless, unthinking, unguided, impulsive (*CW*, II, 897).

Despite this educating episode, the force of her emotional and physical awakenings keeps Edna behind her thoughts rather than before them. For example, when she has resolved to be cool to Robert, it is the result of a "laborious train of reasoning, incident to one of her despondent moods," and her resolve simply "melts" when she sees him. She catches up again only at the end of the novel, when she stays awake all night "thinking"; notably, she is again "despondent." She apparently resolves upon suicide ("she knew a way to elude them") and thus, her thinking now behind her, walks to the sea, "not dwelling upon any particular train of thought" (*CW*, II, 999). For Edna, then, analytical thinking accompanies depression and has little power; forethought is rare since it might conflict with the satisfaction of impulse. Emotion, in short, is more powerful than thought. More importantly, though, one must ask just what the narrator means by the word *thinking*. The concept seems twofold: to Adèle, it means logic, discovering cause and effect; yet to Edna, it means connecting images, finding patterns. Edna's mind works essentially pictorially; when she thinks, she imagines scenes (as she does with Madame Ratignolle's music). Thus the growth of her mind can be better measured by the development of her imagination than by the development of her capacity to reason.

At the beginning of the novel, Edna is familiar with the dual and conflicting realities of an inner self that questions and an outer one that conforms. As her imagination grows in its creative power, she invents realities within and then tests them outside. Within, she has fantasized about the tragedian, the cavalry officer, and an engaged young man. She has been content to keep these fantasies within, believing in a radical split between the imagination and reality. Hence she marries Léonce, feeling that "she would take her place with a certain dignity in the world of reality, closing the portals forever behind her upon the world of romance and dreams," of passion, and "excessive and fictitious warmth" (*CW*, II, 898). In fact, she believes that the inner romantic values "threaten the dissolution" of realistic love.

Yet her awakening—triggered by the swim and by Robert—is (paradoxically) into dream and spirit, as opposed to realities and conditions (*CW*, II, 912). On Grand Isle with Robert and in the water, Edna begins to trust her imagination, her inner life, again. Seyersted rightly, I think, sees her sexual emancipation as "completely interlocked with her spiritual breaking of bonds."[42] In the terms of this analysis, her emotional and physical awareness are necessary conditions for her intellectual and imaginative growth. (Tellingly, Dr. Mandelet sees only the first sorts of growth: "she reminded him of some beautiful sleek animal waking up in the sun" [*CW*, II, 982].)

When she does begin once more to imagine reality, Edna finds that it seems to correspond to actuality, that she can even make it correspond. Thus after re-imagining her childhood trek through the green meadow as an escape from church, she gets up and leaves the Catholic church where she has taken Robert. And just as swimming brought the joyous sense of power and control—swimming that she associates with pushing through the meadow of grass—so leaving the church with Robert takes them into a joyous romantic idyll. The power of the imagination seems confirmed; romantic fiction becomes experienced fact. "She herself—her present self—was in some way different from the other self . . . she was seeing with different eyes and making the acquaintance of new conditions in herself that colored and changed her environment"

(*CW*, II, 921). In short, as her inner self grows, her perception of the outer world necessarily changes. The more that world conflicts with her imagined world, the more alien it appears to her.

What is that imagined world? It begins as the belief that she and Robert can find a world of their own. When he abruptly leaves Grand Isle, Edna nevertheless continues to exert her imagination; she squeezes every bit of Robert she can from conversations, photographs, even the envelope around his letter. By the time she tells her Baratarian story to the people at dinner, her imagination has developed so far as to make "every glowing word seem real" to those who listened. "They could feel the hot breath of the Southern night; they could hear the long sweep of the pirogue through the glistening moonlit water, the beating of birds' wings, rising startled from among the reeds in the salt-water pools; they could see the faces of the lovers, pale, close together, rapt in oblivious forgetfulness, drifting into the unknown" (*CW*, II, 953). Only the doctor, who "knew that inner life which so seldom unfolds itself to unanointed eyes" (*CW*, II, 953), sees that this imaginative creation corresponds to Edna's inner reality; he mistakenly suspects Arobin of being its inspiration.

In the absence of a real Robert, then, Edna continues to imagine him. By the time he returns, we know that "a hundred times Edna had pictured Robert's return, and imagined their first meeting. It was usually at their home, whither he had sought her out at once. She always fancied him expressing or betraying in some way his love for her" (*CW*, II, 982). Yet her imagination does not correspond to actuality: "the reality was that they sat ten feet apart, she at the window, crushing geranium leaves in her hand and smelling them, he twirling around on the piano stool" (*CW*, II, 982). (In *Beulah*, Guy Hartwell's return is the stuff of pure romantic fantasy.) Edna tries to fit reality to her dream. She invites Robert home to dinner that night, seeking to find out his reality: "There is so much I want to ask you," she tells him (*CW*, II, 983); she wants to "know what you have been seeing and doing and feeling out there in Mexico" (*CW*, II, 984). Robert answers her: "I've been seeing the waves and the white beach of Grand Isle; the quiet, grassy street of the Chênière; the old fort at Grande Terre. I've been working like a machine, and feeling like a lost soul. There was nothing interesting." And Edna, matching her inner reality to his with just enough difference to retain individuality, responds to his question, "What have you been seeing and doing and feeling all these days?" with "I've been seeing the waves and the white beach of Grand Isle; the quiet, grassy street of the Chênière Caminada; the old sunny fort at Grande Terre. I've been working with a little more comprehension than a machine, and still feeling like a lost soul. There was nothing interesting" (*CW*, II, 984). But another reality intrudes into this perfect match; Arobin comes in, and Robert's "Vera Cruz girl" suggests that he too has had other affairs. With only that little reality to go on ("how few and meager" his words), Edna again makes up a picture: "a transcendently seductive vision of a Mexican girl rose before her" (*CW*, II, 987). The next morning, she "picture[s] [Robert] going to his business" and tries to understand his reserve, believing it "could not hold against her own passion" (*CW*, II, 987). Yet Robert fails to make her imaginings real; he does not come back. Later, when she accidentally encounters him in Catiche's garden, Edna once again tries to mesh outer with inner reality. She is there because, she says, she likes to walk, an activity from which she can get "so many rare little glimpses of life; and we women learn so little of life on the whole" (*CW*, II, 990). Eager not just to learn about life but also to impress her vision onto it, she again speaks directly to Robert about her feelings. He accompanies her home, and it is then that she kisses him.

But Robert's confession of love reveals an inner reality of his own that radically conflicts with Edna's vision. His "dream" has been of her "some way becoming my wife"; even his diction—he pictures "men who had set their wives free"—reveals that his dream has its roots in the southern patriarchy in which a man owns a wife as he might a slave. Edna tells him that his "dream" is of "impossible things" and tries to persuade him to accept her own, in which, "no longer one of Mr. Pontellier's possessions," she "gives herself where she chooses" (*CW*, II, 992). "If Léonce were to say, 'Here, Robert, take her and be happy, she is yours,' I should laugh at you both," she says. Even more fundamental to Edna's imagined world than the romance with Robert, then, are her freedom and self-control.

Their break is inevitable. Edna wildly exaggerates her earlier "Baratarian" stance: "We shall be everything to each other. Nothing else in the world is of any consequence," and then she immediately contradicts herself with "I must go to my friend" (*CW*, II, 993). She has made her choice. With a desperation that, like Edna's exaggeration, shows he knows the implications of her leaving, Robert begs her to stay. Edna refuses, but she states imperatively, "I shall come back as soon as I can. I shall find you here" (*CW*, II, 993). Despite this final effort, by verbal fiat, to make her imaginative vision become real, Robert really leaves.

Yet despite the reality of the "tearing emotion" at Adèle's *accouchement*, all it takes is Edna's imagination to make it "fall away from her like a somber, uncomfortable garment." Forgetting the conflict implied in their conversation, Edna "pictures" "that hour before Adèle had sent for her" and hopes to "awaken" Robert "with her caresses." The two worlds, thus, are in direct conflict: the inner world of romance, sexuality, freedom, and power, and the outer world of consequences: Robert's possessiveness, Adèle's suffering in childbirth, the presumed suffering of Edna's children should she make this affair real. It is now that Edna thinks through the night, fitting her pictures of romantic possibility to her sense of realistic probability.

Chopin's own apparently double view of reality is suggested by the two scenes with which the novel closes. The first shows two lovers, Victor and Mariequita; in it, the elements of romantic love—jealousy, exaggeration, adultery—are parodied in the conversation and by the extremely realistic setting: they are at work patching a porch. Yet, in the next scene, an amended version of Edna's romantic vision is endorsed without irony, through the symphonic gathering up of the novel's imagery and, most clearly, through the setting itself. A real bird, just as Edna had imagined in "Solitude," flies near the naked woman. But this bird's wing, like Edna's impossibly utopian dream, is broken; the naked man is now a woman. Thus, Chopin shows first the humorous possibilities implicit in the contrast between the wildly romantic dream and actuality. But then she pairs that scene with the final one showing her ultimate sympathy for the tragedy of the dreamer who believes her dream can come true. How close Edna's vision came to Chopin's sense of actuality is represented by the presence of that bird; how far by its injury.

Though Edna's flaw can be seen as a failure of the imagination, this is not to say that her imagination has failed to develop at all through the novel. On the contrary, it has grown—and not, as some critics say, in isolation from and ignorance of reality. As seen in her relationship with Robert, Edna tries with all her energy to make her imagined and her circumstantial, her inner and her outer worlds, consistent. She tries to search out Robert's reality, to adjust her own to his, even to impose hers on him. Yet she will not relinquish the core of her vision, which is not, finally, romance, but rather her own autonomous being. So she freely goes to Adèle, losing Robert; and so she freely goes to the sea, losing her life. But she does not lose her self, the self that has come into being precisely because her imagination, her feelings, and her sense of her body have been set free to express themselves. On the beach the last day, "she understood now clearly what she had meant long ago when she said to Adèle Ratignolle that she would give up the unessential [her money, her life, CW, II, 929], but she would never sacrifice herself for her children" (CW, II, 999). Back at the beginning, this had been "only something which I am beginning to comprehend, which is revealing itself to me" (CW, II, 929). So her mind has grown: she can see what has been revealed.

As in *Beulah*, the home becomes a symbol for the condition of the psyche. The Ratignolles' home, directly above Monsieur Ratignolle's drugstore, demonstrates the "fusion of two human beings into one" (*CW*, II, 938). Mademoiselle Reisz's "apartments up under the roof" keep her in her chosen isolation and permit her a bird's-eye view of the river, exactly the location for an artist who flies above the plain of tradition. The Pontelliers' "very charming home," whose "appointments" are "perfect after the conventional type," is really Léonce's possession: he is "very fond of walking about his house examining its various . . . details. . . . He greatly valued his possessions, chiefly because they were his, and derived genuine´ pleasure from contemplating a painting, a statuette, a rare lace curtain—no matter what—after he had bought it and placed it among his household gods" (*CW*, II, 931). One of those works of art is Edna: "You are burnt beyond recognition," he says to her after a swim at Grand Isle, "looking at his wife as one looks at a valuable piece of personal property which has suffered some damage" (*CW*, II, 882). Thus when the children have gone to their grandmother's, when Léonce has left for New York, Edna "walks all through the house, from one room to another, as if inspecting it for the first time. She tried the various chairs and lounges, as if she had never sat and reclined upon them before. And she perambulated around the outside of the house, investigating, looking to see if windows and shutters were secure and in order. The flowers were like new acquaintances. . . . Even the kitchen assumed a sudden interesting character which she had never before perceived" (*CW*, II, 955). The "radiant peace [that] settled upon her when she at last found herself alone" is immediately and appropriately expressed by this "delicious" repossession of her home, as she is coming to repossess her feelings and her body. Yet the feeling is illusory; after all, as she explains to Mademoiselle Reisz, "It never seemed like mine, anyway—like home. . . . the house, the money that provides for it, are not mine" (*CW*, II, 962). As her reason for moving to the pigeon-house "unfold[s] itself," she realizes that "instinct had prompted her to put away her husband's bounty in casting off her allegiance . . . whatever came, she had resolved never again to belong to another than herself" (*CW*, II, 963).

The double consciousness that Sullivan, Smith, Tompkins, and others see in Chopin's voice in the novel is paralleled by a pervasive fascination with pairing, even, on occasion, with twinning: parrot and mockingbird; lovers and lady in black; naked man on the shore, and naked woman; bird flying high, bird with broken wing; sea and meadow. The Farival twins "could not be induced to separate" during a dance "when one or the other should be whirling around the room in the arms of a man" (*CW*, II, 904). Pairing appears also in the language; Edna matches her words to Robert's, as we saw. Adèle uses almost exactly the same words to chastise Robert and Edna separately for being, like children, without reflection. The narrator similarly creates an almost matched pair of passages beginning "the voice of the sea is seductive" (*CW*, II, 893, and 999–1000), just as she did the passage about giving up the "unessential." And the pairing appears in characters. Married couples can be, like the Ratignolles, a well-matched pair; brothers, Victor and Robert, can serve as a pair of opposites. Certainly pairing is thematically expressed in the notion of a "dual life" (*CW*, II, 893). And, in the development of Edna's imaginative capacity to match her inner and her outer worlds, pairing is, as we saw, a method of growth. So it seems likely to be fruitful both to speculate further on the thematic implications of pairing and to consider in detail two of the most significant pairs: Mademoiselle Reisz and Madame Ratignolle, Edna Pontellier and Robert Lebrun.

Chopin uses pairing for obvious comparison and contrast purposes in cases like the two Lebrun brothers or the caged birds. But the Farival twins express a more subtle thematic implication: the relationship between identity and love. Their depiction suggests that the closest attachments may come from the greatest degree of similarity. This idea finds its fullest treatment in the relationship between Edna and Robert. The obverse follows; opposites like Mademoiselle Reisz and Madame Ratignolle, Victor and Robert, cannot bear to be around one another. In the case of the lovers and the lady in black, the apparent opposition of romantic love and religious commitment reveals itself to be actual similarity at the dinner when Robert announces that he is leaving for Mexico. All respond by staying in their own private worlds; the lovers whisper to themselves, and the lady in black is interested only in the possible indulgence attached to her Mexican prayer beads. Thus they are always seen together, different versions of idealism.

Since Adèle and Mademoiselle Reisz are the two women closest to Edna, a closer examination of that pair should help to show two sides of Edna. It is Madame Ratignolle, the "mother-woman," and Mademoiselle Reisz, the artist, who symbolize the conflict within Edna. Both are closer to her than any other woman, both are more fully realized than other woman characters in the novel, and, importantly, they have practically no relationship with one another. Nor is it likely that they would: where Madame Ratignolle embodies nature redeemed by religion, as represented by her angelic appearance and her fecundity, Mademoiselle Reisz represents the rejection of both qualities—she never goes near the water and she wears artificial violets in her false hair. Where

Madame Ratignolle plays skillfully for social purposes and keeps a piano for the children, Mademoiselle Reisz plays Frédéric Chopin with consummate art and, more important, deep understanding. Madame Ratignolle's "spun-gold hair that comb nor confining pin could restrain; the blue eyes that were like nothing but sapphires; two lips that pouted, that were so red one could only think of cherries" (CW, II, 888) are those of a sensuous Madonna. Mademoiselle Reisz, however, is "strikingly homely" (CW, II, 944); when she plays, her body "settles into ungraceful curves and angles that give it an appearance of deformity" (CW, II, 946). As we saw, Madame Ratignolle responds to others warmly and expresses her responses physically, with a natural sensuousness; it is she who first touches Edna's hand with warmth. Mademoiselle Reisz, on the other hand, "took Edna's hand between her strong wiry fingers, holding it loosely without warmth, and executing a sort of double theme upon the back and palm" (CW, II, 944). Mademoiselle Reisz, as an artist, excludes nature; Madame Ratignolle, as a "natural woman," excludes art.

But art and society are also mutually exclusive. Madame Ratignolle, as a "mother-woman," is at the religious center of the society. Further, she enforces social rules, warning both Robert and Edna on separate occasions of the consequences, personal and social, of their actions. She lays down, in short, the "law and gospel" (CW, II, 900). Mademoiselle Reisz, on the other hand, has apparently no important social or religious function in the community; the artist is neither legislator nor prophet. Madame Ratignolle is wholly integrated into her society, both the family and the larger Creole world. Mademoiselle Reisz chooses isolation, both physical and emotional (she dislikes most people); she is a spinster. But, implies Mademoiselle Reisz, solitude is essential to the artist. And Madame Ratignolle, perhaps because of her thorough meshing with others, leads a "colorless existence," as Edna sees it (CW, II, 938). Society and nature combine to make Madame Ratignolle essentially passive, as expressed most extremely in the occasional public fainting fits she attributes to her pregnancy. Mademoiselle Reisz, on the other hand, is a "disagreeable little woman, no longer young, who had quarreled with almost every one, owing to a temper which was self-assertive and a disposition to trample on the rights of others" (CW, II, 905).

It is to these two women that Edna is drawn, and it is because their characterization is so utterly opposite that we can see her own deeply divided self. The splits in Edna have been resolved or, more likely, have never been felt by the other two women. Edna is torn between nature and art: between the weather and her painting, between her sensuality and her freedom. She is torn between the erratically expressed, but real, love for her children and the relief she feels when they are gone. And she is torn between her feelings for her family, friends, lovers, and her desire to be alone. Madame Ratignolle and Mademoiselle Reisz may have resolved these conflicts; but, if so, each has done so by the process of exclusion. Edna wants more: she says she wants her "self" (CW, II, 929); to do as she "feels" (CW, II, 939); to have her "own way" (CW, II, 996). But to get what she wants means—though Edna does not realize it until the end of the novel—that she must find a workable resolution to the relationship, within her own psyche, of "*Mademoiselle* Reisz" and "*Madame* Ratignolle" (my emphasis). The resolution she chooses, at the end, is to eliminate both.

Perhaps one reason for that choice is that, whereas Adèle's values obviously impede Edna's development away from the role of southern lady, Mademoiselle Reisz's values, more insidiously, also impede her growth, for Mademoiselle Reisz embodies several of the significant masculine values in the novel, values against which Edna is defining herself. First we should look at the men and the masculine "sphere" in the novel, to see what it is Edna wants to reject. Klein's Hotel represents the male universe on Grand Isle; it is where Léonce Pontellier spends much of his time hearing news and gossip, gambling, reading the newspaper, staying late. In New Orleans, the business community is the men's world; after Robert decides to go to Mexico, Léonce runs into him on Carondelet Street, they go for a drink and a cigar, and Robert seems to Léonce "quite cheerful, and wholly taken up with the idea of his trip, which Mr. Pontellier found altogether natural in a young fellow about to seek fortune and adventure in a strange, queer country" (CW, II, 928). Men, then, have a world of their own different from both that of and that with women—and largely inaccessible to women—a world where money provides business and pleasure, a world of conflict, risk, and adventure. What Edna rejects of the man's world is what Chopin called in an early short story titled "Her Letters" the "man-instinct of possession,"[43] an instinct, says Peggy Skaggs, "she apparently believes to be universal, although most fully developed perhaps in a sharply stratified society like that in the South of which she usually wrote."[44] In "Athénaïse," Chopin makes explicit the connections between the possession of a woman and the possession of slaves; Cazeau, recognizing the similarity, resolves never again to force his reluctant wife to come home with him. Clearly the central objection to "possession" is that it deprives the possessed of freedom; as it tramples on her rights, so Edna tramples on her wedding ring.

It is Léonce Pontellier who represents repeatedly and almost flawlessly the typical American (though he is, of course, Creole) man of the period, the man whose obsession with gender-linked "spheres" produced what Henry James called, and Larzer Ziff adopted, the "abyss of inequality" between the sexes.[45] He fits a pattern that has been developing in this study: he is paternalistic and lives in a wholly male universe. Léonce is considerably older than Edna; he protects her ("'You were not so very far, my dear; I was watching you,' he told her" after Edna's first lone swim [CW, II, 909]) and pampers her with gifts, bonbons, and diamonds. The other side of paternalism is clearer, though. Just as he feels she has the duty of ordering the servants, he feels he has the right to order her, and order her he does, from the first scene with Raoul's "fever" through the time when Edna wants to stay outside ("I can't permit you to stay out there all night. You must come in the house instantly" [CW, II, 912]) to the less imperative "don't let the family go to the devil" (CW, II, 939). But even this is not authoritarian enough for Edna's father, who tells Léonce the problem is that "You are too lenient . . . coercion [is] what is needed. Put your foot down good and hard; the only way to manage a wife. Take my word for it" (CW, II, 954).

Léonce is blindly obsessed with the "male sphere" of newspapers, billiards, camaraderie, and, most of all, money. He leaves the domestic sphere to Edna, leaves the children and sends them bonbons, scatters his speech with financial metaphors, sees his house—and his wife—as possessions, objects to Edna's father because he lost a farm in racing bets, and cares about Edna's pigeon-house "*coup d'état*" not because others might think there is a marital breach, but because of "his financial integrity. It might get noised about that the Pontelliers had met with reverses, and were forced to conduct their *ménage* on a humbler scale than heretofore. It might do incalculable mischief to his business prospects" (CW, II, 977).

It is this obsessive concern with money that informs Léonce's definition of the proper role for women: "It seems to me the utmost folly for a woman at the head of a household, and the mother of children, to spend in an atelier days which would be better employed contriving for her family" (CW, II, 939). To him, the woman is only a wife and mother; her job is to sacrifice for "comfort"; failure to do this is, oddly, "folly." But of course it is folly, if one's object is to "keep up with the procession" (CW, II, 932). And that Léonce sees Edna's duties as part of his business is clear in his examination of the calling cards left when she first neglects her Tuesday receptions: "'The Misses Delasidas.' I worked a big deal in futures for their father this morning; nice girls; it's time they were getting married. 'Mrs. Belthrop.' I tell you what it is, Edna; you can't afford to snub Mrs. Belthrop. Why, Belthrop could buy and sell us ten times over. His business is worth a good, round sum to me. You'd better write her a note" (*CW*, II, 933).

The colonel, Edna's father, as has been seen, enforces even more strongly, though for different reasons, the notion that women should be slaves to family. When Edna refuses to go to her sister's wedding, he "reproached his daughter for her lack of *filial* kindness and respect, her want of *sisterly* devotion and *womanly* consideration" (*CW*, II, 954, my emphasis).

Alcée Arobin seems to represent in some points an opposite to these men. Antidomestic, he lives for the favors of married women. Antibusiness, his name is appended to a local lawyer's shingle only for the appearance of a professional life. He lives the fashionable role of a not-so-Petrarchan lover, the dark side of gyneolatry. Yet in his treatment of Edna, we find in Alcée some of the same characteristics seen in her father and husband. He is protective to a fault; he is patronizing towards her, while simultaneously adulating her; he is always the aggressor, the assertive one, and she the passive respondent to his well-polished techniques. And, like them, he defines woman—though his definition differs from theirs, he will not, as has been shown, allow Edna to define herself. When she says she "must think about . . . what character of woman I am," Alcée discourages her: "Why should you bother thinking about it when I can tell you what manner of woman you are," he replies (*CW*, II, 966).

Because Dr. Mandelet possesses, according to the narrator, a kind of "understanding" that very few men possess, and because it is only his offer to talk that Edna sees in her final swim as having been a possibility for salvation, the "wise" doctor presents a puzzle. Despite his insight, his sympathy, his discretion, his generosity—in fact, the "human" values we have seen in both men and women in the first two works considered in this study—he is still a father figure, and he still, like the others, defines "woman." In the very scene (quoted earlier in part) in which he offers to talk, Dr. Mandelet persists, we saw, in calling Edna "my child." And in a conversation with Léonce, he defines woman *his* way: "Woman, my dear friend, is a very peculiar and delicate organism—a sensitive and highly organized woman, such as I know Mrs. Pontellier to be, is especially peculiar. . . . Most women are moody and whimsical. This is some passing whim of your wife . . . let her alone" (*CW*, II, 949). Although his intuition is excellent, then, Dr. Mandelet cannot get beyond the blinders of a kind of paternalism that, for Edna, is retrogressive.

Edna finds very attractive certain of the qualities manifested in these men, and the attraction evokes not simply admiration but emulation from her. Thus when she finds in Mademoiselle Reisz a woman who asserts and defines herself—as do the men—and who, moreover, is courageous and adventurous, journeying essentially alone above the plain of tradition, Edna wants to emulate her. But Edna also sees in Mademoiselle Reisz less appealing elements of the "masculine" character. For example, Mademoiselle Reisz expresses her affection for Edna in a style that Edna rejects in Léonce. She uses the language of slavery and possession: she calls herself a "foolish old woman whom you [Edna] have captivated" (CW, II, 946); later, love's slave, she asks "Can I refuse you anything?" (CW, II, 964). She teases Edna, withholding Robert's letters at first; she encourages Edna's visits with hot chocolate, brandy, coffee, and biscuits, reminiscent of Léonce's bonbons. Unnatural herself, she sees Edna as the "sunlight. . . . Now it will be warm and bright enough; I can let the fire alone" (CW, II, 962). Mademoiselle Reisz at first acts the authoritarian with Edna, from the smallest action—"Don't stir all the warmth out of your coffee; drink it"—to defining for Edna the role of the artist. And, most important, Mademoiselle Reisz's independence has its destructive consequences: along with her "self-assertion," she has a "disposition to trample upon the rights of others" (CW, II, 905). Thus, even though her "divine art" can "reach Edna's spirit and set it free . . . quiet[ing] the turmoil of [her] senses," Mademoiselle Reisz's "personality" remains "offensive" to Edna, insofar as that personality expresses qualities from which Edna is trying to escape.

Because Edna emulates other masculine values, and because (as the pairing pattern suggests) to emulate is to become like, at several key points in the novel Edna sees herself quite literally as a man. Filled with exultation, "as if some power of significant import had been given her to control the working of her body and her soul" that night in the Gulf, Edna wants to "swim far out, where no woman had swum before" (CW, II, 908). Her implicit identification here with the power and control she sees in men follows shortly after the narrator has told us of Edna's picture of "Solitude" as "the figure of a man standing beside a desolate rock on the seashore" (CW, II, 906).

Yet elsewhere the narrator sees "truth" as beyond sex differences. Mademoiselle Reisz's playing, for instance, moves Edna temporarily beyond identifying passions with either sex. "She saw no pictures . . . but the very passions themselves were aroused within her soul, swaying it, lashing it, as the waves daily beat upon her splendid body" (CW, II, 906). The narrator cautiously suggests that "perhaps it was the first time she was ready . . . to take an impress of the abiding truth" (CW, II, 906).

But Edna finally cannot sustain that impress: for her, freedom is defined as escape from womanhood. Thus after she swims beyond, not just the women but everyone, tests her courage and her strength, and has a "quick vision of death," it must be particularly galling for Léonce to remind her of her sex by saying, protectively, "You were not so very far, my dear; I was watching you" (CW, II, 909). Nor is it any wonder that it is for Robert, who has "penetrated her mood and understood" (CW, II, 910), that she now feels the "first-felt throbbings of desire" (CW, II, 911).

A similar pattern of events sends her into the arms of Alcée Arobin. When they go with Mrs. Highcamp to the horse races (where Alcée has met Edna with her father), Edna

> sat between her two companions as one having authority to speak. She laughed at Arobin's pretensions and deplored Mrs. Highcamp's ignorance. . . . She did not perceive that she was talking like her father as the sleek geldings ambled in review before them. She played for very high stakes, and fortune favored her. The fever of the game flamed in her cheeks and eyes, and it got into her blood and into her brain like an intoxicant. . . . Arobin caught the contagion of excitement which drew him to Edna like a magnet. (CW, II, 957)

Filled with a sense of authority, playing and winning at man's money game, Edna unconsciously identifies with her father. And like the freedom that came with candor, the power that came with swimming in the Gulf, this control "intoxicates" her and frees her sexual energy. That night, when she is at home alone, she is "hungry again," so she eats Gruyère and drinks a beer. But she is still "restless and excited . . . she wanted something to happen . . . she did not know what" (CW, II, 958). Although she does not know it, of course, she wants sex; consciously "she regretted that she had not made Arobin stay a half hour to talk over the horses with her" (CW, II, 958). Metaphorically, the control of horses again signifies woman's power; for Edna, though, it is the illusion of control through the economics of gambling—in the novel a specifically male avenue to power that (as Léonce shows) finally fails.

Edna has learned her lesson well by the time Robert returns. Sexuality, power, freedom, control are part and parcel of the male sphere. Thus it is perfectly appropriate that, returning to Robert after Adèle has given birth, Edna should be able to "picture at that moment no greater bliss than *possession* of the beloved one. His expression of love had already *given him to her*. . . . She would awaken him with a kiss" (CW, II, 996, my emphasis). Chopin's irony should be obvious: just hours before, Edna has said to Robert, "I am no longer one of Mr. Pontellier's possessions to dispose of or not. I give myself where I choose" (*CW*, II, 992). In her fantasy, she has become the prince who wakes the sleeping beauty; she becomes the possessor, the taker. Yet just as she cannot accept these qualities in others, Edna cannot sustain this identification, for it conflicts with her growth toward selfhood specifically as a woman—a point she has just demonstrated by leaving her "conquest" Robert to be with Adèle during the most female of actions, giving birth. And selfhood as a woman means to Edna through Adèle—as the children symbolize—the refusal to trample on the rights of others who are weaker. Edna thinks: "It makes no difference to me, it doesn't matter about Léonce Pontellier—but Raoul and Etienne!" (*CW*, II, 999); "I shouldn't want to trample upon the little lives" (*CW*, II, 996). Edna imagines that if she sacrifices mastery, the children will become her masters: "The children appeared before her like antagonists who had overcome her, who had overpowered and sought to drag her into the soul's slavery for the rest of her days" (*CW*, II, 999). She feels caught, her wings pinned and broken. She will not be a slave to anyone, yet she rejects the mirror opposite of that pair: mastery. There seems no other way.

In this light, the pairing, nearly the twinning, of Robert and Edna makes sense. By pairing these two, male and female, Chopin temporarily bridges the "abyss" between the sexual spheres in the novel yet permits individual differences to remain. Beginning with the sexual difference, I think that here Chopin invents her own picture in which she tries to fit heterosexuality with freedom, nature with art, inner life with outer behavior, fantasy with reality. It turns out, she sees, to be an illusion. But it is worth a look, to see what the dream was.

Like Edna, Robert has a real self and a role self. He has played the role of Petrarchan lover for years on the island, even with Madame Ratignolle: adore the woman, let her rule you like a queen, suffer visibly in the anguish of uncompleted love, assume that marriage means the end of love, but never attain the object of love.

Robert's real self, though, like Edna's, begins to emerge on the island and out of a relationship that began as Petrarchan. That real self goes beyond the "feminized" man to the androgynous. He and Edna are alike, surface to core, in ways that permit a genuinely interdependent relationship to unfold. They look alike: "In coloring he was not unlike his companion [Edna]. A clean-shaved face made the resemblance more pronounced than it would otherwise have been" (*CW*, II, 883). "His hair—the color of hers—waved back from his temples in the same way as before" (*CW*, II, 981–82). They instinctively position themselves similarly in this arguably symbolic scene: "When they reached the cottage, the two seated themselves with some appearance of fatigue upon the upper step of the porch, facing each other, each leaning against a supporting post." Shortly, they both "try to relate [a story] at once" (CW, II, 882).

Robert, like Edna, is associated with the sea. After the piano scene when Edna's passions (not just pictures of them) have been aroused by Mademoiselle Reisz's playing, it is Robert who suggests that the group go for a midnight bath, thus precipitating Edna's first important swim. After their day spent at the Chênière, he tells her good night and "did not join any of the others, but walked alone toward the Gulf" (CW, II, 921). Because he shares a love for the sea, Robert is linked with its sensuousness, with solitude, with contemplation.

Robert also shares with Edna the rare privilege of being a person for whom Mademoiselle Reisz likes to play. "Those others? Bah!" says the irascible artist (CW, II, 907). He first meets Edna, after his return from Mexico, at, of all places, Mademoiselle Reisz's home. Both Robert and Edna are independently drawn to the musician, and we are to infer that both of them have some of the sensitivity and courage of the artist, some of the knowledge of the deeper, inner life.

Nor is it Chopin's whim that makes their second accidental meeting occur at the little, simple, unfrequented garden that both, again independently, have discovered. Robert and Edna each love the privacy, the natural beauty, and the simple food there. Their love for beauty, as opposed to utilitarian concerns, earlier merged with their ability to fantasize on the way to the Chênière:

> "Then I'll take you some night in the pirogue when the moon shines. Maybe your Gulf spirit will whisper to you in which of these islands the treasures are hidden. . . ."
>
> "And in a day we should be rich!" she laughed. "I'd give it all to you, the pirate gold and every bit of treasure we could dig up. I think you would know how to spend it. Pirate gold isn't a thing to be hoarded or utilized. It is something to squander and throw to the four winds, for the fun of seeing the golden specks fly."
>
> "We'd share it, and scatter it together," he said. His face flushed. (CW, II, 916)

Given the metaphorical character of the novel as a whole, it is not stretching the imagination to see in Robert's flush a recognition that they have been describing their feelings about sexuality; significantly, it comes as they invent a scene that flouts the worship of capital.

Robert not only lacks the paternalism and, to some extent, the business obsession of his foil Léonce, but he actively participates in and enjoys domestic life. He cooks for Edna on the Chênière; he plays with the children and enjoys it; he helps take care of them: "When Etienne had fallen asleep Edna bore him into the back room, and Robert went and lifted the mosquito bar that she might lay the child comfortably in his bed" (CW, II, 921). The artist tells by structure: she ends chapter 1 with Léonce Pontellier leaving his children, who want to follow him; she ends her second chapter with Robert Lebrun "amusing himself with the little Pontellier children, who were very fond of him" (CW, II, 984).

The pull and tug of Robert's and Edna's relationship derives some of its energy from the two poles of role-playing (on both parts) and genuine sharing of their more inward selves. Before he leaves her (as she will later leave him), that tension has produced a more truly interdependent and simultaneously a more clearly sexual relationship than has been seen heretofore. An example of this delicate motion can be found in the scene when Robert leaves the island. Edna plays the role of the marble lady, imperious and judgmental, until suddenly she blurts out, "Why, I was planning to be together, thinking of how pleasant it would be to see you in the city next winter." Then it is his turn: "So was I. . . . Perhaps that's the—" (CW, II, 926). He cuts it short, returns to formality, and leaves. To follow their relationship up to this point is to see the gradual movement—all unrecognized by Edna—to affection and attraction that are based on shared experiences, values, and compassion. When Edna learns that Robert is leaving, she retreats immediately into a familiar, stereotyped role: "She went directly to her room. The little cottage was close and stuffy after leaving the open air. But she did not mind; there appeared to be a hundred different things demanding her attention indoors. She began to set the toilet-stand to rights . . . gathered together stray garments that were hanging on the backs of chairs, and put each where it belonged . . . went in and assisted the quadroon in getting the boys to bed" (CW, II, 924). The strength of this response, in its rejection of all that she found with Robert outdoors, is an indication of the strength of her feelings for him.

Robert's retreat into the male role—he does business in Mexico—is permanent. He needs to get on in business, to follow the rules of his society; he is shocked and appalled when Edna laughs at his notion of "possession" and does his best to avoid her when he returns to the city. Though Edna wants to "awaken" him, he continues in the dream of masculine values: money, business, possession. Apparently the men's illusions are even harder to break than the women's.

One could argue, finally, that the Creole society, in this novel, offers real possibilities for growth and freedom that are often ignored. As in other works by southern women, the world of fashion is fairly easily dismissed by author and protagonist as a genuine community. Again, too, the nuclear family appears to be less than satisfactory: it is polarized (Pontelliers), boring (Ratignolles), or false (Highcamps). But Creole society—as opposed to the "American" Kentucky that Edna comes from—needs to have a word said for it. Despite the fact that Mademoiselle Reisz sees the people as philistines, selecting only Edna and Robert for an audience, the Creoles are not: "But she [Mademoiselle Reisz] was mistaken about 'those others,'" says the narrator. "Her playing had aroused a fever of enthusiasm. 'What a passion!' 'What an artist!' 'I have always said no one could play Chopin like Mademoiselle Reisz!' 'That last prelude! Bon Dieu! It shakes a man!'" (*CW*, II, 907). Moreover, the Creoles are familiar with the sea: "Most of them walked into the water as though into a native element" (*CW*, II, 908). These two highly charged symbols, then—art and nature—are both valued in the Creole consciousness. The Creoles, including even Mr. Pontellier, talk freely about nearly all subjects—their inward selves conform to their surfaces—and all are sympathetic toward Edna when Robert leaves, recognizing the possibility for profound heterosexual attachments outside of marriage.

But the Creole society has rules, rules that Madame Ratignolle makes clear to Robert and to Edna, and that Edna must fly beyond. Though sensuous, Creoles do not permit sexual intercourse outside of marriage. Chopin did, in "The Storm." Though expressive, they save their most private thoughts for members of the family. Though in some ways the women are like the men, the two sexes clearly have their separate spheres—witness the Tuesday receiving days, for women only; the men are out in the world. Some of Edna's conflicts, then, cannot be resolved by assimilation into this society. She says to Robert in her secret garden-restaurant: "It's so out of the way; and a good walk from the car . . . I always feel so sorry for women who don't like to walk; they miss so much" (*CW*, II, 990). Edna is genuinely a "solitary soul,"[46] as Chopin's intended title would have had it. Thus the original narrative description of the sea—"The voice of the sea is seductive; never ceasing, whispering, clamoring, murmuring, inviting the soul to wander for a spell in abysses of solitude; to lose itself in mazes of inward contemplation" (*CW*, II, 893)—has changed by the time of Edna's suicide: "The voice of the sea is seductive, never ceasing, whispering, clamoring, murmuring, inviting the soul to wander in abysses of solitude" (*CW*, II, 999). It is no longer "for a spell" only; nor is the function of solitude "inward contemplation." The choice has been made; isolation makes for growth, but finally the choice is between the ultimate isolation of death and the deathly assimilation into a society that will not permit Edna to have "my own way" (*CW*, II, 996). Edna's "sea" seems very much like Huck Finn's amorphous "territory," though far more destructive—and, in fact, more real.

But the novel does what Edna cannot. Exploring depths of woman's psyche that heretofore in this study have been only adumbrated, it then (unlike Edna) surfaces, shapes them into a form that has meaning, and continues to live. It is perfectly appropriate to both the author and the character that Edna's death should be shown in a metaphor that shows it coming from a deep level of the self and that it should rehearse, once again, in miniature and in pairs, the stages of the journey she had undertaken: "Edna heard her father's voice and her sister Margaret's. She heard the barking of an old dog that was chained to the sycamore tree. The spurs of the cavalry officer clanged as he walked across the porch. There was the hum of bees, and the musky odor of pinks filled the air" (*CW*, II, 1000). With her last exhausted stroke, Edna moves imaginatively from childhood (Margaret served as surrogate mother) to her first fantasized lover—the chained dog again appears with Cazeau in "Athénaïse"—and finally to a recognition of the purely natural meaning of human sexuality. Male and female, master and dog, bee and pink: Edna could move no further than an awareness of these dualities. She could not resolve the conflicts that such an awakening produced. But for her to have come thus far is an astonishing journey indeed. And Chopin hints, at least, that she sees an "abiding truth" (*CW*, II, 906) beyond all these dualities.

To impose on Edna, then, a model for human growth that is rooted in traditionally masculine—or traditionally feminine—values is to commit as critics an error similar to Edna's own. Failing to find a satisfactory image of freedom and power in the "feminine," Edna turns to the novel's masculine world of risk, possession, and power. Yet the conflict of that world with her own growing sense of herself as a woman—sensual, artistic, emotional, maternal—seems irreconcilable. She withdraws to not caring: "There was no one thing in the world that she desired" (*CW*, II, 999). Imitating the man in "Solitude," she goes to the shore and stands naked. Then, acting in the best way she has discovered to feel power without harming others, she swims into the sensuous sea.

CHAPTER V   **Mary Johnston**
The Woman Warrior

In the year of her death, Edward Wagenknecht said about Mary Johnston that "twenty-five years ago her romances of colonial Virginia were
selling by the hundreds of thousands. Today she is neglected."[1] That
was in 1936; now she is remembered, if at all, for her 1900 tale of colonial Jamestown, *To Have and To Hold*, and for the two films made of the
novel. But in 1936 at least one woman remembered Johnston's Civil
War novels, *Cease Firing* (1912) and *The Long Roll* (1911). Margaret
Mitchell envied Johnston's ability to recapture history and, after reread-
ing the latter work, "found that I couldn't possibly write anything on
my own book. I felt so childish and presumptuous for even trying

to write about that period when she had done it so beautifully, so power-fully—better than anyone can ever do it, no matter how hard they try."[2] Despite her typical evasive effusiveness, Mitchell's feeling here seems to be genuine; she repeated virtually the same story several times in different letters.

But Mitchell never mentions, nor do many now remember, the novel that followed *Cease Firing* by only one year and that astonished John-ston's readers because, although it had a southern setting, it was a "feminist" novel.[3] *Hagar* (1913) came in the middle of a long, prolific, and varied literary career that moved from historical romance to social criticism and then on to mysticism and radical stylistic experiments. The only one of her twenty-two novels she was to set in the realistic present, *Hagar* also is the one which (according to one of Johnston's very few commentators) comes closest to "telling the truth of the inner life" of its author.[4]

Nothing in Mary Johnston's Virginia heritage suggested that John William and Elizabeth Dixon Alexander Johnston would produce such a child. John, a former Confederate artillery major, was a cousin to Gen-eral Joseph E. Johnston; after the war, he became a lawyer, state legisla-tor, and president of the Georgia Pacific Railroad Company. Elizabeth, like her husband, was of Scottish ancestry; at the time of Mary's birth in 1870 they lived at Buchanan, in Botetourt County. John spent several years when Mary was a child working on business in New York; mean-while, Mary, the eldest child of six and frail throughout her life, re-ceived her education at home from a governess and her father's library. About 1886 the family moved to Birmingham, Alabama, and Mary spent the next year at a finishing school from which she came home early because of poor health. Elizabeth Johnston died in 1889, and, as the oldest daughter, Mary took over the running of the home. In 1890 and 1894 she traveled, like her heroine Hagar, with her father. The family lived from 1892 until 1896 in New York City but then returned to Birmingham.[5]

Apparently Johnston's immediate motive in writing her first novel, *Prisoners of Hope* (1898), which dealt with the love of Patricia Verney for an indentured servant, was to help out the family's finances; her fa-ther's multiple business interests had suffered setbacks by then, and the immediate success of the novel must have helped. The year 1900 saw *To Have and To Hold*, and two years later the Johnstons (Mary was now thirty-two) moved back home to Virginia. Mary traveled and con-tinued to read and write, constantly. (In her diary for March 6, 1908, she recorded the books she had read on a recent visit to Nassau: they included, she wrote, "Darwin's *Expression of the Emotions*; Wallace's

Darwin and After Darwin; Lecky's *Map of Life*; Morris, *The Earthly Paradise*; Ellen Glasgow's *The Ancient Law*; Conrad's *Lord Jim*; Haeckle's *Riddle of the Universe*; James's *The Wings of the Dove*; Bain's *The Senses and the Intellect*; Lady Burton's *The Life of Sir Richard Burton*; Cross's *Life of George Eliot, Vol. II*; and McPherson's *Herbert Spencer*."[6]) Their father had died in 1905; in 1911–1913, Johnston and two sisters built Three Hills, a large house on forty acres of land in the mountains near Warm Springs, Virginia, and later took in paying guests to stay solvent. There Johnston lived for the rest of her life, entertaining visitors like Theodore Dreiser and J. Krishnamurti, and joining social movements like the Equal Suffrage League of Virginia (1909), the American Association for Labor Legislation, and the Women's International League for Peace and Freedom. A pacifist during World War I, Johnston later called herself a Socialist. At Three Hills she divided her time among political and social commitments, family and household responsibilities, and her reading and writing.[7]

After the two Civil War novels that Margaret Mitchell so loved and *Hagar*, Johnston turned, in *Foes* (1918), *Michael Forth* (1919), and *Sweet Rocket* (1920), to the dominant theme suggested by her reading of William Blake, Emanuel Swedenborg, Lao Tzu, and theosophy, and adumbrated in the "Fourth Dimension" that she mentions in *Hagar*. Johnston felt she had had a transcendental experience that showed humanity in a new stage of growth, but she never saw herself either as a prophet or as a propagandist: "Mine is no isolated experience," she wrote; "many persons have been and are aware of a widening and deepening of consciousness. My experience is of value to me, but it has no special prominence in that enlargement of life into which we are all sweeping."[8] Wagenknecht seemed to agree: in 1936, arguing that Johnston portrayed the New Man and the New Woman with accuracy, he said that "the age is even now in the process of developing. Here, then, is the tragedy of Mary Johnston—that many readers have already dismissed her as belonging to the past, while the real difficulty is that she has gone so far ahead into the future that they find it impossible to catch up with her."[9] Her mystical works were less popular than her histories; still less popular was *Silver Cross* (1922), a stylistic experiment with its omission of articles and its characters "seen through a kind of opaque mist." Three novels of that period return to her earlier preoccupation with colonial Virginia, adding a psychic dimension: *Croatan* (1923), *1492* (1922), and *The Great Valley* (1926). *The Exile* (1927) is set "on an imaginary island in the later twentieth century"; it and her two last novels attracted few readers. Johnston also wrote a play (*The Goddess of Reason*, 1907; starring Julia Marlowe, it played in Boston,

Philadelphia, and New York), short stories in *Harper's Monthly*, and a volume of the Yale Chronicles of America, *Pioneers of the Old South* (1918). She died in 1936 at sixty-six.[10]

Johnston found her idea of history—which she described as "waves," "direction," "process," and "continuity"—in her examination of the South. Yet in the same place she found a definition of woman that placed her outside of process. Johnston spent much of her artistic life imagining ways to grow away from that side of the South, and the result was a familiar ambivalence. "The American," she wrote in 1905 to Otto Kyllman, "is very like Hamlet's cloud and has as many shapes as the given returns of the last census. He has other haunts than those of Broadway. He dips his sop in the dish of all the philosophies, including one of his own. He will work out. He is not always blatant. See how patriotic I am! And yet—and yet—in spite of all reason and merely an ingrained and hereditary matter, Virginia (incidentally the entire South) is my country, and not the stars and stripes but the stars and bars is my flag."[11]

Nor was her attitude to the South an isolated example of Johnston's self-division. Lawrence Nelson has observed that Johnston's work, albeit various, is characterized thematically by her effort to reconcile the poetic with the historical imagination, the visionary sense of a perfectible future with the tragic sense of a limited past, and the urge toward universality with her loyalty to the South. These tensions in her work produced, he said, writing simultaneously "soft as moonlight" and hard as the rock on which it shines. And they reflected her own private "civil war between the countrywoman and the cosmopolite, the woman [lady] and the feminist, the Virginian and the Universalist." Such divisions found their best expression, Nelson maintains, in the novels whose central metaphor is the historical Civil War: *The Long Roll* and *Cease Firing*. Those novels constitute for him an "authentic embodiment of the Southern Myth" of the "gallant, absurd, proud, foolish, bookish, chivalric, ignorant, sentimental, nostalgic, pastoral, artless Doric Dixieland, with its love of rhetoric, its devotion to family, and its obsessive addiction to tradition and sentiment, piety and violence."[12]

Charlotte Perkins Gilman noticed Johnston's doubleness; she wrote to her in 1913, calling Johnston "You fascinating person. You always make me think of an eagle, delicately masquerading as a thrush—so soft and gentle and kind—and with big *sweepingnesses* in back of it all."[13] Johnston's personal conflict between eagle and thrush—images that invite interpretation as woman and lady—gave her imagination access to the central theme of civil war in her novels, the "idea of spiritual division or dismemberment," which Johnston called a "unity that tears its own flesh." Repeatedly, her "house divided" imagery takes thematic shape as the struggle for power: "Who should rule, and who should be ruled?"[14] Progressively Johnston imagined an alternative to this permanent dialectic of power, a way out of the either/or dilemma implied in her question. The alternative was a form of transcendental unity that would embrace individuality within a great Whole and would replace competition—battle—with creativity. She wrote in 1912: "It has always seemed to me that we might be heroic without fighting. The man or woman that I like is the heroic *builder*."[15]

In *Hagar*, Johnston tried to reconcile these opposites in a new way, combining transcendental oneness with social action. She had just finished the two Civil War novels, which she had written for her father, had set in the southern military past, had filled with allusions to classical and English literature, and through which she had treated what she saw as the simultaneous futility and heroism of war. Perhaps that experience freed her to write the only novel she set in the present, the novel that, as Nelson suggests, comes closest of all to expressing her inner life. *Hagar* tells the story of a southern woman who confronts and then moves away from the South in her mind, in the direction of her dream of becoming "mind undying, self-authoritative and unrelated, the arbiter of her own destiny, the definer of her own powers, with an equal goal and right-of-way" to man's.[16]

Hagar in several ways combines the apparent disparities in Johnston's vision. Her concerns with the South and with the past join here with a vision of the future that is both transcendental and social and that means, in part, fuller humanity for women. Yet many reviewers saw it only as propaganda, an interpretation that perhaps revealed more of the reviewers' biases than of the book's contents. "Her novel is too obviously polemic," said the reviewer for the Boston *Transcript*, hoping that Johnston would return to "romantic tales."[17] "Hagar is too steadily and intensely in earnest; she breathes too constantly the air of a reform movement," the *Outlook* reviewer complained.[18] "I am not saying that the Creator could not make a feminist whom a man could love,—his power is infinite—but that Miss Johnston has failed to do so," said the *Atlantic Monthly*.[19] Other reviewers—including some for women's publications—concurred that Johnston's evident identification with her heroine and with feminism hurt the novel. However, the London *Saturday Review* commended the novel for its realism: "It is a little lacking in humor; but it is real. Hagar is a type of woman that does actually exist. She lives before us, and Miss Johnston has achieved a notable success in presenting us with such a lifelike figure."[20] Charlotte Perkins Gilman agreed when she wrote Johnston about "that strong growing woman

. . . who pushed on through things. That wasn't 'pleasant' to read either, but it was a piece of life. I feel as if, having established your high
reputation in historical novels, you were now doing far better and bigger work. People won't like it as well, of course—but keep on."[21]

Since the novel does concern the state of women, albeit as one element in a larger scheme that includes a vision for humanity and an
analysis of society, it is instructive to note Johnston's own attitude toward the feminist movement, which she called "The Woman's War" in
an article she wrote for the *Atlantic Monthly* in 1910. Apparently per-
ceiving her audience as male (she lists those men who approve of
women's suffrage to include biologists, statesmen, physicians, and moralists, and those who oppose it to include employers of cheap and child
labor, militarists, and the liquor and brothel interest), Johnston presents
a conservative (but not racist) case for giving the ballot to women.[22]

In its analysis of men and women, Johnston's article fluctuates between acceptance of the biological basis for character distinctions and
the endorsement of socio-cultural causality. When she argues for the
biological, Johnston calls the female "cell" "nutritive, constructive"
with "developing and staying power" (561) and the male "cell" "disrup-
tive, destructive, energetic"; the two are not like but equivalent (592),
for the female uses her energy to "bear the human race" and the male
"uses in other ways the energy saved" by building bridges, fortresses,
cathedrals—and poems. The argument that men and women differ in
character because of their biology was a familiar one, used by all sides
in the dispute over woman's role, since just about any observed or fantasized characteristic could be ascribed to the unquestionable difference in anatomy. Like many other writers, then, Johnston moves
from the assumption of cellular differences to statements about the values, positive and negative, of the two types of humans. Man is the
stronger animal; man writes the poems; man has the "brain children"
(569); but man's energy also spills over into "violence, power, lust,
crime" (564). Nevertheless, although "brain children are of great consequence in the future . . . they do not fill the human arms" (569). The
value of women rests in their ability to mother. The "maternal instinct,"
besides providing the world with future poets, will lead women to con-
serve, instruct, and administer better than men, she says; to be the better nurturant force for society. On the other hand, women's weaknesses
include inaccuracy, credulity, inconsequential pursuits like bridge and
gossip, and an "indirect way of approaching and of obtaining the object
or end they desire" (567). (Elsewhere, in a letter to southern novelist
Thomas Nelson Page, Johnston again argued against the notion of
woman's "indirect influence."[23])

As might be expected for a woman who herself is a writer and child-less, Johnston finds it difficult—given her biological assumptions—to explain herself. She does it in two ways. First, she says rather vaguely, if a woman cannot bear a poet, "if she never mates, then, obedient to the spirit of the hive, she will, like the worker-bee, *help*—in how many ways, God who watches only knows!" (562). Second, still relying on bi-ology as destiny, Johnston adopts the position that evolution will even-tually eliminate some of these genetic differences. Since "instinctive growth has become conscious growth" and "conscious growth is in the slow process of becoming rational growth"—from which, eventually, "streams the spiritual" (566)—the way is open for biological change; and women, she claims, are changing. Although Johnston hardly makes a forceful case for it, she implies that if biology *is* destiny, it is also mutable; what we see as eternal sex-linked characteristics may be only a moment in evolution.

Thus, Johnston appears to have found a way out of the popular con-ception of innate differences. Yet scattered through the essay some of her strongest diction indicates a rather different assumption about sex differences than that they are biologically ordained, eternally or tem-porarily. Speaking of woman's manipulative tendencies, for instance, Johnston claims that the press is responsible for making women de-vious. It says, in effect, "Beg; and if refused, manoeuvre!" (568). More-over, the popular touting of woman's "indirect influence" for good really means, she says, "*Make me* [man] *comfortable, and I will see what I can do about it*" (568). Johnston denies that biological differences include differences in brain capacity; she says that although there has been no woman Homer, and although motherhood is itself a poem, nevertheless education and Saint Paul have had something to do with the absence of great women artists. Johnston's semicovert social analysis is revealed by her word choice even when she assumes biology as cause: the "re-productive *sacrifice* is hers" (564, my emphasis), she says, and "the en-ergy of the male, not *sluiced away* as is hers, overflows in art" (564, my emphasis). Social analysis becomes overt in her discussion of working women: "Without strength of arm, without a voice that is counted, un-derpaid, underfed, exploited at every turn, tempted on every side, dis-franchised, held in ignorance—what of the mass of working women?" (564). Johnston goes on to point out that, of the twenty-five million women in America, over five million—more than the total population of the country in 1776—earn wages. Finally, it is impossible not to see her moving toward a social and political rather than a biological analysis when she says that sexual inequality "is used to hide the face of a very human reluctance to share power" (565).

Johnston's ambivalent feelings about her southernness also appear in "The Woman's War." Although she says at the outset that "in the South we are not used to woman's speaking—not, certainly, on the present subject" (550), implying a critique of her culture, later she attacks the growth of cities, ascribing to them the spread of decadence and regretting the loss of the village, "the sanest and sweetest of political units" (565). Johnston's characterization in *Hagar* of the oldest residents at Gilead Balm shows, as we shall see, much the same ambivalence about the South.

Johnston's effort to combine received notions about biology with sociopolitical analysis, and out of this to urge her readers to support women's suffrage, can be seen in *Hagar*. At the outset of the novel, we find what appears to be a sentimentalist's setup. Hagar is twelve, dark-haired and dark-browed, like Augusta Evans' heroines. She is returning with her maiden aunt Serena to her family's home, Gilead Balm, and she sees from the packet-boat a convict whose striped clothing provides her a moment of repulsion, followed by pity and wonder.

Hagar's mother Maria had married into the Ashendyne family, an aristocratic Virginia family that, with the Coltsworths, runs the entire county. Hagar's father Medway has been away from Gilead Balm for many years to travel and study painters; the family blames his behavior on Maria's failure to conform to the role of southern lady. Maria is now sickly, both emotionally and physically. The family at Gilead Balm includes Medway's parents, the Colonel and Old Miss; his sister, Miss Serena; and his father's brother, Captain Bob. Also living on the plantation are the former overseer's family, the Greens, and at least one black family, who have a daughter called Mary Magazine (probably Magdalen). Hagar, Thomasine Green, Mary Magazine, and other children in the area spend most of their time playing together; Hagar's interests differ from the others' mainly in that she enjoys both boys' and girls' games.

In an important early scene shortly after her return on the packet-boat, Hagar, pretending to give a tea party to assorted flowers on the far side of a hill near the house, hears rustling in the bushes. It is the convict, Denny Gayde, who has escaped. He tells Hagar that his crime involved hitting someone at a dance in the rural community where he grew up. Hagar shares her food with him, feeling this time no repulsion, only pity and incomprehension; he leaves, and she remembers the incident.

Hagar's mother soon dies, and Hagar is sent to Eglantine, a school for young ladies. At home, she had read forbidden authors, such as Hawthorne (*The Scarlet Letter*) and Darwin. At Eglantine, run by Mrs. LeGrand, she differs from the other students in her preference for seclusion and in her love for educating her mind as well as her social graces; nevertheless, she has friends. She hears Socialist and feminist doctrines discussed for the first time by a Fabian Englishwoman, a writer who calls herself "Roger Michael" and who has been invited by the teachers to give a talk. They consider her subject a bit indelicate but soon forget it; Hagar, however, keeps it in the back of her mind.

Then, in a moment of romantic feeling that comes while they are reading poetry, Hagar and a young professor at the school, Mr. Laydon, fall in love. Soon they are engaged; their first disagreement comes when Hagar insists upon telling her family and Laydon resists. She "wins," both family and school are scandalized, and Hagar is sent home. Here a sentimentalist might glory in the agonies of separated lovers; instead, Johnston has Hagar discover that what she had believed to be love was actually a temporary infatuation.

Hagar and Laydon meet again at the resort New Springs, where Hagar has gone for a vacation. There, Hagar tells Laydon what she has learned about her feelings for him; he is upset but finds her revelation not too difficult to accept, for apparently he has felt some qualms as well. While she is at New Springs, Hagar meets Elizabeth Eden and Marie Caton, feminist settlement workers from New York. The reader is also introduced to Molly Josslyn and her husband Christopher; Molly is the only woman at the resort who, like the men, enjoys fishing, a clue to her eventual development. Hagar has been interested in writing for a long time and has won a prize in a short story contest; she takes the opportunity to find out more about publishing from the two New York women, who also write.

After she finishes at Eglantine, Hagar goes to New York with a fellow student to visit a southern family, the Powhatan Maines, and to see the city. Although she enjoys the cultural events they have planned for her, Hagar is more impressed by the poverty she sees and by the work in the settlement house.

News arrives at Gilead Balm that Hagar's father Medway, since remarried, has lost his wife and his health in a boat accident in the Mediterranean. Hagar and her grandfather the Colonel set out for Egypt to nurse Medway; Hagar decides to stay with her father, and after he recovers, they spend several years traveling around the world together. Hagar continues her writing and gains wide fame because of it; Medway remains essentially a dilettante. In London, Hagar goes to a party given by Roger Michael, where she meets the Josslyns again. There is much talk about reform and the plight of an avant-garde playwright, talk that confirms Hagar in her growing commitment to social growth and specifically to the cause of women.

Later, while she and her father are in the Bahamas (he has found an old artist friend and settled there for a while), Hagar once again meets the convict, Denny Gayde. He has dedicated his life to his Socialist newspaper and married Rose Darragh, a well-known feminist; now he is taking a few weeks' rest in the islands. For several idyllic weeks (to which the tropical and sea imagery that also inform *The Awakening* contribute), the two spend much time together, talking about ideas and exploring the island. When Denny is about to leave, Hagar realizes she is close to being in love with him; she resolves to suppress the sensual element of her love.

Hagar's father dies two years later in Washington, D.C., leaving his money to her. Against the wishes of the Ashendynes, she gives the money to reform groups and returns to New York, renewing her friendship with the Maines' daughter, Rachel Bolt, and Rachel's two children. Soon Hagar meets (and likes) Rose Darragh; she commits herself to reform work, including helping in settlement houses and feminist public speaking, while still continuing her writing. Hagar is now in her early thirties and lives in an apartment where she employs Thomasine Green as her secretary and Mary Magazine as her housekeeper. When Hagar learns that the Colonel is seriously ill, she goes home once again to Gilead Balm, a trip that clarifies the points of contrast between the values she was trained to hold and those to which she is now committed.

After her grandfather's death, Hagar returns to the city, working long hours toward her vision of a fully humane and egalitarian world. An old school friend introduces her to John Fay, a bridge-builder who is taking six months off after finishing a project in South America. He is converted to Hagar's feminist cause and begins to fall in love with her. Hagar goes to France for a holiday; Fay follows her there and proposes marriage. One day while they are out sailing, a storm comes up that seems certain to kill them. The crisis brings Hagar to commit herself to John. The last few pages of the novel show them safely on shore, talking about the ways they will accommodate one another's needs for work; their marriage will be based on friendship as well as sexual and romantic love. By the end of the novel, the time is the "present," 1913.

Whereas Chopin's *The Awakening* is so richly metaphoric that it approaches the genre of poetry, *Hagar*'s density is not of metaphor but of intellectual analysis. If Chopin seemed to be operating within what Samuel Coleridge called the "imagination," Johnston's plotting, tone, style, and at times her imagery seem to reflect the mind of the essayist.

Yet it is entirely appropriate that this be the case. For *Hagar* is a *Bildungsroman* that tells the story of the growth, not only of a girl to womanhood, but of a society toward maturity. And in the scheme of growth outlined in the novel, thought comes after dream, analysis after metaphor: "She dreamed and imagined still, but the thinker within her rose a step, gained a foot on the infinite, mounting stair" (110). Moreover, for the artist in this scheme, growth means movement toward action: "She had, in her place, served beauty and knowledge. But the hunger grew to serve more fully. Knowledge, knowledge—wisdom, wisdom—action. . . ." (270). Leo Tolstoy becomes the model for Hagar, an artist-heroine who clearly has her author's sympathies. Hagar has met Tolstoy at Yasnaya Polyana; reflecting upon the master, she thinks: "*Non-resistance*—but his mind, through his pen, was not non-resistant! It acted, it scourged, it fought, it strove to build and to clear the ground that it might build. He deceived himself, the tremendous old man. He thought himself quietist as Lao-Tzu, but there in that bare, small study he cried, *Allah! Allah!* and fought like a Mohammedan" (273). Thought and action take priority in *Hagar* over image and dream.

Despite their novels' differences in quality and style, Evans, Chopin, and Johnston treat similar subject matter; the experience of southern womanhood is central to the meaning of each writer's work. The virtue of Johnston's novel lies precisely in its consciousness. Because the scheme displayed by the novel is also endorsed by characters within it—because analytical thought is seen as a higher step than dreaming for both individual and societal growth—Johnston directly articulates and analyzes patterns that were only indirectly demonstrated and described by the writers discussed earlier in this study. Her analysis of the condition of women, and of southern women in particular; of the "old" and the "new" man; and of society, especially that in the South, sound remarkably modern. Although contemporary reviewers attacked the book as "only" a feminist novel and hoped Johnston would return to more popular historical romances, the very qualities that they saw as condemning it might well today recommend the novel. *Hagar* deals explicitly with the position and the future of the South and espouses causes broader than but symbolized by women's emancipation. *Hagar's* author and its heroine are Virginia women; and its concern, in large part, is the relationship of the southern ethos—particularly but not only as it defines womanhood and manhood—to American, even world, society.

Johnston chooses to put the old prescription for womanhood, for manhood, and for the relationship between the sexes into the mouths and actions of southerners, both men and women. The roles of the "new" woman and the "new" man are not prescribed overtly at all; instead, they are demonstrated and discussed, mostly by nonsoutherners, including one Englishwoman. Only one committed reformer, Marie Caton, is even half-southern; other southern women, like Hagar's mother Maria and the Maines' daughter Rachel, provide models of frustrated transition from the mold of the past to the possibilities of the present. Yet it is the southern woman Hagar whose journey we see and who finds a resolution that is not tragic but satisfyingly happy, at least to herself and apparently to her author. Thus Johnston clearly links the perpetuation of what she sees as destructive definitions of woman (and, as we shall see, man and society) to the perpetuation of the culture of the South, specifically that of the Virginia aristocracy.

The southern women who articulate the definition of southern womanhood in words are more important as characters and in number than are those who simply act it out. Primary among these verbal ladies are Old Miss, Miss Serena, and Mrs. LeGrand. As befits the Darwinian thesis of the novel itself, the differences among generations are important: in time we see the changes wrought by evolution's selection of the fittest to survive. For Johnston, however, it is not the physically fittest who will overcome; it is those who endorse the more fully humane vision and who act upon it.

Old Miss, Hagar's grandmother, is a woman of the Old South who has been changed by the Civil War. She is both "comely" and "authoritative" (376); even with great age, she retains her dignity. Old Miss is quite clear about what a woman should be: woman has a "natural sphere" (118) that she should never desert. That sphere includes "fitness, propriety, meekness, and modesty, consultation with those to whom she owes duty, and bowing to what they say" (118). Primary among those to whom the woman owes duty are "family": "You are getting to be a woman and must consider the family. Ashendyne and Coltsworth women, I am glad to say, have always known their duty to the family and have lived up to it" (71). Within the family structure, the duty of the woman is not simply to the man, for the "family" is extended, not nuclear; hence, her duty is to her elders, male or female. Old Miss (and any older woman) not only "bows" but is bowed to; she enjoys power derived from a hierarchy of age and sex within the family. When Old Miss acts, it is within her prescribed role: she works extremely hard around Gilead Balm, knitting, putting up preserves, arranging proper marriages. Her deeds are necessary to the life of her family, as were those of earlier southern women and of women during the war: she lives out that tradition. If problems arise with the woman's role—for, no matter her age, she is still subservient to the male—she must endure; this is God's will: "the Lord, for his own good purposes,— and it is *sinful* to question his purposes,—regulated society as it is regulated, and placed women where they are placed. No one claims . . . that women as women do not see a great deal of hardship. The Bible gives us to understand that it is their punishment. Then I say take your punishment with meekness" (16). Sanctioned by religion, Old Miss's view of woman's place is indeed old; in fact she sees it, as she sees the Bible, to be eternal truth.

But there is a flaw in this view, despite the powers it gives to women and the dignity the author ascribes to its believer. The flaw comes with the corollary definition of man. Old Miss tries to work it all out:

> Hagar's very actual detachment and independence, name and prestige and personality, failed to count with Old Miss.
>
> Such things counted in other cases; they counted in Ralph's case. But Hagar was of the younger, therefore rightfully subordinate, generation, and she was female. Ralph was of the younger generation, also, and as a boy, while Old Miss spoiled him when he came to Gilead Balm, she expected to rule him, too. But Ralph had crossed the Rubicon. As soon as he grew from young boy to man, some mysterious force placed him without trouble of his own in the conquering superior class whose dicta must be accepted and whose judgment must be deferred to. He came up equal with and passed ahead of Old Miss, elder generation to the contrary. (311)

The mysterious operations of the passage of time turn a boy into a dominant man but keep a girl a subordinate female. True to the ethos she endorses, Old Miss, as a rule, dislikes women: "She was not patient with women generally. She thought that, on the whole, women were a poor lot—*witness Maria*" (310). In this passage, Old Miss blames all on Maria, who is in fact a victim, as we shall see. Medway's leaving home, the absence of Ashendyne-Coltsworth grandchildren, the "wilful piece" that is Hagar—all are considered Maria's fault because she did not "know her duty." The rare woman like Old Miss who fills the prescription enforces it in turn by judging other women.

When Hagar confronts her grandmother with the contradictions implicit in her schema, asking whether Old Miss had ever realized that she had "made her mind submissive" only to men and men's ideas, never to women, Old Miss is startled. Then she represses thought with faith: "What Moses and St. Paul said and the way we've always done in Virginia is good enough for me" (312).

Stubbornly holding the past to dictate eternity, Old Miss sees Hagar's rejection of her neighbor and suitor Ralph Coltsworth only as the loss of a "prize" in what is implicitly—and necessarily, given Old Miss's premises—a contest between women for a man. But Old Miss's intractability and clarity give her a genuine dignity. Where Old Miss is "regent," her daughter, Serena, is merely petulant. Where Old Miss dresses sensibly, her aging daughter follows fashion. Where Old Miss knits, Serena knots macramé lambrequins and gilds milking-stools. Where Old Miss reads the Bible, Serena reads sentimental novels.

Most centrally, Old Miss's prescription for the southern lady rests, finally, on action. To *make* one's mind submissive is to presuppose that it might rebel and to choose a course of action. Hagar herself endorses this value, the value of self-control. Serena's prescription, on the other hand, rests on a series of passives. Don't read Darwin or *Tom Jones*; don't ask questions (7); don't "rebel and disobey . . . be forward and almost fast" (105); don't act on your own judgment, for "how can you know that your judgment is good?" (305). In Miss Serena we have purity, piety, submissiveness, and domesticity carried out to the point of rottenness; purity has become prudery, piety religiosity, submissiveness a nearly complete lack of self-confidence and domesticity a literal and perpetual childhood in the home of her birth.

One who cannot act on her own judgment must act, presumably, on *some* basis; just as Serena has contributed to the feminization of American culture with her useless needlework projects, so she has contributed to the cult of gentility by following convention wherever it leads her. Her responses never search beneath the surfaces of appearances— hence her reaction to the convict: "But if he is a convict, he probably did something very wicked" (5). And her reaction to Hagar's appearance in white after Medway's death: "Hagar refuses to put on black. . . . I don't see that she's got a tender conscience" (301). Although she claims that she actively "suppresses" (13) parts of herself, there is no evidence that Serena is not satisfied with her lot. But Serena's role is the logical consequence of Old Miss's beliefs, as becomes apparent when she tells her mother, "You can't say that I haven't honoured father and mother" (117). Old Miss agrees, and grumbles about the younger generation; then the narrator says, "it might almost have seemed that such forthright ductility and keeping of the commandment as had been Miss Serena's had its side of annoyance and satiety" (118). Old Miss is not entirely satisfied with what she has wrought.

That Serena is the pathetic result of a set of dehumanizing beliefs is made clear near the end of the novel. Then Serena says, painfully, that she had almost written a story herself, thirty years ago—but the publisher in Richmond had said she would have to pay to get it printed. In a final narrative description, we see the self-perpetuating cage her life has become: "That night in her bedroom, plethoric with small products of needle, crochet-needle, and paint-box, Miss Serena drew down the shades of all four windows preparatory to undressing. She was upstairs, there was a thick screen of cedars and no house or hill or person who could possibly command her windows, but she would have been horribly uneasy with undrawn shades. Ready for bed, she always blew out the lamp before she again bared the windows" (306). Serena has found the peace after which she was named only externally and at great psychic cost.

Of the three major prescriptive characters in *Hagar*, Mrs. LeGrand has the most power over the most people and is the least sympathetically portrayed. Intelligent and analytical where Serena is not, "despotic" where Old Miss is queenly, Mrs. LeGrand enforces the same prescriptions for women and men as do Old Miss and Serena, but she does so with a clearly pragmatic intent that differs from Old Miss's in its self-indulgence, its compromising hypocrisy, and its lack of religious foundation. Severed from a family role by her husband's death in the war, Mrs. LeGrand found an occupation that was "both ladylike and possible"—a girls' school, Eglantine. There she trains girls for what she sees as essentially a social role, one that she herself embodies in her actions, her name, and that of her school. Her prescription for womanhood is familiar: "compliance . . . feminine sweetness . . . unselfishness" (44); "every girl's duty to her family was paramount" (107); "her 'duty' is to see that her father was wise for her. If he was content there's surely no reason why she should not be so!" (302); "where money comes in . . . I always act under advice. Women know very little about finance, and their judgment is rarely to be trusted" (300); "women's place is the home. And we can surely trust *everything* to the chivalry of our Southern men" (317); "ladies in the South certainly don't need to come into contact with the horrors they talked about [at a feminist meeting in Baltimore]" (319); and finally, appealing to social class, "if a girl knows how to make the best of herself, there inevitably arrives her own establishment and the right man to take care of her. . . . Gentlewomen in reduced circumstances [such as after the war] may have to battle alone with the world, but they do not like it, and it is only hard fate that has put them in that position. It's an unnatural one" (76).

At Eglantine, Mrs. LeGrand puts these "principles" into practice. The teachers she chooses offer surface culture; she calls the unfortunate evening during which Roger Michael speaks to the girls about reform "indelicate"; and the girls are hedged in literally from the outside world and figuratively from anything remotely resembling sexuality. "The place was sweet. M. Morel, the French teacher, who was always improving his English . . . once said in company that it was saccharine" (57). Like Old Miss, though for different reasons, Mrs. LeGrand actively enforces the double standard. Dramatically this is best shown when the romance between Hagar and Laydon is broken up: Hagar is sent home, Laydon retains his position at the school. Always a compromiser, Mrs. LeGrand suggests that Hagar both keep her inheritance and give it away; she almost excuses suffrage on the grounds that "some of them [the suffragists] are pretty and dress well and have a good position" (316). Devious herself, Mrs. LeGrand makes her comments about women's role often enough in the presence of men whom she knows to agree that we suspect a bit of the Machiavel in her. Inwardly, she deplores Hagar's honesty, though outwardly she says nothing. Mrs. LeGrand states outwardly that she prefers men to women, yet she insults Hagar by calling her "intensely unwomanly," just as Grace King's slave characters are insulted by someone who considers herself "too good" to keep slaves. In short, Mrs. LeGrand accepts the conventional prescription for womanhood and manhood and does her best to make capital from it, emotionally and economically; yet, of course, since she accepts a definition of herself that is less than flattering, she becomes an unattractive character. Mrs. LeGrand's final pragmatism is shown in what is for her a remarkably open statement to Hagar: "All these theories that you women are advancing now-a-days— if they *paid*, if you stood to gain anything by them . . . people ridiculing you, society raising its eyebrows, men afraid to marry you—! . . . I like the forms we've got. Perhaps they're imperfect, but the thing is, I feel at home with imperfection" (320). Mrs. LeGrand's world view prescribes as much dependence on others as does Serena's; she is simply smarter, less interested in ethics, and more comfortable living off the generosity of others—which is how she spends all her time away from the school.

Two minor characters—both of Hagar's generation—embody but do not advocate the conventional prescription for the southern lady. Lily, who as a student at Eglantine was hypochondriacal and weak in true nineteenth-century fashion, says much later to Hagar: "There isn't much to tell . . . I've been quite sheltered. For years I was ill, and then I grew better. I've travelled a little, and I like Maeterlinck and Vedanta and Bergson, and I play the violin not badly, and Robert, my husband is very good to me. I haven't grown much, I am afraid, since I was at Eglantine. But more and more continually I want to grow" (348).

Sylvie Maine, "as sweet and likeable as sugar, but not interested in anything outside of the porcelain world-dish that held her," cares about clothes, young gentleman callers, shops, and plays; she finally marries Ralph Coltsworth. Thus the last of the sweet southern làdies marries the last good old boy.

So Johnston sees it, at least in her evolutionary vision. Two victims of that evolutionary process, Rachel Bolt and Hagar's mother Maria, have urgings to become new but are trapped by circumstance. Rachel describes her marriage as typical, that is, bad; she found that her husband wanted only sex, and not with her alone. Her second child was born blind because of his father's syphilis. Yet she recovers, and by the end of the novel her flashing moodiness and bitterness have been replaced by the conviction that she will raise her children in a new, more humane way than she had been raised, with her ignorant fantasy of "expecting men to fall in love with me and ask me to marry them—and expecting to choose one, having first, of course, fallen in love with him, and be married in white satin and old lace, and be romantically happy and provided for ever after! Isn't that the thinking role for every properly brought-up girl?" (215).

Maria's life is even more tragic. Ill at the outset of the novel, she soon dies; we see little of her, but that little illuminates. "If I gave way less. . . . Well, yes, I do give way. I have never seen how not to. I suppose if I were cleverer and braver, I should see—" she says (16) in response to Old Miss's stoical injunction. Clearly Maria is speaking of a vision different from Old Miss's about what it is to which she should not give way. She articulates it: "If I were wiser and stronger and more heroic, I suppose I should break through it. I suppose I should go away with Hagar. I suppose I should learn to work. I suppose I should somehow keep us both. I suppose I might live again. I suppose I might . . . even . . . get a divorce—" (18). A final insight into the character Maria might have been appears late in the novel, when Old Miss tells Hagar, "Don't . . . talk to me! When you're wrong, you're wrong, and that's all there is to it! Maria used to try to explain, and then she stopped and I was glad of it" (318). The echoes of Robert Browning's "My Last Duchess" are clear.

Since Johnston uses southern women to provide the only female voices that actually prescribe, instead of offering or describing or simply acting, a role for women, it is interesting to note that those southern women who do not come from or pretend to aristocracy are treated quite differently. Mrs. Green, the former overseer's wife, is perfectly aware of the conventional prescription: "It ain't so easy for women to make money. . . . It's what they call 'Sentiment' fights them. Sentiment don't mind their being industrious, but it draws the line at their getting money for it" (112). She also sees before anyone else the truth about Hagar's character:

> "I wonder now [she tells the child] if you're goin' to grow up a rebel? Look-a-here, honey, there ain't a mite of ease and comfort on that road."
>   "That's what the Yankees called us all," said Hagar. "'Rebels.'"
>   "Ah, I don't mean 'rebel' that-er-way," said Mrs. Green. "There's lonelier and deeper ways of rebellin'. You don't get killed with an army cheerin' you, and newspapers goin' into black, and a state full of people, that were 'rebels' too, keepin' your memory green,—what happens, happens just to you, by yourself without any company, and no wreaths of flowers and farewell speeches. They just open the door and put you out." (35)

Yet she is herself curious to know about the outside world, an astute observer, and though nurturant, maternal with a twist: she gives Hagar an apple, an act that, given the biblical metaphors that pervade the novel, clearly implies the giving of knowledge. Similarly, Mary Magazine is close to Hagar, observant, and ends up in New York earning her living as Hagar's housekeeper. Thomasine, a Green of Hagar's generation, moves to New York even before Hagar first visits there; by the end of the novel, she, too, is working for Hagar as a live-in secretary. Johnston seems to retain a class bias in her plotting, though she permits these women insight.

Almost without exception, the "new" women in *Hagar* are not southern. Of course, this reflects the historical truth that southerners were late and few to come to specifically women's movements such as suffrage, settlement houses, and the WCTU. Lily's comment—"We're so far South that as a movement it's all as yet only a rather distant sound" (342)—reminds us of Roger Michael's earlier observation that southern girls are different. They are, she says, pretty without the New England girls' "colour" and "stronger frame" that reflect exercise, without the "certain boyish alertness and poise" that she has seen elsewhere; but they have "more grace and slowness, manner and sweetness," a "dim sweetness of expression," an "added control of speech," a greater concern for clothes (63). They sound, in fact, like the girls in "Monsieur Motte."

What is remarkable about these new women—Roger Michael, Elizabeth Eden, Marie Caton, Molly Josslyn, Rose Darragh—is the variety of their origins, their life styles, and their politics. Roger Michael is English; she lives with her adopted children as a single parent in London, writes, and entertains in an English version of the salon. "The fare that she spread was very simple; it was enough and good; it gained that recognition, and then the attention went elsewhere" (250)—to science, plays, politics, the women's movement. Roger Michael's politics are Fabian; from that position, she includes feminism. Elizabeth Eden and Marie Caton, both American, live (apparently together) in New York. Committed to austerity, they work at their settlement house, and Elizabeth writes about sociology and economics. The centrality of sisterhood is shown in Elizabeth's study, with its "small bronze Psyche, a photograph of Botticelli's Judith, a drawing of Florence Nightingale" (208). They come to the "Woman Movement" by way of, and not excluding, an urge to aid the victims of industrialization. Molly Josslyn, whom we first meet at New Springs, simply acts as she feels: she is the only woman who likes to fish; she loves to swim and hates to spend "pretty nearly a whole three-quarters of an hour out of every twenty-four . . . in brushing and combing and doing up hair!" (145); she is a "strong, rosy blonde" (146); and she is very happily married. Her political awakening comes late, with the news of the 1902 Boer War concentration camps; her pity is for the "women and children" in the camps and for the prostitute she has seen the night before. (Her husband Christopher shares her ideals: "Women and men. . . . They're waking, but it's slow, it's slow, it's slow" [245].) Rose Darragh, Irish-American, is another sensuous woman like Molly; her marriage to Denny Gayde, however, defines itself differently from Molly's: they are more apart, each doing his or her work, than together, but both are satisfied with the marriage. Rose's feminism is activist; she is a Socialist agitator and writes for reform publications.

All these women are committed to an egalitarian and most to an androgynous society. Their tactics differ; yet they all come increasingly to see that the most immediately important goal is the emancipation of women. "Behind all that [helping the suffering poor], in the place where I myself live," says Marie Caton, "I am fighting to be myself! I am fighting for that same right for the other woman! I am fighting for plain recognition of an equal humanity!" (331). The process by which they come to this decision is similar. Some books that Hagar reads articulate what "had been in me a long time, only I didn't know it, or called it other names" (209). Molly's experience is similar; an anonymous woman reformer tells her, "It is like that with almost every one. Diffused thought—and then, suddenly one day something happens or another mind touches yours, and out of the mist there gathers form, determination, action" (253).

Once committed, the "new" women face similar problems. As Marie says, "We say the truth, and then we bring in 'charm' and sandpaper it away again" (151). They also analyze society's predominant roles in a similar way. Rose Darragh's analysis is most powerful. Seeing a typical family in a restaurant, she calls the women a "sucking wife and daughter" who are "daughters of the horse leech." Given the premise that the man must shelter, protect, and provide for woman, the husband "looks haggard, and at the moment he's probably grinding the faces of no end of men and women—not because he's got a bad heart and really wants to,—but because he's got to 'provide' for those two perfectly strong and healthy persons in jewelry and orchids!" But he is cowed into his position by tradition, she adds, and moreover can't "keep his cake and eat it too" by asking his women to change; he *wants* them that way. In fact, that very man, Rose adds, will be the first "to strike the table with his fist and violently to assure you that God meant Woman, lovely Woman! to be dependent upon Man . . . Woman, Wife and Mother, God bless her!" (336–37).

These women's vision of the women's movement brings new ideas to the larger movements in which they are involved. Molly tells Hagar: "The movement goes without high priests and autocrats and personifications. We haven't, I suppose, the Big Chief tradition. Perhaps women's individualism has a value after all. It's like religion when it really is personal; your idea of good remains your idea of good; it doesn't take on a human form. Or perhaps we're merely tired of crooking the knee" (328). In the "old" tradition, women did not merely crook their knees to higher male authorities; they fought one another for the privilege. In what Molly calls the "rocking-chair-and-gossip" land, everybody "in a petticoat" who isn't there is "hanged, drawn, and quartered" (145). Why? According to Marie, all people are "waking," but "it wasn't just natural sleepyheadedness with women. They've been drugged—given knock-out drops, so to speak" (330). Who did this, and why, in Johnston's view, will be discussed in the section on society.

However, the novel is not primarily about the "Woman Movement" or even about cultural analysis; it is, as the title suggests, about the growth of one woman, Hagar. Hagar (*Genesis* 16) is the name of Abraham's mistress, Sarai's Egyptian maid whom Sarai gave to her husband so that he could produce a child. Hagar responded to this elevation with what Sarai saw as contempt. Bernhard Anderson glosses the passage from *Genesis*: "The inferior Hagar felt superior to Sarai and threatened to take her mistress's place as the ancestress of Israel."[24] Sarai "dealt harshly with her, and she fled from her" (*Gen.* 16:6), but not before she had conceived a son: Ishmael. Hagar and Ishmael return and stay with Abraham and Sarai until Sarai bears Isaac; then Sarah (as she now is called) says, "Cast out this slave woman with her son; for the son of this slave woman shall not be heir with my son Isaac" (*Gen.* 21:10). God, however, saves mother and son, who live in the wilderness and later found twelve tribes of Ishmaelites, like the later twelve tribes of Israel.

Since characters in the novel refer, albeit elliptically, to Hagar's strange name, it seems probable that Johnston intended certain parallels between her fictional character and the biblical Hagar. Johnston's Hagar, like the biblical one, rises up against a culture that she feels enslaves her; like the original, the fictional Hagar lives "in the wilderness" outside the South; like the original, her society is finally a wandering, free people. Johnston's Hagar does not bear a child; at the end of the novel, however, she indicates that she hopes to do so.

When the novel begins, Hagar is twelve; as a child-woman, she fulfills all the traditional pieties for women and children (which, of course, are similar). She is pious; she says grace before her tea party. She is pure; she doesn't fear the wild face that Denny presents to her, nor is she attracted to it in any way other than as an object of her curiosity. She is domestic, making her little imaginary home and being a good child in her real one. And she is submissive, following the orders of Old Miss not to visit her mother and the orders of Serena not to read "bad" books. Hagar names her paper dolls after the heroines of "women's" novels (one, incidentally, after Augusta Evans' *Vashti*). When she first falls in love at eighteen, it is in a dreamlike trance, like that of Grace King's debutantes, and she worships Laydon as though he were a "demigod." Clearly Johnston has given her character a familiar heritage, out of which a conventional sentimental novel could have been written.

Other elements in Hagar's early character are equally familiar. Certain qualities that appeared in the background of, for instance, *Beulah*, undercutting its ostensible message, now take the fore. Like Beulah, Hagar is considered plain-looking; but "for all her plainness, Hagar's got distinction" (59). She insists on reading, despite the interdict, books like Darwin's *Descent of Man*, Shelley's poetry, and *The Scarlet Letter*. Her intelligence makes her question her world, allows her to analyze it, and provides her with the power to filter her feelings and urges through thinking before she acts. Hagar is also sensitive to beauty and ugliness; this permits an early repugnance to Denny's position as a convict on the grounds of his ugly clothing and a later revulsion to the slums of New York. Beauty for her is best seen in nature, from the "far country" across the hill at Gilead Balm, to the sea and lush land in the Bahamas, to the sky that she turns to as an adult for a sense of peace. Imaginative, too, the child Hagar yokes together opposites in her fantasies: "a favorite haunt was a palm-fringed, flower-starred lawn reached only through crashing leagues of icebergs" (67).

It is these atypical qualities that permit Hagar to grow. Johnston is careful—as is Kate Chopin in *The Awakening*—to show the reader the difference between Hagar's stages of growth and the stages of her awareness. Unlike Edna Pontellier, however, Hagar catches up with her thoughts; and after her first experiences in New York, the narrator no longer distances herself from her character, as she does in early passages like these:

> She came slowly, after many years, into that much knowledge of herself. Today she was but an undeveloped child, her mind a nebula just beginning to spiral. (12)

> Of how youth of all the ages surged, pulsed, vibrated through her slender frame, she had, of course, no adequate notion. (68)

> How much was love [for Laydon], and how much outraged pride and a burning sense of wrong, she was not skilled to know, nor how much was actual chivalric defence of her partner in iniquity. (108)

Because Hagar has these qualities, and because by going to New York and later around the world she finds an environment that will not, like a board on grass (Johnston's image), destroy them, she grows into a woman of honesty, courage, intelligence, self-reliance, sensitivity—and into an artist.

To map the progress of Hagar's fiction is to see in miniature the growth of Hagar's self. Her first, prize-winning story is fantasy "about fairies and a boy and a girl, and a lovely land they found by going neither north nor south nor east nor west, and what they did there" (113). From this inchoate dream of romantic travel and adventure that asserts in its fairy-tale character its own impossibility, Hagar moves to some very practical considerations. "I've read all kinds of useless things and so little useful! For instance," she asks Elizabeth Eden, "is it wrong to write on both sides of the paper?" (153). After she has been in New York, she resolves to reread William Morris' *News from Nowhere*; it satisfies her desire that "people might work, work well and enough, and yet there be for all beauty and comfort and leisure and friendliness" (175). Although this fantasy is more adult, it remains, of course, a utopian vision that in fact appears nowhere. After she has gained fame and critical acclaim for her work, she re-examines it: "For years she had taken now this, now that filament-like value and with skill and power had enlarged, coloured, and arranged it so that her great audience might also see; and she had done, she thought, service thereby" (270). Apparently Hagar's work has moved toward W. D. Howells' sort of realism; its didacticism lies in its power to make people see, to serve beauty and knowledge. And its goal is service: one remembers Beulah's writing in the service of God.

But Hagar finds in this type of writing a fault in herself, one that she calls the "Brahmin" in her that "hate[s] the tumult and the shouting while the people are yet bewildered"—a fear of participation and uncertainty. Henceforth, she resolves, "If that's the Brahmin in me, I am going to sacrifice him. I am going where the battle is" (291). In a later statement about her work, Hagar believes that her job is "communication—ways and means of reaching minds" with a "statement" that is "social." "The inner urge would send the marchers somehow on, but there is needed interpreting, clarifying, articulation" (356). From romantic personal fantasy Hagar has moved through social fantasy to a Howells-like moral realism. Killing her distaste for "the battle," she moves finally to a more Dreiserian participation in reality, but she never relinquishes her fundamentally social purpose for writing.

Fully the most complex character in the novel, Hagar deserves extended analysis that is impossible here. Suffice it to say that, unlike her mother, she both loves Gilead Balm and hates it; she loves her father and hates his hedonism; she loves her mother and hates her circumstantial tragedy; she travels worldwide and settles in her own home; she works with others and requires solitude; she loves women and she loves men; as she says to Denny, "I can be opposites" (287).

And the opposite to women, at Gilead Balm, is men. Once again, it is the southern men who provide overt prescriptions for southern women and who demonstrate the contingency of those prescriptions upon their definition of man. The "new" men, like the "new" women, discuss instead of dictating their definitions, and only one, Denny Gayde, is a southerner.

Like Old Miss, Colonel Ashendyne (Hagar's grandfather) exemplifies in his words and actions the virtues and the failings of the Civil War South. In certain important ways, his expectations of both men and women are similar. He expects responsibility and obedience from both, castigating his son Medway on both counts. He respects mind—he is quick to sniff out "surface culture" in Laydon—and enjoys Hagar's and even Maria's minds (222). He acts upon his values: "I always wanted to travel," he says, "but I never could. I had a sense of responsibility" (222). And he protects his library—in which Hagar finds those forbidden books—from the embroidering hands of Serena.

Yet the differences between his ideal man and ideal woman produce inevitable conflicts. Hagar is forbidden to go to her "far country" over the hill, because it is too "unsettled" for a girl, whereas boys are encouraged to explore. Purity is expected of women: "a young girl may be pardoned anything short of the irrecoverable" (102), he says, indicating a different set of sexual rules for young girls. He also judges women by different aesthetic and intellectual standards. Here is the Colonel on Hagar's writing: "There have been women who have done very good work of a certain type. It's limited, but it's good of its kind. As letter-writers they have always excelled. Of course, it isn't necessary for you to write, and in the Old South, at least, we've always rather deprecated that kind of thing for a woman" (223)—deprecated it because, in part, it might indicate a failure on the part of her men, whose duty it is to be responsible for her. Hence, "There again was a mistake—to let women come of age. Perpetual minors—" he expostulates. He condemns the "modern, unwomanly type . . . [that] professes to see something degrading in the subordination that God and Nature have decreed for women! Gallant! That's just what I am. Knights and gallantry were for the type that's vanishing, though" (303). Of course, the advantage to the man of gallantry was not just the reinforcement of the values he had set for himself, but the power to order when gallantry failed to elicit the desired response: "Hagar! say after me to this gentleman, 'Sir, I was mistaken in my sentiment toward you, and I here and now release you from any fancied engagement between us.'—Say it!" (102). Hagar refuses. By the last fourth of the novel, her actions make the Colonel reject "ever giving property unqualifiedly into woman's hands, and . . . encouraging occupations outside the household, and so breeding this independent attitude" (300).

Despite the limitations he places on the female sex, the Colonel is, for the narrator, an attractive and complex character. His voice is described as being "rich as old madeira, shot like shot silk with curious electric tensions and strains and agreements. . . . It went with his beauty, intact yet at fifty-eight, with the greying amber of his hair, mustache, and imperial . . . with the height and easy swing of his body that was neither too spare nor too full" (6). The narrator also admires his eyes, "in which a certain bladelike keenness and cynicism warred with native sensuousness" (126). Despite his quarrel with Hagar, the Colonel always calls her, fondly, "Gipsy"; one guesses that, just as his wife is not wholly pleased with the cipher that her daughter Serena has become, so the Colonel is not wholly displeased with his rebellious granddaughter.

Rebellious is a key word. Hagar reminds her grandfather and his friends that they, too, rebelled in the Civil War; yet revolt of any kind is, *ipso facto*, anathema to them now. The Judge berates Ibsen for "overturning all our concepts, criticizing supremacies" (148) and describes the effect of the shift in woman's place on him thus: "Poor homeless, friendless sailor with the pole star mysteriously shifted from its place" (150). Similarly, a bishop at New Springs urges Hagar to play with a doll instead of reading Darwin, lest she develop a "hard heart" or, more importantly, disrupt received notions. After all, the reader must remember, these men rebelled to preserve a society premised on a hierarchy of power within which rebellion was considered the worst threat of all.

The Colonel's conflicting views of womanhood obviously produce a bind for the actual women of his family. In a model of self-contradiction that is explicable only if one accepts the notion that women are inferior, he exclaims about Maria: "Gad! I wish she would complain. Then one could tell her there was nothing to complain about. I hate these women who go through life with a smile on their lips and an indictment in their eyes—when there's only the usual up and down of living to indict. I had rather they would whine—though I hate them to whine, too. But women are all cowards. No woman knows how to take the world" (10). Given his prescription, no woman could ever learn. His final, dying confusion shows us once again the bind: he thinks Hagar is Maria and accuses his family of hiding Hagar (the "child") from him: "That woman's my daughter-in-law—my son's wife, dependent on me for bread and shelter and setting up her will against mine . . . [Hagar's] not your child, it's Medway's child! That's law. You ought to be whipped!" (379). If we substitute "slave" where he speaks of and to Maria, the point becomes still more apparent: the Colonel exhibits both the genial and the malignant sides of paternalism.

Yet the Colonel's dying words show him in a near-tragic light. "The wide ocean . . . the wide ocean . . . '*Roll on, thou deep and dark blue ocean, roll!*' That's Byron, you know, Gipsy. . . . The wide ocean" (381). The link between the Colonel and Hagar is clear in the reference to Byron and in the fantasy of sea travel; the Colonel has died in a dream that his own ethos disallowed.

In a similar paradox, the other men of his generation—the Judge and General Argyle—although they decry the new freedom of women, enjoy hours discussing just that issue with Elizabeth Eden and Marie Caton. And when they make the unsettling discovery that not needle-work ("woman's touch") but apples are in the women's basket, they eat.

Johnston's vision of men, displayed in her characterization, grows both darker and brighter with succeeding generations; it becomes, in fact, polarized—just as does her view of women. The next generation is represented by Captain Bob and Hagar's father, Medway. Captain Bob, like Miss Serena, is pathetic. We see him, unimaginative, stolid, sad, always accompanied by a female dog: first Luna, who dies, then Lisa, who can never fully mean to him what Luna had. It is Captain Bob who gets to the heart of the conflicts Johnston discusses when he suggests in his modest way that everything would be all right if people married only their cousins. This would effectively, of course, exclude anything new, even genes.

Medway is indeed midway, caught between his conscious beliefs and his knowledge in an era that permits him greater freedom than his fa-ther, the Colonel, had enjoyed. In some ways Medway is like Mrs. LeGrand; both are wanderers with no purpose but self-indulgence, both lack ethical codes, both nevertheless prescribe roles for people based on their gender, and both exploit those roles.

Medway is happy that his daughter is being raised in the South; of all the cultures he has seen, the order of life at Gilead Balm comes closest to France and China in its preservation of the *jeune fille* (156). Given that the women's movement is called China Awake later in the novel, we can assume that the *jeune fille* is, like those blades of grass, more crushed than the average American girl. Indeed, Medway remarks (half humorously) that "the pivotal mistake was letting women learn the al-phabet" (261). The context of this remark is Hagar's decision to leave her father, to "grow in [her] native forest." "This comes," says her father, "of the damned modern independence of women. If you couldn't write—couldn't earn—you'd trot along quietly enough!" (261). This is precisely what his second wife Anna did. Medway has a proclivity for "annex[ing] all possible things . . . that could serve him" (257). Al-though he studies art, he is not a painter; although he prescribes a role for women, it is clearly and consciously for self-serving purposes. Med-way is incapable of commitment. Although he loved Maria, he grew "bored" with home life; on the other hand, when his second wife dies and leaves much of her fortune to the improvement of workingmen's housing, he raises no objections. That marriage worked, he tells his daughter, because Anna was tolerant and unexacting; because, in fact, each lived a life without what the Colonel would have called respon-sibility to one another.

Like Mrs. LeGrand, Medway argues that "all life . . . is based upon compromise" (262). Were he more fully drawn, we might see an early Rabbit running. As it is, Medway finally finds the semblance of a home in the Bahamas, where, in a suggested homosexual attraction, he finds his artist friend Greer and they set up a salon of sorts, admitting only men. There he argues his case: "Well, I've known a good many philosophers—but none that were irreducible. Every heroic, every transcendental treads at last the same pavement. 'I love and seek the street called pleasure. I abhor and avoid the street called pain.' Therefore the *summum bonum*—" (291). It is appropriate that Medway die midway between New York and Gilead Balm, in Washington, D.C., for he has lived his life—handsome, debonair, dominant, pleasureful—between two worlds.

The more modern male products of the South stand, although with some discomfort, squarely in the modern world. Where the southern women of Hagar's age become either near-ciphers or feminists, the southern men—in the persons of Laydon and Ralph Coltsworth—have capitulated, in their differing styles, to capitalism or, like Denny Gayde, become Socialists. Economics determines the male character; sexual identity determines the female. Yet the connection between capitalism and women's lack of selfhood, on the one hand, and socialism and freedom for women to grow, on the other, is implicit.

Laydon, a teacher at Eglantine, has a veneer of culture laid over a core of opportunism. In some ways he resembles Mrs. LeGrand more profoundly than does the more harmless Medway, for he teaches the young. Laydon's rhetoric about men and women—"All the sons were brave and all the daughters virtuous"—(137) rings hollow in his actual distortion of what once were real, if sexist, values. For him, honor means expediency and love becomes a trade-off—"the home you would make—the love and protection I should give you" (140)—that is stated explicitly as such. Women should not work, he says, because they would "compete" with men. Laydon prides himself on his intelligence and insight, yet he fails entirely to comprehend Hagar's reasons for wanting to tell her family about their engagement. Seeing her as a typical female who fears desertion by the man, he demonstrates not just his incapacity to comprehend simple straightforwardness, but also his presumption of female dependency. And Laydon promotes that dependency: all he wants from Hagar, he says, is that she be beautiful and love him. If she likes, she can work in a settlement house, since "Charity and Woman—they're almost synonymous" (135). It is impossible for him to comprehend Marie Caton's response to his comment: "Charity in your sense—is one of woman's worst weaknesses" (135).

Informing most of Laydon's prescriptions and descriptions of the female gender is his personal ambition; he thinks he is too good to be teaching at a female seminary and aspires to the university—a comment both on his own values and on the education actually offered at female seminaries in that period. Laydon loves to display his intellect; after he takes Hagar tò see *Romeo and Juliet*, he analyzes it in a voice loud enough to attract interested listeners. Yet Laydon's love for the theater is narcissistic; he cares more about his own ideas than he does about the play. During the performance, Hagar, absorbed in the drama, has to spend her time turning away his hand and his whispered comments to her. Moreover, Laydon cannot apply his intelligence to his own life. When Hagar explains her reasons for turning down his marriage proposal, he cannot comprehend that an infatuation is not love, nor basis for marriage, so he soothes himself by rationalizing: "On the whole, she, poor little thing! had probably suffered the most of the two. . . . *He had come off pretty well, after all*" (143, Johnston's emphasis). Laydon's confusion of love with acting and of acting with academic qualifications comes clear in his memory of a conversation with Hagar:

> . . . a strange half-hour . . . with, on his part, Byronic fervour, volcanic utterances. Had he not gone over them to himself afterwards, in his homely, cheerfully commonplace room in the brown cottage outside the Eglantine grounds? They had been fine; from the point of view of Belles-Lettres they could not have been bettered. He felt a glow as he recognized that fact, followed by a mental shot at the great Seat of Learning where he wished to be. "By George! that's the place I'm fitted for! The man they've got isn't in the same class—" (108–109)

In the end, Laydon seems only pitiable because of his ignorance.

Ralph Coltsworth, on the other hand, who starts off as a conventionally handsome rake, ends up provoking Hagar to anger and hatred. Coltsworth—the name again is pointedly chosen—is the scion of the other half of the county, run by his dominating family from their home, Hawk Nest. It is Ralph to whom Old Miss wants to marry Hagar. Ralph's definition of woman is succinct and to the point: woman is made for man. Piety, purity, domesticity—all take a back seat to the primary rule for the female: submit. The narrator makes it clear that this is not a rule invoked only by Ralph and only against women; it is a Coltsworth family trait, the need to rule others—all others. It follows, then, that Ralph would not even be bothered by the suffrage movement. He sees it as a *divertissement* like bridge, something to keep women from interfering with men (317). Ralph is used to getting what he wants; he believes he can *make* a woman fall in love with him, and he sees his role as another version of the old story of man conquering:

> "If I had been my father, I could have waved my sword and gone charging down history—and if I'd been my grandfather, I could have poured out Whig eloquence from every stump in the country and looked Olympian and been carried in procession (I don't like politics now; it's an entirely different thing):—and if I'd been my great-grandfather, I could have filibustered or settled the Southwest; and back of that I could have done almost any old thing—come over with the Adventurers, seized a continent, shared England with the Normans, marauded with the Vikings, whiled through Europe with Attila, done almost anything and come out with a name and my arms full! Now you can't conquer things like that, but, by George, you can corner things!" (290)

Ralph, of course, wants "riches and power," and he will get them in the old way, with a new twist, cornering the market instead of conquering land.

When it comes to Hagar, Ralph will not accept or even acknowledge any refusal. For years he hounds her, though in every conversation he does almost all the talking and she the listening. Finally, in a scene that directly links his ambition to his "love," he corners her with a literal twist: "'By God!' said Ralph, and quivered, 'I wish that we were together in a dark wood—I wish that you were in a captured city, and I was coming through the broken gate—' Suddenly he crossed the few feet between them, caught and crushed her in his arms, bruising her lips with his. 'Just be a woman—you dark, rich thing with wings—'" (369). It certainly takes no special insight to see that Ralph is contemplating rape, or to see that he has merged the angel with the sex object in his imagination. And, of course, rape is the logical outcome of Ralph's point of view, which in turn is the logical product of centuries of male power, male conquest, and male possession. It is no accident that Ralph is described by another character as more American than southern; he has taken his "feudal" values (368) into the "free" marketplace.

For Ralph, there are drawbacks. In this particular scene, "Hagar had a physical strength for which he was unprepared" (370). She hits him; he leaves. But there are subtler drawbacks: we are told that he is in New York after a trip around the world—"his physician had sent him off because of a threatened breaking-down. Apparently that had been staved off, pushed at least into a closet to stay there a few years" (364).

By the end of the novel, he has married Sylvia Maine, like him a last vestige of the traditional southern definitions of male and female, and we learn no more about his fate.

Although Denny Gayde is southern, from "way out in the mountains, the other end of nowhere" (40), his early enactment of a violent southern creed sent him to prison, where he learned how innocent he had actually been: "I hadn't meant to do all that, but still I had done it. So I said, 'I'll take it. And I won't give any trouble. And I'll keep the rules. If it's a place to make men better in, I'll come out a better man . . . I'll study, and I'll keep the rules and try to help other people, and when I come out, I'll be young and a better man.' . . . You see, I didn't know any more about that place than a baby unborn!" (42–43). Later, at a Socialist meeting, he describes the time he spent in prison as a period when he felt more and more like Ishmael. The adult Denny, however, has used those experiences to inform his activist politics. Described by one watcher as a "worn warrior angel," Denny has married the activist feminist Rose Darragh and, when he and Hagar meet in the Bahamas, is about to edit a Socialist newspaper.

Denny, who gives off more light than heat (350), is an ascetic; although his marriage with Rose is physically passionate, and although he comes close to reciprocating Hagar's growing and partly physical love for him, he has "eyes that carried a passion for something vaster than the flesh" (281). Clearly his absence of a verbal definition of woman is replaced by his actions—marrying a woman whose commitment to work equals his own, living a spartan existence, going on separate journeys while remaining faithful to his wife. For Denny, life is a series of periods of growth for all people; since growth requires "upheaval," it is best, he thinks, to direct it with consciousness and thus prevent what might be explosive rather than evolutionary social events. He feels close to Hagar on the island and later; his actions toward and with her are those of a friend, with an undercurrent of sexuality. Thus, the "new" man he represents directs his own life, expects women to direct theirs, and shares with all people the communication appropriate to friendship.

Christopher Josslyn, Molly's husband, takes a slighter role than does Denny. When we see him, it is in conversations with his wife Molly, which in content and structure differ from Ralph's with Hagar as the day from night: the content is the future of humanity, the structure a dialogue. He commits himself to feminism along with his other progressive beliefs: "I do not see how a man can endure to say to a woman, 'You are less free than I am, but be satisfied! you are so much freer than that wretch over there!'" he says. The Josslyns' marriage is the most conspicuously happy in the novel.

John Fay is the man Johnston constructs to be the nameless "comrade" to whom Hagar had once said she would open her home. He reminds Hagar of Medway, in his good looks and his sense of humor: "John Fay had a long and easy figure, a bronzed, clean-shaven, humorous face and sea-blue eyes" (348). Johnston creates in John Fay an enlightened capitalist, an engineer with the values of William Morris. Fay, in the depths of South America building bridges, has clipped pictures of leading writers and intellectuals (among them Hagar Ashendyne); he perceives their work to be the same as his, but on a different plane of reality. As for his workers, he deals with the problem of hierarchy by envisioning that one day "they'll work as artists. . . . And to give the artist component in the mass of humanity a chance to strengthen and come out is, I take it, the . . . work" for the next century or two (353).

Personally, Fay sees himself as continually growing. One mark of this is his speech at a feminist rally, a speech, he tells Hagar, that was provoked not by love for her but by belief that he spoke the truth. The relationship that develops between the two is a dialectic: Hagar wishes, she says, that she could build "great bridges across deep rivers" (352), and he wishes that he could write as she does. Their complementarity will be effected after marriage; she will continue to write (apparently until a child comes); and he will build bridges in America.

The "new men," then, share more characteristics with the "new women" than there are differences between them. Sexuality is not destroyed but enhanced by this identification, and all believe, in varying forms, in a sort of evolutionary optimism about human possibilities.

Johnston's attitude toward the "new men" she creates, and toward the "old," is most clearly embodied in the series of rejections that Hagar ends with her acceptance of Fay, and in the narrator's manipulation of setting and its implications. Briefly, Hagar rejects first Laydon as her permanent companion, then Denny, Medway, the Colonel, and Ralph, before she accepts John Fay "into her home." Of course, only two of these men offer marriage proposals; but each of them expects something from her that she cannot or will not give, for reasons that vary importantly. Laydon she must reject, for by the time they meet again in New Springs, she has learned that her infatuation was just that; she has thought through the relationship and in so doing has grown beyond him. With Denny, the situation is different: what Hagar must do, alone at night in her room, is consciously and actively to suppress her growing feelings of love. Although she could have loved him in the "old immemorial way," she says, she must not let her passion control her; Denny is happily married to a woman she admires. Hagar never wholly rejects Medway; after her initial refusal to go to Bogotá, she stays nevertheless, he has a second stroke, and she nurses him in Washington until his death two years later. Yet while she continues to love him and to see strong parts of herself in him, she rejects him psychologically. What she must reject is his aimless hedonism, for it has provided her with a way to grow but, unchecked, will lead her to the same waste of self that Medway has found.

She rejects the Colonel along with all the family at Gilead Balm: "You're all opponents. . . . Alike you worship God as Man, and you worship a static God, never to be questioned nor surpassed. You have shut an iron door upon yourselves. . . . One day you who shut it, you alone— you will open it, you alone. But I see that the day is somewhat far" (321). As we later see, at the Colonel's death, Hagar never stops loving him, but she rejects his way of life because it prevents hers. Ralph she rejects for obvious reasons, at least on the surface: no woman, one would suppose, wants a rapist. This fact may be obvious, although it is not to the hundreds of writers and thousands of readers who still devour the vaguely disguised rape scenes in sentimental literature—nor is it to the women who love to see Rhett Butler haul Scarlett up the stairs. After all, what Ralph offers Hagar in exchange for her surrender or, alternatively, as reparation after his conquest, is a total definition of herself, adorned with "orchids and pearls," wealth and vicarious power. He offers, in short, to take her over; this is the symbolic meaning of the rape. It is a definition of woman passed on to Ralph—as he knows— through generations of southern gentlemen who, in turn, in their Anglophilia, took John Donne's metaphor seriously: "She's all States, and all Princes, I."[25] It is a measure of Hagar's growth from Laydon to Ralph to Fay that she rejects Ralph so unequivocally; it is also a measure of the power of that image of masculinity that Johnston saved this choice for so late in the novel, when Hagar's identity is already strong.

So Hagar finally accepts Fay. They discuss the terms, they make mutual accommodations, they love one another with both physical and "spiritual" love. As Robert Lebrun resembles Edna Pontellier, John resembles Hagar.

In part, and appropriately to the themes of the novel, it is through the process of rejecting men that Hagar herself grows. But it is equally important to note that the reasons for and extent of each rejection differ precisely as her relationship with each man differs; she learns, among other things, the art of careful discrimination. Johnston's own definition of woman seems then essentially to define man: both are creatures with the urge to grow, and with differing but not sex-based capacities both to express and repress that growth.

Not just Hagar's rejections, but Johnston's use of setting contributes to the development of her image of the "new man." It is interesting,

in the light of the works already examined, to note that the major romantic scenes in this novel all take place at or near water. Hagar rejects Laydon at New Springs, where she finds new springs in herself
through talking with Elizabeth and Marie. The lengthy scenes with
Denny in the Bahamas are lush with the growth and the sounds of the
sea that were so prominent in *The Awakening*; Hagar's sensuality, like
Edna's, is aroused in part by the setting. Her romance with Fay occurs
on the coast of Brittany, beside a cold, though refreshing, sea; and a
nearly fatal storm precipitates Hagar's decision to marry him. Johnston
seems to imply that the natural forces represented by the sea are present in their relationship, but without the illusory eternal summer of the
Bahamas and its concomitant perpetual passion. In this light, it is important that Hagar herself is sexually assertive for the first time in Brittany, and that the two lovers, in the end, walk away from the sea to an
ancient circle of stones—the creation of human beings like themselves
who hope both to stay in touch with and to control the forces of nature.

A final note before moving on to *Hagar*'s vision and analysis of society. Sexuality in this novel is diffused. Johnston is fully conscious of
this; when women are attracted to women, or men to men, she ascribes
it through the narrator to a "pure, detached" love for beauty. However,
in most cases, it is the people whom her characters love regardless of
sex that they find attractive in a sensual way. Love, sex, and beauty are
thus implicitly linked. Perhaps, too, the diffused sexuality is a function
of the analysis, critique, and vision of community implicit in the novel.
For, as we have seen in *Beulah*, Grace King's stories, and *The Awakening*, when the prescriptive community conflicts with the sense of community felt by a character, the body may often protest while the conscious mind submits.

In any case, Johnston's analysis and critique of Western society in its
broad dimensions attacks capitalism and replaces rugged individualism
with a blend of enlightened self-interest and socialism. In its more precise form, the form presented by metaphor, structure, and characterization rather than by speeches, her critique focuses on southern society.
Johnston spends most of her imaginative energy displaying a form of
community that, because of its own definition of itself, must die. As she
sees the South, it is bound for suicide.

Gilead Balm becomes one of Johnston's symbols for the South; Hawk
Nest completes the county, which is, in turn, a larger symbol. Eglantine, too, stands for specific characteristics of the South. The only symbol not yet touched upon in this study is the South as represented by
the Maine family's home in New York.

If Hawk Nest represents the fierceness of the South, the toughness that sends Hotspur Ralph Coltsworth galloping eagerly into the New South, Gilead Balm is its serenity, the balm or Beulah land that its inhabitants believe has already been found before the Civil War. In one sense, Gilead Balm is the feminine South and Hawk Nest the masculine; that is why Johnston has Old Miss eager and determined to marry Hagar of Gilead Balm to Ralph of Hawk Nest. But the critique of Hawk Nest is clear and relatively simple and is shown in the fate of Ralph, as we have seen. It is upon Gilead Balm that most of the attention rests, because this home symbolizes for Johnston the core of the southern ethos.

Informing the community at Gilead Balm, above all other values, is the need for order, apparently a consequence of fear of change. Hence the people living there perceive their particular form of social organization as eternal and as ordained by God. Captain Bob, in his role as unconscious parodist, expresses it this way: "Nobody dies at Gilead Balm—hasn't been a death here since the War" (47). Old Miss, in her stubborn refusal to admit the defeat of her plan to marry Hagar to Ralph, expresses more intelligently her assumption that the way things are is the way they should, and always will, be. The fear we saw expressed by the Colonel's generation showed in its language—the shifting of a "pole star," the sense that something beyond human power to change had, horrifyingly, been changed. Indeed, Gilead Balm is the sole center of stasis in the growth pattern of the novel; each time Hagar comes home, everything is still the same, the same behavior, the same ideas. The one part of life that cannot be controlled, that must change, however, is, of course, the individual's own life: one is born, grows, dies. In an all-but-conscious recognition of this flaw in the eternal scheme of things, Gilead Balm has provided an elaborate set of socializing techniques to ensure that each generation will carry on the same as the one before it.

The particular form that the society of Gilead Balm takes relies on "blood." It is essential that the right "blood" stay in the right "place" for the old order to be preserved; Coltsworths and Ashendynes *must* marry because they embody the specific form that order takes in the South, the order of hierarchy and levels of dominance. "Gilead Balm has always inculcated reverence for dominant kin and family authority. It had been Gilead Balm's grievance, long ago, against Hagar's mother that Maria recognized that so poorly" (101–102). The hierarchy obtains both within the family and without it: hence for the "bottom rail" to be on "top" is as threatening as for a wife to fail to defer to her husband or a child to his or her parent. Although the lower-class whites and the blacks who live at Gilead Balm are treated with affection, the lines of division between Ashendyne and Green, and between white and black, are broken only by the children, who learn that as adults they will have to give up the egalitarian relationship of their childhood. The Ashendynes reject out of hand the notion that Hagar give Medway's inheritance to the Greens and to various social causes. Within the Ashendyne family, the lines of dominance and hierarchy, as has been shown, are clear if occasionally conflicted: God (male) first, then race (white), then sex (male), then age (older) have the power, in that order, to make their wills prevail. It is perfectly logical, then, that Old Miss would link "Women Righters and Abolitionists!—doing their best to drench the country with blood, kill our people and bring the carpetbaggers upon us! Wearing bloomers and cutting their hair short and speaking in town-halls and wanting to change the marriage service—Yes, they do wear bloomers! I saw one doing it in New York in 1885" (316). This is spoken in about 1903; Old Miss has clearly neither forgotten the massive disordering of the Civil War nor abandoned her belief that change itself is bad.

The difficulties with Gilead Balm's notion of community, besides the sexual, economic, and racial injustices that have been noted, come precisely as a result of its definition of community as eternal and as hierarchical. On the one hand, any change that does occur within the community will not be evolutionary; it will be an "explosion." (Denny Gayde, of course, described societal growth as a series of upheavals that must be both encouraged and directed, in order to avoid the damages caused by "explosions.") And that is how the Ashendynes react to Hagar's joining the suffrage movement: they explode (313). On the other hand, since the system itself does not countenance change— since its rigidity excludes flexibility—it is doomed, as Johnston envisions it, to atrophy. Like the body physical, the body social, contends *Hagar*, must grow or decay. Johnston gives the reader clues to this; each time Hagar returns, although all is—like Poe's House of Usher— formally the same, Gilead Balm shows subtle signs of giving up. Near the end of the novel, Hagar says about going to her old home: "Grandmother and grandfather and Aunt Serena said some hard things, but I think they enjoyed saying them, and I could ramble over the old place, and, indeed, I think, though they would never have said so, that they were glad to have me there. I will not quarrel. They are so feeble—the Colonel and Old Miss. I do not think they can live many years longer" (366). Nor can Gilead Balm, as an emblem of the South. To make it clear that she is seeing in the Colonel's death both a personal and cultural end, Johnston has him say, in almost his last words: "Wasn't the

Canal good enough? Who wants their Railroad—damn them! And after the Railroad there'll be something else. . . . Public Schools, too! . . . This country's getting too damnably democratic!" (380). His last words, as has been seen, show that Johnston sees the demise of both person and culture as tragic. At the same time, she seems to hope that her readers will learn from that tragedy and refuse to repeat the flaw.

One facet of the southern ethos, the ethos that contains its own destruction, is seen at Eglantine. Eglantine is a community unlike Gilead Balm in that it excludes more than does Gilead Balm. Whereas Hagar's home keeps out ideas that might incite change, Eglantine keeps out people—blacks, lower-class whites, and men. The adjectives (sweet, smooth) tell the story, as do the metaphors (the high hedge, the portrayal of the girls as Sleeping Beauties). Roger Michael's speech was a mistake, understandable because the Anglophilia of the school would permit an Englishwoman into the grounds assuming she would speak only of received notions. Laydon is allowed only because he contributes to the training of the young women in that "surface culture" so essential to getting a man. It is in this hothouse that southern girls are prepared for their place in the social hierarchy.

By putting a southern family, the Powhatan Maines, into New York City, Johnston comes closest to examining southern culture, its virtues, and its flaws. First of all, it is important that she chose a family, for, as was the case with Gilead Balm, it is kinship that forms community. Moreover, the family is not nuclear; it is extended, including Rachel Bolt and her two children and the cousins and friends who come to visit for various lengths of time. The Maine household is a little South in New York: they live well, "in our quiet, homelike Southern fashion, of course" (157). The house itself

> was deep and for a New York dwelling wide, cool, high-ceilinged, and dark, with a gleam of white marble mantel-pieces and antiquated crystal chandeliers, with some ancient Virginia furniture and some ebony and walnut abominations of the 'seventies. Everything was a little worn, tending toward shabbiness; but a shabbiness not extreme, as yet only comfortable, though with a glance toward a more helpless old age. There were a fair number of books, some portraits and good, time-yellowed engravings. There were four coloured servants beside the nurse for Mrs. Bolt's children. (163)

Like the house, the inhabitants are declining types. Mrs. Maine is "extremely good-natured," though some see her as "indolent"; "no one ever hinted at her intellectuality," and she was "not, apparently, socially ambitious" (162). Nevertheless, many people (mostly southerners) gravitate to the Maine house, where Mrs. Maine is "as unobtrusive and comfortable to get on with as the all-pervasive ether" (163). Mrs. Maine is the southern woman at her most extreme; her submissiveness has made her a nonentity. Powhatan, on the other hand, represents the end of southern manhood: a failing lawyer, he "told good war stories and darky stories" (163). Mrs. Maine's major activities consist of eating chocolates and knitting baby sacques; Mr. Maine keeps her in chocolates regardless of the family's financial condition.

> The beating of the waves of the year was not loudly heard in the Maines' long, high-ceilinged parlour . . . the table was still good and plentiful, and the coloured servants, who were fond of him and he of them, smiled and bobbed, and he had not felt it necessary to change his brand of cigars, and the same old people came in the evening. Mrs. Maine never read the newspapers. She rarely read anything, though once in a while she took up an old favourite of her youth, and placidly dipped now into it and now into her box of chocolates. (185)

As one might expect, the Maines expect the visiting Hagar to act like a proper southern lady—to see the opera, not the slums; to go out with gentlemen, not alone. But, as one might also expect from their characterization, they do little to enforce such expectations; their energies atrophied, the Maines simply act out what is for Johnston an outworn creed. The style persists; years later, Hagar comes for a visit to find "it was all just the same, only the tone of time was deeper, the furniture more worn, the prints yellower" (323). There is a "slight difference in the cast of talk. They all seemed uneasily aware that the world was moving. Mostly they disapproved and foreboded. . . . They sighed for the halcyon past" (323–24).

Johnston refuses, however, the simplistic solution of finding the answer to all social ills in the North. Hagar's first impressions on coming to the city at eighteen are shocking to her; she sees the slums and considers poverty: "she had been brought up on the tradition of the poverty after the war—but that had been heroic, exalted poverty, in which all shared, and where they kept the amenities. Then, when that had passed, there were the steadygoing poor people in the country—those who had always been poor. . . . But it did not seem to hurt so in the country, and certainly it was not so ugly" (174). Besides poverty, in New York (and around the world when she travels with Medway) Hagar finds the sorts of injustice and dehumanizing patterns of behavior that turn her into a Socialist of sorts. She does not forget that it is the South whose ground has nurtured her. In a conversation with Denny, Hagar describes the ideas and attitudes she has had to grow away from and into:

> My own sharp inner struggle was for intellectual and spiritual freedom. I had to think away from concepts with which the atmosphere in which I was raised was saturated. I had to think away from creeds and dogmas and affirmations made for me by my ancestors. I had to think away from the idea of a sacrosanct Past and the virtue of Immobility;—not the true idea of the mighty Past as our present body which we are to lift and ennoble, and not Immobility as the supreme refusal to be diverted from that purpose,—but the Past, that is made up of steps forward, set and stubborn against another step, and Immobility blind to any virtue in Change. I had to think away from a concept of woman that the future can surely only sadly laugh at. I had to think away from Sanctions and Authorities and Taboos and Divine Rights—and when I had done so, I had to go back with the lamp of wider knowledge, deeper feeling, and find how organic and on the whole virtuous in its day was each husk and shell. The trouble was that in love with the lesser we would keep out the stronger day . . . and there was everywhere a sickness of conflict. I had to think away from my own dogmatisms and intolerances. I'm still engaged in doing that. . . . What has come of it all is a certain universal feeling. (284–85)

This passage shows not only Hagar's (and Johnston's) analysis and critique of southern society, but also shows Hagar's refusal to dismiss the past utterly, describes the process by which she has grown, and suggests what will become her final vision of community. When Hagar says this to Denny in the Bahamas, her terminology is highly abstract; later, she comes back to the particular, to Gilead Balm itself, and experiences once again the intellectual evolution described above:

> Hagar leaned back in her chair and regarded the circle of her relatives. . . . She felt trapped. Then she realized that she was not trapped, and she smiled . . . she was not by position Maria, she was not by position Miss Serena. Before her, quiet and fair, opened her Fourth Dimension. Inner freedom, ability to work, personal independence, courage and sense of humour and a sanguine mind, breadth and height of vision,

tenderness and hope, her waiting friends . . . her work. . . .
She crossed the border with ease; she was not trapped. (318)

Hagar's community, her "waiting friends," are neither literally nor figuratively in the South. The very definition of southern community would
not permit what she calls her "Fourth Dimension"—a set of values
clearly reminiscent of those submerged or apparent in the earlier works
discussed in this study. The South has shut an iron gate on itself and
will smother itself to extinction, despite its earlier usefulness. Moreover, the definition of southern community would leave out Hagar's
own vision of future community: "The world one home, and men one
man, though of an infinite variety, and women one woman, though of
an infinite variety, and children one child, and the open road before the
three. And back of the three, Oneness. The Great Pulse—out, the
Many; in, the One" (357).

Johnston, therefore, has criticized through Hagar the South's definition of community, shown how and whom it dehumanizes, and offered
a global vision of unity. Practically speaking, of course, that vision must
remain only a dream, and Johnston's characters recognize this. Hence
they devise a variety of forms of social organization, from the con-
ventlike settlement houses, to the "new" marriage of Denny and Rose,
to the "new" family suggested for John Fay and Hagar Ashendyne at the
end of the novel—from the single person living alone, to the single parent, to the same sex living together, to opposite sexes living together.
Whatever the unit of social cohesion, the actual links between units are
not blood or class or race or money; they are similarity of ideas. In common among all the characters Hagar thinks of as her "friends" is a commitment, not to identity of goals but to mutual understanding and support, not to identity of talents but to the rejection of hierarchies. What
Hagar fervently wishes, to be "glad when I get out of fractions" (169),
Ralph Coltsworth, the last powerful southerner, sees as the "age of the
cuckoo" when "cuckoos are laying their eggs in abler folks' nests"
(302).

Like Kate Chopin, but with less artistry, Johnston ends her novel not
with a didactic statement but with a set of images: "The grey-green silent heath stretched away to the shining sea. The grasses waved around
and between the grey altars of the past, and the sky vaulted all, azure
and splendid. Two sea-birds passed overhead with a long, clarion cry.
Two butterflies hung poised upon a thistle beside them. The salt wind
blew from the sea as it had blown against man and woman when these
stones were raised. They sat and talked until the sun was low in the
west, and then, hand in hand, walked back to the village" (390). De-

spite its relative obviousness, the passage bears comparison with Chopin's conclusion to *The Awakening*. Instead of swimming out to sea to drown, Hagar moves from the sea to the ancient circle of stones, then to the village. Instead of making her journey alone, Hagar is now with her "true mate," having lived alone with dissatisfaction. Instead of dogs, spurs, bees, and pinks, we have twinning—for sea-birds, butterflies, and people.

And instead of the imaginative power of "There was the hum of bees, and the musky odor of pinks filled the air," we have the happy couple walking together into the sunset. Where *The Awakening* succeeds as art, *Hagar* fails. Artistically, the work does not satisfy because of what is ultimately a failure of realism to hold its ground against the force of authorial hope. Among the symptoms of that failure are characters who are occasionally little more than mouthpieces; dialogue that could never occur naturally; a failure to imagine sufficiently potential conflicts in the "new" community and between the "new" man and the "new" woman; a failure to treat with dramatic surety the problems of blacks, of sexuality, of children, of the world outside the "Fourth Dimension." In *Hagar*, the covert again undercuts the overt apparent intent of the author, with the opposite effect to that in *Beulah*. But that is precisely the point. The terms, the design, of the dream are in central ways similar—whether overt or covert—to the dream adumbrated for women, men, and society in the fiction of the preceding southern women writers.

Mary Johnston's papers contain correspondence that indicates she was part of a network of supportive relationships among women writers, especially southerners. Johnston seemed to evoke a particularly strong maternal feeling from her friends, but the mother/child relationship pervades these literary friendships, permitting both roles to each individual and creating a remarkable sense of caring and intimacy. Rebecca Harding Davis, for example, wrote to Johnston that "I always feel as if I should like to put you in a cradle and rock you or mother you in some way."[26] And Ellen Glasgow wrote, "I want you to know and feel how my love goes out to you. It always seems to me that I should like to take you in my arms and shield you."[27] Reciprocally, Johnston wrote to console Glasgow in 1929: "I dreamed of you the other night. I was in a house over against your house. It was night time, very quiet, very still, and I looked out of my window across to your window and saw that it was lighted—not a strong light, but a light turned low, and I thought, 'Ellen is there, sorrowing for Jeremy.'"[28]

Though in their affections these women writers seemed to act for one another as both mother and daughter, as intellectuals and artists they acted as equals and shared a common bond of passionate commitment to the life of the mind. Johnston's diary reports in some detail the conversations she had with Glasgow, conversations that invariably concerned books and ideas. On January 2, 1907, for instance, "Ellen and I talked books; Webster, Ford, Congreve, Swift, Steele, and Addison, Chapman's Homer, Dickens, etc." On February 25, they argued about Henry James's *Turn of the Screw* (Johnston found it "a putrescent thing seen by a blue light"). And on May 12 of the same year she talked with Ellen's sister Cary of writers like Augusta Evans—"The very remarkable trash we all read [as children], *The Wide, Wide World, The Children of the Abbey, Home Influence*, and *Mother's Recompense*, etc., etc."[29] Glasgow wrote to Johnston that "in order to compose my soul I have been reading Spinoza and Plotinus. . . . I can't tell you, dear, how I have wanted to be with you. Next [autumn?] let us hope we'll have a chance to talk."[30]

More than their reading, though, their writing occupies the minds of these correspondents. Through letters, they compare the experience of writing and provide support for it. Charlotte Perkins Gilman, claiming she is "no novelist" after seven tries, still confesses to Johnston that she wants to try another, with a "new" woman who loves an "old" style man, "he pushing his suit on the old basis of conquest; she must 'surrender'—and she, loving him in all ways, holding out steadily for an equal union of strong souls with only the mutual concessions of faithful love and parentage."[31] Addressing Johnston as "my dear fellow craftsman," Ellen Glasgow expressed anxieties about the method of her own work ("sudden spurts and inevitable reactions") and tries to quell Johnston's fears ("it may be that the book will grow faster than you think").[32] Whereas Johnston and especially Glasgow saw their identities as inseparable from their writing, Rebecca Harding Davis, apparently failing to understand, called Johnston's writings "vampire children" who "have been draining your life for years" and hoped that Johnston would forget them, remembering "only that there is a tired little woman going to find health and happiness in the care of a Heavenly Father who loves her"—a sentiment that Johnston did not share.[33]

The combination of shared intellectual excitement, the common bond of serious writing, and mutual maternal support meant, in at least the case of Glasgow and Johnston, a profound sense of closeness. Glasgow wrote to Johnston early in the relationship that "I feel that I should be as glad as possible to know you better—to stand within the gate. Yes, I daresay we are different in many ways—it will be interesting, don't you think, to learn *how* different. And the main thing, perhaps we both have." And a year later, she recalled that "when I first knew you, do you know, I thought that I could never come quite close to you—that your reserve would be so great, and I am very thankful that I have at last found that there was a way through it. You are different from me in many ways, and particularly in as much as you keep your impulses so firmly in hand while mine do often carry me breathlessly away. And then you have such courage, and suffering, which makes me impatient and ready to rend the universe, has given you a peaceful and strong composure. Well, well, do you remember the Buddhist proverb— 'There are many paths down into the valley, but when we come out upon the mountains we all see the self-same sun.'"[34]

Those paths apparently diverged still further for Johnston and Glasgow after the early years of most of these letters. Yet this literary friendship—which flowered also into political activism when, in 1909, they worked in the Virginia Equal Suffrage League's earliest days—filled important personal and professional needs for both during the crucial period of their thirties, keeping them tied to their southern sense of the past and giving them company as each imagined a freer future.

Charlotte Gilman saw Mary Johnston to be an eagle within; Ralph Coltsworth saw Hagar with wings. Ellen Glasgow wanted to "stand within the gate" of Mary Johnston's self; Ralph Coltsworth wanted to push through the "broken gate" to Hagar. If we put together the images, the metaphor of a caged bird emerges. But two very different stances are taken toward the southern women so imagined. Ralph, the good old boy, can understand that creature only as an animal, fundamentally sexual, and requiring dominance, ultimately violence, from the man. Glasgow and Gilman, on the other hand, see the opportunity for intimacy and closeness through acting on the values of parity, nurturance, cooperation, mutual intellectual interests, and trust. The cage cannot be stormed, they imply, to reach the creature within: an eagle, even a caged one, never surrenders. And that is precisely the happy ending that Johnston hands to Hagar in the form of John Fay, the gentle man who combines male sexuality with what are here female values— the values that Johnston envisioned as transcendent and universal.

CHAPTER VI

Ellen Glasgow
The Perfect Mould

Mary Johnston published *Hagar* in 1913. In the same year, Ellen Glasgow—who was to become by far the better-known writer—published her own study of southern womankind. While *Hagar* looked to the future, though, *Virginia* looked to the past to examine what Glasgow believed was a dying breed: the Southern Lady.

Published in the year she turned forty, *Virginia* was Ellen Glasgow's tenth novel in nearly sixteen years. Yet its author claimed, and critics have often concurred, that it was the "first book of my maturity." Perhaps the recent death of her beloved sister and intellectual companion Cary, who was "closer to [her] than anyone else" and to whom Glasgow dedicated the novel, pushed her toward that maturity. Glasgow wrote in her memoir that she "used to think that [she] could never write another line if [she] were to lose her,"[1] yet write she did, and this was the novel. Perhaps, too, the artist's maturity came with her first full and conscious effort to exorcise the saint-figure of her mother in fiction, for, like Virginia, Anne Jane Gholson Glasgow was "the perfect flower of Southern culture."[2] Virginia's story shows the inevitable fading of that flower. Inescapably the victim of her own premises, Virginia banks all on love and loses: her loving parents die, her husband leaves her for another woman, and her children grow up and go away.

Whether that saint was exorcised for all time represents one of the disagreements that Glasgow's name still provokes. It is her mother who, more than anyone else, gave to Ellen Glasgow a sense of the dying aristocratic South that some critics say she clung to sentimentally throughout her life, and others say she fought fiercely with her realism. Whatever the case, as late as 1944 Glasgow stood by her conscious belief that "everything in me, mental or physical, I owe to my mother" and that "I inherited nothing from [my father], except the color of my eyes and a share in a trust fund." In a famous bit of self-analysis, Glasgow added: "It is possible that from that union of opposites, I derived a perpetual conflict of types."[3]

Her parents were indeed of different and conflicting types. Francis Thomas Glasgow, born in western Virginia, came from Scottish and Irish ancestors. Settling in Rockbridge and Botetourt counties in the middle of the eighteenth century, the Glasgows and Andersons produced a state supreme court judge, Francis Thomas Anderson, and a successful pre–Civil War industrialist, General Joseph Reid Anderson, owner of the Tredegar Iron Works in Richmond. Glasgow's father operated Tredegar from 1849 to 1912; during the Civil War, it became the Richmond Arsenal of the Confederacy. In a kinder moment than most, Ellen described her father as "stalwart, unbending, rock-ribbed with Calvinism";[4] for the most part, her memoir shows a man who, like Cyrus Treadwell in *Virginia*, lacked even a modicum of sensitivity. Yet, as Marjorie R. Kaufman puts it,

> Disclaim this heritage though she might, Ellen Glasgow received more than financial independence from these [Glasgow and Anderson] men; she had also their business acumen, their competitiveness, their determination to succeed by creating a respectable product which could command recognition and a fair reward. . . . With [these qualities] she was able to shepherd her reputation with the same attention that

she gave her novels, and thus in the years before her death to enjoy the honor she had long felt her work deserved.[5]

Glasgow's mother, on the other hand, came from Tidewater aristocrats who thought Richmond far enough west to settle. An Episcopalian—her ancestor William Yates had been seventh president of William and Mary College and rector of Bruton Parish Church from 1761–64—Anne Gholson had a genealogy that included some of the oldest colonial families of the state. When her mother died young and her father finally did move west, later to become a justice of the Ohio Supreme Court, Anne Gholson stayed in Richmond to be reared by her great-uncle, Chancellor Creed Taylor of the Superior Court of Law and Chancery, judge, commissioner of the University of Virginia, and founder of the law school at "Needham." Kaufman notes Glasgow's relationship to her aristocratic mother: "The novelist's public image, which emerges from even the earliest interviews she gave the press and is supported by her friends' accounts, is that of her being her mother's daughter—gentle, fragile, hospitable, gay, yet brave and enduring."[6] This image is indeed close to that of Virginia Pendleton in Glasgow's novel. Glasgow sustains this image of her mother in her memoir, *The Woman Within*. During Anne Gholson Glasgow's periods of severe depression, periods that emerged when Ellen was still a child, Mrs. Glasgow used to bring her daughters' beds into the room with her for comfort during the night. Ellen's reaction to this rather strenuous demand upon little children was, she said, simply to feel agonized for her mother.

Born in 1873, the eighth of ten Glasgow children, Ellen had what she remembered in her somewhat self-pitying memoir as a painfully lonely but occasionally blissful childhood. Kept from school by emotional and physical frailty, she read widely—including *Fanny Hill*—in her father's library,[7] roamed the streets and the countryside with her black mammy, and felt cut off even from most members of her immediate family. By the age of seven, said Glasgow in *The Woman Within*, "I became a writer . . . . I had created Little Willie and his many adventures, [and] I beg[a]n to pray every night, 'O God, let me write books! Please, God, let me write books!'"[8] This rather melodramatic beginning culminated in 1897 with her first published novel *The Descendant* (Glasgow burned the first novel she wrote, *Sharp Realities*) and came to an end only in 1966, with the posthumous publication of her twentieth, *Beyond Defeat*.

Ellen Glasgow's private life seemed doomed to a series of deeply felt tragedies. Her mother (like Mary Johnston's) died when the daughter was twenty; her father lived to be eighty-six. Her beloved brother-in-law, Cary's husband Walter McCormack, killed himself when he was twenty-six; her brother Frank killed himself when he was thirty-nine. Both had been sensitive, intelligent, helpful friends. Then Cary died of cancer, soon followed by another sister, Emily. A love affair with "Gerald," reported in *The Woman Within* but not yet understood in much detail, ended when he died. It is no wonder that Ellen Glasgow turned to animals (like her dog Jeremy) for companionship and grieved at their loss.

Apparently, however, the urge to survive stayed alive within her. Only once, during a long and reportedly mediocre love affair with lawyer Henry Watkins Anderson, did she try to kill herself. And her writing served a therapeutic purpose; with *Barren Ground* (1925), for instance, Glasgow said she had "found [her] self."[9] Moreover, the social life she led from her home in Richmond demanded time, tact, and energy that she was more than willing to give, despite her recurrent hearing problems, in exchange for a sense of community. Glasgow lived for periods in New York—the longest 1911 to 1916—and took trips through Europe; gradually, however, she settled into the family home in Richmond where, after years of heart trouble, she died in 1945. She was seventy-two.

That Ellen Glasgow was a southerner not only by birth and rearing, but by some fairly deep level of choice, is clear not just from her geographical roamings and homings. It is clear also in the springs for her art. Unlike the novelist who must leave to gain detachment, Glasgow had to come home. For example, after living in New York for some time, she returned to Virginia so that she could stay in Petersburg ("Dinwiddie") long enough to imagine the characters and setting of *Virginia*. She spoke about and for the South in brief nonfiction prose. And, as the title of *Virginia* suggests, the body of her fiction is, in effect, the body of the South, living, dead, and moribund. C. Hugh Holman, in fact, sees as her great theme the southern Tidewater tradition as it adjusts to and shapes life.[10]

Early in her career, Ellen Glasgow made the famous remark that what the South needed was "blood and irony. Blood it needed because southern culture had strained too far away from its roots in the earth; it had grown thin and pale; it was satisfied to exist on borrowed ideas, to copy instead of create. And irony is an indispensable ingredient of the critical vision; it is the safest antidote to sentimental decay" (*ACM*, 28). Critical discussion concerning her relationship with her region never questions that she cared about it. Instead, it divides over how far she endorsed and how far rejected the mores of the traditional Tidewater aristocracy. Taking a position early on was Alfred Kazin; comparing her to Tolstoy, he said she "knew only one society and spent [her] life quarreling with it." [11] In his 1972 biography, E. Stanly Godbold took the middle ground: "Ellen herself was one day an old fashioned Southern girl and the next day a modern intellectual in total rebellion against the traditions of the past. In all of her life she was not able to shed either role, nor was she able to reconcile them. She was both 'the mould of perfection' and the one who cast it away." [12] Louis D. Rubin, Jr., has argued that the southern woman beat out the intellectual in her, and the sentimentalist the realist. [13]

The terms of dispute about her fiction are similar to those about her life: to what extent did realism "cross the Potomac . . . going North" (*ACM*, 62) in 1900 when Ellen Glasgow was publishing her early novels? Was Glasgow, in fact, a realist at all? In her nonfiction, Glasgow rather clearly saw herself as a realist of a special sort. In the revision of her 1928 *Harper's* article, "The Novel in the South," which she published in *A Certain Measure* as the preface to *The Miller of Old Church*, Glasgow deals with the question that bothered Allen Tate in "The Profession of Letters in the South": why has there been no great southern literature? She sees the pre–Civil War literature of the region as moralism, becoming more strident as slavery needed increasingly to be defended. "The Protestant Episcopal Church," among other offenders, "was charitable toward almost every weakness except the dangerous practice of thinking" (*ACM*, 136). Moreover, the mores of the time required that one be "amusing" and "agreeable"; "generous manners exacted that the artist should be more gregarious than solitary" (*ACM*, 136–37).

After the war, she argues, "to defend the lost became the solitary purpose and the supreme obligation of the Southern novelist." Thus the tradition became a "sentimental infirmity," "true, not to experience, but to the attitude of evasive idealism" (*ACM*, 139). Glasgow concludes by finding hope in the then-current Southern Renaissance. Yet her realism takes a southern turn. Glasgow warns that in the urge to escape from the sentimental tradition, writers should not become the servants to a new master, "patriotic materialism" (*ACM*, 144). Glasgow rejects "Americanism": "the ambition of the New South," she regrets, "is not to be self-sufficing, but to be more Western than the West and more American than the whole of America" (*ACM*, 145–46). She objects to the "mediocrity" of Americanism: "The Americanism so prevalent in the South today belong[s] to that major variety which, by reducing life to a level of comfortable mediocrity, has contributed more than a name to the novel of protest." (Glasgow interestingly includes Margaret Mitchell among the novelists of protest.) "Americanism" also has meant, Glasgow says, a "decrease in that art of living, which excels in the amiable aspects of charm rather than in the severe features of dogmatism," and whose loss results in the rise of "a new class" "to the surface if not to the top" (*ACM*, 147–48). "It is this menace not only to freedom of thought, but to beauty and pleasure and picturesque living that is forcing the intelligence and the aesthetic emotions of the South into revolt" (*ACM*, 147). Thus, when she was confronted, not with sentimentality of the old sort, but with the "uniform concrete surface" of modern culture (*ACM*, 147), Glasgow resorted to an appeal to elements of the very tradition she had rejected: class, charm, amiability, even "picturesque living." Surely here again Ann Gholson's amiable charm, rather than Francis Thomas' severe dogmatism, receives Glasgow's endorsement.

Finally, in this essay she urges a move from immersion in the culture to a "detached and steadfast point of view," for "it is only with the loss of this charm and the ebbing of this sentiment that [the southern novelist] has been able to rest apart and brood over the fragmentary world he has called into being" (*ACM*, 149–50). So she returns, if reluctantly, to the ironic necessity that the southern tradition must die in order for its great literature to be born.

Thus in "The Novel in the South" Ellen Glasgow reveals the same ambivalence to her region seen in her life. There is no question that her novels, too, are deeply informed by the South; whether it was James Branch Cabell's idea or her own, Glasgow in 1938 eagerly called her earlier works an intended "social history of Virginia" (*ACM*, 3). In *Life and Gabriella*, the protagonist must make one final trip to Virginia—after eighteen years' absence—in order to exorcise the South within herself. And in *Virginia*, the state takes the body of a woman.

Nor was Glasgow's art the impersonal vision of any twentieth-century southerner: it was the work of an aristocratic southern woman. And if Kazin is right in saying that the chivalric myth of southern womanhood was the most fervid, the "crowning unreality"[14] of the southern tradition, then perhaps it took a southern woman to write about it realistically. Glasgow certainly hinted as much when she wrote about the literature of the Old South: "Here, as elsewhere, expression belonged to the articulate, and the articulate was supremely satisfied with his own fortunate lot, as well as with the less enviable lot of others. Only the slave, the 'poor white,' or the woman who had forgotten her modesty, may have felt inclined to protest; and these negligible minorities were as dumb and sterile as the profession of letters" (*ACM*, 135–36). The word *inarticulate* appears repeatedly, almost repetitiously, in *The Woman Within*. Glasgow associates it each time with a person or an animal who is a victim of cruelty, whether it be social or personal. And cruelty, she says, is not only the worst of the vices, but provides her the very motivation to write. Although she never, in that work, directly connects suffering, womanhood, and keeping silent, the threads that associate the concepts are there.

In *Virginia*, the connections among these concepts are explicit. First love renders Virginia speechless: "Had her life depended on it, she could not have uttered a sentence . . . yet she would have given her dearest possession to have been able to say something really clever." [15] Though Virginia—like Annie Hall—thinks Oliver is judging her a "simpleton," in fact he—like Alvy Singer—is "not thinking of her wits at all, but of the wonderful rose-pink of her flesh" (64). When they meet later at Abby Goode's party, "her tongue was paralyzed; she couldn't say what she felt. She wondered passionately if he thought her a fool, for she could not look into his mind and discover how adorable he found her responses. The richness of her beauty combined with the poverty of her speech made an irresistible appeal to . . . his imagination" (141–42). When Oliver comes to propose, again Virginia is struck dumb; yet he "became aware that her stillness was stronger to draw him than any speech" (169). In contrast to Virginia's wish for a voice, it is her silence that attracts Oliver; Abby Goode's voice, "high, shrill, and dominant" (145), can be heard above the crowd at the party and helps to keep her single. To be mute, then, is to marry. Thus it is ironic that this same lack of communication later destroys the Treadwells' marriage, and that Oliver makes his living as a playwright, by his words. Keeping quiet finally makes woman suffer. At the end of the novel, Virginia, despairing and isolated, boards the southbound train alone in New York and sits "speechless, inert, unseeing," almost like the corpse she wishes she were (476). On the other hand, Abby Goode grows into energetic womanhood to marry—apparently happily—in her forties.

Certainly Glasgow personally remained highly conscious of and, for the most part, faithful to her region's definition of womanhood. She modeled her life after her mother's; when she died, even her room was arranged like her mother's. The entertaining that became a hallmark of her home in Richmond came from the tradition of southern hostesses; even in so apparently minor a detail as makeup, she seems to have overstated rather than understated her femininity. The descriptions of her love affairs—with "Gerald," with "Harold"—tend towards the melodramatic and romanticized: she calls the chapter about "Gerald" "Miracle—Or Illusion?" and describes their first meeting this way: "One moment the world had appeared in stark outlines, colorless and unlit, and the next moment, it was flooded with radiance. I had caught that light from the glance of a stranger, and the smothered fire had flamed up from the depths."[16] The relationship seems quite similar to the early love of Virginia and Oliver Treadwell in *Virginia*, a love Glasgow intentionally romanticized in passages like this: "His look made the honeysuckle-trellis, the yellow lanterns, and the sky, with its few soft stars, go round like coloured balls before her eyes. The world melted away from her . . . as if she had escaped from the control of ordinary phenomena and stood in a blissful pause beyond time and eternity. It was the supreme moment of love" (140). That romance reappears in *Life and Gabriella* "under a yellow lantern, with the glow in his eyes, and a dreamy waltz floating from the arbour of roses at the end of the garden."[17] And it was a quarrel with "Harold" that led Glasgow to take an overdose of sleeping pills. Virginia, too, is tempted to suicide over the loss of love; both are fundamentally romantic reactions.

Perhaps this clinging in Ellen Glasgow to elements of the tradition she otherwise despised helps to explain both the patterns of female characterization in her novels and the half-committed feminism of her nonfiction. For, although Glasgow's time and place could produce a Mary Johnston and her *Hagar*, it also was an environment in which, according to Godbold, "young ladies still were expected to endure a useless and unhappy life."[18] Ellen Glasgow herself had attended a school that resembled Miss Priscilla Batte's academy against reality, so ironically described in *Virginia*: "[Miss Priscilla Batte's] education was founded upon the simple theory that the less a girl knew about life, the better prepared she would be to contend with it. Knowledge of any sort (except the rudiments of reading and writing, the geography of countries she would never visit, and the dates of battles in ancient history) was kept from her as rigorously as if it contained the germs of a contagious disease. . . . To solidify the forces of mind into the inherited mould of fixed beliefs was . . . to achieve the definite end of all education" (20). Thus when it came to the "crowning unreality" of the southern tradition, the southern lady, Glasgow came closest to her most personal material—and, perhaps, never really resolved it in fiction or in fact.

In fiction, her heroines have been the occasion for quite a lot of critical skepticism. James Branch Cabell, her long-time friend, with some sarcasm called her entire opus "The Tragedy of Everywoman, As It was Lately Enacted In The Commonwealth of Virginia."[19] Louis Rubin points out that Cabell thought she was "a Virginia gentlewoman . . . and she wrote and thought like a Virginia gentlewoman—which is to say, with more than a little romance and sentimentality about her."[20] Elsewhere, Cabell said:

> You will note that almost always, after finishing any book by
> Ellen Glasgow, what remains in memory is the depiction
> of one or another woman whose life was controlled and
> trammeled and distorted, if not actually wrecked, by the
> amenities and the higher ideals of Southern civilization. The
> odd part of this is that it so often seems a result unplanned by
> the author, and more often than not, a result which by no
> system of logic could result from the formal "story" of the
> book. It is merely that, from the first, Ellen Glasgow has
> depicted women, and in some sort all women, as the pre-
> destined victim of male chivalry.[21]

Though Cabell's description of his marriage to Priscilla Shepherd (re-
hearsing as it does so closely the characterization of Virginia and Oliver) reinforces one's sense that he may have lacked insight on a sensitive point, Cabell does not differ except in breadth and simplification
from what some other critics have said. Louis D. Rubin, Jr., hit the
same trail in *No Place on Earth*, when he said Ellen Glasgow "generally
depicted life through the eyes of a highly feminine, subjective perci-
pient, one who had indeed suffered as a woman and whose work was
written in large measure out of that suffering and took much of its character from it." Yet he goes too far when he suggests that "the valuation
given to persons and events by the novelist is so heavily freighted with
the writer's private feminine desires and needs that the reader may find
it all but impossible to accept Miss Glasgow's version of experience."[22]
For the problem is not her "private feminine" version of experience—it
is a version shared by other writers and a large percentage of her readers—but her occasional failure to use that version as a method for analysis, as did Mary Johnston.

Critics have noted that some of Glasgow's female characters tend to
take on dimensions disproportionate to their apparent function in the
conscious design of her novels. Others have observed that there is rarely
a satisfying marriage in Glasgow's novels; moreover, often the women
who are depicted as self-sufficient and independent become, some argue, finally cold and hard, taking satisfaction in their revenge upon
men. Moreover, add Glasgow's critics, the male characters—who say,
in novel after novel, that they wish their perfect southern lady wives
were not so perfect—are themselves imperfectly conceived, sometimes
wooden, often contrived. Marie Fletcher pointed out in her 1963 dissertation that even the women who rebel do so not by thought but by "sensibility."[23] It seems reasonable to suggest that, in Glasgow's otherwise
quite sensible protest against the female practice of staking life on the

single emotion of love, she still retained an obsession with that emotion. Clearly very few of her characters end up being women who, like Gabriella, are both sensuous and sensible, capable of loving and thinking, of dependence and independence. Those few, in *Virginia*, do not take center stage. And even Gabriella, at the end of her story, chooses to surrender, in the old-fashioned way, to a man she believes is superior.

On the other hand, Glasgow also founded the Virginia Equal Suffrage League, was fascinated by Henrik Ibsen, and wrote on feminism for the New York *Times*. At least two critics have examined her as a feminist, neither persuasively. In *The Faith of Our Feminists*, Josephine Jessup rather simplistically argues that Glasgow's "mission was to magnify women."[24] And in a more recent article, "Ellen Glasgow as Feminist," Monique Parent Frazée, apparently setting aside Ben O'Hara in *Life and Gabriella*, claims that Glasgow, "like the radical feminists . . . tends to deny the existence of the species" of what Frazée calls "true men." Frazée adds that in Glasgow's insufficient male characters "we face a bias common to most women novelists, even more flagrant with feminists, this more or less conscious determination to belittle man in order to magnify woman."[25]

A brief look at Glasgow's New York *Times* article should help to clarify her position. The article concentrates primarily on literature by men about women. Tracing the "feminine ideal" from *Clarissa* to Thomas Hardy, Glasgow finds that Richardson's title character "belongs not only to the evolving novel, but to the evolving masculine ideal of woman."[26] Even "so great a writer as Thackeray went to life for his heroes and to the Victorian pattern of femininity for his heroines"; only the old, ugly, or wicked women in Dickens are alive, she says, and that is because they "cease to be valued as witnesses of the achievements of others" (656). Other characteristics of that ideal heroine include passivity and the hatred of change: "she lived for man, and failing this, she died for man" (656). Once the ideal had been formulated by men, women adopted it; by now, Glasgow contends, ages of "false thinking" have made woman think falsely, too, for "she has denied her own humanity so long and so earnestly that she has come at last almost to believe in the truth of her denial" (656).

To explain the invention and perpetuation of the myths of womanhood, Glasgow turns to a form of evolutionism. Shifts in sex roles, first from the matriarchy to the patriarchy, and now into equality, have been nature's way to preserve the race. Man therefore is not "a conscious tyrant but . . . a victim to the conditions of social evolution," just as woman has been, and the mistake of male novelists has been to treat women as the sole exceptions to the "natural" "law of development" (656).

The new feminism, because its "hunger for freedom" is "bound up with the imperative striving for life" (657), is natural. Yet in feminism, which she defines as "a revolt from a pretense of being . . . a struggle for the liberation of personality" (656), Glasgow sees dangers. Although it is good that "the world . . . has outgrown the belief that the worship of a dissolute husband is an exalted occupation for an immortal soul," it would not be good for women to become now "priggish," for "the irritating assumption of woman's moral superiority to man. . . . sounds out of place, though not without humor, on a woman's lips" (656). In this, Glasgow is reminiscent of Kate Chopin's satire of the Miss McEnderses of the nation. The position against moralistic womanhood appears in *Life and Gabriella* as well. Like Chopin in another respect, Glasgow urges neither sex to reject the other, for "just in measure as the sexes fall away from love and understanding of each other do they fall away from life into the futility of personal ends" (657; here Glasgow quotes from Catherine Gallichan's *The Truth About Women*).

For the future, she urges that woman be freed from her old self; thus a "womanhood so free, so active, so conquering" may develop that *woman* will gain an entirely new meaning. The next period may therefore be one of neither the mother nor the father, but of a spiritual force that will simultaneously uplift women and place both sexes together in the home *and* "in the larger home of the State" (657). The most important specific element in traditional womanhood, says Glasgow, is female passivity; history reveals a correlation between that passivity and man's need for a passive woman, but since man no longer needs a passive woman, she believes that this quality will die off, presumably like the appendix.

Critics of Glasgow have usually seen her feminism as temporary, "spiritual," and apolitical, and her article "Feminism" is indeed nonpolitical in tone or content. Yet it is remarkably thorough and consistent; as literary analysis it anticipates contemporary analyses and themes. Written in 1913—the same year Glasgow embalmed and enshrined the southern lady in *Virginia*—it reflects many of the novel's concerns. And it shows clearly that Glasgow sees an important connection between a writer's sex and his or her artistic vision.

It is finally in her own artistic vision and her memoir that we must seek Ellen Glasgow's most profound statement on being southern and a lady; she saw herself not as an activist or an essayist but as an artist. Glasgow saw imaginative writing as a series of raids on the inarticulate inner self. Hence, despite her realism, Glasgow's primary commitment was to a subjective truth. "I was never a pure romancer any more than I was a pure realist," she said; she called herself a "verist" since "the whole truth must embrace the interior world as well as external appearances" (*ACM*, 27–28). Thus one primary function of art for Glasgow was to force herself to articulate her self, to tell her own story.

In her revision of "One Way to Write Novels" for *A Certain Measure*, Glasgow commented upon the subjectivity of writing: "Because of some natural inability to observe and record instead of create, I have never used an actual scene until the impression it left had sifted down into imagined surroundings . . . [living] values must be drawn directly from the imagination and indirectly, if at all, from experience" (*ACM*, 197). "As time moves on, I still see life in beginnings, moods in conflict, and change as the only permanent law. . . . these qualities . . . are derived, in fact, more from temperament than from technique" (*ACM*, 209). But for Glasgow, the imagination, here the temperament, was profoundly affected by experience: "A novelist must write, not by taking thought alone, but with every cell of his being, that nothing can occur to him that may not sooner or later find its way into his craft. Whatever happened to me or to Mammy Lizzie happened also, strangely transfigured, to Little Willie" (*ACM*, 293). The process of art becomes, then, the process of transfiguration; the figures of experience sift into the brain and down to the "creative faculty (or subconscious mind)" (*ACM*, 194) and emerge only by letting that mind be free, by leaving it alone. Glasgow said that when she "tried to invent, rather than subconsciously create, a theme or a character, invariably the effort has resulted in failure. These are the anemic offspring of the brain, not children of my complete being; and a brood whom I would wish, were it possible, to disinherit" (*ACM*, 194). Elsewhere, Glasgow called the process "intuition," even "a state of immersion" in which characters became "more real to me than acquaintances in the flesh" (*ACM*, 205).

Since both her biography and her published works show that a determining element in Ellen Glasgow's mind was her own femaleness, it is not surprising to find the birth metaphor, both in the quotation above and in the following examples: "The true novel . . . is . . . an act of birth, not a device or an invention. It awaits its own time and has its own way to be born, and it cannot, by scientific methods, be pushed into the world from behind. After it is born, a separate individual, an organic structure, it obeys its own vital impulses" (*ACM*, 190). Nor does the author-mother regret this "loss" of her children: "[*They Stooped to Folly*] in company with all my other books that had gone out into the world . . . became a homeless wanderer and a stranger. It had ceased to belong to me. I might almost say that it had ceased even to interest me. The place where it had been, the place it had filled to overflowing for nearly three years, was now empty" (*ACM*, 202–203).

But it was not only her unconscious self that made Glasgow's articulation take female shapes. As can be seen in "Feminism," she consciously looked to a tradition of female writers for inspiration, if not for models. In the preface to *The Sheltered Life*, she reiterated this concern, saying about Emily Brontë that "it is doubtful if either the exposed heart of Byron or the brazen trumpet of D. H. Lawrence contained such burning realities as were hidden beneath the quiet fortitude of Emily Brontë" (*ACM*, 197). And in the preface to *They Stooped to Folly*, she added that Jane Austen was "that delicate iconoclast" (*ACM*, 232). Seeing that women novelists have something different to show the world, Glasgow ends the latter essay with an example:

> It is seldom in modern fiction that a friendship between two women, especially a pure and unselfish friendship, with both women loving the same man, has assumed a prominent place. Although such an association appears to be not uncommon in life, the novelist, since he is usually a man, has found the relationship to be deficient alike in the excitement of sex and the masculine drama of action. But more and more . . . women are coming to understand their interdependence as human beings; and without an example of this, a picture of our time . . . would be wanting in complete veracity. (*ACM*, 245)

Just as she felt certain experiences to be specifically within the purview of the woman writer, so she believed (as she stated in "Feminism") that the notion that the works of men writers are universal in meaning, particularly when they speak about women, is foolish. As late as 1938, Glasgow noted that the female image in novels written by men after World War I showed the same simplifying tendency as before, but that the later novels depicted an opposite, and darker, side of the feminine character: "In a large majority of post-war novels [by men], a woman or two women or even three women thrust themselves between almost every male character and some bright particular moon for which he is crying" (*ACM*, 233). Men writers still, she claimed, seemed to agree that "while man desires more than woman, woman desires only more of man" (*ACM*, 234). It is no surprise that, given Glasgow's commitment to her sex, both conscious and unconscious, and given her jibes at men's "realism," male writers—and critics—would take offense. Hence James Branch Cabell interpreted her search for "fame and daily applause" to be "an atoning for the normal pleasures and the normal ties and the normal contacts with her fellow beings which circumstances had denied her," an atoning that she "tacitly and sullenly demanded of heaven."[27] What is expected of men—success—is abnormal for Glasgow, according to Cabell.

To be a southern writer added to the complexity of Glasgow's commitment to womankind. For if, as Glasgow suggests, the problems of the southern writer have to do with moving beyond feeling and regional chauvinism to develop the powers of observation, analysis, and detachment, on the one hand, and with, on the other hand, imagining actively and remaining faithful to one's subjective vision instead of passively flowing with tradition (literary or otherwise), then the problems for a southern woman writer are compounded. Born to become a southern lady, the southern woman who writes has been taught that emotion, not thought, is feminine; that regional patriotism, not universalism, is moral; that passivity, not active assertion, is ladylike; and that she should sacrifice her subjective self to uphold tradition. Most of all, she has been taught by southern tradition that she, as a southern lady, is its finest flower: thus to attack tradition is suicidal. To such an inarticulate woman of the South, Virginia Pendleton Treadwell, Ellen Glasgow gives a momentary voice in *Virginia*; then she consigns her to silence. And to Gabriella Carr, southern woman in New York, she assigns the apparently impossible task of killing the flower of southern womanhood and surviving the operation.

When *Virginia* opens in 1884, Virginia Pendleton and Susan Treadwell have recently finished their schooling at Miss Priscilla Batte's Dinwiddie Academy for Young Ladies, an education based on the belief that the best preparation for a woman's life is ignorance: "Knowledge of any sort . . . was kept from [girls] as rigorously as if it contained the germs of a contagious disease" (20). Virginia, the daughter of a saintly minister, Gabriel Pendleton, and his sacrificing wife, Lucy, is a model of fragile beauty, the feminine ideal of the time. Her friend Susan, a stronger and hence less "feminine" girl, is the daughter of the town's plutocrat, miserly but determined Cyrus Treadwell, and of an embittered aristocrat, Belinda Bolingbroke Treadwell. Susan's cousin Oliver has bewitched Virginia, and she him. Oliver is young, idealistic, and artistic; he wants to write great plays and argues against his uncle's materialism.

Virginia and Oliver marry after a brief, breathless, and inarticulate courtship; to support his wife, Oliver takes a bank job from his hated uncle Cyrus, and the young couple moves to West Virginia. Through a chapter composed of Virginia's letters home to her parents, Glasgow informs the reader of Virginia's discomfort in the ill-mannered frontier town, of the conflicts in her marriage, which Virginia mentions but glosses over, and of the births of her four children, the last of whom dies an infant. After the family returns to Dinwiddie, Oliver loses his early idealism about playwriting. His first, honest work is performed in New

York and fails; Virginia goes to New York in a misguided belief that she can help him, and Oliver goes back to work for the bank. By this time, Virginia is losing what Oliver thinks are her most essential possessions: her youth and her beauty. But she does not care, nor is she as aware of her loss as Oliver is, for she has directed all her energy into the children and can comprehend neither Oliver's moodiness nor his waning interest in her. Similarly, he neither understands nor approves the changes in Virginia.

While working in Dinwiddie, Oliver takes up fox hunting, riding with Virginia's old rival Abby Goode. Not until her mother insists that the neighbors are gossiping about Oliver's rides with Abby does Virginia decide to do something; then, taking up the sport again, she rides, wins the fox tail, and regains Oliver's admiration—but feels the victory worthless. She plans a weekend trip with Oliver and Abby; then, suspecting that her four-year-old son Harry is sick, she stays at home when they leave. His illness, it turns out, is diphtheria, and Virginia nurses him through it, castigating herself for even considering leaving and offering her life to God if He will only save Harry.

Oliver determines that he will write plays that sell, even if he thinks they are trash, and, true to his Treadwell genes, he succeeds. Now a famous playwright, he spends most of the year in New York. Virginia's father dies, simply and heroically. A black man, grandson of one of Gabriel's former slaves, has been accused of touching a white woman; three white men are harassing him. Gabriel goes into the fray and dies defending him. Only months later, Lucy Pendleton, her reason for living and her home (the rectory) gone, quietly fades into a death she has longed for. The children are grown, and Virginia is left virtually alone.

Virginia is finally persuaded to go to New York for the opening of one of Oliver's plays. There, she discovers that her Dinwiddie fashions are hopelessly out of style. Her childish excitement in the city is destroyed by the accidental discovery that Oliver is in love with his leading actress, Margaret Oldcastle. Virginia goes to confront her, but, too much a lady, cannot reveal her feelings. Her world crumbled, she comes home on the train in a state approaching insanity, and once home she rarely leaves the house. Back in Dinwiddie, it seems she will now live entirely with despair: one of her daughters has married a widower and moved away; the other, a student at Bryn Mawr, is turning into an intellectual and a reformer; Harry is in England; and Oliver has asked for his freedom. On a desperate impulse, Virginia goes to New York a third time, believing that if Oliver sees her, he will know that he still loves her. She goes to his hotel and stands in front of it so long that someone finally asks her what she wants. She turns, goes back to the train, and "speechless, inert, unseeing" (476), comes home to death-in-life. Yet in the last line of the novel, she seems to be "saved": Harry sends a telegram saying he is coming home to her.

In her preface to the novel, written years later, Ellen Glasgow remarked that the tone of the novel had begun as ironic and then, as her sympathy for Virginia grew, become more and more compassionate. She described the conflict in the story as that between Virginia's "pure selflessness" and the world's "self-interest" (ACM, 83) and elsewhere as that between tradition, or a "dream," and the present, or reality. Glasgow claimed that in the novel she demonstrated, not without regret, that "change only endures, and the perfect mould must be broken" (ACM, 91). The novelist as realist spoke more wisely than the critic, however; for Glasgow shows clearly in her fiction that Virginia's selflessness is not absolutely pure and that the "perfect" mould breaks not by anyone's choice but because of its own imperfections. Though Virginia indeed perfectly satisfies the idea of womanhood endorsed by her culture, that idea contains the seeds of its own destruction.

On the other hand, Glasgow as a romantic novelist tries in *Virginia* to make, of the very ideal she realistically rejects, a mode for growth and heroism. Glasgow's effort to redeem her central character within the limits she has set for her is joined with an effort to redeem romanticism itself. The idealism of Dinwiddie society takes several forms, one of which is the view that the imagination can triumph over material circumstance, if only by ignoring it. At best, though,—for example, in love—the imagination can find the larger world in the individual case through symbolism. In Glasgow's society, women are particularly well equipped for this romantic feat. Their world is already narrow; they look out of windows and travel only to shop at the old slave market. They already see, in their homes, the universe. Although Glasgow as realist sees such narrowness of vision to be false and dangerous, she refuses to condemn it utterly. Instead, she grants to such narrowness an intensity, a concentration, that can under great pressure permit insight, the growth of character, heroic actions, and the birth of genuine symbols rather than illusory fictions.

Finally, however, Glasgow rejects romanticism both as a literary form and as a social and personal stance. No matter how strongly Virginia believes in the significance of specifics as symbols—Gabriel's death, Oliver's betrayal—they make no difference to the world of the novel. More frequently, characters use the imagination only to avoid reality, in what Glasgow called "evasive idealism." Instead, Glasgow gives to forces of natural and social evolution the final power to shape reality.

Thus, in the difference between the women who survive and are part of the life force, and those who do not and are not, lies the difference between a society based on romanticism and one based on Glasgow's form of realism.

Those women who adhere to traditions for women, the traditions that formed the heart of the old romantic South, by no means act out consistently the role they voice. That role breaks up the romantic equation of truth, beauty, and goodness: whereas beauty and goodness are valued, truth is not. "To acknowledge an evil is . . . to countenance its existence," maintains one character; thus "a pretty sham has a more intimate relation to morality than has an ugly truth." Since truth is not valued, the perpetrators of "evasive idealism" do not even know that they are being untruthful; in fact, "they called the mental process by which they distorted reality, 'taking a true view of life'" (32). Since women are the South's symbol of itself, as human beings they are praised for physical beauty and the Christian virtues of faith and sacrifice, but they are forbidden to search for truth. "A natural curiosity about the universe is the beginning of infidelity" (20), so curiosity is denied; analysis might lift the "veil of appearances" that is the Episcopal Church, so the capacity to reason is suppressed.

Although nearly all southerners in *Virginia* split truth from virtue and beauty, only southern ladies embody further the definition of beauty as one's physical self and of goodness as sexual purity. Thus the lady is vulnerable to the natural process of aging, which will fade her beauty, while at the same time she must reject the natural process of sex by spiritualizing it. Men may express their sexuality with women outside the dominant southern culture—Cyrus with the black woman Mandy, Oliver with the New York actress Margaret—and thus retain the image of their ideal southern lady.

The prescription for the woman also includes a belief in another of the "fundamental verities . . . the superiority of man" (11). Inferior herself, like the former slaves and the animals with whom she unconsciously identifies, the southern lady compensates by serving man, both literally and as his symbol for the ideal. According to Miss Priscilla Batte, "what [Oliver] needed was merely some good girl to take care of him and convert him to the Episcopal Church" (125).

Miss Priscilla Batte, Lucy Pendleton, Belinda Treadwell, and Mrs. Peachey all subscribe to the formula. Each, however, knows far more than she claims is proper for the woman to know. Miss Priscilla has the knowledge that permits her to tell when her students are moving beyond the pale of acceptable knowledge. "I wonder if she can be getting to know things?" (21) she thinks about Virginia's spirited early defense of Oliver's opinions. Lucy, Virginia's mother, also understands more than she wants her daughter ever to know. In choosing her daughter's library, "she did not honestly believe that any living man resembled the 'Heir of Radclyffe,' any more than she believed that the path of self-sacrifice leads inevitably to happiness; but there was no doubt in her mind that she advanced the cause of righteousness when she taught these sanctified fallacies to Virginia" (49). Similarly, Belinda Treadwell is fully conscious of, if petty and bitter about, the realities of her life and its contrast to her dream: she points out, for instance, that her husband hasn't spoken to her unless he had to for twenty years. Finally, the last of the old guard, Mrs. Peachey, whose husband lives on alcohol and memories of war heroism, is perfectly aware of what she is doing; she manipulates her husband by "pretending to let him have his way" (112) and handles even Cyrus Treadwell through coquetry. Thus, none of these women is as genuinely ignorant as is Virginia.

Moreover, only one of these four—Lucy Pendleton—actually serves a man in a traditional and happy marriage. Mrs. Peachey is the real head of her household; Miss Priscilla, despite her *Beulah*-style matchmaking, never marries at all; and "the unkempt, slack figure" of Belinda Treadwell, "with her bitter eyes and her sagging skirt, pass[es] perpetually, under the flickering gas-jet, up and down the dimly-lighted staircase" of her house-cage (162).

It is not surprising to find that these "model" women have divided selves. Lucy Pendleton not only does her housework before dawn; she also has a "fine invincible blade in the depths of her being [that] had never surrendered" (36). Similarly, Belinda shows Oliver "an inner life as intense, as real, as acutely personal as his own," destroying (temporarily) his "delusion that it is possible for a woman by mere virtue of being a woman to suffer in sweetness and silence" (104). Consistent with the pattern, the black woman Mandy, too—described usually as a tamed animal—has two selves. Her cry "of an animal in mortal pain" at Cyrus' refusal to help their illegitimate son is "strangled by that dulled weight of usage beneath which the primal impulse in her was crushed back into silence" (335). She reverts immediately to her "normal" self-deprecating manner, as Edna did when Robert first left her, and as Marcélite did when she lost Monsieur Motte.

Despite their knowledge, these women ignore certain very important realities in the process of "evasive idealism." One of those realities is history. Both Miss Priscilla and Lucy Pendleton are explicitly characterized as lacking any sense that they are within, not outside, history. So, too, Virginia ignores her mother's historical precedent.

Their evasive idealism serves most of all to permit these women to avoid seeing the reality of their own lives as women; since they are the symbols of tradition, they must ignore history. Looking down at the former slave market, where they shop, the true southern woman sees not "an overladen mule with a sore shoulder . . . straining painfully under the lash," but "the most interesting street in the world, filled with the most interesting people, who drove happy animals that enjoyed their servitude and needed the sound of the lash to add cheer and liveliness to their labours. Never had the Pendleton idealism achieved a more absolute triumph over the actuality" (60). Glasgow's ironic touch is sure: in case we missed the connection between women, animals, and slaves, she has Oliver first speak to Virginia at the slave market—"the last place on earth where I expected to find you" (64), he says. But Oliver, blinded by his need for the ideal, learns nothing; neither do the women themselves. On only one occasion, Lucy doubts the value of what she is teaching her daughter to be. Suspecting that her own happiness was largely a product of Gabriel's idiosyncratic goodness and innocence, she wonders whether she had been wise in telling Virginia to "sacrifice herself" for Oliver. After all, Gabriel has reciprocated Lucy's sacrifices. Yet the doubt "could not struggle against her inherited belief in the Pauline measure of her sex" (182).

More of the female characters in *Virginia* deviate from the norm of evasive idealism than follow it, however. Although Frederick McDowell suggests that the "broadened horizons of Virginia's children . . . indicate that considerable progress has been made by the early twentieth century in the emancipation of women,"[28] there is ample evidence that women of both Virginia's and her mother's generation could lead satisfying lives apart from the prescription. Miss Willy, her mother's and Virginia's seamstress, skips "for pure joy" in the spring, despite—perhaps because of—her lack of a husband and family to sacrifice herself to, and despite, or because of, her need to support herself (188). Late in the novel, Virginia envies her, saying, "She's never had anything in her life, and yet she is so much happier than some people who have had everything" (413); still later, the narrator explains Miss Willy's happiness: "Failing love, she had filled her life with an inextinguishable *curiosity*; and this passion, being independent of the desires of others, was proof alike against disillusionment and the destructive process of time" (421, my emphasis). Mrs. Payson in West Virginia, who, like Miss Willy, is older than Virginia, also leads a satisfying life outside convention. Though she was educated in the North, wears bright colors, speaks for women's rights, and is "horsey," her husband, while officially disapproving of her, actually adores her (199). Oliver, too, likes her; even Virginia finds her a true friend when she is in labor with her first child. Abby

Goode, less flatteringly characterized as an unintelligent scatterbrain, man-crazy, loud, coarse, and dominant, mellows as the novel continues, so that her appearance in the fox-hunting episode is less that of a man-chasing vixen than of a woman having a good time. And, in what the novel seems to endorse as a generally positive move, she "finally" gets married. Margaret Oldcastle, the serious one of this pair of rivals for Oliver's attention, is depicted almost entirely positively. She has "scarcely a beautiful face, but in its glowing intelligence, it was the face of a woman of power. . . . The woman was not a pretty doll; she was not a voluptuous enchantress; the coquetry of the one and the flesh of the other were missing. . . . She had come out of poverty not by the easy steps of managers' favours, but by hard work, self-denial, and discipline" (402). When Virginia visits her, Margaret Oldcastle opens the window in February to get some sun; she embodies the youth, not of the body, but of the spirit; she is a "free woman" (442). Yet Margaret Oldcastle's "freedom, like that of man, had been built upon the strewn bodies of the weaker. . . . she was one with evolution and with the resistless principle of change" (442). Underlining the ambiguity of her depiction of Oldcastle, Glasgow further makes her the heroine not of her own but of Oliver's plays—speaking, but in his words. And those words are, in his eyes, worthless. It is only her acting, he thinks, that redeems his plays. The pattern sounds familiar: the southern lady after the war was the central redemptive symbol for the outdated drama of the South.

The most fully developed "free woman" in the novel is a southerner, Susan Treadwell. She is intelligent and intellectual. In an early outline for the novel, Glasgow had her "even read[ing] Browning for pleasure."[29] Oliver senses that she would make a good wife but can't fall in love with her; she lacks ideal physical beauty, the sine qua non for the southern gentleman. Glasgow lets Susan sacrifice the hope of her life, college, to care for her sick mother; she postpones her marriage to John Henry for the same reason. Moreover, John Henry, though he is a good man, is not nearly as intelligent as Susan. After giving up so much, Susan is finally rewarded by an "abundant life" with a happy family and an existence that is not absorbed by caring for it. In her second preliminary outline, Glasgow explained that "Sue, with her six children, had kept her youth and her interests; but then, Sue had never given herself—The inviobility [sic] of her soul had preserved the freshness of her body—"[30] This sounds remarkably like Edna Pontellier, who would give her life for her children, but would not give herself.[31] Interestingly, the verb *want* is consistently applied to Susan and rarely to the other women. And, like Beulah and Edna, Susan is associated with horses:

Oliver thinks "she looked as if she could ride life like a horse, could master and tame it and break it to the bridle" (93).

All of these deviating women, regardless of their final life-styles, and despite Glasgow's equivocation, share a commitment to life, a refusal to be formed by a mould, a fighting spirit. Like the women who prescribe the traditional role, they think on their own; unlike them, though, they carry their reasoning through to logical conclusions: Susan warns Virginia, for instance, not to spoil Oliver. Unlike the traditional women, too, their minds are not always and only on men. Even Abby enjoys the hunt for its own merits. Moreover, at least Susan sees herself in history, the "enigma of time" (409). Finally, all eventually reject the belief that they should sacrifice themselves in the service of others, though, as we saw with both Margaret and Susan, Glasgow retains the notion of sacrifice of other sorts. Interestingly, both speaking another's words and giving up college are sacrifices of the mind.

Like the first group of women who believe in the feminine ideal, Virginia does not see herself as a creature within history (51, 177). Hence, although Virginia finds her mother's life "pathetic" (56), she is incapable of making the connections between that reality and her own dream of love. Even as a child, the virtual lack of any curiosity or sense for reality in Virginia is clear on her bookshelf; she never rejects the romantic fictions there or tries to read anything else (48–49). Thus Virginia's mind remains unanalytical and uncritical; she can never understand her husband's attitudes towards playwriting or discuss his ideas with him.

Just as Virginia's training suppresses her mind, so it represses her sensuality. When first she falls in love with Oliver, her interest is described in physical terms: "Everything about him, his smile, his clothes, the way he held his head and brushed his hair straight back from his forehead, his manner of reclining with a slight slouch on the seat of the cart, the picturesque blue dotted tie he wore, his hands, his way of bowing, the red-brown of his face, and above all the eager, impetuous look in his dark eyes—these things possessed a glowing interest which irradiated a delicious excitement over the bare round of living" (29). Yet Virginia is unaware of her own erotic interest in Oliver: "She was as ignorant that she offered herself to him with her velvet softness, with the glow in her eyes, with her quivering lips, as the flower is that it allures the bee by its perfume" (65). Nevertheless, the "age-long [women's] dissatisfaction with the physical end of love" (144) prevails; though indirectly, we learn that she and Oliver no longer make love.

Despite this "unnatural" eventuality, Virginia's life is consistently described in metaphors of nature. Yet they reflect a special sort of nature;

she is compared to a rose, product of years of human biological engi-
neering, and to a canary, caged to amuse human beings. Thus Virginia
represents nature radically shaped by civilization. Moreover, she can
accept only the pleasant elements of nature; Glasgow changed a rau-
cous parrot to a canary for the final version of the novel. Virginia tries to
immobilize nature to keep it perfect. For instance, she cannot admit
that Oliver is still growing—that would make him imperfect—so she
simply declares him, in her mind, perfect, rejecting her mother's and
Susan's insights into his character. She keeps her hair always in the
style she wore as a girl. And since it is the past for her that is perfect,
she hopes the paulownias in the rectory garden, symbols of an earlier
age, are never cut down, because she likes to snuggle in their roots
(24–25). Finally, Virginia's response to the canary in Miss Priscilla's
cage shows the lack of development in her character. Virginia first
gazes at the bird, thoughtfully (15) but with no insight; next Miss Priscilla consciously justifies putting women in a "cage"; and finally Virginia wants to be a "wounded bird" (473). Described as "Eve" early in
the novel (47), Virginia wants to stay in an eternally springlike Eden;
her necessary aging, then, is a fall from grace, unlike Susan's growth
into maturity.

   Yet the times when Virginia rebels against her role are also linked
with nature. While she and Oliver are courting, she once throws the
rose in her hair onto the ground, in a gesture that implies her anger at
Oliver—and her rejection of the season and the role the rose signifies.
When, as a married woman, she breaks her sacrificial habits to buy
some blue silk for herself, it is "hyacinth-blue," like her eyes (290). And
when her son is sick, she cries "like a savage" (320) in a clear allusion
to the savage cry of the black woman Mandy. Each of her rebellions
against the way things are is a protest of nature-as-growth against her
imposition upon nature of an illusory eternal spring.

   Yet Virginia finally sacrifices herself to Margaret Oldcastle, who represents the very principle of natural growth. "Though [Virginia] was
wounded to the death, she could not revolt, could not shriek out in her
agony, could not break through that gentle yet invincible reticence
which she had won from the past" (450). Thus submitting her questioning mind to the Episcopal Church and her natural body to the eternal virginity of spring, Virginia has little self left. At the end of the novel,
when even that last element of the female prescription—devotion to a
superior man—is stripped from her, there is virtually no self left. She
goes nearly mad; she can no longer distinguish subject from object,
projects her feelings without control onto the world, and loses feeling,
sensation, even the instinct for food.

Nevertheless, Virginia has had moments of insight. Those moments are associated with the eruption within her of a deeper sort of "nature," a nature that is both sexual and aggressive. It is important to remember that she is attracted to Oliver in the first place by his defiant mind and his appealing body; Oliver's free-thinking triggers, on several occasions, her own independent ideas, just as his sexual self awakens her own. This sort of "nature" sends Virginia into "battle." For example, when aroused by jealousy of Abby Goode, she joins the fox hunt and, her hair flowing free, conquers the fox. When Harry is sick, she fights for his life, praying "not with the humble and resigned worship of civilization, but . . . to an idol who responded only to the shedding of blood" (320). The battle for Oliver's affections teaches her that "her unselfishness had been merely selfishness cloaked [as] duty" (311). And the battle for Harry's life teaches her why her mother made "no further demands on life after the great demands had been granted her" (324).

Elsewhere, Virginia sees something of the truth about Cyrus (58), about womanhood (138–40, 288, 473), about love and unselfishness (262, 312–13, 326), about Oliver (269), and even about "the very structure of life" (442). In each instance, however, she must finally cut off or repress the process of insight. First of all, she has not been trained to analyze; the very process feels foreign and even masculine to her. She believes that to think of oneself is indiscriminately selfish; hence she must block what could be healthy introspection. Secondly, those "primitive" feelings linking aggression with insight must be curbed; she is a lady. Like the lady in Glasgow's preface (viii), she can enter only "righteous conflict"; hence she tries to make housework an "adventure" (186) and is permissibly thrilled by her first trip to New York because she is there out of duty to Oliver (249–51). And, finally, the clues she does get in those rare moments tell her that her entire life has been wasted, even destructive. Hence, when she sees that in fighting Margaret Oldcastle she is fighting life itself, she both avoids the implications and makes a statement about her vision of life by going out to buy a doll for Lucy's daughter, another act of apparent unselfishness that ironically expresses her own role.

In her truncated way, nevertheless, Virginia is quite powerful, if unconsciously so. Ellen Glasgow protested in her later preface that Virginia was not only strong, but the emblem of the eternally good and the beautiful in a changing world. However, a look at the action of the novel indicates that Virginia's power is exerted largely for harm, not good—if good is defined as growth to maturity—and that her destructiveness extends not just to herself but to her family as well. Because she sees gender roles as ahistorical and good, Virginia does not let Oliver help with housework (197) in the belief that such work is not "manly"; later, she cannot understand his lack of interest in domestic matters. From Matoaca City she writes home about Oliver's unfortunate tendency to overspend, for which she compensates by scrimping on her own funds; by the middle of the novel, she has decided that overspending is a virile quality and saving is feminine (267). She discourages Susan from going to college, just as years later she exerts all efforts to send Harry to school, never thinking that a daughter might be better suited for academic life (as indeed Jenny turns out to be). Her most dangerous power is precisely her greatest strength, the strength of love. Virginia defines those she loves as those who need her, and as one might expect, she is forced relentlessly into the position (though she is unaware of it) of *making* people need her. The best way to do this is to turn them into children, for she cannot consciously admit to other kinds of needs, for sex, imagination, or insight—needs that Margaret Oldcastle finally fills for Oliver. So she tries to infantilize Oliver himself, calling him a "boy" (287) when they are both in their forties and trying to protect him from the moral consequences of his relationship with Margaret Oldcastle (445).

The character most clearly victimized by Virginia's need to be needed is Harry, her son. The special relationship that had always existed between mother and son is enhanced by Virginia's vigil during Harry's struggle with diphtheria. As Harry grows older, writing her a letter like a lover's (411) and eventually taking over the emotional place of his father in her psyche (412), Virginia grows more possessive. She is jealous of the mention of a possible wife for Harry (409), says she will live after the Oldcastle affair only because it would "hurt Harry" should she die, and finally admits (463) that she needs Harry's love. The last line of the novel is a telegram from Harry to his mother:

> Dearest mother, I am coming home to you,
> HARRY.

It is the perfect touch of irony for the novel, but it is questionable that Glasgow intended it as irony. Although she never publicly stated her intent, there is reason to suspect that she wanted to evoke a sentimental response. For Glasgow, developing greater sympathy for Virginia as she wrote, could well have seen Harry's act as kind and even as Virginia's vengeance on his father. But the novel's logic leads to irony. Just as Virginia has been destroyed by banking all on love, just as Oliver has been spoiled by too much "love," so Harry will be stunted by the inappropriate channeling of love. Love, for Virginia, becomes a need, not a pleasure; only Harry is willing to give himself up to her need. Clearly

Glasgow wrote what she increasingly thought was a compassionate portrait of a dead ideal. Yet she found herself split, both praising and damning a single woman without ever, perhaps, finally understanding her.

Because they play less important roles in the novel, the men's characterizations often approach stereotyping. Cyrus Treadwell and Gabriel Pendleton, for instance, are almost mirror opposites. Blindly centered on the "dominant motive" of his life, financial success, Cyrus is isolated on the height of his triumph over the old traditional values. He spits into his wife's flowerbed and "live[s] only in his office" (69); he gets Mandy pregnant with Jubal, yet sees as his own blood only his nephew Oliver (158). Cyrus' contempt for women keeps him almost entirely away from them; his only soft spot comes with his memories of soldier days in the Civil War, when he and Gabriel fought together. In Glasgow's original outline, Cyrus played a much greater role; she apparently shifted her thematic interest to Virginia as the novel developed.

Cyrus likes to recall the Civil War days because they were his only moment of idealism; Gabriel likes them because they permitted him to be aggressive. Gabriel dies, in fact, fighting—again for the right—but loving the fight for itself. In that fight, Gabriel does his and Glasgow's best to redeem the romantic South. Here beauty and goodness join with truth. Reality is not evaded but seen quite clearly: the black man is suffering unjustly. Thus idealism becomes not evasive but transforming in intent. Yet Gabriel dies in the effort. More important, his heroism makes no difference to the town. Thus Glasgow shows the end of even heroic romantic idealism. More often, Gabriel presents an image opposite to Cyrus'. Like his wife a master of evasive idealism, he prefers sweet, clean, moral plays and encourages Oliver to write like this. Innocent all his life, he trusts women with a simple trust and believes without question that they are essential to prevent men from returning to savagery. Even his body is androgynous (31, 337).

Though each man seems to fill a stereotype, the rugged individual and the feminized minister, both show opposite characteristics; finally, however, Gabriel seems to stand for the old days and Cyrus embodies the new. And though their versions of southern ladyhood differ only in attitude, they do not differ in prescription. Cyrus refuses to see how his treatment has helped turn Belinda into a whining child; Gabriel never sees Lucy cleaning house before dawn. Though he represents the New South, Cyrus "stood equally for industrial advancement and domestic immobility. The body social might move, but the units that formed the body social must remain stationary" (330).

Three minor figures embody character patterns that Glasgow apparently did not find sufficiently interesting or relevant to her theme to develop more fully. Tom Peachey, for instance, finds sublimity in his memories of the Civil War and in alcohol (167); the doctor, on the other hand, retains the pattern that members of his profession have been given in most of the novels studied: he is godlike—paternal and protective, stern and supportive simultaneously—and he is, most important, there when Virginia needs him. (Oliver is off with Abby.) John Henry Pendleton, the man Glasgow designs to marry Susan, is notable for two qualities: his kindness and his flexibility. With "kind, ox-like eyes" (58), he has the sense to bend with the times, selling bathtubs for a living; despite his early gallantry of the old style (expecting neither intelligence nor responsibility from a woman), he comes to recognize the worth of both in his love for Susan. Yet his mind, as we saw, can never match hers.

Harry begins as a rogue-child, mischievous, imaginative, selfish—perhaps the truest characterization in the novel. Very early in his life, he learns to manipulate his parents; recognizing that his mother prefers him to his sisters and his father does not, he uses every opportunity to take advantage of the family pattern, driving a deeper wedge between Oliver and Virginia and finally falling victim himself to the manipulative techniques that characterize the family. From the genetic best of both Pendleton and Treadwell lines (366), he turns into a mama's boy.

But it is Oliver to whom the author directs most of her attention; one suspects that on her mind as much as the analysis of the southern lady was the analysis of the man who would marry one. It is a mark both of Oliver's strength and of his weakness that he chooses Virginia. As a youth, he defies his Treadwell blood, loving beauty over practicality; that is why he loves Virginia, not Susan. And he wants her for her goodness: "To have her always gentle, always passive, never reaching out her hand, never descending to his level, but sitting for ever aloof and colourless, waiting eternally, patient, beautiful and unwearied, to crown the victory;—this was what the conquering male in him demanded" (143).

But Oliver has the capacity to know how foolish his choice is. Early in the novel, he believes that woman's role is restrictive (65, 101) and knows that Virginia unquestioningly accepts it. Yet he never confronts the contradiction. Finally his egocentricity—what will later be his love for "comfort"—wins; Virginia will take care of his needs, and he will remain a true Treadwell, a "conquering male." But after he wins this ethereal creature, of course, what he had thought her very best qualities—unselfish waiting and serving his physical needs—are those most destructive to him. And he chooses destruction: he wants comfort over conviction, writes plays that he does not like but that will sell, and surrenders any power or status in his own home. Glasgow does not give Oliver credit for developing in insight and maturity (and hence in his expectations of women); for Oliver, Margaret's central virtues are not her intelligence and her strength, but her youth and her beauty. Appropriately for a man who combines such characteristics and embodies such conflicts, his body is androgynous (63–64).

Society conspires with nature in *Virginia* both to produce a perfect flower of womanhood and to direct her behavior. Early in the novel, Priscilla Batte opens Oliver's eyes to Virginia's infatuation. Mrs. Peachey ensures that the two will marry when she goes to Cyrus to see that Oliver will get a job. By supporting the traditional role of women, by depriving women of any privacy for selfhood, and by rejecting the realism of Oliver's first play, Dinwiddie society molds the inevitable tragedy.

One of the characteristics of "evasive idealism" and, more specifically, of the feminine ideal for women, is ignorance of the larger world; hence Lucy Pendleton, for instance, sees the world as ending at the limits of the state of Virginia. Dinwiddie as a community provides the setting for most of the novel; West Virginia and New York exist mainly as contrasting societies. Most generally, the novel seems to attack provincialism, particularly the provincialism of perfervid regionalism. When Virginia goes to West Virginia to live, she finds it impossible to accept the different life-styles and mores she finds there; though she is excited by New York, and though New York forces knowledge upon her that she might have been protected from in Dinwiddie, she ultimately rejects that community too, coming home finally, motionless, on a train heading South.

Within Dinwiddie, the subcommunities divide rather strictly along sexual, and less so along racial and class, lines. In the foreground of the novel is the community of women, who share more than separates them. Susan and Virginia have a relationship that is closer than any other in the novel (27, 189–90). The links between mothers and children transcend even those between husband and wife, as Virginia shows in her letters home and in her treatment of Harry, and as Susan shows in caring for her own benighted mother. Miss Willy is the mobile unit in a community that joins Lucy, Belinda, and the other matrons in the town. The symbolism of the slave market, where they all meet, is reinforced by the ties that exist between black and white women. Despite obvious differences in their daily lives, the parallels between women's experience and that of the slaves, as we have seen, are clear. Mandy makes it explicit when she says to Cyrus through a look: "Am I not what you have made me? Have I not been what you wanted? And yet you despise me for being the thing you made" (159). These words could as easily have been spoken by Virginia to Oliver. Marthy, the "ignorant mulatto girl," shows Virginia that the grief of women over suffering children transcends race and class: "A wave of understanding passed between [Virginia and Marthy], whom [Virginia] had always regarded as of different clay from herself. With that miraculous power of grief to level all things, she felt that the barriers of knowledge, of race . . . had melted back into the nothingness" (323). Not just mutual experience, but a shared and ironically self-destructive dream unites women into a community that transcends class and race, if sporadically. Miss Willy's "sickly, sallow-faced" assistant (178) is visibly moved by Virginia's impending wedding and wants the same dream for herself.

The community of men, though not so well developed, also exists in the novel; but it is a community based largely on the experience of the Civil War and ignorance of the female mind, rather than on any contemporary mutuality of experience and feeling. Cyrus most overtly is a man's man; he understands men but not women (163). Neither Gabriel in his trusting of females nor Oliver in his final pity for Virginia understands women well, especially the southern lady. Just as the women's expectations for other women differ to some extent from the men's, so the men in the novel share an ethos of masculinity that differs both from the ethos of womanhood and from what the women expect and want from the men. And just as the women's society incorporates black and poor women, so the male society includes blacks and the poor; Gabriel dies defending a black man against white outsiders, and Cyrus supports Oliver because he has Treadwell blood. It is no wonder, in a world so stratified by sex, that almost the only points of contact between the sexes are biological: love is, in the case of Virginia and Oliver, rosy eroticism, and children ultimately provide the only bonds between them, between Cyrus and Belinda, and even between Gabriel and Lucy.

Nor is any hope available from the larger community of the South: it is characterized largely as being unthinking (12–13), as opposing introspection because it assumes that what is secret must be evil (170), and finally as moved by neither love nor death (353). As has been seen, Virginia learns about the affair between Margaret Oldcastle and Oliver only in New York, where the people are different. Moreover, Oliver's sense of the realistic in art seems to be linked to his life abroad; his wider experience certainly permitted him to like Mrs. Payson long before Virginia did. Despite its provinciality, the world of the South is a place for southern men to work in, to roam in, to live in—even if they never get beyond its geographical or psychic boundaries. For southern

women, the world is their men: Virginia writes from West Virginia that
Oliver "is the whole world to me" (199); when the men fail, or when the
women have children, the world expands only to include those children—and other women.

In *Virginia*, Ellen Glasgow started out to define and to embalm the
southern lady of the 1880s. She ended up almost enshrining her. In the
ironic conclusion, her art told more than she seems to have known; and
in the characterization of Susan Treadwell, she seems to have been at a
loss to imagine adequately. Yet Susan, I think, is the character (with the
possible exception of Virginia's intellectual daughter Jenny) closest to
the self-perception of Ellen Glasgow herself. Glasgow wrote in 1913
that "woman has become at last not only human but articulate."[32]
Finally, however, it seems that Glasgow has become only partially
articulate.

Three years after *Virginia*, in 1916, Ellen Glasgow published her next
novel, called *Life and Gabriella*. This novel shows a southern lady rebelling, like Hagar, against her role, living in New York, working in a
hat shop, raising two children alone, and finally rejecting a southern
gentleman in favor of a brawny Irishman. The novel is rarely discussed;
it is not considered one of Glasgow's important works. Yet it forms a perfect companion for *Virginia*, paralleling, reversing, developing, and, in
a central and probably unintentional way, reinforcing the patterns in
Virginia.

The parallels are striking. Both novels begin with an old-fashioned
southern romance. Even the setting is the same: the garden at night, a
face beneath a yellow lantern, a trellis of flowers, and music (252). The
lovers marry, bear children, and grow apart; the husband, through an
affair with another woman, breaks up the marriage. In both, the relationship between mother and son takes on special depth. Both are set in
Virginia and New York; both end with significant train rides. In both,
metaphors from nature and from the military are central. Thematically,
both novels concern romance and realism, ideals and facts: *Virginia*'s
three sections are "The Dream," "The Reality," and "The Adjustment,"
while *Life and Gabriella* is divided into "The Age of Faith" and "The Age
of Knowledge." Both concern the relationship between southern tradition and contemporary business and industrial "progress." And both
novels develop these themes by centering on the question of gender
and love.

Yet in *Life and Gabriella*, almost every element that parallels *Virginia*
is turned inside out or upside down. Here, the marital rift occurs, not at
the end, but at the beginning of the story. Here the woman survives

while the man destroys himself. Mother and son are saved from mutual idolatry. Here the setting—for most of the novel and for eighteen years after the marriage—is in New York; the train ride South, at the end, never takes place. Nature—still expressed in images of flowers and birds—expands to include the wilderness, desert, mountain, and sea. In this novel, Glasgow finds romanticism and realism not to be mutually exclusive, but inclusive, since reality includes romantic possibilities. Similarly, the future is envisioned optimistically as a blend of the best of southern love of nature, northern love of business, and western directness and simplicity. And, where *Virginia* told the story of a southern lady, the attainment of an ideal, *Life and Gabriella* tells the story of a southern woman who tries to root out final traces of that ideal from her inner self. Finally, the focus of this novel shifts from the conflict between ideal and real woman to that between ideal and real man, as Gabriella searches for the man to equal her emergent self.

Gabriella Carr, who inherits Virginia's story, is ten years younger than her prototype and has, moreover, a "vein of iron," inherited from her Berkeley ancestors—inborn strength, independence, and moral courage—and a talent for design and color. In the first scene, her sister Jane, a sentimental heroine, has run home to her mother from her drinking and philandering husband. Gabriella resolves to go to work in a local clothing store, Brandywine's, for Jane's children's sake; the sacrifice appeals to her, she is "sick of being dependent" (28), and she wants money, for her family is postwar poor.

Over the family's objections—they prefer that she teach or sew— Gabriella takes the job and thereby enters the battle against "decay and inertia" (75) that will continue throughout her life. She asserts her vitality in yet another way, by breaking off a two-year engagement to the perfect southern gentleman Arthur Peyton and marrying instead the object of her sexual passion, George Fowler. For Gabriella, the excitement of sexuality is that of surrender; elevating her physical attraction into the ideal of love, she finds herself willingly surrendering to George in other areas of their life as well.

The couple soon settle, against Gabriella's will (she wants a separate apartment), with George's parents, who are Virginians in New York. George soon reveals himself to be incompetent, unintelligent, spoiled, and irresponsible. Two children, Fanny and little Archibald, are born while the two "still made love," though "they had ceased . . . to make conversation" (126). Then George comes home very drunk one evening and (apparently) rapes Gabriella; her disgust destroys the last of his appeal for her. Months later, he takes up publicly with an old school friend of Gabriella's, Florrie Spencer. In one crucial day, his father throws

2

George out of the house, loses his fortune, and dies. Mrs. Fowler goes home to the South to live, George vanishes, and Gabriella is left alone with her two children, "fatherless, impoverished, and unprotected, dependent on her untried labour for their lives and their happiness" (273).

Freed from the bonds of marriage, the "net of passion" (180), and the fulltime demands of babies now that hers are older, Gabriella feels a release of energy and excitement. She never goes home to Virginia; instead, she takes rooms on the West Side near Columbus Avenue, sets up a household with the help of her Richmond seamstress, Miss Polly, and wins herself a position at Madame Dinard's fashionable clothing and millinery shop. Simultaneously, she nurtures the memory of Arthur Peyton's perfect love for her. Originating in her desperate need to believe at least one man could love her, the Dream soon becomes for her a symbol of all that is good and beautiful (if not true) about the South and the past.

Gabriella brings both good business sense (one remembers the biographer's comments about Glasgow's own competence and competitiveness) and honesty to her work, a profession that trades in self-deception and camouflage; she makes herself, over the years, so indispensable as to be Madame Dinard's logical successor.

After ten years, the children are adolescents: Fanny is a flighty, shallow beauty like her father, and Archibald a strange, dark child with sensitive eyes and a love for poetry—and football. The three of them (with Miss Polly) move to a house on West Twenty-Third Street which, with its flowers and old-fashioned façade, reminds the two women of Richmond. Gabriella, who has grown steadily away from tradition, still feels she has missed the "best of life" (367). Living downstairs is a big, red-headed Irishman, Ben O'Hara, whose depth of character, Gabriella slowly finds, more than compensates for his lack of culture and education. Ben, who was born in a cellar and has made millions out West, persuades Gabriella to relinquish her protective hold on her son, introduces Archibald to a man's world, and inspires in Gabriella a vision of national community that shows her as a part of, not above, humanity—Italians, Jews, rich and poor. One winter night, George reappears, drunk, violent, and dying of pneumonia. Gabriella courageously takes him in, but then summons O'Hara, who takes "everything . . . out of her hands—everything" (446).

Gabriella still retains one illusion: that she thoroughly understands men. As a result, she plays a somewhat flirtatious and disingenuous role, at times, with Ben. Thus when, at a moment that seems appropriate to him, Ben kisses her "against her will and without warning," she responds as if to an insult, with a more profound anger than she has ever felt. She tells him she loves Arthur, her Dream; Ben leaves, and—making a gesture "as of one escaping from bondage"—Gabriella decides to return to Richmond for the first time in eighteen years.

In Richmond (which is now in the thrall of modernization and "progress") she finds Arthur handsomer than ever but drained of energy and mobility. She spurns his carefully phrased suggestion that they begin their romance again, realizing that she is "in love not with a dream, but with a fact, that she is in love not with Arthur, but with O'Hara" (521). She feels she must choose "without reserve or evasion" (524). So she returns to New York, where she faces her final conflict: the lady in her prefers to wait for Ben to come to her, but the woman knows that unless she races to the train station where he is about to leave New York, he will be lost forever. At the station, she tells him simply and directly, "I came back to you. I wanted you." He asks, "And you'll marry me now—to-morrow?" Seeing this as the "ultimate test," she whispers, "But the children?" and he laughs, "Oh, the children are always there. We're not quitters." She stretches out her hands, watches the "light break on his face," and tells him she'll "come with you now—anywhere—toward the future" (529).

Authorial assertions to the contrary, the light that breaks on Ben O'Hara's face is very like the light that broke on Guy Hartwell's. And Gabriella—deprived of help, friends, and money, alone in the world—has made it on her own much as Beulah did before she, too, won the right to submit to a fine, strong man. Yet this is the novel about which Ellen Glasgow said, "The present work is concerned with woman as a reality; and it is concerned, too, with the complete and final departure from that great Victorian tradition" (ACM, 97). But more interesting and more important than the fact that the novel ends as sentimentally as the most Victorian of novels is the manner in which Glasgow defined and resolved the problems raised in it. Glasgow places her protagonist into a professional all-female world, a subculture of women, as an alternative to returning her to the dying South. Then, by contrast, she develops a hero who is all male, part of a world entirely alien to Gabriella. The confrontation results not in mutual reeducation or equality—as both at least once hope it will—but in Gabriella's loss of power and willing capitulation to Ben's masculine ethos. Thus Glasgow has her protagonist, who has "disciplined her mind as well as her body to firmness and elasticity of fiber" (334), who has independently grown away from stultifying traditions, revert to what Glasgow elsewhere called ironically the finest act of the southern lady, devotion to a superior man. And Gabriella does this, in a final irony, out of precisely her profound desire not to be a southern lady. Glasgow herself suggested that she knew she had failed to exorcise the lady when she remembered her "old friend, James Lane Allen, dissenting across the years: 'Would any Southern lady have so far forgotten herself as to run after a wild Irishman?' Well, perhaps. Or perhaps not. But I have noticed that Southern ladies, even in the novels of James Lane Allen, have had a way of doing unaccountable things" (*ACM*, 101). Instead of eradicating the lady, Glasgow here implies, she has shown how one can both be a lady and be free.

Yet certainly the old-fashioned sentimental lady gets short shrift in *Life and Gabriella* when she is a minor character. Jane, who develops from a "waxlike infant" to a "pressed flower" (16, 502), cries, clutches, and clings to the very husband she tries to leave; she can't bear him as he is, but, worse, when he reforms, giving up drink and other women, she can't bear the loss of her moral mission and her martyred role. Gabriella's and Jane's mother, an old-fashioned heroine of a different stripe, is the perfect "evasive idealist," keeping up appearances even to herself, loving manner more than matter, her furniture more than her children, and revealing the petulant narcissism of the powerless, depressed, dependent, self-styled martyr. Of all the characters, Mrs. Carr depends most on men—"if the bread didn't rise, mother sent for Cousin Jimmy" (464)—and prescribes most unequivocally the separate spheres for men and women. George's mother, though she scrimps on underwear to pay for lavish parties, also is an evasive idealist who usually dominates her husband but rejoices when she can surrender to him, papers all reality with "pleasantness," and tries to impose a sentimental interpretation onto the ugly realities of her son's character and marriage.

With these more or less scathing portraits, it would seem improbable for Glasgow to endorse the very values such women embody. A look at Gabriella's own development shows that Glasgow seems to have wanted her heroine to have developed a self strong and independent enough by the end both to confront the lady within her and to shape a new kind of relationship with a man. But the choice of a medium for this growth— work in a fashionable clothing store in New York—helped lead Glasgow into an untenable position. For the clothing business works because it appeals not to woman's "actual substance but to some passionately cherished ideal of herself which she had stored in a remote and inaccessible chamber of her brain" (282–83). It is the business of inventing womanhood. As the "artist in clothes" (295), then, Gabriella is directly analogous to her author, who consciously works at reinventing the ideal of southern womanhood in her novel.

Madame Dinard, whose name is really O'Grady, frankly exploits women in her own quest for men and money. Inwardly believing that men should work and women should marry rich men, she runs a slovenly but profitable business and trusts no one. She despises women because "they were poor workers, because they were idlers by nature, because they allowed themselves to be cheated, slighted, underpaid, underfed, and oppressed, and, most of all, . . . because they were the victims of their own emotions" (255). Her prosperity—"flourishing, but shallow-rooted"—depends on her principles: "to sell gowns and hats at treble their actual value, to cajole her customers into buying what they did not want and what did not suit them, to give inferior goods, inferior workmanship, inferior style wherever they would be accepted, and to get always the most money for the least possible expenditure of ability, industry, and honesty" (263). Madame Dinard's duplicity is apparent not only in her name and strategy, but in her makeup: her face is "so thickly covered with rouge and liquid powder that it was as expressionless as a mask; [she] turned its hollow eyes on a funeral which was slowly passing in the street" (257). Later in her life, she wheezes into the store, and, "like some fantastically garlanded Oriental goddess of death, her rouged and powdered face nodded grotesquely beneath the flowery wreath on her hat" (352). Paralleling such falseness are the artificial rosebushes in her salon, which nature-lover Gabriella hates, and "from which the dust was never removed" (264).

Gabriella intends to clean up this mess. Her strategy is to make herself indispensable; to exert authority by restraining her feelings and impulses; and to manipulate customers by knowing which to "encourage" and which to "crush" (286). Her standards include efficient business methods and, most important, intelligent and honest help to customers searching for an image. Gabriella believes that clothing should "suit" the customer—that character and manner should be consistent. The crisis occurs when a wealthy patron cannot be persuaded to buy Madame Dinard's most expensive dress. Gabriella is called in and commits the heresy of telling Mrs. Pletheridge that the gown "doesn't suit her at all." Mrs. Pletheridge storms out to a competitor, and Gabriella belatedly realizes how deliberate, and how dangerous, her reply had been. She has risked her own and her children's living on the truth. "I ought to have been evasive, I suppose," she thinks regretfully. "But how could I have been?" (308). The next day, Mrs. Pletheridge returns, asks for Gabriella (who has the "true eye of the artist"), tells her, "I know you will tell me what you really think," and—after receiving Gabriella's intelligent, sympathetic, and competent attention—gives the largest order the house has ever received. Such are the rewards, one supposes, for honesty in art and integrity in womanhood.

But despite her desire to transcend (through honesty) methods that exploit women's self-delusions, Gabriella is by definition an artist of illusion, who must better nature by covering it up. She is not so distant, in this sense, from the duplicitous Madame Dinard: her mask, perhaps, is less blatantly forced over reality, but it is there. When she arrives in New York, one of her first observations (like Virginia's) is that she is dressing "wrongly." She soon adjusts and eventually finds her own style. Always fashionably dressed, she appeals to "older men who like an air, who admire grace . . . and [to] women. . . . But she is not the sort to have followers" (278). If Gabriella, herself her own objet d'art, parallels Glasgow and her novel, then this statement estimates the artist's audience: selective, tasteful, and female in sensibility. Glasgow said about her heroine that she intended to do away with any "exceptional advantages. Yet I lacked, since this is a frank confession, the daring to make her simply plain and good. . . . since Jane Eyre, no novelist has had the courage to make a heroine good and plain and beloved" (*ACM*, 102). Thus she gave to Gabriella, as Gabriella gives to Mrs. Pletheridge, an appearance that is part charm, part natural beauty, and part artifice. That composite identity is reflected much later in the novel, when Gabriella announces, with authority, "I am Madame Dinard" (473).

As Gabriella, throughout the novel, acquires a new self, she acquires a new appearance that reflects it: "experience had added a rare spiritual beauty to her face, and she was far handsomer than she had been at twenty" (332). To find the new self, she has had to drop, like layers of clothing, "illusion after illusion" as she grew "farther and farther away from tradition, from accepted opinions, from the dogmas and the ideals of the ages" (386). She has stripped away the "gauzy fabric" of dreams (392). Of course Gabriella's new self—as with Mrs. Pletheridge—is reflected not only in her body, but in her clothing. For Gabriella never rids herself of the artist's desire to trick bare bones up in some kind of finery, to embroider upon reality. And when the objet d'art of the artist is oneself, such a habit keeps open the possibility for duplicity. When Ben tells her she seems "so strong, so successful, so happy," Gabriella thinks, "A good deal of that is in the shape of my face and the way I dress." But "instead of speaking sincerely," she makes a trite response (469). Again, when Ben compliments her on keeping her "charm"— something working women often lose, he says—she thinks, "Heaven knows I've tried to [keep it]!" but replies evasively (471). Just as Mrs. Fowler let that "look of artificial pleasantness" drop "like a veil" over her anxiety (197), Gabriella at one point dresses herself as a southern lady in order to "diffuse an air of fashion" and thereby gain power over Ben.

Ben has nothing to do with all of this sleight of hand. Open, direct, honest, uneducated, and unsophisticated, he is only "perplexed and embarrassed" by Gabriella's high fashion—symbolically by the lady in her character—and blinded (471) by her less-than-ingenuous responses. Since Glasgow chooses to make Ben's values the moral center of the novel, she must show Gabriella learning directness and honesty and eliminating the ladylike habits of evasiveness and duplicity. But by the terms set in the novel, this entails eliminating—along with duplicity—Gabriella's profession, and indeed art itself. Confronted with the wideness and variety of Ben's male experience, Gabriella feels that her own life has been not only very small and unimportant, but that "the world she had been living in was *merely* a fiction" (413, my emphasis). She jokes lightly about her work rather than taking it seriously when she talks with him. Moreover, Ben, the symbol of American energy, honesty, and possibility—nature untutored—cannot be shaped by Gabriella: "It was impossible to make him over because he was so completely himself . . . to change him, except in trivial details, was out of her power. . . . He couldn't see, however hard he tried, the things she wanted him to look at" (478–79). Gabriella's artistic power stops with her own sex. In an establishment entirely run by women, whose business is to fabricate identities for women, Gabriella brings new vision: she reshapes the definition of womanhood, giving it more integrity. But confronted with the principle of pure virility, she can only be shaped. And virility is a principle that denies the very value of artifice and culture. As a woman writer, Glasgow too reshapes womanhood, in the novel. Interestingly, she used clothing metaphors to describe her own creative process in this letter to Joseph Hergesheimer: "I have always looked through a veil of irony even in the days when all fiction wore fancy dress."[33] One wonders whether, like Gabriella, Glasgow occasionally saw—and devalued—her work as part of an "all-female" tradition and whether she suspected that, open to what she saw as the wide spaces of masculine vision, it too would lose its power.

In any case, Glasgow's efforts to pull away the fabric of illusion by satirizing the old style of womanhood as evasive, parasitic, and lethargic, and by creating a new kind of woman, an honest, self-reliant, energetic creator, end in her capitulation—rather, her "surrender"—to a superior man.

Part of the novel's accomplishment is the anatomy and dissection of the southern gentleman, as Glasgow had done for the woman in *Virginia*. Such an anatomy gains its intensity in the novel not just because of the interdependence of male and female identity structures but also because Glasgow is searching for a national image to reunify the feminized South with the rest of the nation.

Arthur Peyton and George Fowler continue the Shakespearean tradition noticed by William R. Taylor in literature before the Civil War. Arthur is a Hamlet whose indecision eventuates in atrophy. His face is "grave, gentle, and thin-featured, with its look of detached culture, of nameless distinction. [Gabriella] recalled the colour of his eyes, as clear and cool as running water, his sensitive lips under the thin, brown moustache, and his slender aristocratic hands, with their touch as soft and as tender as a woman's" (252–53). Appropriately for a Hamlet figure, the death of his mother causes his own morbidity: "'I have seemed only half alive since I lost her,' he said; and the words were like a searchlight which flashed over his character and illumined its obscurities. Did his whole attitude of immobility and negation result from the depth and the intensity of his feeling, from the exquisite reticence and sensitiveness of his soul?" (516). Also appropriately, his mother is the only effective—rather than evasive—idealist in the novel. "The beauty which all her life she had created through faith awoke in Arthur's suffering heart while she spoke to him. She demanded nobility of being, and it existed; she exacted generosity of nature, and it was there. By her mere presence, by the overflowing love in her heart, she not only banished jealousy and envy, but made the very idea of them unthinkable" (95). As a symbol for the Old South, Arthur shows the desiccating effects on men of its near-worship of woman. Without his dream of womanhood, he has "dried through and through, like some rare fruit that has lain wrapped in tissue paper too long" (519).

Nevertheless, Arthur retains the beautiful manners, the civilizing culture, and the sense of order, proportion, restraint, and history that, for Glasgow, characterized the Old South: "Like [his] house, he was always in perfect order; and everything about him, from his loosely fitting clothes and his immaculate linen to his inherited conceptions of life, was arranged with such exquisite precision that it was impossible to improve it in any way. He knew exactly what he thought, and he knew also his reason, which was usually a precedent in law or custom, for thinking as he did" (34).

On George, the Hotspur of the novel, these habits never took. Impulsive and violent, George's charm is his flaw. He is the "eternal boy" (174). Like a child, he wants his own way regardless of the facts; thus it is "an act of disloyalty for [Gabriella] to be right at his expense" (106). His boyish inarticulateness becomes a "veil in which [Gabriella] struggled as helplessly as a moth in a net" (149). Sexually adolescent, he equates femininity with submission: "He abhorred independence in a wife; and Gabriella's immediate and unresisting acquiescence in his desire appeared to him to establish the fact of her essential and inherent femininity. Had not all laws, as well as all religions, proclaimed that woman should be content to lay down not only her life but her very identity for love; and that Gabriella was womanly to the core of her nature, in spite of her work in Brandywine's millinery department, it was impossible to doubt while he kissed her" (99). Although fundamentally unintelligent, George does not take long to learn wherein his power over Gabriella lies. "He was testing his power to dominate her; and never had she felt it so vividly, never had her will been so incapable of resisting him as at that instant. Moving slightly in his arms she looked at the clear red brown of his throat, at his sensitive mouth, with the faint dent in the lower lip, at his bright blue eyes, which had grown soft while he pleaded. His physical power over her was complete, and he knew it. Her flesh had become as soft as flowers in his arms, while her eyes, like dark flames, trembled and fell away from his look" (109). Like his pre–Civil War southern prototype, this Hotspur destroys himself with excess while his Hamlet brother dies of disuse. Both reveal themselves quintessentially in their attitudes to Gabriella: George rapes her, and Arthur makes an altar to her in his bedroom.

Glasgow does not find in the South an image of manhood that can heal by unifying energy and virtue, physical potency and intelligence, nature and culture. That is Ben O'Hara's role. Born in New York City, in poverty, deprived of family and tradition, he has developed independently the ideal combination of force and direction. He now prefers the Far West, for its clarity, space, and fundamental natural power. Physically, Ben is as big as Gabriella's heroic Confederate cousin Micajah Berkeley had been; his thick red hair expresses his vitality, and he has the "look of exuberant vitality which accompanies perfect physical condition" (388). And all this strength is channeled for the good, which Glasgow sees as courage, truthtelling, fidelity, generosity, compassion, and creativity—"experimental, not established virtues" (479). He saves a family from a fire; the "large free movement of his arm expresse[s] a splendid scorn of small things, of little makeshifts, of subterfuges and evasions" (396). He stayed loyal to a wife who was a "drug fiend" for twenty years; he cooks for and serves Gabriella food; he builds railroads that cross the desert. O'Hara's character shows the wide virtues of the side of nature he knows best: "He had lived so long in touch with the basic realities—with vast spaces and the stark aspect of desert horizons, with droughts, and winds, and the unquenchable pangs of thirst and hunger, with the vital issues of birth and death in their most primitive forms—he had lived so long in touch with the simplest and most elemental forces of Nature, that his spirit, as well as his vision, had adjusted itself to a trackless and limitless field of view" (478–79). The contrast Gabriella sees between Ben's wilderness soul and her own limited one is reminiscent of lines from Louise Bogan's poem, "Women":

> Women have no wilderness in them,
> They are provident instead,
> Content in the tight hot cell of their hearts
> To eat dusty bread.

> They do not see cattle cropping red winter grass,
> They do not hear
> Snow water going down under culverts
> Shallow and clear.[34]

Ben O'Hara shows not only the tonic of the wilderness but also the broadening that comes from experiences open only to men. In almost a heroic catalogue, Ben lists his achievements for Gabriella: "I've cut corn and ploughed fields, and greased wheels, and chopped wood, and mended machinery, and cleaned the snow away, and once out in some little town in Arizona, I even dug a grave because the sexton was down with pneumonia. I've been brakesman, and freightman, and, after that, freight agent. That was just before I struck it rich in Colorado" (415).

But O'Hara's experience with women is as limited as his experience with men and nature is wide. "I've men friends scattered everywhere," he says. "But I don't believe I ever had a woman friend in my life" (462). He treats Gabriella with a combination of the candor of two men friends and the chivalry he showed to his wife, whom he married because "she was a poor little creature that didn't have any man to look after her" (456). On the one hand, he believes that men and women are "all alike" (417); in this vein, he suggests that Gabriella design clothes that—unlike the fashionable hobble skirt—will "make [women] more comfortable" (460). (Gabriella only jokes in response.) On the other hand, he shows a "spark of his unquenchable Western chivalry" when he can't bear to think of Gabriella's "ever having worried" (470).

Just as Gabriella finds the image of security in Arthur and of sensuality in George, she responds to the fundamental realities of Ben's character: she learns assertiveness and direct speech from him, on the one hand, and, on the other, plays lady to his knight. Thus it is that Glasgow can snatch the lady from the jaws of death. It is at the implicit cost, however, of her protagonist's psychic integrity. Already good at surrendering, at being "weak" with men; already good at conquering, at being "strong" in a world of women; Gabriella now confronts the dual necessity of alternately "capturing" the object of her "quest" (473) and surrendering to a superior man. This surely is a division that will require the covering of a mask, or a veil.

But Glasgow did create a woman in *Life and Gabriella* who, with her series of lovers, goes so far beyond convention as to be "as far removed as one could imaginably be from the repentant Magdalen of tradition" (492). This character, Florrie Spencer, the old Richmond girl who won George away from Gabriella in New York, seems to exert a fascination for Glasgow. In several respects, her character and experience parallel and mirror Ben's. Red-headed like him, "vulgar" and "common" like him on her mother's side, she has his energy and vitality as well. Moreover, in refusing to suffer, she has "blunted every weapon with which Nature might have punished her in the end" (492)—and, we remember, Gabriella hates willing victims. She is, in short, a winner, "glowing, sparkling, prosperous, victorious" (491). And she shares Ben's direct speech, too—"her frankness, like her sensuality, was elemental in its audacity" (494).

But this kind of elemental nature Glasgow rejects. She designed the novel so that a scene between Florrie and Gabriella occurs just after that in which Ben kisses Gabriella and she leaves him, insulted. Florrie comes into Gabriella's shop, where she finds—significantly—"exactly what I've been looking all over New York for" (491): Gabriella's style of womanhood suits her. They then recognize one another. Florrie, remembering that "we were chums long before either of us ever thought about a man" (494), asks if Gabriella wants to keep on being friends, despite the affair with George. Gabriella responds very much as she has just done to O'Hara's kiss: "The barefaced effrontery!" she thinks (495). And then she refuses this offer as she had refused Ben's, saying simply, "You aren't good" (494); "Somehow I don't seem able to forgive you for being what you are" (495).

Glasgow's sympathies here are unequivocally against Florrie. Yet the many parallels to the preceding scene with O'Hara, parallels of structure, plot, and characterization, raise the obvious question: why is O'Hara the hero, and Florrie the villain, in this melodrama? Florrie seems set up to be Glasgow's new image of womanhood, beyond the lady, the woman to whose freedom, contact with elemental forces of nature, and wide experience Gabriella aspires—when they are Ben's. But Florrie's freedom, unlike Ben's, is sexual; like Edna Pontellier, she knows that "today it is Arobin; tomorrow it will be some one else." [35] And in Glasgow's imagination, such freedom is incompatible with morality; it conflicts with loyalty, and deprives the relationship between man and woman of the basic structure of values. Thus, despite the chance, Florrie is consigned to minor, deviant status and made an unthinking fool, a simple embodiment of nature, rather than someone tutored by her familiarity with primal forces.

So far Glasgow's imagination stretched, and no further. Yet in *Life and Gabriella*, she has transformed if not destroyed the lady. For Gabriella gives up, through the relationship with Ben, the imperiousness, the evasiveness, the narrow hierarchical vision, the obsession with family, and the cultural snobbery that characterize other southern women in the novel. In her conscious choice of a man who lacks family, status, and class, she is reminiscent of Augusta Evans' Edna Earl, who wept (articulately) into her pillow, "Commit me rather to the horny but outstretched hands, the brawny arms, the untutored minds, the simple but kindly-throbbing hearts of the proletaire!"[36] Edna demonstrates, presumably, as does Gabriella, her own moral merit in this rejection of the southern class taboo. And Gabriella does find new values to replace the old. Dropping her defensive, commanding, "marble-lady" look, she finds herself to be "for the first time . . . feeling and thinking in unison with the multitude" (427). And she decides, with Polly, that Ben's golden-oak hatrack is acceptable, since character transcends culture. After all, Ben has "been his own Hamlet" (427); he doesn't need to read or see the play. Nature and culture, reality and romance, are one—in him.

The tension between romanticism and realism occupied Ellen Glasgow's mind for the rest of her life. She saw the conflict as characterizing southern history, as her comments about *Virginia* indicate: "My *Virginia* is as realistic as any production of the Middle West—only realism of that period in Virginia was tinctured with romantic illusion."[37] Late in life, she saw the conflict as continuing to characterize southern literature as well as history: "For all the weeds that grow and run wild in Southern soil, plain truth is the most difficult to serve without sauce. Moreover, there does not exist in the South today, nor has there ever existed at any time, a treatment of truth in fiction so plain and broad that it could be called, with fairness, a school of realism. . . . We remain incurably romantic. Only a puff of smoke separates the fabulous Southern hero of the past from the fabulous Southern monster of the present—or the tender dreams of James Lane Allen from the fantastic nightmares of William Faulkner."[38]

In sum, Glasgow used gender definitions and romantic love as a way of exploring the tension between romanticism and realism. The South already provided, in the "perfect mould" of southern womanhood into which it poured its white women, an image of the romantic ideal. The experience of a southern woman like Virginia, who is caught between her human needs and wants and her acceptance of the imperative to be a lady, thus provided Glasgow with a way to symbolize what she saw and felt as the larger southern conflict between actual and ideal. She wrote to Allen Tate in 1933 about *Virginia*: "The theme of the book is concerned with the fate of perfection in an imperfect world. Virginia is the incarnation of an ideal, and the irony is directed not at her, but at human nature which creates an ideal only to abandon it when that ideal comes to flower." [39] When she wrote from the point of view of the emancipated southern woman, however, she focused the conflict between real and ideal on the object of her protagonist's desire. The sort of man Gabriella chooses for her own romantic love-ideal thus expresses Glasgow's symbolic representation of the mind of the South. In her notes for *Virginia*, she had suggested the problem: "Love him but don't think about him—*That's* the whole trouble—"[40] To love *and* to think would unify romance and realism by joining feeling with analysis. Rejecting the idealist Arthur Peyton as well as the sensualist George Carr, both of whom evoke love from her (albeit of different sorts) but not thought, Gabriella settles on an Irishman who makes her think, whose life is itself art, who is epically heroic, and who is not a southerner at all. Perhaps aware that she had failed to resolve the conflict she saw at the heart of the South, Glasgow never again turned to a male protagonist who was not from the South. Nor did she complete the third "feminine biography" she had apparently originally projected. In a 1916 interview, she was reported to have described the three this way: "Virginia . . . was the passive and helpless victim of the ideal of feminine self-sacrifice. The circumstances of her life first moulded and then dominated her. Gabriella is the product of the same school, but instead of being used by circumstances, she uses them to create her own destiny." The third was to be "a woman who faces her world with the weapons of indirect influence or subtlety."[41] In this account, the crucial question of the third novel's tone—whether ironic or sentimental—is left unanswered, leaving us no closer to understanding whether or how Glasgow resolved these questions of romance and realism.

Whether or not the sentimentalist won out over the ironist in Glasgow, the romancer over the realist, she apparently found the friendship of other southern women writers helpful in her quest. In 1912, *Collier's Magazine* published a bad but revealing poem of hers, "The Call," in which she traces the "history" of woman's relationship to woman. This excerpt begins with the third stanza:

Queen or slave or bond or free, we battled,
Bartered not our faith for love or gold;
Man we served, but in the hour of anguish
Woman called to woman as of old.

Hidden at the heart of earth we waited,
Watchful, patient, silent, secret, true;
All the terrors of the chains that bound us
Man has seen, but only woman knew!

Woman knew! Yes, still and woman knoweth!—
Thick the shadows of our prison lay—
Yet that knowledge in our hearts we treasure
Till the dawning of the perfect day.

In the last stanza, Glasgow looks to the future:

Woman calls to woman to awaken!
Woman calls to woman to arise![42]

And in her correspondence with other women writers like Mary Johnston and Marjorie Kinnan Rawlings, that "woman knowledge" particularly surfaces: relationships to ideas, to work, to men, and to one another are openly and passionately discussed. The intensity and importance of these literary friendships are apparent as early as 1906, when Glasgow wrote to Mary Johnston,

I want to work—work—work for at least six quiet months.
   Your letter, dear, was like a song of joy, so overflowing with renewed vitality and a high heart for life. I know, I *know* it all, for a year ago I passed through exactly the same awakening of myself, though from different causes. . . . We suffered in different ways, but we both suffered to the death—each of us saw at the end of her road the mouth of hell—and each of us turned and struggled back to life—you along your steep path and I along mine. . . . I have come at last into what Whitman calls "the me myself," that is behind and above it all. . . . Our temperaments, our inheritances, our attitudes even may be different—but it is love, after all, that smooths away the edges of personality and makes one *know* another by intuition rather than by knowledge.[43]

Almost thirty-five years later, Glasgow and Marjorie Kinnan Rawlings, author of *The Yearling* (a book Ellen Glasgow said she loved), developed a friendship that seems to have made up in depth what it lacked in time spent together. In 1939, Glasgow invited Rawlings to stop by for a visit in Richmond on her next trip north; Rawlings did, and the ensuing letters show a relationship that went immediately to the center of each woman's self. As with Johnston, the question of common identity arose. Rawlings wrote to Glasgow in 1940: "Reciprocal admiration among writers is so rare a thing that after many years of devotion to your work, I find myself totally unprepared for your liking mine. Superficially, our aims and our material would seem so divergent that one could not conceive of common ground. Yet . . . it seems to me possible that our object has been more or less identical: to present human beings, as you know one type and I another, struggling against whatever is inimical within themselves or in their background."[44] Elsewhere in their correspondence, Rawlings worries about the difficulty of combining writing with housekeeping and, repeatedly, about the quality of her work. After Glasgow had apparently written to her in 1945 about her own inability to work, Rawlings responded, just days before Glasgow died, "How I suffer with you, for [being unable to work] puts one into an acute state of melancholy and frustration. Being obliged to write is a strange curse. . . . I am in a dreadful state of mind, from being unable to do anything with a novel that has been long on hand. . . . In one version, I did about a quarter's book-length, and was so depressed that one night I tore it all into irretrievable shreds. And felt much better."[45]

Earlier, they had discussed the "man question." Rawlings, now married to a "dear close friend," had been through an "oppressive and almost entirely hideous" fifteen-year marriage and then had lived for years in solitude "punctuated by emotional entanglements"; she says she knows Glasgow must be "familiar with the pain of these." And she comments on the relationship between work and love: "Long independence, and above all, the peculiar mental independence of the creative worker, is not the best of bases for a successful marriage." She has hopes for her present marriage, however, because "the man too is accustomed to independence," is "so generous, so tolerant, and so tender," and because "we care for each other in so deep and quiet a way, that being with him is like coming into harbor after long storms."[46]

But the most remarkable of the correspondence between Marjorie Rawlings and Ellen Glasgow came in 1941, after they had met only once, and when Rawlings was in her early forties and Glasgow nearing seventy. When Rawlings had arrived for her visit, Glasgow had been in bed, recovering from a heart attack and correcting proofs. They were, Glasgow said, immediately drawn to one another. Several months later, Rawlings wrote that she had had the following dream about Glasgow:

You came to live with me. I was away when you came, and on my return, to one of those strange mansions that are part of the substance of dreams, you were outside in the bitter cold, cutting away ice from the roadway and piling it in geometric pattern. I was alarmed, remembering your heart trouble, and led you inside the mansion and brought you a cup of hot coffee. You had on blue silk gloves, and I laid my hand over yours, and was amazed, for my own hand is small, to have yours fit inside mine, much smaller. You chose your room and suggested draperies to supplement a valance. The valance was red chintz and you showed me a sample of a heavy red brocade of the same shade. I told you that from now on I should take care of you, and you must not do strenuous things, such as cutting the ice in the roadway. James Cabell came into the room and asked what the two of us were up to. (As of course he would!)[47]

Glasgow was so taken with this that she responded immediately that it had brought a "thrilling sense of friendship and sympathy. . . . Ever since I finished 'In This Our Life' I have felt as if I were drifting in an icy vacuum toward something—or nothing. . . . But the dearest part of your dream was the way you brought me in. . . . And the warmth of the red curtians [sic] and the valance! . . . Ever since you came to see me, so strong and warm and vital, I have felt very near to you, and you have had your own chosen place in my life, just as I had in the house of your dream."[48] The next day she wrote a note to herself that she wanted to include the letter in her autobiography, adding that "after publishing In This Our Life, which [Marjorie] liked and understood, as deeply as I loved and understood The Yearling, I sank down into an icy vacuum, that living death, when I told myself that, within, I was caught in the midst of frozen fields, and could not escape. Then, last night, I had this letter from Marjorie telling me of her singular dream. I cannot explain it."[49] On August 1, she wrote to Cabell, using the same metaphor: "I have not broken away from that icy vacuum, which, if nothingness has a superlative, grows deeper and deeper. I know that I am over and done with, and I cannot reconcile myself to being merely a shell with an inadequate heart. . . . May you never know the horror of coming to the end of your work before your life is finished. . . . Remind me, if and when I return in the autumn, to tell you of a singular dream Marjorie Kinnan Rawlings had about me a few days ago."[50]

The metaphors in this episode are everywhere richly suggestive. If

Glasgow had hoped to "stand within the gate" of Johnston's inner self years before, she is here welcomed into her own room in Rawlings' "mansion." The reds may suggest (as in Jane Eyre's red-room [51]) a particularly female self. And the icy fields, in which Glasgow feels herself trapped, and out of which she is cutting (in Rawlings' dream) geometric pieces, bear an obverse resemblance to the fields and finally the sea through which Edna Pontellier ran and swam so ambiguously for freedom. Certainly the split between feeling and form, heart and head, is here, as well as Glasgow's dogged persistence in working despite the damage to the sources of imaginative power in her "inadequate heart." But these are speculations. Most important, the impression overall is that of a kind of empathy, even identity, between these two southern women writers, a mutual understanding of their most private selves that offered to Rawlings, writing in Florida, and to Glasgow, ill and depressed in Maine, a sense—temporary, perhaps, and in certain respects illusory—but a sense of a sustaining community.

CHAPTER VII   **Frances Newman**
The World's Lessons

The change in mores that characterized the United States after World War I was hardly remote from the South. Zelda Fitzgerald, probably the most famous flapper of all, was born and raised in Alabama. And the novels of another southern woman, Frances Newman, reflect culturally relaxed attitudes towards sexuality in their very titles: she called her first novel *The Hard-Boiled Virgin* and her second (and last) *Dead Lovers Are Faithful Lovers*. But, just as the titles, brassy and impertinent though they appeared, imply a type of freedom that the novels themselves do not embody, so the twenties for women in the South gave more the appearance of liberation than the fact. This was true nationally; historians have noted that, after a few years of wild living, the lost youths of the period rather unequivocally returned to traditional sex roles after they had flung their flings. Newman herself seems to have embodied some Jazz Age conflicts, though she acted them out on a plane more sophisticated and eccentric than most. All her life she wore purple. In her letters—written on lavender paper—and her conversations, she affected a tired, bored, and bitingly caustic persona. Yet in her novels, she examined with increasing seriousness the continuing difficulties unique to those who were born southern, white, and female—difficulties that were not very different from those faced by Evans' Beulah almost three-quarters of a century before, and that, for Newman, were only compounded by sexual freedom.

The paucity of materials concerning Frances Newman's life and work indicates the virtual oblivion into which, until quite recently, she has fallen. Neither the *Literary History of the United States* nor Jay B. Hubbell's *The South in American Literature* mentions her; Margaret Mitchell's biographer Finis Farr and Richard Harwell, editor of the *"Gone With The Wind" Letters*, note only that Newman wrote for the Atlanta *Journal* while Mitchell was reporting for that paper.[1] In fact, since Hansell Baugh edited *Frances Newman's Letters* (1929),[2] very little attention has been paid to this extraordinary woman. Nevertheless, her life, expressing as it did the changed mores of the post–World War I period, and her works, concerned as they so obsessively are with the role of the southern lady, deserve to be reexamined. Elizabeth Hardwick indicated this when she chose Newman's novels as two of her eighteen-book "personal selection" of rediscovered fiction by American women.[3] Most of my information about her life comes from John E. Talmadge's contribution to *Notable American Women*[4] and Hansell Baugh's gloss to *Frances Newman's Letters*, and from the special collections of the University of Georgia.

Frances Newman was born the last of five children to a family that had moved from Tennessee to Atlanta after the Civil War. Her father, William Truslow Newman, fought with the Second Tennessee Cavalry and lost his arm in battle in 1864. Her mother, Frances Alexander Percy, to whom she dedicated her first novel, was one of a prominent Knoxville family that included the city's founder and his son, Senator Hugh Lawson White. Although both parents came from pioneer stock, when they moved to Atlanta it was not to seek a new territory, but to become a part of the old. By the time Newman was born in 1883, her father was city attorney (later to be U.S. district judge), and both parents were active in social and civic circles.

The similarities between Newman's life and that of Katharine Faraday, protagonist of *The Hard-Boiled Virgin*, are striking. Both were the youngest children in their families and were considered rather unattractive physically; both had older sisters whose beauty was their most important asset. Both responded to their somewhat inferior positions in the family hierarchy by spending hours in their fathers' libraries. Both Katharine and Frances attended public schools in Atlanta and then went to boarding schools in Washington, D.C. Newman was also sent to a boarding school in New York and spent a year at Agnes Scott College. Unlike her first novel's heroine, Frances Newman became a librarian; she spent a year (1913) as librarian in Tallahassee at Florida State College for Women and then returned to Atlanta to work first at the Carnegie Library and later at the Georgia Institute of Technology. Like Katharine Faraday, Newman traveled to New York and abroad, committed herself to the study of European literature, and carried out the profession of southern lady of letters.

Newman made her debut in the American literary world with book reviews and some "corrosive and sparkling essays in literary criticism"[5] that were published in the Richmond-Chapel Hill *Reviewer* and in New York newspapers. James Branch Cabell and later H. L. Mencken, attracted by her writing, encouraged her. Mencken mentioned her in a 1922 column called "Violets in the Sahara"; then in 1924, he published her short story, "Rachel and Her Children," in his *American Mercury*. The story revealed both her profound concern with the dehumanizing effects of the role of southern lady and her ability to write fairly traditional sentences—an ability that came under some ironic question later. The story won an O. Henry Prize, which Newman said she "accepted . . . with some misgivings because of her 'detestation of O. Henry as a writer.'"[6] (Newman found O. Henry's style "shrill" and his stories "cut by a pattern. . . . which could be fitted to any theme, and which is just beginning to wear along its edges."[7]) Also in 1924 a highly praised collection of short stories that she had selected, introduced, and translated appeared from B. W. Huebsch, James Joyce's American publisher at the time. *The Short Story's Mutations: From Petronius to Paul Morand* included Joyce's "Ivy Day in the Committee Room," Henry James's "The Private Life," and Anton Chekhov's "The Darling."[8] In fact, Newman was a pioneer in support of Joyce's works; she understood both his ambivalence to the culture that bore him and his "delight in technical problems."[9] Her primary American literary interest, she said, was in "the stories of those authors who know that Freud and Tchekhov have crossed the ocean, and who try to see below the surfaces of their characters and to find for every theme the precise form that it requires."[10] In her commentary for *The Short Story's Mutations*, she explained the modern "preoccupation with form" as "necessarily more serious than the interest of those centuries which had one unyielding form for each art—a dramatist like Euripides, who knew that he could have only three actors on his stage at any one moment, and a poet like Boileau, who knew that his first iambic hexameter could not run over into the iambic hexameter which completed his inevitably rhyming couplet, were far freer from technical problems than a Chekhov, who created for each new play and each new story the form that its emotion demanded."[11] Thus she gave O. Henry some credit for teaching the American masses that "the way of telling a story may be as important as the story itself."[12] Though her own literary efforts reflect this commitment to form with varying degrees of success, her models were modernists like Virginia Woolf. Thus, no doubt, she took it as praise in 1928 when the New York *Times* reviewer called her own work "ever [that of] the artificer, the artist, the craftsman. Nothing extraneous to her structure is admitted."[13]

By 1924 her mother had died, and Newman more or less settled in Atlanta with her former mammy, Susan Long, and her nephew, Louis Rucker, for whom she took responsibility when his mother died. Thereafter she left Atlanta periodically: she lived in New York and Paris, and spent two summers at the MacDowell Colony in Peterborough, New Hampshire. She joined, in fact, at least the periphery of an international community of artists. Early in her literary career (1921), she had attacked F. Scott Fitzgerald's first novel, *This Side of Paradise*. Fitzgerald wrote to her, very angry; she sent his letter to James Branch Cabell, adding that "I feel as if I had pulled a spoiled baby's curls and I made him cry. Please send it back—first blood, you know." Cabell rapped her on the wrist: he replied, "I think you dealt over-harshly with him,"[14] and the episode ended. While writing *The Hard-Boiled Virgin* (1926) at the MacDowell Colony, she befriended Thornton Wilder, a "very amusing man . . . very good looking," who "thinks I will be horrified by the amount of wicked publicity it [her novel] will get," but who praised it himself by saying he "feels like a woman as well as a man since he read it." From Paris in 1923, she wrote that "[James] Joyce's eyes are very poorly, so I haven't seen him, and I'd forgotten all about Ezra [Pound], but I'll inquire after him."[15] Five years later, again in Paris, she wrote that she went to a party at Ford Madox Ford's, that the Louis Bromfields gave a party for her, and that she had a long conversation with Paul Morand at a tea in the home of painter Hélène Pédriat. She corresponded for years with Compton Mackenzie, whom she visited in England; in some respects, her closest and longest friends were James Branch Cabell and H. L. Mencken.

Newman apparently felt deeply ambivalent about moving in these circles. On the one hand, her first summer with other writers at the MacDowell Colony was extraordinarily productive: it was a "lovely smiling country and a perfect place to work"; "I probably rather bubble here because the atmosphere seems to be encouraging. . . . Willa Cather is coming Saturday," she wrote to a friend.[16] On the other hand, because she so badly wanted approval and acceptance by the largely male literary world and because she never quite trusted or felt that she understood men, Newman varied between terrible insecurity in her letters to men who were artists and, as with Fitzgerald, surprising cockiness. It is apparent that she identified herself as part of a male literary tradition, hoping to be accepted within it, while at the same time paradoxically asserting that her own literary value rested in her distinctly female voice.

Newman consistently believed that men were more powerful in most spheres than women. "No woman ever believes that a man can't do something," she wrote, "because, as you must know, nothing stops them from doing what they want to do." Therefore she sought their approbation: to a journalist writing about contemporary southern rebels, for instance, she said, "I am frightfully anxious to be one of your royal flush. After all, you can't have one without a lady."[17] Her own literary favorites were almost all male, among them Voltaire, Maupassant, James, Chekhov, Beerbohm, Huxley, Joyce, Lawrence, Morand, Giraudoux, Pirandello, and Proust.

Consistent with her eagerness to be accepted by the literary patriarchy, she had "no . . . great opinion" of women herself. She saw herself as an exceptional woman, but even then she thought that "between the ordinary man and the ordinary woman there is little choice, except that the woman is always anxious to assume a culture though she have it not. . . . It is exactly between the exceptional man and the exceptional woman that there is a gulf most mortifying to a woman."[18] Newman's own acceptance of her credo of female inferiority is apparent in her choice of *mortifying*—it is the woman who is to blame for her position. And in her fiction, as will be seen, Newman consistently satirized women at the same time that she called *The Hard-Boiled Virgin* "the first novel in which a woman ever told the truth about how women feel."[19] Newman called herself a feminist and had affectionate relationships with other literary women, nevertheless; she helped Julia Peterkin, knew Ellen Glasgow, and admired the writing of Virginia Woolf, Rose Macauley, Katherine Mansfield, and Colette. Her relationships with other women seem from her letters to be emotionally open, affectionate, and unquestioningly supportive, but not very interesting; few of her letters were written to women. By contrast, her relationships with men offered excitement, wit, and the shared anxieties of creation and judgment.

As a woman artist in a world whose values and experiences seemed to be so rigidly divided by sex, Newman felt handicapped by a lack of skills and training more easily accessible to her masculine counterparts. To write, she needed authority and control over her words to "make . . . language ride bare-backed and leap unscathed through paper hoops, to touch words and make them obey"; yet, without a college education, she felt that she had "never enjoyed the advantage of having my five-finger exercises ordained by authority or corrected by authority." [20] Newman more than compensated for her lack of training, however; she taught herself the literature of seven languages, and her obsession with style (about which more will be said later) may well reflect her desire to be faultlessly in linguistic control.

Newman's relationships to men affected her work in at least two other significant ways. According to her letters, she seems to have fallen in love several times quite intensely, but each time she did, her work stopped. "I've fallen violently in love—for the last time [this is a refrain]—and am entirely unfit for letters and work and everything," she wrote in 1925.[21] These relationships, though intense, were somewhat brief; in between, she worked on her fiction. In fact, she saw the men as muses. Mary Johnston had called her muse the "old man of the sea"; he "climb[ed on] her shoulders" and stayed there until she finished a piece.[22] Newman believed that "a woman can't write a book without a father for it any more than she could have a baby—I think of writing an essay on that subject some time," she wrote to Edith Stern in 1928. "Anyway, all three of mine have had fathers as different as the fathers of Isadora Duncan's children. But I suppose you can have legitimate literary children, too." [23] Not only did Newman, in her female imagination, see her literary children as bastards; she—like her predecessor Anne Bradstreet [24]—also saw them as deformed or at best badly clothed. Asking to see her *Short Story's Mutations*, Cabell referred to it as "that, as you call it, hare-lipped child." [25] The connection of that condition with the power to speak can hardly be fortuitous.

In a rare direct and personal moment in her letters, Newman questioned her own writing:

> And why, after all, should I struggle to "write"? I don't ever
> like what I do write. I used to think writing would make me
> know interesting people, but it doesn't seem to. . . . I feel
> quite craven about taking the library [job at Georgia Tech],

and as if I'd be silly not to take it. . . . Books and stories and even reviews aren't *in* me. I have to create them with terrible agony and terrible work. But I don't mind that as I mind the horrid indignities of being a literary woman—it's rather worse, I think, than running for office, and worse in very much the same way.[26]

Though here she may have been thinking of the public exposure, running for office also requires intelligence and charm. Newman was torn through much of her life by a conflict between the two qualities that to her seemed contradictory.

As a southern woman, she was expected to be charming; as a writer, she wanted to be intelligent. Newman well knew, growing up in the South, that one of charm's charms is the conspicuous absence of assertive intelligence, or, in more sophisticated circles, its harmless use for entertainment as cleverness or wit. Newman's mind, however, thrived on adversity; she loved a battle, and she loved to win. Hence, at one point, she said, "I can stand being called no lady much more cheerfully than I can stand being called a fool," and at another she hid behind her southern charm: "I looked so nice at the [Paris] Woman's Club that it didn't matter what I said. . . . I had a little hat dyed precisely to match [her cyclamen crêpe frock] with a little feather almost completely blotting out the right side of my face, and I behaved as sweetly and ingenuously and gaily as a Lanvin frock demands." She described the Atlanta reception of her book, the product of her brain, to be "as important a social event as a wedding—almost." And in writing to a woman friend, she said that she valued the rare combination of intelligence and good manners: "I want people to be clever and to have the kind of manners I think of as good manners—somebody I can enjoy talking to in both ways. You are one of the very few women like that."[27] A journalist described her in 1928 as a "strange mixture of Southern romantic, aristocratic ladyhood and modern sophistication," who said, "I have a quaint preference for ladies and gentlemen."[28] This split between lady and mind, thematically central to her novels, appears as well in the paradox of southern woman writing: she mentioned in another letter that her character Katharine Faraday had to discover "one may be born in the South and still write something."[29]

Newman also felt a great deal of ambivalence about living and working in the South. She clearly identified herself as a southerner. In an interview, she said she "loved the Southland which was her birthplace and her home for most of her life, and she was proud of its chivalry and gallantry."[30] She and Emily Clark, editor of *The Reviewer*, planned one year a Christmas annual open only to "writers born below Mason and Dixon's line and resident there until their eighteenth year"—yet she "emigrated" to New York in 1926 to get away from Atlanta. There, "about every two days I get so homesick that I think I will come back to Atlanta as soon as I live up my month's rent, and then I see a copy of the Atlanta paper and feel that I never can stand it again." However, in New York she feared becoming an "intellectual air-plant, instead of profiting by the example of those eminent novelists who have remained where they had roots." Nor did the environment of the MacDowell Colony at Peterborough satisfy her after that first blissful summer. By 1927 she said, "I do write very slowly here [Atlanta] but I can't write at all in New York, and I don't believe I can ever bear the exposure of Peterborough again."[31]

Despite Newman's love for southern chivalry, she told in her novels some unpleasant truths about the South, and, as James Branch Cabell said after her death, "a hyper-sensitive South objected, as a matter of course, to her truth-speaking."[32] Earlier, in a review of *Dead Lovers Are Faithful Lovers*, southern writer Donald Davidson had said ambiguously, "perhaps the South deserves [Newman] as the United States deserves Sinclair Lewis."[33] *Saturday Review*—referring to both Newman and Glasgow—said with less ambiguity that "the South must begin to realize that its only salvation lies in taking the girl babies of good family who look as if they might have brains, and drowning them as soon as possible after birth."[34]

Newman attributed her capacity to know and speak the truth to her mammy, Susan Long. She lived with Long most of her life; one letter to Susan assures her that the money for a lawyer to defend the cook Elizabeth (who had shot another black woman) would be raised, and another, consoling her in grief, says, "Louis and I are your family, and . . . we both love you more than anybody in the world. . . . I never realize how much I love you until I am away like this."[35] Here she tells what she learned as a child from Susan Long:

> I think she must be mostly responsible for my lack of a southern lady's traditional illusions. When I was a little girl, she used to tell me about slavery times, and I thought Miss —, her old mistress, was a woman and the devil was a man, and that was the only difference between them. If you grow up hearing of mistress's sons who set dogs on a little girl three years old to see her run, who beat the slaves, and who didn't tell them they were free, you can't admire the antebellum south completely. But even that didn't depress me

like the tale about how she ran away because Miss —'s daughter threatened to have her mama whip her for losing a string, how she got away to the nearest town and was protected by the Freedmen's Bureau, and when Miss —'s husband couldn't take her back, he took the little yellow-spotted dress that was the pride and joy of her life—she can't have been more than about eight.[36]

Days before her death, when Winifred Rothermel called on her for an interview, Newman "summoned 'mammy' to have me [Rothermel] meet her, saying, 'You really must meet "mammy," for no one could know me without knowing my "mammy."'" Rothermel observed that Mammy's "faith in her charge" and her role fending off distractions were invaluable to Newman throughout her professional life.[37]

Newman's novels were efforts to resolve some of these conflicts. Although she claimed once that "the peculiarities of my own style are caused by the necessity of circumventing the Atlanta papers,"[38] when *The Hard-Boiled Virgin* appeared, Cabell wrote her, "You have arrived with all the reticence and the amiability of a thunder-bolt. I can think of no book ever written by any woman which I like better. This appears to me the most brilliant, the most candid, the most civilized, and . . . the most profound book yet written by any American woman."[39] She had succeeded, then, in charming him with her kind of intelligence.

After her two novels were published, Frances Newman went to Paris to work on Jules Laforgue, planning to translate several of his stories. "La Forgue is not known in this country," she said later, "and I do not expect to make money from translating his stories. They are literary masterpieces, and I love them. And I did them simply because I wanted to."[40] When she developed a painful eye problem, she returned to the United States and continued translating despite continuous headaches and undiagnosed difficulty with vision. A devastating parody of her latest novel, *Dead Lovers Are Faithful Lovers*, appeared in the *Vanity Fair* for November, 1928; called "Dead Novelists Are Good Novelists," it told of a narcissistic woman writer who goes to a New York agent on October 20 to proffer her book full of "delicately curved allusions" and "voluptuous paragraphs," as though it were her body. When the man is not in (he plans to avoid her), she despairs and throws herself out of his window, thinking of the flowers he will bring to the funeral.[41]

On October 22, Frances Newman was found dead in her room at the Hotel Schuyler in New York. The New York *World* claimed on October 26 that Newman had killed herself; a Hearst paper claimed by November 3 that she had died of an overdose of Veronal; another paper claimed the autopsy had been performed at its instance. Interpretations of the presumed motives for her "suicide" exploited Newman's variance from the norms of womanhood. One person claimed she had "succumbed to futility, heightened by spinsterish complications"; another summarized her life with these sexual innuendoes: "Miss Newman, a 44-year-old spinster, became an author late in life and her undoubtedly brilliant mind expressed itself in strange circumlocutions of language and with an unusual emphasis on sensual superficialities." A literary critic of some eminence, H. E. Dounce, called her "pathetic" and at times "preposterous," and identified her with her protagonist Katharine Faraday, whom he described as "a miserable and pitiable creature, 'fixated,' mired in 'narcissism' to the most tormenting degree—one whose suicide, whenever a last illusion should shatter and leave her bankrupt, might be logical even without much immediate cause. Especially had she gone on and become famous, and as a public character challenged scathing criticism by being herself scathingly critical, and by artificialities got herself known of as something of a comic figure." [42]

Agonized, her friends—among them Hansell Baugh, Adrienne Battey, and Frank Daniel—apparently did what they could to find out and present the truth. An incomplete typescript, possibly by Frank Daniel, accuses the New York *World* October 26 report of a "triumphal contempt": "I cannot see why the apparent fact that Miss Newman was a spinster was of such vital news value that this condition must be mentioned three times," the author wrote. Moreover, the document concludes, the suicide scandal was "ridiculous"; doctors had already diagnosed inflammation of the optic nerve, and her death came as a result of a cerebral hemorrhage. In a November 3 letter, Frank Daniel said that "Atlanta is even yet taking its revenge against Katharine Faraday." [43]

Newman's first try at fiction, "Rachel and Her Children," takes its title from a minister's remark in the story that old Mrs. Overton (Sally) weeps "like Rachel weeping for her children" [44] at the funeral of her daughter. In Genesis 30, the Rachel to whom the minister probably refers weeps because she has no children (her sister Leah, on the other hand, has given their mutual husband several sons). Rachel first gives her maid to Jacob, then seeks out mandrakes to try to conceive. When she finally bears Joseph, Rachel says, "God has taken away my reproach" (Genesis 30:23). Rachel dies giving birth to her second son, whom she names Benoni ("son of my sorrow"); Jacob renames him Benjamin ("son of the right hand," or "son of the South"). [45] Newman is ironic here, for Sally Overton is weeping not as a mother for her (now both) lost children, but for her own lost self. And—given that *The*

Hard-Boiled Virgin shows more than once a minister preaching from a text whose meaning he misses—she is taking a shot at the church as well.

The setting of "Rachel and Her Children" is a church in the South: "The society of Colonial Dames was there, in a body, and the Daughters of the Confederacy were there, in a body, and even the Chamber of Commerce was there, in a body. There was all of the Social Register which did not happen to be on its yachts, or in sanitoria, or abroad" (92). The story shows what takes place behind Sally Overton's expensive black crepe veil, ironically contrasting her inner self to the pious and conventional assumptions about her feelings made by the congregation at her daughter's funeral.

Behind her veil, Mrs. Overton remembers when she was sixteen in 1864. She had "fairly ached with adoration" of Captain Ashby, who had black hair, black eyes, and a "wound in some vaguely invisible spot that no Southern lady could even think about" (92). Well-read in Dickens, Thackeray, and Scott, she had "never been allowed," however, to read *Jane Eyre*. Thus when Ashby, her Rochester, kissed Sally not "respectfully on the forehead" but passionately "under her soft chin," she knew he did not love her: none of her fictional heroes would do such a thing, and her mother "confirmed Sally's belief that she had been insulted" (93). Though Sally sighed for the dashing captain, she acceded to her mother's plan to marry her to the elderly widower Colonel Overton, thinking that she would at least have the freedom to talk when and with whom she chose and to sit at the head of her own table.

No one had prepared her for marriage: "People hardly talked then of the boredom of sitting at the other end of the table from the wrong man every morning; certainly they never talked of the occasions when there wasn't a table between one and the wrong man" (93). Sally became "an old man's slave, a carefully treasured harem of one" (94). Moreover, when Cornelia, their daughter, grows old enough, she takes on the characteristics of her grandmother, Sally's domineering mother, doing "the correct thing, in all matters from sleeves and shoes to husbands and religions" (94). Thus Cornelia takes over Mrs. Overton's life just as Mr. Overton and, before him, Sally's mother had done.

One untouched family topic is the colonel's generosity to a "prepossessing colored—just barely colored—nurse, who had been the comfort of his declining years" (94); he leaves her most of his estate, and Sally must move in with her daughter. While Sally is living there, Cornelia is "thrown into such a state" by her mother's desire to marry Mr. Robinson, with whom—despite his lower social class—she would "at last have been able to talk to the people she wanted to talk to about the things she wanted to talk about," that Sally feels "obliged to give up the idea" (95).

Since then—she was under forty—Mrs. Overton has existed as an adjunct to her children's lives. Only when Cornelia, now Mrs. Foster, becomes lingeringly ill does Mrs. Overton have a chance to act—to go to the market alone, to go shopping alone, to run the household. During the funeral, Mrs. Overton (tearless) thinks of her future with her daughter's widower, living an active social and familial life. But then she notices young and recently widowed Mrs. Turner looking at Mr. Foster and "suddenly felt cold and forlorn" (96). So when she leaves the funeral, "shaking with bitter sobs," she is weeping for the loss not of her child but of her self. She will probably now "go back to the side of another Mrs. Foster's table" (96).

The point of the story is clear. However Mrs. Overton defines the power to run her life, it is a power that she has lost; she has never been able to become a person in her own right. Hemmed in by literary and social convention, by mother, by daughter, by husband, and never quite strong enough to defy them (and indeed it would require the strength of an Amazon), Mrs. Overton will die without having lived, and knows it, behind her veil.

"Rachel and Her Children" sets the tone and the theme for Newman's later work, even to specific images. For example, "old Mrs. Overton was seventy-four years old; she belonged to a generation which believed that dreaming of a funeral was a sign of a wedding, and that dreaming of a wedding was a sign of a funeral. She had never read the works of Dr. Sigmund Freud" (92). That her equation of marriage with death is not really a generational problem is clear when Newman has young Katharine Faraday, the hard-boiled virgin, believing the same dream-sign. For Newman sees an almost Kafka-like power in the persistence of southern mores; she shows the pathetic and desperate struggles of women who have internalized the South's definition of the lady and find themselves dying from its effects. Thus, if, as Maxwell Geismar claims, the "weakness as well as the charm of the generation of the twenties lay in its indifference to its own past,"[46] then Newman's heroines contradict the pattern; their weakness—and their charm—are explicitly linked to a tradition that is regional in nature.

In Newman's somber vision, the vitality of southern forms has been vitiated by time; yet the husks now exert more power than the original ethos ever had. Sexual purity has become a willed and alienating innocence from which the only escape is prurience. Religious piety has become a matter of social class and social climbing through church-going. The prime goal of the woman in the home has turned into a loveless pressure to place herself, her husband, and, most destructively, her children into the Piedmont Driving Club. And submission to a husband has become self-immolation before all men, a surrender to which the only conceivable alternative is victory through proving one's superior intelligence. The strength of the Civil War woman, seen affectionately but rejected by Mary Johnston, has become trivialized into the power to enforce the rules of society. And the rules of society have become not the rules of an organic community of individuals but mere techniques: for women, the techniques of getting and keeping a man; and for men, the techniques of getting money and social status. The result is alienation and narcissism. Newman's vision terrifies. In her South, "southern ladies and gentlemen respect the polite fictions of society";[47] if they do this in ignorance (as most do), they destroy any inner life; if they do this in conscious choice, they become hard and privately bitter. Unlike the world of *Hagar*, there is no exit from those fictions; unlike the world of Ellen Glasgow, this evasive idealism retains no genuine ideals.

An apparently puzzled contemporary reviewer called Frances New-man's *The Hard-Boiled Virgin* a novel "for the critic rather than the general reader."[48] The novel has no dialogue whatsoever. Its division into dozens of minute chapters seems designed more to provide relief than to guide the reader, though Newman claimed that she made "each episode one paragraph . . . to get a perfect sequence and—if possible—a perfect sequence of the reader's attention."[49] All the action comes to the reader not just through the point of view of its heroine, Katharine Faraday, but through the voice of an omniscient but circumlocutory and ever-apparent narrator. Allusions to works of literature and other forms of art are so frequent and so completely unexplained in the text as to require a highly educated reader or alienate a less well-informed one.

And diligence is required to drag sense from the prose itself. New-man repeatedly uses double, even triple, negatives in a single sentence. An example from early in the novel: "She did not like to feel the emotion she did not know was called pity, and she did not understand how her father could have reached such age and such eminence without learning that all mothers are as infallible as any pope and more righteous than any saint" (10). A second repeated device is the conditional: "But if Katharine Faraday had ever heard of a writer called George Meredith, and if she had known that she was not created to enjoy a wider circulation among human beings than his novels enjoyed, her peculiarities would hardly have been lessened by learning her destiny from a little girl whose divine commission had no external symbols except an aquiline nose, a crimson crepe de chine frock pleated like an accordion, and the carefully curled hair of an oldest daughter" (18). These linguistic habits demand and demonstrate both cleverness and indirection. Newman's famous "obscenity"[50] even requires ingenuity to find. Never once does she use a word like *masturbation, syphilis, menstruation, penis,* or even *sex*—yet what these words mean forms a major theme of the novel.

Not only is the style sardonically euphemistic in its diction and wittily contorted in its syntax; it perambulates in exposition. In one section, for instance, the narrator discusses Katharine Faraday's mother's definition of charity as the "social ladder with the smoothest rungs" (188), comparing it to the more modern penchant for climbing by means of gardening, then moves to the mother's feelings about flowers, then to the flowers that two men have sent for what they think is Katharine's twentieth birthday but is actually her twenty-first, then to Neal Lumpkin's faux pas of sending her crimson roses (now considered unfashionable for brunettes), and only then to the center of the chapter—Katharine's visit to her friend, the new mother, Sarah Rutledge Simpson. Such a structure has in fact an organic unity perceptible after close reading. Newman was very interested in stream of consciousness, was highly conscious herself of form, and was familiar with—in fact, considered herself and was considered part of—the experimental avant garde of the period. No critics have yet paid the novel's structure the careful attention it deserves, however.

Although it was banned in Boston, *The Hard-Boiled Virgin* did receive some good notices. Rebecca West credited the book with a "very high degree of literary accomplishment"; Grant Overton called it a "novelists' novel, in the sense that Proust is a novelists' novelist." Reviewers were most impressed with the style, the implicit sexuality, and the attack on southern conventions. Finding a comparison to Charlotte Brontë's *Villette,* the New York *Times* reviewer applauded Newman for her "authentic style, atonic as anything Jane Austen ever wrote, dry to astringency and with true ironic inflection." Others found less to praise in the style. Although H. E. Dounce said after her death that he had felt the emotional effect of the novel was "enhanced by the style, mocking tone, and defiant technique," its title, he thought, was a "brass shield for diffidence." And the *New Republic* agreed; the "defensive panoply" of flippancy and the "ribald ruthlessness" wouldn't fool a baby, the reviewer said; the paradox was that a woman of such talent, whose creative instincts led her to invent a sensitive, tragically unfulfilled character—demanding "simplicity, sincerity, and freedom" in style—should instead turn to cleverness.[51]

Some, particularly in the South, were offended by the "bawdy of the most impertinent and allusive order." On the other hand, Elizabeth Hardwick recently pointed out that the novel is "a work of intellectual and social skepticism rather than one of sexual astonishment." In 1926, Rebecca West, too, found the theme to be not bawdy but a "study of the extreme discomforts and humiliations inflicted on women in any society where they are treated as the protected sex." Elmer Davis pinpoints the society more precisely: "Only a Southerner," he said, "can appreciate it fully." As an intellectual history of "spiritual escape from the too, too solid South and the Lost-Cause psychosis," it is "treason against her fatherland," and every line is "grounds for lynching."[52]

Whether Newman's experimentation produced a work of art, and whether her work would survive, seemed to have been answered by the almost total absence of criticism and readers for her work from the time of her death until the very recent past. It is possible that Newman will eventually share the reputation of some of her literary friends. But whether she ultimately succeeded or failed in her efforts to fit style to theme is not the issue here; my interest is rather in what Newman's work says concerning, not modernism, but men, women, and the society they made in the South.

Katharine Faraday (always referred to by her full name—for distance, said Newman) journeys from childhood to her mid-thirties in the novel. Born in Atlanta as the "sixth pledge" of her parents' "love" (9), she is the youngest child in three sets of girl-boy pairings, if not literal twins. Her oldest sister Marian is a great beauty and consequently a great belle; Marian's counterpart George is equally "so beautifully brought up that [he] never had any ideas more unusual than the ideas of Peachtree Street, on which they were born" (12). Eleanor and Arthur, "less well brought up" (12), still endorse the conventions constantly taught by their mother. Katharine and Alex are "not brought up" at all (12); nevertheless, they too become victims to the social conventions of the "world" created for the Faraday children. The novel is set in the period preceding and just following World War I.

That Katharine differs from the rest of her family—she has dark hair, reads in her father's library chair, and has to be sent away to boarding school to learn grace and bellehood—is either her curse or her blessing. The reader must decide carefully when and if the author's sympathies are with her protagonist, for the tone varies from trenchant satire to apparent affection for Katharine Faraday. Autobiographical elements in the novel lead to speculation about the author's detachment, which seems so carefully aimed for; it is possible that the fluctuation in tone reflects the uncertainty in Frances Newman's feelings about herself.

In any case, Katharine Faraday forms her ideas about the world—

particularly about human sexuality—mainly from fiction, ranging from *Elsie Dinsmore* to *Doctor Faustus*. Occasional brushes with reality, like seeing her brother George drunk and apparently naked, traumatize her. Katharine Faraday, then, has little or no preparation for actual experience either from her books or from her family, most of whom do their best to protect themselves and her against it. She learns a little from her contemporaries, with whom she discusses birth, love, and what the first night of marriage must be like. Troubled by the conflict between what she reads and what she suspects, young Katharine takes to fantasizing. She invents plays, in each of which she takes the leading role; she never, however, transcribes the plays from her head to the page.

Katharine goes to public school in Atlanta (her mother grudgingly admitting that God seems to have become more democratic), then to Miss Randolph's in Washington. While there, she is invited to West Point; knowing such a coup is essential for a southern lady, she goes and falls for her blind date, the handsome James Fuller. Unable to sustain the intensity, Katharine abruptly ends the relationship. Later, in Charleston for the Saint Cecilia Ball, she falls for Edward Cabot, and he takes over James's part in what the narrator calls one of Katharine's plays. The plays have several themes, but they are all romances; Fuller and Cabot are interchangeable actors in a specifically military romance.

At a North Carolina mountain resort with her family, Katharine (now about eighteen) spends a lot of time with Robert Carter, an older man (in his thirties) who discusses literature with her and enjoys it, who causes her "fountain" to rise and fall and drop its "electric spray through her thin brown body" (75), and who is married. His wife develops high blood pressure (the ironic euphemism, as always, is clear), and they leave. Katharine Faraday dreams and mourns, not realizing that Robert has just been the first actor in another romance, that of Katharine Faraday and the scholar. As she grows older, making her debut, touring Europe, returning to Atlanta as an aging belle, various men take over the parts in Katharine's romances. Despite her fantasies, she hangs on to her physical virginity from her profound fear of actual (rather than imagined) sex and the pains of childbirth.

Katharine finally does write; it is an essay called "Virginal Succession," whose thesis is that a woman must remain celibate to be an artist. Although its publication begins a friendship of sorts with Virginia Wise (possibly based on Emily Clark or Ellen Glasgow) and provides an entrée into southern literary circles, Katharine's efforts to prove that she can be simultaneously very clever and a southern lady continue. The roles, as one might expect, conflict; the narrator here describes Katharine's strategic but self-destructive resolution: "And since she had already discovered that a southern lady's charms are estimated entirely by their agreement with tradition and that her intelligence is judged entirely by her ability to disagree with tradition, she told him that she thought there was a great deal to be said for the Old South, but not nearly as much as people had already said" (244). Out of Katharine's conflicting behavior—aping men and then trying to prove that she is smarter then they, combining and sometimes confusing a concern for style in dress with a concern for style in her writing, developing conversation as a social technique and then trying to say something real—Newman creates the tension that moves her heroine through an almost endless series of men with her virginity still intact.

Near the end of the novel, Katharine seems to have found a "world" (of writers) that is larger than her own fantasies. She has lost her virginity, but without even the pleasure she gets from a kiss and with the added agony of waiting to find out whether she is pregnant. And she has succeeded in writing and having produced a real play, *No Sheets*, about "a girl who could not face the idea of marriage or even of seduction, and whose young man thought she might manage to lose her virtue if the scene were part of the evening instead of being part of the night" (257–58).

Katharine remains confused about the meaning of her writing precisely because she can stop neither writing nor being a southern lady. The end of the novel finds her back in the endless cycle of her private, personal plays. *No Sheets* is a success; she has found public acclaim and the approbation of writers whom she respects; and an apparently much younger man comes to praise her. The tables are turned. Whereas Katharine has imitated men's language, now he uses her words; whereas she has been the ingenue, now he is innocent of the inevitable pattern of romantic development with which she is so familiar. Yet she determines to become involved with him—only to the point of sexual intercourse, when she will say good-bye. Because now that she knows exactly what she is doing, Katharine can see with the despair implicit in the last paragraph of the novel that "she would go on discovering that one illusion had been left to her a minute before, and that she would discover it everytime she heard another illusion shattering on the path behind her" (285).

Emphasizing not the content of experience, but the manner in which it is expressed, Newman explained that it was "her determination" in this novel "to express things only as a woman—as distinct from a man—could express."[53] A closer look at art as a theme in the novel will lead us to the heart of the matter, for it is precisely with the issue of style that Newman presents her theme most clearly.

As a conscious artist, Katharine Faraday rejects her own first novel, *Deeper Depths*, at age ten, because she finds the "literature of her own country unbearable" (13) and wants a European style. "Virginal Succession" she considers to be legitimately an "essay" precisely because "she thought [its] style was more important than [its] subject" (235). Katharine likes the idea of *No Sheets* partly because "her characters would take the responsibility for her American sentences" (257), which she still considers less stylish, and in her conversations with the great literary people she comes to know, the subject most often is style. The significance of this concern for style derives from a determination that manner be taken for matter, that a felicitous style disguise the more genuine subject. An "American" style might reveal too much truth. Art thus becomes a metaphor for that element of experience within a specifically southern society that prefers style to truth. Moreover, to write like a woman, for Newman, is to write with an even greater sensitivity to style. All her life Newman manifested enormous concern over her own appearance. She said, "Oh, you might consider me frivolous and vain if I tell you what importance I attach to personal dress. But it is not at all strange to me that persons who love the beautiful in art and music should love beautiful dress, for dress in itself is an art. One should wear colors and styles which reflect the personality of the wearer."[54] Newman was so well known for this concern that, as we saw, Corey Ford parodied her novelistic style by comparing it with a woman's makeup. In her novel, although writing does become Katharine's means of growth on the one hand, insofar as it permits her to say the truth, it also becomes, on the other hand, a means of self-destruction insofar as it permits her to hide behind the "makeup" of a stylish *persona*. Her private "art," her mental plays, perform the same function, with this major difference: because no one else can see them, she is less vulnerable than she can be as a productive artist. Yet on a less conscious level, Katharine Faraday recognizes the limits of mere style. Katharine says at one point to one of her actual romantic heroes that "her social and aesthetic conscience were both unhappy when she stayed with Virginia Wise, because she felt that the butler and the two footmen and the maids were always giving a carefully rehearsed and directed play" (255). This comes after Katharine has learned that the test of intelligence for a southern lady is her ability to criticize tradition (here the role of blacks). Thus her saying this to Samuel King is partly another step in the ritual of proving herself to be "intelligent." But more important, Katharine here sees the blacks as doing exactly what she does—acting in a "carefully rehearsed and directed play"—and she is disturbed by it. Although Katharine makes this intuitive connection with black servants, she does not recognize why she does it, for she, like them, is part of a dominated subculture that finds a way of survival in playing a role at the cost of some personal awareness.

In addition to creating a protagonist who is herself a writer, Newman gives thematic weight to literature, journalism, and conversation. The literature that Katharine reads teaches her about "reality": she ironically takes its content far more seriously than its style and learns, for example (like Sally Overton), that an honorable man never kisses a lady before proposing marriage. Thus, her trust in art as a guide to behavior produces problems. Newman sees journalism as more likely to present truth, although not stylishly; some of her more trenchant narrative satire attacks the falsity with which newspapers report reality ("journalists who described dances were not yet allowed the pleasure of choosing any of their adjectives on the impolite side" [129]). Conversation, on the other hand, is regarded as style without content—or so it is prescribed by Katharine's world. Katharine first fails at the art of saying nothing gracefully, then she discovers, through Robert Carter and later other artists, that one can discuss real things. Yet she persists in forming her conversations out of subjects in which she believes men will be interested, in using their words and ideas instead of her own, and in refusing to speak what is really on her mind. Katharine's growth can be marked by the degree to which she finds herself courageous enough to care more about subject than style, whether it be in her writing, her mind-plays, or her conversation.

The absence of meaning and its replacement by manner in art, and the absence of knowledge and its replacement by willful ignorance typify the culture in which Katharine is brought up—the specific southern world of fashion. Newman's manipulation of the narrator's point of view exemplifies this theme. Since she persistently describes Katharine as *not* knowing various things, we may infer that what the narrator says Katharine does not know, the narrator *does* know. Therefore, we can trace Katharine's development by looking for "she felt" or "she knew" to replace "she did not know she felt" or "she thought she knew." The effects of the South's denial of truth, particularly to its women, provide the central axes of the novel and its final point: alienation produces narcissism, and narcissism destroys life. Katharine Faraday is alienated from her family, from her society, from women, from men, and from herself, precisely because she is raised to believe that the inner life should be kept utterly private and that the outer life is an elaborate dance whose steps one must learn and which has no relationship to the inner self. Like Edna Pontellier, she leads a "dual life—that outward existence which conforms, the inward life which questions." [55] Unlike

Edna, however, a significant part of Katharine's inner life *is* the outer life that conforms; she has internalized the prescriptions of her culture so thoroughly that her growth, compared to Edna's, is stunted. For example, when she is lonely, she is not simply lonely; she is "mortifyingly lonely" (182). Katharine can never fully separate her own feelings from the approbation of the world around her, but to some extent she does grow out of the extreme alienation from even her own feelings that is the result, for her, of accepting the ethos of the southern lady.

Katharine is alienated, in part, because she is blind to reality (as, of course, her society prescribes that women should be); the awful result of her blindness—which is to both external and to internal reality—is that she makes up her own world and cannot even discriminate the true from the false within it. Hence, again, the narrator must constantly tell us what Katharine does not know.

To say that Katharine makes up her own world because of her alienation is to say that she has become a narcissist, "that paradoxical condition of self-regard in which absorption with the self speaks to an absence of the self." [56] If a healthy self-image derives from an individual's successfully unifying her sense of inner experience with her "perception of . . . self as an object" in an external world, then a radical contradiction between the messages from inner and outer worlds will impede the development of a self. A narcissist may then overvalue her inner life of wish and thought—as Katharine does her mental "plays"—and devalue objective information. [57] Thus, as Vivian Gornick explains, a narcissist experiences the external world "solely as a source of gratification or deprivation. . . . [hence] genuine engagement with the objective world is precluded." [58] Freud thought women and artists, as classes of people, were particularly susceptible to extremes of narcissism. And in *The Feminization of American Culture*, Ann Douglas links blacks, women, and ministers as out-groups in her discussion of cultural causes for narcissism:

> Such subculture groups, past and present, evince certain inherent patterns. Most simply, one might say that a society forces members of a subculture at any moment of intersection with the larger culture into a constant, simplified, and often demeaning process of self-identification such as a punitively generalized mode of self-description. . . .
>
> Naturally those belonging to a subculture will themselves be preoccupied with who they are, often in equally simplistic and distorted terms. They will struggle obsessively, repetitiously, and monotonously to deal with the burden of self-dis-

like implied and imposed by their society's apparently low estimation of them. In a sense, they will be forced into some version of narcissism . . . best defined not as exaggerated self-esteem but as a refusal to judge the self by alien, objective means, a willed inability to allow the world to play its customary role in the business of self-evaluation. . . . The narcissist must always by definition be self-taught, because the world's lessons are inevitably unacceptable to his ego. He is committed not only to an underestimation of the force of facts, but, in Freud's words, to an "over-estimation of the power of wishes and mental processes. . . . a belief in the magical virtue of words and a method of dealing with the outer world—the art of magic." Narcissism can necessitate the replacement of society by the self, reality by literature.[59]

Newman's choice of narrative point of view, as already noted, enhances the reader's sense that Katharine is an isolated consciousness whose anxious task it is to learn, throughout the novel, lessons from the objective world whose learning can only teach her to devalue herself still further. Interestingly, Katharine writes a poem in Venice that describes the town as Narcissus, admiring its own reflection in the canals. Newman follows this episode with the following: "She felt obliged to smile across a narrow canal at a young man who looked like a young gentleman and who was singing to his guitar. He dropped his guitar and answered her smile by a deliberate exposition of the mysteries George Faraday had already revealed to her accidentally" (211). Narcissism as writing *about* narcissism is followed by an effort, however reluctant (note "obliged"), to move out of the "self" and "literature" into "society" and "reality." But the equally narcissistic young man, "singing to his guitar" as she is to her notebook, quite literally exhibits himself to the fragile Katharine. Thenceforth, Katharine cannot even read books about Venice: the "world's lessons" that she is a sexual victim are "unacceptable."

Douglas' definition, though it helps considerably to explain Katharine, is rather too extreme, because at other times Katharine does emerge, with less traumatizing effects, from her (false) self. Although terrified of the real world, outside as well as inside herself, Katharine seeks it. But it is precisely her identity as a female (in both the biological and the southern social sense) that makes Katharine a narcissist and that provokes Newman to her most trenchant satire on the South. This satire is clearly directed at the society, for the reason for Katharine's failings is traced most frequently to her "upbringing." A closer look at the women, the men, and the society as they are depicted in the novel will demonstrate how clearly Katharine's alienation and narcissism are the result of being raised to be a southern lady in the early twentieth century.

Katharine's mother, Mrs. Faraday, identifies herself clearly as a southerner. No presentable man was ever born in Connecticut, she says (231), and she "had heard in her cradle that a nation which could prefer a Lincoln to a Breckinridge was unlikely to return to the conviction that elegance is the greatest of human virtues, and she had even heard delicate suggestions that a God who could look down unmoved on the triumph of a Grant over a Lee could hardly expect to be acquitted of increasingly democratic sympathies" (17). Mrs. Faraday never questions what she learned in her cradle. Her role in the novel is to prescribe and supervise the behavior of her daughters, to teach them how to be southern ladies. One refrains from talk about religion, reads only the right books, remains in the "state of innocence" that "good breeding" requires (55), seeks an education only because a wife with class should read and converse, works constantly to improve her looks, chooses friends who are from the "right" society. As to men, Mrs. Faraday instructs her daughters that a woman must live for her husband. "A woman's success is her husband's success" (173), hence she "must always persuade a man to talk about the subject he is interested in" (73). The premise that a woman's consuming goal is to find a correct husband is so completely accepted that Mrs. Faraday feels no need to mention it. Marriage, however, has its drawbacks: "Since her mother had never suspected that Katharine Faraday might ever be interested in any subject a man could be interested in, she had told her that a woman must always expect to be bored. Her mother had also told her that no southern lady had ever sat in a hammock with any man" (73–74). A southern lady, according to Mrs. Faraday, not only must endure and never enjoy conversation and sex with her husband, but she must also show no affection for him: the "discussion of religion on week-days [is] as unbecoming a southern lady as affection for her husband" (50).

Given this set of injunctions, it is difficult to see how a southern lady could survive. She gives up her self to her husband and then cannot even enjoy the fringe benefits of marriage because she is so radically different from him. Her consolation is not philosophy; it is social status. The self-esteem that is inevitably lost in the alienating process described above can be regained by an all-consuming passion for receiving the approbation of the public—that is, the public of the socially elite. There logically follows the elaborate set of games that women play with other women to prove their place in the pecking order.

Katherine's two sisters are adept at this game. In it, the woman prefers the attention of men to that of women but invites women to lunch and other female gatherings in order to fulfill and incur "obligations" and to make connections with "important" families. The subjects of conversation—the latest shows and fashions, how to decorate a home— provide a medium through which women can exert their power plays. Katharine's oldest sister Marian clearly is raising her daughter in her mother's tradition when she takes the child home from Europe because "she had already discovered that men are not made precisely like women and that all women do not dislike being kissed" (265). Eleanor, too, instructs her sister Katharine in the proper role: to hide "her more elaborate mental processes" (124) and to become aware of the "damaging effects of [honest feeling such as] Katharine Faraday's entirely unconcealed affection for Edward Cabot" (154).

The necessity of concealing the truth is integral to the definition of the southern lady. Most things she is not supposed to know about in the first place, so being honest only reveals a lack of gentility. Katharine's female friends illustrate this doubleness. All of her friends are southerners. One had a great-grandmother who "had proved herself [Richmond's] ideal of southern womanhood by combining a degree of beauty which charmed George Washington with a degree of intelligence which refused the hand of George Washington," a combination of charm and intelligence that is precisely what Katharine—and Newman—find so hard to attain (132–33). Another, a Charlestonian, tells Katharine the rules for the Saint Cecilia Society ball: don't wear red, don't go outside the Hibernian Hall with a young man. Although Katharine does talk with her friends about "real" things to some extent, there is no bond of affection between them, for they are all in pursuit of the same goal: a man. Hence they are competitors, and hence a button from a West Point jacket is described as a "trophy" (117). Of course, this competition is one thing never discussed—unless it involves a third party not present. One character who appears late in the novel shows the awful alternative to marriage. Catherine Robinson, forty, is "too unhappy to endure being alone . . . does not enjoy sharing a room with a woman . . . and is sure she would not enjoy sharing it with a man" (266).

Not just mother, sisters, and friends elaborate the rules of behavior and the goals of a southern lady. More generally, the culture of Atlanta and the South makes its idea clear; men as well as women, of course, comprise that culture. It is understood, for instance, that if a girl is smart she will be ugly and that "the stupidest girl with a short upper lip and curly golden hair is born to a social situation much pleasanter than the social situation of the cleverest girl with a long upper lip and straight black hair" (30). Moreover, "any boy is born to a more honourable social situation than any girl" (30). In school, for instance, both boys and girls are rewarded for academic performance. But the highest-scoring boys all sit in the front row, even if their marks are lower than those of the highest-scoring girls, who sit in the second row. And the privileges of such achievement are appropriately symbolic: the boy may open the school door if he thinks he hears a knock, and the girl gets to carry out the trash. "In Georgia no lady was supposed to know she was a virgin until she had ceased to be one," Katharine knows. Yet the double standard is clear. One of her beaux, Neal Lumpkin, conducts his campaign for the state legislature on the argument that the age of consent should not be raised: "Raising the age of consent meant increasing the possibility that perfectly respectable young Georgians—who might even be sons and grandsons of the heroes who wore the gray—would be hanged for nothing more than the violation of fourteen year old virgins" (174). Of course, Katharine cannot discuss the issue with Lumpkin, for she must pretend ignorance about the very subject. According to her mother's ideas, she should not even be interested.

Given the definitions of southern lady and gentleman in the book, it is no wonder that from a very early age Katharine follows a narcissistic pattern. She tries to kiss her elbow—to change her sex. She finds consolation in literature, for there she finds, for instance, that some women with her "high forehead and her straight nose and her long upper lip" have been brilliant (40). When she is quite young, her instinctive values are intellectual (25), egalitarian (26), and antifashion (27). Coming of age for Katharine, however, means accepting the dictates of her culture, from which she knows no possible deviations. Then she becomes snobbish; she feels as "publicly depraved" as Hester Prynne when she and her boarding-school friends have tea with some nice boys to whom they have not been "introduced." She becomes increasingly concerned with her looks and her clothing; she betrays her girl friends by telling them they look good when they don't. She believes she has a "destined husband" and makes sure she is knowledgeable about subjects in which she thinks potential mates are interested, regardless of her own interest. She never asserts herself, she reads Darwin only because he is "celebrated," and she even makes up her own rules about conversation: "The first rule forbade her to ask a question unless she was sure she was asking it of a man who would enjoy answering it . . . the second forbade her to make a remark merely for the pleasure she found in saying something aloud" (220–21).

Simultaneous with her public conformity, however, Katharine develops an inner life that, unlike the inner life of her "plays," reflects a growing desire to teach herself what is real. Her body comes first; as she matures physically, she notices a "delicate line which was slightly browner than the area she thought was her stomach" (35) and is pleased when her turn comes to get her "feet wet" (the euphemism for menstruation). She rejects the Presbyterian church's theology, minister, and social graspers; at her first communion she is astonished that she does not fall dead for her apostasy.

But these and other choices and awarenesses remain private. Perhaps the radical split between public and private existence helps to explain a gradual intensification of the violence of her private fantasies. They include making a wax doll of Robert Carter's wife and sticking pins into its blue veins, responding to her brother Arthur's death only with the hope that it will force her most recent beau to write to her, and an increasing consideration of suicide. The two sides of her inner self— and the complicated tone of the narrator—can be clearly seen when Katharine learns that David Hoffman has had another son: "she felt a sickness . . . and she sank down into it while she wondered if she should throw herself down among the hydrangeas or whether she should only throw down the fuchsia crepe" (264).

Katharine, then, becomes adept at acting in a way different from her feelings: "she felt again that their reunion was a miracle, but she looked as calm as the green laurel-tree which had seen Daphne pursued by Apollo one minute before, and she took his hand as she might have taken the high-veined hand of Mrs. Randolph's oldest gentlewoman" (119–20). But she retains the need for some kind of integrity, which, along with her narcissist self, can be seen in her writing. The act of writing in her notebook (in response to a marriage proposal) that she would rather earn her living by day than by night permits what the narrator calls a "new birth" (198). And her professional writing brings her into contact with people among whom she comes closest to being and becoming herself.

Yet any form of verbal expression that is real and not part of her social role continues to threaten her throughout the novel. Katharine learns that a real dialogue with a man may well mean something different to him; it may be taken as a sexual overture. She learns that "a woman who hopes to enjoy life must turn her back on life and pay no attention to it" (227); her insight contradicts the very notion of having insight. Moreover, her lady-self is a self-censor: "she would not have elaborated with an unladylike idea [such as comparing a bride to Titania] even in a notebook" (217). So writing remains for her as much a part of a game as a means of expression of honest thought and feeling—hence her never-ending concern for style, akin (as with Newman herself) to her concern for dress style. Finally, threading through the entire novel is a profound fear of public ostracism, a fear that extends to the act of writing. As a child, Katharine drinks water from a rusty cup so that she won't risk not being chosen for a game of Prisoner's Base; that fear extends to the publication of "Virginal Succession," an act that she sees as safer than marriage only because it does not expose her directly in front of other people. The greater the bifurcation between her fantasy life and her expression of it, the more outrageous become her fantasies and the more profound her fear of rejection. Caught, she equivocates; she writes, but with a purple pencil; she talks, but with an elliptical style; she acts, but never lets herself be "swept away" (as no southern lady should). One guesses that there is very little of a genuine self to be swept away.

The authorial narrator, despite her own similarities to Katharine Faraday, is more explicit. The two clearest paths to narrative stance consist of direct attacks on her culture and the subtle but careful repetition of phrases that threads a tone of seriousness through the satirical portrait of this southern belle. Newman directly attacks female education: it "extracts" or "paralyzes" the brains of southern women (58). Hitting next the victims of that education, she attacks female wiles: for instance, women know that wearing "perpetual black and white can always delicately suggest a perpetual rival in heaven" (72) and keep a man on the hook. She compares checking off "safely partnered dances" at a ball to convicts checking off "days without lashes" (138). The double standard evokes an acid tone: "Southern gentlemen consider alcoholic beverages unsuited to the fragile organisms which are capable of nothing more energetic than producing twelve babies" (111). On the other hand, the girls "of [Katharine's] world did not often think of being interested by the things which the necessity of being interesting made them talk about to men, [so] no sensible girl ever damaged her fragile reputation by talking to a man through the bars of matrimony" (185). Neither southern gentlemen nor southern ladies, then, are exempt from the sarcastic voice of the narrator. But the sharpest—and the most numerous—barbs are reserved for the culture of the South. Besides the passage on southern gentlemen and rape quoted above, Newman mocks the sanctimonious worship of the Church of England and of England itself, of ancestors, of blood, of southern history. Katharine is probably aware of the irony of what she is doing when her author makes her please the "Virginian pride of Isabel Ambler's aunt by pointing out the strange resemblance between the most plebeian English features and the most aristocratic Charlestonian features" (214). But it is the narrator's direct voice that speaks of "a thin young man called Grantland Lamar as evidence that his grandfathers had both shed blood of the best quality on the red clay of half the counties to which their grandfathers had given their names, but that one of his great-grandfathers had known better than to buy any of the bonds printed by the Confederate States of America" (132). As we shall see, many of the men in Newman's world are Lamars living in Grant's land—blue bloods pursuing the almighty dollar.

Of Newman's repeated phrases, some are satirical in intent and some apparently quite serious. Variations upon the phrase "Katharine Faraday's world" seem to indicate the narcissism, the self-production of that world, and simultaneously its links with the "larger" and thus implicitly narcissistic world of the South. Repeatedly, the narrator expresses Katharine's waxing and waning "confidence in the world's ability to appreciate her charms." The satire is clear when, after several men have been defined as her first "real" love, Katharine still finds it a "miracle" that she should see each of her latest loves as once again the first.

Yet the persistence of the reference to Prisoner's Base reveals a darker and more serious thread; Katharine's deepest fears are never satirized. Most important, although she uses the repeated question, "Why do fathers love their children?" as a semi-intentional device to get a man to show that he can love her, Katharine's question appears often enough and in enough different contexts to let us see in it a buried pulse in the novel. On one of its deepest and perhaps least conscious levels, the novel is about a woman's fears and questions about her body and the male body, about sex and birth, about isolation and suffering, and about the possibility of love. In her insistence on repeating this question, Newman hints at a web of concerns about men and women that —like Katharine's mind—remains private, divorced from the more apparent social satire of the novel.

Perhaps the ambiguous concluding sections reflect the central ambivalence of their author. Each of Katharine's insights is tempered or contradicted by other elements in the story. By page 246, for instance, Katharine has found that she can no longer act what she does not feel; though a negative statement, it represents a positive stage of growth. Perhaps, one thinks, she will be able to act what she *does* feel. Yet on the following page she "dreamed dreams which she thought were giving her an insight into a nature very unlike the nature a southern lady should have had" (247). By the end of the next section, she "had begun to fear that she was really a southern lady and that she would never be swept off her feet" (253). She has retreated into passivity once again: whether she is or is not "swept," she will continue to be an object, rather than a subject, of action.

Elsewhere, Katharine discovers that "she had been right when she had thought she was not brave enough not to be virtuous" (276); then the success of her play gives her a sense of power, so that she "had be-gun at last to feel that a peg has at least as much right to be square as a hole has to be round" (281). Yet the belief that she has attained con-fidence and a sense of identity is mitigated at the end of the novel by her behavior with Philip Cobb. Though the male and female roles are now reversed—this younger man will sit "at her feet and by her side at the same time" (283), just as she and Virginia Wise have done with male writers—nevertheless it is the same play. She has found adulation and even, in a striking metaphor, a baby: "he would put out his hands to her as blindly as a baby reaching out his hands and his mouth for his mother" (284). But the reversal of roles only saddens her; there is no way out of the utter predictability of the relationship. Instead of creat-ing a definition of woman, Newman has tried to expose one. Only in the inferences drawn from her satire and from the serious verbal threads in her novel can we find hints of what she would actually prefer.

The men in Newman's novel vary more than do the women. Some, like Marian's husband, reveal the arrogance of caste; he speaks "with the conscious infallibility of a man who knows that his mortal remains will be buried in a vault" (115). Some are pure consumers, like Elea-nor's husband, who builds their house as a frame to show off his wife's beauty (152); she is only one more pretty possession. Some are overtly misogynic: Arthur Faraday is "sure that men would never publicly admit that they had seen their best days by inviting women into the polls women had nothing at all to do with inventing" (158); some are simply knee-jerk sexists, like Neal Lumpkin, who believes "all the faiths of his fathers which concerned God and women and negroes and cotton" (177) and who gives Katharine a copy of Buckle's *History of Civiliza-tion in England* "as the basis of education for an enlightened states-man's wife" (180).

On the other hand, the only really sympathetic characters in the novel are men like Robert Carter, who enjoys learning even when his name and his fortune don't require it (73), or James Fuller, whose good looks are matched by his sensitivity to Katharine's feelings. More im-portant, it is only male characters whom the narrator, by dropping her narrative "thoughts" and "felts," allows to understand Katharine: Hoffmann, for instance, "understood her well enough to tell her she was always writing her emotions down in black and white without waiting for either tranquillity or a pencil" (259). And Samuel King had "shown his insight into feminine characters by telling her that she did not like women" (266). Despite these two instances—or perhaps because their insights are rather depressing—Katharine's attitude toward men remains until the end a combination of a rather desperate search for love (whether from a father or a husband or a son is ambiguous, as we have seen), a decreasing but persistent inability to comprehend the male psyche, a strong need to compete with men and to prove her "cleverness" to them, and a simultaneous need to assimilate herself into the men she is with, even to the point of total identification. Men for Katharine—and ultimately for the author—are good or bad, attractive or unattractive; only very rarely can they be friends and equals, full characters.

The principal notion of community in the novel finds itself in the neo-aristocratic society of the South. Even the southern artists depicted in the novel make disparaging comments like Frederick Thomas' "no New Englander ever had been a gentleman and . . . no New Englander ever would be a gentleman" (245). There are distinctions among regions in the South; Sarah Rutledge from Charleston is astonished that Atlanta can value "frocks, houses, even brains" more than ancestors (11). The history of this South seems rather like *Hagar*'s: the "great-grandfathers had given their names to the counties of the more distinguished southern states," whereas the fathers know "on Wednesday what the price of cotton would be on Thursday" and the sons are "members of the Piedmont Driving Club" (57–58). The male South has moved, as Mary Johnston put it, from conquering the land, to cornering the market, to cornering the social scene. Meanwhile, women's history is static: the "mothers would be arranging careful dinners and dances and lunches" (58), just as—with the exception of the Civil War period and the earlier pioneer days—the women had done for generations and would continue to do in the future.

The family as community is roundly rejected by the depiction not just of the loveless Faradays but of Katharine's married contemporaries' blossoming mediocrity. Katharine, like Hagar, finds a community that transcends sex and region, a community of artists, of her "own small circulation" (265). Yet because—unlike Hagar—the baggage that Katharine carries into her community includes not just her writings but the habits of a southern lady, she encourages the male writers she meets to talk only of themselves, effacing herself. (The writer Virginia Wise, too, can give a man the feeling that "she was sitting at his feet and by his side and on his knee at the same time" [249].) The contradiction implicit in the images of the southern lady and the intelligent woman, the belle and the intellectual, charm and intelligence is never resolved, even in the community of artists. With this in mind, it is especially intriguing to note Newman's dedication of the book to her mother, the "charming lady who gave me a great deal more than her name." *The Hard-Boiled Virgin* may well be the answer to what that "great deal" was.

When *The Hard-Boiled Virgin* was published, Atlanta was "shocked almost into convulsions over it, and," said Newman, "I hadn't a particle of character left. Lots of people apparently think I've done everything in it, and although I point out that Hawthorne was never the mother of an illegitimate daughter . . . it doesn't do any good. However, all of it sells the book, I gather, so I bear up."[60] She was apparently encouraged enough to continue writing. Two years after *The Hard-Boiled Virgin*, Frances Newman published her second and last novel, *Dead Lovers Are Faithful Lovers*. Though less well known than her first novel, it deserves a careful look. Difficult to read though it, too, is, several of the stylistic mannerisms that made her first novel almost undecipherable are weeded out of Newman's second. Gone are the multiple negatives, the elaborate conditionals, the hundreds of literary references, and the heavy use of narrative distancing. Nevertheless, Newman retained and refined the technique of indirection that had contributed both to the first novel's density and to its point. For example, it takes a careful reader to sort out the chronology, and one must be on one's toes even to recognize that Charlton Cunningham, the central male in the novel, never actually completes a sexual relationship with his supposed "mistress," Isabel Ramsey.

Furthermore, influenced by her reading of Virginia Woolf, Newman refined and expanded her manipulation of point of view. Here we have not one but two characters' minds expressed in their inmost workings. The split between them slices the novel in half (though Newman considered it a "modulated" shift), giving the first half to Cunningham's Richmond wife, born Evelyn Byrd Page, and the second to his Georgia love, Isabel Ramsay. The end of the novel shifts back to Evelyn's point of view; we never see Isabel's reaction to Charlton's death, and we learn of Charlton's death only in the last three words. Newman's method of making points that are inaccessible to the minds of her two women is, again, repetition. She repeats phrases, word clusters, sentences, images, so that the reader can see connections that the characters cannot. One obvious example occurs when Charlton is reported as saying to each woman that "human speech is not one of the languages of love"; it shows us consistency in his persona and deepens the irony that, although each woman hopes she is his one real love, both probably are. (Both women even receive the same postcard of a statue showing a man and a woman embracing.)

One might speculate that the virtual absence in *Dead Lovers Are Faithful Lovers* of the satirical tone that riddled *The Hard-Boiled Virgin* threw reviewers off when they read Newman's second novel in 1928. The notices are less flattering than were those for her first novel, and in some cases they simply miss the point. In the *Nation*, A. B. Parsons noted Newman's "satiric gift" and her "eye for color," for "social niceties," and for "social slips." But, he claimed, "this book does not demonstrate . . . that she knows the difference between a novel and a bag of parlor tricks . . . the repetition of a once good joke can not make a distinguished literary style." John Macy found the story original, sharp, tragic, and true, but said it "suffers from being berouged, lip-sticked, toilet-watered . . . on almost every page, [Newman] puts too much make-up on, and does it in public." The Springfield (Illinois) *Republican* again claimed that her "real flair is satirical. Her observation often plays over the surface of life with a zest that the reader can share, as he can share her covert antagonism to various social forms and conventions of the older South, despite their accompanying humaneness. But her understanding of emotions is limited." The august London *Times Literary Supplement* complained that the novel was "quite flat— readable only for the ingenuity of the style and the sophisticated ingenuousness of her allusions." And the *Independent* dismissed it as the "spiritual jeremiad of a near-neurotic Southern lady." [61]

Many of these reviews sound in fact as though their subject should be *The Hard-Boiled Virgin*. Closer to an accurate appraisal of the novel's tone was T. S. Matthews' statement in the *New Republic* that "the cumulative effect of this story is considerable: it has moments of poignancy, and its tragedy is genuine, implicit and restrained." And Isabel Patterson, writing for the New York *Herald Tribune*, came closer to an accurate description of the novel's content—and possibly an explanation for the befuddlement of some of its reviewers: "It will give offense. It is meant to. . . . The head of its offending is that it shows women as autonomous emotional beings. . . . But it does stultify the charge that women writers spend their powers in imitation of men writers. No man could have written it. Most men will be unable to read it. It says a good many of the things men have tried by every social and economic device to avoid hearing." [62]

Between the publication of *The Hard-Boiled Virgin* and that of *Dead Lovers Are Faithful Lovers*, Newman changed her purpose in writing the second novel. In November, 1926, she said she wanted "to write about a woman who lets herself be entirely absorbed by love—lets it eat up everything she has in her, simply sinks down into it. I could do that myself, I feel some times." By May 28, 1927, she had "entirely changed" her plan for the novel. "I am trying to do a certain type of man, first from the point of view of his wife, and then from the point of view of a girl with whom he falls in love about ten years after he is married. I wouldn't think of trying to do a man at any closer range, because although I know what they will do under certain circumstances, I have no idea why." Her publishers, Boni and Liveright, said they preferred this novel to *The Hard-Boiled Virgin*; but "I don't," Newman wrote in January, 1928, "and I don't think any women will, but all the men who have read it so far like it better. I suppose they enjoy seeing two women so idiotically in love with a man, and altogether, men don't come off so badly in it, and women do. I think it's better prose, and I think it's rather neat technically, but I don't think it's anything of a mutant."[63] *Dead Lovers Are Faithful Lovers* is certainly a book *about* women; probably—though, oddly enough, given the antifemale sentiment of the major female characters—it is *for* women as well. Like the sentimentalists in their very different way, Newman here tells women who they are and speaks with particular accuracy to and about southern women.

The novel begins in 1910 at the end of Evelyn Cunningham's honeymoon with her husband Charlton, a promising counsel for the Southeastern Railway. In a sleeping compartment on the train, they are approaching Atlanta, where they will set up their household. If there were a word for women that means what *uxorious* does for men (later in the novel Evelyn remembers her father said that the word was *wife*),[64] it would describe Evelyn's mind and behavior. From the first scene, when we learn that she always wakes up before her husband so she can prepare her body—combing her hair, touching her skin with perfume, arranging her nightgown for his awakening—we see her sexual hunger for her husband, enhanced by love (or permitted by it) and turning into dependence. Her infatuation is so profound that she thinks of him constantly, worries about his possible infidelity, and makes a profession of making herself attractive to him. As her father has told her, "You reckon from Charlton Cunningham exactly as the rest of the world reckons from Greenwich" (53).

It is no wonder that she is so attracted to him; Charlton is what Isabel Patterson called the "feminine ideal of a man."[65] He is tall, with a thin face, dark eyes, and a striking manner of holding his right shoulder high while he expresses himself with his hands. Not only does he look much like her father, John Rolfe Page, but he talks and thinks like him, too, with an epigrammatic style and an intelligent eye for the reality behind his culture's pleasant fictions; he lacks only a degree of moody acerbity to be a latter-day Rhett Butler. Moreover, though Evelyn is sure that she loves him more than she has any other man, she is equally sure that Charlton does not love her more than any other man has. And she takes to heart her mother's warning that, in marriage, a wife's love always grows and a husband's always wanes.

In Atlanta, Evelyn spends her days while Charlton is at work doing what every proper southern lady should: entertaining callers (all women), playing bridge, discussing social niceties. But within, she is thinking about Charlton, what he is doing at three o'clock, what he is thinking at four. Her father had called her "probably the last of the Virginia belles" and thus "was afraid you could never fall in love" (20). Nevertheless, she has gone beyond Katharine Faraday to find what she thinks is a reciprocal love. However, she feels that Charlton quite literally has given her her body: when he kissed her ("twice") and proposed at Greenbrier, "this strange figure had united with her familiar head and . . . had become her body" (51). Because of her consequent dependence on him, she plays all the games she has been taught will ensure his continuing love: flirting with other men, never letting "her head lie against her husband's shoulder so long as he wanted it to lie there" (66), never failing to see a "man or a woman whose interest in her could make her seem more important to him" (67). The subject invites satire, but Newman's tone is compassionate, if controlled; one emerges from Evelyn's section of the novel moved by pity and perhaps by fear.

To achieve such a tone with this particular character is a considerable accomplishment; with equal skill, however, Newman creates the mind of the other heroine as well, the "other woman," Isabel Ramsay. Clearly autobiographical, at least in broad outline, Isabel is single, Atlanta-bred, a librarian, well-read (in 1922 she has read T. S. Eliot's "The Waste Land"), and intelligent. Moreover, she is beautiful with a dark-haired elegance that, like a Gutenberg Bible under glass, draws men to admire but not to touch. Charlton Cunningham, however, "certainly looked at her as if she were a woman instead of a Holy Bible . . . lying remotely inside a glass cage" (203). Isabel meets Charlton at the library where he has come to look up some information about Hugo Grotius; she is twenty-seven, he has been married about ten years (so Evelyn is about thirty-five), and it is around 1920. By now he and Evelyn have moved to Richmond, where, Evelyn has thought, "she would certainly be important to her husband in a town where he would be slightly more important because he was Evelyn Byrd Page's consort than he would be because he was a vice-president of the Southeastern Railway" (114). He is now the youngest president the railway has ever had.

Isabel's and Charlton's relationship begins cautiously and with propriety—a lunch and, months later, a dinner in New York. It is while all three are at a New York flower show that the two women see each other for the first time and the point of view shifts to Isabel; the last time the two women see one another is again in New York, as Charlton is dying in the Plaza Hotel. Evelyn never suspects that any real woman, much less this one, has come close to actualizing her dread of Charlton's infidelity. Isabel becomes, however, almost as obsessed as Evelyn is with a consuming desire for Charlton; the reader observes her go agonizingly through a day of waiting for mail deliveries while at work in the "feminine" Carnegie Library. (Here Newman drew on her own experiences at the Atlanta Carnegie Library and later at Georgia Tech, for Isabel has been offered a job at a "masculine" university library and has accepted.) Despite her obsession, Isabel can, unlike Evelyn, escape from it at times. She is more analytical, more intelligent, has more information—in short, she has some experience of the world that gives her a context into which she can, if need be, place her pain.

The romance with Charlton grows. Isabel lives in New York for some months doing library work, and they dine and kiss but never make love; he is, as she sees it, "saving her from himself for himself" (266). On the night when she thinks he might give in, he arrives at her apartment ill. The novel ends with his corpse in a coffin, on a train again with Evelyn, going this time to Richmond. Isabel, we presume, will go to a better job in that "masculine" university library. Evelyn feels, along with her grief, an unconscious triumph: "the pain . . . did not tell her that she felt herself walking at last on the green oasis of a memory over which she was dropping the victorious curtain of her very long black crape veil" (295). She will live with her father and can still fulfill her own goal to become an "*impregnable* great lady" of Virginia (29, 100, 131, my emphasis)—a goal that as a young woman she "did not suspect" required "admiring their [men's] world enough to accept its verdict on love and on religion, and on the status of women and of negroes, and on books and music and on a tariff for revenue only" (29–30). It is now 1922.

By expressing with delicacy, poignancy, and truth the minds of these two southern women, Newman has both implicitly and explicitly presented a critique of the society that produced them. Both women lead two lives, the inner one passionate and the outer decorous; the daily life of each is typically southern and is spent in the company of women; both find, aside from Charlton, their best avenue to reality and their deepest mutual affection in their fathers.

The women come from two Souths. Evelyn's is Richmond, a culture that treasures "blood" so much that her uncle wanted her to marry a certain George because he was "the only living grandson of two Confederate generals" (25). Her parents have the same grandfather. It is a South of careful attention to caste, where the distinctions between the

North Carolina Pages and the Virginia Pages are considered as important as the distinction between Methodist Episcopal and Protestant Episcopal, yet where "overseers and sheriffs and hereditary followers of John Wesley" are lumped together (136). Evelyn's mother gives her daughter Sheraton furniture and a family letter from Lafayette to prove her genealogy to the parvenu Atlantans; her aunt warns that she "will find herself in a town where people have no ancestors and no manners of their own. . . . They invite people to dinner for business reasons" (26). Mrs. Page even sends down a "primrose"-colored servant; the Atlanta servants are too dark. It is a South where a daughter's first duty is deference—to parents, to tradition, to husband, to God—and her first goal is perfection, outwardly demonstrated in manners, appearance, and (not so paradoxically) self-deprecation. Evelyn's God is, as she first sees him, "omniscient but inexperienced and masculine" (17); He, like the men in *The Hard-Boiled Virgin*, is "pleased by her silent quotation from his literary works" (114). Although God "could interfere with the laws of nature . . . to raise men and women from the dead . . . he could not interfere with the social dogmas of Virginia" (132). John Rolfe Page, Evelyn's father, takes an ironic view of this culture; for example, he says about George that "every time I see his chin rushing away from his profile into his collar, I remember that Confederate armies were led into unusually bloody battles by the men who begot his father and mother. And I am afraid of understanding why the Confederacy is a lost cause" (25–26). Evelyn thinks of writing to her father to remind him of the time when "your brother Lee was putting all of Charlton's fellow-citizens into one class. And I remembered his face when you told him that all Englishmen put all Americans in the same class—Americans. And when you told him that Mr. Balfour would probably find a Shonts or a Harriman just as well-bred as a Page of Shadwell or a Middleton of Middleton Place" (42). But Mr. Page's failure to act on his insight into southern culture has destroyed the inner life of his marriage: his affections for Mrs. Page "had not survived the birth of his daughter" (84); he sees his wife in the traditional southern way, as a "mere object of respectful veneration" (85). As for Mrs. Page, her adherence to the traditions of caste and of the "four kinds of hot bread" cooked for her husband every morning "shorten[ed] the interval between the two dates on the grey stone" under which she is buried (132).

Isabel's South, of course, is Atlanta, a society that apes the mores of Richmond with only little success and, simultaneously, in its obsessions with money and commerce, is determined to "grow as far as possible towards New York" (227). Her father takes as jaundiced a view of the mores of the South as does John Rolfe Page. Walter Wingfield Ramsay, a newspaper editor, believes heretically that "the dipping of cattle [is] more beneficial to the state of Georgia than the baptism of men and women and infants" (267) and does not believe in the God "about whom he had written so deferentially and so frequently" (267). Like Page, he hides his true opinions, endorsing editorially what he privately abhors, writing "only the words he had known his paper would print" (210) partly because he "had never felt that the father of two daughters" (231) could afford to take any greater risk. (His daughters, to pay homage to his convictions, refuse to wear black to his funeral.) Unlike Evelyn, Isabel inhabits a larger world than either Atlanta or Richmond, thanks to her education. Working in the library has taught her, through "eating daily apples from the tree of the knowledge of good and evil" (218). Hence she notices, for example, that nineteenth-century romances "seem to punish a villainess for wanting the very things with which the writers are preparing to reward a heroine for not wanting them" (215); the women are punished, in short, not for the objects of their desire but for having a desire at all. Even when she is swept away by Charlton, Isabel's mind keeps working. He has said that he now knows why "the heroine of the story is always the one who doesn't see the hero until after she belongs to a King Mark or a Karenin" (253). What Charlton doesn't realize is that because it is he, not she, who belongs to another, there is a world of difference. Isabel's mind slips "down pages of alphabetical dictionaries of heroines . . . she saw Fiora and Francesca da Rimini and Guinevere and Helen and Isolde and Anna Karenina and Melisande standing on the side where Mr. Charlton Cunningham might have been standing beside a tall fair-haired man, and she saw herself standing alone until her mind dropped down all the alphabetical pages to Zaza" (254). The literary omens for a single woman's carrying on with a married man are not good; and, as was the case for Katharine Faraday, literature has a great deal to do with life for Isabel Ramsay. Despite her intelligence, Isabel's daily life is almost as exclusively feminine as is Evelyn's, and the duties of her job—patience, deference, altruism, endurance—are close to those of a wife. And like Evelyn, though for different reasons, Isabel learns to dislike women.

Despite the differences between these two Souths—in effect, between the Old and the New South—the similarities are more important, and the difference between the South and the North far deeper than any regional distinctions within the South. Although the Atlantan "Mrs. Jordan seems to be so important that she enjoyed the right to be as rude as most of Evelyn Page's relations had waived their right to be in Virginia" (90), and although it is hinted that New Orleans grants women far less inhibition of sexuality, knowledge, and verbal expression (138–39), the South as a whole is characterized as sharing certain values, particularly toward its women. It trusts, for instance, "the virtue of any custom which had happened to coincide with its own youth" (177). Atlanta has a procession to honor the Confederate dead. Charlton smiles when he sees the statue of Sherman in New York, because it is "fading" (282). And in the South as a whole, "courageous convictions do not take precedence over politeness" (220). Most important for women, the South is still a patriarchy; a woman is known by her father or her husband and is shown a deference proportional to his or their importance to the South.

The narrator herself resembles the two divided fathers she describes, for although she can satirize the South, when she places her most worldly character Isabel in New York, she has her react very strongly against it. New York, as described by the narrator and as seen by Isabel, is a very unpleasant place; unlike southern cities, it is ugly, its people all seem to be nearly criminal, the only things natural to it are snow and rain, and even the fruits are imported. Isabel feels alien in this environment; it "gnaws away" at her repeatedly. She feels, in fact, that "she would always be gnawed on in a town where eyes were thrust forward by brains which were straining towards sights that she would have run away from" (286). Isabel is no Hagar, and southern men and women, for Newman, place their southernness—despite its drawbacks—at the forefront of their identities.

So the paradox for the southern woman remains that to define herself as a southerner is to accept a definition of herself that dehumanizes. The women whom Isabel and Evelyn so dislike are superficial (one conversation concerns "whether a butler should offer a silver platter of squabs and wild rice first to a hostess or first to a guest of honour" [97]) because they have never questioned their world's verdict "on the status of women" (30). And that status relegates them precisely to superficiality, to the state of an ornament. There are hints that even Evelyn might have grown beyond the confines of her life. She does, unlike Katharine Faraday and the traditional lady, allow herself sexual feelings; moreover, she has a talent for painting and once considered settling "down to a lifetime of painting landscapes" (95). But the professions open to women are few—men, gardening, God, teaching, or the library—and all demand the "feminine" rather than "masculine" qualities of character. The segregation of character qualities by sex is virtually complete; hence the only situations where each woman can express her intelligence or humor are when she is alone, with a very unusual man (Charlton or father), or in a "masculine" institution. Evelyn constantly *wonders* whether other women's masks hide the same fears she has; Isabel thinks she does understand other women. But there are no woman-woman friendships, no sharing of the "inner life" between women (or between men, so far as we see them)—with one all-important exception: the author's own intimacy with her two characters.

Out of a stereotyped plot and stereotyped female roles, Newman wrote in *Dead Lovers Are Faithful Lovers* what is perhaps only a minor novel, but an absorbing and finally truthful one. In her last work of fiction, Newman came to a vision that once again overlaps that of her literary predecessors. The central women are treated sympathetically, despite the one simple fact between them—Charlton Cunningham—that might for another writer have meant limitation to a single point of view. Although female sexuality is endorsed, its risks are made clear. And by depicting the suffering that both women feel at their constant waiting, waiting for Charlton and by giving to men almost all the "experience" of the world that deflects one's energies from a monomaniacal infatuation, Newman implicitly endorses the value of a broad experience for all people.

Female intelligence is unequivocally endorsed; Isabel's psyche and her future are in better shape than Evelyn's because she lets herself think. In fact, this might have been what attracted Charlton to her in the first place. Clearly thinking of Evelyn, he says to Isabel at one point that he wishes Charleston men would "bind their women's feet instead of their brains. Of course, they do all those things in Richmond, except eating rice—though I don't think binding the women's brains has often been really necessary in either town" (274). Yet Charlton's insight is limited, as the narrator shows when Evelyn demonstrates her own intelligence, well-hidden from her husband because of the very values he holds so dear. She decides not to tell him that "he would soon be like the man her father had convicted of admiring only girls like the girls who had been belles of the finals in the year of his graduation" (291), an insight that Charlton demonstrates in his choice of the considerably younger Isabel. Thus Newman shows the effects of binding a brain. It does not atrophy; it simply remains hidden or is employed in the service of trivial goals that do not seem to require intelligence.

Though men in this novel are attractive both physically and intellectually, they are seen with a tinge of either envy or condescension. Evelyn somewhat enviously wonders what a man finds for satisfaction in his work; Isabel is exasperated by the dullards who fall in love with her. Nevertheless, Newman seems to believe that the closest relationship possible between human beings is that between man and woman. The only thoroughly close relationships depicted in this novel are between father and daughter, probably because the family ties both permit greater freedom of expression and prohibit the danger of sexual victimization. The closeness between man and woman who are not father and daughter, though, is threatened by the imbalances produced by a society that separates and demeans its women. The Cunningham family library is exclusively Charlton's domain and is the place where he entertains only men—we remember Beulah. On the other hand, the training of women takes place not in the library, but with a mother, who teaches her daughter to say "the things which make desirable young men want to marry her" and later the "things which will make elderly and influential gentlemen show enough interest in her to make her seem important to her husband" (73). Men are trained for professions; women are trained for men—or, failing that, for a womanly job. As Isabel says, "men and women usually believe that a man is suited to any official position he has managed to slip into, and . . . men and women seem to believe that even a woman is suited to her official position if a woman has managed to slip into it before" (192).

One way this gender separation demeans women, as we saw, is to make them narcissists, and a final comment on Newman's treatment of narcissism in this book seems in order. First of all, she sees not just women but the entire culture as narcissistic: the audience at an opera applaud *"themselves* for seeing a little stick held in the right hand of the world's most celebrated conductor of operas" (94; my emphasis). Of the women, Evelyn is the most obvious narcissist; she constantly gazes at herself in mirrors. That there are fewer mirror images involving Isabel is a mark of her lesser narcissism and her larger world.

Yet Evelyn's obsession with seeing herself is, just as Douglas' definition states, hardly "exaggerated self-esteem," but an absorbing concern with her body because it is all she has to hold Charlton. Cosmetics become quite explicit elements in Evelyn's religion, in which Charlton is her God. To be cut off from God is the worst form of alienation; Evelyn recognizes this in one dark moment when she realizes that "she was walking into a house which was Charlton Cunningham's house . . . walking up stairs which were Charlton Cunningham's stairs . . . looking at a telephone which was Charlton Cunningham's telephone. And when she laid the face she could not hide from him in a bowl of cold water, she remembered that it was Charlton Cunningham's water, she felt as lonely as she had felt" when she first went away to boarding school (107–108). Because she sees her psychic and economic survival as contingent upon Charlton's approbation, she uses every trick possible to keep that approbation, as has been seen; when she finds that a man is most helpless in the horizontal position, she tries to get him there as often as she can. Yet Evelyn realizes how risky her whole pro-fession is. She knows that Charlton loves her more for the "gold and scarlet glamour of the homage which had painted the footlights of the beautifully set stage where he had first seen her" (44) than for herself; he "could hardly have begun his wedding-night with a woman who was less known to him" (44), and she knows it. Hence she cannot be honest with him; she must continually create new stages, perpetuate the bridal night, preserve the bridal body—the body he "gave" her. And since her society requires of its women self-deprecation, she cannot use even the experiences she has had in the larger world: she must deny what she knows beyond the world of getting and keeping a man.

Because the novel shows that Evelyn's best moments with Charlton are carefully created (by Evelyn) and because it shows that Isabel's re-lationship with Charlton consists of fragments separated by long peri-ods of absence, *Dead Lovers Are Faithful Lovers* seems to imply that the best relationship with a man that a woman can have, given the prem-ises of this culture, is not a long-standing and growing love, but a single instant—constantly re-created or perpetually postponed—of intensity. It is no wonder that by the end of the novel, Evelyn is alienated not just from her husband and her society, but from her religion: "she could not say anything to an inexperienced masculine god who could not possibly know what she was feeling, and she knew that even if she had not been such a very Protestant Episcopalian, she could not have said anything to the Blessed Virgin Mary whose gospel did not record any unusual affection for her husband, or even for the father of her most celebrated son" (293).

The gruesome effects of southern ladyhood on southern women, Newman says, leave the women utterly alone. Evelyn replaces "society by the self," and Isabel, to some extent, replaces "reality by literature," because the normal mode of human development, learning from the "world's lessons,"[66] can teach them only that they should not be fully human.

For Elizabeth Hardwick, all of Newman's fiction exposes radical con-trasts between the "proprieties of Southern manners for women and the anarchic urgency of their feelings."[67] Those contrasts produced, as we have seen, conflicts between inner imperative and outer restraint that are complicated for Newman's protagonists by the depth of their acceptance of the propriety of the very restraints against which they re-bel. Newman explained it this way, discussing *The Hard-Boiled Virgin*: "I discovered that I was going to write a novel about a girl who began by believing every thing her family and her teachers said to her, and who ended by disbelieving most of those things, but by finding that she couldn't keep herself from behaving as if she still believed them—about a girl who was born and bred to be a southern lady, and whose mind never could triumph over the ideas she was presumably born with, and the ideas she was undoubtedly taught."[68] The complex inner battle that results is at the center of Newman's vision. Using just such imagery, Rebecca West faulted Newman in 1926. Fine novels show a battlefield, West argued, but a battlefield that is under an "overarching sky" that can provide a sense of harmony, beauty, and rest against which the characters' misery and struggles are an offense, yet to which those struggles are the only avenue of approach. "The trouble with Miss Newman," West concluded, "is that she has not enough sky."[69]

At the time of her death, Newman planned to continue to wage that war in fiction. She had completed her translations of Laforgue (Horace Liveright published them in 1928 as *Six Moral Tales from Jules Laforgue*). And she had discussed in print and in private a collection of biographies, a book of criticism, a play, two short stories, and two novels. The biographies—of Leonardo da Vinci, St. Francis of Assisi, Jane Austen, Cardinal Newman, and Henry James—were to be entitled *Eminent Virgins, So-Called*. The criticism, *A History of Sophistication*, was to treat her favorite periods in literature, those "when wit and cynicism combined." The play, set aboard the *Ile de France*, involved the heroine with detectives who were investigating a U.S. senator traveling with a beautiful woman.[70]

In the short stories and novels, Newman's concern with the contingency of female identity, particularly its contingency on men, emerged most clearly. One short story was to tell of a woman in heaven who finds her satisfaction in boasting of her husband's grief, until one day she looks down to see him in the arms of a second wife. Another, "Mr. Prioleau's Deceased Wife's Sisters," was to show two unmarried sisters who have "merg[ed] their individuality so thoroughly that finally a single visiting card is sufficient for both." A third, married sister dies; competition for her widower wrenches the merger apart, so that "each becomes a personality, vying for Mr. Prioleau's affection."[71] When he chooses neither, the two again become one identity.

The novel *She Ascended into Hell* was to touch again on the theme of the survival of a woman's identity after her husband's death. (Interestingly, Newman was especially concerned to write this novel so that readers could not tell the author's sex.) The widow of a young artist, Cordelia is determined to establish his reputation, does so at first out of genuine love, and then finds she loves the public adulation she receives for her work. She forms an artists' colony in his memory, where she rules as an "implacable empress."[72] Finally envious even of the respect she has elicited for her dead husband, Cordelia finds her doom in her sister, who gives the colony enough money to deprive Cordelia of her reason for getting the public attention she so values.

Newman's other projected novel, *There Is a Certain Elegance About Celibacy*, was to return Katharine Faraday to the scene as a successful writer. She and several other women writers were to pay court to and assemble around a brilliant unmarried man who had produced one great novel, and who, instead of writing more, was to spend the rest of his life trying to perfect it.[73] Newman herself, of course, lived to write none of these ideas into prose; in none of them, though, does there appear to be much clear blue sky.

CHAPTER VIII

Margaret Mitchell
The Bad Little Girl
of the Good Old Days

There is little doubt that Margaret Munnerlyn Mitchell knew what it meant to be a southern lady. She was born to the role, reared to it, and to a great extent lived it, in Atlanta, as Mrs. John R. Marsh. In a telegram to Marsh just after his wife's death in 1949, President Harry S. Truman said that "the author of *Gone With the Wind* will also be remembered as a great soul who exemplified in her all too brief span of years the highest ideals of American womanhood."[1] Truman may have been thinking of her dedicated war work. Mitchell herself had, years earlier, expressed a rather different perception of herself as an American woman: "Being a product of the Jazz Age, being one of those short-haired, short-skirted,

hard-boiled young women who preachers said would go to hell or be
hanged before they were thirty, I am naturally a little embarrassed at
finding myself the incarnate spirit of the Old South!"[2] In fact, Margaret
Mitchell was simultaneously an unreconstructed southerner—a believer in the traditional values of the southern lady—and a new kind of
rebel. And out of the tension produced by the conflict of different definitions of southern women, her life—and her novel—grew.

Born in 1900 in Atlanta, Mitchell came from generations of southerners. Her lawyer father Eugene was a fifth-generation Atlantan; her
mother, Maybelle Stephens, came from Irish Catholic roots that resemble Gerald O'Hara's in *Gone With the Wind*. As a child, Margaret read
voluminously, listened to tales of the Civil War and Reconstruction (she
claimed she thought Lee had won until she was ten), and wrote stories
and plays, keeping a running notebook of ideas.

Mitchell attended Atlanta's Washington Seminary (1914–18), where
she finished a novel about girls in a boarding school, *The Big Four*, and
the story of "Little Sister," who hears her older sister being raped and
shoots the rapist. In 1918, she entered Smith College. In her words, "I
hoped to study medicine but while I was at Smith College my mother
died and I had to come home to keep house."[3] Eugene Mitchell wanted
his daughter to take a role in upper-crust Atlanta society; she followed
his wishes, making her debut in 1921. In 1922, she married Berrien K.
Upshaw; he left after several months apparently due to his own emotional instability, and she divorced him in 1924. Shortly after her marriage, Mitchell began reporting. In addition to hundreds of feature stories, many with by-lines, she also began a novel about adolescent life in
the 1920s and completed a novelette, later rejected by Macmillan,
called 'Ropa Carmagin. The subject of the short novel was the love of a
southern white girl for a mulatto man. With the exception of "Little Sister," none of these fictional works is apparently now available; all reports indicate that Mitchell destroyed some of them herself and ordered
others to be destroyed after her death.

In 1925, Mitchell married John Marsh, a public relations writer for
the Georgia Power Company who had been best man at her first wedding. After several months, she quit her newspaper job; she cited an
ankle injury that would not heal properly and added that there was
room for only one career in a family. She began writing *Gone With the
Wind* in 1926, working on a portable typewriter at home for three years,
and writing the last chapter first, others at scattered intervals. Substan-
tially complete by 1929, the novel sat in coat closets and propped up
furniture, filed by chapter in manila envelopes. In April, 1935, she reluctantly and impulsively showed the manuscript to Macmillan editor

Harold S. Latham, who was on a writer search in Atlanta. *Gone With the Wind* was accepted in July, and Mitchell spent the next year rewriting, editing, adding the first chapter, and checking the historical accuracy of the work.

Gone With the Wind sold a million copies in six months. The reviews were almost uniformly good, and the novel became a national fad. For the rest of her life Margaret Mitchell was absorbed in what she called "cleaning up after *GWTW*."[4] The debris included international copyright difficulties, contractual misunderstandings, plagiarism cases, thousands of letters and callers, impostors, rumors about her life, and requests for articles and appearances (most of which she turned down). In 1937 she received the annual award of the American Booksellers Association (now the American Book Award) and the Pulitzer Prize; in 1939 Smith College conferred upon her an honorary degree and the movie was released, winning ten Academy Awards.

During World War II, in addition to steering through the wake of *Gone With the Wind*, Mitchell worked for the war effort and nursed her ill father. In 1945 her husband suffered a heart attack; she nursed him at home for months. She wrote to Harper's in 1949 to correct a statement that she would never write again, but on August 11, she was hit by a car. She died on August 16 and was buried in Atlanta's Oakland Cemetery.

"If I did any *thinking* [my emphasis] about writing," she had said in 1936 when *Gone With the Wind* was published, "it was about a novel which I never wrote and never will write."[5] Mitchell's reticence as a writer was paralleled by her reticence about her life. It extended far deeper, apparently, than a simple dislike of public performance or a need to preserve privacy in the face of the *Gone With the Wind* publicity—so deep, in fact, that some of her closest friends claimed they were never sure they really knew her. Ralph McGill said that she "never, at any time or to anyone, fully revealed herself, not even to John Marsh. She was never the marble statue of the symbolic Confederate woman. She was always flesh and blood. But she could keep her counsel and be as reticent as ice."[6] Richard Harwell says in his *Margaret Mitchell's "Gone With the Wind" Letters: 1936–1949* that "she wrote full and charming letters, personalizing them while seldom revealing her private self."[7] She allowed only one radio interview about the novel, shortly after publication and conducted by a close friend. She stopped giving speeches after one prepublication talk in Macon, Georgia, and quit autographing books when she saw how much time it was going to require—though she usually took the time to write a letter to explain why she could not sign her book.

Because of her dislike of exposure, the public image of Margaret Mitchell probably says more about contemporary beliefs and expectations than it does about the writer herself. Most of the rumors have in common the effect of taking away from her image the quality of competence and substituting for it the more "feminine" virtue of passivity; the legends that do ascribe competence to Mitchell do so with such wild romanticism as to cause one to wonder if they might have been a response to the myth of incompetence. In any case, the public found it incongruous that a small woman could write a large, popular, and financially successful novel. "Why, lady," said one gas station operator to the author herself, "you're not big enough to write a book. That's a famous book—making a lot of money." [8] Rumors flew that not she but her husband, her father, her brother, even Sinclair Lewis had written the novel; that she was going blind, had leukemia, had a wooden leg, and wrote the novel stretched out, an invalid, in bed. [9] Women even followed Mitchell into the dressing room of a clothing store, marveling at her size (about five feet tall).

One of Mitchell's strategies for reconciling her desire for personal privacy with the need for some social relationships and some public statements was to create a persona. That persona is evident in her letters. Mitchell uses the same structure, the same anecdote, even identical phraseology in several different letters to different people. Naturally, this expedited her writing, especially since she barely knew many of the people to whom she wrote. In addition, though, the repetitions clearly constitute the formation of a written personality. Her persona was designed to convey to her reader the impression of a woman who is witty and sensitive but self-deprecating. Here, she describes a speech she gave in Macon, Georgia: "When I rose trembling I had a vague memory of how horses (lock) their knee joints when they go to sleep standing up and fearing that I'd fall on the floor, I locked my knee joints and took a good grip on the table and also on some whipped cream on the table cloth. Don't ask me what I said. I haven't much idea. . . . I never went through such a horrible experience in my life (except when I dropped my drawers in the church aisle when I was six or seven)." [10] (In fact, as Marian Elder Jones remembers the speech, it was consummately delivered, alternating between wit and seriousness, and it captivated the audience.) [11] But in telling her version, Mitchell made herself the butt of her joke. Whatever real fear, sense of unworthiness, or pride Mitchell took in her ideas must be left for guesswork; the persona she created must be analyzed as a mask that let her use language more often as a mode of reticence than as one of expression.

Yet despite lost manuscripts, restrictions on her personal letters and papers,[12] and her untrustworthy persona, it is possible to piece together the evidence to find something of how Mitchell thought of herself. First of all, Margaret Mitchell saw herself primarily not as a woman but as a southerner, and her novel not about womanhood but about the South. She claimed that she wrote *Gone With the Wind* because "when I was a child I had to hear a lot about the Civil War on Sunday afternoons— when I was dragged hither and yon to call on elderly relatives and friends of the family who had fought in the war, or lived behind the lines . . . the gathering spiritedly refought the Civil War. . . . I heard everything in the world . . . except that the Confederates lost the war."[13] It was only following southern tradition, then, for her to transcribe and transmute these tales into fiction. And in the following summary of her novel, she puts geography before character: "It is a book about Georgia and Georgia people—especially north Georgia people. There are incidents in the book which take place in Savannah and Charleston and Macon and New Orleans, but nearly all of the action takes place in Atlanta, and at Tara, the plantation home of Scarlett O'Hara, the heroine."[14] Atlanta seems to be the main character, with Scarlett only the city's human symbol, a passive recipient of history:

> she experiences what Atlanta experiences during the war years, the thrills and excitement of the boom town that Atlanta became when the war changed it from an obscure, small town into one of the most important cities in the South; then the increasing hardships as the Confederate Cause waned; then the alarm of Atlanta people as they saw General Sherman's army advancing steadily on the town; finally the terrifying days of the siege, the capture of Atlanta by Sherman, and the burning of the town.
>
> Scarlett O'Hara goes through all these experiences and, after the war is over, comes back to Atlanta and does her part in the rebuilding of the city. She lives through the terrible days of Reconstruction and the story carries her, and Atlanta, up to the time when the carpet baggers had been run out of Georgia and people could begin living their normal lives again.[15]

This summary of *Gone With the Wind* was made on a radio interview; her careful focus on history, to the exclusion of character, may have revealed Mitchell's assumption as to where her audience's interests lay. (It may also have been an effort on her part, similar to the invention of her persona, to evade discussion of the more personal and emotional

elements in the novel.) And finally, a southern image provided the
theme of the novel, as Mitchell said she intended it:

> Her mother would take her for a drive into the countryside,
> and stop on a back road when a ruined chimney could be
> seen above the scrubby second-growth timber. Pointing to
> the column of blackened brick, Mrs. Mitchell would say,
> "That is one of Sherman's sentinels." Then she would give
> Margaret the familiar speech about the difference between
> the people who had been, so to speak, defeated by defeat and
> those who refused to "go down in the world and disappear."
> One's obligation to life was to turn in a good performance;
> that was the hard path, and the only path, by which one at-
> tained validity and self-respect.[16]

Margaret Mitchell was loyal to and could be defensive about the
South. Her Macon speech ended "on a serious note. She said that we
must tell the truth, we writers of the South, we must give a true interpretation of our section, and so set our Southland right with the
world."[17] Earlier in the same speech, Mitchell remembered the occasion of her showing the manuscript of *Gone With the Wind* to Harold
Latham: "Something that he said got my fighting blood up. . . . When I
told him that my book was about the South he wanted to know if it was
a story of degeneracy. This question with its implication had struck fire
in my mind and I answered him, 'No! My story is not about degeneracy.
It is about a tough-skinned people who could take it on the chin.'" According to this report, Latham replied, "If Southerners want to stand
right before the world, why don't they themselves write the truth?"[18]
The challenge to the South from a northern publisher, like Grace King's
from Richard Watson Gilder, provoked an angry response; because of it,
she agreed to let him read *Gone With the Wind*.

Mitchell's politics took a traditional southern form. Like many southerners, she disliked Roosevelt and his "pushy" wife Eleanor; she wrote
to columnist Westbrook Pegler (so he claimed) that she viewed the Roosevelt "spirit" as similar to that of the Carpetbaggers' regime. She supported Wendell Willkie's aborted campaign in 1940 and thought it
"strange" that the Democratic party was the "colored man's party" in
1944, when "old-fashioned Democrats" (including, presumably, herself) were used to thinking of the Republican party as the party of
blacks.[19]

Like the public Grace King, Mitchell shared the unreconstructed
southerner's view of blacks. She loved Bessie Parker, who was her cook

for many years; she daily visited the hospital when Parker was sick and left her a house in her will. She was part of a "group" that "took up for Negroes, who were much oppressed by the local police of that day,"[20] and she originated the idea of a separate hospital for blacks who were not poor enough to go to Grady, the free hospital.[21]

Mitchell's southernness included its quota of damn Yankeeism, too. In a letter to Leodel Coleman, she recalled a "tacky party" for which they were supposed to dress tastelessly:

> I enjoyed that tacky party enormously. . . . Do you remember how I knocked on your door to see if you were ready and you two came roaring out looking like Tobacco Road or something William Faulkner wrote about, and chased me, screaming, down the hotel corridor, making gestures at me with jug and fishing pole?
>
> My own costume, as you recall, of hoop skirts and plumed hat and large doll, was a bit strange to see. And just then those Yankee tourists got off on the wrong floor and caught a glimpse of us and decided that everything they had ever read about the South was true.[22]

There is an echo here of the southern tall tale, the hoax on the city slicker, the last laugh. Though Mitchell could laugh at Yankees for their credulity, she was more cautious with her fellow southerners. The audience whose criticism she feared most was that of the South. After the novel was accepted for publication, she spent an entire year searching out names and facts and places to be sure that no Atlanta names were duplicated and all facts were entirely accurate. In a letter to a West Coast critic, she described her feelings about the "probable reception my book would have in the South and at the hands of Southerners. . . . I was a little frightened because, while I had written nothing that I could not prove and much that I had heard, as a child, from eyewitnesses of that era, I feared some of it would not set well upon Southerners. I suppose Southerners have been lambasted so often and so hard, in print, that they have become unduly sensitive."[23] Only after the South had clearly accepted the novel could she afford to drop a little of this seriousness. When the movie was released, three years after publication of the novel, she objected to the cinematic Tara as "much too grand," not the "upcountry functional" she had in mind, and she was relaxed enough to "scream with laughter" at Hollywood's version of Twelve Oaks.[24]

In fact, Margaret Mitchell thoroughly believed her novel to be a real-

istic depiction of the South, the antithesis of what she called (scorn-
fully) a "Thomas Nelson Pagish" novel. She considered the plantation
myth of the Old South to be Hollywood's creation:

> I believe we Southerners could write the truth about the an-
> tebellum South, its few slaveholders, its yeoman farmers, the
> rambling, comfortable houses just fifty years away from log
> cabins, until Gabriel blows his trump—and everyone would
> go on believing the Hollywood version. The sad part is that
> many Southerners believe this myth even more ardently
> than the Northerners. A number of years ago some of us
> organized a club, The Association of Southerners Whose
> Grandpappies Did Not Live in Houses with White Col-
> umns. . . . Its membership would be enormous if all the eli-
> gibles came in. Since my novel was published, I have been
> embarrassed on many occasions by finding myself included
> among writers who pictured the South as a land of white-col-
> umned mansions whose wealthy owners had thousands of
> slaves and drank thousands of juleps. I have been surprised,
> for North Georgia certainly was no such country—if it ever
> existed anywhere—and I took great pains to describe North
> Georgia as it was. But people believe what they like to believe
> and the mythical Old South has too strong a hold on their
> imaginations to be altered by the mere reading of a 1037-
> page book.[25]

Though no naïve idolator of the South, Mitchell was nevertheless
fundamentally a southerner. Yet that regional identity conflicted with
her sense of herself as a woman, more specifically as a southern lady.
For "southern" breaks down, under even the most superficial analysis,
into southern ladies and southern gentlemen. In a 1949 effort to praise
her, for instance, the Atlanta *Journal* focused not on her southernness
but on her sex: "Even her last moments of conscious behavior were
those of an ordinary American housewife" who had "escaped the label
of the usual 'woman author' even in the matter of attire, never dressing
either ostentatiously or resorting to the equally distressing device of
sloppiness."[26]

Mitchell had at least three objective definitions of the southern
woman with which to deal. One came fully embodied in her mother,
Maybelle Stephens, and in other women in her family who resembled
Old Miss in *Hagar*. A second was the more conventional definition of
her southern culture, the still powerful vestiges of the helpless, depen-

dent, ornamental version of femininity. And a third came straight from her own American peers: the flapper, product of the Jazz Age, an ideal that superficially seemed to promise the independence of those older southern women, but that failed to challenge and in fact often reinforced the separation of the sexes by role and responsibility.[27]

In her fiction and in her life, these contradictory and confusing definitions produced conflict within Margaret Mitchell that she seemed unable to resolve. As an artist, she had to kill Melanie for Scarlett to live; all her life she issued conflicting statements about Scarlett's character. In her own life, Mitchell deployed several strategies for dealing with this conflict, from identifying with men, to self-deprecating wit, to her evasive public persona.

If Scarlett O'Hara is the more "masculine" woman in the novel, and Melanie Wilkes the more "feminine," then their author led a childhood that let her go both ways. According to her brother, Margaret was a tomboy who also played with dolls. Certainly two of her main loves were riding horses (twice the cause of serious injury) and putting on plays that she herself wrote and for which she organized the neighborhood children into productions. Her awareness that there were sexually based behavior distinctions, distinctions that she breached, appears in this memory of a source for *Gone With the Wind*:

> I remember that when I was a little girl and rode my pony every afternoon, my boon companion was a fine old Confederate veteran. He looked exactly like a stage Confederate—white hair and goatee, jimswinger coat, and a habit of gallantly kissing ladies' hands, even my own grubby six-year-old hand. He and a young lady who had reached the beau age were the only two people in my part of town who owned horses. And we three went riding together. . . . Frequently we had several veterans with us. The families of the veterans and my mother encouraged us to ride together in the belief that we'd keep each other out of mischief. . . .
>
> I regret to say that we didn't. There was still plenty of fire and dash left in the old boys. They still had hot tempers and bullheads and they still dearly loved a fight. The day seldom passed that they didn't have a heated argument about the Civil War. And the day seldom passed when the young lady who accompanied us didn't turn her horse and race for home. She realized, even if I didn't, that the company of quarrelsome old gentlemen was no place for a lady.

But Margaret didn't go home, because

> at the age of six I was not concerned about being a lady. Be-
> sides I was too fascinated by the way the veterans shouted at
> each other. On these occasions, too, I was seen and not
> heard, even if I had wanted to speak, for it would have taken
> the lungs of the bull of Rashan to be heard above their tu-
> mult. . . . The language they used was highly entertain-
> ing and instructive to a small but interested girl. . . . The
> young lady who went riding with us always turned her horse
> toward home when they got onto the subject of Recon-
> struction.[28]

There is a clear sense in this passage that it may be a shade improper
but that it is certainly a lot more fun to be a grubby, asexual six-year-old
than a beau-age young lady: the one role at least permits observation of
the "rough male world," the other shuns it. Mitchell's "regret" is clearly
ironic, yet she knew she was to grow up into one of those young ladies.

The sense of forbidden fruit that is freely available to men also pervades this story of her childhood reading: "They [stories by Beatrice
Grimshaw] were published in magazines like *Argosy* and *Cavalier* in
the days when those magazines were better thought of than now. I was
not supposed to read them, but an uncle of mine loved them and hid
them behind the haybales in the loft of his carriage house. I used to
read them there, wickedly smoking cigarettes made of rabbit tobacco
rolled in toilet paper."[29] Other favorite reading when Margaret Mitchell
was young included the boys' stories written by George Alfred Henty
and the Tom Swift and Rover Boys series. From this reading, incidentally, she culled her lasting belief that it was plot and character, not
style, that mattered in a story.[30]

Maybelle Stephens Mitchell was not one to put up with ladylike conventions when they went against her practical sense. When she was
three or four, Margaret's skirts caught fire over an open grate: "Thereafter until she was old enough to go to school her mother dressed her in
pants, as if she were a little boy. The neighbors called her 'Jimmy,' after
a fancied resemblance to a little boy by that name in a comic by Swin-
nerton."[31] Perhaps that experience helped to produce this attitude:
when she worked on *Gone With the Wind* at her typewriter, she always
wore boys' corduroy pants—"definitely not [women's] slacks," she
said.[32]

Maybelle Stephens Mitchell was not an ordinary southern lady; in
fact, she was one of Georgia's first suffragists. "My earliest memories,"
said Margaret Mitchell, "are of my mother and the woman's suffrage

movement."³³ The first time Margaret got to stay up after six P.M. was for a suffragist rally: "Mother tied a Votes-for-Women banner around my fat stomach, put me under her arm, took me to the meeting, hissing blood-curdling threats if I did not behave, and set me on the platform between the silver pitcher and the water glasses while she made an impassioned speech. I was so enchanted at my eminence that I behaved perfectly, even blowing kisses to gentlemen in the front row. I was kissed by Mrs. [Carrie Chapman] Catt, if it was she, and called the youngest suffragette in Georgia and the future of our cause."³⁴ It is interesting that the memory of Margaret Mitchell should imagine perfect behavior at a suffragist rally to be blowing kisses at the men. But it is probably more important that she saw her mother as a forceful, vital, decisive woman, one who "made an impassioned speech" urging that women should have more political power.

Mitchell's mother died during her daughter's freshman year at Smith, and most of the memories Margaret Mitchell chose to record of her mother took place when Margaret was considerably younger than eighteen. It is these childhood events that Mitchell repeatedly cited as the wellsprings for *Gone With the Wind* or as its themes or its ideas. Clearly, long after her death, Maybelle continued to have a serious impact upon Margaret and *Gone With the Wind* is linked in important ways to Margaret Mitchell's relationship with her mother. We have seen the virtue of "good performance" extolled in Maybelle's "Sherman's sentinels" speech: that competence earns "validity" and "respect," regardless of sex. And in several other ways Maybelle Stephens Mitchell disregarded traditional sex boundaries in her own values and those she taught her daughter.

Courage, Maybelle observed, was "the only virtue worth worrying about, for it comprehended all the others."³⁵ Courage is a virtue required rather clearly in battle; Maybelle Mitchell's imagination turned inevitably to war for images and values. How deeply the idea of the Civil War affected her can be seen in the conclusion to her "sentinels" speech, as her daughter remembered it:

[My mother] talked about the world those people had lived in, such a secure world, and how it had exploded beneath them. And she told me that my own world was going to explode under me, some day, and God help me if I didn't have some weapon to meet the new world. She was talking about the necessity of having an education, both classical and practical. For she said all that would be left after a world ended would be what you could do with your hands and what you had in your head. "So, for God's sake, go to school and learn something that will stay with you. The strength of women's hands isn't worth anything, but what they've got in their heads will carry them as far as they need to go." [36]

The difference in being a woman is in physical strength only, Maybelle believed, not in intelligence or courage.

Maybelle felt a particular loathing for passive women. "Nothing infuriated her as much," Margaret later remembered, "as the complacent attitude of other ladies who felt that they should let the gentlemen do the voting." Yet her own actions were on behalf of others. She died because she caught the flu when she was already "worn and weak from nursing others." [37]

Maybelle Mitchell made no bones about calling reality as she saw it, either. Stephens Mitchell recalls that "she knew the world and its perils and was willing to speak of them in a day and time when things were done but not spoken of." In perhaps the clearest divergence from the culture's image of the lady, Maybelle gave her children advice about drinking and sex. Prohibition would make a "dull world," she thought, but drink had its dangers, so she taught her children to drink and to "be mannerly about it." "She realized the strength of sex," according to Stephens, "and had only one suggestion for control of it—early marriage." [38]

Courage, action, competence, drinking, sex, directness in speech— all are traditionally "masculine" virtues. It is not surprising, then, that Margaret Mitchell would later identify with men who embodied these values.

One of these men was her father. She "loved and respected [her] father, though she resembled him too closely for complete understanding," Farr says, adding that they shared a love of history and truth, a sense of humor, and a conviction as to the inviolability of contracts. Unlike Maybelle, though, Eugene seems to have been cold and judgmental. Margaret was extremely wary of criticism from her father: he had "withheld praise from her" when she was a child, and later, criticism would "make [her] sense of independence flare." [39] When Margaret married John Marsh (who, Ralph McGill suggests, provided a "father image"),[40] the relationship with her father apparently became smoother. Even then, much of the rest of her life was spent nursing her father, emotionally and physically.

Her father was not the only male ancestor with whom Margaret Mitchell identified. She apparently loved the story of the "not too far distant ancestor" to whom she felt "very sympathetic" and about whom her mother had once said "there was only one person in the family

[Margaret] had ever shown the slightest resemblance to, and it was that bewhiskered old wretch." This gentleman "didn't want anyone to know about his business and . . . couldn't bear to have a house full of women gabbling and quacking about his activities."[41]

Margaret Mitchell herself had very little tolerance for many types of women, especially those she called "weak-minded." And there are hints that many types of women had very little tolerance, reciprocally, for Margaret Mitchell. As early as her days at Washington Seminary in Atlanta, she "did not get an invitation to join any of the school sororities," according to her brother, because "she had made enemies as well as friends." This enigmatic comment is reinforced by an equally baffling choice of phrase much later in Farr's biography, when he makes the odd point that Margaret's "sense of fun" explained her popularity with men, but that she "took pains" to preserve her friendships with women and was "grateful for" her women friends. It is unclear whether Farr's preconceptions or Margaret's are showing here, but the distinction between male fun and female dullness is apparent. Margaret did, however, have several close women friends in her adult life, such as newspaperwoman Medora Perkerson and Macmillan editor Lois Cole. There is probably some significance to the fact that they were both women committed to careers and that they both had a sense of humor. Lois Cole recalls first meeting Margaret Mitchell at a bridge luncheon where they were partners. When she asked Mitchell whether she followed any conventions, Mitchell replied, " 'Conventions? I don't know any. I just lead from fright. What do you lead from?' 'Necessity,'" Cole told her. They both grinned.[42]

Certainly Mitchell's work at the Atlanta *Journal* both demonstrated and reinforced her male-centered universe. In a memoir of her days at the *Journal* by William S. Howland, the period is described as "days of rugged, masculine news staffs." The staff was almost entirely male; in fact, Peggy Mitchell's original desire to be a reporter was thwarted because, said the city editor, "We felt the time was not ready for the *Journal* to hire regular women reporters." Consequently, Mitchell was assigned to the magazine section staff, where she did in fact prove herself according to the "hard working, hard hitting" terms of the paper and did, as Howland puts it, "make the team." She "wrote like a man," he adds. When it came to using the dictionary—essential, of course, to a writer—she had a problem. Too short to reach it without stretching and thereby exposing "an inch or so of white skin above tops of her rolled stockings," Margaret was soon admonished to stop using her reference tool: said the city editor, "You're upsetting my young men."[43] There is no indication that she protested or that alternative arrangements were offered. The evidence suggests that, admiring "masculine" virtues, working in a male-dominated profession, and simultaneously identifying with men and flirting with them, as she loved to do, Mitchell would have accepted the rules of a game she most likely felt lucky to be able to play at all.

Had Mitchell's mother been a more typical southern lady, Margaret Mitchell would surely have had more problems with her sexual identity than she apparently did. As it was, enough of what her culture saw as the "male" virtues were embodied in her mother and in other female family members to prevent too easy an identification of sex with specific values. Other women who fitted this pattern included Margaret's unmarried aunts, Mary and Sarah Fitzgerald, who lived on a farm in Clayton County. These women were alive but very old when Margaret was a child. They exerted much power in their community and family, power that was largely moral. They were devout and strict Catholics and had what Mitchell ascribed to all southern women of generations previous to her own—the "quality of rising to any situation which the good Lord saw fit to send their way." [44] Mitchell wrote in 1948 that her mother "often remarked that my Aunt Mary could sit on her back porch shelling a panful of butterbeans and if the President of the United States or the King of England or the Pope of Rome drove up into the back yard she could rise and greet them and make them feel at home. And I hope you will notice that Mother took it for granted that the King of England the President and the Pope would be good enough Georgians not to come and ring the front door bell but would drive up into the back yard." [45]

In a 1936 letter to a West Coast critic, Mitchell elaborated her vision of the women who survived the Civil War:

> I'm sure, if you are Southern born, you must have seen many of the old ladies who had lived through that era who could scare the liver and lights out of you with one word and blast your vitals with one look. They owned their negroes still and their children and their contemporaries' children too. And they were the bossiest, hard boiledest bunch of old ladies I ever saw. And they could be so plain spoken, upon occasion, that they made the brashest flapper blush. But they never got too old to be attractive to the gentlemen. . . . I felt certain that people who were like that in old age couldn't have been completely Thomas Nelson Page in their youths. [46]

But, as Mary Johnston's *Hagar* shows, there are conflicts implicit in this very ideal, admirable though Johnston too saw it to be. The toughness of these ladies conflicts with their acceptance of the old adage that the husband and the wife are one, and the husband is the one. Hence they valued without question such particularly feminine virtues as self-sacrifice, loyalty to family before self, and the perpetuation of manners.

We see even Maybelle Mitchell consciously endorsing the ideal of feminine self-sacrifice in the last letter she wrote to Margaret:

> However little it seems to you I got out of life, I have held in my hands all that the world can give. I have had a happy childhood and married the man I wanted. I had children who loved me, and, as I loved them, I have been able to give them what will put them on the high road to mental, moral, and perhaps financial success, were I to give them nothing else.
>
> I expect to see you again, but if I do not I must warn you of one mistake that a woman of your temperament might fall into. Give of yourself with both hands and overflowing heart, but give only the excess after you have lived your own life. This is badly put. What I mean is that your life and energies belong first to yourself, your husband and your children. Anything left over after you have served these, give and give generously, but be sure there is no stinting of love and attention at home. . . . Care for your father when he is old, as I cared for my mother. But never let his or anyone else's life interfere with your real life.[47]

Yet a careful reading of this letter reveals what appears to be a central ambiguity. First of all, one must ponder what Maybelle means by "all the world can give"; a more predictable turn of phrase might have been "all I have wanted." Then, after warning her daughter to give of herself only "the excess after you have lived your own life," Maybelle pauses and reconsiders. As the statement stands, it would undercut decades of self-sacrifice and resemble Edna Pontellier's statement that she would give anything to her family, including her life—but not her self. So the phrase bothers Maybelle Mitchell. She then defines "your own life" as the lives of Margaret, Margaret's (expected) husband, and their children. And, in the next sentence, it is clear who comes first in that triad: "anything left over after you have served these, give . . . but be sure there is no stinting of love and attention at home." It is doubtful that Mrs. Mitchell meant love and attention to oneself. The rest of the letter leads one to believe that Maybelle is worried that her widower will burden her daughter and damage her potential marriage and family. But "your real life" remains intriguingly undefined.

The letter consciously enjoins upon Margaret other traditional female virtues: loyalty to family before self and the home before outside work. In fact, such loyalty is assumed, as Maybelle tries to help her daughter define how much to give to which members. And although Margaret Mitchell "fell out" with various members of her extended family during her life, she nevertheless remained loyal to her kin. Her way of showing that loyalty came in sacrificing her own goals to their needs. She gave up the dream of a career in medicine to come home and keep house for her brother and father after Maybelle died. She entered "society" at her father's wish. And she insisted on putting her husband's profession first, by quitting her *Journal* position and later, after *Gone With the Wind* was published, by refusing to let her fame affect her often deferential attitude to John's work. Her biographer said she "hoped and believed that John would become an important man, and held that one career in a family was enough"[48] when she stopped work at the *Journal*; Farr suggests that she kept *Gone With the Wind* from publishers because "if she became the author of a successful novel, she would advance beyond her husband in the world's estimation. And this was not Margaret's idea of a suitable turn of events."[49] She said throughout her life: "A married woman must be first of all a wife. I am Mrs. John R. Marsh."[50]

Mrs. John R. Marsh, like her mother, kept good manners. "I was brought up to consider it better to commit murder than to be rude," Margaret remembered as an adult.[51] And it might indeed have been a little emotional murder when her mother "refused to allow her daughter to indulge in reticence at the expense of courtesy," as Farr stoically phrased it.[52] Apparently Margaret was a shy child; her mother's remedy was to smack her with a slipper.

Thus Maybelle Stephens Mitchell and the other women of her own and earlier generations left Margaret Mitchell with a heritage that she tried her best to meet, a heritage that had its own built-in conflicts. By the time Mitchell came of age, however, these two strands of womanhood—velvet and steel—had separated within her immediate culture into, on the one hand, the admonition of traditionalists that women be dependent, sacrificial, pious, pure, and self-deprecatory; and on the other, into the Jazz Age "freedom" that loosened the straitjacket of "hard-boiled" women's sexuality and language. Again, Margaret Mitchell seems to have tried to follow both prescriptions.

> "I don't believe anybody in the world is afraid of me," says Peggy with a smile. "People ask me to do anything and everything, from writing a history paper for a 12-year-old son to

collaborating on a novel for which I am promised 10 percent of the proceeds."

Peggy would like to do all the things she is asked—all the reasonable things. She started out trying to.[53]

This was written in December, 1947. Certainly Mitchell's voluminous *Gone With the Wind* correspondence attests to just one way in which she tried to "do for others." Much earlier, as a debutante, she had ascribed to her in a news story all the qualities appropriate for a southern lady of the helpless sort:

> Margaret Mitchell must be the shy and shrinking violet of the club, for when you urge her to talk of herself, of her preferences in the catalog of pleasures and of the things which fill her with abhorrence she will at once tell you a funny story, or something about "Court's" [a friend, Courtney Ross] approaching wedding, or in some other charming way divert your attention from herself. Was this the breadth of vision which her college life engendered? Or is it just Margaret's unselfishness in loving to exploit the attractions of those she loves.[54]

Mitchell's self-deprecation has already been noted; it is, of course, part of this traditional strand of southern ladyhood. When Lois Cole asked Mitchell about her (as yet unpublished) novel, Mitchell responded, "It stinks—and I don't know why I bother with it, I've got to do something with my time." Cole also remembers a conversation the two had a couple of years after *Gone With the Wind* was published: "Then a faraway look came into her blue eyes. 'You know, I always liked the book I wrote before "Gone With the Wind" better.' I took a firm clutch on the arm of the sofa and said as calmly as I could. 'How nice. And where is the manuscript now?' 'Oh, I burned it up when it was finished. I just wrote it for fun. I never thought of having it published.'"[55] Although Mitchell may have had "fun" writing the unnamed work, it seems reasonable that burning it indicated more serious levels of feeling; certainly it was with utmost seriousness that Mitchell instructed, in her will, that all her papers and manuscripts be destroyed after her death.

Thus Margaret Mitchell participated to some extent in the traditional southern lady image prescribed in part by her mother and to a greater extent by her culture. On the other hand, her experiences at the *Journal* led her once to say that "if more women, when they were girls, were in a position to see—as a newspaper girl is—the inside of jails, the horrible things Travelers' Aid discovers, the emergency rooms of Grady

Hospital and those sad, desolate sections which used to be fine homes but now are rookeries and rabbit warrens—if more people knew the sad things and the horrible things that go on in the world, there would be a darned sight less complacency and probably not so many of those sad sights and horrible things."[56] The Jazz Age, in fact, had endorsed more assertive behavior, and Margaret Mitchell saw herself to be, as we saw, a "hard-boiled" "product of the Jazz Age." She chose, at another time and in a different context, the same term—"hard-boiled"—to describe the Civil War women whom she so admired. It is conceivable that Mitchell and other southern women saw in the changed mores of the twenties the possibility that qualities they admired in an earlier genera-tion could be resuscitated and reincorporated into their culture.

But, milder version though she was, Margaret Mitchell faced the cold stare of society when she indulged in her Zeldaesque adventures. At one of the debutante balls, Margaret and her escort danced the "Apache dance," and the older ladies at the ball had a fit. The dance, a "rough dance of Paris hoodlums," was considered daring; Farr suggests that this was precisely why Margaret did it. She was a good dancer; the dance was complicated and involved hard work, which she loved; and she knew it would be an "irritant to the elderly."[57]

About the same time, several debutantes, among them Margaret Mitchell, objected to the "unquestioned authority" of the senior com-mitteewomen of the Debutante Club. They were especially disturbed that these ladies had sole authority in choosing which charities would receive the proceeds from the debs' ball. "Margaret's argument," says her biographer, "was that the girls did the work, and so should have the privilege of allocating the funds."[58]

The results of these attacks on authority were disastrous to Mar-garet's march into society. The normal next step for a "certified debu-tante" was an invitation to join the Junior League. Margaret Mitchell didn't get one. Farr says it must have been an "intentional omission, and in Margaret's case especially pointed because some of her relatives were members. . . . Recognized authority had closed a conventional door in her face."[59]

"Society," interestingly, proved after the Junior League incident to be largely composed of women. The Junior League ban, according to Farr, did not hurt Margaret Mitchell's confidence or her popularity with men; in fact, he suggests that "Margaret enjoyed flaunting her popularity with men before the girls and women who disapproved of her."[60] And one suspects that she experienced a certain pleasure twenty years later, on the night before the world premiere of David Selznick's film of her novel, the night of the Junior League ball—which Margaret Mitchell refused, with no explanation, to attend.

Her failure to "enter society" did not, of course, make Margaret Mitchell a social pariah. But it is interesting to speculate on the relationship between these episodes and two highly significant and often played-down acts of her young adulthood: her first marriage and her decision to work as a newspaperwoman. Little is known about her first marriage, but what information is available indicates that the "handsome fraternity man," Berrien Kinnard Upshaw, was as different from John Marsh as Rhett Butler is from Ashley Wilkes. Farr explains Mitchell's attraction to him by saying that while he was courting Margaret, Upshaw was "in one of his good periods" and the "uncontrollable factors in his personality remained out of sight." A "dangerously unstable man," the "big and broadshouldered" Upshaw married Margaret Mitchell over the objections of her father and brother, who sensed "something wrong about Upshaw."[61] It was a conventional home wedding; an Episcopalian minister officiated, Margaret having practically abandoned her Catholicism (in fact, her religion) by then; and, of course, Marsh was best man.

This marriage fell apart quite soon. The couple moved in with Margaret's father and brother, possibly the first mistake. Then "Berrien Upshaw's performance as a breadwinner was sketchy, his temper grew uncertain, and within a few months he left . . . Atlanta," years later to be found "dead on the ground below a hotel window in the Middle West." How Margaret felt about all this—even the details of what actually happened—are now highly speculative. Even if her personal letters and manuscripts were available, it is doubtful that much could be learned from either, for this was among the most private areas of a private person's life. Given her intelligence and perception, though, one guesses that Mitchell was not totally blind to Berrien's "instability"; given her relatively recent ouster from "society," it may have been one of his charms. Whatever the case, she seems to have changed her mind: she kept a loaded pistol by her bed, so the story goes, until she knew he was dead.[62]

But if this first marriage was a "flapperish" reaction to rejection for "flapperish" actions, it was also the act of a woman who, unlike most girls of either the traditional or the Jazz Age sort, looked at marriage with a highly pragmatic and calculating eye. Mitchell saw clearly that marriage was a job like any other and that bagging a husband was the equivalent of getting a promotion. Note her military imagery here: "When a girl is making a social career," she wrote, "clothes are a uniform, to be worn like a soldier's—always well done—never sloppy."[63] In college, "Margaret made a private estimate of each young man she met—a measurement against specifications of an acceptable husband." She wrote asking her parents to "look up" one suitor, for he might be a "rough neck."[64]

Mitchell's reaction to the emotionally tearing experiences of her adolescence and young adulthood—the death of her mother, the sacrifice of her education, the snub by Atlanta society, the divorce—was to get a job in one of the most thoroughly antifemale fields she could have picked. There, at the newspaper, she began to cultivate the persona that she would maintain for the rest of her life. She never sought entrance into society thereafter; her friends came mainly from work. Yet the limits of her rebellion became apparent with her marriage to John Marsh, who was apparently gentle, quietly witty, and entirely predictable. One night, Margaret "yelled" (as she put it) at the Capital City Club that "I thought the duty of a citizen involved, too, the calling of sons of bitches 'sons of bitches' every time they acted like sons of bitches."[65] This may be freedom, but it is freedom *within* the Capital City Club. William Chafe points out that the freedom of language and sexuality that characterized the 1920s did not change the role of wife for most American women; Mitchell seems perfectly to exemplify this in her own limited rebellion. Thus how far Margaret Mitchell stood outside her culture's values and whether she questioned specifically and seriously its definition of woman are questions answerable only indirectly. What does seem clear is that the confusions of being an Atlanta woman growing up in the 1920s, with the conflicting definitions of family heritage, traditional ladyhood, and contemporary mores, produced conflicts in Mitchell that, though strategically circumvented and possibly buried, surfaced from time to time throughout her life and affected her imagining of the South during the middle nineteenth century in *Gone With the Wind*.

A woman she found obnoxious said once that Margaret really wasn't "serious" enough to be a novelist. Mitchell later recalled that she "got so mad that I began to laugh, and I had to stop the car because I laughed so hard. And that confirmed their opinion of my lack of seriousness. And when I got home I was so mad still that I grabbed up what manuscript I could lay hands on, forgetting entirely that I hadn't included the envelopes that were under the bed or the ones in the pot-and-pan closet, and I posted down to the hotel and caught Mr. Latham just as he was about to catch the train."[66] Mitchell switches anger into laughter and makes her novel's publication seem contingent on an impulse. For the women of her culture, the expression of direct feeling—especially anger—and professional achievement outside the home were forbidden. Thus it is hard to know just what Margaret Mitchell realistically expected, when she said to Faith Baldwin in 1937 that what she most desired in life was "freedom . . . freedom to think what you want to think, privacy of the spirit, and freedom to do what you want to do, within the law, the usages and customs of civilized society."[67] For she must have known by then that freedom and "the usages and customs" of Atlanta were incompatible.

It may be that her novel was her ultimate strategy, her way of being both free and acceptable. For despite Margaret's frequent disparaging remarks about Scarlett O'Hara, Maybelle Mitchell and the Jazz Age had a lot to do with that character's imagining; and, despite Mitchell's ironic jabs at twentieth-century society, Melanie Wilkes comes right out of the South's expectations for its young ladies as late as the 1930s. Two parts of a complicated vision of southern women, Scarlett and Melanie show that Margaret Mitchell found it imaginatively impossible to unify her conception of woman. In a telling comment on the writing of the novel, Margaret Mitchell said that "she began to wonder . . . what the ladies of the Daughters of the Confederacy organizations, and the Civil War veterans would say about her making a woman like Scarlett the heroine of her novel. . . . she had meant for Melanie, the ideal Southern woman, to be the leading character, but . . . somehow Scarlett had simply taken over."[68]

She kept the writing of the novel secret from almost all her friends; only John read anything of it before publication, and only a few other people even knew what she was up to during those long years. The split between her public and private lives seemed complete. She was satisfying her need to have work to do and to do it well, and her need to assert herself, for she could create and control the universe of that book according to her own lights. Yet it need never see the light of day; after giving the manuscript to Latham, Mitchell sent him a famous telegram saying that she had changed her mind and asking him to send it back. He didn't, and Mitchell spent the rest of her life trying to fend off the public world that so liked her private one.

At the premiere of the film of *Gone With the Wind*, the Hollywood women who attended, like Carole Lombard, wore sophisticated clothes: black velvet dresses, sables, silver fox, jewels, orchids. Suffering privately from an injury for which, because of delays in the movie, she had repeatedly postponed seeking medical attention, Margaret Mitchell made her appearance in a bouffant pink gown—the dress of a demure southern girl. She was then thirty-nine. There, it would seem, is her paradox: the ultimate cause of all the glory and glamour, in disguise as an innocent southern belle. Despite her efforts, once again, to create a public persona, the novel itself—if not the film—reveals a test of gender-based southern tradition that its writer could never articulate in any other language.

Margaret Mitchell took the title for her novel from Ernest Dowson's poem, "*Non sum qualis Eram bonae sub regno Cynarae*" ("I am not what I was under the rule of the good Cynara"): "I have forgot much, Cynara! gone with the wind,/Flung roses, roses riotously with the throng." Though Margaret Mitchell and most critics have maintained that the only relationship between the poem and the novel is in the four key words, it is not hard to find other reasons why the poem itself might have appealed to the novelist. Surely Cynara in the poem resembles the set of values in the novel that Scarlett "forgets" and that are, for her, best represented by her memory of Ellen O'Hara, the Cynara of the novel. The lines quoted and the title of Dowson's poem, in fact, could well have come from Scarlett at the end of the novel, as could the conclusions of each stanza in Dowson's poem, "I have been faithful to thee, Cynara! in my fashion."

In any case, it was certainly in Mitchell's own fashion that she wrote the novel. Most important for critical analysis is that she said she wrote the last chapter first, probably in 1926, and the first chapter last, apparently just after the novel had been accepted for publication ten years later in 1936. The last chapter left many readers hanging with the question that expressed what concerned them most about the novel: the love story. "Does Scarlett get Rhett back?" Mitchell was asked for years, by telephone, telegram, letter, and in person. She replied, consistently, that she did not know. The fact that she had ten years to decide—or to find out—indicates that Mitchell fully intended to leave the question moot.

On the other hand, chapter one, with its famous opening line ("Scarlett O'Hara was not beautiful, but men seldom realized it when caught by her charm as the Tarleton twins were" [3]) and its entry into the world of the novel by way of the Tarleton twins' college predicament, was written quite hastily, some say in only a day. In that chapter, one may reasonably expect to find Mitchell's last imaginative vision of her novel, those concerns that still—after ten years—informed her pen. And central to that chapter, as is the case with the entire novel, is a probably less than conscious but certainly quite pronounced obsession with gender roles.

Before proceeding to a detailed discussion of the novel, a brief summary of its action may point out some differences between the written and the filmed versions—differences that are often overlooked because the film so nearly recapitulated the novel. *Gone With the Wind* begins on Sunday, April 14, 1861. Georgia has seceded; General Beauregard has fired on Fort Sumter two days earlier; and the next day Lincoln will call up a 75,000-man militia for the U.S.A. All this is of little concern or interest to sixteen-year-old Scarlett O'Hara, whose eyes are focused on the Wilkes family picnic the next day and what she sees as her own central role there. She will use her charms once again to prove her popularity with the men, particularly with Ashley Wilkes, whom she secretly loves. When her Clayton County neighbors Stuart and Brent Tarleton tell her that Ashley is to marry his cousin Melanie, Scarlett faces for the first time in her pampered life a fact that she both does not like and cannot control. Control it she tries, though, at the picnic at the Wilkeses' plantation, Twelve Oaks: she announces her love to Ashley in the library, but he turns her down. Meanwhile, the catlike Rhett Butler overhears the entire scene and is attracted by her directness.

The narrator explains Scarlett's character partly by heredity and partly by environment. Her father, whom she most deeply—and increasingly—resembles, is an Irishman of sixty whose gambling and drinking skills won him the land he had always wanted and whose sheer luck (or so he thinks) won him the hand of Ellen Robillard, a Savannah aristocrat of French heritage. Ellen, now only thirty-two, married Gerald as the only alternative she saw to entering a convent after her real and, as it turns out, only love, her cousin Philippe, had been exiled to and killed in New Orleans. By now she has borne six children, first Scarlett, then the snippy and petty Suellen, then Carreen, a gentle, mystical girl, and then three boys who all died young and were buried under gravestones marked Gerald O'Hara, Jr. Scarlett, seen by her father as a sort of son-substitute, hides Gerald's impetuous, assertive, unanalytic, and occasionally thoughtless but soft-hearted nature under a veneer of southern ladyhood taught her by Ellen, whom she reveres, and Mammy, who understands Scarlett as few others do.

At the picnic, the news about Lincoln's call to arms overshadows the announcement of Ashley's and Melanie's engagement. After her fruitless effort to convince Ashley to give up Melanie (and despite her own obvious ambivalence), Scarlett immediately accepts the marriage proposal of Melanie's brother, Charles Hamilton.

Both couples marry. The men go off to war; at home, Scarlett soon learns of her husband's death by pneumonia and, a few months later, gives an easy birth to their son Wade Hampton Hamilton. Miserable because she is bored by her new role as a widow and mother (though others blame grief), Scarlett goes to Atlanta to stay with Melanie and the silly Aunt Pittypat. There, although she performs the war work expected of southern ladies, she continues to chafe at the restrictions put on her by widowhood. At a charity ball, Scarlett dances with Rhett Butler, to the scandal of society. Rhett, an aristocrat from Charleston, has become the black sheep of his family. Expelled from West Point, he then spent an evening unchaperoned with a young woman yet failed to ask her to marry him; now he makes money from blockade-running. He is attracted to Scarlett apparently as much from a recognition of kindred character as from physical desire. But Scarlett continues to think only of Ashley and devises plans for making her fantasies real, despite Melanie's public support and private affection for her.

Atlanta falls; as the Confederates burn their ammunition warehouses, Rhett helps Scarlett, Wade, Melanie, Melanie's newborn son, and Prissy (Scarlett's maid) to escape, then leaves them behind Union lines to search out Tara among the other burned and ruined homes, while he goes off to join the Confederate artillery.

Tara has survived (thanks in part to good Yankees), but Ellen is dead from typhoid caught while she was nursing the trashy Slatterys; Scarlett's two sisters are weak, recovering from the same disease; Gerald has gone senile from the shock, and the few blacks who remain look to Scarlett for guidance. She takes over with an unnecessary asperity that demonstrates her insecurity. Through her energy and work, the household survives even a lone Yankee deserter, looter, and would-be rapist, whom Scarlett kills, and a troop of Yankees who steal goods and set the house on fire. The household at Tara eventually includes Will Benteen, a gentle and responsible Cracker who decides to stay after convalescing there, and Ashley, who comes home from a federal prison in Illinois.

But problems only intensify with the end of the war. In order to raise the exorbitant taxes required by the Reconstruction government, Scarlett ingeniously dresses up in the velvet draperies, goes to Atlanta to take up Rhett's earlier proposition that she become his mistress, and finds him in jail, where he is first pleased and then angered by her appearance: he discovers her purpose and declines. Failing this, when Scarlett accidentally meets Suellen's beau Frank Kennedy and discovers he owns a store and is buying a sawmill, she manages to convince him that Suellen has married another and that she, Scarlett, should be his wife. Once married, they stay in Atlanta, and Scarlett defies convention by supervising first the store and then the mill, work interrupted only briefly by her second pregnancy and the birth of her daughter Ella. Scarlett not only is good at business; she loves it and will take almost any risk to continue it and to prosper, including hiring convict labor and riding about town alone. During one ride, she is attacked by two men, one black and one white, in Shantytown; Big Sam from Tara saves her, but in the evening's reprisal, Frank Kennedy and his fellow members of the Ku Klux Klan (including Ashley) are shot at, and Frank is killed. Once again, Rhett—still socially ostracized by all but Scarlett and Melanie—saves the day by pretending the men were all at a brothel belonging to his mistress, Belle Watling.

Widowed a second time, Scarlett begins to respond to Rhett's courting, to change her mind about the once-despised Melanie, and to lose some of her passion for Ashley. She agrees (under some duress) to marry Rhett; they go off on a lavish honeymoon to New Orleans and return to build a huge house that is both ostentatious and tasteless but is what Scarlett wants. Deciding to make the best of the Reconstruction, Scarlett chooses her friends from among the Carpetbaggers, and her southern acquaintances snub her; only Melanie remains faithful. Pregnant once again, she considers abortion, but Rhett forbids it, and Bonnie Blue Butler is born. The marriage worsens; both continue playing roles and turn to alcohol. Scarlett insists on separate bedrooms, saying she wants no more children.

On the afternoon of what will be Ashley's first birthday party since the picnic at Twelve Oaks so long ago, Scarlett talks with him at the lumber mill, where, over his protests, she has employed him. The relationship appears to resolve itself into a deep but passionless friendship; as they embrace as friends, however, three people see them and report it to the town. Nevertheless, Melanie asks that Scarlett receive with her at the party—to which Rhett has forced Scarlett to go—and after the party, Rhett carries her upstairs to have sex forcibly. Scarlett actually enjoys this, but, out of mutual vulnerability, the two never talk about it. Instead, angry at Rhett's simulated nonchalance about the episode some time later, Scarlett strikes at him; he sidesteps and she falls down the huge staircase, later miscarrying the child conceived the evening of Ashley's party, and nearly dying. As the marriage continues to falter, Rhett gives to his daughter (who resembles Gerald O'Hara even more nearly than does Scarlett) the affection and the expectations he had had for his wife, grooming her to be a part of the finest old Atlanta society. Then Bonnie is killed, like Gerald, jumping her pony over too high an obstacle, and Rhett goes temporarily insane, refusing to let the child's coffin out of his bedroom. Scarlett, saner but now more cruel, tells Rhett he killed Bonnie.

At the end of the novel, Rhett calls Scarlett back from a visit elsewhere in Georgia; Melanie is dying of a miscarriage. On her deathbed, Melanie asks Scarlett to care for her more or less helpless son and husband and to be kind to Rhett, for, she says, he loves Scarlett. Next, in a conversation with Ashley, Scarlett learns that he is a child like herself. She leaves to go home, in a mist identical to that of a recurring nightmare; unlike the nightmare, she finally sees lights and runs for Rhett. But it is an illusion of security: Rhett listens patiently to her telling him that she finally knows she loves him, but then he says the relationship has simply worn out for him. He will return to Charleston society, to the forms of the old days; Scarlett resolves to begin again, at Tara, and to get him back—somehow—for "after all, tomorrow is another day" (1037).

No brief summary, of course, could do justice to Mitchell's long novel. Nevertheless, even the barest summary reveals a central concern with the definition and role of women, men, and community. It is the mores and biology of being female that shape Scarlett's life: incompatible cultural definitions of femininity and masculinity as well as her three unwanted children help to make of Scarlett the tragic figure she in some sense becomes. Similarly, Melanie's meshing with and ultimately redefining her culture's prescription for womanhood give her security and nobility, but finally death.

Even the first paragraph of the novel indicates that the concern will be gender and its relationship to action, for after the famous first sentence Mitchell continues to describe Scarlett's face as "too sharp" a blend of her mother's feminine features and her father's masculine ones. The definition of masculinity in Clayton County soon follows: "raising good cotton, riding well, shooting straight, dancing lightly, squiring the ladies with elegance and carrying one's liquor like a gentleman were the things that mattered" (4) to men such as the Tarleton twins who sit with Scarlett. And Scarlett, true to southern ladyhood, rejects any discussion of politics, threatening (in an appropriately "feminine" symbolic gesture) to "go in the house and shut the door" behind her if the Tarleton twins keep up the talk about war (5).

Although the twins accept the cultural division between masculine and feminine, their own mother bridges the gap by her concern with horses and her ability to control them. That this is perceived as unusual behavior for a woman is clear in the narrator's comment that "the County could never get used to the way small Mrs. Tarleton bullied her grown sons" (6) and in one twin's comment that Mrs. Tarleton's daughters won't let her ride her new stallion to the picnic: "They said they were going to have her go to one party at least like a lady" (7).

Scarlett calls Charles Hamilton a "sissy" (9), revealing her attitudinal grounding in gender roles; yet her difference from the usual female type is what attracts the twins: she doesn't "hold herself in" or "go around being cold and hateful when she's mad" like most girls do (11).

Nevertheless, the twins, like Scarlett, normally think in terms of gender. Trying to explain her sudden quiet after hearing about the engagement, they fall back on "girls set a big store on knowing such things first" (12), and in discussing Cathleen Calvert's recent trip to Charleston, they bet that "all she'll know about is the balls she went to and the beaux she collected" (15). Ashley doesn't fit their definition of "masculine" because he is "kind of queer about music and books and scenery" (16), whereas Able Wynder, though poor, is a "real man" because he is "the best shot in the Troop" and "knew all about living outdoors" (18).

It is no accident that the novel begins with so many references to gender distinctions. Although *Gone With the Wind* deals directly and overtly with several themes, the one issue that unites them and of which its author appears to be ironically least conscious is precisely the concern for gender. Mitchell herself intended the novel's subject to be the conditions for survival: who makes it through a traumatic, world-destroying event, who doesn't, and why. As a novel whose subject is southern history, *Gone With the Wind* describes the downfall of the Old South and the beginnings of the New; looked at from this angle, the characters embody historical forces. Scarlett, for example, represents Atlanta, the New South, and finally post–Civil War America. Yet Mitchell's history, as Floyd Watkins and others have pointed out, is faulty, at best accurate in minor details rather than persuasive as a major interpretation of the period.[69] Hence its historicalness becomes more interesting as historiography—how one twentieth-century southern woman envisioned her past—than as scholarship; and Mitchell's vision is, rather inescapably, banal. Moreover, though her own view that the novel's theme is personal survival comes close to the heart of her work by emphasizing individual psychology, it is rather imprecise.

Gone With the Wind itself presents a far more interesting and complex problem: it questions not only the means but the value of sheer survival and defines survival quite clearly as psychological and ethical as well as physical. The axes on which Mitchell imagined survival (in this larger sense) to balance are self-reliance and dependence. Carried to its extreme, self-reliance becomes isolation and even solipsism; dependence, at its worst, becomes the loss of selfhood. Because both the culture Mitchell lived in and the culture she imagined placed these specific values upon one or the other sex, the novel becomes a study of gender roles, of what it means to be a man or woman. And, of course, *Gone With the Wind* remains highly ambivalent on the issue. Although the novel is Scarlett's story, she is, as Charles Everett pointed out in 1936, "an unsympathetic character [used] to arouse sympathetic emotions."[70] And although Rhett is finally a broken man, returning to the shell of the very culture he has rejected, it is, for the most part, the male point of view as most strongly expressed by Rhett that the narrator herself overtly endorses. Thus neither womanhood nor manhood is unequivocally imagined; certainly neither "wins," and in fact the ambiguous narrative stance remains largely unresolved.

Nevertheless, we can see with some clarity the terms and nature of the conflict as well as the narrative's efforts to resolve it. One example both of the gender conflicts implicit in the novel and of narrative and structural efforts to resolve them comes in the collapsed parallelism among the four central characters. In various ways too numerous to discuss here, the novel (like *Hagar* and *The Awakening*) endorses similarity rather than complementarity as the ideal for husband and wife. Ellen's true love is her Low Country cousin Philippe; Suellen and Frank Kennedy are tediously meant for one another; Rhett and Scarlett are thoroughly "like"; Ashley and Melanie share values, experience, and genes. Yet marriage of like to like leaves both yearning for what is missing, and (one would presume) for both partners the values that are missing are also similar. Indeed, just as Scarlett nurses a love for the complementary Ashley that lasts until nearly the end of the novel, so does Rhett maintain a love for Melanie that continues indefinitely; for both, the unattainable man or woman represents a set of values that Rhett and Scarlett find equally unattainable. Similarly, Ashley the dreamer sustains a certain attraction to earthy Scarlett that is formed partly of physical lust and partly of admiration and envy of her physical and psychic strength. And Melanie responds to worldly Rhett on the same grounds: physical reaction to his maleness and awe of his strength. Yet the parallelism falters. Melanie's response is revulsion, not attraction, for Rhett's body. Moreover, though Rhett (and the reader) constantly wishes Scarlett to rid herself of the Ashley in her mind (Rhett's jealousy of Ashley quite specifically provokes him to want to rape his wife as punishment), Scarlett never feels, much less expresses, jealousy of Rhett's feelings for Melanie, who quite clearly is the object of his adoration, the "only great lady" he knows. Instead, her envy is reserved for Belle Watling, the object of his physical rather than spiritual love, and the keeper of a whorehouse. While Rhett's love is for two different dream women, whom he sees as the virgin (Melanie) and the whore (Belle), Scarlett fuses physical attraction and idealism in her love for Ashley. Rhett is acting out of a specifically male tradition, and Scarlett out of a different female one. Similarly, Ashley's physical attraction to Scarlett and Melanie's physical revulsion from Rhett come from traditions specific to gender, though Melanie's (ladyhood) differs from

Scarlett's. Thus the narrative efforts to pursue the notion of male-female similarity that are implicit in the novel's matchmaking founder when the partners in those ideal matches begin to dream their separate southern man's and southern woman's dreams.

But let us back up for a look at other ways in which the novel comes to confront issues specific to cultural gender definitions. There is certainly no question that the novel presents a prescription for southern ladyhood, from which the major characters deviate. It appears as early as Ellen's famous comment that her

> life was not easy, nor was it happy, but she did not expect life to be easy, and if it was not happy, that was woman's lot. It was a man's world, and she accepted it as such. The man owned the property, and the woman managed it. The man took the credit for the management, and the woman praised his cleverness. The man roared like a bull when a splinter was in his finger, and the woman muffled the moans of childbirth, lest she disturb him. Men were rough of speech and often drunk. Women ignored the lapses of speech and put the drunkards to bed without bitter words. Men were rude and outspoken, women were always kind, gracious and forgiving.
>
> She had been reared in the tradition of great ladies, which had taught her how to carry her burden and still retain her charm, and she intended that her three daughters should be great ladies also. (58)

The tone of anger is not Ellen's; it is the narrator's, and it rarely reappears in the novel. Instead, Mitchell created a woman whose ladyhood was only a veneer and then observed what happened to her. As one might expect, Scarlett successively finds bellehood a trap (79), marriage a trap (101), and widowhood a trap (134); there is no female role in which she is happy. So she adopts the male role, as indicated by her looking more and more like Gerald and by the narrator's insistence that the Gerald in her soul won over the Ellen. But by the end of the novel, the prescription still remains, consciously still endorsed, in Scarlett's mind: "What would have happened to me, to Wade, to Tara and all of us if I'd been—gentle when that Yankee came to Tara? I should have been—but I don't even want to think of that. And when Jonas Wilkerson was going to take the home place, suppose I'd been—kind and scrupulous? Where would we all be now? And if I'd been sweet and simple minded and not nagged Frank about bad debts we'd—oh, well. Maybe I am a rogue, but I won't be a rogue forever, Rhett" (775). But it is not by the masculine term *rogue* that her society refers to Scarlett; they call her "unwomanly" and "unsexed" (947). For that society has carried through the war and into the Reconstruction period its old traditions, including that of the southern lady:

> The old usages went on, must go on, for the forms were all that were left to them . . . the leisured manners, the courtesy, the pleasant casualness in human contacts, and, most of all, the protecting attitude of the men toward their women. . . . the men were courteous and tender and they almost succeeded in creating an atmosphere of sheltering their women from all that was harsh and unfit for feminine eyes. That, thought Scarlett, was the height of absurdity, for there was little, now, which even the most cloistered women had not seen and known in the last five years. . . . But . . . they remained ladies and gentlemen. (608)

It is significant that none of these ladies is a central character in the novel, with the exception of Ellen. For, if the novel's theme were truly survival, as Mitchell said, then the Atlanta women like Mrs. Elsing, Mrs. Meade, and Mrs. Merriwether, all of whom worked after the war (sewing, painting china, or making pies for sale) and all of whom kept up the traditions and survived, would be the heroines. Even Ellen, at the extreme of ladyhood, and Belle Watling, apparently at the other extreme as a madam, stay within the traditional scheme. Because Ellen dies before the war ends, we do not see what Scarlett's model of the great lady would do after the war, and we are left only with the prewar vision of sacrificial acceptance. And because Belle Watling (despite her donations to the Confederacy) knows her "place" and stays in it, even refusing to permit Melanie to address her on the street, she too endorses traditional definitions of ladyhood.

It is also significant that northern ladies are perceived not just by characters but by the novel as a whole to be very different from (and not as sympathetic as) southern women. Southerners in the novel believe northern women to be direct in speech, assertive, rich, and unlucky in love: their men, says Mammy at one point, marry them only for money. The northerners who actually appear in the novel are excluded from and by southern society. In Clayton County, the northern-born Mrs. Calvert is reduced to weeping over her inability to figure out southern forms, and the Yankee women who move South after the war are depicted as fascinated by southern women but vulgar themselves. Only Melanie has a good word for northern women, when she pleads that there must be some good northern women who care for southern soldiers' graves. At the very least, the distinctions indicate that *Gone With the Wind* perceives the southern lady to be a genus separate from American women generally; were Scarlett raised in the North, the novel implies, she would have had no problems being herself—but then there would have been no novel.

Scarlett and Melanie both deviate in important but very different ways from the societal definitions of southern ladyhood. Though even before the war Scarlett's ladyhood is only a surface form of behavior, it is possible that without the war, she could have continued to fit into the expected forms. Yet because the war forces her to become "head of the house now" (484), the dependence forced on her by her gender role is replaced by the opportunity to express the "masculine" side of herself. She uses her "sharp intelligence hidden beneath a face as sweet and bland as a baby's" (59), an intelligence that, it is repeatedly pointed out, is masculine because it can figure out dollars but not folks. She shows her headstrong, impetuous assertiveness, masculine because it came from Gerald. And she reveals her desire to get out into the world, a masculine desire because, when she is literally out, she almost gets raped. Although Scarlett's character is complicated (her obstinacy, for instance, cannot be described as gender-specific), it is precisely her stereotypically masculine desires and behavior that form the central conflict within her and within the novel. For these desires and behavior push her towards autonomy and beyond, to the love of power and control of others as well as of the self. Once forced, at Tara, to run a small universe, later, in Atlanta, she enjoys running the sawmill and, still later, cannot stop her obsession with working harder and harder to earn more and more money and to control more and more people.

Yet there is another side to Scarlett, the stereotypically feminine side that does not simply endure but enjoys dependence and a sense of an outer force that provides stability. It is evident most consistently in her memories of Ellen, particularly of Ellen's office, the calm functional center of order at Tara. Not by accident does Mitchell describe Scarlett's final dream of Tara—to which she will respond by returning—by saying "she thought of Tara and it was as if a gentle cool hand were stealing over her heart" (1036). That hand, throughout the novel, is Ellen's; and immediately after thinking of Tara, Scarlett "suddenly . . . wanted Mammy desperately, as she had wanted her when she was a little girl, wanted the broad bosom on which to lay her head . . . Mammy, the last link with the old days" (1037). Scarlett's desire for dependence comes through clearly and consistently, too, in her recurring nightmare. In it, she is running through a heavy mist, alone, chased by an unknown presence, and looking for some haven. At one point, she interprets the elusive haven as "Ashley." When she tells Rhett and Melanie about the dream, Melanie responds by offering her support, but Rhett fails to comprehend it. By the end of the novel, Mitchell has the dream become real: as Scarlett goes home from Melanie's deathbed, she begins to run through the heavy fog and sees lights. "In her nightmare, there had never been any lights, only gray fog. Her mind seized on these lights" (1020), for "lights meant safety, people, reality" (1020). The lights are those of her home; now, says the narrator, "she knew the haven she had sought in dreams. . . . It was Rhett" (1021). But Scarlett's moment of enlightenment does not give her the haven she has sought, for Rhett no longer gives a damn about her; hence, her turn to Tara and Mammy.

Scarlett vacillates between these two extremes of self-reliance and dependence, never able to reconcile them. Because she has gone so far in the direction of self-reliance, for her sex and her period, she has made impossible the fulfillment of her need for dependency; for instance, she allows herself to recognize the role Melanie has played to support her only after Melanie dies. Her conscious independence and less conscious dependence affect centrally Scarlett's attitudes towards children, men and women, and sexuality. Children she cannot abide; some of the narrator's most powerful language is spent in showing her revulsion at Wade's hiccoughs, whining, and clinging to her skirts. It is because they are so dependent upon her that Scarlett dislikes children: she does not mind actual responsibility for them, but she resents being reminded of her own childish needs, and, when reminded, she does not like the idea of anyone else's competing with her for a "haven." Some of her vitriol towards blacks (specifically towards Prissy) takes its energy from precisely the same source; Scarlett is repulsed by incompetence and total dependency because she has had to fight to repress those very things in herself. Women she dislikes too, as a group, because she thinks they are spineless and weak, dependent. Only when Melanie appears at the top of the stairs prepared to kill the Yankee marauder with a sword does Scarlett begin to have respect for her; eventually she learns that Melanie's courage, though differently expressed, is quite as real as her own, and Melanie becomes perhaps the only character in the novel with whom Scarlett begins to have an interdependent relationship. She perceives other women either as totally powerful, like Ellen and Mammy, or utterly boring, like her sisters and the Atlanta women, because they continue to observe the old forms.

It is with men, and specifically in her sexual relationships with them, that the conflict between control and dependence becomes most clear and affects most centrally Scarlett's behavior. Ashley and Rhett, the two men for whom she feels physical desire, are the two men she cannot control. Immediately after losing Ashley, she marries the boy Charles Hamilton with his "calf" eyes; immediately after Rhett tells her he has no money for Tara, she turns to the "sissy" Frank Kennedy. Rhett calls her, at one point, a "bully" who will run all over anyone she can; this includes her own children and two of her husbands, for neither of whom she feels any physical attraction. Yet Scarlett is by no means "frigid," as her author once said. Certainly the scene when she and Ashley meet in the orchard at Tara is a scene of mutual passion (532–33); Scarlett looks over his body with love and "pleading," and when he kisses her, he feels "her change within his grip and there was madness and magic in the slim body he held and a hot soft glow in the green eyes . . . the lips . . . were red and trembling" (533). Until now, Scarlett has consistently viewed Ashley as her Perfect Knight, the living embodiment of stability who is also, fortunately, male. Hence she can have both erotic and dependency fantasies about this blond, beautiful man. When he comes home for furlough during the war, Scarlett crams the weeks with "incidents to remember . . . from which she could extract every morsel of comfort." Here are those events: "dance, sing, laugh, fetch and carry for Ashley, anticipate his wants, smile when he smiles, be silent when he talks, follow him with your eyes so that each line of his erect body . . . will be indelibly printed on your mind" (271).

If this sounds like a happy slave, it should; for Scarlett's erotic fantasies are inextricably linked with her desire for a benevolent paternalism. Hence it is no surprise that, in the famous scene with Rhett which is so much like rape, Scarlett feels the "wild thrill" of "joy, fear, madness, excitement, surrender to arms that were too strong, lips too bruising, fate that moved too fast" (940), that she feels the "ecstasy of surrender" to someone "who was bullying and breaking her" (941). Not only is Rhett the tower of strength that Ashley has been; in his brutality, he is paying her back, punishing her, for her own bullying and breaking of others. This is no traditionally erotic scene: a "terrifying faceless black bulk" (933) speaks with "violence as cruel as the crack of a whip" (935); his eyes glowing "redly like twin coals" (935), he threatens to tear her to pieces and to smash her head like the shell of a walnut (937). Furious about Ashley, Rhett carries Scarlett upstairs, declaring, "By God, this is one night when there are only going to be two in my bed" (939); the way to accomplish this, he thinks, is force. Elsewhere in her relationship with Rhett, each time Scarlett feels physical desire for him it is precisely because Rhett has shown he can overpower her. And the animal imagery that pervades the novel supports this connection: men are associated either with dogs and calves—and asexuality—or with horses, panthers, and leopards—and sexuality.

Scarlett, then, can find no satisfactory reconciliation between her need for self-reliance and that for dependence. As the one becomes more extreme, so does the other, until finally she finds it equally exciting to rule like a dictator and to be raped. Mrs. Tarleton and Aunt Pittypat represent the two extremes in two objectified characters. Mrs. Tarleton, with her love for horses, her earthy talk, and her bullying of her sons, is the only fully dominating woman in the novel; Aunt Pittypat, on the other hand, is the purely dependent woman, so dependent that the word *baby* is consistently used to describe her.

Like Scarlett, Melanie rebels against the conventional mores that define the lady. Yet, unlike Scarlett, her revolt takes the form not of defying but of transcending those mores. Melanie defends Scarlett against the opprobrium of Atlanta, saying that people simply don't like smart women. She, too, works in the fields until she drops, is ready to kill the looter, puts out the fire in the kitchen, and saves Scarlett from burning to death. Each time she goes against her culture, though, she does it for a higher, more "Christian" ideal, whereas Scarlett rebels for materialistic, "selfish" reasons, quite like the southern idealism and northern materialism counterpointed in other novels. Moreover, Melanie's differences with the definition of lady depend on her special limited vision, a view of reality that finds and believes only the good about those she loves. Both Rhett and Scarlett, for instance, feel it necessary to protect her against the knowledge that Ashley and Scarlett really had something going on between them. Her goodness depends on ignorance; it is prelapsarian in nature. And it is also prepubescent. Melanie's body is consistently described as that of a child, a girl; she dies because her pelvis is too narrow to deliver children. When her sexual ignorance is tested, when she is alone with Rhett after Bonnie's death, she is repulsed: Rhett's body, hairy and muscular, frightens her and she turns away. The novel implies, also by her death in the larger plot, that Melanie's sort of goodness and strength, real though they are, are limited to a world that is neither virile nor evil.

Yet the world, as Mitchell envisions it, is both virile and evil. In fact, the two qualities are virtually equated. For example, the one activity that gives Frank Kennedy a sense of masculinity and hence dignity— and the one activity from which Scarlett feels herself utterly excluded—is violence, the violence of the Ku Klux Klan. More important, the characterization of Rhett Butler has a massive dose of the devil in it. Much like the nineteenth-century dometic novelists' Guy Hartwells and St. Elmos, Rhett has spent a life traveling and engaging in shady deals. But he is also described physically as a devil: his eyes glint, he watches Scarlett like a cat watching a mouse hole, he prowls with a contained ferocity, and he has an uncanny ability to read other people's minds. Most striking of all is Rhett's astonishing ability to appear on, and to leave, the scene at exactly the right moment. To choose only a few examples: he manages to appear just as Scarlett is sobbing over Ashley during the war; just as the family appear at the train station to find out the casualties; just as they prepare to evacuate the city; and just as the last of Aunt Pittypat's chickens is cooked.

Margaret Mitchell endows this character with such remarkable powers of knowledge that it is easy to make the mistake of thinking that he is her authorial point-of-view character; indeed, the narrator herself often agrees with his perceptions when they conflict with others' and enhances our sense of his infallibility by never directly entering his mind, as she does with almost every other character. And, in various contexts in the novel, it becomes clear that cold objective knowledge and concern with larger issues are exclusively the province of males. Hence, in his constant ratiocination, in his near-telepathy, and in his large, very male body, Rhett Butler is the principle of masculinity. And in his hidden emotions, his violent nature, and his grasping opportunism, he is simultaneously the figure of evil.

Mitchell, however, is too good a novelist to permit a character to be as one-dimensional as this. Rhett has lips and feet like a girl's, understands "folks," joins the Confederate army, is gentle towards Melanie, supports his mother and sister, grieves over Bonnie. However, Mitchell is too poor a novelist to envision fully how such an oddly androgynous man would tick: hence she never explores his mind. Rhett lies somewhere between Joyce Carol Oates's Arnold Friend (in "Where Are You Going, Where Have You Been?") and Ashley Wilkes.

If Rhett Butler is Mitchell's dark devil, Ashley Wilkes is her fair angel. Yet once again, Mitchell is too good a novelist to let Ashley remain so simple as Scarlett initially perceives him. Though a dreamer, he is also a realist: he knows exactly what has happened to the South and joins the Confederate army in the knowledge that the war will solve nothing and the chances of victory are slim. Though he lacks the push of Rhett or Scarlett, he knows full well that he must define himself through some independent action. When he agrees to work for Scarlett, it is only because Melanie and Scarlett join forces, and, as he says, he can't fight both of them. He would prefer to go North on his own, to start over with his family. So, although his "mainspring is broken," like the other "non-survivors" Mitchell planned to write about—though he is, as Scarlett finally perceives, a child like herself—he is also an adult in his knowledge of reality.

And it is knowledge of a specific sort that the novel finds to be the link between the two men and an important distinction between men and women. Although Scarlett has the "male" mind for business, although Rhett has the "female" mind for character, no women in the novel can see—as can Rhett and Ashley—the larger implications of history and of their actions. No woman can think abstractly. In a novel written by a woman (who of course imagines their abstract thinking), this reinforces once again the suspicion that Mitchell sees her voice as essentially "masculine," just as she has Scarlett wanting not just to have or to love but to *be* Ashley and Rhett.

Other men in the novel are treated with less sympathy. Dr. Meade, as the voice of the Old South, is consistently mocked for his imperception: he does not fit the image of the typically imagined doctor in southern women's fiction, the nurturant androgyne. Charles and Frank are trivialized by "feminization"; and Gerald O'Hara is finally revealed as fundamentally weak. Ellen is the true head of the household at Tara, whereas Gerald is consistently described as a "boy"; Gerald's mainspring is broken at Ellen's death.

Yet Mitchell seems to do an about-face. Though she identifies the forces of knowledge and power and truth with Rhett and Ashley, both these men, like Gerald, are finally brought to their knees by women; Ashley by Melanie's death, Rhett by Bonnie's. The definition of manhood is contingent upon that of womanhood. The woman must be protected, but the man, too, needs someone to protect; the woman must be dependent, but the man needs someone to depend upon him. Mitchell is quite explicit about this. For instance, she has Melanie and Scarlett plot together—while Melanie is dying—to protect Ashley and simultaneously to keep him ignorant of the protection, for the sake of his "masculine pride." We have already seen Frank become manly when he has the chance to protect, by force, his family; more important is the revealing speech Rhett makes when he tells Scarlett why he turned to Bonnie Blue:

> "I wanted to take care of you, to pet you, to give you everything you wanted. I wanted to marry you and protect you and give you a free rein in anything that would make you happy—just as I did Bonnie. . . . I wanted you to stop fighting and let me fight for you. I wanted you to play, like a child—for you were a child, a brave, frightened, bull-headed child. I think you are still a child. . . . I liked to think that Bonnie was you, a little girl again, before the war and poverty had done things to you. She was so like you . . . and I could pet her and spoil her—just as I wanted to pet you."
> (1030–31)

Genuine and tender though his feeling is—and Scarlett feels honestly sorry for him, without contempt—it is a desire that, the reader knows, could never come true. For Scarlett has come through the war and through poverty and has emerged, not a child, but "a woman" (420). Because the code insists that manliness is a product and result of woman's weakness and childishness, men are excruciatingly vulnerable to women who are strong.

Society in the novel is that of "old" Atlanta. Within that society, these gender definitions are so overt and so rigid that to breach them is to face not just the cold stare of society but the alienation and isolation that can come with exploration into unknown territory alone. It is only Melanie's perceptive but simultaneously ignorant support that lets Scarlett stay sane—as Scarlett realizes at the end of the novel—for it is only this support that keeps up even the façade of Scarlett's connection to others. There are other societies depicted in the novel—that in New Orleans, for instance, composed of Civil War profiteers, and that in postwar Atlanta, composed of Yankees come South to profit and rule. Yet neither of these groups greatly concerns Mitchell: she dispenses with both in rather little space (despite the fact that in them Scarlett might have found a sense of community).

Mitchell's concern here is to see whether the traditional South can absorb new modes of behavior. That it ultimately cannot is clear in the conclusion. The two who rebel most against their society finally turn back to it, Scarlett in her return to the "old days" at Tara, and Rhett in his return to Charleston, where he wants "the outer semblance of the things I used to know, the utter boredom of respectability—other people's respectability, my pet, not my own—the calm dignity life can have when it's lived by gentle folks, the genial grace of days that are gone. When I lived those days I didn't realize the slow charm of them—" (1034).

If there is a winner in *Gone With the Wind*, it is the "old days." Fight as the four major characters do to find a way to live in the new, and different though their tactics may be, all are finally defeated. Scarlett and Rhett come closest to inventing a new pattern of life; but they so deeply incorporate contradictory elements of the old, particularly those that defined men and women, that they both are doomed to failure. Perhaps this is what makes the novel both peculiarly southern and internationally popular. It articulates, challenges, and finally confirms the traditional view of the nature and roles of the sexes. Perhaps that is the price Mitchell felt she had to pay to stay in the South. She believed that she "couldn't live anywhere else in the world except in the South. I suppose, being adaptable, I *could* live elsewhere, but I probably would not be very happy. I believe, however, that I see more clearly than most peo-

ple just what living in the South means. There are more rules to be followed here than any place in the world if one is to live in any peace and
happiness. Having always been a person who was perfectly willing to
pay for anything I got, I am more than willing to pay for the happiness I
get from my residence in Georgia."[71]

Gary Kissick

CHAPTER IX.

Conclusion
Tomorrow Is
Another Day

By the time Scarlett says "tomorrow is another day" for the last time near the end of *Gone With the Wind*, the phrase has accrued at least two sorts of meaning. As a girl infatuated with Ashley and unduly confident of her power to control her own life, Scarlett used these words evasively. When she said them, the reader knew she was avoiding reality, fooling herself in the belief that what was put off until tomorrow would take care of itself. By the end of her *Bildungsroman*, however, Scarlett has become an adult. She has lost Rhett, Bonnie Blue, and most of her illusions about money, love, and her own power. Hence when she says that "tomorrow is another day," while thinking of her imminent and final return to Tara, it expresses not only a desire to evade the present but also a sense of faith in the future, a faith strained by experience but also taught by it. Her return to Tara will be not solely to the dream of the secure world of her childhood, but also to a reality that, during and after the war, she shaped as she would and could.

If one adds a third possible meaning to the phrase, that tomorrow is just another day like the last, that the future admits of no change, then these words—evasion, hope, despair—together describe the works of the seven novelists in this study. The authors of *Beulah, Monsieur Motte,* and *Life and Gabriella* offer their protagonists hope for the future by evading the implications of the fiction. *The Awakening, Virginia,* "The Little Convent Girl," and Newman's two novels approach despair: Edna, Virginia, Evelyn, and the little girl are psychically or physically destroyed, and Isabel and Katharine survive at the cost of bitterness. Only *Hagar* presents a wholly optimistic vision for its southern woman protagonist and, as we saw, this was at the cost of imaginative complexity.

Despite their somewhat variant tones, these writers analyze women, men, and community in the South using values and terms that are essentially similar. Moreover, they share some ambivalence about the nature of art itself, an ambivalence deepened by their perception that the woman in the South—like a work of art—served as symbol and object of beauty, in particular of a beauty that is pure, fragile, and finally irrelevant. This perception of the self as symbol complicates critical efforts to define the literature as either realistic or romantic, since for these women even the most prosaic understanding of reality must take account of the symbolic function of women. In their works can be found, as well as similar values and characterizations, similar patterns of imagery.

Women characters from Beulah to Scarlett find that appropriate behavior is demanded by a source outside themselves, sometimes by men and sometimes by other women. The particulars of that code do not change much from Mrs. Asbury's articulation in *Beulah* to Mrs. Merriwether's in *Gone With the Wind.* They demand that a southern woman be compliant, deferential, sacrificial, nurturant, domestic, quietly and uncontroversially intelligent, chaste, beautiful, cultured, religious, and loyal to her region and to its definition of herself.

Yet in each novel and story, the models and injunctions for southern ladyhood have been directly or indirectly challenged. Most apparent, the conventions of behavior are breached. Central to those conventions is the role of the angelic wife and mother, sacrificial, submissive, and dependent. Many characters reject the traditional role altogether, substituting for it the self-reliance of remunerated work. Beulah teaches school and writes, Madame Lareveillère runs a school, Marcélite is a hairdresser, Bonne Maman and her granddaughter sew; Thérèse sells her lumber, Edna her paintings, Hagar her stories and articles, and Katharine her play; Gabriella runs a hat and dress shop; Isabel works in a library, and Scarlett runs Tara and then the sawmill. Yet each writer apparently finds that she must confront the inevitable conflict between the values shaping marriage and motherhood and those required by work outside the home—in short, between dependence and independence. When Beulah converts to Christianity and marries Guy, Augusta Evans resolves the conflict by simply wrenching her heroine out of character and into the expected happy ending. Grace King moves into more complexity with Madame Lareveillère, who must make an adult choice to risk love again and whose work apparently does not conflict with love, perhaps because the school is already so much like a conventional home. Edna Pontellier's painting is never at the heart of her quest for independence; her awakening sexuality, however, founders her with the logic of its conclusion in motherhood. Hagar simply rewrites the rules of marriage so that Johnston avoids the conflict between work and mothering. Of the protagonists who do not work for pay, Virginia makes motherhood into her work and thereby destroys her marriage, herself, and quite probably her son; and Evelyn Cunningham makes her husband into her work and thereby destroys her sense of larger reality. Defining womanhood by designing fashion seems to Gabriella mean and small in comparison with Ben's heroic endeavors; thus for her, work loses its function of teaching self-respect. Isabel's work, on the other hand, gives her the confidence that comes from a sense of the reality Evelyn avoids. In an interesting variant, Scarlett marries three times, but never for love, nor does she care for her children. Yet when she does recognize her love, she loses its object: work and love again seem incompatible, unless the love is of the work, as at Tara.

Such a conflict, between independence and dependence, expressed in terms of work alone outside the home and work for a family within the home, is not unexpected for any woman writer. More than the role of wife and mother, however, these southern writers criticize the conventions that prescribe specifically southern womanhood. When Virginia lives in a world of "evasive idealism," and when Melanie steps out of her role as wife and mother to perform acts of transcendent self-sacrifice and courage, these protagonists are acting in the context of the southern brand of womanhood.

In contrast to the docile wit and unquestioning faith prescribed in the image, these writers place the free and imaginative use of intelligence high among their priorities. It is the source of Beulah's interest, of Claire's growth, of Hagar's salvation, of Scarlett's survival, of Marcélite's invention, of Susan Treadwell's calm, of Isabel's strength. The absence of reflection and analysis, on the other hand, helps to destroy Virginia, Edna, and Evelyn, and the conflict between intellect and submission informs Katharine Faraday's character. On the other hand, not one character—except the utterly selfless little convent girl—is conventionally Christian. In fact, Marcélite and Edna (at her dinner party) are described as pagan goddesses.

In contrast to surrounding characters with others who need them, almost every writer isolates her central character, whether in a pigeon-house, a cottage, an empty dormitory, a black ghetto, an apartment in New York, or a dense fog. Though no writer endorses isolation as a way of life (Mademoiselle Reisz demonstrates the witchlike risks of that choice), the necessity for each protagonist to find herself alone in order to achieve insight and growth is in part, no doubt, a reaction to the pre-scription that southern women always care for and think of others first.

In contrast to the deference and compliance of the ideal southern woman, these writers show their characters deepening a sense of self and growing stronger by speaking from and for that self. Beulah, Mar-célite, Edna, Hagar, Gabriella, and Scarlett all act on the basis of inter-nal direction, often at the risk of social disapproval.

In contrast to symbolizing beauty as purity and fragility, as the south-ern lady should, these protagonists have dark eyebrows and strong bodies. Probably because their values—free intelligence, aloneness, self-assertion—are traditionally masculine, the physical appearance of the protagonists is often atypical, even androgynous. Edna, Scarlett, Katharine, Beulah, Hagar, and Gabriella are all described as striking but not beautiful: they have "character." On the other hand, to Oliver, Virginia appeared fragile and delicate, her skin like magnolia blossoms. Moreover, many characters feel and express their sexuality, from the adolescent Claire's emerging sensuousness, responding to the dancing in the streets, to Calixta's full adult pleasure in the act of sex.

And not one character, from Beulah, whose environment could be al-most anywhere, to Scarlett, who finds the Civil War boring, feels an abiding loyalty to the South.

The androgynous character, expressed in physically androgynous characteristics, extends also to the men in a number of the works. Often enough to be interesting, the most sympathetic men in the novels are the protagonists' lovers and have some of the traits, even certain physical characteristics, stereotypically associated with women. Clearest examples are Monsieur Goupilleau, Robert Lebrun, and Ashley Wilkes, with their poets' eyes. But John Fay, Charlton Cunningham, and Oliver Treadwell, too—even Guy Hartwell and Rhett Butler—have a "feminine" sensitivity of feeling and appearance. For Ashley and Robert, this is associated with a lack of force and of fulfilled sexuality; but most of these men combine sexuality with feminine values. In a variation, Glasgow splits Gabriella's intended lover into two, the ultra-"feminine" southerner and the ultra-"masculine" westerner. Fathers also fit this pattern, but remain relatively powerless: think of Gerald O'Hara, Gabriel Pendleton, and Medway Ashendyne. (Mothers, on the other hand, tend not to exist at all: Beulah, Claire, Marie Modeste, Edna, Melanie, and Isabel are motherless; Hagar and Scarlett lose their mothers early in the novels. And black women—Mammy, Marcélite, the little convent girl's mother—may serve as mothers, but where there are significant white mothers, daughters come closest to becoming the ideal, as in Virginia and Evelyn Cunningham. The pattern implies that the protagonist's growth is somehow contingent upon the absence of a southern lady mother.)

Opposite to the androgynous figures is the dark seducer, even the rapist, like Ralph Coltsworth and Alcée Arobin, or the militaristic father, like the Colonel in *The Awakening*; they represent both the threat of superior physical power and the promise of sexuality, raising the conflict for women between satisfying their sexuality and retaining their freedom. Guy Hartwell and Rhett Butler, despite their feminine characteristics, retain this element of latent violence.

Most writers limit the narrator's point of view so that she does not enter the minds of significant men; although the writers apparently wanted to invent an ideal man, one who was both humane and sexually attractive, most chose not to or perhaps could not show his mind in its privacy.

Because the expected definitions of women and men are challenged directly or changed indirectly, the vision of society in this fiction also takes an unexpected turn. The family unit is not the center of interest in these communities; not only are protagonists orphans or near-orphans, but their own families either collapse (Edna, Virginia, Gabriella, Scarlett, Evelyn, the little convent girl), or we do not see beyond the happy beginnings at the end (Hagar, Beulah, Marie Modeste, Gabriella). Despite this lack of interest in (and perhaps implicit indictment of) the traditional family, some of the roles of members of a family are often filled by people not of the class or race of the protagonist, who act, for instance, as ideal mothers (Mammy) or fathers (the steamboat captain), sisters (Thomasina), or brothers (Will Benteen). Beyond the family unit, society is seen to be rigidly organized in the South, by class and race as well as sex. These writers are particularly ambivalent about the upper class, which Evans condemns but marries Beulah "up" into, which Gabriella makes clothes for but finally rejects by marrying Ben, and which Scarlett perpetually horrifies, as she in turn (claimed her creator) horrified Margaret Mitchell. With less ambivalence, these writers reconstruct racial relationships such that black and white women, especially, find themselves in both literally and symbolically significant relationships, often as one another's hidden self. Community is thus ultimately redefined for several protagonists in a way that avoids or undercuts the rigidities of southern hierarchies. It is the community of the like-*minded*—often intellectual, interregional, and even international, but certainly crossing racial and economic barriers—that many of the writers present as the antithesis to the ossified community of the traditional South. Here Beulah spends much of her adult life, King ends *Monsieur Motte*, and Hagar travels. Gabriella finds this community in Ben, Katharine joins it as a writer, Isabel has access to it in the library, and even Oliver's mistress is part of it. Not surprisingly, in several of the plots, the world outside the South (especially New York) offers knowledge and experience inaccessible to these women at home.

To come to terms with the question of realism and romanticism in the tradition of these southern women writers requires, first of all, a recognition that the South itself has, as a culture, a romantic tradition. American literary romanticism generally assumes a unified real world of idea that lies beyond the material world and that may be benevolent or malevolent. The material world, nature, in turn expresses and is contingent upon the ideal; nature is evocative and symbolic. When this romantic idea loses its complexity and stringency, it can be debased into a sentimental dream of a better world elsewhere whose existence justifies ignoring palpable realities such as racial injustice. Mark Twain saw this decadent romanticism as a southern habit of mind and called it (after Sir Walter Scott) the "Sir Walter disease"; Ellen Glasgow called it "evasive idealism."

On her pedestal at the center of the South's particular romantic dream stood, of course, its central symbol: the southern lady. Like the dream world itself, she was beautiful, fragile, good, and ultimately irrelevant to actuality. She was, as William Taylor early noted, simultaneously overvalued and devalued. More than—or at least differently from— Mark Twain and other southern men, therefore, southern women writers participated in the reality that they described, analyzed, and perhaps defied in their fiction. Through their authorial voices, the silent symbol spoke, and what it said, whether disguised in convention or plain and direct, was rarely fragile and good, and usually relevant to actual experience. The protagonists in their fiction, too, experience a kind of doubleness as both actual person and symbol of the South; Scarlett is Atlanta, Virginia is Virginia.

Given their experiences with southern cultural symbolism, it might seem likely that southern women writers would reject romanticism wholesale, choosing instead the demythologizing possibilities of realism, to expose the earth from which the pedestal rose. Before going further with this line of thinking, however, and because the terms are variously understood, let me clarify what I mean by *romanticism* and *realism*. First, I follow Jacques Barzun when he distinguishes between "two distinct fields of application" for such terms. "In one sense [they refer] to human traits which may be exhibited at any time or place. In the second sense [they are names] given to a period in history because of the notable figures that gave it its peculiar character."[1] These southern women writers, I believe, can be better understood on their own terms as confronting a perpetual choice between the romantic and the realistic vision than by trying to place them into the dominant literary tradition of their various periods in history. What then was that choice?

Corollary to the romantic's faith in an ideal world is the belief that, seen correctly, the natural world can reveal the ideal and can provide connection for the isolated self. In a pond, a blade of grass, or New England mud can be found the infinite. For these southern women writers—or at least their protagonists—access may be through the sensuous gulf or the red Georgia dirt. Not only nature, but the ideal human being (of the opposite sex), can also show the way; Hartwell heals the heart, and Ben brings to Gabriella a masculine nature that symbolizes vaster realities than she has known. Whether through nature or through a man, however, such insight into reality can be gained only by the educated eye—Emerson's "transparent eyeball"—and the tutored heart. Romantics assume that an inner self exists and that it can grow into fuller awareness through the exercise of the imagination. Having discovered (and, perhaps, half-created) the real self within, an individual can express that self in action. A particularly appropriate act is the creation of art, for art not only shows but embodies the transcendent unity of all that is real, self and nature, material and ideal.

As a consequence of these notions, the protagonist in romantic fiction may often be heroic, the setting expressive, and the plot ideally resolved. Inner, subjective conditions are more important to characters than their social or economic conditions; the theme is the development of the entire self by liberating the feelings and the unconscious and by defying oppressive external authority. A romantic narrator typically has no qualms about intruding into the narrative to point out a moral or interpret a symbol; after all, the story is meant to be expressive, not simply reportage.

But what seems insight to the romantic sensibility is illusion to the realist. For the realist assumes that only the empirical is real, that what we call the ideal has been invented by human beings, for personal, social, or biological gain that can be measured and understood. Dr. Mandelet sees romantic love, for instance, as a "decoy to secure mothers for the race."[2] Arguing against the romantic view that the material subserves and expresses the ideal, the realist believes that the ideal subserves and expresses underlying material conditions, which he or she calls "real." For the romantic, nature is symbol; for the realist, it is mere fact.

In order to see the truth, a different kind of vision is required. Realism trusts the photographic eye rather than the transparent eyeball. The careful, detached, objective eye of the observer replaces the imaginative vision of the romantic; that reportorial eye focuses on the material world and reports just what it sees. Such a view reveals the ugliness, the injustice, and the sordidness of society, which romanticism can pass over. It may also reveal people who are self-deluded romantics, like Virginia. and such a focus protects the viewer himself or herself from self-delusion and helps him or her to reach an adult accommodation with the outer world. The tutored self, then, is not the romantically self-created self but the self that has been educated, even chastened, by the world. That world may in fact be all there is; subjectivity itself may be only an illusion, a byproduct of biochemical processes subject to natural law.

Though it may seem self-contradictory, fiction is possible for the realist; it can tell the truth by replicating as closely as possible what is real. Protagonists thus will be ordinary people, not heroes. The setting may well have a powerful effect on people, but (with the possible exception of natural law) it does not express a world beyond the material. Plots may be episodic; they do not in any case follow improbable and wish-fulfilling literary conventions such as the comedic marriage. And the narrator keeps herself or himself carefully detached from the tale; reality is not symbolic in character, hence it needs no intrusive interpretation. It speaks for itself.

There is little written evidence from the writers in this study of systematic thinking about the choice between romance and realism. Ellen Glasgow and Frances Newman are exceptions; Glasgow called herself a realist, and Newman located herself in the vanguard of postrealistic modernism. Kate Chopin made a point (perhaps with a touch of irony) to describe her work, on the other hand, as entirely unself-conscious and unreflective; "I am completely at the mercy of unconscious selection," she wrote.[3] A lack (studied or not) of apparent aesthetic self-consciousness should not, however, be assumed to indicate lack of interest in the issues. For one condition required of the woman writer was that she be perceived and indeed perceive herself as the passive vessel for the muse, rather than an active creator with artistic strategies and tactics. Nevertheless, for whatever reasons, we lack the tellers' theories.

But we do have their tales. And a look at them reveals no obvious choice of either realism or romanticism, in any of the time periods covered and even for Glasgow, Newman, and Chopin, but rather a persistent dialectic between the two human impulses.

Why did these writers diverge in this way from dominant literary tradition? A look at the implications of each artistic option will suggest reasons. Because the realist depicts the actual daily experience of ordinary persons, realism would have appealed as the literary method for debunking the ideal of the southern lady. It would thus serve as a corrective for the entire society of the South, in exposing the romantic illusion of the marble lady. With more subtlety, the techniques of realism could also operate as a corrective for the romantic dreams of a woman protagonist herself; such illusions plague Edna Pontellier, for instance. More extremely, the southern woman as narcissist—who, it will be remembered, must reject the lessons of the world—can be healed by an accommodation to reality, should a realistic author so permit. If her narcissism results from the unacceptability of society's devaluation of her, then she can find a real material world whose lessons she can accept because they permit self-respect—so Katharine Faraday, for example, chooses intellectual and artistic circles over the social whirl of Atlanta.

Yet there are persuasive reasons why southern women writers might choose the romantic vision after all—in addition to the simple fact that, as southerners, they grew up with it. To start with, the "lessons of the world" devalue but also overvalue and idealize southern womanhood, in a complication of the narcissistic pattern described by Ann Douglas. Thus, to take the romantic route may be to substitute for material reality a dream that is, paradoxically, more "realistic" than objective reality. This is, in fact, what these writers do when they dream up characters who are neither beautiful nor fragile, conventionally good nor powerless. But more than this, the romantic idea includes, along with the notion of the superiority of dream to dull fact, powerful corollaries that validate subjectivity, individualism, freedom, the unconscious, and the revolt against authority. Given the particular constraints of the image of womanhood, including denial of the self and submission to authority, each of these romantic ideas would seem likely to appeal to the southern woman writer. In fact, where there has been a decipherable *Bildungsroman* in these works, its stages have moved exactly in the direction of these values.

Perhaps because both options exerted their own particular attractions, these writers found themselves squarely in both camps. Glasgow's *Virginia* is the clearest example in this study of the conflict between the impulses to romanticism and to realism. Begun as a realist's effort to depict with documentary accuracy the process by which the South makes an individual woman into a symbol, the novel shifts from an objective to a sympathetic tone, culminating in an ambiguous conclusion that might well be seen as romantic, even sentimental. The conclusion to the realistic novel *Life and Gabriella*, with its symbolic union of male and female, South and West, is without question romantic. Johnston and Evans, too, fall into the romantic temptation at the ends of their otherwise nonromantic novels; in both, not only is the plot ideally resolved but the setting itself is evocative, even symbolic. In "The Little Convent Girl," Grace King layers a realistic story over the romantic notion that within nature (here, the river) the self meets itself. The story can be seen thematically as about the conflict between romance and realism: confronted with actuality (her mother is black), the girl chooses against it and, in the choice for romance, finds a deeper, inner life in the other mother of the river—but in so doing dies.

Ironically (given their official statements), Kate Chopin exerted more control over her material than did Ellen Glasgow; hence the tension between romance and realism is sharper and clearer, apparently less the result of a fall into romantic temptation than of a truly double vision. Ultimately, I have argued, Chopin opts for the romantic view in *The Awakening* by permitting her natural setting to express a meaningful reality beyond itself, darker and more tragic than Edna's fantasies, but no less romantic. Elsewhere, Chopin chooses to expose the decadent romance of southern womanhood by realistically depicting women who see themselves as symbols; Thérèse Lafirme and Miss McEnders are two.

To look at *Gone With the Wind* in this light is to see its problem in a new way. Mitchell treats Scarlett, her realist, with thorough accuracy, from her thoughts to her actions. Thus the woman who is confronted with the chance to become a symbol and rejects it (never unequivocally) is herself treated from a realistic point of view. In her characterization of Melanie, though, Mitchell is tempted into romance. For Melanie consistently, in word and act, expresses and thus validates the existence of a transcendent and ideal reality. The narrator, instead of giving us access to her private thoughts, keeps Melanie at a distance, a symbol of the ideal. The failure of Melanie's death to redeem the world of the novel (compare Gabriel Pendleton's death) suggests a rejection of the romantic. Yet that death does inspire Scarlett's inner (and romantic) growth, first in her recognition of her love for Rhett, and then in her choice to return to the healing world of Tara, a romantic dream tempered by the realism of the war. Mitchell leaves it to the reader to compare the clearly evasive idealism of Rhett's desire to return to the old days in Charleston with Scarlett's arguably more realistic romanticism in returning to Tara, that plain upcountry functional.

In each writer, then, the realistic impulse is ultimately superseded by some form of romanticism, pure or muddied into sentimentality. Even Frances Newman, whose modernism is evident in her self-consciousness, her experimental form, and her astringent voice, found her choice to lie in some respects between the romantic dream of growth (which she found illusory) and the reality of modern southern mores. Nearly alone among the writers in this study, however, Newman opts finally for realism. This is apparent not only when she leaves Katharine Faraday depressed but recognizing that she must continue to lose her illusions, but also when she treats Evelyn's choice of the dream world behind the crepe veil of a widow with the irony apparent in the novel's title.

Besides sharing a certain ambiguity about the values of romance and realism, these writers also share a pool of images that surface in their fiction from 1859 to 1936. Of natural symbols, the sea appears most prominently, from Beulah's storm-tossed ocean to Edna's and Hagar's sensuous gulf to Hagar's cold north sea—and perhaps to the little convent girl's river of hidden self. In each case, water is connected with the evolution of identity, a fact unsurprising to those familiar with traditional romantic symbolism. Animals trot, leap, and fly through the fiction; in particular, horses consistently are associated with power and energy, hence with issues of control. Birds seem to represent the possibilities of the female psyche, from isolated eagle to domestic canary to strong or broken seagull.

The home takes on special significance as an image both of internal order and of real and ideal community; these writers rearrange the home as a metaphorical way to reorganize society, sometimes taking the domesticated woman out of her traditional role (and home) and sometimes putting surprising collections of people into the big house.

As images, black people and children of both races represent for the writers both the appeal and the threat of oppression. The physical bodies of men and women express character; the frequent androgynous bodies thus reflect values that transcend traditional sexual distinctions.

Consequently, traditional images of the beauty of the southern female are, in almost every work, scorned or ignored. Beginning by discarding the fragility of skin like magnolias and eyes like violets, these women writers are inventing through imagery their own definitions of southern womanhood.

The ambivalence they feel in that process appears perhaps most clearly in the imagery of clothing, masks, and veils. Because appearance is so important to the ideal of southern womanhood, clothing becomes a vital symbol. In the hands of these revisionists, clothing can disguise and protect, as for Beulah when she covers herself with a veil to go to her publisher, or for the little convent girl on the frightening boat. Yet clothing can also suffocate—think of those sleepers Adèle Ratignolle makes for her children—and drown: her skirts pull the little convent girl to her death. Hence to strip off clothing (Edna on the beach, Marie Modeste in her dormitory) or to resent its confines, as Scarlett O'Hara does, may be a way to freedom and integrity. Hawthorne appealed to precisely this imagery when he praised the work of Fanny Fern. For the southern woman, however, the risks of nakedness, whether it is emotional, physical, or intellectual, are apparent in Edna's fate. An alternative is to use clothing to create the appearance that one desires: to get what one wants, as Scarlett does when she makes a dress out of velvet curtains, or to express one's inner self, as Gabriella tries to do in her clothing shop. Each tries to gain control of her world by controlling the way she presents herself, in effect manipulating her prescribed symbolic function as southern beauty.

Just as they found themselves both romanticists and realists, then, these seven southern women writers find themselves, at one point, "strip[ping southern life] of the veil with which ethical and conventional standards have draped it"[4] and, at others, carefully draping the figures they create. By the same token, the masks they wear as authors, the personae they create, half reveal and half disguise the truth within their fictions. Yet perhaps their ambivalence should be forgiven; it is quite a magician's trick, after all, to make a marble statue live and move, and then to make it speak.

Notes

Chapter I

1. Lucian Lamar Knight, Introduction to Mrs. Bryan Wells Collier, *Biographies of Representative Women of the South*, quoted in Anne Firor Scott, *The Southern Lady: From Pedestal to Politics, 1830–1930* (Chicago: University of Chicago Press, 1970), 221–22.

2. Fred Powledge, *Journeys Through the South* (New York: Vanguard, 1979), 235.

3. On the question of the relationship of southern womanhood to other types of American womanhood, Nancy F. Cott wrote "the Northern 'cult of true womanhood' and the Southern image of the lady may be seen in at least three relations. They could neither be indigenous but both be 'the nineteenth century's' conception of the female role. . . . They could be separate traditions depending on the same or similar patterns of causation, with perhaps different timing. Or they could be separate, indigenous traditions with different origins. I tend to support the last view. . . . The Southern image . . . rested on the purposive establishment of a slaveholding 'cavalier' society . . . rather than an ongoing social transformation. It seems to me highly possible that the Southern tradition influenced Northern conceptions of women's roles more than vice versa; that would explain why by mid-century Northern rhetoric on woman's role sounded increasingly like Southern." Nancy F. Cott, *The Bonds of Womanhood: "Woman's Sphere" in New England, 1780–1835* (New Haven: Yale University Press, 1977), 11 n. This is an important footnote, for here Cott revises her earlier opinion that the "myth of southern womanhood in the antebellum South was an exaggerated version of the romantic, inspirational aspects of the cult of true womanhood." Nancy F. Cott (ed.), Introduction, *Root of Bitterness: Documents of the Social History of American Women* (New York: Dutton, 1972), 15.

4. Sandra Gilbert and Susan Gubar, *The Madwoman in the Attic: The Woman Writer and the Nineteenth-Century Literary Imagination* (New Haven: Yale University Press, 1979), 34.

5. The standard histories of the South, for the most part, omit southern women almost entirely, treat them only stereotypically, or spend an "extra" chapter on them. E. Merton Coulter, in *The South During Reconstruction: 1865–1877* (Baton Rouge: Louisiana State University Press, 1947), spends more pages—four—on women's fashions than he does on any other topic relating to women. Second comes women as authors; each writer's husband (if she married) receives as much emphasis as her writings. Although C. Vann Woodward, in *Origins of the New South, 1877–1913* (Baton Rouge: Louisiana State University Press, 1951), describes Ellen Glasgow's *Virginia* and *Life and Gabriella* as expressing the "feminist revolt against chivalry" (p. 436), he does not discuss that revolt. Woodward discusses women in the Grange,

the "labor force," and factories in a total of four pages. George B. Tindall describes *The Emergence of the New South, 1913–1945* (Baton Rouge: Louisiana State University Press, 1967), but in it southern women do not emerge from the blank of history. In fact, the organized women's suffrage movement is treated as a foreign influence: in Tindall's view the movement "had invaded the South in the 1880's and 1890's, but remained relatively dormant until the progressive era" (p. 222). Wilbur Cash sees the importance of women to the mind of the South, but his assumption that the mind of the South is male (though unconscious) prevents him from seeing beyond women's importance to men in the South. When he ventures to describe the mind of the southern woman, he falls into banality: if a white woman even suspected that some man in her family was having sexual relations with a black woman, he says, "why, of course she was being cruelly wounded in the sentiments she held most sacred" (Wilbur J. Cash, *The Mind of the South* [New York: Vintage, 1941], 88). Discussing the post–Civil War fears of rape, Cash adds, "And there were neurotic old maids and wives, hysterical young girls, to react to all this in a fashion well enough understood now" (p. 118): Cash speaks from, as well as about, the myth of the southern lady.

Histories of women, on the other hand, tend to see New Englandly. Not atypical is Mary P. Ryan, who warns in her introduction to the first edition of *Womanhood in America from Colonial Times to the Present* (New York: Franklin Watts, 1975) that "whole groups and sections fail to make even a fleeting appearance" in the book; one of those groups is southern women (p. 16). Nor does the second edition put them on stage. Gerda Lerner points out that "regional differences [are] largely ignored" and that "the South [is] left out of consideration entirely because its industrial development occurred later" (Gerda Lerner, "The Lady and the Mill Girl: Changes in the Status of Women in the Age of Jackson," *Mid-Continent American Studies Journal*, X [1969], 5). Although by no means a comprehensive survey of the southern woman in histories, these examples suggest that there is as yet no history of the southern white woman. (Interestingly, just as histories of the South deal extensively with blacks, so histories of women tend to deal in some depth with black women in the South.)

6. Walker Percy, *The Moviegoer* (New York: Noonday Press, 1961), 241–42, 224, 228, 183, 182, 197, 234, 228.
7. John Carl Ruoff, "Southern Womanhood, 1865–1920: An Intellectual and Cultural Study" (Ph.D. dissertation, University of Illinois, 1976), 18. Throughout I will use "womanhood" to refer to an image or idea, as distinct from actual women. Sara Evans points out, with others, that "few Southern women actually lived the life of the lady or fully embodied her essential qualities." Sara M. Evans, "Women," in *The Encyclopedia of Southern History*, ed. David C. Roller and Robert W. Twyman (Baton Rouge: Louisiana State University Press, 1979), 1353–55.
8. Evans, "Women," 1353.
9. George Fitzhugh, *Sociology for the South, or the Failure of Free Society* (1859; reprint ed., New York: Burt Franklin, n.d.). See 86, 105. Quotations are from 214.
10. Cash, *The Mind of the South*, 118.
11. Ruoff, "Southern Womanhood," 133.
12. Cott, *The Bonds of Womanhood*, 11n.
13. Jacquelyn Dowd Hall, *Revolt Against Chivalry: Jessie Daniel Ames and the Women's Campaign Against Lynching* (New York: Columbia University Press, 1979), 155.
14. Scott, *The Southern Lady*, 14.
15. *Ibid.*, 16, 17.

16. Cash, *The Mind of the South*, 118.
17. Lillian Smith, *Killers of the Dream* (Revised ed.; New York: Norton, 1961), 121.
18. William R. Taylor, *Cavalier and Yankee: The Old South and American National Character* (New York: George Braziller, 1961), 146, 148.
19. Sara Evans, *Personal Politics: The Roots of Women's Liberation in the Civil Rights Movement and the New Left* (New York: Alfred A. Knopf, 1979), 26.
20. Taylor, *Cavalier and Yankee*, 175, 174.
21. Scott, *The Southern Lady*, 21.
22. Eugene Genovese, *The World the Slaveholders Made: Two Essays in Interpretation* (New York: Pantheon, 1969), 201, 198.
23. Ruoff, "Southern Womanhood," 184, 128, 18, 19, 47.
24. Evans, "Women," 1353.
25. Carl Carmer, *Stars Fell on Alabama* (New York: Farrar & Rinehart, 1934), 14–15.
26. Quoted in Hall, *Revolt Against Chivalry*, 203.
27. Scott, *The Southern Lady*, 82.
28. Wilbur Fisk Tillett, "Southern Womanhood as Affected by the War," *Century*, XXI (November, 1891), 9, 10, 16, 12.
29. According to Ruoff, Edward A. Pollard's *The Lost Cause, A New Southern History of the War of the Confederates* "gave its name to a congeries of conceptions of the antebellum South and the Civil War which defined for postbellum southerners the nature of the South and its relation to the North and industrialization." Ruoff finds three sets of concepts, one rejecting the New South, one advocating it, and one avoiding the issue by focusing on the courage of the Confederate troops. Southern womanhood was at the center of the first two. Ruoff, "Southern Womanhood," 77, 78, 84.
30. *Ibid.*, 85, 87–88. Throughout his thesis, Ruoff establishes a distinction between two types of southern womanhood. Evangelical Womanhood, middle-class and Methodist, perpetuated the "Cult of True Womanhood," as Barbara Welter described it in "The Cult of True Womanhood: 1820–1860," *American Quarterly*, XVIII (Summer, 1966), 151–74: it endorsed purity, piety, submissiveness, and domesticity. On the other hand, Traditional Womanhood, says Ruoff, "generally ignored religion, encouraged a chaste coquettishness, inculcated submission to men as a traditional and familial duty, and fostered a domesticity concerned largely with the direction of an efficient and gracious household." Ruoff, "Southern Womanhood," 49. However, since the types so often seem to merge in the southern imagination, I have found the distinction not to be of sufficient usefulness to pursue in my analyses of the novels. Ruoff seems on occasion to conflate the two himself, for example, in his discussion of the role of southern womanhood in the Lost Cause (pp. 77–106). Interestingly, Edwin Mims made a similar distinction between the two types of southern womanhood in his *The Advancing South: Stories of Progress and Reaction* (Garden City, N.Y.: Doubleday, Page, 1926), 224–26.
31. *Ibid.*, 107, 112, 128.
32. Hall, *Revolt Against Chivalry*, 149.
33. Scott, *The Southern Lady*, 167.
34. Laura Sterrette McAdoo, "Woman's Economic Status in the South," *Arena*, XXI (1899), 747, 748, 743.
35. Julie Roy Jeffrey, "Women in the Southern Farmers' Alliance: A Reconsideration of the Role and Status of Women in the Late Nineteenth-Century South," *Feminist Studies*, III (Fall, 1975), 74, 85, 84.
36. William Henry Chafe, *The American Woman: Her Changing Social, Economic, and*

Political Roles, 1920–1970 (New York: Oxford University Press, 1972), 96.

37. Cash, *The Mind of the South*, 339.

38. *Ibid.*, 347.

39. Anne Firor Scott, "After Suffrage: Southern Women in the Twenties," *Journal of Southern History*, XXX (November, 1964), 316.

40. John Donald Wade, "The Life and Death of Cousin Lucius," in Louis D. Rubin, Jr. (ed.), *I'll Take My Stand: The South and the Agrarian Tradition, by Twelve Southerners* (New York: Harper & Row, 1962), 273, 279, 300, 289.

41. "Eliza Heard" [Virginia Foster], "In the Name of Southern Womanhood," *New South*, XVII (November–December, 1962), 18, 17.

42. Sam J. Ervin, Jr., to Peter W. Rodino, Jr., June 19, 1978, in *Congressional Record-Senate*, 95th Cong., 2nd Sess., S16667 (daily edition, September 29, 1978).

43. Scott, *The Southern Lady*, xi.

44. Ruoff, "Southern Womanhood," 188.

45. Scott, *The Southern Lady*, xi.

46. Quoted in Taylor, *Cavalier and Yankee*, 238.

47. Louis D. Rubin, Jr., *William Elliott Shoots a Bear: Essays on the Southern Literary Imagination* (Baton Rouge: Louisiana State University Press, 1975), 27.

48. Taylor, *Cavalier and Yankee*, 336.

49. *Ibid.*

50. Conversations with Bruce Clayton, May–June, 1980. See his *The Savage Ideal: Intolerance and Intellectual Leadership in the South, 1890–1914* (Baltimore: Johns Hopkins University Press, 1972).

51. John William DeForest, *A Union Officer in Reconstruction*, quoted in Scott, *The Southern Lady*, 101.

52. Belle Kearney, *A Slaveholder's Daughter* (1900; reprint ed., New York: Negro University Press, 1969), 71–72.

53. Conway Whittle Sams, *Shall Women Vote? A Book for Men*, quoted in Ruoff, "Southern Womanhood," 181.

54. Scott, *The Southern Lady*, 229.

55. *Ibid.*, 18.

56. Taylor, *Cavalier and Yankee*, 167–68.

57. Ernest R. Groves and William F. Ogburn, *American Marriage and Family Relationships*, quoted in Scott, *The Southern Lady*, 220.

58. Robert Afton Holland, "The Suffragette," *Sewanee Review*, XVII (July, 1909), 284, 282, 275, 277, 278, 287–88, 281, 280.

59. Jeffrey, "Women in the Southern Farmers' Alliance," 72.

60. Scott, "After Suffrage," 317.

61. Anne Firor Scott, "The 'New Woman' in the New South," *South Atlantic Quarterly*, LXI (Autumn, 1962), 481.

62. Walter Hines Page, "The Last Hold of the Southern Bully," *Forum*, XVI (November, 1893), 303. However, at the end, Page blames lynching not on "that much-discussed worthy, 'the old Southern gentleman,'" but on "this imitator of [his] faults and pretender to [his] traditions," the southern bully.

63. Kearney, *A Slaveholder's Daughter*, 109.

64. Francis Pendleton Gaines, *The Southern Plantation: A Study in the Development and the Accuracy of a Tradition* (New York: Columbia University Press, 1925), 180, 178.

65. Scott, *The Southern Lady*, 64, 61.

66. Evans, *Personal Politics*.

67. Quoted in Anne Firor Scott, "Women, Religion, and Social Change in the South, 1830–1930," in Samuel S. Hill, Jr. (ed.), *Religion and the Solid South* (Nashville: Abingdon Press, 1972), 99.

68. Diary of Myra Smith, April 17, 1851, quoted in Scott, "Women, Religion, and Social Change," 97.

69. Sarah M. Grimké to Mary S. Parker, 1837, in Sarah M. Grimké, *Letters on the Equality of the Sexes and the Condition of Woman, Addressed to Mary S. Parker, President of the Boston Female Anti-Slavery Society* (1838; reprint ed. New York: Burt Franklin, 1970), 51.

70. Lucilla McCorkle Diary, December 1, 1850, quoted in Scott, *The Southern Lady*, 12.

71. Caroline Gilman, *Recollections of a Southern Matron*, quoted in *ibid.*, 8–9.

72. Lucilla McCorkle Diary, May, 1846, quoted in *ibid.*, 11.

73. Percy, *The Moviegoer*, 239, 233.

74. Kate Chopin, "Emancipation. A Life Fable," in *The Complete Works of Kate Chopin*, ed. Per Seyersted (2 vols.; Baton Rouge: Louisiana State University Press, 1969), I, 37–38.

75. Scott, "Women, Religion, and Social Change," 96.

76. Gilman, *Recollections*, quoted in Scott, *The Southern Lady*, 9.

77. Kate Chopin, *The Awakening*, in *Complete Works*, II, 893.

78. Scott, *The Southern Lady*, 8.

79. Lerner, "The Lady and the Mill Girl," 15.

80. Kearney, *A Slaveholder's Daughter*, 3.

81. Mary Boykin Chesnut, *A Diary from Dixie*, ed. Ben Ames Williams (Boston: Houghton Mifflin, 1949), 186.

82. Bell Irvin Wiley, *Confederate Women* (Westport, Conn.: Greenwood Press, 1975), 174.

83. Ruoff, "Southern Womanhood," 26–27.

84. Quoted in Scott, *The Southern Lady*, 38.

85. *Ibid.*, 37.

86. Chesnut, *Diary from Dixie*, 21–22. Chesnut's passionate writing here apparently evoked the following intriguing image of woman writing, *i.e.*, creating rather than absorbing: "I think this journal will be disadvantageous for me, for I spend my time now like a spider spinning my own entrails, instead of reading as my habit was in all spare moments" (p. 22).

87. Amory Dwight Mayo, *Southern Women in the Recent Educational Movement in the South*, ed. Dan T. Carter and Amy Friedlander (1892; reprint ed., Baton Rouge: Louisiana State University Press, 1978), 65.

88. Quoted in Scott, *The Southern Lady*, 64.

89. Ruoff, "Southern Womanhood," 29.

90. Eudora Ramsay Richardson, "The Case of the Women's Colleges in the South," *South Atlantic Quarterly*, XXIX (April, 1930), 126–39.

91. Caroline E. Merrick, *Old Times in Dixie Land: A Southern Matron's Memories* (New York: Grafton Press, 1901), 16.

92. Anne Firor Scott, "Women's Perspective on the Patriarchy in the 1850s," *Journal of American History*, LXI (June, 1974), 59.

93. Wiley, *Confederate Women*, 156.

94. Scott, "Women, Religion, and Social Change," 100.

95. Irving H. Bartlett and C. Glenn Cambor, "The History and Psychodynamics of Southern Womanhood," *Women's Studies*, II (1974), 20, 19, 11.

96. Sarah Grimké diary, 1827, quoted in Gerda Lerner, *The Grimké Sisters from South*

Carolina: Rebels Against Slavery (Boston: Houghton Mifflin, 1967), 23.

97. Scott, "Women's Perspective on the Patriarchy," 62.
98. All quoted in Scott, *The Southern Lady*, 47, 48, 49.
99. L. Minor Blackford, *Mine Eyes Have Seen the Glory: The Story of a Virginia Lady, Mary Berkeley Minor Blackford, 1802–1896, Who Taught Her Sons to Hate Slavery and to Love the Union* (Cambridge, Mass.: Harvard University Press, 1954), 47.
100. Grimké, *Letters on the Equality of the Sexes*, 51–52.
101. E. G. C. Thomas Diary, quoted in Scott, *The Southern Lady*, 50.
102. Chesnut, *Diary from Dixie*, 49, 486.
103. Quoted in Scott, *The Southern Lady*, 53.
104. Catherine Edmonston, "Diary of Looking Glass Plantation," quoted in *ibid.*, 60.
105. Quoted in *ibid.*, 41.
106. Wiley, *Confederate Women*, 89, 109, 138, 120, 122, 110, 125, 138.
107. *Ibid.*, 146.
108. John Andrew Rice, *I Came Out of the Eighteenth Century*, quoted in Scott, *The Southern Lady*, 100.
109. Merrick, *Old Times in Dixie Land*, 108.
110. Scott, *The Southern Lady*, 93.
111. Quoted in *ibid.*, 217.
112. John Dollard, *Caste and Class in a Southern Town* (1937; reprint ed., Garden City, N.Y.: Doubleday, 1957), 136–37.
113. Ruoff, "Southern Womanhood," 136.
114. Scott, *The Southern Lady*, 139, 143, 141.
115. Ruoff, "Southern Womanhood," 161.
116. *Ibid.*, 101.
117. Mrs. J. C. Croly, *The History of the Woman's Club Movement in America* (New York: Henry G. Allen, 1898), 1082.
118. Scott, *The Southern Lady*, 147.
119. *Ibid.*, 170.
120. Ruoff, "Southern Womanhood," 180.
121. *Ibid.*, 148, 155.
122. Hall, *Revolt Against Chivalry*, 169–70.
123. *Ibid.*, 170.
124. Hope Summerell Chamberlain, *This Was Home*, quoted in Scott, *The Southern Lady*, 72–73.
125. Quoted in *ibid.*, 169.
126. Sue Shelton White to Mary Dewson, November 23, 1928, quoted in *ibid.*, 206.
127. *Ibid.*, 191.
128. Quoted in Mims, *The Advancing South*, 241.
129. Scott, *The Southern Lady*, 225.
130. Ruoff, "Southern Womanhood," 182*n*.
131. Hall, *Revolt Against Chivalry*, x, 127.
132. Smith, *Killers of the Dream*, 144.
133. Hall, *Revolt Against Chivalry*, 248, 144, 71, 190, 255.
134. Chopin, *The Awakening*, in *Complete Works*, II, 893.
135. Quoted in Scott, *The Southern Lady*, 216.
136. *Ibid.*, 46.
137. Quoted in *ibid.*, 75.
138. *Ibid.*, 138.
139. Quoted in Rufus B. Spain, *At Ease in Zion: Social History of Southern Baptists,*

1865–1900 (Nashville: Vanderbilt University Press, 1967), 171. Ruoff, "Southern Womanhood," 163, adds that the speaker, Tiberius G. Jones, "was addressing the Virginia Baptist General Association Meeting of 1888."

140. Scott, *The Southern Lady*, 140.

141. Mrs. J. J. Ansley, *History of the Georgia Woman's Christian Temperance Union from 1883 to 1907*, quoted in *ibid.*, 149.

142. Croly, *History of the Woman's Club Movement*, 227.

143. Kearney, *A Slaveholder's Daughter*, 107–108.

144. Merrick, *Old Times in Dixie Land*, 127–28.

145. Ruoff, "Southern Womanhood," 152, 153, 154.

146. Gilbert and Gubar, *The Madwoman in the Attic*, 73–74.

147. Elaine Showalter, *A Literature of Their Own: British Women Novelists from Brontë to Lessing* (Princeton: Princeton University Press, 1977), 13.

148. Ann Douglas, *The Feminization of American Culture* (New York: Alfred A. Knopf, 1977).

149. Jay B. Hubbell, *The South in American Literature: 1607–1900* (Durham, N.C.: Duke University Press, 1954), 536.

150. *Ibid.*, 358.

151. Louis D. Rubin, Jr., and C. Hugh Holman (eds.), *Southern Literary Study: Problems and Possibilities* (Chapel Hill: University of North Carolina Press, 1975), 120.

152. Genovese, *The World the Slaveholders Made*, 96, 242, 126, 124–25.

153. Lewis Simpson, "The South's Reaction to Modernism: A Problem in the Study of Southern Letters," in Rubin and Holman (eds.), *Southern Literary Study*, 63–64, 65.

154. Hubbell, *The South in American Literature*, 753.

155. *Ibid.*, 740.

156. Angelina Weld, "Appeal to the Christian Women of the South," in Gail Parker (ed.), *The Oven Birds: American Women on Womanhood, 1820–1920* (Garden City, N.Y.: Doubleday, 1972), 105–43.

157. Hubbell, *The South in American Literature*, 842.

158. C. Hugh Holman, *The Roots of Southern Writing: Essays on the Literature of the American South* (Athens, Ga.: University of Georgia Press, 1972), 194.

159. Tillie Olsen, *Silences* (New York: Dell, 1978), 16, 17, 18.

160. Hall, *Revolt Against Chivalry*, 167.

Chapter II

1. Nina Baym, *Woman's Fiction: A Guide to Novels by and about Women in America, 1820–1870* (Ithaca: Cornell University Press, 1978), 11. "Woman's fiction," Baym's term, refers to the "large body of once popular but now neglected American fiction, the many novels by American women authors about women, written between 1820 and 1870."

2. Hubbell, *The South in American Literature*, 699.

3. Quoted in Caroline Ticknor, *Hawthorne and His Publisher* (Boston and New York: Houghton Mifflin Company, 1913), 141–42.

4. Dee Garrison, "Immoral Fiction in the Late Victorian Library," *American Quarterly*, XXVIII (Spring, 1976), 72, 73.

5. Mary Kelley, "The Sentimentalists: Promise and Betrayal in the Home," *Signs*, IV (Spring, 1979), 434.

6. Ann Douglas Wood, "The 'Scribbling Women' and Fanny Fern: Why Women Wrote," *American Quarterly*, XXIII (Spring, 1971), 4, 7.

7. Baym, *Woman's Fiction*, 18, 12.
8. See Herbert Ross Brown, *The Sentimental Novel in America, 1789−1860* (Durham: Duke University Press, 1940), and Fred Lewis Pattee, *The Feminine Fifties* (New York: D. Appleton-Century, 1940).
9. Baym, *Woman's Fiction*, 17.
10. Helen Waite Papashvily, *All the Happy Endings: A Study of the Domestic Novel in America, the Women Who Wrote It, the Women Who Read It, in the Nineteenth Century* (New York: Harper & Brothers, 1956).
11. Garrison, "Immoral Fiction," 88.
12. Kelley, "The Sentimentalists," 435, 444.
13. Quoted in Ticknor, *Hawthorne and His Publisher*, 142.
14. Augusta Jane Evans, *Beulah* (1859; reprint ed., New York: Hurst & Co., n.d.), 431−32. All subsequent quotations from this work are taken from this edition.
15. Carl N. Degler, *Out of Our Past: The Forces That Shaped Modern America* (Rev. ed.; New York: Harper & Row, 1970), 182.
16. William P. Fidler, "Augusta Jane Evans Wilson," in Edward T. James (ed.), *Notable American Women 1607−1950: A Biographical Dictionary* (3 vols.; Cambridge, Mass.: Harvard University Press, 1971), III, 625.
17. Quoted in Papashvily, *All the Happy Endings*, 157.
18. *Ibid.*, 154.
19. Hubbell, *The South in American Literature*, 613.
20. Papashvily, *All the Happy Endings*, 154.
21. Hubbell, *The South in American Literature*, 611.
22. Augusta Jane Evans to General Beauregard, March 17, 1863, quoted in Katharine M. Jones (ed.), *Heroines of Dixie: Spring of High Hopes* (New York: Ballantine, 1955), 228.
23. Quoted in William Perry Fidler, *Augusta Evans Wilson: 1835−1909* (University, Ala.: University of Alabama Press, 1951), 86.
24. Quoted in *ibid.*, 119.
25. Augusta Jane Evans to A. W. Seaver, January 13, 1867, in the Clifton Waller Barrett Collection, Alderman Library, University of Virginia, Charlottesville.
26. Alexander Cowie, *The Rise of the American Novel* (New York: American Book Co., 1948), 412.
27. Augusta Jane Evans, *St. Elmo* (New York: Dillingham, 1866), 394−95.
28. Fidler, "Augusta Jane Evans Wilson," 626.
29. Hubbell, *The South in American Literature*, 612.
30. Papashvily, *All the Happy Endings*, 183.
31. Fidler, *Augusta Evans Wilson*, 79.
32. Quoted in *ibid.*, 80.
33. Quoted in *ibid.*, 48, 54.
34. *Ibid.*, 48.
35. Baym, *Woman's Fiction*, 283.
36. See *ibid.*, 35−44.
37. Quoted in Fidler, *Augusta Evans Wilson*, 63.
38. Quoted in *ibid.*, 64.
39. Cott, *The Bonds of Womanhood*, 1.
40. Fidler, *Augusta Evans Wilson*.
41. Quoted in *ibid.*, 66.
42. *Ibid.*, 22.
43. *Ibid.*, 38.

44. *Ibid.*, 40.
45. Evans persistently uses "idols" to refer to human objects of love. There is no apparent irony intended.
46. Quoted in Fidler, *Augusta Evans Wilson*, 51.
47. Mary Elizabeth Massey, *Bonnet Brigades* (New York: Knopf, 1966), 15.
48. Hubbell, *The South in American Literature*, 376.
49. Baym, *Woman's Fiction*, 282.
50. *Ibid.*, 24–25.
51. Evans, *St. Elmo*, 565.
52. Baym, *Woman's Fiction*, 286.

Chapter III

1. Rayburn S. Moore, "Grace Elizabeth King," in James (ed.), *Notable American Women*, II, 331; Edmund Wilson, *Patriotic Gore: Studies in the Literature of the American Civil War* (New York: Oxford University Press, 1962), 292; Robert Bush (ed.), *Grace King of New Orleans: A Selection of Her Writings* (Baton Rouge: Louisiana State University Press, 1973), 3. Moore suggests 1853, Wilson 1852, and Bush 1851.
2. Bush (ed.), *Grace King of New Orleans*, 31.
3. Louis D. Rubin, Jr., *George W. Cable: The Life and Times of a Southern Heretic* (New York: Pegasus, 1969), 21.
4. *Ibid.*, 22.
5. Grace King, *Creole Families of New Orleans* (New York: Macmillan, 1921), vii–ix.
6. George W. Cable, *The Creoles of Louisiana* (New York: Scribner's, 1889), 139.
7. Grace King to Edwin Anderson Alderman, February 11, 1903, quoted in Bush (ed.), *Grace King of New Orleans*, 388.
8. Cable, *The Creoles of Louisiana*, 262.
9. Moore, "Grace Elizabeth King," 331.
10. Grace King, *Memories of a Southern Woman of Letters* (New York: Macmillan, 1932), 7. Subsequent references to this edition are in the text in parentheses.
11. Bush (ed.), *Grace King of New Orleans*, 6.
12. *Ibid.*, 10.
13. Moore, "Grace Elizabeth King," 331.
14. Quoted in Bush (ed.), *Grace King of New Orleans*, 6.
15. Quoted in *ibid.*, 28.
16. *Ibid.*, 8, 12, 26, 28.
17. Quoted in *ibid.*, 12.
18. *Ibid.*, 15.
19. Quoted in *ibid.*, 390.
20. Grace King, "Monsieur Motte," in Bush (ed.), *Grace King of New Orleans*, 57. Bush chose to include the revised version of this story that King wrote for her novel, *Monsieur Motte*; he omitted a transitional passage that King inserted to connect "Monsieur Motte" to its sequel. Subsequent references to this edition are in the text in parentheses.
21. Quoted in *ibid.*, 14.
22. Quoted in *ibid.*, 14–15.
23. Quoted in *ibid.*, 14.
24. See Papashvily, *All the Happy Endings*.
25. Grace King, *Monsieur Motte* (New York: Armstrong, 1888), 104. Subsequent references to this edition are in the text in parentheses.

26. Grace King, *Tales of a Time and Place* (New York: Harper & Bros., 1892), 86. Subsequent references to this edition are in the text in parentheses.
27. Quoted in Bush (ed.), *Grace King of New Orleans*, 388.
28. In between she had published *Tales of a Time and Place* (1892), *Balcony Stories* (1893), a number of stories in *Harper's* and *Century*, a biography of Jean Baptiste le Moyne, founder of New Orleans (1892), and a textbook history of Louisiana (1893).
29. King, *Memories of a Southern Woman of Letters*, 76–78.
30. Quoted in Bush (ed.), *Grace King of New Orleans*, 18.
31. *Ibid.*, 20.
32. Grace King, "The Little Convent Girl," in Bush (ed.) *Grace King of New Orleans*, 150. All subsequent references to this edition will appear in the text in parentheses.
33. Bush (ed.), *Grace King of New Orleans*, 131.
34. Quoted in *ibid.*, 14.
35. Quoted in *ibid.*, 29.
36. *Ibid.*, 24.
37. Quoted in *ibid.*, 24.
38. *Ibid.*, 23.
39. *Ibid.*, 30.
40. Quoted in *ibid.*, 390.
41. Robert E. Spiller, *et al.* (eds.), *Literary History of the United States* (3rd ed., rev.; New York: Macmillan, 1963), 858; Ann Douglas Wood, "The Literature of Impoverishment: The Women Local Colorists in America, 1865–1914," *Women's Studies*, I (1972), 17.
42. Quoted in Bush (ed.), *Grace King of New Orleans*, 389.
43. Quoted in Gregory Paine (ed.), *Southern Prose Writers* (New York: American Book Co., 1947), 207.
44. Bush (ed.), *Grace King of New Orleans*, 9, 16.
45. Quoted in *ibid.*, 17.
46. *Ibid.*, 6.
47. Wilson, *Patriotic Gore*, 575–76.
48. Bush (ed.), *Grace King of New Orleans*, 26.
49. Quoted in *ibid.*, 14.
50. Quoted in *ibid.*, 399.
51. Quoted in *ibid.*, 380.
52. Quoted in *ibid.*, 398.
53. Quoted in *ibid.*, 386.

Chapter IV

1. Per Seyersted, *Kate Chopin: A Critical Biography* (Baton Rouge: Louisiana State University Press, 1969), 14.
2. *Ibid.*, 17, 21, 20.
3. Quoted in *ibid.*, 27.
4. Quoted in *ibid.*, 29.
5. C. L. Deyo, review of *The Awakening*, St. Louis *Post-Dispatch*, May 20, 1899, quoted in Kate Chopin, *The Awakening: An Authoritative Text, Contexts, Criticism*, ed. Margaret Culley (New York: Norton, 1976).
6. Seyersted, *Kate Chopin*, 40–42.
7. *Ibid.*, 46–53.
8. Chopin, *Complete Works*, II, 741. All subsequent references to both volumes of this edition will appear in the text in parentheses.

9. Lewis Leary, "Kate Chopin's Other Novel," in *Southern Excursions: Essays on Mark Twain and Others* (Baton Rouge: Louisiana State University Press, 1971), 189.

10. Seyersted, *Kate Chopin*, 63, 66.

11. See, for example, Cynthia Griffin Wolff, "Thanatos and Eros: Kate Chopin's *The Awakening*," *American Quarterly*, XXV (October, 1973), 449−72.

12. Seyersted, *Kate Chopin*, 67.

13. Quoted in *ibid.*, 67−68.

14. Chopin, *The Awakening*, ed. Culley, 159.

15. Quoted in Seyersted, *Kate Chopin*, 51.

16. *Ibid.*, 91, 96.

17. Seyersted makes this point in *ibid.*, 114.

18. Emily Toth, "Kate Chopin's *The Awakening* as Feminist Criticism," *Louisiana Studies*, XV (Fall, 1976), 241.

19. Otis B. Wheeler, "The Five Awakenings of Edna Pontellier," *Southern Review*, XI (January, 1975), 128.

20. Seyersted, *Kate Chopin*, 138.

21. James H. Justus, "The Unawakening of Edna Pontellier," *Southern Literary Journal*, X (Spring, 1978), 112.

22. Wolff, "Thanatos and Eros," 471.

23. Willa Cather, review of *The Awakening*, Pittsburgh *Leader*, July 8, 1899, quoted in *The Awakening*, ed. Culley, 153.

24. C. L. Deyo, "The Newest Books," St. Louis *Post-Dispatch*, May 20, 1899, quoted in *ibid.*, 149.

25. "Fresh Literature," Los Angeles *Sunday Times*, June 25, 1899, quoted in *ibid.*, 152.

26. "New Publications," New Orleans *Times-Democrat*, June 18, 1899, quoted in *ibid.*, 150.

27. Ruth Sullivan and Stewart Smith, "Narrative Stance in Kate Chopin's *The Awakening*," *Studies in American Fiction*, I (Spring, 1973), 63, 72−73.

28. Jane P. Tompkins, "*The Awakening*: An Evaluation," *Feminist Studies*, III (Spring− Summer, 1976), 24, 27, 28.

29. Sullivan and Smith, "Narrative Stance," 73.

30. Seyersted, *Kate Chopin*, 153.

31. Peggy Skaggs, "Three Tragic Figures in Kate Chopin's *The Awakening*," *Louisiana Studies*, XIII (Winter, 1974), 346.

32. Emily Toth, "Timely and Timeless: The Treatment of Time in *The Awakening* and *Sister Carrie*," *Southern Studies*, XVI (Fall, 1977), 271, 275.

33. Leary, *Southern Excursions*, 169−74.

34. Quoted in *The Awakening*, ed. Culley, 134−38.

35. Justus, "The Unawakening of Edna Pontellier," 112.

36. John R. May, "Local Color in *The Awakening*," quoted in *The Awakening*, ed. Culley, 191.

37. Margaret Culley, "Edna Pontellier: 'A Solitary Soul,'" in *The Awakening*, ed. Culley, 224.

38. Seyersted, *Kate Chopin*, 157.

39. Wheeler, "The Five Awakenings of Edna Pontellier," 123.

40. Seyersted, *Kate Chopin*, 159.

41. See, for instance, Tompkins, "*The Awakening*: An Evaluation," 22.

42. Seyersted, *Kate Chopin*, 145.

43. Chopin, *Complete Works*, ed. Seyersted, I, 401.

44. Peggy Skaggs, "'The Man-Instinct of Possession': A Persistent Theme in Kate

Chopin's Stories," *Louisiana Studies*, XIV (Fall, 1975), 277.

45. Larzer Ziff, *The American 1890s: Life and Times of a Lost Generation* (New York: Viking, 1966), 275.

46. Chopin may have intended to entitle the novel *A Solitary Soul*. See Culley, "Edna Pontellier: 'A Solitary Soul,'" 224–28.

Chapter V

1. Edward C. Wagenknecht, "The World and Mary Johnston," *Sewanee Review*, XLIV (April–June, 1936), 188.

2. *Margaret Mitchell's "Gone With the Wind" Letters, 1936–1949*, ed. Richard Harwell (New York: Macmillan, 1976), 8.

3. "Mary Johnston," in James (ed.), *Notable American Women*, II, 283.

4. Lawrence G. Nelson, "Mary Johnston and the Historic Imagination," in R. C. Simonini, Jr. (ed.), *Southern Writers: Appraisals in Our Time* (Charlottesville: University Press of Virginia, 1964), 71.

5. "Mary Johnston," *Notable American Women*, II, 283.

6. Mary Johnston's diary, March 6, 1908, in Mary Johnston Papers (3588), Alderman Library, University of Virginia, Charlottesville.

7. "Mary Johnston," *Notable American Women*, II, 283.

8. Quoted in *ibid*.

9. Wagenknecht, "The World and Mary Johnston," 191.

10. "Mary Johnston," *Notable American Women*, II, 283.

11. Mary Johnston to Otto Kyllman, February 1, 1905, in Johnston Papers (5967).

12. Nelson, "Mary Johnston and the Historic Imagination," 76, 101, 89–90.

13. Charlotte Perkins Gilman to Mary Johnston, October 15, 1913, in Johnston Papers (3588).

14. Quoted in Nelson, "Mary Johnston and the Historic Imagination," 91, 78.

15. Mary Johnston to Mrs. C., January 27, 1912, in James A. Walker Papers, Southern Historical Collection, University of North Carolina at Chapel Hill.

16. Mary Johnston, *Hagar* (Boston: Houghton Mifflin, 1913), 274. Subsequent references to this work are in the text in parentheses.

17. E. F. E., review of Mary Johnston's *Hagar*, Boston *Transcript*, October 25, 1913, p. 8.

18. "Five New Novels by Women," review of Mary Johnston's *Hagar*, *The Outlook*, November 15, 1913, p. 571.

19. "Recent Reflections of a Novel-Reader," review of Mary Johnston's *Hagar*, *Atlantic Monthly*, CXIII (April, 1914), p. 491.

20. "Novels," review of Mary Johnston's *Hagar*, *Saturday Review of Politics, Literature, Science and Art* (London), CXVI (November 15, 1913), 623.

21. Charlotte Perkins Gilman to Mary Johnston, October 18, 1917, in Johnston Papers (3588).

22. Mary Johnston, "The Woman's War," *Atlantic Monthly*, CV (April, 1910), 565. Subsequent references to this article are in the text in parentheses.

23. John R. Roberson (ed.), "Two Virginia Novelists on Woman's Suffrage: An Exchange of Letters Between Mary Johnston and Thomas Nelson Page," *Virginia Magazine of History and Biography*, LXIV (July, 1956), 287.

24. Herbert G. May and Bruce M. Metzger (eds.), *The Oxford Annotated Bible with the Apocrypha* (New York: Oxford University Press, 1965), 18.

25. John Donne, "The Sunne Rising," in *The Songs and Sonnets*, ed. Helen Gardner (Oxford: Clarendon, 1965), 72–73.

26. Rebecca Harding Davis to Mary Johnston, March 20, [1904?], in Johnston Papers (3588).

27. Ellen Glasgow to Mary Johnston, Thursday [1905?], in *ibid.*

28. Mary Johnston to Ellen Glasgow, September 27, 1929, in Ellen Glasgow Papers (5060), Alderman Library, University of Virginia, Charlottesville.

29. Mary Johnston's diary, in Johnston Papers (3588).

30. Ellen Glasgow to Mary Johnston, Thursday [January, 1905?], in *ibid.*

31. Charlotte Perkins Gilman to Mary Johnston, October 18, 1917, in *ibid.*

32. Ellen Glasgow to Mary Johnston, March 22, 1904; Sunday midnight [January, 1905?], in *ibid.*

33. Rebecca Harding Davis to Mary Johnston, January 28, [1904?], in *ibid.*

34. Ellen Glasgow to Mary Johnston, March 22, 1904; February 3, 1905, in *ibid.*

Chapter VI

1. Ellen Glasgow, *The Woman Within* (New York: Harcourt, Brace, 1954), 187, 188.

2. Ellen Glasgow, *A Certain Measure: An Interpretation of Prose Fiction* (New York: Harcourt, Brace, 1943), 90. Subsequent references to this work will be given in parentheses in the text.

3. Glasgow, *The Woman Within*, 16.

4. *Ibid.*

5. Marjorie R. Kaufman, "Ellen Glasgow," in James (ed.), *Notable American Women*, II, 45.

6. *Ibid.*

7. Louis D. Rubin, Jr., note to the author, October, 1977.

8. Glasgow, *The Woman Within*, 36.

9. *Ibid.*, 243.

10. C. Hugh Holman, "Ellen Glasgow and the Southern Literary Imagination," in Simonini (ed.), *Southern Writers*, 106.

11. Alfred Kazin, *On Native Grounds: An Interpretation of Modern American Prose Literature* (New York: Harcourt, Brace, 1942), 258.

12. E. Stanly Godbold, Jr., *Ellen Glasgow and the Woman Within* (Baton Rouge: Louisiana State University Press, 1972), 99.

13. Louis D. Rubin, Jr., *No Place on Earth: Ellen Glasgow, James Branch Cabell, and Richmond-in-Virginia* (Austin: University of Texas Press, 1959), 44–47.

14. Kazin, *On Native Grounds*, 261.

15. Ellen Glasgow, *Virginia* (1913. Old Dominion Edition; Garden City, N.Y.: Doubleday, Doran, 1929), 64. Subsequent references to this work will be given in the text in parentheses.

16. Glasgow, *The Woman Within*, 154.

17. Ellen Glasgow, *Life and Gabriella: The Story of a Woman's Courage* (Garden City, N.Y.: Doubleday, Page, 1916), 252. Subsequent references to this work will be given in the text in parentheses.

18. Godbold, *Ellen Glasgow*, 260.

19. Quoted in Rubin, *No Place on Earth*, 11.

20. *Ibid.*

21. Quoted in Marie Fletcher, "The Southern Heroine in the Fiction of Representative Southern Women Writers, 1850–1960," (Ph.D. dissertation, Louisiana State University, 1963), 190.

22. Rubin, *No Place on Earth*, 12, 13.

23. Fletcher, "The Southern Heroine," 188.

24. Josephine Lurie Jessup, *The Faith of Our Feminists* (New York: Richard R. Smith, 1950), 38.
25. Monique Parent Frazée, "Ellen Glasgow as Feminist," in M. Thomas Inge (ed.), *Ellen Glasgow: Centennial Essays* (Charlottesville: University Press of Virginia, 1976), 185.
26. Ellen Glasgow, "Feminism," *New York Times Book Review*, November 30, 1913, p. 656. Subsequent references to this article will appear in the text in parentheses.
27. James Branch Cabell, *As I Remember It: Some Epilogues in Recollection* (New York: McBride, 1955), 232.
28. Frederick P. W. McDowell, *Ellen Glasgow and the Ironic Art of Fiction* (Madison: University of Wisconsin Press, 1960), 253.
29. Oliver Steele, "Ellen Glasgow's *Virginia*: Preliminary Notes," in *Studies in Bibliography: Papers of the Bibliographical Society of the University of Virginia*, ed. Fredson Bowers, Vol. XXVII (Charlottesville: University Press of Virginia, 1974), 282.
30. *Ibid.*, 285.
31. Kate Chopin, *The Awakening*, in *Complete Works*, II, 929.
32. Glasgow, "Feminism," 656.
33. Ellen Glasgow to Joseph Hergesheimer, January 7, 1924, in Ellen Glasgow, *Letters of Ellen Glasgow*, ed. Blair Rouse (New York: Harcourt, Brace, 1958), 70.
34. Louise Bogan, "Women," in Florence Howe and Ellen Bass (eds.), *No More Masks! An Anthology of Poems by Women* (Garden City, N.Y.: Doubleday, 1976), 71.
35. Chopin, *The Awakening*, 999.
36. Evans, *St. Elmo*, 120.
37. Ellen Glasgow to Joseph Hergesheimer, in Glasgow, *Letters*, 70.
38. Rejected chapter for *The Woman Within* (Chapter XIV, "Random Thoughts on the Artist and the Scholar"), in Glasgow Papers.
39. Ellen Glasgow to Allen Tate, April 3, 1933, in Glasgow, *Letters*, 134.
40. Notes on *Virginia*, in Glasgow Papers.
41. Florence Finch Kelly, "Some Novels of the Month," *Bookman*, XLIII (March, 1916), 80.
42. Quoted in Godbold, *Ellen Glasgow*, 92-93.
43. Ellen Glasgow to Mary Johnston, September 15, 1906, in Glasgow, *Letters*, 55-57.
44. Marjorie Kinnan Rawlings to Ellen Glasgow, May 30, 1940, in Collection 7225-B, Alderman Library, University of Virginia.
45. Marjorie Kinnan Rawlings to Ellen Glasgow, November 9, 1945, in Glasgow Papers.
46. Marjorie Kinnan Rawlings to Ellen Glasgow, November 11, 1940, in *ibid.*
47. "An Exchange of Letters Between Ellen Glasgow and Marjorie Kinnan Rawlings," Atlanta *Journal*, April 28, 1946, p. 5.
48. *Ibid.*
49. Note concerning *The Woman Within*, in Glasgow Papers.
50. Ellen Glasgow to James Branch Cabell, August 1, 1941, in James Branch Cabell Papers, Alderman Library, University of Virginia.
51. See, for instance, Showalter, *A Literature of Their Own*, 114-17.

Chapter VII

1. Finis Farr, *Margaret Mitchell of Atlanta: The Author of "Gone With the Wind"* (New York: William Morrow, 1965), 68; Harwell (ed.), *Margaret Mitchell's "Gone With the Wind" Letters*, 223n.
2. Hansell Baugh (ed.), *Frances Newman's Letters* (New York: Horace Liveright, 1929).

3. Frances Newman, *The Hard-Boiled Virgin*, ed. Elizabeth Hardwick (1926; reprint ed., New York: Arno, 1977); Frances Newman, *Dead Lovers Are Faithful Lovers*, ed. Elizabeth Hardwick (1928; reprint ed., New York: Arno, 1977).

4. John E. Talmadge, "Frances Newman," in James (ed.), *Notable American Women*, II, 623.

5. Baugh (ed.), *Frances Newman's Letters*, v.

6. Hardwick, introduction to Newman, *The Hard-Boiled Virgin*, i.

7. Frances Newman, "The American Short Story in the First Twenty-Five Years of the Twentieth Century," *Bookman*, XLIII (1926), 188.

8. Frances Newman (ed. and trans.), *The Short Story's Mutations: From Petronius to Paul Morand* (New York: B. W. Huebsch, 1924).

9. James Penny Smith, "Frances Newman and James Joyce," *James Joyce Quarterly*, XII (Spring, 1975), 309.

10. Newman, "The American Short Story," 190.

11. Newman (ed. and trans.), *The Short Story's Mutations*, 5–6.

12. Newman, "The American Short Story," 188.

13. "*We Are Incredible* and Other New Works of Fiction," review of *Dead Lovers Are Faithful Lovers*, *New York Times Book Review*, May 6, 1928, p. 8.

14. Baugh (ed.), *Frances Newman's Letters*, 44; James Branch Cabell to Frances Newman, March 7, 1921, in *ibid.*, 44.

15. Frances Newman to Lamar Trotti, July 14, 1926, Frances Newman to Horace Liveright, July 16, 1926, and August 19, 1926, Frances Newman to Hansell Baugh, April 23, 1923, all in *ibid.*, 195, 197, 205, 97.

16. Frances Newman to Delia Johnston, July 2, 1926, Frances Newman to Mrs. Fred McCormick, August, 1926, both in *ibid.*, 194, 200.

17. Frances Newman to Tom Y. Horan, May 9, 1927, in *ibid.*, 254; Frances Newman to A. B. Bernd, October 10, 1924, in *ibid.*, 135.

18. Frances Newman to James Branch Cabell, April 14, 1921, and August 10, 1921, both in *ibid.*, 49, 59.

19. Frances Newman to Horace Liveright, August 17, 1926, in *ibid.*, 205.

20. Frances Newman to the editor of the Emory *Phoenix*, November, 1924, in *ibid.*, 148–50.

21. Frances Newman to Hansell Baugh, April 2, 1925, in *ibid.*, 171.

22. Mary Johnston diary, February 20, 1907, in Johnston Papers.

23. Frances Newman to Edith Stern, February 2, 1928, in Baugh (ed.), *Frances Newman's Letters*, 310.

24. See Anne Bradstreet's "The Author to Her Book," in *The Works of Anne Bradstreet*, ed. Jeannine Hensley (Cambridge, Mass.: Belknap Press of Harvard University Press, 1967), 221.

25. James Branch Cabell to Frances Newman, November 17, 1924, in Baugh (ed.), *Frances Newman's Letters*, 141.

26. Frances Newman to Hansell Baugh, October 24, 1924, in *ibid.*, 140.

27. Frances Newman to A. B. Bernd, February, 1925, Frances Newman to Hansell Baugh, May 16, 1928, both in *ibid.*, 346; Frances Newman to Hansell Baugh, December 6, 1924, in *ibid.*, 151; Frances Newman to Sylvia Chatfield Bates, February 28, 1928, in *ibid.*, 324.

28. Winifred Rothermel, "Aristocratic Writer, Daughter of the South, Taken by Death in Gotham," Birmingham *News—Age-Herald*, October 28, 1928, p. 4.

29. Frances Newman to Frank Daniel, July 14, 1926, in Baugh (ed.), *Frances Newman's Letters*, 196.

30. Rothermel, "Aristocratic Writer," 4.

31. Frances Newman to Hansell Baugh, October 6, 1924; Frances Newman to Delia Johnston, February 16, 1926; Frances Newman's "niece's biographical sketch"; Frances Newman to Hansell Baugh, October 6, 1924, all in Baugh (ed.), *Frances Newman's Letters*, 131–32, 187, 184, 131–32.

32. James Branch Cabell, "A Note on Frances Newman," *ibid.*, vii.

33. Quoted in Frances Newman to Lamar Trotti, August 7, 1928, in *ibid.*, 356.

34. Elmer Davis, "Candid Miss Newman," *Saturday Review of Literature*, III (December 18, 1926), 449.

35. Frances Newman to Susan Long, May, 1927, in Baugh (ed.), *Frances Newman's Letters*, 254.

36. Frances Newman to Hudson Strode, September 2, 1927, in *ibid.*, 273.

37. Rothermel, "Aristocratic Writer," 4.

38. Frances Newman to A. B. Bernd, November 23, 1924, in Baugh (ed.), *Frances Newman's Letters*, 144.

39. James Branch Cabell to Frances Newman, October 5, 1926, in *ibid.*, 213.

40. Rothermel, "Aristocratic Writer," 4.

41. "John Riddell" [Corey Ford], "Meaning No Offense: Parody Interviews in the Respective Manners of Frances Newman and Carl Van Vechten," *Vanity Fair*, November, 1928, p. 89.

42. Adrienne Battey Collection, University of Georgia Library, Athens; H. E. Dounce, quoted in William Soskin, "Books on Our Table: A Communication on the Death of Miss Frances Newman," New York *Evening Post*, November 9, 1928 (n.p.), in Battey Collection.

43. Battey Collection; Frank Daniel to Adrienne Battey, November 3, 1928, in *ibid*.

44. Frances Newman, "Rachel and Her Children," *American Mercury*, II (1924), 92. Subsequent references to this story will appear in the text in parentheses.

45. May and Metzger (eds.), *The Oxford Annotated Bible with the Apocrypha*, 44–45n.

46. Spiller *et al.* (eds.), *Literary History of the United States*, 1296.

47. Frances Newman, *The Hard-Boiled Virgin* (New York: Boni & Liveright, 1926), 51. Subsequent references to this work will appear in the text in parentheses.

48. Matilda L. Berg, review of *The Hard-Boiled Virgin*, in Marion A. Knight (ed.), *The Book Review Digest* (New York: H. W. Wilson, 1927), 517.

49. Baugh (ed.), *Frances Newman's Letters*, 210.

50. Review of Frances Newman's *The Hard-Boiled Virgin*, in Springfield (Illinois) *Republican*, December 5, 1926, p. 7F, quoted in Knight (ed.), *Book Review Digest*, 517.

51. Rebecca West, "Battlefield and Sky," review of *The Hard-Boiled Virgin*, in New York *Herald Tribune Books*, November 28, 1926, p. 1; Grant Overton, review of *The Hard-Boiled Virgin*, in *Literary Review*, December 18, 1926, p. 1; "Frances Newman Cuts a New Caper in the Novel," review of *The Hard-Boiled Virgin*, in *New York Times Book Review*, December 12, 1926, p. 12; H. E. Dounce, quoted in Soskin, "Books on Our Table"; E. B. H., "Fiction Notes," *New Republic*, XLIX (January 5, 1927), 202.

52. "Frances Newman Cuts a New Caper in the Novel," 12; Hardwick, introduction to *The Hard-Boiled Virgin*, ii; West, "Battlefield and Sky," 4; Davis, "Candid Miss Newman," 449.

53. Hardwick, introduction to *The Hard-Boiled Virgin*, ii.

54. Rothermel, "Aristocratic Writer," 4.

55. Chopin, *The Awakening*, in *Complete Works*, II, 893.

56. Vivian Gornick, "Female Narcissism as a Metaphor in Literature," in her *Essays in Feminism* (New York: Harper & Row, 1978), 219.

57. Edith Jacobson, *The Self and the Object World* (New York: International Universities Press, 1964), 20, 4.

58. Gornick, "Female Narcissism," 220.

59. Douglas, *The Feminization of American Culture*, 347–48, note 11.

60. Baugh (ed.), *Frances Newman's Letters*, 226.

61. Alice Beal Parsons, "Setbacks and Style," review of *Dead Lovers Are Faithful Lovers*, *Nation*, CXXVI (June 6, 1928), 648; John Macy, "Women Are Witches," review of *Dead Lovers Are Faithful Lovers*, *Bookman*, LXVII (June, 1928), 429, 432; review of Frances Newman's *Dead Lovers Are Faithful Lovers*, in Springfield (Illinois) *Republican*, May 26, 1928, quoted in Knight (ed.), *Book Review Digest*, 570; "New Books and Reprints," review of *Dead Lovers Are Faithful Lovers*, in London *Times Literary Supplement*, June 14, 1928, p. 452; "New Books in Brief Review," review of *Dead Lovers Are Faithful Lovers*, in *Independent*, CXX (June 9, 1928), 560.

62. T. S. Matthews, "Fancy Goods," review of *Dead Lovers Are Faithful Lovers* in *New Republic*, LV (June 27, 1928), 153; Isabel Patterson, "Phantom Lover," review of *Dead Lovers Are Faithful Lovers*, in New York *Herald Tribune Books*, May 6, 1928, p. 3.

63. Baugh (ed.), *Frances Newman's Letters*, 222, 263, 309.

64. Frances Newman, *Dead Lovers Are Faithful Lovers* (New York: Boni & Liveright, 1928), 133–34. Subsequent references to this work are included in the text in parentheses.

65. Patterson, "Phantom Lover," 4.

66. Douglas, *The Feminization of American Culture*, 348, note 11.

67. Hardwick, introduction to *Dead Lovers Are Faithful Lovers*, ii.

68. Quoted in Robert Y. Drake, Jr., "Frances Newman: Fabulist of Decadence," *Georgia Review*, XIV (Winter, 1960), 391.

69. West, "Battlefield and Sky," 4.

70. Frank Daniel, "Miss Newman's Unwritten Books," Atlanta *Journal*, November 18, 1928, pp. 24, 5.

71. *Ibid.*, 24.

72. *Ibid.*

73. *Ibid.*, 5, 24.

Chapter VIII

1. William Key, "Margaret Mitchell and Her Last Days on Earth," *Atlanta Historical Bulletin*, IX (May, 1960), 122.

2. Harwell (ed.), introduction to *Margaret Mitchell's "Gone With the Wind" Letters*, xxxii.

3. *Ibid.*, xxviii.

4. Farr, *Margaret Mitchell of Atlanta*, 154.

5. Harwell (ed.), *Margaret Mitchell's "Gone With the Wind" Letters*, xxx.

6. Ralph McGill, "Little Woman, Big Book: The Mysterious Margaret Mitchell," *Show* (October, 1962), 72.

7. Harwell (ed.), *Margaret Mitchell's "Gone With the Wind" Letters*, xxxiv.

8. Edwin Granberry, "The Private Life of Margaret Mitchell," *Collier's*, March 13, 1937, p. 6.

9. Farr, *Margaret Mitchell of Atlanta*, 154–55.

10. *Ibid.*, 118.
11. Marian Elder Jones, "'Me and My Book,'" *Georgia Review*, XVI (Summer, 1962), 180–87.
12. Although Stephens Mitchell has donated most of Margaret Mitchell's papers to the library of the University of Georgia in Athens, access to these materials is at the time of writing carefully restricted.
13. Medora Field Perkerson, interview with Margaret Mitchell, Atlanta *Journal Magazine*, May 23, 1937, p. 1.
14. *Ibid.*, 2.
15. *Ibid.*
16. Farr, *Margaret Mitchell of Atlanta*, 30.
17. Jones, "'Me and My Book,'" 186.
18. *Ibid.*, 184.
19. Westbrook Pegler, "A Soliloquy on Margaret Mitchell," Atlanta *Constitution*, n.d. (1949?).
20. Norman Shavin and Martin Shartar, *The Million Dollar Legends: Margaret Mitchell and "Gone With the Wind"* (Atlanta: Capricorn, 1974).
21. "Margaret Mitchell in Public Affairs," *Atlanta Historical Bulletin*, IX (May, 1950), 29–30.
22. Caroline Bernd, "GWTW Words Echo Its Author's Letters 80 Years Later," Savannah *Morning News*, March 3, 1974, p. 1B.
23. McGill, "Little Woman, Big Book," 71.
24. Farr, *Margaret Mitchell of Atlanta*, 198–99.
25. *Ibid.*, 199.
26. Atlanta *Journal*, August 16, 1949, p. 2.
27. Chafe, *The American Woman*, 94–98.
28. Perkerson, interview with Margaret Mitchell, 2.
29. Bernd, "GWTW Words Echo Its Author's Letters 80 Years Later," 1B.
30. Farr, *Margaret Mitchell of Atlanta*, 31.
31. Stephens Mitchell, "Margaret Mitchell and Her People in the Atlanta Area," *Atlanta Historical Bulletin*, IX (May, 1950), 15.
32. Robert L. Groover, "Margaret Mitchell, the Lady from Atlanta," *Georgia Historical Quarterly*, LII (March, 1968), 61.
33. Farr, *Margaret Mitchell of Atlanta*, 22–23.
34. *Ibid.*
35. *Ibid.*, 24.
36. *Ibid.*, 30–31.
37. *Ibid.*, 23, 43.
38. *Ibid.*, 23.
39. *Ibid.*, 19, 87.
40. McGill, "Little Woman, Big Book," 73.
41. Farr, *Margaret Mitchell of Atlanta*, 166.
42. *Ibid.*, 182, 38, 223, 80.
43. William S. Howland, "Peggy Mitchell, Newspaperman," *Atlanta Historical Bulletin*, IX (May, 1950), 50, 47, 54, 56, 63.
44. Farr, *Margaret Mitchell of Atlanta*, 16.
45. Quoted in *ibid.*
46. Harwell (ed.), *Margaret Mitchell's "Gone With the Wind" Letters*, 8.
47. Quoted in Farr, *Margaret Mitchell of Atlanta*, 43–44.
48. Quoted in *ibid.*, 74.

49. *Ibid.*, 88.
50. Quoted in *ibid.*, 74.
51. Quoted in *ibid.*, 142.
52. *Ibid.*, 13.
53. Medora Field Perkerson, "Why Margaret Mitchell Hasn't Written Another Book," Atlanta *Journal Magazine*, December 14, 1947, p. 6.
54. "Polly Peachtree," "Chatter by Polly Peachtree," *Hearst's Sunday American*, October 17, 1920, p. 1C.
55. Lois Dwight Cole, "The Story Begins at a Luncheon Bridge in Atlanta," *New York Times Book Review*, June 25, 1961, p. 7.
56. Quoted in Farr, *Margaret Mitchell of Atlanta*, 68.
57. *Ibid.*, 53–54.
58. *Ibid.*
59. *Ibid.*
60. *Ibid.*, 55.
61. *Ibid.*, 56.
62. *Ibid.*, 57.
63. Quoted in *ibid.*, 50.
64. *Ibid.*, 47–48.
65. Shavin and Shartar, "The Million Dollar Legends."
66. Cole, "The Story Begins at a Luncheon Bridge in Atlanta," 7.
67. Faith Baldwin, "The Woman Who Wrote *Gone With the Wind*: An Exclusive and Authentic Interview," *Pictorial Review* (March, 1937), 4.
68. Jones, "'Me and My Book,'" 185.
69. Floyd C. Watkins, "*Gone With the Wind* as Vulgar Literature," *Southern Literary Journal*, II (Spring, 1970), 86–103.
70. Farr, *Margaret Mitchell of Atlanta*, 97.
71. Quoted in *ibid.*, 165.

Chapter IX

1. Jacques Barzun, *Classic, Romantic and Modern* (Boston: Little, Brown and Co., 1961), 4.
2. Chopin, *Complete Works*, II, 996.
3. *Ibid.*, II, 722.
4. *Ibid.*, II, 692.

Bibliography

Abernathy, Mollie C. (Davis). "Southern Women, Social Reconstruction, and the Church in the 1920s." *Louisiana Studies*, XIII (Winter, 1974), 289–312.

Adams, J. Donald. "A Fine Novel of the Civil War." Review of *Gone With the Wind* by Margaret Mitchell. *New York Times Book Review*, July 5, 1936, p. 1.

Allen, Carolyn. "Mary Johnston." *American Literary Realism*, VIII (Autumn, 1975), 293.

Alman, David. "The Legend of Southern Womanhood." *Negro Digest*, VI (November, 1947), 72–76.

Angell, Susan, Jacquelyn Dowd Hall, and Candace Waid, eds. *Generations: Women in the South. Southern Exposure*, IV (Winter, 1977).

Arner, Robert. "Kate Chopin." *Louisiana Studies*, XIV (Spring, 1975), 11–139.

Bailey, Hugh C., and William Pratt Dale. "'Missus Alone in de "Big House,"'" *Alabama Review*, VIII (January, 1955), 43–55.

Bain, Robert, Joseph M. Flora, and Louis D. Rubin, Jr., eds. *Southern Writers: A Biographical Dictionary*. Baton Rouge: Louisiana State University Press, 1979.

Baldwin, Faith. "The Woman Who Wrote *Gone With the Wind*: An Exclusive and Authentic Interview." *Pictorial Review*, March, 1937, p. 4.

Barrett, Clifton Waller. Collection of papers relating to American literature. Alderman Library, University of Virginia, Charlottesville.

Bartlett, Irving H. and C. Glenn Cambor. "The History and Psychodynamics of Southern Womanhood." *Women's Studies*, II (1974), 9–24.

Barzun, Jacques. *Classic, Romantic and Modern*. Boston: Little, Brown, and Co., 1961.

Battey, Adrienne. Papers. University of Georgia Library, Athens.

Baym, Nina. *Woman's Fiction: A Guide to Novels by and about Women in America, 1820–1870*. Ithaca: Cornell University Press, 1978.

Benet, Stephen Vincent. "Georgia Marches Through." Review of *Gone With the Wind*, by Margaret Mitchell. *Saturday Review*, July 4, 1936, p. 5.

Berg, Matilda L. Review of *The Hard-Boiled Virgin*. In Marion A. Knight, ed., *The Book Review Digest*. New York: H. W. Wilson, 1927.

Bernd, Caroline. "GWTW Words Echo Its Author's Letters 80 Years Later." Savannah *Morning News*, March 3, 1974, p. 1B.

Bishop, John Peale. "War and No Peace." Review of *Gone With the Wind*. *New Republic*, LXXXVII (July 15, 1936), 301.

Blackford, L. Minor. *Mine Eyes Have Seen the Glory: The Story of a Virginia Lady, Mary Berkeley Minor Blackford, 1802–1896, Who Taught Her Sons to Hate Slavery and to Love the Union.* Cambridge, Mass.: Harvard University Press, 1954.

Blanchard, Christina G., Judith V. Becker, and Ann R. Bristow. "Attitudes of Southern Women: Selected Group Comparisons." *Psychology of Women*, I (Winter, 1976), 160–71.

Boatwright, James. "Reconsideration: Totin' de Weary Load." *New Republic*, September 1, 1973, pp. 29–32.

Bogan, Louise. "Women." In Florence Howe and Ellen Bass, eds., *No More Masks!: An Anthology of Poems by Women.* Garden City, N.Y.: Doubleday, 1976.

"Books: Backdrop for Atlanta." Review of *Gone With the Wind*. *Time*, July 6, 1936, p. 62.

"Books in Brief." Review of *Dead Lovers Are Faithful Lovers*. *Christian Century*, XLV (June 7, 1928), 737.

"Books in Brief." Review of *Gone With the Wind*. *Christian Century*, LIII (July 22, 1936), 1017–18.

[Brickell, Herschel.] "The Literary Landscape." Review of *Gone With the Wind*. *Review of Reviews*, LXXIV (August, 1936), 8.

————. "Margaret Mitchell's First Novel, *Gone With the Wind*, a Fine Panorama of the Civil War Period." Review of *Gone With the Wind*. New York *Post*, June 30, 1936. Margaret Mitchell Marsh Estate Papers, Atlanta.

————. Review of *Dead Lovers Are Faithful Lovers*, by Frances Newman. *North American*, July, 1928, p. 226.

Brown, Herbert Ross. *The Sentimental Novel in America, 1789–1860.* Durham, N.C.: Duke University Press, 1940.

Bukoski, Anthony. "The Lady and Her Business of Love in Selected Southern Fictions." *Studies in the Humanities*, V (January, 1976), 14–18.

Bullis, Helen. "A Feminist Novel." Review of *Hagar*. New York *Times*, November 2, 1913, p. 591.

Bush, Robert, "Charles Gayarre and Grace King: Letters of a Louisiana Friendship." *Southern Literary Journal*, VII (1974), 100–131.

————. "Grace King (1852–1932)." *American Literary Realism*, VIII (Winter, 1975), 43–51.

————. "Grace King: The Emergence of a Southern Intellectual Woman." *Southern Review*, XIII (April, 1977), 272–88.

Cabell, James Branch. *As I Remember It: Some Epilogues in Recollection.* New York: McBride, 1955.

————. Papers. Alderman Library, University of Virginia, Charlottesville.

Cable, George W. *The Creoles of Louisiana.* New York: Scribner's, 1889.

Carmer, Carl. *Stars Fell on Alabama.* New York: Farrar & Rinehart, 1934.

Carr, Lois Green, and Lorena S. Walsh. "The Planter's Wife: The Experience of

White Women in Seventeenth-Century Maryland." *William and Mary Quarterly*, XXXIV (October, 1977), 542–71.

Carroll, Berenice A., ed. *Liberating Women's History*. Urbana, Ill.: University of Illinois Press, 1976.

Cash, Wilbur J. *The Mind of the South*. New York: Vintage, 1941.

Chafe, William Henry. *The American Woman: Her Changing Social, Economic, and Political Roles, 1920–1970*. New York: Oxford University Press, 1972.

———. *Women and Equality: Changing Patterns in American Culture*. Oxford: Oxford University Press, 1977.

Chamberlain, John R. "Six Months in the Field of Fiction." Review of *Dead Lovers Are Faithful Lovers*. *New York Times Book Review*, June 24, 1928, p. 26.

Chesnut, Mary Boykin. *A Diary from Dixie*. Edited by Ben Ames Williams. Boston: Houghton Mifflin, 1949.

Chopin, Kate. *The Awakening: An Authoritative Text, Contexts, Criticism*. Edited by Margaret Culley. New York: Norton, 1976.

———. *The Complete Works of Kate Chopin*. Edited by Per Seyersted. 2 vols. Baton Rouge: Louisiana State University Press, 1969.

Clark, William Bedford. "The Serpent of Lust in the Southern Garden." *Southern Review*, X (October, 1974), 805–22.

Clayton, Bruce. *The Savage Ideal: Intolerance and Intellectual Leadership in the South, 1890–1914*. Baltimore: Johns Hopkins University Press, 1972.

Cole, Lois Dwight. "The Story Begins at a Luncheon Bridge in Atlanta." *New York Times Book Review*, June 25, 1961, p. 7.

Commager, Henry Steele. "The Civil War in Georgia's Red Clay Hills, Vividly Told from the Viewpoint of the Women Left Behind." Review of *Gone With the Wind*, by Margaret Mitchell. New York *Herald Tribune Books*, July 5, 1936, p. 1.

Congressional Record, Senate. 95th Cong., 2nd Sess., S16667 (Daily edition), September 29, 1978.

Coon, David L. "Eliza Pinckney and the Reintroduction of Indigo Culture in South Carolina." *Journal of Southern History*, XLIII (Fall, 1976), 61–76.

Cooper, Frederic Taber. "Inconclusiveness and Some Recent Novels." *Bookman*, XXXVII (June, 1913), 536–37.

Cornillon, Susan Koppelman, ed. *Images of Women in Fiction: Feminist Perspectives*. Bowling Green, Ohio: Bowling Green University Popular Press, 1972.

Cott, Nancy F. *The Bonds of Womanhood: "Woman's Sphere" in New England, 1780–1835*. New Haven: Yale University Press, 1977.

———, ed. *Root of Bitterness: Documents of the Social History of American Women*. New York: Dutton, 1972.

Coulter, E. Merton. *The South During Reconstruction: 1865–1877*. Baton Rouge: Louisiana State University Press, 1947.

Cowie, Alexander. *The Rise of the American Novel*. New York: American Book Co., 1948.

Cowley, Malcolm. "Going with the Wind." Review of *Gone With the Wind. New Republic*, LXXXVIII (September 16, 1936), 161.

Croly, Mrs. J. C. (Jennie June). *The History of the Woman's Club Movement in America.* New York: Henry G. Allen, 1898.

"Current Fiction." Review of *Hagar. Nation*, XCVII (October 30, 1913), 410.

"Current Fiction." Review of *Life and Gabriella. Nation*, CII (February 17, 1916), 197.

"Current Fiction." Review of *Virginia. Nation*, XCVI (May 22, 1913), 524.

Daniel, Frank. "Miss Newman's Unwritten Books." Atlanta *Journal*, November 18, 1928, pp. 5, 24.

————. "Simplicity, Loyalty and Love Produced *Gone With the Wind.*" Atlanta *Journal*, August 17, 1949, p. 6.

Dashiell, Margaret May. Papers. Southern Historical Collection, University of North Carolina at Chapel Hill.

Davis, Elmer. "Candid Miss Newman." Review of *The Hard-Boiled Virgin. Saturday Review of Literature*, III (December 18, 1926), 449.

Degler, Carl N. *At Odds: Woman and the Family in America from the Revolution to the Present.* New York: Oxford University Press, 1980.

————. *Out of Our Past: The Forces That Shaped Modern America.* Rev. ed. New York: Harper & Row, 1970.

————. *Place Over Time: The Continuity of Southern Distinctiveness.* Baton Rouge: Louisiana State University Press, 1977.

————. "The South in Southern History Textbooks." *Journal of Southern History*, XXX (November, 1964), 48–57.

————. "What Ought to Be and What Was: Women's Sexuality in the Nineteenth Century." *American Historical Review*, LXXIX (December, 1974), 1467–90.

DeGraffenried Family Collection. Southern Historical Collection, University of North Carolina at Chapel Hill.

DeGraffenried, Thomas P. *The DeGraffenried Family Scrap Book, 1191–1956.* Charlottesville, Va.: University Press of Virginia, n.d.

Diamond, Arlyn, and Lee R. Edwards, eds. *The Authority of Experience: Essays in Feminist Criticism.* Amherst: University of Massachusetts Press, 1977.

Dollard, John. *Caste and Class in a Southern Town.* 1937. Reprint. Garden City, N.Y.: Doubleday, 1957.

Donald, David. "Scarlett Fever." *Book Week*, January 23, 1966, p. 5.

Douglas, Ann. *The Feminization of American Culture.* New York: Alfred A. Knopf, 1977.

Dounce, H. E. Review of *Dead Lovers Are Faithful Lovers*, by Frances Newman. New York *Evening Post*, May 5, 1928, p. 8.

Drake, Robert Y., Jr. "Frances Newman: Fabulist of Decadence." *Georgia Review*, XIV (Winter, 1960), 389–98.

————. "Tara Twenty Years After." *Georgia Review*, XII (1958), 142–50.

Duus, Louise. "Neither Saint Nor Sinner: Women in Late Nineteenth-Century Fiction." *American Literary Realism*, III (Summer, 1974), 276–78.

E. B. H. "Fiction Notes." Review of *The Hard-Boiled Virgin*. *New Republic*, XLIX (January 5, 1927), 202.

E. F. E. Review of *Hagar*. Boston *Transcript*, October 25, 1913, p. 8.

Eleazar, R. B. "Southern Women Against the Mob." *Southern Workman*, LX (March, 1931), 126–31.

Ellman, Mary. *Thinking About Women*. New York: Harcourt, Brace, Jovanovich, 1968.

Evans, Augusta Jane. *Beulah*. 1859. Reprint. New York: Hurst & Co., n.d.

———. *Inez*. 1856. Reprint. New York: New York Book Company, 1911.

———. *Augusta J. Evans Wilson Letters*. Clifton Waller Barrett Collection. Alderman Library, University of Virginia, Charlottesville.

———. *Macaria*. 1863. Reprint. New York: Dillingham, 1887.

———. *St. Elmo*. New York: Dillingham, 1866.

Evans, Sara. *Personal Politics: The Roots of Women's Liberation in the Civil Rights Movement and the New Left*. New York: Alfred A. Knopf, 1979.

"An Exchange of Letters Between Ellen Glasgow and Marjorie Kinnan Rawlings." Atlanta *Journal*, April 28, 1946, p. 5.

Fanning, Clara Elizabeth, ed. *The Book Review Digest*. White Plains, N.Y.: H. W. Wilson, 1913.

Farr, Finis. *Margaret Mitchell of Atlanta: The Author of "Gone With the Wind"*. New York: William Morrow, 1965.

Faust, Marie Elisabeth. "In Memoriam: Grace King." *Bookman*, LXXV (August, 1932), 361.

Ferguson, Mary Anne, ed. *Images of Women in Literature*. Boston: Houghton-Mifflin, 1973.

"A Few of the Season's Novels." Review of *Virginia*. *Review of Reviews*, XLVII (June, 1913), 762.

Ficklen, John Rose. Papers. Southern Historical Collection. University of North Carolina at Chapel Hill.

Fidler, William Perry. *Augusta Evans Wilson: 1835–1909*. University, Ala.: University of Alabama Press, 1951.

Fiedler, Leslie A. "Fiction of the Thirties." *Revue des Langues Vivantes*, Special U.S. Bicentennial Issue (1976), Année 42, pp. 93–104.

Fitzhugh, George. *Sociology for the South, or the Failure of Free Society*. 1859. Reprint. Burt Franklin: New York, n.d.

"Five New Novels by Women." Review of *Hagar*. *The Outlook*, November 15, 1913, pp. 570–72.

Fletcher, Marie. "The Southern Heroine in the Fiction of Representative Southern Women Writers, 1850–1960," Ph.D. dissertation, Louisiana State University, 1963.

Flexner, Eleanor. *Century of Struggle: The Woman's Rights Movement in the United States*. Cambridge, Mass.: Harvard University Press, 1959.

Follett, Wilson. "Sentimentalist, Satirist, and Realist: Notes on Some Recent Fiction." Review of *Life and Gabriella*. *Atlantic*, CXVIII, (October, 1916), 501.

Foster, Virginia. "The Emancipation of Pure, White, Southern Womanhood."

New South, XXVI (Winter, 1971), 46–54.

"Frances Newman Cuts a New Caper in the Novel." Review of *The Hard-Boiled Virgin. New York Times Book Review*, December 12, 1926, p. 12.

Friedman, Jean E., and William G. Shade, eds. *Our American Sisters: Women in American Life and Thought.* 2nd ed. Boston: Allyn and Bacon, Inc., 1976.

Fryer, Judith. *The Faces of Eve: Women in the Nineteenth-Century American Novel.* New York: Oxford University Press, 1976.

Gaillard, Dawson. "*Gone With the Wind* as Bildungsroman, or Why Did Rhett Butler Leave Scarlett O'Hara?" *Georgia Review*, XXVIII (1974), 9–18.

Gaines, Francis Pendleton. *The Southern Plantation: A Study in the Development and the Accuracy of a Tradition.* New York: Columbia University Press, 1925.

Garrison, Dee. "Immoral Fiction in the Late Victorian Library." *American Quarterly*, XXVIII (Spring, 1976), 71–89.

Geismar, Maxwell. *Rebels and Ancestors: The American Novel, 1890–1915.* Boston: Houghton Mifflin, 1953.

Genovese, Eugene. *The World the Slaveholders Made: Two Essays in Interpretation.* New York: Pantheon, 1969.

Gilbert, Sandra, and Susan Gubar. *The Madwoman in the Attic: The Woman Writer and the Nineteenth-Century Literary Imagination.* New Haven: Yale University Press, 1979.

Ginsberg, Elaine. "The Female Initiation Theme in American Fiction." *Studies in American Fiction*, III (Spring, 1975), 27–37.

Glasgow, Ellen. *A Certain Measure: An Interpretation of Prose Fiction.* New York: Harcourt, Brace, 1943.

———. *The Collected Stories of Ellen Glasgow.* Edited by Richard K. Meeker. Baton Rouge: Louisiana State University Press, 1963.

———. "Feminism." *New York Times Book Review*, November 30, 1913, pp. 656–57.

———. *Letters of Ellen Glasgow.* Edited by Blair Rouse. New York: Harcourt, Brace, 1958.

———. *Life and Gabriella: The Story of a Woman's Courage.* Garden City, N.Y.: Doubleday, Page, 1916.

———. Papers. Alderman Library, University of Virginia, Charlottesville.

———. *The Sheltered Life.* New York: Doubleday, Doran, 1932.

———. *Virginia.* 1913. Old Dominion Edition. Garden City, N.Y.: Doubleday, Doran, 1929.

———. *The Woman Within.* New York: Harcourt, Brace, 1954.

Glenn, Isa. "What a Young Wife—?" Review of *Dead Lovers Are Faithful Lovers. Saturday Review of Literature*, IV (May 12, 1928), 861.

Godbold, E. Stanly, Jr. "A Battleground Revisited: Reconstruction in Southern Fiction, 1895–1905." *South Atlantic Quarterly*, LXXIII (Winter, 1974), 99–116.

———. *Ellen Glasgow and the Woman Within.* Baton Rouge: Louisiana State University Press, 1972.

Godwin, Gail. "The Southern Belle." *Ms.*, IV (July, 1975), 49–52, 84–85.

"*Gone With the Wind* and Its Author Margaret Mitchell." New York: Macmillan, 1961. Advertising booklet for 25th anniversary edition.

Gornick, Vivian. *Essays in Feminism.* New York: Harper & Row, 1978.

———, and Barbara K. Moran, eds. *Woman in Sexist Society: Studies in Power and Powerlessness.* New York: New American Library, 1971.

Granberry, Edwin. "The Private Life of Margaret Mitchell." *Collier's,* March 13, 1937. Margaret Mitchell Marsh Collection, Atlanta.

Grantham, Dewey S. "History, Mythology, and the Southern Lady." *Southern Literary Journal,* III (Spring, 1971), 98–108.

Gray, Virginia Gearhart. "Activities of Southern Women: 1840–1860." *South Atlantic Quarterly,* XXVII (July, 1928), 265–79.

Green, Michelle. "Guarding the Gates at Tara." Atlanta *Constitution,* October 1, 1979, p. 1-B.

Grimké, Sarah M. *Letters on the Equality of the Sexes and the Condition of Woman Addressed to Mary S. Parker, President of the Boston Female Anti-Slavery Society.* 1838. Reprint. New York: Burt Franklin, 1970.

Groover, Robert L. "Margaret Mitchell, the Lady from Atlanta." *Georgia Historical Quarterly,* LII (March, 1968), 53–69.

"*GWTW* Interview Reproduced." Atlanta *Journal,* December 15, 1939, p. 51.

Hagood, Margaret Jarman. *Mothers of the South: Portraiture of the White Tenant Farm Woman.* 1939. Reprint. New York: W. W. Norton, 1977.

Hall, Jacquelyn Dowd. *Revolt Against Chivalry: Jessie Daniel Ames and the Women's Campaign Against Lynching.* New York: Columbia University Press, 1979.

Hansen, Harry. Review of *The Hard-Boiled Virgin.* New York *World,* November 18, 1926, p. 10M.

Hardwick, Elizabeth, ed. and intro., *Dead Lovers Are Faithful Lovers,* by Frances Newman. 1928. Reprint. New York: Arno Press, 1977.

———, ed. and intro. *The Hard-Boiled Virgin,* by Frances Newman. 1926, Reprint. New York: Arno Press, 1977.

Hart, James D. *The Popular Book: A History of American Literary Taste.* New York: Oxford University Press, 1950.

Hartley, L. P. "New Fiction." Review of *Dead Lovers Are Faithful Lovers. Saturday Review* (London), CXLVI (July 14, 1928), 56.

Hartman, Mary S., and Lois Banner, eds. *Clio's Consciousness Raised: New Perspectives on the History of Women.* New York: Harper, 1974.

"Heard, Eliza" [Virginia Foster]. "In the Name of Southern Womanhood." *New South,* XVII (November/December, 1962), 16–18.

Heilbrun, Carolyn. *Toward a Recognition of Androgyny.* New York: Knopf, 1973.

Henry, Josephine K. "The New Woman of the New South." *Arena,* XI (February, 1895), 353–62.

Hentz, Caroline Lee. *The Planter's Northern Bride.* 1854. Reprint. Chapel Hill: University of North Carolina Press, 1970.

Hesselbart, Susan. "Attitudes Toward Women and Attitudes Toward Blacks in a Southern City." *Sociological Symposium,* XVII (Fall, 1976), 45–68.

Heustis, Rachel Lyons. Papers. Southern Historical Collection, University of North Carolina at Chapel Hill.

Hogeland, Ronald W. "'The Female Appendage': Feminine Life-Styles in America, 1820–1860." *Civil War History*, XVII (June, 1971), 101–14.

Hoffert, Sylvia D. "Mary Boykin Chesnut: Private Feminist in the Civil War South." *Southern Studies*, XVI (Spring, 1977), 81–89.

Holland, Robert Afton. "The Suffragette." *Sewanee Review*, XVII (July, 1909), 272–88.

Holman, C. Hugh. *The Immoderate Past: The Southern Writer and History*. Athens, Ga.: University of Georgia Press, 1977.

————. *The Roots of Southern Writing: Essays on the Literature of the American South*. Athens, Ga.: University of Georgia Press, 1972.

————. *Three Modes of Modern Southern Fiction: Ellen Glasgow, William Faulkner, Thomas Wolfe*. Athens, Ga.: University of Georgia Press, 1966.

Hooker, Brian. "Twelve Books of the Month." Review of *Hagar. Bookman*, XXXVIII (December, 1913), 591.

Horan, Tom. "Cabell Talks of Frances Newman." Atlanta *Journal*, October 16, 1932, p. 6.

Howland, William S. "Margaret Mitchell—Romantic Realist." In *Margaret Mitchell Memorial of the Atlanta Public Library*, pp. 1–16. Atlanta: Atlanta Public Library, 1954.

————. "Peggy Mitchell, Newspaperman." *Atlanta Historical Bulletin*, IX (May, 1950), 47–64.

Hubbell, Jay B. *The South in American Literature: 1607–1900*. Durham, N.C.: Duke University Press, 1954.

"Humor and Pathos in a Woman's Life." Review of *Life and Gabriella. New York Times Book Review*, January 16, 1916, p. 1.

"The Hundred Best Books of the Year." Review of *Virginia*. New York *Times*, November 30, 1913, p. 665.

Hutchinson, Joanne. "All in the Family: Innocent Incest in Victorian Fiction." Paper read at the annual meeting of the Northeast Modern Language Association, May, 1977, in Pittsburgh, Pennsylvania.

"I. M. P." "Turns with a Bookworm." Review of *Gone With the Wind. New York Herald Tribune Books*, October 25, 1936, p. 26.

Inge, M. Thomas, ed. *Ellen Glasgow: Centennial Essays*. Charlottesville: University Press of Virginia, 1976.

Jackson, Margaret, ed. *The Book Review Digest*. White Plains, N.Y.: H. W. Wilson Co., 1917.

Jacobson, Edith. *The Self and the Object World*. New York: International Universities Press, 1964.

James, Edward T., ed. *Notable American Women 1607–1950: A Biographical Dictionary*. 3 vols. Cambridge, Mass.: Harvard University Press, 1971.

James, Mertice M., ed. *The Book Review Digest*. New York: H. W. Wilson Co., 1937.

Jeffrey, Julie Roy. "Women in the Southern Farmers' Alliance: A Reconsideration of the Role and Status of Women in the Late Nineteenth-Century South." *Feminist Studies*, III (Fall, 1975), 72–91.

Jessup, Josephine Lurie. *The Faith of Our Feminists*. New York: Richard R. Smith, 1950.

Johnson, Guion Griffis. "Feminism and the Economic Independence of Woman." *Journal of Social Forces*, III (May, 1925), 612–16.

———. "The Changing Status of the Southern Woman." In *The South in Continuity and Change*. Edited by John T. McKinney and Edgar T. Thompson. Durham, N.C.: Duke University Press, 1965.

Johnson, Kenneth R. "Kate Gordon and the Woman-Suffrage Movement in the South." *Journal of Southern History*, XXXVIII (August, 1972), 365–92.

Johnston, Mary. *Hagar*. Boston: Houghton Mifflin, 1913.

———. Papers. Alderman Library, University of Virginia, Charlottesville.

———. *The Witch*. Boston and New York: Houghton Mifflin, 1914.

———. "The Woman's War." *Atlantic Monthly*, CV (April, 1910), 559–70.

Jones, Katharine M., ed. *Heroines of Dixie: Spring of High Hopes*. New York: Ballantine, 1955.

Jones, Marian Elder. "'Me and My Book.'" *Georgia Review*, XVI (Summer, 1962), 180–87.

Justus, James H. "The Unawakening of Edna Pontellier." *Southern Literary Journal*, X (Spring, 1978), 107–22.

Kazin, Alfred. *On Native Grounds: An Interpretation of Modern American Prose Literature*. New York: Harcourt, Brace, 1942.

Kearney, Belle. *A Slaveholder's Daughter*. 1900. Reprint. New York: Negro Universities Press, 1969.

Kelley, Mary. "The Crisis of Domesticity: Women Writing of Women in Nineteenth Century America." Unpublished book-length manuscript, Dartmouth College, Hanover, N.H.

———. "The Sentimentalists: Promise and Betrayal in the Home." *Signs: Journal of Women in Culture and Society*, IV (Spring, 1979), 434–46.

Kelly, Florence Finch. "Some Novels of the Month." Review of *Life and Gabriella*. *Bookman*, XLIII (March, 1916), 80.

Key, William. "Author Was Always Reporter at Heart: Margaret Mitchell Wore Fame Casually as an Old Garment." Atlanta *Journal*, August 16, 1949, p. 2.

———. "Margaret Mitchell and Her Last Days on Earth." *Atlanta Historical Bulletin*, IX (May, 1960), 108–28.

King, Grace. *Balcony Stories*. New York: Macmillan, 1925.

———. *Creole Families of New Orleans*. New York: Macmillan, 1921.

———. *Grace King of New Orleans: A Selection of Her Writings*. Edited by Robert Bush. Baton Rouge: Louisiana State University Press, 1973.

———. *Memories of a Southern Woman of Letters*. New York: Macmillan, 1932.

———. *Monsieur Motte*. New York: Armstrong, 1888.

———. Papers. Microfilm, Southern Historical Collection, University of North Carolina, Chapel Hill.

———. *The Pleasant Ways of St. Médard*. New York: Macmillan, 1916.

————. *Tales of a Time and Place.* New York: Harper & Bros., 1892.

Kinnel, Ellen. "Contributions to the History of Psychology: XXIV. Role of Women Psychologists in the History of Psychology in the South." *Psychological Reports,* XXXVIII (April, 1976), 611–18.

Knight, Marion A., ed. *The Book Review Digest.* New York: H. W. Wilson, 1927, 1929.

Kolodny, Annette. "The Land-as-Woman: Literary Convention and Latent Psychological Content." *Women's Studies,* I (1973), 167–82.

————. "Some Notes on Defining a 'Feminist Literary Criticism.'" *Critical Inquiry,* I (Autumn, 1975), 75–92.

————. "'Stript, Shorne and Made Deformed': Images of the Southern Landscape." *South Atlantic Quarterly,* LXXV (Winter, 1976), 55–73.

Koloski, Bernard. "The Structure of Kate Chopin's *At Fault.*" *Studies in American Fiction,* III (Spring, 1975), 89–94.

Kondert, Nancy T. "The Romance and Reality of Defeat: Southern Women in 1865." *Journal of Mississippi History,* XXXV (May, 1973), 141–52.

Kraditor, Aileen S. "Tactical Problems of the Woman-Suffrage Movement in the South." *Louisiana Studies,* V (Winter, 1966), 289–307.

————, ed. *Up From the Pedestal: Selected Writings in the History of American Feminism.* Chicago: Quadrangle, 1968.

Lasch, Christopher. *The Culture of Narcissism: American Life in an Age of Diminishing Expectations.* New York: Warner Books, 1979.

Latham, Harold. *My Life in Publishing.* New York: Dutton, 1965.

L. C. "Modified Feminism." Review of *Life and Gabriella. New Republic,* VI (March 18, 1916), 194.

Leach, Anna. "Literary Workers of the South." *Munsey's Magazine,* XIII (April, 1895), 57–65.

Leary, Lewis. "Kate Chopin, Liberationist?" *Southern Literary Journal,* III (Fall, 1970), 138–44.

————. "Kate Chopin's Other Novel." *Southern Literary Journal,* I (December, 1968), 60–74.

————. *Southern Excursions: Essays on Mark Twain and Others.* Baton Rouge: Louisiana State University Press, 1971.

Lebsock, Suzanne D. "Radical Reconstruction and the Property Rights of Southern Women." *Journal of Southern History,* XLII (May, 1977), 195–216.

Lerner, Gerda. *The Grimké Sisters from South Carolina, Rebels Against Slavery.* Boston: Houghton Mifflin, 1967.

————. "The Lady and the Mill Girl: Changes in the Status of Women in the Age of Jackson." *Mid-Continent American Studies Journal,* X (1969), 5–15.

Link, Arthur S., and Rembert W. Patrick, eds. *Writing Southern History: Essays in Historiography in Honor of Fletcher M. Green.* Baton Rouge: Louisiana State University Press, 1965.

McAdoo, Laura Sterrette. "Woman's Economic Status in the South." *Arena,* XXI (1899), 741–56.

McDowell, Frederick P. W. *Ellen Glasgow and the Ironic Art of Fiction.* Madison: University of Wisconsin Press, 1960.

McGill, Ralph. "Little Woman, Big Book: The Mysterious Margaret Mitchell." *Show* (October, 1962), 69–73.

Macy, John. "Women Are Witches." Review of *Dead Lovers Are Faithful Lovers. Bookman*, LXVII (June, 1928), 429–32.

"Margaret Mitchell in Public Affairs." *Atlanta Historical Bulletin*, IX (May, 1950), 29–30.

"Margaret Mitchell Memorial Issue." *Atlanta Historical Bulletin*, IX (May, 1950).

"Margaret Mitchell Memorial Issue." Atlanta *Journal Magazine*, December 18, 1949.

"Margaret Mitchell Memorial of the Atlanta Public Library, Dedicated Dec. 15, 1954." Pamphlet. Atlanta: Atlanta Public Library, 1954.

Martin, Wendy, ed. *The American Sisterhood.* New York: Harper & Row, 1972.

Massey, Mary Elizabeth. *Bonnet Brigades.* New York: Knopf, 1966.

———. "The Making of a Feminist." *Journal of Southern History*, XXXIX (February, 1973), 3–22.

Matthews, T. S. "Fancy Goods." Review of *Dead Lovers Are Faithful Lovers. New Republic*, LV (June 27, 1928), 153.

May, Herbert G., and Bruce M. Metzger, eds. *The Oxford Annotated Bible with the Apocrypha.* New York: Oxford University Press, 1965.

May, Robert E. "*Gone With the Wind* as Southern History: A Reappraisal." *Southern Quarterly*, XVII (Fall, 1978), 51–64.

Mayo, Amory Dwight. *Southern Women in the Recent Educational Movement in the South.* 1892. Reprint. Edited and with an introduction by Dan T. Carter and Amy Friedlander. Baton Rouge: Louisiana State University Press, 1978.

Mendenhall, Marjorie Stratford. "Southern Women of a 'Lost Generation.'" *South Atlantic Quarterly*, XXXIII (October, 1934), 334–53.

Meriwether, James B., ed. *South Carolina Women Writers. Proceedings of the Reynolds Conference, University of South Carolina, October 24–25, 1975.* Transcript of the "second of a series of annual conferences dealing with various aspects of South Carolina intellectual and cultural history made possible by the generosity of Mrs. John S. Reynolds." Columbia: Southern Studies Program, University of South Carolina, 1979.

Merrick, Caroline E. *Old Times in Dixie Land: A Southern Matron's Memories.* New York: Grafton Press, 1901.

Mims, Edwin. *The Advancing South: Stories of Progress and Reaction.* Garden City, N.Y.: Doubleday, Page, 1926. See especially Chapter IX, "The Revolt Against Chivalry," pp. 224–56.

———. "The Southern Woman: Past and Present." *Bulletin* of Randolph-Macon Woman's College, I (July, 1915), 3–17.

Mitchell, Eugene M. "Atlanta During the 'Reconstruction Period.'" *Atlanta Historical Bulletin*, II (1936), 18–25.

Mitchell, Margaret. *Gone With the Wind.* New York: Macmillan, 1936.

————. Letter to Miss Martin, February 17, 1937. Miscellaneous Letters #516, Southern Historical Collection, University of North Carolina Library, Chapel Hill.

————. "Little Sister."*Facts and Fancies* (Annual of Washington Seminary, Atlanta, Georgia), 1917.

————. *Margaret Mitchell's "Gone With the Wind" Letters, 1936–1949.* Edited by Richard Harwell. New York: Macmillan, 1976.

————. Margaret Mitchell Marsh Papers. Manuscript Department, University of Georgia Library, Athens.

Mitchell, Stephens. "Margaret Mitchell and Her People in the Atlanta Area." *Atlanta Historical Bulletin*, IX (May, 1950), 5–26.

Mitchell, Stephens, Literary Rights Collection, Atlanta, Georgia.

Moers, Ellen. *Literary Women: The Great Writers.* Garden City, N.Y.: Doubleday, 1976.

Mott, Frank Luther. *Golden Multitudes: The Story of Best Sellers in the United States.* New York: Macmillan, 1947.

Murphy, Sara. "Women's Lib in the South." *New South*, XXVII (Spring, 1972), 42–46.

Myrdal, Gunnar. *An American Dilemma: The Negro Problem and Modern Democracy.* Twentieth Anniversary Edition. New York: Harper & Row, 1962.

"The New Books." Review of *Hagar. Independent*, LXXVI (October 30, 1913), 218–20.

"The New Books." Review of *Life and Gabriella. Independent*, LXXXV (February 28, 1916), 316.

"New Books and Reprints." Review of *Dead Lovers Are Faithful Lovers.* London *Times Literary Supplement*, June 14, 1928.

"New Books in Brief Review." Review of *Dead Lovers Are Faithful Lovers. Independent*, CXX (June 9, 1928), 560.

"New Books in Brief Review." Review of *The Hard-Boiled Virgin. Independent*, CXVII (December 18, 1926), 716.

"New Books Reviewed." Review of *Virginia. North American Review*, CXCVII (June, 1913), 856–57.

"The New Novels: Romance Unending." Review of *Gone With the Wind.* London *Times Literary Supplement*, October 3, 1936, p. 787.

"The Newest Fiction." Review of *Life and Gabriella. Review of Reviews*, LIII (March, 1916), 377.

Newman, Frances. "The American Short Story in the First Twenty-Five Years of the Twentieth Century." *Bookman*, XLIII (1926), 186–93.

————. *Dead Lovers Are Faithful Lovers.* New York: Boni & Liveright, 1928.

————. "Elizabeth Bennet's Gossip." Atlanta *Journal*, January 1, 1928, p. 14.

————. *Frances Newman's Letters.* Edited by Hansell Baugh. New York: Horace Liveright, 1929.

————. *The Hard-Boiled Virgin.* New York: Boni & Liveright, 1926.

————. Assorted papers. Adrienne Battey Collection, Manuscript Department, University of Georgia Library, Athens.

————. "Rachel and Her Children." *American Mercury*, II (1924), 92–96.

————. *The Short Story's Mutations: From Petronius to Paul Morand*. New York: B. W. Huebsch, 1924.

————, ed. and trans. *Six Moral Tales from Jules Laforgue*. New York: Horace Liveright, 1928.

"Novels." Review of *Hagar*. *The Saturday Review of Politics, Literature, Science and Art* (London), CXVI (November 15, 1913), 623.

O'Brien, Michael. *The Idea of the American South, 1920–1941*. Baltimore: Johns Hopkins University Press, 1979.

Olsen, Tillie. *Silences*. New York: Dell, 1978.

"On the Liberation of Women: A Special Double Issue." *Motive*, XXIX (March/April, 1969).

O'Neill, William L. *Everyone Was Brave: The Rise and Fall of Feminism in America*. Chicago: Quadrangle, 1969.

Overton, Grant. *Cargoes for Crusoes*. New York: D. Appleton, 1924.

————. Review of *The Hard-Boiled Virgin*. *Literary Review*, December 18, 1926, p. 1.

————. *The Women Who Make Our Novels*. Revised ed. New York: Dodd, Mead, 1928.

Page, Walter Hines. "The Last Hold of the Southern Bully." *Forum*, XVI (November, 1893), 303–14.

Paine, Gregory, ed. *Southern Prose Writers*. New York: American Book, 1947.

Pannill, Linda. "The Artist-Heroine in American Fiction, 1890–1920." Ph.D. dissertation, University of North Carolina, 1976.

Papachristou, Judith, ed. *Women Together: A History in Documents of the Women's Movement in the United States*. New York: Knopf, 1976.

Papashvily, Helen Waite. *All the Happy Endings: A Study of the Domestic Novel in America, the Women Who Wrote It, the Women Who Read It, in the Nineteenth Century*. New York: Harper & Brothers, 1956.

Parker, Gail, ed. *The Oven Birds: American Women on Womanhood, 1820–1920*. Garden City, N.Y.: Doubleday, 1972.

Parsons, Alice Beal. "Setbacks and Style." Review of *Dead Lovers Are Faithful Lovers*. *Nation*, CXXVI (June 6, 1928), 648–49.

Pattee, Fred Lewis. *The Feminine Fifties*. New York: D. Appleton Century, 1940.

Patterson, Isabel. "Phantom Lover." Review of *Dead Lovers Are Faithful Lovers*. *New York Herald Tribune Books*, May 6, 1928, p. 3.

Patton, Frances Gray. "Anatomy of the Southern Belle." *Holiday*, XXVI (November, 1959), 76–77, 120–26.

"Peachtree, Polly." "Chatter by Polly Peachtree." *Hearst's Sunday American*, October 17, 1920, p. 1C.

Pegler, Westbrook. "Margaret Mitchell Disliked Roosevelt." Charlotte *Observer*, January 20, 1956, unpaginated clipping in the personal collection of Stephens Mitchell.

————. "A Soliloquy on Margaret Mitchell." Atlanta *Constitution*, unpaginated and undated clipping.

Percy, Walker. *The Moviegoer*. New York: Noonday Press, 1961.

Perkerson, Medora Field. Interview with Margaret Mitchell. Atlanta *Journal Magazine*, May 23, 1937, pp. 1–2.

──────. "Was Margaret Mitchell Writing Another Book?" Atlanta *Journal Magazine*, December 18, 1949, p. 4.

──────. "When Margaret Mitchell Was a Girl Reporter." Atlanta *Journal Magazine*, January 7, 1945, pp. 5–7.

──────. "Why Margaret Mitchell Hasn't Written Another Book." Atlanta *Journal Magazine*, December 14, 1947, pp. 5–7.

Poussaint, Alvin. "The Stresses of the White Female Worker in the Civil Rights Movement in the South." *American Journal of Psychiatry*, CXXIII (October, 1966), 401–407.

Powledge, Fred. *Journeys Through the South*. New York: Vanguard, 1979.

Putnam, Emily Jane. *The Lady: Studies of Significant Phases of Her History*. Chicago: University of Chicago Press, 1910.

Raper, Julius Rowan. "Ambivalence Toward Authority: A Look at Glasgow's Library, 1890–1906." *Mississippi Quarterly*, XXXI (Winter, 1977–78), 5–16.

──────. *Without Shelter: The Early Career of Ellen Glasgow*. Baton Rouge: Louisiana State University Press, 1971.

"Recent Novels." Review of Augusta J. Evans' *Infelice*. *Nation*, XXII (February 3, 1876), 84.

"Recent Reflections of a Novel-Reader." Review of *Virginia*. *Atlantic Monthly*, CXII (November 13, 1913), 690.

Reed, John Shelton. *The Enduring South: Subcultural Persistence in Mass Society*. Chapel Hill: University of North Carolina Press, 1975.

Review of *Dead Lovers Are Faithful Lovers*. Springfield (Illinois) *Republican*, May 26, 1928. In *Book Review Digest*, 1928.

Review of *Gone With the Wind*. *Time*, December 25, 1939, pp. 30–32.

Review of *Hagar*. *Saturday Review*, November 15, 1913, p. 623.

Review of *The Hard-Boiled Virgin*. Springfield (Illinois) *Republican*, December 5, 1926. In *Book Review Digest*, 1926.

Review of *Life and Gabriella*. London *Times Literary Supplement*, June 22, 1916, p. 299.

"Reviews of New Books." Review of *Hagar*. *Literary Digest*, XLVII (November 15, 1913), 954.

"Reviews of New Books." Review of *Virginia*. *Literary Digest*, XLVII (September 6, 1913), 388.

Richardson, Eudora Ramsay. "The Case of the Women's Colleges in the South." *South Atlantic Quarterly*, XXIX (April, 1930), 126–39.

──────. "The South Grows Up." *Bookman*, LXX (January, 1930), 545–50.

"Riddell, John" [Corey Ford]. "Meaning No Offense: Parody Interviews in the Respective Manners of Frances Newman and Carl Van Vechten." *Vanity Fair*, November, 1928, pp. 89–108.

Ringe, Donald A. "Cane River World: Kate Chopin's *At Fault* and Related Stories." *Studies in American Fiction*, III (Summer, 1975), 157–66.

Roberson, John R., ed. "Two Virginia Novelists on Woman's Suffrage. An Exchange of Letters between Mary Johnston and Thomas Nelson Page." *Virginia Magazine of History and Biography*, LXIV (July, 1956), 286–90.

Roller, David C., and Robert W. Twyman, eds. *The Encyclopedia of Southern History*. Baton Rouge: Louisiana State University Press, 1979.

Rothermel, Winifred. "Aristocratic Writer, Daughter of the South, Taken by Death in Gotham." Birmingham (Ala.) *News—Age-Herald*, October 28, 1928, p. 4.

Rouse, Blair. *Ellen Glasgow*. New York: Twayne, 1962.

Ruark, Robert C. "Will the Critics Now Get Around to Admitting 'GWTW' Is a Great Novel?" Atlanta *Journal*, August 19, 1949, n.p. Margaret Mitchell Marsh Papers, University of Georgia Library, Athens.

Rubin, Louis D., Jr. *George W. Cable: The Life and Times of a Southern Heretic.* New York: Pegasus, 1969.

———. *No Place on Earth: Ellen Glasgow, James Branch Cabell, and Richmond-in-Virginia*. Austin: University of Texas Press, 1959.

———. "Scarlett O'Hara and the Two Quentin Compsons." In *The South and Faulkner's Yoknapatawpha: The Actual and the Apocryphal*, edited by Evans Harrington and Ann J. Abadie, pp. 168–94. Jackson: University Press of Mississippi, 1977.

———, and C. Hugh Holman, eds. *Southern Literary Study: Problems and Possibilities*. Chapel Hill: University of North Carolina Press, 1975.

———. *William Elliott Shoots a Bear: Essays on the Southern Literary Imagination*. Baton Rouge: Louisiana State University Press, 1975.

———, ed. *The Writer in the South: Studies in a Literary Community*. Athens: University of Georgia Press, 1972.

Ruoff, John Carl. "Frivolity to Consumption: or Southern Womanhood in Antebellum Literature." *Civil War History*, XVIII (September, 1972), 213–29.

———. "Southern Womanhood, 1865–1920: An Intellectual and Cultural Study." Ph.D. dissertation, University of Illinois, 1976.

Ryan, Mary P. *Womanhood in America from Colonial Times to the Present*. New York: Franklin Watts, 1975.

Santas, Joan Foster. *Ellen Glasgow's American Dream*. Charlottesville: University Press of Virginia, 1965.

Schnell, Jonathan. "Books: A Causerie." Review of *Gone With the Wind. Forum*, XCVI (August, 1936), iv.

Scott, Anne Firor. "After Suffrage: Southern Women in the Twenties." *Journal of Southern History*, XXX (November, 1964), 298–318.

———, ed. *The American Woman: Who Was She?* Englewood Cliffs, N.J.: Prentice-Hall, 1971.

———. "Making the Invisible Woman Visible." *Journal of Southern History*, XXXVIII (November, 1972), 629–38.

———. "The 'New Woman' in the New South." *South Atlantic Quarterly*, LXI (Autumn, 1962), 473–83.

———. *The Southern Lady: From Pedestal to Politics, 1830–1930*. Chicago: University of Chicago Press, 1970.

———. "Women, Religion, and Social Change in the South, 1830–1930." In

Religion and the Solid South, edited by Samuel S. Hill, Jr. Nashville: Abingdon Press, 1972.

———. "Women's Perspective on the Patriarchy in the 1850s." *Journal of American History*, LXI (June, 1974), 52–64.

Scott, Evelyn. "War Between the States." Review of *Gone With the Wind*. *Nation*, CXLIII (July 4, 1936), 19.

Scura, Dorothy McInnis. "The Southern Lady in the Early Novels of Ellen Glasgow." *Mississippi Quarterly*, XXXI (Winter, 1977–78), 17–'32.

Segal, Miriam, and Shanna Richman. "The BEM Sex-Role Inventory: A North/South Comparison." *Psychological Reports*, XLIII (August, 1978), 183–86.

Seyersted, Per. *Kate Chopin: A Critical Biography*. Baton Rouge: Louisiana State University Press, 1969.

Shavin, Norman, and Martin Shartar. *The Million Dollar Legends: Margaret Mitchell and "Gone With the Wind."* Atlanta: Capricorn, 1974. Unpaginated pamphlet.

Shelby, Annette N. "Southern Feminist Rhetoric: A Search for Its Roots." Paper presented at the annual meeting of the Southern Speech Communication Association, April, 1976, in San Antonio, Texas.

Showalter, Elaine. *A Literature of Their Own: British Women Novelists from Brontë to Lessing*. Princeton: Princeton University Press, 1977.

Simkins, Francis Butler. *A History of the South*. New York: Alfred A. Knopf, 1956.

Simonini, R. C., Jr., ed. *Southern Writers: Appraisals in Our Time*. Charlottesville: University Press of Virginia, 1964.

Simpson, Claude M., Jr. "Grace King: The Historian as Apologist." *Southern Literary Journal*, VI (Spring, 1974), 130–33.

Simpson, Lewis. "The South's Reaction to Modernism: A Problem in the Study of Southern Letters." In *Southern Literary Study*, edited by Louis D. Rubin, Jr., pp. 48–68. Chapel Hill: University of North Carolina Press, 1975.

Skaggs, Peggy. "'The Man-Instinct of Possession': A Persistent Theme in Kate Chopin's Stories." *Louisiana Studies*, XIV (Fall, 1975), 277–81.

———. "Three Tragic Figures in Kate Chopin's *The Awakening*." *Louisiana Studies*, XIII (Winter, 1974), 345–64.

Smith, Henry Nash. "The Scribbling Women and the Cosmic Success Story." *Critical Inquiry*, I (September, 1974), 47–70.

Smith, James Penny. "Frances Newman and James Joyce." *James Joyce Quarterly*, XII (Spring, 1975), 307–309.

Smith, Lillian. *Killers of the Dream*. Revised ed. New York: W. W. Norton & Co., 1961.

———. *The Winner Names the Age: A Collection of Writings by Lillian Smith*. Edited by Michelle Cliff. New York: W. W. Norton & Co., 1978.

Smith-Rosenberg, Carroll. "The Female World of Love and Ritual: Relations Between Women in Nineteenth-Century America." *Signs*, I (Autumn, 1975), 1–29.

Soskin, William. "Books on Our Table: A Communication on the Death of Miss

Frances Newman." New York *Evening Post*, November 9, 1928, n.p. Adrienne Battey Collection, University of Georgia Library, Athens.

Spacks, Patricia Meyer. "'Ev'ry Woman Is at Heart a Rake.'" *Eighteenth-Century Studies*, VIII (Fall, 1974), 27–46.

———. *The Female Imagination*. New York: Knopf, 1975.

Spain, Rufus B. *At East in Zion: Social History of Southern Baptists, 1865–1900*. Nashville: Vanderbilt University Press, 1967.

Spiller, Robert E., *et al.*, eds. *Literary History of the United States: History*. 3rd ed. New York: Macmillan, 1963.

Spruill, Julia Cherry. *Women's Life and Work in the Southern Colonies*. 1938. Reprint. New York: Norton, 1972.

Steele, Oliver. "Ellen Glasgow's *Virginia*: Preliminary Notes." In *Studies in Bibliography*, edited by Fredson Bowers, pp. 265–89. *Papers of the Bibliographical Society of the University of Virginia*, XXVII. Charlottesville: University Press of Virginia, 1974.

Stern, Jerome. "*Gone With the Wind*: The South as America." *Southern Humanities Review*, VI (Winter, 1972), 5–12.

Stuckey, W. J. *The Pulitzer Prize Novels: A Critical Backward Look*. Norman, Okla.: University of Oklahoma Press, 1966.

Sugg, Redding S., Jr. "Lillian Smith and the Condition of Woman." *South Atlantic Quarterly*, LXXI (Spring, 1972), 155–64.

Sullivan, Ruth, and Stewart Smith. "Narrative Stance in Kate Chopin's *The Awakening*." *Studies in American Fiction*, I (Spring, 1973), 62–75.

Taylor, Lloyd C., Jr. "Lila Meade Valentine: The FFV as Reformer." *Virginia Magazine of History and Biography*, LXX (October, 1962), 471–87.

Taylor, William R. *Cavalier and Yankee: The Old South and American National Character*. New York: George Braziller, 1961.

———, and Christopher Lasch. "Two 'Kindred Spirits': Sorority and Family in New England, 1839–1846." *New England Quarterly*, XXXVI (March, 1963), 23–41.

Ticknor, Caroline. *Hawthorne and His Publisher*. Boston and New York: Houghton Mifflin Company, 1913.

Tillett, Wilbur Fisk. "Southern Womanhood as Affected by the War." *Century*, XXI (November, 1891), 9–16.

Tindall, George B. *The Emergence of the New South: 1913–1945*. Baton Rouge: Louisiana State University Press, 1967.

Tompkins, Jane P. "*The Awakening*: An Evaluation." *Feminist Studies*, III (Spring–Summer, 1976), 22–29.

Toth, Emily. "The Independent Woman and 'Free' Love." *Massachusetts Review*, XVI (Autumn, 1975), 647–64.

———. "Kate Chopin's *The Awakening* as Feminist Criticism." *Louisiana Studies*, XV (Fall, 1976), 241–51.

———. "Timely and Timeless: The Treatment of Time in *The Awakening* and *Sister Carrie*." *Southern Studies*, XVI (Fall, 1977), 271–76.

Van Alen, Eleanor L. Review of *Gone With the Wind*. *North American Review*,

CCXLII (Autumn, 1936), 201–203.

Van Auken, Sheldon. "The Southern Historical Novel in the Early Twentieth Century." *Journal of Southern History*, XIV (May, 1948), 157–91.

Wade, John Donald, "The Life and Death of Cousin Lucius." In *I'll Take My Stand: The South and the Agrarian Tradition, by Twelve Southerners*, edited by Louis D. Rubin, Jr. New York: Harper and Row, 1962.

Wagenknecht, Edward C. "The World and Mary Johnston." *Sewanee Review*, XLIV (April–June, 1936), 188–206.

Walker, James A. Papers. Southern Historical Collection, University of North Carolina at Chapel Hill.

Walters, Ronald G. "The Erotic South: Civilization and Sexuality in American Abolitionism." *American Quarterly*, XXV (May, 1973), 177–201.

Wasserstrom, William. *The Heiress of All the Ages: Sex and Sentiment in the Genteel Tradition*. Minneapolis: University of Minnesota Press, 1959.

Watkins, Floyd C. "*Gone With the Wind* as Vulgar Literature." *Southern Literary Journal*, II (Spring, 1970), 86–103.

Watson, Annah Robinson. "The Attitude of Southern Women on the Suffrage Question." *Arena*, XI (February, 1895), 363–68.

"*We Are Incredible* and Other New Works of Fiction." Review of *Dead Lovers Are Faithful Lovers. New York Times Book Review*, May 6, 1928, p. 8.

Weeks, Edward. "What Makes a Book a Best Seller?" *New York Times Book Review*, December 20, 1936, p. 2.

Weld, Angelina Grimké. "An Appeal to the Christian Women of the South." In *The Oven Birds: American Women on Womanhood, 1820–1920*, edited by Gail Parker. Garden City, New York: Doubleday, 1972.

Wells, Charles E. "The Hysterical Personality and the Feminine Character: A Study of Scarlett O'Hara." *Comprehensive Psychiatry*, XVII (March/April, 1976), 353–59.

Welter, Barbara. "The Cult of True Womanhood: 1820–1860." *American Quarterly*, XVIII (Summer, 1966), 151–62, 173–74.

West, Rebecca. "Battlefield and Sky." Review of *The Hard-Boiled Virgin*. New York *Herald Tribune Books*, November 28, 1926, p. 1.

Wheeler, Otis B. "The Five Awakenings of Edna Pontellier." *Southern Review*, XI (January, 1975), 118–28.

Wiley, Bell Irvin. *Confederate Women*. Westport, Conn.: Greenwood Press, 1975.

Williams, Michael. "Romance of Reality." Review of *Gone With the Wind. Commonweal*, XXIV (August 28, 1936), 430.

Wilson, Edmund. *Patriotic Gore: Studies in the Literature of the American Civil War*. New York: Oxford University Press, 1962.

Wolff, Cynthia Griffin. "Kate Chopin and the Fiction of Limits: 'Desiree's Baby'." *Southern Literary Journal*, X (1978), 123–33.

———. "Thanatos and Eros: Kate Chopin's *The Awakening*." *American Quarterly*, XXV (October, 1973), 449–72.

Wood, Ann Douglas. "'The Fashionable Diseases': Women's Complaints and

Their Treatment in Nineteenth-Century America." *Journal of Interdisciplinary History*, IV (Summer, 1973), 25–52.

————. "The Literature of Impoverishment: The Women Local Colorists in America, 1865–1914." *Women's Studies*, I (1972), 3–45.

————. "The 'Scribbling Women' and Fanny Fern: Why Women Wrote." *American Quarterly*, XXIII (Spring, 1971), 3–24.

Woodward, C. Vann. *The Burden of Southern History*. New York: Vintage, 1960.

————. *Origins of the New South, 1877–1913*. Baton Rouge: Louisiana State University Press, 1951.

Ziff, Larzer. *The American 1890s: Life and Times of a Lost Generation*. New York: Viking, 1966.

Index

Allen, James Lane, 257, 265
Ames, Jessie Daniel, 13, 14, 36, 37, 50
Anderson, Bernhard, 202
Anderson, Sherwood, 125–26
Androgyny: as theme in fiction by southern women, 55, 354–55, 361; Grace King admires, 131
—as attribute of fictional characters and situations: in *Beulah*, 74, 88; in *Monsieur Motte*, 106, 112, 115, 117; in "Charlie," 142, 143, 144; in "Athénaïse," 150; in *The Awakening*, 158, 159, 175–76, 177, 178, 180, 182; in *Hagar*, 201, 224; in *Virginia*, 249, 251; in *Gone With the Wind*, 347, 348
Animal imagery, in fiction, 361; in *Beulah*, 69, 80–81, 82, 83, 84; in *Monsieur Motte*, 107, 108, 110; in *The Awakening*, 162, 169, 170, 171; in *Virginia*, 246; in *Gone With the Wind*, 345
Art and artists: approach to, of southern women writers, 352; Kate Chopin on, 144–45, 146, 147, 148, 153; Augusta Evans on, 70; Grace King on, 127, 128, 132, 133, 134; Ellen Glasgow on, 229, 230, 235–36, 238; Frances Newman on, 274; mentioned, 137
—nature of, discussed in fiction, 352, 357; in *The Awakening*, 154, 160, 162, 170, 171, 172, 176, 179, 181; in *Hagar*, 193, 205, 213; in *Virginia*, 252; in *The Hard-Boiled Virgin*, 287, 288, 289
Association of Southern Women for the Prevention of Lynching, 36. *See also* Lynching; Women's clubs
Atlanta *Journal*, 272, 320, 325, 329
Atlantic Monthly, 187, 188
Austen, Jane, 237, 284
Authority: patriarchal, of slaveowners, 10, 11–12, 13, 16, 18–19, 20, 21, 28,

42, 43–44; relinquished by southern lady, 8
—figures of, in fiction, 355, 357; in *Beulah*, 76, 77–78, 79, 84, 87, 89, 157; in "Athénaïse," 149, 150; in *The Awakening*, 159, 161, 163, 168, 170, 174–75, 176; in *Hagar*, 195, 206, 207, 210, 214, 217, 224; in *Virginia*, 249, 250; in *Life and Gabriella*, 254, 256, 260, 261–62; in *The Hard-Boiled Virgin*, 299; in *Dead Lovers Are Faithful Lovers*, 307; in *Gone With the Wind*, 344–45
Awakening, The: discussed, 154–82; synopsis of, 154; title of, 374n46; publication of, 139; Chopin on, 146; critics on, 154–58, 165, 169, 170; compared with *Beulah*, 157, 158–59, 160, 161, 162, 167, 170; male characters in, 173–75, 178–80, 355; imagery of, 157, 158–59, 162, 163, 169, 170, 181, 192, 215, 221, 222, 361; mentioned, xii, 24, 46, 48, 136, 137, 139, 141, 142, 143, 144, 150, 204, 242, 244, 270, 289, 290, 327, 340, 352, 353, 354, 355, 358, 359, 360, 362. *See also* Chopin, Kate

Baldwin, Faith, 333
Bartlett, Irving H., 29
Barzun, Jacques, 357
Battey, Adrienne, 280
Baugh, Hansell, 272, 280
Baym, Nina, 53, 55, 61, 86, 91
Beauty: definition of, in southern culture, 41–42
—as theme in fiction, 352, 362; in *Beulah*, 62, 63, 67, 77, 79, 83, 86, 88; in *Monsieur Motte*, 101; in *Hagar*, 203–204; in *Virginia*, 238, 241, 244, 250, 251; in *The Hard-Boiled Virgin*, 293

292, 294, 296; in *Monsieur Motte*, 102;
in *The Pleasant Ways of St. Médard*,
132; in *Virginia*, 232, 238, 241–42
Eliot, George, 61
Elliott, William, 18
Emerson, Ralph Waldo, 18, 28, 44, 45,
62, 85, 357
Equal Rights Amendment, 17, 34
Ervin, Senator Sam, 17
Evans, Augusta Jane: family and biography of, 57–61; southern self-identification of, 47, 57, 58–59, 60; literary
career of, 58, 59, 60, 61, 70–71; subject matter of, 193; on her own work,
68–69, 70; religious beliefs of, 81;
mentioned, 40, 46, 47, 48, 49, 51, 52,
99, 101, 108, 117, 120, 121, 190, 223,
265, 353, 356, 360
—works of: *At the Mercy of Tiberius*, 60;
Devota, 60; *Macaria*, 47, 59; *Inez*, 58,
70; *Infelice*, 52, 60; *St. Elmo*, 28, 58,
59–60, 90–91, 265, 346; *Vashti*, 60,
203. *See also* Beulah
Evans, Sara, 8, 11, 12, 22, 45, 364n7
Everett, Charles, 339–40

Family: role of, in lives of women writers,
49; of Grace King, 95–96, 130; of Mary
Johnston, 185, 223; of Ellen Glasgow,
226–27, 228; of Frances Newman,
274; of Margaret Mitchell, 328
—as theme in fiction, 355–56; in *Monsieur Motte*, 99, 100, 101, 104,
106–107; in *The Awakening*, 174, 175;
in *Hagar*, 194, 216, 218, 221; in *The
Hard-Boiled Virgin*, 299; in *Dead
Lovers Are Faithful Lovers*, 309
Farmers' Alliance, 16, 21
Farr, Finis, 272, 325, 328, 330, 331
Fashion: Newman on, 288
—as metaphor in fiction, 362; in *Beulah*,
76–77; in *Monsieur Motte*, 100, 101;
in *The Awakening*, 181; in *Hagar*, 196;
in *Life and Gabriella*, 257, 259, 353; in
The Hard-Boiled Virgin, 289
Faulkner, William, xii, 265
Feminization of American Culture, The
(Douglas), 41, 196, 290–91
Fidler, William Perry, 60
Fitzgerald, F. Scott, 274, 275
Fitzgerald, Zelda Sayre, 16, 271, 330
Fitzhugh, George, 8, 11, 19
Fletcher, Marie, 233
Ford, Ford Madox, 274
Frazée, Monique Parent, 234

Freeman, Mrs. Julia D. ("Mary Forrest"),
44
Freeman, Mary Wilkins, 146
Freud, Sigmund, 290, 291
Fuller, Margaret, 28

Gaines, Francis, 22
Gallichan, Catherine, 235
Garnett, Edward, 126–27
Garrison, Dee, 54
Gayarré, Charles, 130
Geismar, Maxwell, 282
Genovese, Eugene, 11, 42–43, 54
Gentility, cult of, 196, 293
Gilbert, Sandra, 40–41
Gilder, Richard Watson, 48, 96, 97, 99,
318
Gilman, Caroline, 23, 24
Gilman, Charlotte Perkins, 158, 186, 187,
223, 224
Giraudoux, Jean, 275
Glasgow, Ellen: family and early life of,
225–28; literary career of, 225, 227; on
her own work, 223, 229, 235–36, 268,
269, 358, 360; critics on, 225, 226,
228, 229, 230, 232–33, 234, 235, 237,
278; southern self-identification of, 47,
226, 228, 230, 235; on fiction, 229,
230, 234, 235, 236, 237, 238, 265;
southern tradition as major literary
theme of, 228–29; "evasive idealism"
as theme in work of, 240, 283, 356; on
values of the South, 229–30; feminism
of, 232, 234, 235, 237, 253; as southern lady, 231, 232, 238; female characters of, 232–34; male characters of,
234; friendships of, with other women
writers, 224, 266–69, 275; mentioned,
42, 44, 45, 46, 47, 48, 49, 135, 222,
223, 224, 286, 359, 360, 363n5
—works of: "Feminism," 234–37; *The
Woman Within*, 227, 228, 230–31; *A
Certain Measure*, 229, 230, 236; "The
Call," 266–67; novels, 227, 228, 236,
237, 269. *See also Life and Gabriella*;
Virginia
Godbold, E. Stanly, 229, 232
Gone With the Wind: discussed, 334–49,
360–61; synopsis of, 334–38; writing
and publication of, 314–15, 318, 319,
328, 332, 333, 334; title of, 334;
Mitchell on, 315, 317, 318, 319, 320,
321, 329, 333, 334, 345; critics on,
339–40; treatment of southern history
in, 339; survival as theme of, 339, 342,

Faithful Lovers, 307; in Gone With the Wind, 341

Women's Christian Temperance Union, 33, 38. See also Women's clubs; Reform movements

Women's clubs: in liberation of women, 32–34, 36, 38. See also Reform movements

Wood, Ann Douglas. See Douglas, Ann

Woodward, C. Vann, 363n5

Woolf, Virginia, 275, 300

Woolson, Constance Fenimore, 52

Work: and ideal of southern ladyhood, 15, 16, 20, 22, 25, 26, 34; of southern women, during Civil War, 13, 14, 25, 31–32; acceptable professions for southern ladies, 34, 254, 307; Mary Johnston on, 189

—professions of southern women writers: Newman, 272, 273, 276–77, 304; Chopin, 137; Mitchell, 48, 314, 325–26, 329–30, 331, 332

—depicted in fiction, 353; in Beulah, 64, 353; in "Bonne Maman," 118, 119–20, 353; in "Miss McEnders," 147, 148, 360; in Hagar, 200, 353; in At Fault, 353; in Monsieur Motte, 97, 98, 100, 102, 353; in The Awakening, 160, 161, 353; in Virginia, 243, 244; in Life and Gabriella, 254, 255, 256, 258, 259, 260, 353; in Dead Lovers Are Faithful Lovers, 303, 304, 306, 307, 353; in

Gone With the Wind, 336, 342, 343, 353; in The Hard-Boiled Virgin, 353

Writers, southern women: history of, 41, 44, 51–52; place of, in southern society, 39–40; regional identification of, 47; critics interpret novels by, 52–54; seen as different from male writers, 125–26, 132, 133–34, 206, 234, 235, 237; models for, 45, 237; themes of, 39, 44, 45–46, 52–53; backgrounds of, 46–47; reasons for writing, given by, 47–48, 71; on writing, 223, 236, 237, 268, 277; characteristics of works by, 352–62 passim

—fictional allegories of: in "The Little Convent Girl," 124

—as characters in fiction, 39; in Beulah, 56, 64, 65, 66, 70, 71, 72, 73, 74; in Hagar, 191, 192, 204–205, 206; in The Hard-Boiled Virgin, 286–87, 288–89, 295, 296, 299; in "Charlie," 142, 143

Writing: as "safe" mode of expression for southern women, 24, 39–41; and ideal of southern ladyhood, xi, xii, 5, 44–46, 124, 125, 237–38, 367n86; as suitable profession for southern ladies, 5, 34; problems of, for women, xi, 40–41, 44, 189, 359

Ziff, Larzer, 174

Zola, Emile, 148